SAGE was founded in 1965 by Sara Miller McCune to support the dissemination of usable knowledge by publishing innovative and high-quality research and teaching content. Today, we publish over 900 journals, including those of more than 400 learned societies, more than 800 new books per year, and a growing range of library products including archives, data, case studies, reports, and video. SAGE remains majority-owned by our founder, and after Sara's lifetime will become owned by a charitable trust that secures our continued independence.

Los Angeles | London | New Delhi | Singapore | Washington DC | Melbourne

Financial Planning

Financial Planning

Theory and Practice

Sid Mittra, Ph.D., CFP®
Emeritus Professor of Finance, Oakland University, Michigan

Shailendra Kumar Rai, Ph.D.
Assistant Professor of Finance, Management Development Institute, Gurgaon

Anandi P. Sahu, Ph.D.
Professor and Chair of Economics, Oakland University, Michigan

Harry Starn, Jr., MBA, MS, CFP®
Executive Faculty, California Lutheran University, California

SAGE | TEXTS

Los Angeles | London | New Delhi
Singapore | Washington DC | Melbourne

First published in 2012 by American Academic Publishing

This South Asia adaptation published in 2015; fifth impression 2022

SAGE | TEXTS

SAGE Publications India Pvt Ltd
B1/I-1 Mohan Cooperative Industrial Area
Mathura Road
New Delhi 110 044, India

Published by Vivek Mehra for SAGE Publications India Pvt Ltd.

ISBN: 978-93-515-0250-0 (PB)

Brief Contents

Detailed Contents

Foreword

Financial planning is an area that the average person has started to give serious attention to only in the last few years. Recognizing the necessity to educate and inform such persons, a number of attempts have been made, including through the medium of publications, to explain fundamental concepts and to enable the taking of appropriate financial decisions. However, the need has always been felt for a detailed exposition of both the theory and the practice of financial management. It is this requirement that the present book *Financial Planning—Theory and Practice* co-authored by Mittra, Rai, Sahu and Starn, Jr. addresses admirably.

Conceptual clarity is an important ingredient in facilitating the correct investment decision. Yet, many persons with investible surpluses choose the wrong asset classes because of being misled by product pushers masquerading as investment advisors. In a country which has an acute shortage of appropriately qualified investment advisors, this book is, to put it briefly, a timely offering. Comprehensive in content and with simplicity of language that helps to demystify theoretical concepts with the help of illustrations, this book is invaluable for persons who wish to know where they are on the financial planning curve, and where they need to get to, in order to address the requirement of the future through appropriate savings and investments strategies. It takes note of the ground realities of the Indian context as also the regulatory and legislative framework within which the game of financial management is played out, and the fundamentals that an average person needs to understand and factor into her investment decisions.

The authors deserve our unstinted gratitude for the enormous wealth of facts and advice put together between the two covers of this book. This is the kind of book that should be referred to by persons who encounter doubts and difficulties in regard to planning the investment of their resources.

The effortless manner in which the book straddles the twin worlds of theory and practice, with a number of illustrations, is truly commendable.

M. Damodaran
Former Chairman, SEBI, UTI, and IDBI
Chairperson, Excellence Enablers Private Limited

Preface to the First Indian Edition

Years ago, Philosopher Russell A. Kemp published the following ageless poem in *Daily Word* (A Unity Publication, January 1, 1969):

Wonderful, wonderful, fortunate you,
this is the year that your dreams come true!
This is the year that your ships come in;
this is the year you find [joy] … within.
This is the year when you know the truth;
this is the year when you find new youth.
Wonderful, wonderful, fortunate you,
this is the year that your dreams come true!

It is phenomenal that, in 2014, Kemp's prediction for India literally came true. We will share with you the reason for our optimism. But first let's recount a little bit of history.

In America, initially the financial planning movement began in 1972 when the College for Financial Planning (a private institution) was established with the objective of granting the certified financial planner (CFP) mark. But the CFP designation granting power remained in the domain of a *private* institution almost for a decade. And in a true sense, the planning movement came of age only in 1985 with the establishment of a *national* board titled *International Board of Standards and Practices of Certified Financial Planners* (subsequently the name changed to CFP Board). This Board was founded as a national nonprofit organization in order to serve the public interest by promoting the value of professional, competent, and ethical financial planning services to be performed by the holders of the CFP® certification. This organization (of which coauthor Mittra was a founding board member), then, literally marked the beginning of a national financial planning movement in the USA.

We believe that a comparable unique moment has finally arrived in India. In the recently concluded Lok Sabha elections, that is, 2014, people of India spoke with a unified voice, a phenomenon rarely experienced in its 67 years of existence as an independent nation. And that has placed India on the verge of a renaissance, paving the way for the country to emerge as an awakening giant in the 21st century.

Like the early US experience, financial planning—which was officially introduced in India by the *Financial Planning Standards Board India*—has thus far remained nascent. However, we feel that with the new ruling party coming to power with a clear majority, and its powerful and inclusive message of hope captivating the nation, a solid foundation has finally been created for bringing the financial planning movement into the mainstream. Buoyed by this realization, we decided to become active participants in this exciting national movement by publishing an Indian version of our leading (in the USA) financial planning text entitled *Practicing Financial Planning for Professionals* in 2014 (originally published in the USA in 1990 by Prentice Hall). We remain convinced that this new era will rapidly open up significant opportunities for middle- and upper-income families to reap enormous benefits by engaging financial planners to help them reach their financial goals.

We sincerely hope that this book will play a significant role in exposing financial planning professionals in India to the state-of-the-art theoretical and practical foundations so that they would feel equipped to help people in India convert their lofty dreams into reality.

About the Authors

Sid Mittra holds the title of Emeritus Professor of Finance at Oakland University, Michigan. He was a board member of the International Board of Standards and Practices of Certified Financial Planners. He has been regularly invited to offer seminars at the World Congress of the International Association for Financial Planning, including those in Japan and Australia. Mittra is in several prestigious listings, including: International Authors' Who's Who, American Men of Science, and Who's Who in Finance and Industry. Also, he has published a dozen books, including *Practicing Financial Planning: A Complete Guide for Professionals*, which enjoys wide acceptance among top universities and trade associations.

Mittra uniquely combines conceptual and theoretical knowledge in financial management with communicative skills. He frequently speaks on financial economics, money, and financial management. He also advises corporations, partnerships, and closely held corporations in financial matters.

Shailendra Kumar Rai, Ph.D., is an Assistant Professor of Finance at the Management Development Institute (MDI), Gurgaon, and a General Fellow of Indian Council of Social Science Research. He has published numerous articles on finance, financial institutions, and entrepreneurship in national and international journals. He is actively involved in joint research at the national and international levels.

Dr Rai has extensive teaching and research experience both in India and abroad, including the USA, Germany, Sweden, Portugal, Belgium Greece, Lithuania, and Taiwan. Also, he has worked as a consultant and conducted training for corporations—such as Life Corporation of India, Bharat Electrical Ltd, and Canara Bank—as well as for various government departments, including the Department of Science & Technology, Indian Railways, and Indian Armed Forces.

In addition to serving as a visiting professor, Dr Rai has addressed many Indian and global audiences, and is widely considered as a highly regarded speaker.

Anandi P. Sahu is a Professor and Chair of Economics at the School of Business Administration, Oakland University, Michigan. He obtained an MA degree and a Ph.D. degree in economics from Washington University in St. Louis in 1985. He has concentrated his research efforts in three fields: macroeconomics, monetary theory, and finance.

Dr Sahu has published numerous articles in scholarly and professional journals. His journal publications include articles in the *Southern Economic Journal*, *Financial Services Review*, *Quarterly Journal of Business and Economics*, *Review of Business and Economic Research*, *Eastern Economic Journal*, *Journal of Economics and Finance*, *Journal of Applied Business Research*, *Public Finance Quarterly*, *AAII Journal, and Personal Financial Planning*. He is also a coauthor of four books: *The Economic Legacy of Reagan Years: Euphoria or Chaos?* (1991), *Defense Spending and Economic Growth* (1993), *Understanding Macroeconomics* (2006), and *Practicing Financial Planning for Professionals* (2007). He is also the author of *An Agenda for a Great America* (2008)—a book on long-term US public policy.

Harry Starn, Jr., is an Executive Faculty Member in California Lutheran University's MBA in Financial Planning Program and serves as the Associate Director of its California Institute of Finance. He earned a Bachelor of Science Degree from the United States Military Academy at West Point and a Master of Science Degree in Finance from the University of Colorado in Boulder. He holds professional credentials as a CFP® and Chartered Financial Analyst (CFA).

Mr Starn has over 20 years of experience in the financial services industry. He formerly operated his own fee-only financial planning practice, Action Financial Planning, LLC. Prior to starting his own practice in 1996, he worked as a registered representative with Financial Network Investment Corporation and later served as the manager of special directors' services with Lipper Analytical Services, Inc.—a consulting department to the mutual fund industry.

In 2010, the United States Distance Learning Association (USDLA) presented him with a bronze award for excellence in distance teaching. He was honored with a two-year appointment to the CFP Board's Council on Education (2012 and 2013) and also served on the board of directors of the Ventura Chapter of the Financial Planning Association (FPA).

Acknowledgments

The coauthors of this textbook express their gratitude toward many individuals, all of whom have made significant contributions to enhance the quality of this book.

Although somewhat unconventional, the authors would like to begin by expressing their gratitude to highly recognized financial planning professionals around the globe who have been associated with this book in various capacities since the first U.S. edition was published (1990) almost a quarter of a century ago. Any personal financial planning text must have the depth, the breadth, and the technical sophistication needed to prepare financial planning professionals for meeting the challenges of the time. In preparing the Indian version of our text, as was also the case with multiple editions published in the USA, we felt that no one person, no matter how competent or astute, could satisfactorily produce such a textbook. Consequently, in this Indian edition, we have continued our non-traditional policy of publishing a collaborative textbook by building on the base established with the 11th edition of the textbook published in the USA. In fact, like all the U.S. editions, this text is a truly multi-authored book that reflects the contributions of many financial planning practitioners who have generously given their time and talent to enhance the overall quality of this text. All the coauthors of this text are truly grateful for their significant contributions.

Next, we are thankful to **Mr M. Damodaran** for his willingness to write the foreword to this book. He is former Chairman, SEBI, UTI, and IDBI, and Chairperson, Excellence Enablers Private Limited. It is extraordinary that despite his extremely busy schedule and the tight publication deadline imposed on him, Mr Damodaran generously accepted the invitation to write the foreword and met the publisher's deadline with grace.

The authors acknowledge the contributions made by **Professor Rajesh Kothari**, R.A. Podar Institute of Management (Faculty of Management Studies, University of Rajasthan, Jaipur) as an academic consultant, improving the overall quality of the textbook. It is clear that the textbook has gained in various ways because of the advice we received at various stages from Professor Kothari.

It has been a matter of great delight to work with various members of SAGE's Editorial and Production team. While we have been directly exposed to only a few of them, we express our sincere thanks to everyone who diligently worked on this project.

We would like to extend our special thanks to Amit Kumar, Publishing Editor, Indrani Dutta, the Development Editor, and Vandana Gupta, Associate Production Editor (Books). All of them as well as their associates worked tirelessly to make the textbook project a great success.

Sid Mittra
Shailendra Kumar Rai
Anandi P. Sahu
Harry Starn, Jr.

PART 1

INTRODUCTION TO FINANCIAL PLANNING AND BASIC TOOLS

1 Emerging Role of the Financial Planner*

AN AWAKENING GIANT

In India, in May 2014, a new beginning was ushered in when the Bharatiya Janata Party (BJP) was elected as the majority party in the 16th Lok Sabha elections (winning 282 out of 543 seats) and became the first party since 1977 to win a majority in the Parliament. In taking his oath of office, the newly elected Prime Minister Narendra Modi made unequivocal promises to invigorate and energize the whole country. These included a seven-point rainbow principle for India—namely, culture, youth power, women's empowerment, agriculture, natural resources, democracy, and knowledge. Equally important, the government decided to forge ahead with policies aimed at developing the five proverbial "Ts": *T*alent, *T*rade, *T*radition, *T*ourism, and *T*echnology.

Commenting on the current state of affairs prevailing in India today, T.P. Srinivasan, a former Indian ambassador, eloquently stated:

> India has never had it so good. Change in India is coming more rapidly than most people seem to realize. It is true that in the old days India's policy of nonalignment brought her some respect. But even then, the world powers never provided this country with as much space as they are creating now. Every day we find a major country lining up to establish economic and strategic partnership with India. An economic and political miracle is truly taking place before our very eyes.

For the first time in many decades in India, change is in the air and people's expectations are skyrocketing. While that does not guarantee success by any means, it does lay the foundation for establishing a "New India," where achievements meet expectations, especially when it comes to improving the well-being of all segments of the population and becoming one of the dominant players in the fast-changing world.

A key aspect of this exciting change is the new challenges that financial planners face in becoming an integral part of this development process. It is, of course, true that many years ago, for the benefit of all Indians in general, and the middle- and high-income families in particular, the U.S. Certified Financial Planner Board introduced the personal financial planning discipline in India. While that was a welcome beginning because of myriads of financial, social, and structural problems, thus far financial planning as a discipline in India has remained at the introductory level. But now, with the country triumphantly entering a new era of political and economic change, and the affluent Indians fast becoming the dominant players and key engines of rapid economic growth, financial planners are now being called upon to get on the bandwagon and playing a critical role in this rapidly developing society.

And so, against this backdrop of an awakening giant, we say to the personal financial planning community in India, *Welcome Aboard!*

* At the start of this book project, Professor Rajesh Kothari of R.A. Podar Institute of Management, Jaipur, served as an academic consultant.

CHALLENGES FOR THE FINANCIAL PLANNING COMMUNITY IN INDIA

The verdict is finally in: The 21st Century is undeniably going to be one of the *most underappreciated* periods in human history.

On one hand, life appears to be shooting through with wonder. Even the awesome achievements of the 20th century—technological marvels, sophisticated communications, artificial intelligence, walking on the moon, deep probes of faraway planets, and, most amazing of all, cloning life itself—appear pale by comparison. Now, 50 new planets have been found outside our solar system, one of them orbiting two suns! And that is not all. Scientists now claim that subatomic particles have shattered the speed of light. This claim, if confirmed, will literally redefine the word, *impossible.*

On the other hand, *everything-will-go-wrong* mentality pervades the entire country. This mentality includes: fear of living too long, agony of suffering from catastrophic illness—another major depression leading to a collapse of the world economy—widespread poverty after retirement, inadequacy of the pension system, and concerns over continuing bureaucratic problems and lackluster development of the country's infrastructure. Everyone seems to be besieged by pessimism about the dismal future.

We keep hoping that a statesman will suddenly rise up to the occasion and passionately convince the skeptical public that in India, in multiple dimensions, the situation is dramatically improving. As Charles Kenny of Center for Global Development rightly observes, people are living longer, food is becoming more plentiful, infant mortality is improving steadily, human slavery is disappearing from earth, and the rights of minorities are gaining more respect every day. Unfortunately, we do not see such a statesman appearing on the scene to help us move to a higher plane, no matter how excruciatingly painful the journey might be.

This, then, is the environment in which professional financial planners must pledge to assist their clients in achieving their goals, operating in an environment of unprecedented opportunities and fearfully difficult challenges.

According to the latest census data available (2011), the total population in India is 1.2 billion. The population is divided almost equally between male (51 percent) and female (49 percent). The national literacy rate is 73 percent (for women being only 65 percent). Although there are no accurate data available, the traditional joint family system (many generations living under the same roof) is very much on the decline, with single family units becoming the norm in all sections of the country. In a joint family system, the family is headed by a patriarch, usually the oldest male called "Karta," who makes all final decisions on economic and social matters on behalf of everyone. By contrast, in the case of single households consisting of married couples with children, typically the head of the household (and often the couple) makes all the financial decisions for the entire family.

Interestingly, single-unit families are progressively becoming less capable of financially assisting their aging parents and their children. The implications are enormous. In contrast to a society that traditionally buttressed each individual with a network of family support, this century is marked by an increasing need for individuals and single families to take full responsibility for meeting their own financial goals.

Indian Economy and the Financial Sector

India is the second most populous country in the world, with over 1.21 billion people (2011 census), growing at an annual rate of 4.7 percent. Currently, the country is young and vibrant, with more than 65 percent of its population being below the age of 35. India has numerous ethnic groups, and unlike most other countries, in India every major religion is represented. And that is not all. There is great variation across this nation on social parameters, such as income, education, health, and opportunities for personal development. The economy of India is the 10th largest in the world as measured by nominal Gross Domestic Product (GDP) and the 3rd largest when judged by the purchasing power parity index. The country is already recognized as one of the G-20's major economies, a member of BRICS (Brazil, Russia, India, China, and South Africa), and a developing economy that is among the top 20 global traders.

The agriculture sector is the largest employer in India's economy but contributes to a declining share of its GDP (only 13.7 percent in 2012–13). India's manufacturing industry has held a constant share of its economic contribution, while unequivocally the fastest-growing part of the economy now is its services sector that includes construction, telecom, software/information technologies, infrastructure, tourism, education, health care, travel, trade, banking, and others components of its economy. In recent years, India's economic growth has slowed to 4.7 percent; however, the 2014 election has brought new hopes for a revival of the annual GDP growth rate to around 9 percent.

As the 2014 general elections got under way, the biggest economic problems that the country was facing were its sluggish economic growth (at 4.7 percent), a record high current account deficit, and a declining value of rupee (US$1 = ₹60+). There was a serious lack of even a minimum amount of infrastructure investment, and the government continued to provide huge amounts of subsidies it could ill afford. Finally, to top it off, the traditional policymaking inertia coupled with an inefficient and ineffective bureaucratic juggernaut continued to haunt the lack of progress of the country. All of this contributed to the defeat of the ruling party and a landslide victory of BJP—a clear winner of the 2014 elections.

THE NEW INDIAN DREAM

In May 2014, India's 1.21 billion people handed a landslide victory to Narendra Modi and his party. And with that people expressed their deep aspirations for a major structural change in the country's developmental paradigm, thereby laying a solid foundation for forcefully bringing the country into the 21st century. A wave of optimism has already begun across all sections of the country: urban, rural, and even tribal areas. In fact, the collective dream of a billion-plus people was recently summarized by a native social thinker saying, "Indians are looking for employment and not doles; empowerment and not entitlements; growth and not mere distribution and transfers; good governance and not an executive devoid of direction and purpose."

Clearly, these are exploding aspirations, but the challenges are also frightfully enormous. Still, since achieving her independence in 1947, for the first time the country is solidly in the grips of such powerful optimism. Buttressed by the collective action of all segments of the society, the country is poised to become a major player among the world's leading nations.

As is commonly recognized, this election appears to have replaced India's traditional dynasty-based, pseudo-secularist economic model with a novel brand of the free enterprise system. The ultimate goal of New India, then, is to make the benefits truly inclusive, based on sharing the fruits of a broadly and rapidly expanding economy rather than distributing stagnant wealth by continuing the old policy of growth-restricting entitlements and bureaucratic nightmares. Clearly, the journey has only just begun, and the burden of delivering on these hopes and aspirations is squarely on the shoulders of the new government and the powerful private sector. Equally challenging is the fact that India is a highly diverse country on all conceivable fronts. Hence, as the country moves forward, what is urgently needed is the launching of a creative model based on the proverbial platform with four pillars of *D*emocracy, *D*iversity, *D*evelopment, and *D*etermination; that is, of course, a tall order. Still, there is plenty of hope for optimism. As Orison Swett Marden puts it: "There is no medicine like hope, no incentive so great, and no tonic so powerful as expectation of something tomorrow."

India's Middle Class

India's middle class (families with an annual income of ₹3.4–17 lakh based on 2009–10 prices) is exploding. Currently, India has 31.4 million middle-class households, or 160 million individuals falling in this category. But the National Council for Applied Economic Research estimates that by 2015–16, India will be a country of 53.3 million middle-class households, translating into 267 million middle-class people. Prediction for such a phenomenal growth is based on a number of factors, such as the country's potential GDP growth, projected to approach 9 percent, and the escalating high growth rate of urbanization. If this upward trend continues, conventional wisdom suggests that by 2025–26 the number of middle-class households in India would be more than double, approaching a whopping half a billion individuals. Put differently, the percentage of the middle class in the country's total population is predicted to reach 20.3 percent by 2015–16 and to an unimaginable 37.2 percent by 2025–26. These are mighty impressive developments, all of which translate into a surge in demand for consumer products such as automobiles, TVs, computers, air-conditioners, microwave ovens, and a great deal more.

Incidentally, as impressive as this upward trend toward the ever-expanding middle class is, it still tells only part of the story; the rest is equally revealing. The middle class that represents only 13.1 percent of India's population currently owns 49 percent of automobiles, 21 percent of TVs, 53 percent of computers, 53 percent of air-conditioners, 38 percent of microwaves, and 46 percent of credit cards. A recent official report also revealed that a typical middle-class household spends only half of the total income on family budget, saving the rest for the future. The inevitable conclusion to which one reaches from this observation is that these families not only possess a strong purchasing power to be spent on consumer goods and services but also act as the primary source of the country's investable funds. These elements have enormous implications for the future potential economic growth of the country.

Not everything associated with this income group is rosy, however. It is widely reported that over the last two decades the inequality in earnings of this group has doubled. The top 10 percent of wage earners now make 12 times more than the bottom 10 percent, up from a ratio of 6 in the 1990s. In addition, wages are not smoothly spread out even within this group. The top 10 percent of earners make almost five times more than the median 10 percent, but this median 10 percent makes only 0.4 times more than the bottom 10 percent. There is also other evidence of the growing concentration of wealth among the elite. For instance, the consumption of the top 20 percent of households grew at almost 3 percent per year in the 2000s (as compared to 2 percent in the 1990s), while the growth in the consumption of the bottom 20 percent of households remained unchanged at 1 percent per year. A continuous rise in income inequality, of course, can have a far-reaching adverse impact on the overall economic development of the country.

Not everyone is impressed with the prowess of the middle class, however. A recent article entitled, "India's Middle Class: Growth Engine or Loose Wheel" sums up the country's dilemma. On one hand, despite them being only 25 percent of the population (as compared to 63 percent in China), it is customary to brand the middle class as the "bird of gold," the movers and shakers of the modern India. These people play by the rules of the global free enterprise system and lead the country's rapid economic growth. And despite the fact that they represent only 25 percent of the population, they hold enormous economic power and can drive the growth engine faster than anyone ever expected. The fate of the middle class and that of the Indian economy are in lockstep: The hope is that their rising incomes will fuel consumption, which will drive demand and productivity, leading to more employment and a further rise in incomes, including those of the poor.

On the other hand, when the prevailing structural weaknesses and social barriers are taken into account, some of the glamor of the middle class as the mavericks of new India is invariably diminished. For instance, it is estimated that almost 80 percent of the middle-class Indians are in the lowest income bracket, many without proper education and adequate social safety nets. Another problem with this group is that most by nature do not belong to the entrepreneurial middle class and, hence, are not the creators of jobs and other opportunities for the rest of India. These cultural weaknesses of course can be traced back to India's feudal social structure and the formation of the colonial middle class in the mid-19th century. Naturally, times have significantly changed since then, but in a traditional country like India the wheels of change can be expected to move ever so slowly.

Life after Retirement

Retired people in India present a different set of challenges for financial planners. That should not come as a surprise, given that major changes are afoot both in social and financial lives of India's aging population.

In India, the size of the elderly population (age 60 or above) has been steadily growing, from 7.4 percent of the population in 2000 to almost 10 percent today. That fact itself creates multidimensional socioeconomic problems. These include, but are certainly not limited to, the following: pension outlays, health care expenditures, financial expenditures, personal savings, and family sickness and other emergencies. Clearly, the financial planning community needs to provide multiple levels of assistance to people who are contemplating retirement or are already retired.

Statistics relating to old people in India are truly sobering. The old-age dependency ratio climbed from 11 percent in 1961 to an estimated 15 percent today. About 65 percent of the aged are dependent on others for their day-to-day maintenance. Among the economically dependent elderly men, almost 85 percent are financially supported by their own children. Finally, perhaps the most sobering statistic is that 60 percent of the people who wish to retire are *forced* to continue working, a clear sign of inadequate retirement planning.

In India where the majority of the population is young, the rapidly rising percentage of senior citizens presents yet another vexing problem. As the country continues its quest for faster economic growth, the aging population is likely to fall further and further behind. After attaining the age of superannuation varying between 60 and 65 years, most people who worked in organized sectors receive sizeable pension and other retirement benefits. But those who had worked for the central and state governments receive only nominal (₹75–150 per month) old-age pension coverage. Of course, government does provide a few other additional benefits for the elderly, but these benefits largely turn out to be insufficient. For these people, medical and other expenses continue to accelerate, leading progressively to increased dependency on children and relatives for physical, mental, and economic support. It is, therefore, no exaggeration to argue that much more needs to be done for the nation's aging population.

At a different level, the problem of low literacy rate of the retired people is no less vexing. Statistics reveal that only 50 percent (20 percent for women) have received formal education in school. Hence, during working years, at best they superficially manage their own financial resources with the result that they are rarely ready for retirement. And at worst, many of these people, being vulnerable to bad financial advice, witness their retirement dreams going up in smoke.

In this area, a relatively recent (1999) development of considerable importance is the passage of the National Policy on Older Persons (NPOP) designed to ensure the well-being of India's growing retired population. The Policy directs individual states to protect the financial and food security of older persons and to meet their health care, shelter, and other needs. It also directs the government to allocate resources to help in improving the quality of life of India's senior citizens. This indeed marks a good beginning; but sadly it still is just a beginning. Today, with the country moving rapidly toward a new horizon, the urgent need for the financial planning community to help India's growing senior citizens in particular, and all citizens in general, and to achieve their financial and retirement goals cannot be overemphasized.

A Summary View

Current trends suggest that the future will offer the people of India unparalleled opportunities in all areas of life. But to exploit these opportunities, rather than relying on traditional sources of assistance, individuals will have to assume increasing responsibility for their own financial well-being. The process of making the most of one's money is both an arduous and a technically oriented endeavor. Therefore, it is best to recognize that the future, however distant it may seem, is *now*. Fortunately, people no longer need to face these challenges alone. Professional financial planners, who only recently were practically unknown even to sophisticated individuals, are slowly being recognized by the general public as invaluable partners in planning for their financial future. And so, there is no denying that *personal financial planning profession* has definitely passed the adolescent age and is poised to reach the age of maturity in the foreseeable future.

CONCEPT OF FINANCIAL PLANNING

The term *personal financial planning* has been loosely and broadly applied to a wide range of advisory services and financial products' sales efforts. While many financial planning professional organizations have defined the term to foster a unified financial planning profession, the most comprehensive definition has been developed by the Certified Financial Planner Board of Standards. In its Code of Ethics and Professional Responsibility, the Board presents the following definition:

> "Personal financial planning" or "financial planning" denotes the process of determining whether and how an individual can meet life goals through the proper management of financial resources. Financial planning integrates the financial planning process with the financial planning subject areas. In determining whether the certificant (*planner*) is providing financial planning or material elements of financial planning, factors that may be considered include, but are not limited to the:
>
> 1. Client's understanding and intent in engaging with the certificant.
> 2. Degree to which multiple financial planning subject areas are involved.
> 3. Comprehensiveness of the data gathering.
> 4. Breadth and depth of the recommendations.[1]

Financial Planning Process

Financial planning is a *process* and not a *product*. It may lead to the recommendation of investment, insurance, or legal products; however, a financial planner should never act as an order taker, merely using life insurance or mutual fund investment as a panacea for solving all problems. Instead, financial planning should be thought of as a *process* for helping people achieve their financial goals either through the development of integrated, comprehensive planning solutions or through the use of a segmented approach for solving specific problems. Thus, it is the skillful use of the process that elevates an individual to the level of a professional financial planner.

In its *Standards of Professional Conduct*, the CFP Board offers the following definition of the planning process:

> "Personal financial planning process" or "financial planning process" denotes the process which typically includes, but is not limited to, some or all of the six steps:
>
> 1. Establishing and defining the client–planner relationship.
> 2. Gathering client data including goals.

[1] *Standards of Professional Conduct*, Certified Financial Planner Board of Standards.

3. Analyzing and evaluating the client's current financial status.
4. Developing and presenting recommendations and/or alternatives.
5. Implementing the recommendations.
6. Monitoring the recommendations.[2]

The financial planning process and associated job tasks will be discussed at length in Chapter 2.

Financial Planning Subject Areas

Financial planners should be well versed in all aspects affecting their clients' lifetime financial decisions and especially in the following core planning areas:

1. Cash management, savings, credit, and debt planning.
2. Funding for educational need.
3. Risk management and insurance.
4. Investment planning.
5. Income tax planning.
6. Retirement and employee benefit planning.
7. Estate planning.

A useful image of "material elements" within comprehensive planning is presented in Figure 1.1. While financial planners may have expertise in only a few of these areas, they must have a clear understanding of all of these areas so that they can effectively work with other professionals while servicing their clients.

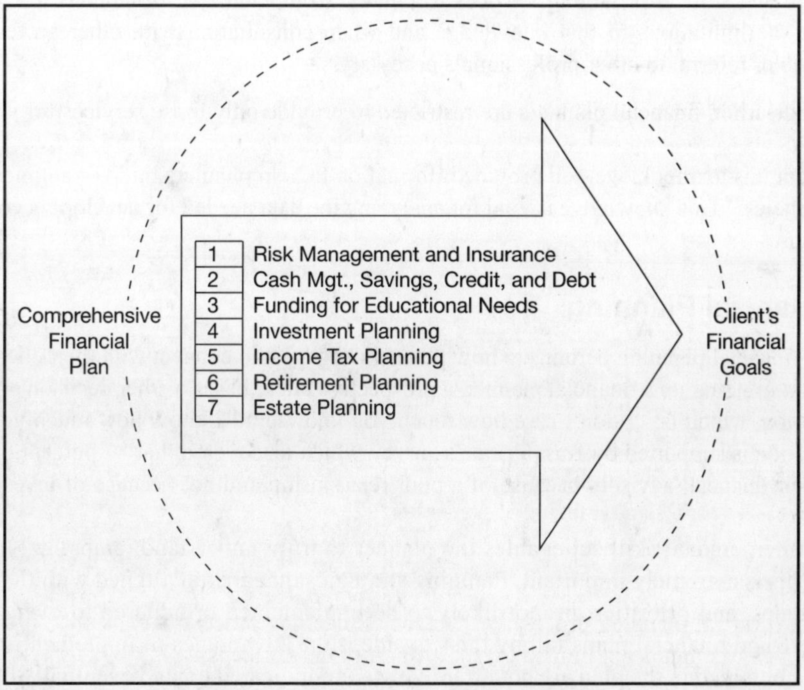

Figure 1.1 *An Overview of a Comprehensive Financial Plan*

[2] *Standards of Professional Conduct*, Certified Financial Planner Board of Standards.

SCIENCE AND ART OF FINANCIAL PLANNING

Financial planning is both a science and an art. It involves skillfully moving the core pieces of the financial planning puzzle in tandem, better known as integrative planning. Efficient use of this technique helps motivate clients to take the actions necessary to reach their desired goals.

Science of Financial Planning

The "science" of financial planning pertains to technical competencies and practical knowledge within the core topic areas—cash and debt management (including financial statement analysis and cash flow projections), risk management and insurance, investment planning, funding for education, income tax planning, employee benefit analysis, retirement planning, and estate planning. Armed with a solid technical background, the planner is able to assess the data, synthesize strategies, and identify products that will improve the client's probability of reaching the stated goals. For example, when offering purely investment advisory services, the planner assesses the client's goals, risk tolerance, time horizon, preferences, and constraints; develops an appropriate asset allocation strategy; implements the portfolio by identifying suitable investment products; and hedges the portfolio against market volatility. However, if this investment planning is undertaken as part of providing comprehensive planning services, then the planner develops investment recommendations only after taking into consideration income tax implications, cash flow constraints, and the impact of investment decisions on the client's competing or complementary objectives.

The CFP Board describes competency in its *Code of Ethics* as,

> [A]ttaining and maintaining an adequate level of knowledge and skill, and application of that knowledge and skill in providing services to clients. Competence also includes the wisdom to recognize the limitations of that knowledge and when consultation with other professionals is appropriate or referral to other professionals necessary.

As mentioned earlier, financial planners are restricted to provide only those services for which they are duly qualified.

Throughout this textbook, we will provide information to help planners build or augment their "content competencies." This knowledge is vital for analyzing the data needed for developing comprehensive financial plans.

Art of Financial Planning

The "art" of financial planning pertains to how planners engage and connect with their clients. It is commonplace that in sizing up a financial planner, a prospective client bases his/her decision on a simple yet powerful notion, which is: "I don't care how much you know until I know how much you care." This sage observation is supported by Russ Prince's survey which discovered that 87 percent of affluent clients fired their financial advisors because of a poor relationship and not because of investment performance.

A solid, interpersonal skill set enables the planner to truly understand, empathize, and relate to the client. This is extremely important. Planning strategies that are not aligned with the client's core values, attitudes, and priorities are not likely to be implemented or adhered to over the long run. Even the best-laid financial plans fall by the wayside if the advantages of implementing the recommendations contained in the plan are not effectively communicated to, and eventually bought by, the client.

For these reasons, financial planners need to develop a unique set of *communicative skills* in order to interact with their existing and potential clients. Effective communication is established when planners recognize their clients' needs and fears, are able to articulate their short- and long-term objectives, and finally succeed in developing a comprehensive program for meeting these objectives. An integral part of an effective communication, of course, is to help clients understand that financial planning is not an exact science, and that quick fixes or unrealistic expectations are bound to fail. Thus, through proper communication, clients learn that financial planning is a long-term process, and that continuous monitoring by the planner and total cooperation between the two parties are essential for achieving both short- and long-term objectives.

The topic of communication will be discussed in more detail in Chapter 2.

Summary

More than ever before, individuals seek the assistance of financial planners committed to fulfilling their needs with competent care, professionalism, and high moral values. By successfully applying the art and the science of financial planning, planning professionals can effectively communicate to their client that they are:

A: Accountable for all planning-related actions.
B: Both caring and committed for the long term.
C: Competent, both academically and experientially.

THE CLIENT

The Emerging Client

In the United States, from the end of World War II until the beginning of the 1970s, financial planning was relatively simple and straightforward. Starting in the mid-1970s, however, with the advent of double digit inflation, stagflation, high unemployment, massive budget and trade deficits, and frequent tax law changes, financial planning became far more complicated. As a result, consumers in America began demanding comprehensive planning services that were much broader in scope and far more complex than they were provided from their financial planners. And with that, a new breed of planning professionals began to emerge: far more vibrant and professionally astute than their previous counterparts. This trend toward the demand for an ever-more sophisticated financial planning industry continued unabated as the 20th century drew to a close.

With the turn of the 21st century, the nature of complexity of the planning clients rapidly began to change in the western countries. Today, bachelors stay single a lot longer. If two wage earners marry, often their financial plans do not include children. And even where children are included in the plan, each parent may have a prenuptial agreement, thereby making financial planning more complicated. Also, average families who faithfully follow the recommendations of their financial planners often find their financial lives turned upside down as aging—and often ailing—parents move in with them. It is, therefore, little wonder that today the *average client* of the 1970s is practically nonexistent, and that there is no single comprehensive financial plan that fits all situations. Fortunately, even though the nature and complexity of services that today's clients demand have dramatically changed, certain basic financial needs of the public remain intact.

Common Denominators

In India, each client is unique, with his or her own hopes, dreams, priorities, and family circumstances. However, within the "uniqueness" there are some commonalities that provide useful starting points for most planning situations. Three distinct commonalities can be conveniently grouped as follows:

Life Concerns: Three major life's concerns are fear of (a) running out of money before death, (b) dying and leaving the family without financial support, and (c) becoming disabled and losing the ability to generate income for the family.

1. ***Fear of running out of money.*** Many Indians have pension phobia—the fear of not having enough money to retire with peace and dignity. The average life expectancies for men and women (2008) have already reached 64.6 and 67.7, respectively, and these numbers are certain to continue their upward trend. The viability of the pension system is at best tenuous. Catastrophic health care costs threaten to cripple many families, housing markets are skyrocketing, and a collapse of the world economic system—a distinct possibility—can turn the retirement dream into a nightmare.

   Whatever lifestyle a person envisions, the best way to ensure that the retirement goal will be met is to plan early. The primary duty of financial planners is to impress on their clients that the choices they make at a relatively young age will largely determine how well they reach their retirement goals. Once that is accomplished, they can articulate the steps their clients need to take to effectively plan for retirement.

2. ***Fear of dying too young.*** We live in a turbulent society in which the threat of an early death is ever-present. An untimely death of the breadwinner can be catastrophic, and the surviving family may never be able to financially recover from it. Risk management planning involves the transfer of the risk of untimely death to an insurance company by buying adequate life insurance. Such an action presents a major challenge for financial planners for two reasons. First, calculating what constitutes an adequate amount of life insurance coverage is not an exact science, since the quantification of several related variables requires making value judgments. For instance, if a woman with kids is willing and able to join the labor force at an adequate salary level immediately after her husband's death, then her husband would need far less life insurance coverage than in another case where the woman wants to stay at home until her children have completed their high school education. A problem of a different kind is created by high-powered insurance salespersons pushing life insurance policies on unsuspecting buyers, thereby making it difficult for buyers to appreciate the real need for buying insurance. Despite these difficulties, however, risk management planning remains a top priority for everyone.

3. ***Fear of becoming disabled.*** One of the major challenges faced by financial planners is to convince their clients that they should be covered by an effective disability plan. Several reasons account for the universal apathy consumers have toward buying a comprehensive disability policy. Among them are: (a) most people do not recognize that long-term disability poses a real threat in their lives; (b) few people understand that unlike death, where all expenses related to the deceased cease, a long-term disability places a continuing financial burden on the family; (c) many people shy away from purchasing disability insurance because *it appears to be* far more expensive than a life insurance policy. Clearly, people often fail to recognize that the disability policy *appears* to be very expensive only because they naively compare apples and oranges when they uncritically compare the cost of buying life and disability insurance.

The Economic Life Cycle: Every person passes through three broad economic stages: the accumulation stage, the consolidation stage, and the spending/gifting stage. Each presents a totally different set of challenges.

1. ***The accumulation stage.*** This stage describes the "starting out" period. During this phase (generally when adults are in their 20s or 30s), an individual, or a couple, is focused on promoting a career, starting a family, acquiring personal assets, and buying a home. Because people

belonging to this stage earn relatively low incomes but generate large cash outflows, planners serving them should expect to find the following:

(a) Extensive use of credit to buy a home and accumulate personal assets.
(b) Low saving rate.
(c) Educational loan payments.
(d) Need to save for children's education.
(e) Need to hedge income risks through the purchase of life and disability insurance.

2. ***The consolidation stage.*** During this stage, corresponding to middle age (typically 40s and 50s), most people manage to progress in their careers and succeed in generating substantial disposable income. For many of these families, after graduation from college children are gone, leaving behind their parents as empty nesters. During this stage, planners normally expect to notice a shift in clients' priorities toward retirement. However, in some cases clients may divert their attention instead to career changes or to climb up the social ladder by buying bigger homes and embarking on extensive travels. In few cases, during this stage prudent clients become interested in discussing their long-term care needs.

3. ***Spending and gifting stage.*** The postretirement period is characterized by the depletion of assets. During this stage, spending generally exceeds the family's earnings and passive income streams, and the attention is invariably diverted to developing a systematic saving withdrawal strategy. Of course, interests and concerns of the people passing through this stage are hardly uniform. Some plan to spend many *active* retirement years, while others gravitate toward a sedentary existence. Ultimately, however, in almost all cases, people become engrossed with health care concerns. During this stage, the three priority needs that planners expect clients to have are:

   (a) Need to budget retirement expenses.
   (b) Manage health care costs that consume a large portion of the budget.
   (c) Develop an estate plan and a systematic gifting plan.

Special Situations: Similar to life cycle commonalities, there are several special situations that always present some commonalities in terms of needs and planning priorities. Examples of special situations include:

1. Divorce.
2. Loss of spouse (widow or widower).
3. Nontraditional families.
4. Single parenting.
5. Dependents with special needs.
6. Dependent elderly parents.
7. Permanent disability.
8. Terminal illness.
9. Loss of job or job change.
10. Planning for military families.
11. Monetary windfalls (i.e., "sudden money").

Consider, for example, the case of single parents. While every single parent is unique with respect to goals, dreams, interests, values, and experiences, they all have certain common characteristics. These include, but are not limited to, the following: high priority for life and disability insurance coverage, urgent need for updating the will naming a designated guardian for the child, making adjustments in the family budget to allow for escalating childcare costs including higher education and other important tax-related matters. If the single-parent status is the result of a divorce, then a whole slew of other important planning issues surface that need to be considered when planning for these single parents.

COORDINATION WITH OTHER PROFESSIONALS

The profession of financial planning, when compared with accounting and legal professions, is relatively new, and over the years it has evolved as a way of dealing with our modern complex society. Even as late as at the turn of this century, there was little demand for financial planners, and most people were content dealing with their traditional advisors, such as attorneys, accountants, bankers, insurance agents, and stockbrokers. However, as we entered the 21st century, the Indian society slowly started to grow more complex. Clearly, the financial planning profession was ill-equipped to handle the myriad of special financial planning needs of Indian families. So to deal with this challenging situation, recently a "new" financial profession was born in India, marking the beginning of the modern financial planning profession as we know today.

As is generally the case with the emergence of a new discipline, initially people expected financial planners to be *all things to all people*. That expectation, however, was short-lived. Before long it was recognized that consumers' interests would be truly served only if financial planners acted either as a quarterback or as an orchestra leader, coordinating the services of other traditional advisors to provide comprehensive planning services for their clients. For instance, if a client needed an estate plan, an attorney could fulfill that need. A complex tax return could be prepared by a chartered accountant (CA). Life insurance could be purchased from a life insurance professional. Similarly, the investment portfolio could be reorganized with the help of a portfolio manager or a professional investment counselor.

Let there be no misunderstanding, however. To suggest that a financial planner should closely work with other professionals does not imply that the planner cannot—or should not—perform one or more of the tasks just listed. In fact, frequently financial planners are licensed members of one or more of these professions and, hence, can successfully perform the related tasks. For instance, practicing financial planners may also be licensed to sell securities and insurance products. In addition, some planners are CAs, while others are lawyers and licensed to practice law. Nevertheless, most sophisticated financial planners recognize that while it is desirable to be knowledgeable about the key areas of planning, when circumstances warrant, it is best to seek professional services of other advisors. The following is a brief description of the approach taken by each type of professional and the importance of including such a person on the planning team.

A Lawyer

In recent years, a great deal has been written on the client–lawyer relationship and on the legal community's indifferent behavior toward the financial planning community. These writings suggest that at least some of the dissension stems from turf battles. The thinking behind such behavior is not only misplaced, but if allowed to continue, can be counterproductive and ultimately damaging to the client's best interests.

In the context of financial planning, a lawyer's key function is to certify the legality of a proposal developed by a financial planner and to prepare the associated legal documents. For instance, if a charitable trust is recommended, the lawyer would be asked to either confirm the planner's choice of the legal instrument or suggest a better instrument to accomplish the client's objective. The lawyer would then prepare the appropriate legal document to implement the recommendation. The same approach would be used for recommendations relating to education, life insurance, joint ownership, and other types of trust and estate planning issues. Clearly, in the scenario just described, there is no room for turf battles and acrimonious debates, for in this role the lawyer operates not as an adversary but an integral part of the team of professionals.

An Accountant

Traditionally, accountants and CAs have performed two principal functions: maintenance of financial records and preparation of taxes. In addition, occasionally these professionals also perform certain financial planning functions. Whatever be the role, traditionally CAs have commanded the public's respect and admiration primarily because they were not permitted to receive commission on product sales.

With the financial world becoming more complex and financial planners establishing themselves as coordinators of the professional team, the role of accountants has significantly changed. Today, CAs and accountants still perform financial record-keeping and compliance services such as audit and tax preparation. But as team players, they also assume a major role in analyzing the overall tax consequences of buying investment products or transacting investment business. In addition, CAs also provide invaluable assistance to the financial planners by (a) interpreting and evaluating the ever-changing tax laws, (b) recommending ways of taking advantage of these changes in the law, and (c) occasionally computing and monitoring investment results by acting as investment advisors.

A Portfolio Manager

The two most important components of financial planning are the creation and preservation of a client's assets. While a lawyer and a tax professional help preserve the estate, a portfolio manager helps create or build it. This constitutes a two-step process. First, a financial planner creates a target investment portfolio that would help achieve the client's short- and long-term objectives. Second, a portfolio manager identifies appropriate investment vehicles—stocks, bonds, mutual funds, annuities, real estate, gold, and so on—thereby helping the planner complete the investment planning process.

An Insurance Counselor

An important dimension of asset protection is the purchase of life, disability, property, casualty, professional liability, long-term health care, and other forms of insurance. Also, in the event of an untimely death, a life insurance policy provides the liquidity for paying taxes and administrative expenses without imposing undue financial hardship on the surviving family. The financial planner is responsible for developing a coordinated risk management plan covering various types of insurance. The task of an insurance counselor is to select from a wide variety of those insurance products that are suited for the client.

Other Professionals

A financial planner works with other professionals as well, depending on the client's special needs and unique circumstances. These include trust officers, bank and credit advisors, real estate brokers, investment bankers, and human resource department representatives. In each instance, the planner's objective is to seek external assistance in order to enhance the overall value of the financial plan.

Summing Up

By establishing harmonious and productive relationships with traditional advisors, financial planners can provide valuable services for the client. If the activities of these advisors are well coordinated, it is possible to create a productive working environment that would ultimately benefit all parties: the client, the financial planner, and all the traditional advisors.

In an effort to promote a healthy cooperation between the financial planner and the traditional advisors, the financial planner should establish a rapport with the client and the existing advisors. This can be achieved only if the planner makes a firm commitment to the client and coordinates the activities of the traditional advisors to serve the client with distinction.

COMPETENCE

Financial planning continues to be an emerging profession. Consequently, what constitutes a well-qualified, objective financial planner is often debated. In this section, we will discuss this issue in terms of academic degrees, required credentials, and professional experience.

Academic Degrees

The most significant step in establishing financial planners' minimum standards of competence took place in the USA in June 1986 when the International Board for Standards and Practices of Certified Financial Planners (IBCFP) was officially launched. On February 1, 1994, the IBCFP changed its name to Certified Financial Planner Board of Standards, commonly known as the CFP Board. It may still be some time before the CFP Board succeeds in firmly establishing universally acceptable model curriculum guidelines for financial planning degree-granting institutions. Nevertheless, it is worth reviewing the current status of the model curriculum developed by the CFP Board and published in the CFP Board's *General Information Booklet*.

The CFP Board recognizes that in the practice of personal financial planning, the professional planner helps achieve the client's short- and long-range goals. To assume this responsibility, the planner should have a broad understanding of human experience, cultural values in the Indian society, business and finance, planning techniques, counseling issues and skills, and fiduciary obligations. Educational institutions should provide necessary education to develop the financial planners' understanding of such matters.

In order to guide educational institutions in their efforts to develop degree and certificate programs in financial planning, the CFP Board has developed the model curriculum guidelines. These guidelines are broad; they include studies in economics, finance, accounting, communication skills, business ethics, the legal environment of business, taxation, investments, computer sciences, and financial analysis. Subject matter and required competencies derive from a study of the practice of financial planners.[3] At present the completion of this, or a similar, curriculum leads to the granting of an undergraduate or a graduate degree in financial planning. Any person seriously considering financial planning as a career would be well advised to obtain a degree in financial planning. These guidelines, which gave way to job knowledge requirements of the Certified Financial Planner, are revised and updated every five years.

The Credentials

In 1986, when the CFP Board was formed, the CFP certification mark was transferred from the Denver-based College for Financial Planning (which since the 1970s had owned and granted the CFP certification marks) to the CFP Board. Initially, the CFP Board endorsed the passing of the six-part examination as a prerequisite to granting the CFP certification. Subsequently, however, the CFP Board replaced it with a single comprehensive examination comparable to the Bar and certified public accountant (CPA) examinations.

CFP® is not the only valid certification mark for practicing financial planning or providing advice for certain aspects of planning. In the USA there are several other credentials, all of which ensure that whoever possesses any one of them can perform financial planning services. These credentials include: ChFC (Chartered Financial Consultant), PFS (Personal Financial Specialist), and RFP

[3] L. Skurnik, *Job Analysis of the Professional Requirements of the Certified Financial Planner* (Denver: College of Financial Planning, 1987).

(Registered Financial Planner). Other financial services credentials include: CFA (Chartered Financial Analyst), CLU (Chartered Life Underwriter), CPA (Certified Public Accountant), and JD (Doctor of Jurisprudence).

The Experience

A candidate with a baccalaureate degree from an accredited college or university must fulfill the CFP Board's financial planning-related work experience requirement. The experience requirement can be completed either before or after meeting the examination requirement. A complete listing of experience requirements can be found in the CFP Board of Standard's *General Information Booklet.*

For purposes of this requirement, experience is defined as full-time (or equivalent part-time) employment in situations in which the candidate actively uses the knowledge, skills, and abilities required for the certification examination. Under this definition, experiences gained in corporate settings that directly relate to "personal financial planning" (such as those associated with an accountant, lawyer, banker, stockbroker, financial planner, insurance salesman, tax preparer, and so on) are accepted.

Continuing Education

The CFP Board of Standard's Licensee Manual specifies that each CFP licensee is required to fulfill 30 hours of continuing education (2014) every two years by completing programs that meet the specified requirements in two areas: (a) two credit hours in ethics as required by the CFP Board's Code of Ethics and Professional Responsibility and (b) the remaining 28 hours of continuing education in one or more of the following areas: fundamentals of financial planning, estate planning, investments, retirement planning, employee benefit planning, tax planning, and knowledge of the CFP Board's Code of Ethics and Professional Responsibility. Credits must be earned after a licensee's certification date and in the current two-year reporting period. Credits in excess of 30 hours required for the reporting period may not be carried over to the subsequent ones.

All CFP registrants are required to report continuing education credits to the CFP Board. The CFP Board requires satisfaction of the continuing education requirement as one of the standards for continued use of the certification marks, CFP® and Certified Financial Planner™. A specific set of rules has now been developed that automatically qualifies continuing education seminars. The CFP Board has established that the standards of continuing education must be (a) consistent with the standards for certification and marks usages (i.e., quality controlled), (b) meaningful and not financially burdensome or discriminatory, (c) protective of the public interest, and (d) effective as a means of helping so as to ensure continued competency as a financial planner.

Summing Up

A qualified practicing financial planner should: (a) earn an appropriate academic degree in financial planning, (b) possess the appropriate professional certification, and (c) meet continuing education requirements. Of course, these are necessary, but not sufficient, conditions for becoming a professional financial planner. Also, depending on the activities performed, the planner is also required to possess other appropriate licenses required by law.

In the final analysis, competent financial planners are entrusted with collecting detailed knowledge of clients' finances and personal financial goals. Clearly, financial planners are expected to be far more informed about their clients' financial, tax, economic, and legal statuses. Consequently, clients invariably depend on the skills, judgment, and guidance of their financial planners. Only competent financial planners deserve to earn their clients' complete trust.

COMMITMENT TO ETHICS

A *standard* definition of ethics is not very useful in defining the ethical standards by which financial planning professionals should conduct business. The reason is that there are well over 400 national associations, including medicine, law, and public accounting, all of which have published written codes. To this, one would have to add countless numbers of ethics codes among individual business firms, government bodies, and labor organizations in order to obtain a complete list of ethical standards applicable to financial planners.

Let there be no misunderstanding, however. To say that financial planners must maintain the highest levels of ethical standards is not intended to deny the fact that they are also entrepreneurs and profit maximizers. Against that backdrop, it is best to present the ethics in the following manner: A less-than-ethical financial planner concentrates on making money even when engaging in certain activities that could be detrimental to the client. In contrast, an ethical financial planner *always* serves the client's best interests and earns income as a by-product of that service.

We have observed earlier that financial planning is an emerging profession. As this profession continues to mature, a great deal is being written about financial planners' unethical practices, conflicts of interest, and self-serving activities. The water is muddied even further by the prevailing practices among many financial planners of both offering planning services and selling investment and insurance products. The establishment of the Disciplinary and Ethics Commission as an integral part of the CFP Board of Standards is in response to the deep concerns our society has toward unethical practices. However, it is also argued that guarding the sanctity of the CFP® mark and policing the ethical conduct of those who hold the mark are not sufficient to protect the consumer.

Some years ago, the most comprehensive ethical code in the financial planning profession was developed by the CFP Board of Standards. The *Code of Ethics and Professional Responsibility* was designed to provide principles and rules of conduct for all CFP® licensees. It contains principles which express the profession's recognition of its responsibilities to the public, clients, colleagues, and employers. These principles apply to all CFP® designees and provide ethical and professional guidance and ideals for them in the performance of their professional services.

The meaning of each principle is further explained as follows. The rules provide practical guidelines derived from the tenets embodied in the principles. These rules set forth the standards of ethical and professional conduct expected to be followed in particular situations. In addition, it is emphasized that due to the nature of a CFP® designee's particular field of endeavor, certain rules may not be applicable. The Code is structured so as to make parallel presentation of the rules and principles.[4]

It is obvious that the task of policing an unethical, self-designated, financial planners is complicated and should be left in the hands of regulatory agencies. However, we firmly believe that professional financial planners need to go far beyond the compliance of the minimum regulatory requirements. In our considered view, professional financial planners should also be:

E Efficient
T Trustworthy
H Honest
I Ingenious
C Completely loyal
S Sincer

[4] Principles and rules were extracted from the CFP Board's *Code of Ethics and Professional Responsibility*. A copy might be obtained by either calling the CFP Board at (800) 487-1497 or going to the CFP Board's website at www.CFP.net

That is, if financial planners make a firm commitment to be efficient, trustworthy, honest, ingenious, completely loyal, and sincere, then they will automatically maintain the highest levels of ethical standards. If that happens, then financial planning will be universally recognized as a venerable profession.

In order to provide competent and caring service to their clients, financial planners must also recognize the importance of the five "Cs" of financial planning:

Client:	Client interests must always come first.
Communication:	Communication is the key to motivate clients to implement plan recommendations.
Coordination:	Coordination among various professionals provides the highest quality of the overall planning service.
Competence:	Competence based on both education and experience is essential for professional performance.
Commitment to Ethics:	Commitment to ethics and professionalism is the basis for providing quality service.

As previously mentioned, in India personal financial planning is slowly coming of age. Today, the services of highly ethical and competent planning professionals are urgently needed.

In this chapter, we discussed general financial planning issues. The financial planning process and job tasks associated with each step in the process will be presented in the Chapter 2.

2 Personal Financial Planning Process

INTRODUCTION

In Chapter 1, we introduced the six-step financial planning process that is now widely adopted by the planning profession. A pictorial view of that process is shown in Figure 2.1.

In 2009, the US Certified Financial Planning (CFP) Board surveyed financial planning practitioners to gather evidence (CFP Board Technical Standard 14.14) to show that the "knowledge and skills being tested in the CFP® Exam are required for credential-worthy performance." In order to assess the readiness of certified financial planners to serve their clients, the survey asked participating financial planners to identify critical job-task activities in which they engaged in their practice. Based on the statistical analysis of their responses, the CFP Board instituted a major shift in focus in the CFP exam.

The most important shift in focus centered on the assessment criteria. From concentration on technical proficiency in arranging the pieces of the "financial planning puzzle," the focus shifted to the "job-task domain knowledge." The former consisted of the field knowledge of financial principles, insurance planning, investment planning, educational funding, tax planning, retirement planning, employee benefits planning, and estate planning. The focus then shifted to the processes, job-task activities, and content knowledge. Table 2.1

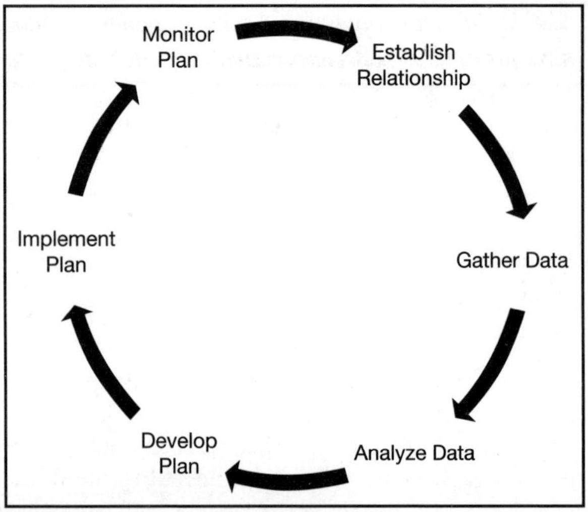

Figure 2.1 *The Six-step Financial Planning Process*

Table 2.1 *The Eight Job-task Domains*

Job-task Domains	
Domain 1	Establishing and defining the client–planner relationship
Domain 2	Gathering information necessary to fulfill the engagement
Domain 3	Analyzing and evaluating the client's current status
Domain 4	Developing recommendations
Domain 5	Communicating the recommendations
Domain 6	Implementing the recommendations
Domain 7	Monitoring the recommendations
Domain 8	Practicing within professional and regulatory standards

summarizes the resulting eight job-task domains, which closely integrate the financial planning process just presented.

In this chapter, we will discuss the nature of the planning process in general and the associated job tasks involved in offering each phase of comprehensive financial planning in particular. In our presentation, we will discuss the issues that arise before engaging the services of a financial planner; we will also analyze the activities related to the maintenance of an ongoing relationship with the client. Finally, to facilitate our discussion, we will wrap the personal financial planning process around 10 distinct steps:

1. Conduct initial interview and sign a formal engagement contract.
2. Gather client's qualitative and quantitative data, and collect the missing data.
3. Formulate reasonable planning assumptions to be used in analyzing the plan.
4. Analyze the current plan.
5. Evaluate alternative strategies and products.
6. Synthesize final recommendations.
7. Communicate final recommendations to the client.
8. Refine plan recommendations based on client feedback.
9. Implement the revised plan.
10. Monitor implementation progress while ensuring that all planning regulations are being met.

NATURE AND STRUCTURE OF ENGAGEMENT

Qualifying Potential Client

A financial planner begins the planning process by performing the initial job task of *qualifying* the potential client. Initially, the planner begins by asking probing questions, such as "Is this someone I wish to work with?" and "Do the needs of the client match my areas of competency and align with my business model?" In general, job-task activities associated with qualifying a potential client include the following:

1. Understanding client's goals, needs, circumstances, and expectations.
2. Describing the financial planning process to the prospective client.
3. Explaining the scope of the services to be provided.
4. Assessing the planner's ability to serve a client's needs.

An important *caveat* should be added here. While every *comprehensive* financial plan should complete all the 10 planning steps listed above, not all engagements have to achieve that level of sophistication. In fact, in the real world, financial planners offer services at different levels of complexity in order to accommodate clients with differing needs and goals. For instance, the American Institute of Certified Public Accountants (AICPA) has identified the following three levels of service: consultant engagements, segment planning engagements, and comprehensive personal financial engagements. Consultation is an informal or unstructured financial planning arrangement which explores the nature and depth of a financial problem by requiring a prospective client to fill out an initial financial profile (or pre-data gathering) form.

The consultation process generally ends with determining whether the client needs a more formal type of engagement, and it is communicated in the form of either an oral or a written report. Individual planners across the country refer to various levels and types of services by names such as retirement planning, investment planning, tax planning, and comprehensive financial planning. Regardless of the level or type of service performed, there is no substitute for a professional approach to every type of financial planning service.

Typically, an initial, informational interview is designed to qualify a potential client. During this interview, the focus is more on understanding qualitative issues (such as core values, goals, dreams, fears, and the degree of sophistication) than on collecting quantitative data (such as bank account values, insurance policies owned, investment portfolio, and so on). During this initial contact the planner might ask questions like the following: (a) What transpired in your life that persuaded you to see me? (b) What are your goals and dreams? (c) What types of people and things are most important to you? (d) What could we do for you so that a year from now you would consider our relationship to be successful? Qualitative questions like these help the planner determine if the profile of the person fits the planner's target clientele.

Of course, in all fairness, during this interview a potential client also has the right to collect critical information about the planner and the practice. For instance, a potential client might ask questions like the following: (a) How does your planning firm operate based on its core values and planning philosophy? (b) How would your planning services help me? (c) Why should I wish to establish of a long-term relationship with your planning practice? (d) Do I have to buy from you all the products that you recommend? In short, the informational interview is a two-way process: In this meeting the planner sizes up the client, while the client also performs due diligence on the planner. Here are two real-life examples that demonstrate the importance of qualifying a prospective client *before* starting the planning process.

Case Number 1

Ranjit Ghosh and his fiancée, Swapna Sarkar, are requesting a financial planner, Bipin Gupta, to develop a comprehensive financial plan for them. For past 20 years Ranjit was a registered pharmacist in Lucknow, but recently for health reasons he has been forced to move to Bengaluru. He has sold his pharmaceutical business in Lucknow and is contemplating buying a suitable business in Bengaluru. Swapna is a tenured school teacher in Agra and currently earns an annual salary of ₹60,000. She participates in the school's retirement benefit plan and enjoys the school's health insurance benefits. Ranjit and Swapna are planning to get married in a few months and settle down in Bengaluru. This is a second marriage for both, and between them there appears to be a great deal of understanding, flexibility, and open communication. Bipin Gupta's responsibility is to develop a comprehensive financial plan by assuming that Ranjit and Swapna are already married, even though officially they will not be married for several months.

The couple's situation is straightforward, or so it seems on the surface. But after the initial interview, Bipin realizes that his responsibility would have to extend far beyond developing a comprehensive financial plan for this couple. Ranjit Ghosh naively assumes that after marriage Swapna will quit her teaching job, lose her annual salary of ₹60,000 plus the associated teachers' fringe benefits, quietly settle down in Bengaluru, and be content playing the role of a full-time, devoted housewife.

Unfortunately, Swapna Sarkar views the situation very differently. She recognizes that after marriage, she will lose all of the following: (a) An annual salary of ₹60,000 plus future increments, (b) school's retirement contribution, (c) all of her fringe benefits, (d) financial independence, (d) her home in Agra, which would have to be sold at a significant loss, and (e) option to retire at the age of 59 with full retirement benefits, currently offered by her school system to all employees with at least 25 years of service. Swapna also resents the fact that Ranjit opposes financing her daughter's education at an expensive school like the IIT in Kanpur where she is confident of getting admission. As a fair compensation for all of the above-mentioned potential losses, before tying the knot, Swapna expects Ranjit to pay her at least ₹2 lakh. The problem with such an expectation is that Ranjit totally rejects that demand and considers that subject out of bounds. The only thing Ranjit is willing to do is to take the financial responsibility for Swapna's daughter, and that too only after marriage.

The potential problem in this case should now be obvious. If Bipin accepts this couple as his client, his task would be far more complicated than what he initially perceived. In fact, he now realizes that by accepting this client he would become loaded with psychological and emotional issues, a task he is ill-equipped to handle. This case clearly illustrates the importance of collecting qualitative data as a prelude to accepting a new client.

Case Number 2

Mohan Kulkarni, 52, and Suvarna Kulkarni, 49, are a happily married couple. They have three children, aged 28, 25, and 23. Both Mohan and Suvarna fear that their financial situation is in shambles, and they strongly feel the need for a financial planner to bring order to their chaotic financial situation. The Kulkarnis are requesting Ram Desai to develop a financial plan for them and are willing to pay a handsome planning fee for that service.

During the initial interview, Mohan insisted that his mother's net worth (in excess of ₹5 lakh) be treated as an integral part of their financial assets. After briefly reviewing Kulkarnis' financial information Ram concludes that, with the exception of Mohan's unusual suggestion, the case appears to be straightforward.

The situation soon begins to get cloudy, however, as the interview progresses, and Ram discovers some very interesting facts. Mohan, now 52, is currently unemployed. Yet, he has no intentions of returning to work, because he claims that since he is the only child, he will inherit his mother's entire estate worth ₹5 lakh. Mohan even argues that since his mother is already 75 years old, he will *soon* have all of her money; hence, it makes no sense for him to go back to work now. But this fact alone has become a source of great friction between the couple. Suvarna strongly believes that Mohan should not count on receiving this money any time soon, if at all, because his mother could still live for a long time and could even lose all of her wealth through bad investments, due to escalating medical expenses, or even through donation to her favorite charity. And that creates a big planning headache: Mohan wants Ram to include his mother's net worth in their plan; Suvarna opposes that idea.

There is yet another family matter that is the source of an enormous friction between Mohan and Suvarna. All three of their children are now grown-up adults and should be settled in their respective lives. Unfortunately, none of them has more than a high school education, regular employment, or even any normal means of support. The oldest one has a complicated health problem, but physically the other two are healthy. All three children live at home and are fully dependent on their parents for financial support. Mohan is very upset with the current situation and believes that the only way to resolve this problem is *to throw the children out of the house and force them to become responsible human beings.* Suvarna, however, feels that since the failure is in fact on the part of the parents, they should set up a separate trust for each of the three children and start funding them.

As if that is not enough, there is also an emotional problem that impacts on the family's current financial situation. Since Mohan is unemployed and Suvarna is compelled to be the sole breadwinner, she wants her salary to be spent solely on herself and does not want it to be used for supporting the family. Mohan disagrees with that approach, since in his judgment, family finances should never be split in that fashion.

And so, judging from the facts just presented, to Ram Desai this case looks like a financial nightmare, with no sensible way of untangling the cobweb that envelops the family. Against this backdrop, Ram needs to decide if he should even consider accepting the Kulkarnis as his long-term clients.

Based on these two hypothetical cases, it is apropos to make a few general observations concerning the running of a successful financial planning practice. Regardless of their orientation and expectations, initially what clients really need is a *subjective*, rather than an *objective*, perspective of their personal finances. Truly speaking, a financial planner should be well versed with the mechanics of plan development and implementation. But, the planner should also be able to blend mechanical expertise with human understanding in developing acceptable solutions that will best serve the clients. In the final analysis, then, the long-term success of a planning process is assured only when a financial planner is able to establish an honest, open, and professional relationship with the *right type of clients.*

Engagement Letter

Once both the financial planner and the prospective client decide to establish a professional relationship between them, it is time to sign a formal contract, commonly known as the engagement letter. This letter should include the following:

1. Client and planner identification and signatures.
2. Documentation of the scope of engagement.
3. List of planner and client responsibilities.
4. Terms of contract and the method of termination.
5. Disclosure of the existing and potential conflicts of interest.
6. Supply of additional relevant material to client.
7. Compensation arrangements.
8. Required disclosures, including applicable regulations.

At this point, the financial planner is obliged to provide the client with a planning brochure. This brochure describes the financial planning services being offered. After the brochure has been supplied, the client can take time to study the contract and, if desired, have it reviewed by an attorney. If the client is fully satisfied with the contract and is ready to sign it, it suggests that both parties have made a decision to establish a long and fruitful relationship. The signing of the engagement letter by both parties completes all the initial signing rituals and signals the initiation of the next phase of the financial planning process.

COLLECT QUALITATIVE AND QUANTITATIVE DATA

The second phase of planning begins with data collection. The nature and extent of data required depend on the desired degree of sophistication of the financial plan. For instance, the collection of data required to create only an investment management plan would be much less extensive than that required to formulate a full-blown comprehensive plan.

Qualitative Data

The first phase of data collection deals with the "inside" or qualitative issues. Each client is unique, and the planner must have a good handle on a client's perspective on financial challenges before collecting "outside" or quantitative data. Typically, qualitative data are collected via free-flowing conversations with a client. For the sake of efficiency, such a conversation can be based on a carefully crafted questionnaire to assist the client think through the key issues on which a planner wishes to concentrate. In most cases, in sizing up a client's overall financial situation, qualitative data may include the following:

1. Client's current core values, beliefs, and attitudes (important and not-so- important items, fears, expectations, and dreams).
2. Prioritized goals.
3. Time horizon for each goal.
4. The level of risk tolerance.
5. Preferences and constraints.
6. Client's knowledge and experience in dealing with financial issues.
7. Special family circumstances.
8. Risk exposures (such as family health history, job security, participation in dangerous hobbies, and so on).

Very early in the planning process, the financial planner needs to develop a clear picture of a client's goals. And since clients rarely face a single goal, an understanding of the client's priorities among multiple goals becomes of paramount importance. In essence, challenging clients to reflect on this financial situation: (a) forces them to think clearly, (b) helps them identify all of their major goals, (c) establishes a rational basis for charting a course of action, (d) encourages them to prioritize their goals, and (e) directs them to articulate their time frame for achieving these goals.

Quantitative Data

Quantitative data provide a detailed view of a client's current and projected financial situation. Typical sources and key documents of quantitative data consist of the following:

1. *Assets, liabilities, and cash flow information:*
   (a) Sources and amounts of income.
   (b) Itemization of outflows.
   (c) Investments (balances, basis, titling, and beneficiaries).
2. *Current account statements:*
   (a) Bank statements.
   (b) Investment and brokerage statements.
   (c) Retirement Accounts Statements .
   (d) Credit card statements.
   (e) Cash value in permanent life policies.
3. *Loan statements (terms, balances, and costs) and leases:*
   (a) Home mortgage.
   (b) Home equity.
   (c) Auto loan.
   (d) School loans.
   (e) Private loans.
   (f) Rental leases.
4. *Insurance policies and employee benefits package:*
   (a) Life insurance contracts.
   (b) Health insurance policies (health, disability, and long-term care).
   (c) Property/casualty policies.
   (d) Liability policies.
   (e) Employer medical benefits package.
5. *Income tax statements (several years with all schedules).*
6. *Employee pension statements and benefits package:*
   (a) Plan statements.
   (b) Employer retirement benefits package.
7. *Estate and legal documents:*
   (a) Latest will.
   (b) Powers of attorney.

(c) Living wills.
(d) Trust agreements.
(e) Prenuptial arrangement.
(f) Divorce decree.

8. *Titling documents:*

(a) Deeds.
(b) Contracts.
(c) Titles.

9. *Business documents:*

(a) Corporation or partnership documents.
(b) Business income tax returns.
(c) Financial statements (balance sheet, income statement).
(d) Stock purchase agreements.
(e) Employment agreements.
(f) Employee medical and retirement benefit programs.
(g) Leases.

Quantitative data are typically collected via a fact-finding questionnaire, samples of which can be easily found on the web.

Collection of Additional Information

Frequently, financial planners discover that major gaps exist in the submitted questionnaire. These gaps must be filled before proceeding further. Since collecting reliable information is of utmost importance, financial planners use a checklist similar to the one listed below:

1. Client circumstances (e.g., family history, prioritized goals and objectives, time horizons, network of friends and associates, and job stability).
2. Data relating to values, beliefs and attitudes, risk preferences, constraints and preferences, and interests and hobbies.
3. Quantitative data for each of the planning areas such as budgeting, risk management, insurance coverage and employee benefits, investment planning, funding for higher education, tax planning, retirement planning and employee benefits, estate planning, and closely held business planning.
4. List of professional advisers such as a chartered accountant, a banker, an insurance professional, and a stockbroker.

As stated, collecting missing data can become a challenging task. The client might have difficulty obtaining the employer benefits package or fail to locate the original investment records. In these and other related instances, recognizing that clients frequently find the task of locating missing data daunting, the planner should assist them in completing the task. Taking the time to explain why these data are vital for developing a plan might alleviate a client's anxiety.

Sometimes even the best efforts to collect the missing data will fall short. In such cases, the CFP Board's guidance published in its Standards of Practice might come in handy:

> If the practitioner is unable to obtain sufficient and relevant quantitative information and documents to form a basis for recommendations, the practitioner shall either (a) restrict the scope of the engagement to those matters for which sufficient and relevant information is available, or terminate the engagement.

DEVELOP ASSUMPTIONS/ANALYZE FINANCIAL DATA

After completing the data collection task, a planner can begin analyzing financial and non-financial data. This requires the development of reasonable and supportable assumptions, indeed a delicate and arduous process.

The process begins by making basic assumptions by either the client or the planner, or both. For instance, in one situation, a client might decide to send his/her son to an expensive school regardless of whether or not he/she can afford it. In another, the client and the planner might choose to jointly map out the nature and the degree of the client's risk tolerance. However, technical assumptions such as investment returns, correlations, inflation-rate expectations, and future costs of health care generally fall in the planner's domain.

It is logical to assume that for every financial plan to be credible and effective, it must be based on *reasonable* assumptions. Aggressive and unrealistic assumptions (such as very high investment growth rate, low education costs, etc.) invariably lead to disappointing outcomes. But if a client still insists on making such aggressive assumptions, a planner must clearly explain the consequences of such behavior.

Here is an example that explains the attendant risk. Based solely on the fact that both his father and grandfather died before 50 of heart attack, a client directs a planner to develop his financial plan assuming that he will die before the age of 60. While that could well turn out to be true, in creating a long-term financial plan it is inadvisable to make such a short-sighted assumption. In such a situation, the planner must use powers of persuasion to change the client's mind.

Modification of unrealistic goals constitutes a serious challenge for a financial planner. This is necessarily so, because to solve these types of problems, psychological, emotional, and social factors may need to be handled, all of which are clearly beyond the expertise of most financial planners. Consider, for instance, a client with a lavish lifestyle who wishes to retire early. While under the right circumstances this might possibly be a lofty goal, it is a prescription for disaster if retirement income and available savings fall short of what is needed to support such a lifestyle. Here again, a serious discussion of all the relevant factors between a planner and a client could possibly save the day.

As mentioned, in developing a comprehensive financial plan, a financial planner, in collaboration with a client, needs to make a set of realistic assumptions. The key assumptions include:

1. *Client-specified assumptions:*

   (a) Goal prioritization.
   (b) Tolerance for risk.
   (c) Special situations (e.g., planning for dependents with special needs).

2. *Budgeting assumptions:*

   (a) Projected incomes (amounts and risk of income volatility).
   (b) Monthly expenses.
   (c) Timing and future cost of planned major expenditures.
   (d) Annual living expense needs.

3. *Health assumptions:*

   (a) Longevity expectations.
   (b) Family health risk factors.
   (c) Projected health care costs.

4. *Economic and investment-related assumptions:*

   (a) Reinvestment rates.
   (b) Future volatility and correlation data.
   (c) Business cycle forecasts.

5. *Inflation and interest rate assumptions.*
6. *Higher education assumptions:*
   (a) Type of school a children (or a child) will attend.
   (b) Client's funding plans.
   (c) Future cost of schooling.
7. *Tax planning assumptions:*
   (a) Change in tax rates and brackets (legislation).
   (b) Charitable wishes.
8. *Retirement planning assumptions:*
   (a) Desired age of retirement.
   (b) Retirement income needs.
   (c) Longevity in retirement.
   (d) Sources and projected level of systematic income.
9. *Estate planning assumptions:*
   (a) Family boundaries.
   (b) Client's distribution and privacy wishes.
   (c) Legacy wishes of client (e.g., rupee amounts).
10. *Business assumptions:*
   (a) Future valuation.
   (b) Disposition wishes.

ANALYSIS OF ALTERNATE SOLUTIONS

CFP Board Practice Standard 400-1 states: "A financial planning practitioner shall consider sufficient and relevant *alternatives* to the client's current course of action in an effort to reasonably meet the client's goals, needs and priorities." Consistent with this mandate, a planner begins by considering alternative ways of accomplishing the stated goals. This is done by running *what if* simulation tests which take the form of analyzing the results of asking, "What is feasible?" Results of these tests help determine the most *efficient* ways of achieving a client's desired objectives; in turn, these results establish a basis for formulating sound planning recommendations. This style of integrated analysis brings the plan to life and makes the planning process truly meaningful.

Job tasks associated with this stage of the process include:

1. Reflection on shortcomings and gaps of the current plan.
2. Alternative strategies and products.
3. Evaluation of the impact of suggested recommendations on other parts of the plan.
4. Management of future uncertainties.
5. Consultation with other professionals.
6. Identification of actions that align with a client's values, attitudes, beliefs, and behavioral finance issues while simultaneously achieving stated goals.
7. Documentation of recommendations.

The following illustrations demonstrate the creative use of the "What is possible?" technique.

of a plan: (a) Strengths and weakness, (b) existing gaps, (c) possibilities that some of the goals would not be attained, and (d) misinterpretation of the nature of a client's risk tolerance, reluctance to effectively move forward with plan implementation, and other key concerns not picked up in previous sessions.

In assessing each content area, planners should employ their content knowledge, and experience; utilize planning tools such as calculators, software programs, ratio analysis, and trend analysis; and employ various planning tools (discussed in subsequent chapters). Following is a demonstration of the application of SWOT (strengths, weaknesses, opportunities, and threats) analysis.

Nita (aged 30) and Nalin Sachdev (aged 32) have engaged Amit Chaudhery to develop a risk-management plan for them. As part of his task on hand, Amit: (a) reviews their individual insurance policies and employee benefit items, (b) identifies glaring gaps in their total risk-management plan, (c) determines if at least the risk-management basics are covered by these plans, and (d) evaluates the current coverage vis-à-vis the clients' specific needs. When analyzing the insurance coverage, Amit critically examines the "red flag" items which include the following:

1. *Life insurance:*
   - (a) Benefit amount too low relative to their needs.
   - (b) Type of plan that does not meet their needs (e.g., term insurance when client has a need for permanent insurance).
   - (c) Coverage dependent solely on continued employment (e.g., group term life).
   - (d) Beneficiary designations that do not reflect a client's wishes.
2. *Health care coverage:*
   - (a) Lack of adequate coverage, creating catastrophic risk exposure.
   - (b) Low lifetime caps.
   - (c) High stop losses.
3. *Disability:*
   - (a) Inadequate income replacement.
   - (b) Insufficient benefit period.
   - (c) Unacceptably long waiting period.
   - (d) Restrictive access to coverage.
4. *Homeowner's coverage:*
   - (a) Home not fully covered.
   - (b) Missing important riders.
5. *Auto coverage:*
   - (a) Inadequate liability coverage for family risk exposures.
   - (b) Insufficient auto coverage.
6. *Liability:*
   - (a) Insufficient coverage based on a client's net worth and exposures.
   - (b) Failure to maintain adequate underlying liability coverage.

Clearly, the "SWOT and gap" analyses provide an efficient means of conducting a systematic review of client's risk-management coverage. In this context, a planner moves through each content area looking for the existing gaps in coverage. That, in turn, helps the planner determine the best means of closing or limiting these insurance-related gaps.

IMPLEMENTATION OF RECOMMENDATIONS

Even the best-laid financial plan falls by the wayside if the benefits of implementing a planner's recommendations are not effectively communicated to a client. For this reason, the planner needs to develop strong oral and written communication skills. In this context, it is best to remember that engagement with a client is a collaborative effort. In the final analysis, the planner needs to wear many hats, including those of a counselor, a teacher, a mentor, an advocate, a sounding board, and of course, an effective communicator.

Important job tasks associated with planners playing these important roles include the following:

1. Plan presentation.
2. Education of a client.
3. Receipt of client feedback.
4. Modification of recommendations based on client feedback and new information.
5. Documentation of recommendations.
6. Discharge responsibility for appropriate disclosures.
7. Verification of client acceptance of recommendations.

PLAN IMPLEMENTATION TIMELINE

In making recommendations a planner should take great pains in emphasizing that his or her conflict of interest played no part in generating plan recommendations and that a client is under no obligation to implement these recommendations through the planner. Additionally, a planner should emphasize that to derive full benefits these recommendations must be implemented in a timely fashion. All too frequently, the ultimate success of a financial plan depends on the speed and the efficiency with which the recommendations are implemented.

Normally, at the time of engagement, a planner agrees to assist a client in implementing plan recommendations. If that is the case, the planner has assumed the following task responsibilities.

1. Creating a prioritized implementation timeline (i.e., an action list).
2. Assigning planner and client implementation responsibilities.
3. Supporting the client (directly or indirectly).
4. Coordinating activities with other parties (as authorized).
5. Defining client and planning monitoring responsibilities.

Plan Revisions

In most instances, following a plan presentation, clients require further clarification and often show resistance to adopting certain recommendations. In these situations, it is best that planners exhibit understanding, empathy, and care. After all, as already stated, the client–planner engagement for the long term is a collaborative process, and feedback and revisions are but an integral part of that process.

Based on the mutually agreed set of revisions, a planner makes the necessary adjustments and resubmits the revised plan to the client for further consideration and final acceptance. In this process, the final step for a planner is to create a detailed checklist (Table 2.2) that specifies what actions need to be taken, when to be taken, and by whom. Once the action plan is formally accepted, the client effectively takes the "ownership" of the plan.

Table 2.2 *Sample of a Detailed Checklist to Be Created by a Planner*

Action Checklist		
Action Items	**By Whom**	**By When**
Purchase ₹1 lakh term life insurance	Client, agent	March 21
Increase personal insurance policy to ₹5 lakh	Client, agent	March 21
Start an educational plan	Client, planner	June 15
Update will	Client, attorney	April 30

MONITOR AND REVIEW THE PLAN

Personal financial planning is an ongoing process. Over time, a client's personal situation, specific goals, financial conditions, and the economic and tax environments—some or all of these—can and do change. Consequently, a client's progress toward achieving short- and long-range goals specified in the plan should be constantly monitored, and the client should be kept abreast of the changes that could affect the plan's progress. In addition, a periodic review and revision of the plan's recommendations are essential for establishing financial planning as a long-term process. There are, of course, no universal guidelines on how frequently these reviews should be conducted. A typical time cycle is an annual update with a provision for more frequent reviews whenever changes in personal, financial, or economic conditions warrant them.

More specifically, a planner should periodically review a plan and determine if changes in one or more of the following factors are likely to change the plan's outcome: tax laws, economic conditions, investment products and techniques, family situation (e.g., birth, death, divorce, etc.), the physical condition of family members (e.g. disability), and employment. In addition, a planner should reevaluate the original objectives to determine whether they, too, have changed. Clearly, the reason for undertaking these periodic reviews should be to ensure that the plan remains current and effective.

Planners accepting the responsibility for monitoring a plan are involved in performing the following job tasks:

1. Assessing changes in client circumstances (e.g., change in employment, change in family boundaries, etc.).
2. Reviewing plan performance.
3. Analyzing plan progress against benchmarks.
4. Monitoring changes in the legal, economic, and tax environments.
5. Providing ongoing client support.
6. Adapting recommendations to changes in client circumstances.
7. Redefining the scope of engagement.

PROFESSIONAL AND REGULATORY STANDARDS

There is an old adage, "Clients don't care how much you know until they know how much you care." Clients expect a planner to take necessary actions whenever conditions so warrant. After all, occasionally the stock market does sell off and publicized improprieties by a few so-called professionals do continue to taint public's trust in financial service industries. For these and other related reasons, clients do tend to seek the assistance of knowledgeable and caring professionals who they can trust on.

Clearly, such an environment creates a unique opportunity for ethical and knowledgeable planning professionals. In offering financial planning services as a CFP® practitioner, a planner is held to a higher fiduciary standard. Operating as a fiduciary sends a strong message to the ever-anxious planning clients. Of course, it is not simply adhering to rules that count, but embracing the professional and regulatory standards protect the public as well.

CFP's job-task domain 8 focuses on the environment in which all financial planners offer their services. Specific job tasks require that planners satisfy the following:

1. Adherence to CFP Board's Code of Ethics, Professional Responsibility, and Rules of Conduct.
2. Understanding CFP Board's Disciplinary Rules and Procedures.
3. Working within CFP Board's Financial Planning Standards.
4. Managing practice management risk (e.g., document client data and communications).
5. Complying with regulatory and legal guidelines.
6. Maintaining an awareness of regulatory and legal issues.

In this chapter, we have presented an overview of the personal financial planning process and associated job tasks. Next, we will undertake a detailed analysis of the time value of money, *a core concept that flows through all aspects of financial planning.*

3 Time Value of Money: The Universal Tool

INTRODUCTION

We have observed that a planner's primary goal is to optimize a client's financial welfare by analyzing seven critical areas:

1. Budget planning.
2. Educational planning.
3. Insurance planning.
4. Investment planning.
5. Income tax planning.
6. Retirement planning.
7. Estate planning.

A common theme permeating these seven planning areas is the calculation of cash flow values over various time periods. In fact, of all the techniques used in financial planning, none is more important than the calculation of the value of money over time, *also known as the time value of money* (TVM) *concept*. In this chapter, we will discuss in detail the conceptual framework of the TVM concept and its critical applications.

SIMPLE INTEREST

Simple interest provides a quick method for calculating the interest charged (or received) on a loan (or investment). It is determined by multiplying the interest rate by the principal amount by the number of periods. Always stated on an annual basis, this interest is calculated by:

$$I = P \times R \times N \tag{3.1}$$

where

I = Simple interest
P = Principal
R = Rate of interest
N = Time period for which the principal is invested or lent.

Thus, the simple interest on ₹1,000.00 for 35 days at 11 percent is ₹10.55:

$$I = [₹1,000.00 \times 0.11] \times 35/365$$
$$= ₹10.55.$$

FUTURE VALUE: FIXED SUM

Multiple Year Annual Compounding

A rupee invested today would earn interest, and next year it would be worth more than one rupee. During the second year, the original rupee would earn interest, and *the interest earned during the first year would also earn interest.* To illustrate this process, called *compounding*, assume Shilpa Sharma deposited ₹1,000 in a bank certificate of deposit (CD) that paid 10 percent interest, compounded annually. How much money would she have at the end of two years?

The future value of a fixed sum is calculated by:

$$FV = PV\,(1+r)^n \tag{3.2}$$

where

FV = The *future value* of the investment at the end of n years
PV = The value of the investment today, or *present value*
r = The interest rate during each compounding period
n = The number of years, or compounding periods.

We can use Equation (3.2) to determine the value of ₹1,000 at the end of two years, compounded annually at 10 percent:

$$\begin{aligned} FV &= ₹1{,}000\,(1+0.10)^2 \\ &= ₹1{,}000 \times 1.21 \\ &= ₹1{,}210.00. \end{aligned}$$

If the CD had a maturity date after 10 years, then the original investment of ₹1,000 would grow to ₹2,593.74:

$$\begin{aligned} FV &= ₹1{,}000\,(1+0.10)^{10} \\ &= ₹1{,}000 \times 2.59374 \\ &= ₹2{,}593.74. \end{aligned}$$

Fortunately, we can use financial calculators to calculate the future values of a fixed sum for various interest rates and maturity periods. Figure 3.1 shows how a fixed sum of money grows over time at various interest rates. As expected, the higher the interest rate and/or the longer the compounding period, the larger is the future value of a fixed sum at the end of the investment period.

At this point, we would like to introduce the topic relating to the use of calculators. The most popular financial calculators are: HP-12C (Platinum), HP-10B II Plus, HP-17B II Plus, and Texas Instruments BA II Plus. In this chapter, for solving various financial problems, we have selected the HP-12C Platinum Financial Calculator because it is considered a classic. This calculator can be efficiently used to answer standard questions in personal finance: How much one has to save to achieve goals like financing college costs or generate retirement income? How big a mortgage should one be able to afford? How would interest rate changes affect monthly payments on an adjustable loan? Is it better to buy or lease a car? Should an investor whose income falls within a certain marginal tax bracket prefer a tax-exempt investment over a taxable investment?

Details regarding features of other calculators (HP-10B II Plus, HP-17B II Plus, and Texas Instruments BA II Plus) can be easily found at their manufacturer's website and on the Internet. Each of them can be used for financial calculations demonstrated in this textbook using the HP-12C Platinum Financial Calculator.

The keyboard of the HP-12C calculator is reproduced in Figure 3.2. The calculator keyboard (not shown in this figure) has three colors: white, gold, and blue. Two keys, one labeled "f" (gold) and the

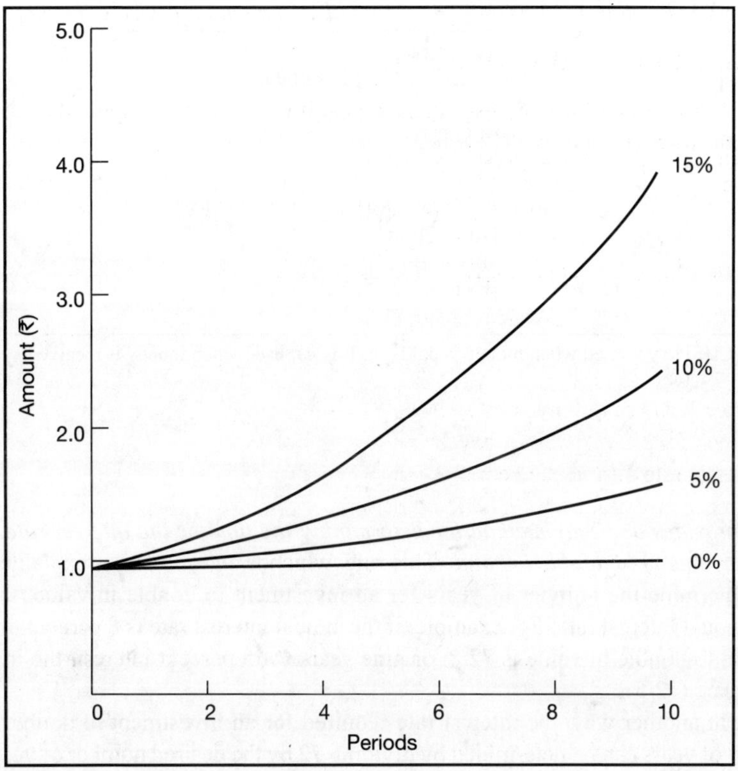

Figure 3.1 *Future Value of a Fixed Sum over Time*

other "g" (blue), match the colors of the keyboard. These keys (shown above the key or the face of a key in the appropriate color code) access specific operation modes of the calculator. The power key is labeled "ON." When the [ON] key is pressed, several zeros and a decimal point (0.00000) appear in the window. The calculator can be cleared by pressing [f] followed by [CLX]. The gold lettering above CLX reads REG. Above this appears a gold bar with the word CLEAR. Knowing that the gold [f] accesses the gold operation mode, it is possible to recognize that **[f] [CLX]** *clears the register (display)*.

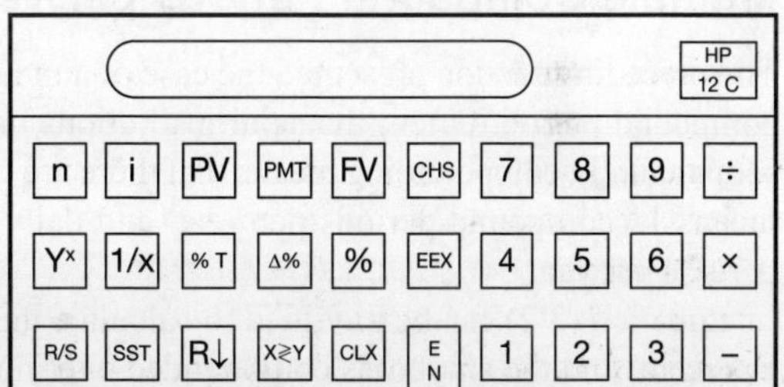

Figure 3.2 *HP-12C Calculator Keypad*

To set the number of decimal places, [f] and the number of decimal places desired are pressed. For example, [f] [4] results in 0.0000; pressing [f] [2] gives you 0.00.

The value of a ₹1,000 CD earning 10 percent and maturing in 10 years can be calculated by using the HP-12C calculator, as demonstrated in Table 3.1.

In a present/future value problem, four variables are involved, namely (a) present value, (b) future value, (c) interest, and (d) number of years (periods). If any three variables are known, the value of the fourth variable can be easily calculated.

Table 3.1 *Finding the Future Value (Annual Compounding) Using a Calculator*

Step 1:	Identify known variables:
	Future value: ₹1,000
	Interest: 10%
	Number of periods: 10 years
Step 2:	Clear calculator [f] [CLX]
Step 3:	Enter data
	Press [1] [0] [0] [0] [CHS] [PV]
	[10] [*i*]
	[10] [*n*]
	[FV]
	Answer: ₹2,593.74

Note: [CHS] key is used when money is paid out. It is *not* used when money is received.

Rule of 72

The Rule of 72 provides a speedy method for determining the time or the interest rate required for an investment (or any index) to double in value. This rule, which is an estimate, is explained next.

In order to determine the number of years for an investment to double in value, the number 72 is divided by the annual interest rate. For example, if the annual interest rate is 8 percent, the time required for an investment to double in value is 72/8, or nine years. At 5 percent interest, the investment would double in 14.4 years (72/5).

Looking at it in another way, the interest rate required for an investment to double in value over a specified number of years can be determined by dividing 72 by the desired number of years. For instance, if Anjan Narasimham wishes to double his investment in 10 years, over that period he must invest the principal to earn an interest rate of 7.2 percent (72/10), compounded annually.

Multiple Compound Periods per Year

The preceding section presented the case of annual compounding, where each year consisted of only one compound period. Often, financial institutions use more frequent compounding periods. For example, semiannually compounding means that there are two compound periods per year, monthly compounding means 12 compound periods per year, and daily compounding indicates that there are 365 compound periods per year.

Equation (3.2) can be modified to calculate the compound value of ₹1,000 after n years if invested at r percent, and the amount is compounded over multiple periods per year (m):

$$\text{FV} = \text{PV}\,(1 + r_{nom/m})^{mn} \tag{3.3}$$

where

r_{nom} = Declared interest rate, or nominal interest rate
m = Number of compounding periods per year
n = Total number of years.

Using Equation (3.3), we can calculate the FV for ₹1,000 after two years, which is invested at 10 percent, compounded quarterly:

$$\begin{aligned}\text{FV} &= ₹1{,}000\,(1 + 0.10/4)^{4\times 2}\\ &= ₹1{,}218.40.\end{aligned}$$

Table 3.2 *Finding the Future Value (Quarterly Compounding) Using a Calculator*

Step 1:	Identify known variables:						
	Present value:			₹1,000			
	Interest:			10%/quarterly (4)			
	Number of periods:			2 years × quarterly (4)			
Step 2:	Clear calculator [f] [CLX]						
Step 3:	Enter data						
	Press	[1]	[0]	[0]	[0]	[CHS]	[PV]
		[10]	[ENTER]	[4]	[÷]	[i]	
		[2]	[ENTER]	[4]	[X]	[n]	
		[FV]					
	Answer: ₹1,218.40						

The same answer could be obtained by using the HP-12C calculator, as demonstrated in Table 3.2.

Note that, as expected, the *quarterly* compounding resulted in a higher value of ₹1,218.40 as compared to the *annual* compounding value of ₹1,210.00. Clearly, the more frequent the compounding period, the larger is the final compound amount, because interest is earned on interest more often. Values of other compounding periods (PV = ₹1,000, $r = 10$ percent, $n = 2$ years) are given in Table 3.3.

Table 3.3 *Values of Other Compounding Periods*

Type of Compounding	Future Value (₹)
Annual	1,210.00
Semiannual	1,215.51
Quarterly	1,218.40
Daily	1,221.37

These relationships are illustrated in Figure 3.3.

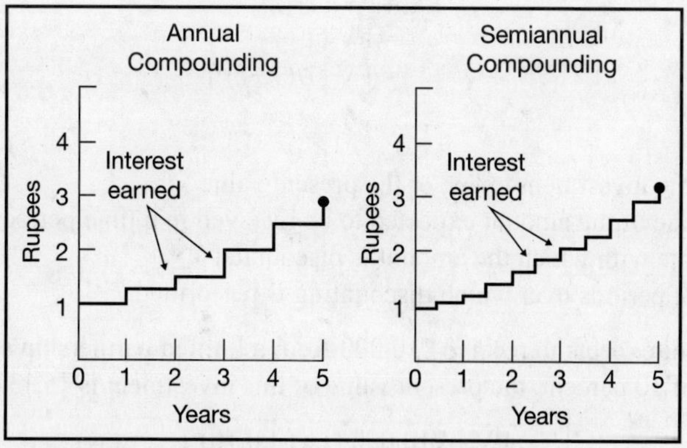

Figure 3.3 *The Future Value of a Fixed Sum Using Multiple Compound Periods per Year*

PRESENT VALUE: FIXED SUM

A rupee in hand today is worth more than a rupee to be received next year because, if gainfully invested, it would earn interest, and the next year it would be worth more than a rupee. For instance, if ₹100 is invested at 5 percent, after one year the amount would grow to ₹105. Put differently, the *present value* of ₹105 expected to be received next year, *discounted* for one year at 5 percent, is ₹100. In general, the present value of a sum invested at y percent and due in n periods in the future is the amount which—if it were on hand today and invested at y percent for n years—would grow to equal the future sum. The concept of discounting a future value to arrive at the present value of a fixed sum is presented in Figure 3.4.

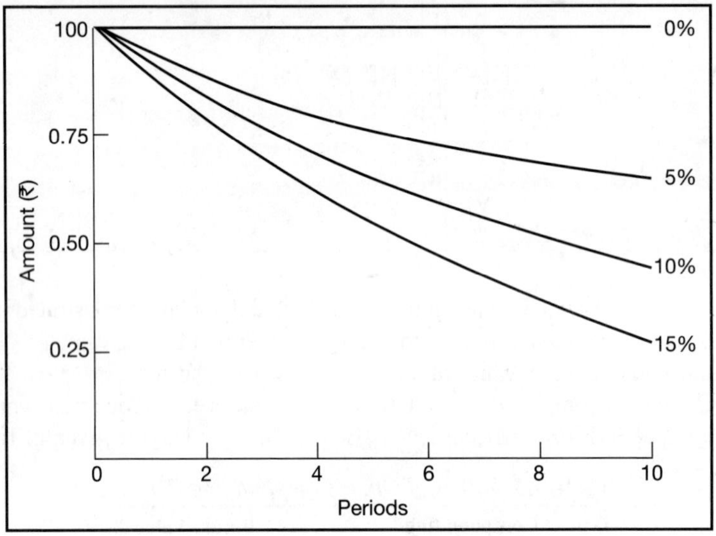

Figure 3.4 *Present Value of a Fixed Sum over Time*

Finding the present value—or *discounting,* as it is technically called—is merely the reverse of compounding. For instance, the future value equation is:

$$FV = PV\,(1+r)^n \qquad \text{(3.2 restated)}$$

Solving for PV, we obtain

$$\begin{aligned} PV &= FV/(1+r)^n \\ &= FV\,(1+r)^{-n} \\ &= FV\,[1/(1+r)^n] \end{aligned}$$

where

PV = The value of the investment today, or the present value
FV = The future value of the amount expected to be received in n time periods
r = The interest rate with which the amount is discounted
n = The number of periods over which discounting is performed.

For instance, an investor expects to receive ₹10,000 from a limited partnership seven years from today. Using a discount rate of 10 percent, the present value of this investment is ₹5,132:

$$\begin{aligned} PV &= ₹10{,}000\,[1/(1+0.10)^7] \\ &= ₹10{,}000 \times 0.5132 \\ &= ₹5{,}132. \end{aligned}$$

As expected, by using the calculator we obtain the same result, as can be seen from Table 3.4.

Table 3.4 *Finding the Present Value of a Fixed Sum (Annual Compounding) Using Calculator*

Step 1:	Identify known variables:	
	Future value:	₹10,000
	Interest:	10%
	Number of periods:	7 years
Step 2:	Clear calculator [f] [CLX]	
Step 3:	Enter data	
	Press [1] [0] [0] [0] [0] [FV]	
	[1] [0] [*i*]	
	[7] [*n*]	
	[PV]	
	Answer: ₹5,131.58	

Note: [CHS] key is used when money is being received.

The PV concept is also useful in determining how much must be invested today at, say, 8 percent in order to accumulate ₹15,000 five years from today to fund a child's education:

$$\begin{aligned} PV &= ₹15{,}000\ [1/(1+0.08)^5] \\ &= ₹15{,}000 \times 0.6806 \\ &= ₹10{,}209. \end{aligned}$$

Since PV is a mirror reflection of FV, ₹10,209 invested at 8 percent should grow to ₹15,000 in five years:

$$\begin{aligned} FV &= ₹10{,}209\ (1+08)^5 \\ &= ₹10{,}209 \times 1.4693 \\ &= ₹15{,}000. \end{aligned}$$

Clearly, if interest was compounded *quarterly* and the investor wanted to find out how much must be invested today at 8 percent to accumulate ₹15,000 five years from today, the PV calculation would be as follows:

$$\begin{aligned} PV &= ₹15{,}000\ [1/(1+0.08/4)^{5\times4}] \\ &= ₹15{,}000 \times 0.6729713 \\ &= ₹10{,}094.57. \end{aligned}$$

The same calculation performed on a calculator is shown in Table 3.5. As expected, since more frequent compounding produces a larger terminal value, the investor needs to invest a smaller amount (₹10,094.57) when quarterly compounding is involved as compared with annual compounding (₹10,209).

The relationship between simple interest, FV, and PV is presented in Figure 3.5. An understanding of these relationships is essential for their effective use as financial planning tools.

FUTURE VALUE: ANNUITY

Frequently, individuals accumulate funds on an *annual* basis. Assume that we wish to know how much money would Rekha Bose have at the end of five years, if she invests ₹2,000 annually in a retirement accounts statement that grows at 10 percent a year? In this case, since the same amount (₹2,000) is invested for more than one year (in this case five years) this investment is called an *annuity*. As revealed

Table 3.5 *Finding the Present Value of a Fixed Sum (Quarterly Compounding) Using a Calculator*

Step 1:	Identify known variables:
	Future value: ₹15,000
	Interest: 8%/quarterly (4)
	Number of periods: 5 years × quarterly (4)
Step 2:	Clear calculator [f] [CLX]
Step 3:	Enter data
	Press [1] [5] [0] [0] [0] [FV]
	[8] [ENTER] [4] [÷] [*i*]
	[5] [ENTER] [4] [×] [*n*]
	[PV]
	Answer: ₹10,094.57

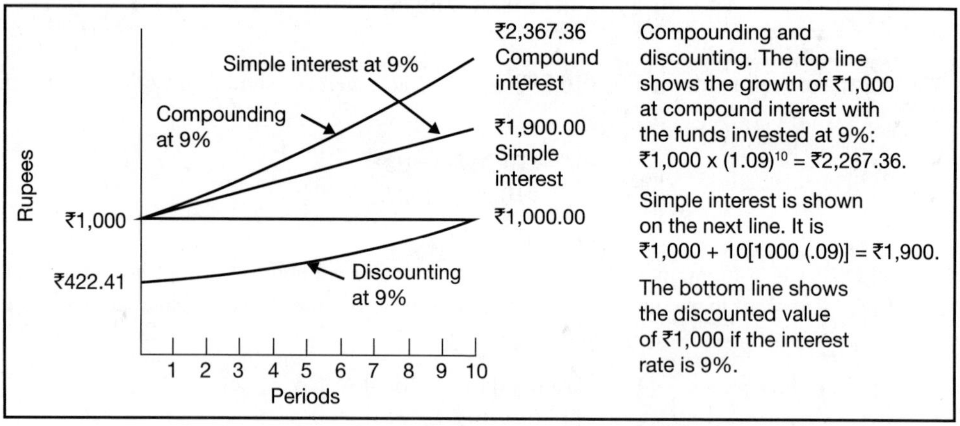

Figure 3.5 *Relationship between Simple Interest, Compounding, and Discounting*

by Figure 3.6, since the IRA funds earn 10 percent annually, at the end of the five-year period this annuity would grow to ₹12,210.20. The future value of an annuity can be calculated by:

$$\text{FVA} = \text{PMT}\sum_{n=1}^{N}(1+r)^{N-n} \tag{3.4}$$

where

FVA = The future value of an annuity
PMT = The payment per compound period
n = The number of compound periods
N = The total number of years.

Equation 3.4 can be used to calculate the future value of an annuity:

$$
\begin{aligned}
\text{FVA} &= ₹2{,}000\,(1+.10)^{5-1} + ₹2{,}000\,(1+.10)^{5-2} \\
&\quad + ₹2{,}000\,(1+.10)^{5-3} + ₹2{,}000\,(1+.10)^{5-4} \\
&\quad + ₹2{,}000\,(1+.10)^{5-5} \\
&= ₹2{,}000\,(1.4641) + ₹2{,}000\,(1.331) \\
&\quad + ₹2{,}000\,(1.21) + ₹2{,}000\,(1.10) + ₹2{,}000\,(1) \\
&\quad + ₹2{,}928.20 + ₹2{,}662.00 + ₹2{,}420.00 + ₹2{,}200.00 + ₹2{,}000.00 \\
&= ₹12{,}210.20.
\end{aligned}
$$

As expected, the use of a calculator yields the same result, as revealed by Table 3.6.

PRESENT VALUE: ANNUITY

Another important financial tool is the *present value of an annuity* (PVA). Financial problems, such as the identification of an undervalued stock, attractiveness of an income-producing limited partnership, or a lump sum versus a pension for life retirement settlement, can be solved by using the PVA concept. The following problem has been solved here by applying the PVA concept.

Question: A valued client has just won a lottery. He is offered the following two alternatives: (a) A four-year annuity with payments of ₹1,000 at the end of each year and (b) a lump sum payment of ₹3,170 today. Which one should he choose? At first blush, either the four-year payment or the lump sum *may*

Table 3.6 *Finding the Future Value of an Ordinary Annuity Using a Calculator*

Step 1:	Identify known variables:	
	Payment:	₹2,000
	Interest:	10%
	Number of periods:	5 years
Step 2:	Clear calculator [f] [CLX]	
Step 3:	Enter data	
	Press [2] [0] [0] [0] [CHS] [PMT]	
	[1] [0] [*i*]	
	[5] [*n*]	
	[FV]	
	Answer: ₹12,210.20	

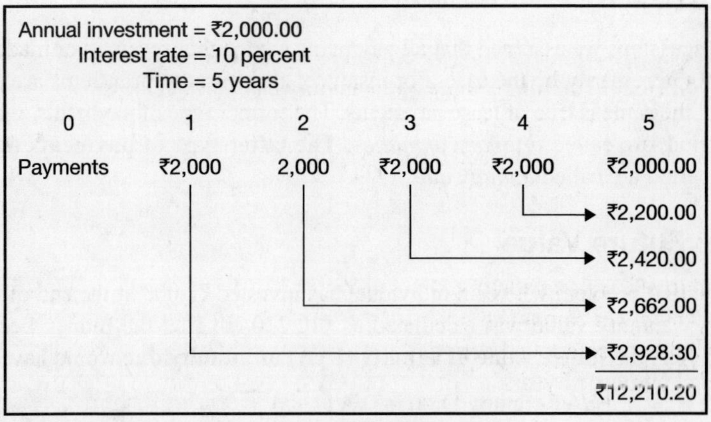

Figure 3.6 *Future Value of an Ordinary Annuity*

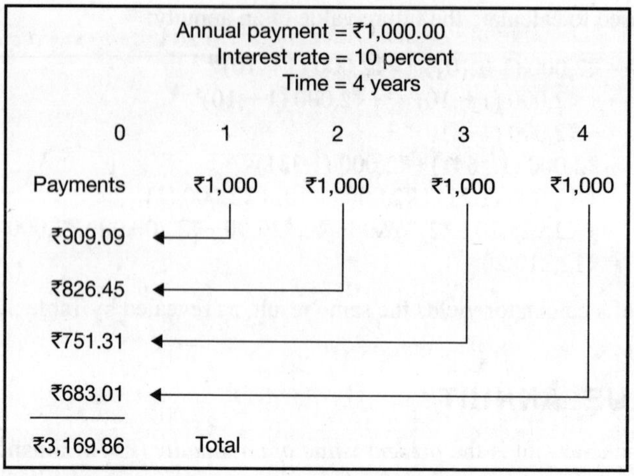

Figure 3.7 *Present6 Value of an Ordinary Annuity*

appear to be more attractive. However, as revealed by Figure 3.7, if the money earns 10 percent per year, *both alternatives are of equal value*. The algebraic equation for calculating the PVA is:

$$\text{PVA} = \text{PMT}\sum_{n=1}^{N}[1/(1+r)]^{n} \tag{3.5}$$

In the preceding example, the PVA equals:

$$\begin{aligned}\text{PVA} &= ₹1{,}000\ [1/(1+.10)]^{1} + ₹1{,}000\ [1/(1+.10)]^{2}\\ &\quad + ₹1{,}000\ [1/(1+.10)]^{3} + ₹1{,}000\ [1/(1+.10)]^{4}\\ &= ₹1{,}000 \times 0.90909 + ₹1{,}000 \times 0.82644\\ &\quad + ₹1{,}000 \times 0.75131 + ₹1{,}000 \times 0.68301\\ &= ₹909.09 + ₹826.44 + ₹751.31 + ₹683.01\\ &= ₹3{,}169.85.\end{aligned}$$

By using a calculator, we obtain the same result as shown by Table 3.7.

ANNUITY DUE: A REFINEMENT

In our previous discussions we assumed that all payments were either received or made *at the end of the year*. That need not necessarily be the case. For instance, all insurance premiums are paid at the *beginning* of the period; the same is true of lease payments. The former type of payments, received or made at the end of the period, are called *ordinary annuities*. **The latter type of payments** due or made at the beginning of the period are called *annuity due*.

Annuity Due: Future Value

Let us revert to the IRA problem where an individual has invested ₹2,000 at the end of each year for five years. The *ordinary* annuity value was calculated as ₹12,210.20. Had the money been invested at the beginning of each year, the **future value of annuity (FVA) or annuity due** would have been as follows:

$$\begin{aligned}\text{FVA (Annuity Due)} &= \text{FVA}\ (1+r)\\ &= ₹12{,}210.20\ (1.10)\\ &= ₹13{,}431.22.\end{aligned} \tag{3.6}$$

Table 3.7 *Finding the Present Value of an Annuity Using a Calculator*

Step 1:	Identify known variables:	
	Payment:	₹1,000
	Interest:	10%
	Number of periods:	4 years
Step 2:	Clear calculator [f] [CLX]	
Step 3:	Enter data	
	Press [1] [0] [0] [0] [PMT]	
	[1] [0] [*i*]	
	[4] [*n*]	
	[PV]	
	Answer: ₹3,169.87	

Note: If the payments were received at the beginning of each period, step 3 would have been modified as follows:

Press	[g] [7]
	[1] [0] [0] [0] [PMT]
	[1] [0] [*i*]
	[4] [*n*]
	[PV]
Answer: ₹3,486.85	

Notes: 1. [CHS] is *not* used since this is money being received, not paid out.
2. [g] [7] is pressed to initiate the "beginning" mode.

Clearly, since the payments were made earlier, the annuity due (₹13,431.22) has a higher value than ordinary annuity (₹12,210.20).

Annuity Due: Present Value

The present value of an annuity due can be calculated by:

$$\text{PVA (Annuity Due)} = \text{PVA}\,(1 + r) \tag{3.7}$$

Referring to the lottery example, the present value of an annuity (PVA) based on ₹1,000 payments received at the *end of the year* was ₹3,169.85. Had the ₹1,000 annual payments been received at the *beginning* of each year, the present value of the annuity due would have been ₹3,486.84:

$$\begin{aligned}\text{PVA (Annuity Due)} &= \text{PVA} \times (1 + 0.10)\\ &= ₹3{,}169.85 \times 1.1\\ &= ₹3{,}486.84.\end{aligned}$$

As revealed in Table 3.7, this was also the result we obtained by using the calculator—the tiny difference is due to a rounding error.

PRESENT VALUE OF PERPETUITY

What is the present value of a preferred stock which has no maturity date and makes dividend (annuity) payments indefinitely? Here, the payments resemble an infinite series, which is defined as *perpetuity*. The present value of perpetuity is given by:

$$\text{PV (Perpetuity)} = \text{PMT}/r \tag{3.8}$$

Assume that IBM Preferred pays an annual dividend of ₹5.00. If the rate of discount is 8 percent, the present value of the IBM Preferred is ₹62.50:

$$\begin{aligned}\text{PV (Perpetuity)} &= ₹5.00/0.08\\ &= ₹62.50.\end{aligned}$$

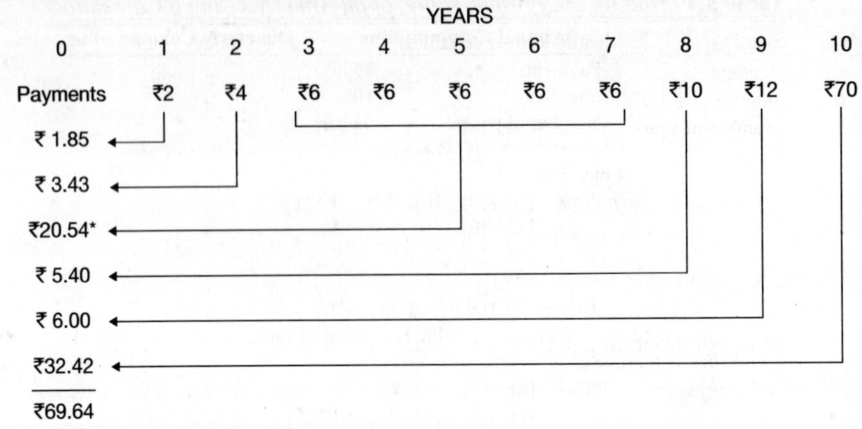

*This figure is calculated in two steps:

Step 1: PV of dividend payments of ₹6 for 5 years, from year 3 through year 7.
PMT = ₹6, n = 5, i = 8%
PV (End of year 2) = ₹23.96 (Referring to Table 3.7)

Step 2: PV of ₹23.96 at present (t = 0)
FV = ₹23.96, n = 2, i = 8%
PV (Beginning of year 0) = ₹20.54 (Referring to Table 3.5)

Figure 3.8 *Present Value of ABC Common Stock*

Present Value of an Uneven Payment Series

In our previous discussions we assumed that the periodic payments were even. This would not be a valid assumption for common stocks that typically declare dividends on an uneven basis. What, then, is the present value of ABC Common Stock which declares uneven dividend payments?

The present value calculation of ABC Common is demonstrated in Figure 3.8. An assumed discount rate of 8 percent is selected for this calculation. Two observations are apropos here. (1) The *PV of an uneven stream of expected future dividends is merely the sum of the PVs of the individual components of the stream*. The PV of each individual dividend payment can be calculated by referring to Table 3.4. If within a series, the dividend payments for two or more years remain constant, as is the case here during years three through seven, steps described in Table 3.7 can be used to calculate the present value of the dividend payments for these years. Assuming that an ABC Common is sold for ₹70 in the 10th year and the future expected dividend payments and the sale price of ABC Common are discounted by an 8 percent discount rate, the PV of ABC Common would equal to ₹69.64.

NOMINAL VERSUS EFFECTIVE INTEREST RATE

Not all payments are received and compounded annually. For instance, bonds make interest payments semiannually, stock dividends are paid quarterly, and banks charge loan interest on a daily basis. As previously demonstrated, quarterly versus annual compounding produces results as shown in Table 3.8.

Since the future values are higher for more frequent compounding, it is appropriate to differentiate between the two by contrasting the *nominal*, or stated, interest rate with the *effective* annual rate (EAR). The EAR can be determined by:

$$\text{EAR} = (1 + i_{nom}/m)^m - 1.0 \tag{3.9}$$

Table 3.8 *Results of Quarterly versus Annual Compounding*

	Annual Compounding	Quarterly Compounding
Amount	₹1,000.00	₹1,000
Interest rate	10%	10%
Number of years	2	2
Compound value	₹1,210.00	₹1,218.40

where

EAR = Effective annual rate
i_{nom} = Nominal, or stated, interest rate
m = Number of compounding periods per year.

Using the preceding example,

$$\begin{aligned} EAR &= (1+0.10/4)^4 - 1.0 \\ &= (1.025)^4 - 1.0 \\ &= 1.1038 - 1.0 \\ &= 0.1038 = 10.38\%. \end{aligned}$$

In this case, the *nominal* interest rate is 10 percent. However, if the amount is compounded quarterly, the EAR, or the rate actually being earned, is 10.38 percent. The solution to this problem with the use of a calculator is presented in Table 3.9.

Table 3.9 *Finding Effective Annual Rate Using a Calculator*

Step 1:	Clear calculator [f] [CLX]
Step 2:	[f] [5]
Step 3:	Effective annual rate PRESS [.] [1] [0] [ENTER] [4] ÷ [ENTER] [4] [Y^X] [1] + [1] – Answer: 0.10380 or 10.38%

Note: [f] [5] will change the key function to 0.00000.

ROLE OF INFLATION IN FINANCIAL CALCULATIONS

In making decisions about future income needs, it is important to take into consideration the effect of inflation. Assume that for the next five years, at the beginning of each year Ram Nath wishes to receive ₹36,000 a year (₹3,000 per month) in today's prices. Ram assumes that the rate of inflation over this period will be 5 percent a year and that on his investments he will be able to generate an after-tax return of 8 percent. He wishes to know how much money he would need to invest *now* to meet his desired goal.

Ram Nath's problem is graphically presented in Figure 3.9. The financial planner feeds this data

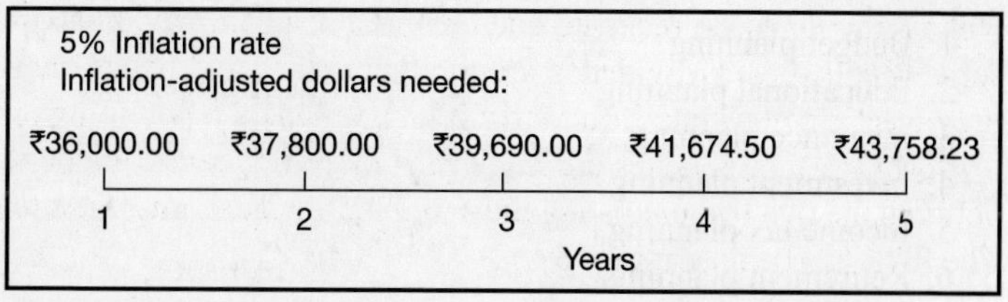

Figure 3.9 *Impact of Inflation on Future Income Needs*

Table 3.10 *Finding Investment Needs in Face of Inflation Using a Calculator*

Step 1:	Identify key variables: Payment: ₹36,000 Interest: 8% after-tax return Number of period: 5 years Inflation rate (r): 5%
Step 2:	Clear calculator [f] [CLX]
Step 3:	Enter data Press [g] [7] [3] [6] [0] [0] [0] [PMT] Note* [1] [.] [0] [8] [ENTER] [1] [.] [0] [5] [÷] [1] [–] [1] [0] [0] [×] [i] [5] [n] [PV] Answer: ₹170,273.94

Note: the following equation is used:

$$d = \left[\frac{1+i}{1+r} - 1\right] \times 100$$

where d = inflation-adjusted interest rate
i = after-tax interest rate
r = inflation rate

into an HP-12C calculator and determines that Ram needs to invest ₹170,273.94 today to meet his objective. This calculation is presented in Table 3.10.

INTERNAL RATE OF RETURN

A valuable investment concept is the *internal rate of return* (IRR). Assume Shakuntala Sachdev wishes to purchase 10, 10-year zero-coupon bonds for ₹250 each, that is, an investment of ₹2,500. Upon maturity, each bond will pay her ₹1,000, or a total of ₹10,000. She is curious to know her rate of return on her original investment of ₹2,500. That is, ignoring taxes and investment fees, she wants to know the IRR on her investment.

The IRR calculation, presented in Table 3.11, reveals that Shakuntala will receive an annual return of 14.35 percent on her investment.

PROBLEM SOLVING WITH THE HP-12C CALCULATOR

In this section, we will demonstrate the use of an HP-12C calculator in solving a variety of financial problems. For clarity, we will select one problem from each of the seven key areas of financial planning:

1. Budget planning.
2. Educational planning.
3. Insurance planning.
4. Investment planning.
5. Income tax planning.
6. Retirement planning.
7. Estate planning.

Table 3.11 *Finding Internal Rate of Return Using Calculator*

Step 1:	Identify known variables:	
	Present values:	₹250 × 10 = ₹2,500
	Future:	₹1,000 × 10 = ₹10,000
	Number of periods:	10 years × semiannual (2)
Step 2:	Clear calculator [f] [CLX]	
Step 3:	Enter data	
	Press [2] [5] [0] [0] [CHS] [PV]	
	[1] [0] [0] [0] [0] [FV]	
	[2] [0] [*n*]	
	[*i*] [2] [x]	
	Answer: 14.35%	

BUDGET PLANNING

Problem I

Tapas Lahiri has approached you with a budgetary problem. He is financing his car with a three-year loan at 10.5 percent, compounded monthly. His car costs ₹7,250 and his monthly down payment is ₹1,500. Tapas wants to know the amount of his monthly loan payment.

Solution to Problem I

The problem can be presented in the following manner:

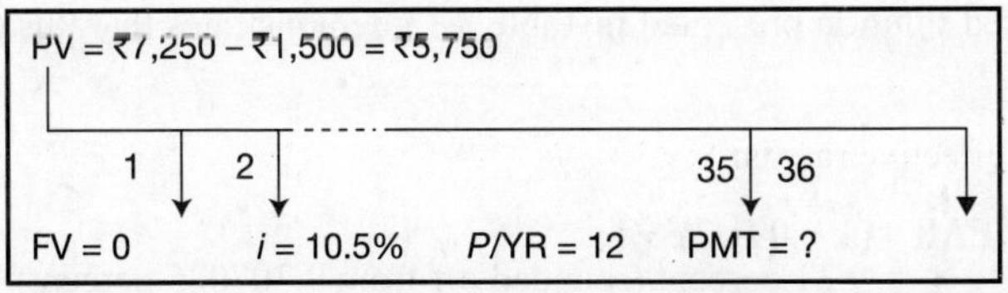

Using Equation (3.5):

$$\begin{aligned} PVA &= PMT \times PVAF \\ \text{or } PMT &= PVA/PVAF \\ &= ₹5{,}750/30.767 \\ &= ₹186.89. \end{aligned}$$

The use of a calculator in solving this problem is demonstrated in Table 3.12. The solution confirms that Tapas will pay ₹186.89 at the end of every month.

EDUCATIONAL PLANNING

Problem II

One common question routinely asked relates to educational planning. Assume Leela Modi's son just turned five. She plans to save for his college education by making equal semiannual deposits in an investment account earning 9.1 percent compounded semiannual return. After her son turns 18, for the next four years Leela expects to finance his four-year college education by spending ₹24,000 per year. Leela wants to know that starting from today how much money she would need to save every six months until her son turns 18 (i.e., for 13 years, or 26 deposits) to reach her education funding goal.

Table 3.12 *Finding the Monthly Car Payment Using a Calculator*

Step 1:	Identify known variables:	
	Present values:	₹5,750
	Interest:	10.5%
	Number of periods:	3 years
Step 2:	Clear calculator [f] [CLX]	
Step 3:	Enter data	
	Press [5] [7] [5] [0] [CHS] [PV]	
	[1] [0] [.] [5] [g] [*i*]	
	[3] [g] [*n*]	
	[PMT]	
	Answer: ₹186.89	

Solution Problem II

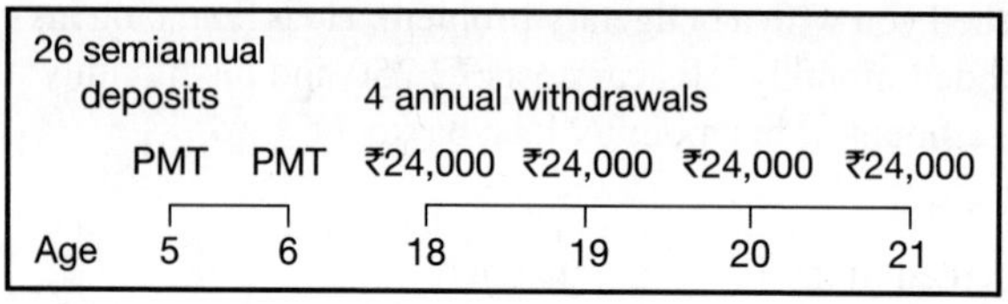

The calculator-generated solution presented in Table 3.13 demonstrates that this problem can be solved in four steps.

Steps 1 and 2. The effective rate is:

$$\begin{aligned} EAR &= (1+.091/2)^2-1 \\ &= 9.31 \text{ percent (rounded off from 9.307025 percent).} \end{aligned}$$

Step 2 in Table 3.13 yields this result.

Step 3. At the age of 18, the present value of four withdrawals at 9.31 percent is ₹77,227.14:

Step 4. To achieve the educational funding goal, the future value of the deposits at the age of 18 must equal to ₹77,227.14. Therefore, the semiannual deposits required, as calculated in step 4 in Table 3.13, is equal to ₹1,611.86.

In this case, if Leela makes 26 semiannual deposits of ₹1,611.86 each earning 9.1 percent interest, after her son turns 18, she would be able to provide ₹24,000 per year for four years to finance her son's education.

INSURANCE PLANNING

Problem III

Shashi and Meena Kapoor came to you for insurance planning. An analysis of their finances produced the result seen in Table 3.14.

Meena is 55 years old and her life expectancy is 80. In planning for future income she does not want to take into account her retirement benefits. Sashi Kapoor wants to know how much additional life insurance he should buy so that if he were to die today, his insurance policy would pay Meena ₹700 per month until she turns 80.

Table 3.13 *Finding Educational Funding Needs Using Calculator*

Step 1:	Clear calculator [f] [CLX]
Step 2:	Enter data
	Press [.] [0] [9] [1] [ENTER] [2] [÷]
	[1] [+]
	[1] [.] [0] [4] [5] [5] [×]
	[1] [−]
	Answer: 9.31%
Step 3:	Enter data
	Press [2] [4] [0] [0] [0] [CHS] [PMT]
	[9] [.] [3] [1] [*i*]
	[4] [*n*]
	[PV]
	Answer: ₹77,227.14
Step 4:	Enter data
	Press [7] [7] [2] [2] [7] [.] [1] [4] [FV]
	[9] [.] [1] [ENTER] [2] [÷] [*i*]
	[1] [3] [ENTER] [2] [×] [*n*]
	[PMT]
	Answer: ₹1,611.86

Note: Since semiannual deposits are made, 9.1%/2 is used rather than the effective annual rate of 9.31%.

Table 3.14 *Shashi and Meena Kapoor's Finances*

Shashi Kapoor: Monthly Shortfall for Meena	
Amount of Current Life Insurance	₹150,000
At Shashi's Death	
Meena's Earned income Per Month Available	₹800
Income Per Month if Insurance Proceeds (₹150,000) are invested at 8%	+ ₹1,000
Total Dollars Per Month Available to Meena	₹1,800
Monthly Income Meena Needs after Shashi's Death	− ₹2,500
Monthly Shortfall for Meena	− ₹700

Solution to Problem III

The problem can be restated as follows: What is the present value of an ordinary annuity (payments to be received at the end of each month) which invested at, say, 8 percent after taxes will produce a monthly income of ₹700 for 25 years (Meena's life expectancy of 80 less her current age of 55)? The solution to this problem is presented in Table 3.15.

This solution suggests that, to achieve his objective, Sashi would need to purchase a ₹91,000 (rounded off to nearest ₹1,000) life insurance policy.

Table 3.15 *Finding Life Insurance Needs Using a Calculator*

Step 1:	Identify known variables:	
	Payment:	₹700/monthly
	Interest:	8%
	Number of periods:	25 years
Step 2:	Clear calculator [f] [CLX]	
Step 3:	Enter data	
	Press [7] [0] [0]	[PMT]
	[8] [.] [g]	[*i*]
	[2] [5] [g] [*n*]	
	[PV]	
	Answer: ₹90, 695.17	

Notes: 1. [g] [*i*] makes adjustment for monthly interest calculations.
2. [g] [*n*] makes adjustment for number of periods (not number of years) calculations.

Table 3.16 *Finding the Present Value of Disability Payments Using a Calculator*

Step 1:	Identify known variables:	
	Payment:	₹3,500/monthly
	Interest:	7%
	Number of payments:	20 years
Step 2:	Clear calculator [f] [CLX]	
Step 3:	Enter data	
	Press	[3] [5] [0] [0] [PMT] [7] [.] [g] [*i*] [2] [0] [g] [*n*] [PV]
	Answer: ₹451,438.77	

Problem IV

You have recommended that your client Rina Raghu, aged 45, purchases a 20-year, ₹3,500 per month disability insurance policy for ₹3,000 annual premium. Rina is shocked to learn that only a ₹3,500 policy would cost her ₹3,000 every year, and has summarily rejected your recommendation. Your task is to explain Rina the *true value* of your recommended policy.

Solution to Problem IV

The problem can be restated as follows: What is the present value of an annuity which invested at, say, 7 percent will produce a monthly income of ₹3,500 for 20 years? First, point out to Rina that the disability income is paid *monthly*, while the insurance premium is paid *annually*. Next, explain that, if disabled today, the company will make *monthly* payments for 20 years until Rina reaches the age of 65. Equally important, disability payments are completely tax free.

The present value of the disability policy is ₹451,438.77 as shown in Table 3.16. By paying ₹3,500 today, Rina is in fact purchasing a *potential value* of ₹451,438.77. If she were to become disabled today, Rita will no longer have to make annual disability premium payments, and she will immediately start receiving ₹3,500 disability checks every month, and these checks will keep coming for 240 months (20 years × 12 months per year).

Problem V

Let us assume that in Problem I, Tapas Lahiri informs you that he cannot pay more than ₹177 per month. What is the highest interest rate he can afford to pay if he still wishes to purchase this car?

Table 3.17 *Finding the Maximum Interest Rate Using a Calculator*

Step 1:	Identify known variables	
	Present value	₹5,750
	Future value:	₹0
	Payments:	₹176.89/month
	Number of periods:	3 years
Step 2:	Clear calculator [f] [CLX]	
Step 3:	Enter data	
	[5] [7] [5] [0] [PV]	
	[1] [7] [6] [.] [8] [9] [CHS] [PMT]	
	[3] [g] [*n*]	
	[*i*]	
	[ENTER] [12] [x]	
	Answer: <u>6.75%</u>	

Solution to Problem V

The solution to this problem with the use of an HP-12C calculator is presented in Table 3.17. Based on this calculation, you could ask Tapas Lahiri to shop around for a specific interest rate which would reduce his monthly payment to, say, ₹176.89 (i.e., ₹10 less than the current monthly payment).

The interest rate associated with the desired monthly payment is 6.75 percent. Therefore, Tapas can purchase this car for ₹7,250 provided he can find a bank that would offer him an interest rate of 6.75 percent on his car loan. Of course, if that is not possible, Tapas would have to either find a cheaper car or make a larger down payment.

Problem VI

Ranjit Gurwal has just joined the brokerage firm of Anand & Co. The company has requested Ranjit to choose between the following two offers: (1) An annual salary of ₹50,000 for the next three years. (2) An initial bonus of ₹50,000 plus an annual salary of ₹25,000 for the next three years. Ranjit needs to decide financially which of the two offers is financially better for him. In your calculation, he wants you to use an interest rate of 16 percent, compounded quarterly.

Solution Problem VI

The solution to this problem with the use of an HP-12C calculator is presented in Table 3.18.

Steps 1–3. First, we need to calculate the EAR so that the rate will be on the same basis as the payments. The EAR is 16.986 percent:

$$\begin{aligned} EAR &= (1 + rnom/m)^m - 1.0 \\ &= (1 + .16/4)^4 - 1.0 \end{aligned} \quad (3.10)$$

restated

$$= 0.1\,6986 = 16.986\%.$$

Steps 1 through 3 in Table 3.18 yield this result.

Step 4. The PV of ₹50,000 for three years with $r = 16.986$ percent is ₹110,504.31.

Step 5. The PV of ₹25,000 for three years is ₹55,252.16. Therefore, the total value of option 2, which includes an immediate bonus of ₹50,000, is ₹105,252.16 (₹55,252.16 + ₹50,000.00). Step 5 in Table 3.18 yields this result.

Table 3.18 *Comparing the Present Value from Two Cash Flows Using a Calculator*

Step 1:	Clear calculator [f] [CLX]
Step 2:	[f] [5]
Step 3:	Effective annual rate
	Press [.] [1] [6] [ENTER] [4] [÷] [ENTER] [4] [Y^x] [1] + [1] −
	Answer = .16986 or 16.986%
Step 4:	Press [5] [0] [0] [0] [0] [PMT] [1] [6] [.] [9] [8] [6] [*i*] [3] [*n*] [PV]
	Answer: ₹110,504.31
Step 5:	Press [2] [5] [0] [0] [0] [PMT] [1] [6] [.] [9] [8] [6] [*i*] [3] [*n*] [PV] [5] [0] [0] [0] [0] [−]
	Answer: ₹105,252.16
Step 6:	Option I (Step 4) = ₹110,504.32
	Option II (Step 5) = ₹105,252.16
	Option I is better.

Note: [f][5] will change the key function to 0.00000.

Step 6. Since the total value of option II is only ₹105,252.16 and the value of option I is ₹110,504.31, the first option of ₹50,000 per year for three years is preferred.

Problem VII

Sudhir Shah wants to purchase a home. He can afford to make a down payment of ₹12,000 and a monthly payment of ₹630. The interest rate on a 30-year fixed mortgage is 11.5 percent. How much mortgage can Sudhir afford to pay on this house?

Solution to Problem VII

The solution to this problem with the use of the calculator is presented in Table 3.19. The present value of a monthly payment of ₹630 for 30 years is ₹63,617.64. Therefore, these payments would have been sufficient to purchase a home valued at ₹63,617.64. However, since Sudhir can make a down payment of ₹12,000, he can afford to buy a home valued at ₹75,617.64 (₹63,617.64 + ₹12,000.00). Step 3 in Table 3.19 yields this result.

INVESTMENT PLANNING

Problem VIII

Rasesh Patbardhan was informed by his broker that a 10 percent, AAA-rated, XYZ bond, with a 10-year maturity, is completely risk free. However, he became totally confused when he attended one of your seminars in which you pointed out that even the AAA-rated bonds are subject to interest rate *risks*. Resesh wants to know if your assertion is valid.

Table 3.19 *Finding Mortgage Size Using a Calculator*

Step 1:	Identify known variables	
	Payments:	₹630/monthly
	Interest:	11.5%
	Number of payments:	30 years
Step 2:	Clear calculator [f] [CLX]	
Step 3:	Enter data	
	Press	
	[6] [3] [0] [CHS] [PMT]	
	[1] [1] [.] [5] [g] [*i*]	
	[3] [0] [g] [*n*]	
	[PV]	
	[Add ₹12,000 down payment] [1] [2] [0] [0] [0] [+]	
	Answer: ₹75,617.64	

Solution to Problem VIII

First, explain to Rasesh that interest rate risk is *different* from default risk. Then, using Table 3.20 demonstrate that if the interest rate rises from 10 to 12 percent, and Rasesh will have to sell his bond, even his AAA-rated bond is likely to incur a loss of ₹114.70.

Table 3.20 *Showing the Effect of Interest Rate on Bond Price Using Calculator*

Step 1:	Identify known variables	
	Future value:	₹1,000
	Payment:	₹100/year
	Interest:	12 percent × semiannual (0.5)
	Number of periods:	10 years × semiannual (2)
Step 2:	Clear calculator [f] [CLX]	
Step 3:	Enter data	
	Press [1] [0] [0] [0] [FV]	
	[5] [0] [PMT]	
	[6] [*i*]	
	[2] [0] [*n*]	
	[PV]	
	Answer: ₹885.30	

Problem IX

Three years ago Ravi Verma bought an investment worth ₹5,000. Since then, it has increased 60 percent in value, and Ravi wants to buy more of this investment. Your task is to calculate the *true* annual return on this investment, given that the current market value of this investment is ₹8,000.

Solution to Problem IX

The calculator-generated solution is presented in Table 3.21. The compounded annual return of an investment that grows from ₹5,000 (PV) to ₹8,000 (FV) in three years is 16.96 percent.

INCOME TAX PLANNING

Problem X

Sharmila Bose, who is in the 28 percent tax bracket, is excited about investing ₹100,000 in a tax shelter. Basically, she is a risk-averse person; however, she wants to purchase this tax shelter because over the next five years she will enjoy a 90 percent write-off on this investment. She wants to know how much money she will have accumulated at the end of five years as a result of these write-offs, assuming that she earns a 9 percent annual interest from this deal.

Table 3.21 *Finding the Rate of Return on an Investment Using a Calculator*

Step 1:	Identify known variables	
	Present value:	₹5,000
	Future value:	₹8,000
	Number of periods:	3 years
Step 2:	Clear calculator [f] [CLX]	
Step 3:	Enter data	
	Press	
	[5] [0] [0] [0] [CHS] [PV]	
	[8] [0] [0] [0] [FV]	
	[3] [*n*]	
	[*i*]	
	Answer: 16.96%	

Solution to Problem X

Assuming that Sharmila is correct in her assumption about the write-offs, the key facts are listed here:

1. Total investment: ₹100,000
2. Write-off (90%): ₹90,000/year for five years.

At her marginal tax bracket of 28 percent, Sharmila's tax savings are ₹25,200 at the end of each year (28 percent of ₹90,000) for five years. So the question is: "What is the future value of a ₹25,200 annuity for five years?" The interest rate that will be used in this case is 9 percent.

The solution is presented in Table 3.22. The future value of a ₹25,200 annuity for five years is ₹150,814.71. Of course, Sharmila should realize that tax write-offs are not guaranteed and the resultant tax savings are merely deferred taxes which become due when the tax shelter is liquidated.

Table 3.22 *Finding the Future Value of a Tax Deferred Investment Using a Calculator*

Step 1:	Identify known variables	
	Payment:	₹25,200/year
	Interest:	9%
	Number of periods:	5 years
Step 2:	Clear calculator [f] [CLX]	
Step 3:	Enter data	
	Press [2] [5] [2] [0] [0] [CHS] [PV]	
	[9] [*i*]	
	[5] [*n*]	
	[FV]	
	Answer: ₹150,814.71	

RETIREMENT PLANNING

Problem XI

Jayant Porwal has been asked by his company to accept a retirement payout of either ₹500,000 or a monthly lifetime annuity of ₹5,000. He is impressed with the half-a-million-rupee lump sum payment, but his wife wants him to go for the lifetime annuity offer. Jayant is seeking your advice.

Solution Problem XI

Solution to this problem is based on the certain key assumptions made. After some discussion, you make the following assumptions:

1. Jayant is 65 and his life expectancy is 82. You assume that Jayant will receive annuity payments for 17 years, or a total of 204 (17×12) monthly payments.
2. If Jayant accepts a lump sum, it is assumed that his retirement money will earn a compounded annual return of 8 percent, which translates into a monthly return of (8/12) 0.6667 percent.
3. You assume that there are no tax consequences to making either choice.

The solution to this problem is presented in Table 3.23. Based on your assumptions and analysis, you recommend Jayant choose the lifetime annuity payment option because the present value of the annuity payments exceeds the lump sum distribution by ₹56,633.67. Of course, Jayant should understand that the outcome could be different if the assumptions were modified.

Table 3.23 *Comparing Lump Sum and Annuity Payments Using a Calculator*

Step 1:		Clear calculator [f] [CLX]
Step 2:	Press	[g] [8]
		[5] [0] [0] [0] [PMT]
		[8] [g] [*i*]
		[1] [7] [g] [*n*]
		[PV]
	Answer:	₹556,633.67
Step 3:	The present value of the annuity payments exceeds the lump sum distribution by:	
		₹556,633.67
		–₹500,000.00
		₹ 56,633.67

Problem XII

Recently, Achyut Rao, a young executive, requested you to develop an early retirement plan for him. He wants to invest ₹5,000 per year with the first deposit beginning on his 30th birthday. For the next 30 years, this investment will be assumed to earn an EAR of return of 9 percent. Beginning at the age of 60, Rao will tour around the world for five years and will need a large sum each year to finance that expensive trip. After completing this tour, Rao wants to receive an annual income of ₹30,000 per year for the next 15 years. Assuming an EAR of 9 percent for the entire time period, what is the maximum amount of capital that Rao can spend on his world tour?

Solution to Problem XII

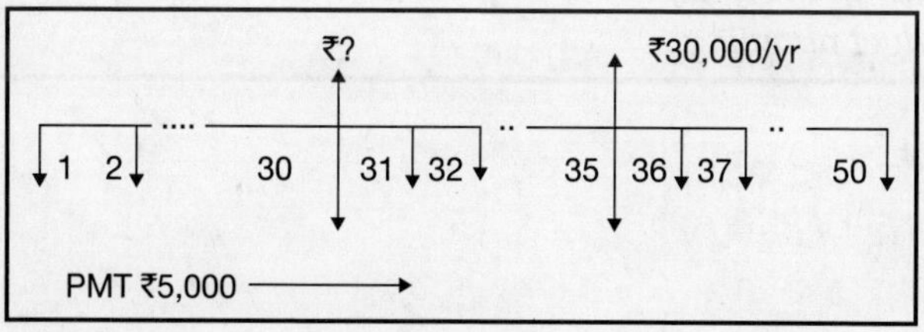

The calculator-based solution to this problem is presented in Table 3.24. This problem should be broken down into six steps.

Steps 1 and 2. The value of annual investments at the age of 60 is calculated in Step 2 in Table 3.24. Rao will have accumulated ₹681,537.69 by the age of 60.

Steps 3 and 4. Next, the PV of ₹30,000 in annual payments for 15 years, starting with year 36 (age 65) is calculated. Step 4 yields the PV of ₹241,820.65.

Table 3.24 *Finding the Residual Left for a World Tour Using a Calculator*

Step 1:		Clear calculator [f] [CLX]
Step 2:	Press	[5] [0] [0] [0] [CHS] [PMT]
		[9] [*i*]
		[3] [0] [*n*]
		[FV]
	Answer:	₹681,537.69
Step 3:		[0] [FV]
Step 4:	Press	[3] [0] [0] [0] [0] [PMT]
		[9] [*i*]
		[1] [5] [*n*]
		[PV]
	Answer:	₹241,820.65
Step 5:	Press	[2] [4] [1] [8] [2] [0] [.] [6] [5] [FV]
		[9] [*i*]
		[5] [*n*]
		[PV]
	Answer:	₹157,166.83
Step 6:		Achyut should be able to spend
		₹681,537.69
		−₹157,166.83
		₹524,370.86

Step 5. The PV of ₹241,820.65 at the age of 60, discounted for five years at 9 percent, is ₹157,166.83.

Step 6. Rao should be able to spend the difference between what he would have at the age of 60 and the amount he would need to generate the current income starting at the age of 65. Specifically,

Amount accumulated by the age of 60	= ₹681,537.69
Amount needed to generate income at the age of 65	= ₹157,166.83
Amount available for world trip	= ₹524,370.86

In this chapter, we have explained the use of the concept of the time value of money and have demonstrated the use of the HP-12C financial calculator in solving different types of financial problems. In the Chapter 4, we will undertake a comprehensive analysis of the issues involving budget planning.

PART 2

RISK MANAGEMENT PLANNING

Chapter 4

Life Insurance: Structure, Concepts, and Planning Strategies

Chapter 5

Health, Homeowner's, Automobile, and Liability Insurance: Structure, Concepts, and Planning

4 Life Insurance: Structure, Concepts, and Planning Strategies

In the first segment of this chapter we will present the structure and key concepts relating to life insurance. Important life insurance planning strategies for individuals and businesses will be presented in the second segment.

Section I: Risk Management

INTRODUCTION

Risk is a fundamental aspect of life. Every day we are faced with the threat of a loss or injury. Acknowledging this reality, our objective shifts from trying to avoid all risk exposures to positioning ourselves to retain only the level of risk that is appropriate. This process is referred to as "risk management," a fundamental aspect of comprehensive financial planning.

The risk-management process comprises several discrete steps. The starting point in this process involves understanding a client's overall risk-management objectives and financial capacity to absorb the loss. Under this lens, the financial planner will seek to:

1. Identify the nature and causes of risk.
2. Assess the probability of loss and quantify the rupee value of the occurrences.
3. Understand the weaknesses and gaps in the current risk-management plan.
4. Evaluate alternative methods for handling exposures.
5. Develop strategy and product recommendations.
6. Implement a risk-management plan.
7. Monitor the situation.

THEORY OF RISK TRANSFER: RISK EVALUATION

In theory, there are five methods of dealing with specific risks: avoidance, retention, reduction, transference, and sharing.

Risk Avoidance

Certain types of risk can be totally avoided. For example, a physician may choose not to practice as an obstetrician to avoid the risk of being sued. An individual afraid of getting injured may choose to avoid high-risk recreational activities such as mountain climbing or skiing. An investor may avoid the risk of losing the principal by not investing in stocks. However, in the real world, it may not be practical to avoid these types of risks altogether.

Risk Retention

At the other end of the risk-management spectrum is risk retention. In this situation, a person assumes the risk (sometimes referred to as "self-insurance"). Risk can be retained on either a voluntary or an involuntary basis. Generally, people who assume risk voluntarily do so because they have sufficient resources to handle the loss. For instance, individuals may decide against purchasing life insurance because they are independently wealthy and the families would be able to maintain the current life style in the event of untimely death. By contrast, involuntary risk assumption occurs when a risk-taker fails to transfer the risk to an insurer. An example of involuntary risk assumption is when a homeowner is unable to obtain earthquake or flood insurance. It is important to point out that retention can only be a viable alternative when the exposure is not catastrophic, either financially or nonfinancially.

Risk Reduction

Another means of handling risk is to reduce the likelihood of the occurrence. This can be accomplished through loss prevention and control. Examples of this approach include: installation of smoke detectors and burglar alarms in homes, installation of a theft alarm in a car, and a commitment to eating healthy and exercising regularly. Insurance companies control their risk exposure by taking advantage of the law of large numbers. By insuring the lives of millions of people, insurance companies dramatically reduce their risk exposure because they know that statistically only a small percentage of insured individuals will die during a given time period.

Risk Transfer

Often the preferred method for handling risk is to completely transfer the risk exposure to a third party. In this chapter and the next, we will explore various insurance policies that enable personal and business risk transfers. Other examples of risk transfer include: hedging (which refers to the simultaneous buying and selling of a contract), a surety arrangement (the individual is bonded against loss), and a "hold harmless" agreement (one person assumes the potential loss of another person).

Risk Sharing

Another method of handling risk is to assume a limited or manageable degree of risk and transfer the balance of exposure to one or more organizations. For example, an insurance company shares risk with its clients by integrating deductibles and coinsurance provisions into the policy. Individuals might decide to hire contractors (who maintain business insurance) to perform construction activities in their homes. A sole proprietor of a business might become a corporation in order to benefit from the corporate shield of limited liability. Insurance companies often mitigate their market risk exposure by purchasing insurance through a reinsurance company. In these situations, risk-takers assume only a manageable degree of risk.

A summary of this discussion is presented in Figure 4.1. As the figure reveals, risk sharing and risk transfer are strategies that lead to the selection of an appropriate insurance company. Examples of risks and risk-management strategies across a variety of personal events are presented in Table 4.1.

Clearly, transferring risk to an insurance company is only one of the many ways of handling risks. Other means of avoiding or reducing risk include: personal savings, security plans, and health-enhancing behavior.

RISK-MANAGEMENT STRATEGY

Two important factors that should be considered when assessing a risk-management strategy are: (a) the frequency or probability of the adverse occurrence and (b) the severity of the loss. In developing a

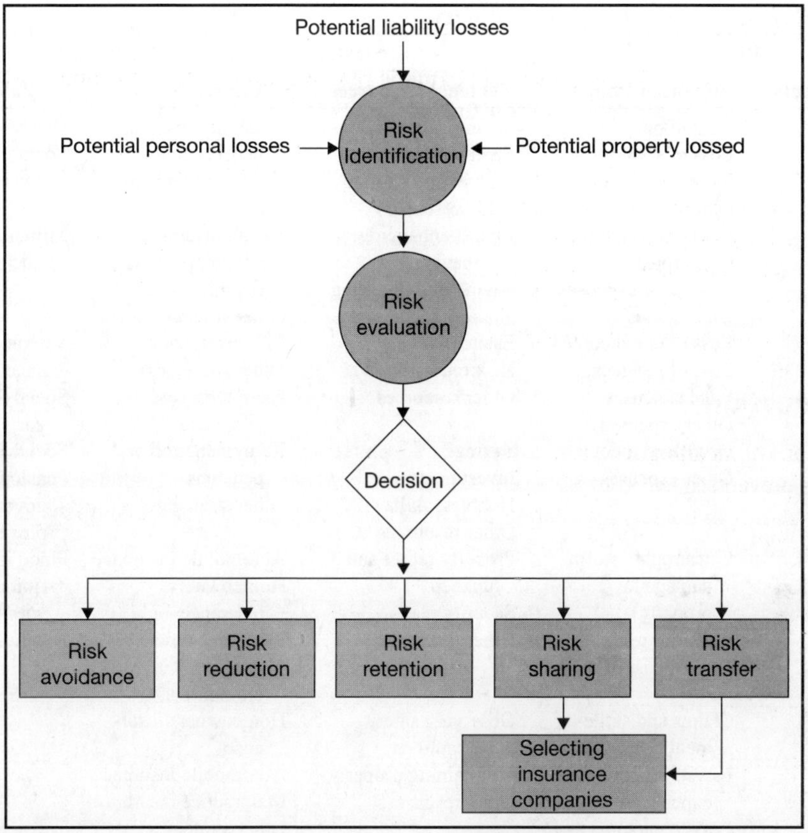

Figure 4.1 *Personal Risk Management: An Overview*

prudent risk-management strategy, it is important to simultaneously assess these two factors. The following guidelines are generally suggested to perform this task.

Transfer high-severity loss/low-probability occurrences. There are two reasons why "transfer" is the preferred method in this scenario. First, it is always desirable to transfer catastrophic losses (e.g., loss of income, high potential liability exposure), if that is at all possible. Second, when losses have a low probability of occurring, it is possible to cost-effectively transfer that risk. Such a transfer makes even more sense when the potential severity of loss is high and its anticipated frequency is low.

Avoid, reduce, or share high-severity loss that has a high probability of occurrence. While it is prudent to transfer "high-ticket" losses, the frequency of those losses impact the feasibility of purchasing insurance. A high frequency of occurrence combined with high expected loss will generally translate into premiums that are cost prohibitive. Typically, the optimal approach is to totally avoid taking the risk; if that is not possible, then it makes sense to share at least a portion of the projected loss.

Low-severity loss/high-probability occurrences. Here again, a high probability of occurrence will most likely make the risk transfer costly. Because the amount of the anticipated loss is low, the preferred strategy is typically to absorb the loss while simultaneously taking steps to reduce the likelihood of such an occurrence.

Low-severity loss/low-probability occurrence. Typically, low-cost risks that occur frequently are retained. The optimal strategy, here, is to retain the risk while taking steps to reduce the chance of occurrence.

Table 4.1 *Risks and Risk-management Strategies*

Risks		Strategies for Reducing Financial Impact		
Personal Events	**Financial Impact**	**Personal Resources**	**Private Sector**	**Public Sector**
Disability	Loss of one income Loss of services Increased expenses Other losses	Savings, investments Family observing safety precautions Other resources	Disability insurance Other strategies Worker's compensation	Disability insurance Social Security Second Injury Funds
Illness	Loss of one income Catastrophic hospital expenses Other losses	Health-enhancing behavior Saving and Investing Nursing home care	Health insurance Health maintenance organizations Other strategies	Military health Medicare, Medicaid
Death	Loss of one income Loss of services Final expenses Other expenses	Estate planning Risk reduction Other resources	Life insurance Other strategies Long-term care insurance	Veteran's life insurance Social Security survivor's benefits
Retirement	Decreased income Other expenses	Savings Investments Hobbies, skills Other resources	Retirement and/or pensions Other strategies	Social Security Pension plan for government employees
Property loss	Catastrophic storm damage to property Repair or replacement cost of theft	Property repair and upkeep Security plans Other resources	Automobile insurance Homeowners insurance Flood insurance (joint program with government)	Flood insurance (joint program with business) Federal Disaster Relief
Liability	Claims and settlement costs Lawsuits and legal expenses Loss of personal assets and income Other expenses	Observing safety precautions Maintaining property Other resources	Homeowners insurance Automobile insurance Malpractice insurance Other strategies	

Source: Adapted from American Council of Life Insurance (1983).[1]

A summary of the four strategies is presented in Table 4.2. As this table reveals that risk sharing and risk transfer are strategies that require insurance company selection. Also, the types of insurance available for covering various forms of risk are illustrated in Figure 4.2.

Section II: Individual Life Insurance Policies

INTRODUCTION

No one knows for sure when, where, and how our lives, and thus our ability to generate income, will end. The risk of permanent loss of family income due to premature death is one of the primary reasons for purchasing life insurance, and the severity of that loss makes life insurance an integral part of a risk-management strategy. Purchasing life insurance effectively converts the uncertainty that a person may not be able to meet all financial obligations, in the event of a possible misfortune, into the certainty that these financial obligations will be fulfilled. Individual uses of life insurance include:

[1] American Council of Life Insurance, *Personal and Financial Family Planning: A Staff Development Workshop for Secondary School Trainers and Teachers* (Washington, D.C.: American Council of Life Insurance, 1983), vi/13d.

Table 4.2 *Various Ways of Handling Risk*

	High Frequency	Low Frequency
High severity	Avoidance	Transfer/Sharing
Low severity	Reduction	Retention/Sharing

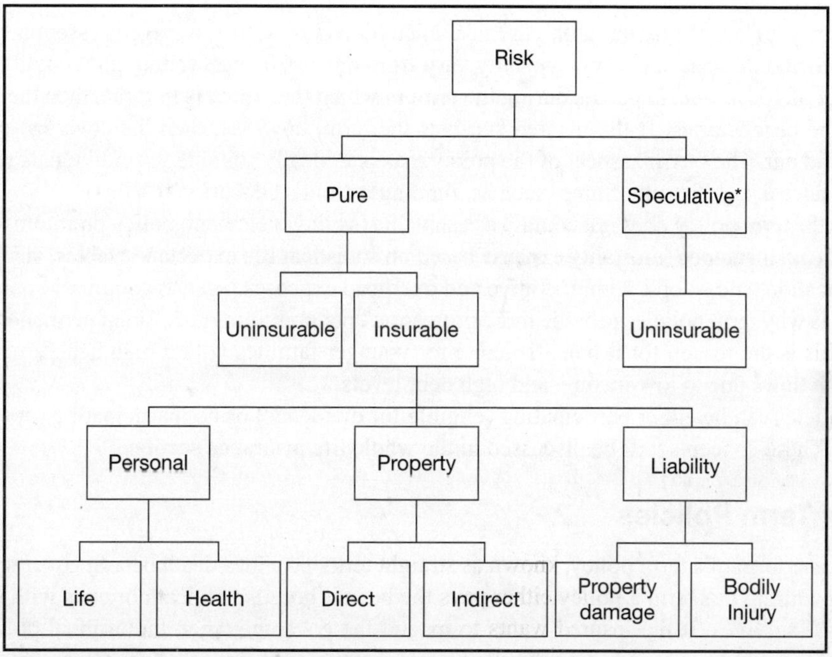

Figure 4.2 *Types of Insurance Available for Certain Risks*

Source: Adapted from David L Bickelhanpt (1979).[2]
Note: *A speculative risk is one in which there is a chance of either loss or gain. Starting a business and gambling are examples of speculative risk.

1. Paying final expenses, including funeral expenses, final health care expenses, federal estate taxes, state inheritance taxes, and administrative costs associated with probate.
2. Providing future income for spouse, children, and other dependents.
3. Furnishing funds for education.
4. Preserving and leveraging the legacy passed on to heirs or charities.
5. Offering the estate with liquidity for paying off final debts, including mortgages, car loans, student debts, and credit card loans.

In the following section, we will discuss different types of life insurance policies, standard policy provisions, policyholder options, policy riders, and taxation of life insurance death benefits and withdrawals.

[2] David L Bickelhanpt, *General Insurance*, 11th ed. (Homewood, IL: Richard D. Irwin, 1979), 11. *Source:* Adapted from David L Bickelhanpt, *General Insurance*, 11th ed. (Homewood, IL: Richard D. Irwin, 1979), 11.

BASIC TYPES OF LIFE INSURANCE POLICIES

There are two major categories or classes of life insurance: term insurance and cash value life insurance. An overview of the various types of life insurance policies, their relative advantages and disadvantages, and their appropriateness based on the needs of different groups of buyers, is presented in Table 4.3.

Term Insurance Overview

A term policy provides the owner with pure insurance protection. The coverage is essentially rented for a specified period of time, and terms typically vary from one to 30 years (although it could extend even up to the age of 100). If death occurs during the term in which the policy is in force, then the face benefit is paid to the beneficiaries. If the insured survives the term, however, then the coverage ends and no benefit is paid out. The "term" aspect of the policy makes it ideally suitable for individuals whose insurance needs have a specific time frame, such as, funding a child's education.

Because the term policy does not contain a cash value (savings) element, policy premiums reflect only the cost of death insurance (mortality expense based on statistical life expectancy tables, insured's health history, avocation, and so on), administrative and overhead expenses, agent's commission, and insurer's profit. That is why term policies provide more protection "per premium rupee" than permanent life insurance, and this is the reason for it being suitable for younger families with a high benefit need but constrained cash flows due to low income and high debt levels.

Term policies can be either participating (eligible for dividends) or nonparticipating (not eligible for dividends). These concepts will be discussed in the whole life insurance section.

Types of Term Policies

The most basic form of a term policy, known as straight term, provides death benefit coverage for a one-year period. During this term a policy either pays the benefit because of death or ends with no payment if the insured survives. If the insured wants to extend the coverage when the original policy expired, another application would have to be submitted. Note that the premium of a new policy would be higher because the risk of insuring an older person would be higher.

Term policies can differ significantly from one another, partly because they come with different options and features. Today, most term policies are issued for a number of consecutive periods and often contain provisions that allow for renewability beyond the initial period as well as convertibility to a cash value policy. Term policies that are typically offered by insurers include the following:

Level premium term policy. In this type of policy the coverage extends beyond the one-year period (5-, 10-, 20-, and 30-year terms or to a stated age). During the duration of a multiyear period policy, both the benefit and the premium remain level or fixed. In order to compensate the insurance company for increasing levels of mortality risk, the premium payments in the early years are higher than necessary to meet the anticipated claims, while the premium payments in later years are lower than would be required to cover the higher risk. Generally, these policies are not considered attractive at advanced ages because of their prohibitively expensive mortality costs.

Renewable term policy. This type of term policy includes a provision that guarantees the insured the right to renew the policy for another year, period of years, or a number of subsequent periods without providing further evidence of insurability. For example, an individual who purchases a five-year renewable term policy at an age of 35 will have the option of renewing the policy at the age of 40 for another five-year term. However, upon each renewal the insurance company will have the right to determine a new premium rate. In most cases an insurance company will set an age cap (e.g., 65 years) after which further renewals would not be automatically permitted. Note that the renewability

Table 4.3 *A Overview of Life Insurance Policies*

Type	General Description	Investment Products	Flexibility of Investment	Safety of Cash Value	Potential Rate of Return	Death Benefit
Term: annual renewable and convertible	Quality term. After-tax life insurance. Pure life insurance with no cash-value element.	None	NIA	NIA	N/A	Fixed, level or decreasing
Whole life	Basic coverage. dividends add flexibility. guarantees	Long-term 1 bonds and mortgages.	None Alternative is to borrow from policy and invest.	High	Low to moderate	Fixed, level
Interest sensitive Whole life	Combination or universal life and whole life.	Interest-sensitive investments	Same as universal life.	High	Moderate	Fixed, level
Adjustable life	Similar to whole life, except may adjust death benefit and premiums	Interest-sensitive investments.	Same as universal life.	High	Moderate	Adjustable
Universal life	Flexible Premium Payments.	Interest-sensitive investments.	None Insured may borrow from cash value or withdraw capital.	High	Moderate	Adjustable
Variable life	Investment selected by insured.	Stocks. bonds. mutual funds. zero coupons. money market. instruments, etc.	Excellent Insured directs movement of funds.	Low to moderate	High	Usually guaranteed minimum. can increase with investment performance.
Universal variable life	Combination of universal and variable life.	Combination of universal and variable life.	High Insured direct movement of Funds.	Low to moderate	High	Adjustable can increase with investment performance.
Survivorship/ whole life	Payment upon second death.	Long-termbonds and mortgages.	None	High	Low	Fixed. level

Note: Survivorship life may be funded with variable, universal, or variable–universal life.

(Continued)

Table 4.3 (*Continued*)

Flexibility of Premium	Alteration of Death Benefit	Advantages	Disadvantages	Appropriate Buyer
None Increases periodically.	None	Lower initial cost. Rupees can be invested elsewhere. Pure death protection.	No savings element. Expires after specified period. Cost increases.	Young couples who need a large amount of insurance. People who do not want to invest in an insurance vehicle. People whose insurance needs will decrease over time. People who have temporary needs.
None Premium fixed, dividends can lower or eliminate payment. Loans available.	None	Lifetime coverage. Savings element. Loan privileges. Variety of premium payment plans.	Higher cost of death protection. Low rate of return. Lack or flexibility. May not keep pace with inflation.	People who need forced Savings, lifetime coverage, estate liquidity.
None May change based on insurer's experience.	Same as universal life.	Level fixed premiums between each redetermination period, forced savings element.	Policyholders bear more risk of adverse trends in mortality and expenses. Considerable loss if surrendered first several years.	People who need forced savings for a period of time and who want the potential for better investment results than those guaranteed in traditional policies.
High	Same as universal life.	Flexibility with premium face amount.	Direct recognition method used to calculate dividends.	People who want flexibility and forced savings.
High Maximum: Allowed by law. Minimum: To cover mortality and expenses.	Excellent. Amount can be increased or decreased as desired.	Flexibility Potentially higher rate of return. Pull disclosure of fees. loads, proportion invested.	No forced savings. Potential drop in rate of return. Not the most competitive investment vehicle.	People who want choice and flexibility. People who want a cash value fund with a higher rate of return.
None	None	Potentially high rate of return. Control of investments. Pull disclosure required by law. Cash values are held in separate accounts which are segregated from the insurer's general investment portfolio.	No guaranteed cash value. Element of risk borne by policyholder. Need for familiarity with investments. Generally high expense ratio.	People who are investment-oriented and want a higher rate of return and/or want flexibility.
Flexible at option of policy owner.	Same as universal life.	Cash values are held in separate accounts which are segregated from the insurer's general investment portfolio.	No guaranteed cash valve. Element of risk borne by policyholder. Need for familiarity *with* investments. Generally high expense ratio.	People who are investment oriented and want a higher rate of return and/or want flexibility.
None	None	Lower insurance cost than insurance on each insured.	Low return. Lack of flexibility. Long period before death benefit becomes due.	People seeking funds for paying estate taxes upon second death.

Source: Adapted from Don Johnson and Cheryl Toman-Cubbage(1986)[3].

[3] Don Johnson and Cheryl Toman-Cubbage, "Have Your Cake…," *Financial Planning* (January 1986), 191.

feature is a valuable risk-management tool because it ensures coverage for the subsequent period even if the insured person has become uninsurable.

Convertible term policy. A convertible term policy grants the insured the option to exchange the policy for permanent life insurance without incurring a penalty or having to provide evidence of insurability. The date, by which the conversion must occur, is clearly specified in the contract. Obviously, a longer conversion period (e.g., until the age of 65) is more valuable than the one that expires early. If a policyholder eventually expects to convert the term policy into a cash value building policy, then the insured should ensure that the insurance company offers such a policy as well. Similar to the renewal policy, the conversion right in this type of policy is a valuable risk-management option.

Decreasing term policy. This policy offers a level premium payment plan but the face value of the policy's benefit continues to decrease throughout the term. A commonly used form of a decreasing term policy, known as mortgage redemption insurance, provides a benefit sufficient to pay off the remaining mortgage debt at any given time during the covered period. So if the insured survives the term, then both the insurance policy coverage and the need for mortgage protection simultaneously expire. On the other hand, should the insured die during the term the death benefit payment would match the remaining mortgage owed.

Many insurers allow policyholders to reduce their coverage and premium without having to apply for a new policy or pay additional fees. This may be helpful if a policyholder anticipates that the insurance needs will continually shrink until they finally disappear. As the needs decline, it might be prudent for a policyholder to reduce the coverage, thereby reducing the premium payments. Of course, in reducing the coverage, a decline in the value of the rupee due to inflation should be taken into account.

In selecting a term policy, it is generally desirable to assume the worst-case scenario. For instance, if a person is considering a 10-year level premium term policy but expects the need to continue for an additional 5–10 years, cost estimates should be based on the assumption that, for medical reasons, upon renewals a policyholder would have to pay a higher level of premium. In the final analysis, all else being equal, the best strategy is to purchase a term policy that is marketed by a quality company, is expected to be relatively inexpensive over the long term, and offers the most attractive options.

Cash Value Insurance Overview

Cash value or "permanent" life insurance is designed to provide for the lifetime benefit needs of the insured. As long as the required annual premiums are maintained, a policy will not expire and death benefits will be paid to the beneficiaries upon the insured's death. Cash savings build up in the policy because the premium payments in the beginning years are much higher than that required to buy an equivalent amount of term insurance. The additional premium payments are credited to the insured's account and are invested to earn interest. Figure 4.3 offers a graphic depiction of how the level premium of a permanent policy compares to the annual premiums for a series of one-year term policies.

The role played by a cash value type of policy is clearly demonstrated in Figure 4.4. As cash value builds up in the account, a gradually declining amount of term insurance (net amount at risk) is needed to supplement the savings to produce the debt benefit or the face value of the policy. Note that only the declining term portion, and not the policy's face value, truly represents the liability of an insurance company. For example, consider a situation where the insured dies owning a ₹10 lakh whole life policy with a cash value of ₹600,000. In this case, the benefit to the beneficiaries would consist of the ₹600,000 of cash value plus the additional ₹400,000 generated by the term portion. This is why every cash value insurance policy is presumed to be a combination of term insurance and a long-range savings plan known as cash value.

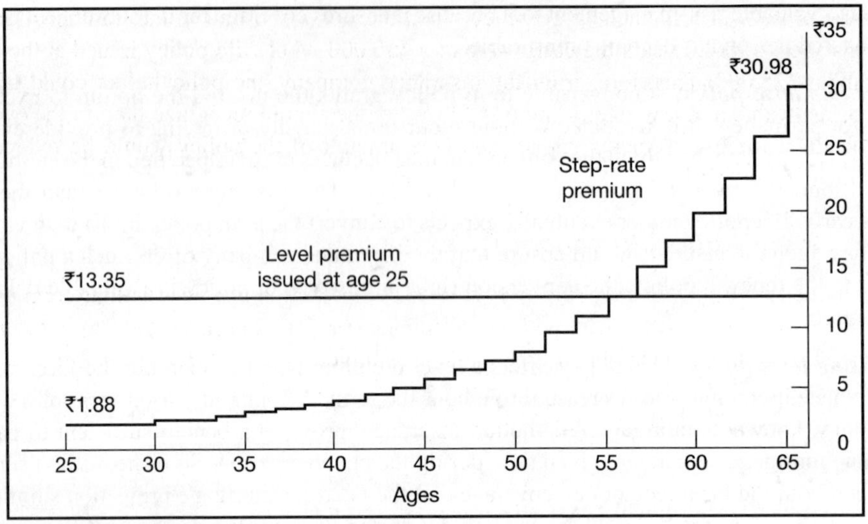

Figure 4.3 *Comparison of Level Premiums for ₹1,000 Insurance*

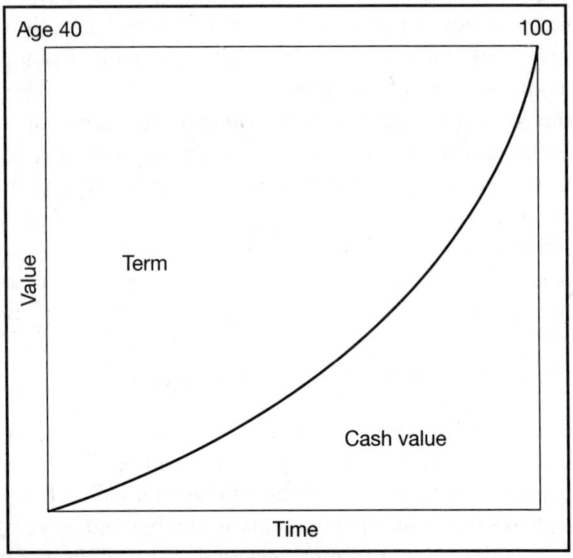

Figure 4.4 *Cash Value Insurance*

In buying a permanent (cash value) policy, the insured can make premium payments: (a) for a lifetime, (b) for a predetermined number of years, (c) up to a certain age, or (d) as a lump sum. The choice of the premium payment plan should be based on the current financial condition and the tax situation of the insured. Similar to term policies, cash value policies can be purchased on a participating (par) or nonparticipating (non-par) basis. In a non-par policy, the company fixes the premium at a rate sufficient to cover the cost of death protection and promised cash value savings. Consequently, there is no provision in these policies to return in the form of dividends the over-collection of premiums.

By contrast, in the case of a par policy, the insurance company initially charges a higher premium rate, but plans to return the overpayment of premiums in the form of dividends. A policyholder of a par policy may elect to use dividend payments in one of the five ways: (a) receive dividends in cash, (b) invest dividends with the insurance company at a specified interest rate, (c) purchase additional paid-up insurance, (d) reduce future premiums, or (e) buy additional one-year term insurance (known as fifth dividend option).

At the age of 100, the cash value policy is considered to be "paid up." At that point, the insured may withdraw the benefit as a lump sum or in installments. Prior to being "paid up," the insured is entitled to take a loan against the policy's cash value. For instance, if a policyholder wishes to tap the cash value to make a premium payment, the insurance company can advance a premium loan to continue the protection, and the loan can be repaid at a later date. The cash value accumulated inside an insurance policy might also be tapped for a financial emergency when there is a shortfall in the traditional emergency fund. For instance, after 20 years the cash value of a ₹50,000 whole life policy issued at the age of 45 might be about ₹25,000. Therefore, from the insurance company, the policyholder could take a loan against this cash value at a low rate of interest. However, he should recognize that, in the event of the insured's death, if the loan remains unpaid, the face amount of the policy would be reduced by the amount of the outstanding loan.

Types of Cash Value (Permanent) Policies

Cash value policies are ideally suitable for individuals whose insurance need is long term and whose cash flow situation can accommodate the higher premium cost (as compared to term insurance). Four common varieties of cash value policies are: whole life, universal life (UL), variable life, and variable–universal life.

Whole Life

Whole life insurance was originally devised as an alternative to the increasing premium payments associated with term insurance. Straight or ordinary whole life offers guaranteed fixed premiums, a guaranteed interest rate on savings, and a fixed death benefit. Because premiums are paid continually throughout the insured's life (until paid up at the age of 100), the premium rupee amount is lower than that of other types of whole life policy. Straight life policy is one of the most widely purchased types of permanent policies because, to most families, it offers a fine balance between protection and cash accumulation.

In a whole life insurance policy, the insured does not control the investment vehicle. Instead, premiums are invested in long-term bonds and mortgages, and held in an insurance company's general account. Because of regulatory pressures to play it safe, these companies generally limit their portfolio holdings to bonds of shorter maturity and high-quality mortgages, which produce relatively modest investment returns. Still, the "guaranteed" aspect of the policy makes it quite suitable for conservative investors and individuals with limited investment experience.

Variations of the straight whole life policy include the following:

Limited-pay whole life. This form of whole life policy differs from a straight life policy in three respects. (a) Although these policies provide a lifetime protection, premium payments cease after a period of 10, 20, or 30 years, or at a certain age (usually 65), depending on the insurance contract selected. (b) Since the premium-paying period is limited, the premium rate is higher than that for a whole life policy. (c) Because of the higher premium rate and the shorter payment period, these policies build up cash values faster than those in a whole life policy. A limited-pay whole life policy is generally preferred by persons who prefer receiving high earnings during the early periods of their lives so they could build a nest egg faster should their earnings significantly drop later in life, as would be the case in retirement.

Modified or graded-premium whole life. Premiums in this type of policy start at a low level and then increase incrementally during each period until they reach the required premium level. Once that level is reached, the premium remains fixed for as long as the policy remains in force.

Single-premium whole life. Single-premium whole life (SPWL) is a whole life insurance policy for which the lifetime premium is paid upfront as a lump sum. However, the difference between a traditional whole life and an SPWL is more than that implied by the method of premium payment. The compelling reason for buying an SPWL is to use a life insurance policy as a tax-deferred investment.

Endowment life. Endowment life policy is similar to whole life as in this policy the annual premium remains fixed, savings continue to accrue, and the policy becomes paid up at maturity. However, unlike a whole life that is "paid up" at the age of 100, the endowment could become paid up in 10 or 20 years, depending on how it was originally structured. The policy pays a guaranteed face benefit either at maturity or earlier if a policyholder dies before the maturity date.

Other variations of the whole life policy include the following:

Current assumption whole life. This type of policy (also referred to as the interest-sensitive whole life [ISWL] policy) combines the attractive features of both whole life and UL insurance policies. As with the traditional whole life policy, an ISWL policy has fixed premium payments and a guaranteed death benefit. However, unlike a whole life policy, in this case, after an initial guarantee period, every year (referred to as the redetermination period) the insurance company is permitted to use modified assumptions relating to mortality costs and interest rates. Any changes resulting from using these modified assumptions are then reflected in the accumulation of the cash value, and a higher growth in cash value results in pushing the death benefit above the stated minimum. Note that the interest rate used for calculating the cash value build-up is tied to a prespecified rate, although a minimum interest rate is always guaranteed. As with other types of insurance policies, if prematurely canceled, ISWL policies impose back-end surrender charges for an extended period.

Return-of-premium whole life. Upon the death of the insured, this type of policy pays the face death benefit *plus* the value of the premiums paid by the insured. In selecting this policy, effectively, a person purchases two whole life policies; one designed to accumulate the value of the death benefit and the other to accumulate the value of premiums. It is important to point out, however, that in viewing the return-of-premium option some people might be led to believe that they are "getting something for nothing." That is simply not the case.

Put differently, the key difference between a traditional plan and this plan is that upon maturity, the beneficiary receives the face value as well as all the premium payments that were made by the insured. It is also important to remember that the entire payment made by the insurance company is tax free.

An example should make this clear. Puja Bhatia, a 30-year old, buys a ₹12 lakh return-of-premium whole life policy. The annual premium for this policy is ₹9,000 (around ₹6,000 for a traditional policy). If Puja dies after, say, 20 years, the beneficiary will receive, tax free, ₹12 plus lakhs an additional ₹180,000 (₹9,000 per year × 20 years).

At present there are only a few companies that market this product. Examples include: LIC's New Bima Kiran, ICICIPru Lifeguard with return of premium, and Birla Sunlife's Premium Back Term Plan. Premium payments associated with these products vary, so it is best to compare them carefully before signing off on the dotted line.

Universal Life Policies

A UL policy is a flexible form of life insurance. It permits a policyholder to either increase the death benefit coverage with satisfactory evidence of insurability or decrease the coverage if warranted by changed circumstances. It also allows the policyholder to increase or decrease the amount or frequency of premium payments so long as the accumulated cash value is sufficient to cover the cost of continuing the policy. This flexibility permits individuals to tailor the coverage to their changing financial needs and situation, a privilege the whole life policyholders never enjoy.

A UL insurance clearly discloses how each premium payment is applied by unbundling an insurance company's operating expenses, mortality charges (protection component), and the cash value (savings component). Annual statements typically state: the death benefit, cash value, interest earned during the period, deductions for mortality expenses, deductions for insurance company expenses, loans outstanding, and withdrawals. This high level of policy transparency makes it easy for insurance professionals to determine the true performance of a UL policy. It also helps a policyholder understand how changes will impact the future cost of coverage.

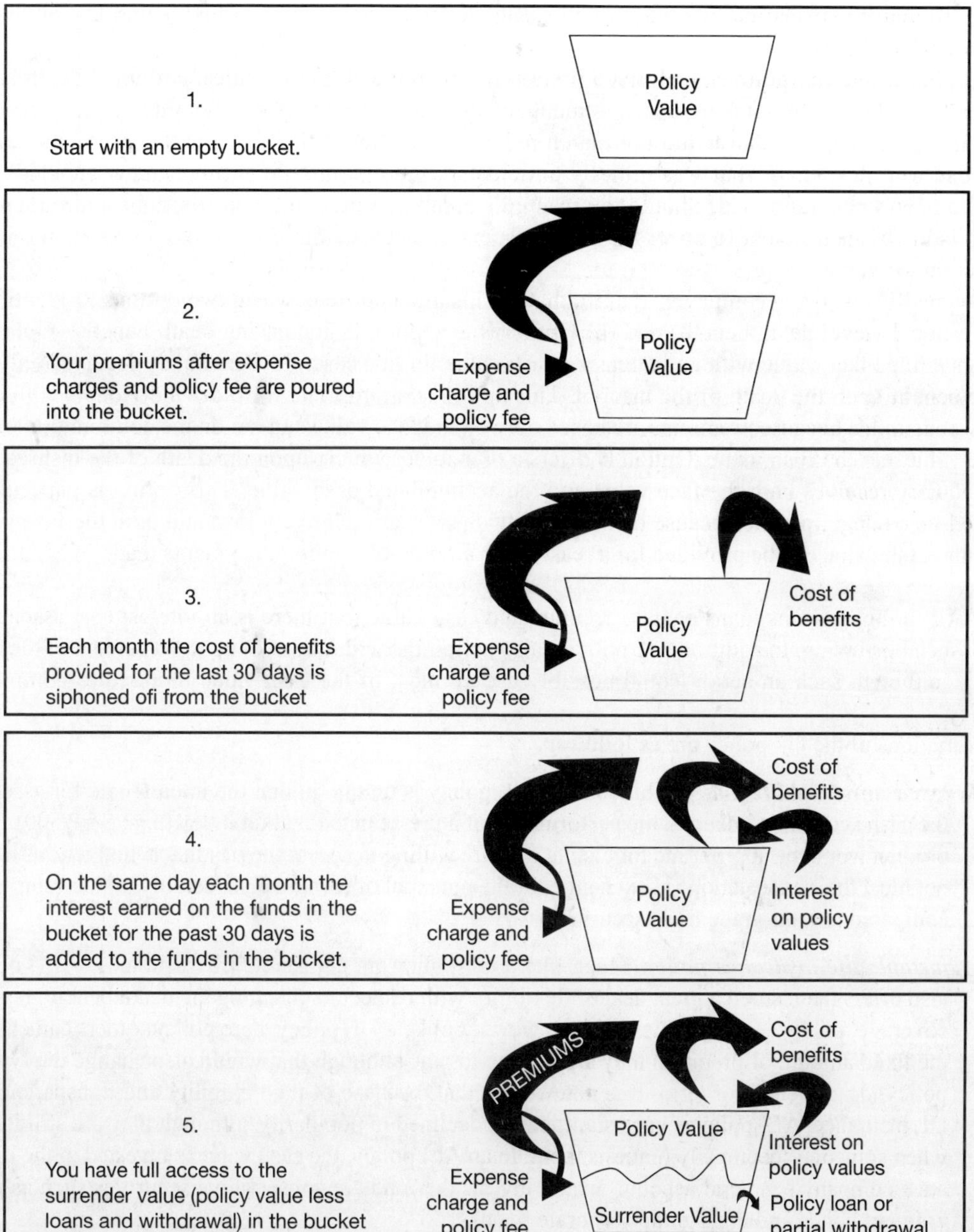

Figure 4.5 *How Universal Life Insurance Works*

Source: TMG Life Insurance Company.

Figure 4.5 demonstrates how a UL policy works. As depicted, one part of the premium covers the cost of insurance, the other part flows into a cash accumulation fund. Interest payments in excess of the guaranteed interest rate are deposited into the cash accumulation fund. In effect, the insured invests the funds with the insurance company which, in turn, invests them in fixed-rate short-term debt instruments paying competitive interest rates. Each policy has an account value and a cash surrender value.

The difference between the two values represents deferred sales charge, which could last anywhere from 10 to 20 years.

Unlike whole life policies with fixed premiums, guaranteed interest rates, and fixed death benefits, a UL policy shifts some of the investment and mortality risk to the policyholder. If, for example, the actual investment returns did not match policy-illustration projections, or the premium contributions were less than what was initially anticipated, there would be an investment shortfall that would need to be addressed. Should the insured's combined premium contributions and remaining cash value be insufficient to cover the costs associated with maintaining it, the policy would lapse ("run out of gas").

Typically, insurance companies require that the insured choose between two options: (a) Option A or Option 1 (level death benefit) and (b) Option B or Option 2 (increasing death benefit). Option A offers a fixed face value with an increasing cash value. In this case, the beneficiary receives only the face benefit upon the death of the insured. This option is appropriate for older individuals with cash flow constraints because premiums are based only on the face value and not on the combination of the face value and the cash value. Option B offers a plan under which, upon the death of the insured, the beneficiary receives both the face value and the accumulated cash value. This option is particularly suited for younger people because their mortality charges are relatively low, and both the face value and the cash value can be provided for a reasonable amount of premium payments made over a longer time.

A UL policy permits loans against accumulated cash value, but there is an interest cost associated with such borrowing. In addition, UL policies also permit the withdrawal of up to 90 percent of the cash value, although such an action could possibly use up most of the cash value required to continue a policy.

Variations of the UL policy are as follows:

Indexed universal life policy. This form of UL policy is unique in that the interest rate for assets in the cash account is linked to the performance of a pre-selected market index (e.g., S&P 500). This product would be appropriate for clients who are willing to accept the risk that actual returns might not meet their expectations in exchange for the potential of earning considerably higher returns (as compared to high-grade fixed securities).

Adjustable life insurance policy. Much like a UL policy, an adjustable life insurance (ALI) policy also offers the insured a great deal of flexibility with respect to changing the death benefit, term of coverage, policy type, or policy mix. However, unlike a UL policy, here policyholders can change the fixed amount of premium they are willing to pay, although that would also change the type of policy, death benefit or term. It is noteworthy that, because of the flexibility and transparency of UL insurance, ALI policies have significantly declined in popularity, although they are still issued when someone specifically requests them. In an ALI policy, the cash value is invested in the insurance company's general account, which invests the funds in conservative securities such as government bonds and high-grade corporate bonds.

In this connection, it is important to note that in November 2010 the Insurance Regulatory and Development Authority (IRDA) announced that henceforth UL products would be known as variable insurance products (VIPs), and that they would be offered exclusively to the non-unit linked platform.

Variable Life Policies

Variable life insurance is a type of cash value policy in which a policyholder can play an active role in making appropriate investment decisions. A policyholder's cash value is diverted to "separate accounts" of an insurance company and the insured is permitted to direct some or all of the policy's cash value to the securities markets primarily through mutual-fund-like investments. One of the benefits of a variable life policy is the potential benefit of long-term growth associated with equity securities, although under this arrangement significant investment risks are shifted to the policyholder.

Essentially, a variable life policy is similar to a tax-deferred mutual fund charging management and administration fees. This type of policy offers a variety of investment choices consisting of stock and bond mutual funds, fixed income products, and money market instruments. After the initial investment process is completed, switching between these products is permitted. In addition to mutual fund advisory and administration fees of a mutual fund, a policyholder is also charged the normal expenses associated with a life contract (insurance company expenses, load fees, and mortality expenses).

When a portion of the cash value is invested in a portfolio consisting of financial securities such as equities and lower rated bonds, the death benefit and the cash value fluctuate up or down, depending on the performance of the investment portfolio. Note that in most instances an insurance company guarantees the initial face amount of the policy so long as scheduled fixed premiums are paid and there is sufficient cash value to keep the policy in force. So, in a real sense, what fluctuates in a variable life policy is the cash value. For this reason, Indiana University's insurance professor, Joseph Belth, has observed: "If you invest in a variable life policy, your beneficiary's best hope is that you will die on an uptick."

The variable life product is most appropriate for individuals with investing experience and acumen, a tolerance for risk, and a desire to hedge against the risk of inflation. An interesting variation of this policy is the *single-premium variable life*. In this type of life policy, covering a person younger than 45 years of age, the minimum guaranteed amount is greater than ₹50,000 or 10 times the annualized premium. For people older than 45, the payout is higher than ₹50,000 or seven times the annualized premium.[4]

There are two types of variable life insurance policies—participating and nonparticipating. While the former offers only a guaranteed return, the latter offers both a guaranteed return and year-end annual bonuses.

Single-premium variable life policy. This type of policy is suitable for those who prefer tax-deferred investments and desire to use life insurance as a vehicle for earning a highly competitive tax-deferred rate of return.

Variable Universal Life Policies

A variable UL policy, also known as flexible-premium variable life or universal life II, combines the flexibility of premium payments and death benefit (offered by UL) with investment flexibility (offered by variable life). This broad flexibility shifts all of the account risk to the policyholder, and there are no guarantees except the right to keep the policy in force. The variable–UL product is appropriate for individuals who can anticipate changing needs and funding ability, possess investment acumen and experience, and exhibit a tolerance for market volatility. Variable–UL policies can only be offered by prospectus.

No-lapse guarantee option. Some insurance companies offer a no-lapse guarantee option, which guarantees that during the stated guaranteed period the policy would not lapse so long as the accumulated premiums, less any loans or withdrawals, equal or exceed the required total minimum premiums. Such an option requires an additional premium payment and may impose certain limitations, such as fewer investment choices, only Option A death benefit, and loan restrictions. The guarantee is available for a lifetime or for a stated number of years (subject to some age restrictions). Of course, if at the end of the

[4] http://articles.economictimes.indiatimes.com/2011-01-10/news/28429102_1_death-benefit-and-savings-new-york-life-insurance-premium (last accessed on October 4, 2014).

guarantee period the cash value turns out to be insufficient to keep the policy in force, the insured would have to either make additional payments within the grace period or extend the no-lapse guarantee option.

A variable life insurance with a no-lapse guarantee seems attractive to those who not only believe in the long-term growth potential of equities but also wish to protect themselves from the potential effects of short-term market volatility on their life insurance coverage. Without such a safety net, significant stock market losses over time could cause a variable life insurance policy to lapse.

Other Forms of Life Insurance

Irrevocable trust. When an irrevocable trust is selected as the policy owner, the insured makes periodic payments to the trust, which are used to pay the premiums. In this case, the trust is also selected as the beneficiary and its instrument specifies how the policy's benefits are to be designated. Incidentally, if the trust is created after the policy is issued, and the policy is subsequently transferred to the trust, the insurance proceeds are added back to the estate if death were to occur within three years following the transfer.

Charity. A policyholder can designate a charity as the policy's owner and beneficiary. Each year the policyholder makes a tax-deductible gift to the charity to pay the policy's premium. Upon the second insured's death, the charity directly receives the policy's death benefits. Another option for a policyholder is to set up a charitable trust. The policyholder transfers appreciated assets to the trust, which in turn sells these assets to generate funds with which the policy's premiums are paid. And since the assets are sold inside the trust, neither the insured nor the estate becomes liable for taxes generated by the sale of the appreciated assets. In this case, an irrevocable trust can be set up outside the charitable trust to replace the assets going to the charity.

Children. An insured can make his or her children the policy's beneficiaries and owners. When the second parent dies, the adult children receive the face value of the policy free of income taxes. By utilizing the annual gift tax exclusion, parents can give gifts to children without triggering a gift tax, which children, in turn, use to make premium payments.

Joint-life or first-to-die policy. The first-to-die policy, also referred to as the joint-life policy, pays out the income-tax-free death benefit to the survivor upon the death of the first insured person. This type of policy is generally more suitable for dual-income families needing income replacement as well as for people with certain types of business-ownership arrangements. While the premiums associated with the first-to-die policies are higher than the survivor policy, these premiums are still lower than would be the case if two individual policies were issued to both spouses.

Family income policy. The family income policy utilizes the concept of decreasing term insurance to fit a shrinking need for insurance coverage. This type of policy combines some form of permanent insurance like whole life with decreasing term insurance. Upon the death of the insured, the term insurance portion starts making a prespecified amount of payment until a specified date. The sum payable per month is typically 1 percent of the amount of permanent insurance, although many companies offer other options as well.

LIFE INSURANCE CONTRACT

In Chapter 5, it is specified that property and casualty insurance contracts are highly standardized. However, that is not the case with life insurance contracts. Each insurance company has some discretion in developing its own life contract, although by law certain provisions (if and when the items apply) must be present. Moreover, the insurance department of each state must approve the final wording. In this section, we will investigate standard contract provisions and policy riders (endorsements).

Life Contract Provisions

Policy provisions that are commonly included in life policies include:

Entire contract clause. This clause states that the life policy and the insured's application constitute the entire contract.

Ownership clause. This clause defines who has the ownership rights to a policy. Ownership rights include the ability to assign or transfer the policy, use it as collateral for a loan, borrow against the cash value, receive dividends, and designate beneficiaries. Often the insured and the policyholder are one in the same, although that need not always be the case. The owner could be either a separate policyholder (person or entity) or an irrevocable beneficiary.

Incontestability clause. This provision states that an insurance company cannot dispute the validity of the life insurance contract once a policy has been in effect for a period of time even if there was a material misstatement in the application. However, many policies contain an exception that could void the benefit on the basis of fraudulent misstatements. Note that a misstatement of age is no grounds for voiding the contract within that contestability period; rather, the death benefit would be adjusted to reflect what benefit would have been due for the given level of premium payment.

Grace period. Every life insurance policy has a grace period (generally 30–31 days) beyond the premium due date during which a policyholder is permitted to make the premium payment without a lapse in coverage. Should the insured die during the grace period the death benefit would be paid, although the insurer can reduce the benefit by the amount of premium outstanding. While interest might be added to the premium due, generally, insurers do not follow that practice.

Reinstatement clause. The reinstatement clause allows a policyholder, who survived the grace period without payment of the premium, to reinstate a policy within a certain period of time (generally three years or less) with evidence of insurability. In this case, a reinstatement requires payment of back premiums plus interest.

Nonforfeiture options. Several options are available to policyholders wishing to discontinue making premium payments, one of which is to surrender a policy for the nonforfeiture cash value. If, however, the objective is to keep the policy enforced (i.e., not taking a cash payout), then the accumulated cash value could be used to convert the existing policy into either an extended term policy or a paid-up permanent policy. In the former case, the insured would continue to be covered for the original face value, but for a reduced time period. In the latter case, the significantly reduced death benefit would be what the nonforfeiture cash value would fund. Also, some insurance companies might allow the policyholder to purchase an annuity.

Dividend options (participating policies only). As previously stated, participating policies return excess premiums paid by a policyholder as dividend. In such cases, policyholders are entitled to select from a list of multiple dividend payout options. These include: a cash payout, using dividend to reduce the next premium, purchase of a "paid-up" whole life policy, placement in a separate account to accumulate interest, or purchase of a one-year term policy (referred to as the "fifth dividend").

Policy loans (cash value policies only). Cash value growing tax-deferred inside an insurance policy acts as an attractive tax shelter investment. What really makes a cash value insurance policy an attractive savings vehicle, however, is that the accumulated cash value can be withdrawn as a loan, often at a net borrowing cost that is significantly lower than the prevailing rate on unsecured personal loans. Equally important, these policy loans are easy to obtain and their repayments are made quite flexible.

There are some disadvantages associated with taking out a policy loan, however. For one thing, a policy loan automatically reduces the death benefit by the amount of the loan plus the interest due. Still, policy loans remain attractive to those who urgently need the funds or for whom alternative sources of loan are not available.

Settlement Options. A life contract must spell out the nature of settlement options available to policyholders and their designated beneficiaries. These include: cash option (i.e., lump sum), interest-only option, and installment options (e.g., fixed amount, fixed period, and life period).

1. ***Lump-sum payment.*** Cash payments represent by far the most popular life insurance settlement option. A cash settlement enables the beneficiary to retire outstanding debts, pay off administrative and funeral costs, meet tax liabilities, and provide emergency funds. In addition, a lump-sum payment provides funds for creating a diversified investment portfolio to achieve multiple objectives, namely growth, current income, liquidity, and diversification. Of course, it is advisable for a policyholder opting for this type of settlement to ensure that the beneficiary or the associated advisor is sufficiently sophisticated to construct, manage, or oversee the management of such a challenging investment portfolio.

2. ***Interest option.*** In some situations beneficiaries might decide to leave the funds with the insurance company at a guaranteed rate of interest. There might be an option for the beneficiary to withdraw an additional amount each year (e.g., 10 percent of the death benefit). This option is generally not preferred unless it is used to temporarily park the funds with an insurance company.

3. ***Installment payments (annuity).*** For those who do not wish to put enormous burden of investment management on their beneficiaries there are installment options. These options include fixed and variable alternatives.

4. ***Fixed-period option.*** Under this option, first the period of payment is identified (generally 1–30 years), and then for each period the amount of installment or annuity payment is calculated, based on principal and interest expected to be paid at the end of the period. This option is appropriate for providing income for raising children or buying time until the surviving spouse succeeds in joining the labor force.

5. ***Fixed-income option.*** Under this form, first the installment amount is identified, and then payments continue until both principal and interest are totally exhausted. This option is preferred in situations where the main objective is to provide temporary readjustment income for the surviving spouse.

6. ***Straight life option.*** Under the straight life income option the beneficiary cannot outlive the income stream. Annuity payments are based on the age and sex of the beneficiary, and income payments continue even if the beneficiary outlives the life expectancy. This option is appropriate for individuals who are concerned about outliving their financial resources. There are three problems associated with this option, however. (a) If the beneficiary dies at an early age, a substantial portion of the principal would be forfeited. (b) Over time, inflation would certainly erode the value of the monthly income. (c) The recipient is never permitted to invade the principal. For those concerned with these shortfalls, a variant known as life-income- with-installment-certain option is available. This option guarantees that payments will continue for at least a specified period (usually 10, 15, or 20 years) even if the principal beneficiary dies early. Of course, even after the expiration of the minimum guaranteed period the insurance company would continue to make payments for as long as the primary (or secondary in the case of joint life) beneficiary is alive.

7. ***Life with period certain.*** This form of installment payout is a straight life option in which there is also a stated minimum guarantee (e.g., 10 years of payments). If the surviving spouse or the

beneficiary were to die prior to the minimum period, the remaining payments would be made to the named beneficiary. For example, if a widow were to die after eight years where the minimum guarantee period was 10 years, then the beneficiary would receive additional two years of installment payouts. Note that the monthly installment amount for a straight life with period certain would be less than that of a straight life installment because of a greater liability exposure of the insurance company.

8. ***Life income with refund.*** Under this option the payout is a straight life installment with a guarantee that at least the full amount of the premiums paid (without interest) for the life policy will be returned to the beneficiaries. For example, assume that after her husband's death, a widow collected ₹50,000 of installment income and then passed away. If the deceased husband had paid ₹70,000 in premiums, then the beneficiaries would receive an additional ₹20,000 (₹70,000 less ₹50,000) of installment income. As noted above, the monthly installment payout for a life income with refund would be less than that of a straight life installment payout.

Beneficiary Provision. A policy owner is authorized to name both primary and contingent beneficiaries. A policyholder also has the right to change the designated beneficiaries, unless of course a named beneficiary was classified as irrevocable. In that case, the irrevocable beneficiary would have to consent before any such change could be recognized.

Simultaneous Death Clause. If the insured and the beneficiary die simultaneously, it would be presumed that it was the beneficiary who died first. The proceeds will then be paid to the secondary beneficiary or to the estate of the insured, if no secondary beneficiary had been named.

Suicide Clause. This clause states that suicide within one year of the policy in force will completely void the policy.

Conversion Privileges. Some insurers provide a policyholder the right to convert a term policy into a permanent policy within a specified time period.

Alterations Privileges. Generally, a policy document provides the specific terms of a contract. However, if some of these terms are unacceptable or appear unsui, the insurance company may offer the policyholder various alternatives from which he or she can choose. These include, but are not limited to, changes in the following items: basic terms of the plan, name, nominee, mode of premium payment, with or without profit arrangement, and so on. Other changes that might also be approved relate to the settlement option of payments assured by installments, splitting of a policy into more than one policy, alteration in currency and place of policy payments, addition of accidental benefits, and a premium waiver benefit.

Policy Riders

Policy riders that might be added to an insurance policy include the following.

Accelerated death benefit. Some insurance companies offer policyholders a specified portion of the death benefit (e.g., 50 percent of the policy's face value) if they are suffering from a terminal illness, require long-term care, or need to be admitted to a nursing home, and the anticipated death is imminent. While this could be an appealing option, there might also be some risks associated with it. For one thing, the benefit received by a policyholder could be treated by the government as taxable income. For another, if this option were exercised, a policyholder could become disqualified from a variety of government-subsidized programs available to terminally ill patients.

Accidental death benefit. In this policy, if death occurs as a result of an accident, in addition to the death benefit, an additional benefit amount is provided by the insurance company. For example, a "double indemnity" policy provides a benefit equal to twice the face value of the policy. In a situation like this, so long as the cause of death is directly related to an accident, the additional benefit payment would be made even if death occurs after, say, six months. However, the accidental death benefit typically ends at a certain age (e.g., by the age of 65).

Disability waiver of premium. A waiver of premium rider suspends premium payments when the insured becomes totally disabled. In such a situation, a policy would continue as though premium payments were being made and cash value would continue to accumulate. The rider would define disability, which could change over time. For example, one rider might state that during the first five years the insured would be considered totally disabled if he or she could not be employed. This definition, however, might change after five years to something more lenient, such as "any job for which the person is reasonably trained." As stated, disability waivers typically end at a certain age.

Disability income rider. In this case, an insured receives a certain amount of monthly cash flow during the disability period.

Family rider. This rider provides the option of obtaining term insurance on family members (i.e., spouse and children).

Guaranteed insurability option. This option enables the insured to purchase additional insurance at specific times or intervals (e.g., every three years up to the age of 40) without the evidence of insurability. The amount of additional insurance is specified in the provision. This option is valuable in that it offers excellent flexibility for future planning.

Major surgical assistance option. This rider provides the option of financial support during medical emergencies, including surgery. However, claims arising from pre-existing injuries or illnesses and other predefined specific events are typically excluded.

Critical illness rider. This rider covers the insured during critical illness. More specifically, this rider covers: cancer, heart attack, coronary artery bypass, renal failure, paralytic stroke, and major organ transplant.

Return-of-premium rider. Under this rider, at the end of a specified term, all premium payments are returned to the insured. In case the insured dies before the term expires, the beneficiary receives all the premium payments made up to that point.

TAXATION OF LIFE INSURANCE

As previously mentioned, life insurance provides an important source of income for paying final expenses after death, replacing lost annual income, funding education, providing estate liquidity, and paying off debts of the estate. Tax considerations are also important and should be carefully evaluated in a life insurance transaction.

Life insurance has three distinct tax attributes: the increase in a policy's cash value is not considered taxable, transfers between separate accounts are not taxed, and proceeds paid by reason of the insured's death are generally excluded from taxable income. There are, however, exceptions when these tax attributes are lost, especially when an active policy is changed or surrendered. These exceptions, as well as other related tax considerations, are based primarily upon the *tax basis* of a policy.

Income and Estate Taxation of Death Benefits

Following the death of an insured, life insurance distributions to the estate or beneficiaries are generally exempt from income tax. However, whether a policy's death benefit is subject to estate taxes depends on the ownership of the policy.

Gross estate. Life insurance benefits are treated as part of the decedent's gross estate and subject to estate tax liability if the insured was the named beneficiary or if he or she retained incidents of ownership.

Outside the gross estate. Life insurance benefits will be neither a part of the decedent's gross estate nor subject to estate liability if the deceased had no ownership or retained no incidents of ownership in the policy and if the insurance proceeds were not received by the estate. An exception to this rule is when an individual insurance policy was gifted or transferred to a different person or an entity like a trust within three years of the decedent's death; in this case the proceeds are pulled back into the gross estate of the decedent. However, if an irrevocable life insurance trust owns the policy outright, the three-year rule does not apply, since the life insurance was never transferred to the trust.

It is important to note that because life insurance is a contract, so long as the beneficiary is a person or a trust, death benefits completely bypass the probate process. Also, the assignment of a life policy without consideration received generates a gift tax liability. These subjects will be discussed in detail in Chapter 15 (Estate Planning).

Transfer for value. As mentioned, generally death benefits from a life insurance policy are free from federal income taxes. However, there is an important exception that applies if a policy is sold to someone other than the insured, namely a partner of the insured, a partnership in which the insured is a partner, or a corporation in which the insured is a shareholder or officer. If this transfer for value occurs, the amount by which the death benefit exceeds the tax basis of the policy is recognized as taxable income for the transferee (purchaser).

Installment payments to the beneficiaries. Installment payments of the death benefit to beneficiaries are considered partly as a nontaxable death benefit and the rest as taxable interest income.

Distributions during Life

An understanding of the concept of *basis* is necessary to assess the income tax implication of distributions from a life insurance policy during a policyholder's lifetime. The basis of the contract is the total premiums paid, including dividends used to purchase additional insurance, less nontaxable distributions received, if any, in the form of dividends and tax-free withdrawals.

Policy dividends. Dividends distributed in the form of cash, used to purchase additional insurance, or invested in the policy are considered nontaxable return of capital.

Policy withdrawals/loans. Withdrawals after five premium payments are generally considered nontaxable. If that obligation has not been met, the surrender value is added to the insured's taxable income for the year. As already stated, upon maturity, all withdrawals are completely tax free.

Incidentally, withdrawals from pension plans before maturity are treated differently. All premiums claimed as a deduction from income taxes (under Section 80C of the Income Tax Act) become fully taxable. In addition, the entire surrender value is recognized as the income for the year and is fully taxed.

Provisions relating to loans from pension plans are complex. Loans granted from a pension plan cannot exceed 90 percent of the surrender value of that policy (85 percent for paid-up policies including cash value of bonus). The term of a loan must be at least six months long. Each policy specifies in advance whether or not loans can be granted from that policy.[5]

Interest on policy loans. Tax laws distinguish between single premium insurance policies in which substantially all of the premiums are paid within three years of the purchase date and non-single premium policies. In the case of the latter, the tax law does not allow deductions for interest if the loan was taken

[5] https://www.licindia.in/help_us_to_serve.htm (last accessed on October 6, 2014).

against an increase in the policy's cash value. However, in both cases the general limitations on interest deductions apply. For example, if the funds were used to purchase investment securities or personal assets like an automobile, the interest is treated as nondeductible personal interest.

Surrender, sale or disposition, maturity. Insurance contracts are treated as noncapital assets. If a policy is surrendered, sold, or allowed to mature, any cash or value received in excess of the tax basis in the contract is treated as ordinary income. Also, losses generated in this context are not deductible. There are, however, exceptions to this rule.

Accelerated death benefit. An exception to the "transfer for value" rule applies when the insured, who is also the policy owner, is either terminally ill (expected to die within two years) or is chronically ill and needs assets to pay for long-term care. In such a case, the insured is allowed to surrender the policy or withdraw cash value from it without income tax consequences.

Section III: Life Insurance Planning for the Individual

INTRODUCTION

In order to develop a policy recommendation for individual clients, it is important for a financial planner to fully understand: (a) the client's goals and objectives, (b) detailed account of current expenses and outstanding liabilities, (c) the duration of current needs, (d) the client's financial capacity to make future premium payments, and (e) the client's risk tolerance, investment experience, and personal situation. These issues will be explored in the remainder of this section.

CLIENT GOALS

The starting point in any planning process is to understand what the client is trying to achieve. The goals typically fall into five major categories.

1. ***Income replacement.*** Practically, every head of a family dreams that in the event of a premature death the financial lifestyle of the family should not be adversely affected, even if the surviving spouse is unwilling or unable to work. This dream can be realized only if after death the family's current flow of income continues unabated. In order to meet this objective, the following questions would need to be asked: (a) In the event of death, how much income will the family need in order to maintain the desired standard of living? (b) What is the duration of this income need? (c) How much income from Employees' Provident Fund (EPF)/Public Provident Fund (PPF)/National Pension System (NPS)/ other pension schemes will be received until the children are no longer covered? (d) How much income will the spouse need after the children are on their own (e.g., in retirement)? Answers to these questions will provide the basis for determining the life insurance needs of the family.
2. ***Pre-funding education for the children.*** Pre-funding educational costs through life insurance is a way for the income earner to continue playing a role in the children's future even after death. If providing funds for education is a goal, then it is important to inquire about: (a) the preference for a specific (e.g., public, private, in-state, or out-of-state) type of school, (b) the number of years' tuition is to be funded, and (c) other costs that need to be covered (e.g., housing, books, and travel).
3. ***Paying off outstanding debts.*** Another common goal is to provide the surviving spouse with a "clean slate" or a "head start" by paying off all or most of the existing home mortgage, car loans, student debts, and credit card loans. Life insurance is a prudent vehicle for achieving this goal because of the leverage it provides by generating huge benefits relative to the premium costs. If that is a client's goal, then quantitative data would need to be gathered to determine the amounts of all outstanding debts.

4. ***Providing for final expenses and taxes.*** Final expenses might include funeral expenses, final health care costs, and probate-related administrative costs. In order to estimate these final costs, a financial planner would need to assess a client's financial and personal situation and apply reasonable assumptions in estimating the projected expenses.

5. ***Leaving a legacy.*** Sometimes, by providing a legacy, clients may wish to continue playing a role "beyond the grave." This can be the case where a parent's goal is to give his or her children a head start in life by providing funds for buying a home or starting a business. Here, a financial planner would have to estimate the amount that would be needed to achieve this objective. In another situation, individuals who like to play an active role in advocating a cause they believe in might strongly wish to leave a meaningful legacy by creating and funding a charity. If that is the case, a planner would need to ask appropriate questions relating to the amount required to establish that legacy as well as to the specifics of the distributions to the beneficiaries.

CALCULATING LIFE INSURANCE NEEDS

Many "rules of thumb" have been devised to determine the life insurance needs of a family, and clients often receive simple advice on how to allocate their insurance "nest egg" money. For example, one insurance counselor suggests spending annually a sum equal to 6 percent of a breadwinner's gross income, plus 1 percent for each dependent—a total of ₹900 a year for a sales clerk who earns ₹10,000 a year and has a spouse and two children. Another counselor argues that the rule of thumb for coverage is 7–10 times the annual income. A third counselor asserts that 5 percent of one's take-home pay should be used to make life insurance premium payments. Because individual needs vary considerably between families, at best, such guidelines are of limited value.

Two commonly used methods for determining how much life insurance a family needs are the human life value approach and the capital needs analysis.

Human Life Value Approach

This approach is based on the income, or economic loss, potential of a client. It takes into account the future earnings that would be lost if the income earner were to die today. The human life value is typically determined by either (a) aggregating the present values of all estimated earnings, calculated by discounting those earnings by an assumed discount rate, or (b) applying some multiple to the expected annual income. For example, in the case of a client who has an expected annual income of ₹70,000 and wishes to continue working for another 30 years (when his income would disappear), using a discount rate of 6 percent, the human life value would equal ₹963,538 (based on financial calculator inputs of $N=30$, $I=6$, PMT = 70,000, FV = 0, and solving for PV). On the other hand, if a multiple of 12 times the annual income rule is applied, then the human value would equal only ₹900,000 ($12 \times 70{,}000$). Based on these two calculations it might be appropriate to recommend that this client purchases ₹1,000,000 life insurance coverage. Note that if the person already owns a ₹300,000 policy, then it would be appropriate to recommend a supplemental ₹700,000 policy to make up the difference.

A slight variation of this approach would be to reduce the ₹70,000 of the annual income by the portion that can be estimated to be consumed by the breadwinner (e.g., payroll taxes, self-maintenance, and so on). A calculation based on the same present value methodology for a ₹50,000 annual income (₹70,000 less ₹20,000 value of self-consumption) replacement suggests an income replacement need of only ₹688,242 (financial calculator inputs of $N=30$, $I=6$, PMT = 50,000, FV = 0, and solving for PV).

Certain drawbacks exist, however, in using the human life value approach. These include: (a) difficulty in accurately estimating the future lifetime income of a breadwinner, (b) possibility of ignoring existing assets, (c) unrecognized unique lifestyle expense needs of the survivors, and (d) random nature of the selection of discount rates and earnings multiples. Because of these drawbacks, the "capital needs analysis" approach is often considered to be theoretically more accurate for determining the amount of life insurance that a family should purchase.

Capital Needs Analysis

The capital needs analysis focuses on the estimated deficit between the existing assets and future expenses, and cash needs. The three steps involved in this process are as follows.

1. ***Determine expenses and cash needs.*** In the event a breadwinner wishes the family to continue enjoying the current income flow should the income producer pass away prematurely, several important questions should be answered before making an attempt to determine a family's life insurance needs. These questions include: Will the family remain in the same home? Will the surviving spouse be employed, and if so, will day care costs be a new expense factor? Will the lifestyle remain the same or will there be a downward readjustment? How does the client respond to the ideas concerning pre-funding education, paying off existing debts, leaving a legacy, and providing for the estate's liquidity? Clients' responses to these questions will enable a planner to realistically quantify their financial needs.
2. ***Confirm current assets and project future incomes.*** A list should be prepared that documents the family's assets (savings accounts, retirement plans, individual life insurance policies, employer-provided life policies, rental properties, and so on) currently available to shoulder the financial burden. After that, answers to a set of questions should be sought: What future incomes can be projected? How much, and for what duration, if any, the EPF/NPS/pension schemes survivorship benefits will be received? How much income does the surviving spouse expect to earn? What reinvestment rate will be earned on the existing assets? Answers to these questions will help a planner quantify the resources and the expected cash inflows.
3. ***Plan for the deficit.*** Once the values of the existing assets, liabilities, cash inflows, and cash outflows have been determined, capital needs of a family can be calculated, which in turn can be effectively covered by life insurance. Clearly, in calculating the capital needs, several critical assumptions will have to be made. For purposes of making conservative estimates (so the surviving spouse does not run into any unexpected surprises), it is best to ensure that the assumptions are reasonable and fully supportable.

Typical income needs of a family and sources of income expected by the surviving spouse are listed in Table 4.4.

POLICY SELECTION

In selecting a policy the financial planner needs to reflect on several important issues, including: (a) a client's ability to fund premium payments, (b) the policy's suitability for achieving a client's desired objective (while aligning with the client's risk tolerance, duration of the need, and personal situation), and (c) policy replacement.

Client's Ability to Fund Premiums

For the most part, the viability of a life insurance policy is dependent on a client's ability to fund ongoing premiums. If that does not happen, a policy either expires (term insurance) or "runs out of gas" (permanent insurance). Therefore, it is important for the financial professional to consider the client's financial situation when making a life insurance recommendation. For instance, is it reasonable to assume that the insured can continue to make the premium payments? A young couple with children might have to select

Table 4.4 *Expense Needs versus Sources of Income*

Expense Needs	Sources of Income
A. Single-period needs	A. EFP/PPF/NPS: Survivor's income
i. Administrative/Final expenses*	B. Group life insurance
ii. Estate settlement costs*	C. Spouse's earnings
iii. Debt liquidation*	D. Investment income
iv. Emergency fund*	
B. Multiple-period needs	
i. Educational cost	
ii. Surviving spouse's income needs	
iii. Children's income needs	
iv. Retirement needs	

Note: *Life insurance need not cover all of these expenses. These items can be considered optional in determining the life insurance needs of a family.

a renewable term, rather than a permanent policy in order to receive a higher level of benefits with an affordable premium schedule. Although that might not constitute an optimal solution for more affluent families, by doing so this young couple would have the ability to keep the renewable term policy in force.

Some clients with cash flow constraints might prefer a blended solution based on a combination of term and whole life insurance. Assume that a 53-year-old male in need of ₹250,000 coverage blends a ₹100,000 whole life policy with a ₹150,000 term life policy. On the whole life part of the blend, he pays a level premium for life. That guarantee is possible because the associated premium is much higher than that needed to provide coverage in the early years; the excess goes into a side fund used to cover substantially higher mortality costs later in life.

While on the surface this appears to be an attractive option, there might be a catch hiding below the surface which can have serious unintended consequences. In blended policies annual premiums are not guaranteed for life. The more the term life exists in the mix, the lower is the annual premium in the earlier stages, and the greater is the risk of premium escalation in later stages. For this reason, the term–whole life blend can quickly become impractical unless it is combined with the third ingredient of dividends. Whole life policies typically pay annual dividends which can be used to purchase additional whole life insurance. In the blended policy, as the proportion of whole life increases, that of the term life gradually decreases. So in a likely scenario, by using future dividends, in approximately 20 years a 50-year-old male can transform a blended policy into a 100 percent whole life policy under which the premium remains fixed for life.

The blended approach just described works reasonably well only if all the underlying assumptions happen to turn out to be accurate, but that might not always be the case. For instance, over time interest rates might fall causing a company to lower its future dividends. Similarly, increased expenses could compel an insurer to raise his or her term rates or drop the dividends altogether. In situations like these, a blended insurance policy could turn out to be totally unworkable.

Policy Suitability

Earlier in this chapter we presented different types and variations of life insurance policies. Each policy type has its specific purpose, benefits, and drawbacks. In synthesizing insurance policy recommendations, a financial planner should consider the amount of insurance needed, the duration of the coverage intended (permanent or temporary), the critical factors relating to the client (age, risk tolerance, knowledge, and experience), and the available personal and financial resources. If the policy recommendations are out of alignment with one or more of these factors, they will not achieve the intended purpose. Worst still, unless sizable contributions are made to the cash value account, the recommended policy might even lapse before its time.

Consider, for instance, a situation in which an inexperienced and a conservative client is sold a variable life policy based on an illustration using a 10 percent reinvestment rate, distribution of sizable participating dividends, and a death benefit that exceeds the guaranteed face value. In such a case, the client may erroneously believe that this "scenario" policy illustration is in fact guaranteed. Similar issues arise in viewing the policy illustration for a universal product in which unduly aggressive interest rate assumptions are made and the notion of premium flexibility is not clearly underscored. Fortunately, this problem was addressed in 1995 when the National Association of Insurance Commissioners in the U.S. adopted what came to be known as the Life Insurance Illustrations Model Regulation. In order to prohibit the use of misleading illustrations, this Regulation (subject to modification at the state level) requires that all items be clearly labeled as either guaranteed or non-guaranteed.

In a different scenario, assume that the objective of a conservative client is to fund college tuition for his son who enters college in 10 years. That goal has a quantifiable rupee need and a preset time horizon. In this case, a 10-year renewable term policy provides a perfect duration match since it ensures that, even in the case of the father's premature death, the goal of college funding would be achieved. This benefit, of course, would remain guaranteed so long as the annual premiums are paid and the policy remains in force.

Another "suitability" issue revolves around the need for insurance. In that context, it is appropriate to ask: Who in the family really needs life insurance? Following are the different life insurance schemes designed to benefit various members of the family.

Spousal Insurance. A family's sole breadwinner, or a co-breadwinner, has an obvious need for life insurance. Additionally, it is claimed that the economic value of a homemaker, particularly when she or he is also the caretaker of small children, is fairly high. To provide even the minimum of essential services performed by a homemaker, a family would have to hire maids, day care services, baby sitters, or other helpers, all of which would cost a staggering sum. So, in such a situation, a family could protect itself from the risk of losing a homemaker by buying spousal insurance in the form of an annual renewable term or a level term policy.

Juvenile/Child Insurance. Insurance for children represents a huge business for the insurance industry, as is evident by the fact that each year one of four cash value insurance policies is sold to cover the lives of children under the age of 18. Yet, for a compelling reason, the decision to insure a child's life remains controversial. If life insurance is designed for protecting a dependent, it is argued, then why would a parent wish to buy insurance coverage on a child? As a rebuttal, however, for a number of reasons insurance companies strongly recommend the purchase of juvenile policies. First, children's policies cost less than a comparable coverage on adults. Second, getting coverage for children guarantees that they will always have some life insurance, and this is especially valuable if subsequently they become uninsurable. Third, a child insurance plan not only offers a lump- sum payment on the death of the policyholder, but all future premiums are also waived and the insurance company continues to invest the funds on behalf of the policyholder. Fourth, all cash value policies have an investment component. With a typical variable life policy, for example, a portion of the paid premium is invested in a separate tax-deferred account consisting of stocks, bonds, and money markets instruments. A child can borrow part of the policy's cash value often at a low interest rate and use it to pay for college tuition or other big ticket items. Fifth, premiums paid for a child's insurance plan are eligible for tax deduction under Section 80C and any income received from the insurance plan is tax free under Section 10 (10D)—of the Income Tax Act.

There exist equally strong arguments against purchasing a juvenile policy as well. First, because in these policies the liability of insurance companies is extremely limited, juvenile policies can be considered to be very expensive. Second, besides life insurance, other less expensive products are available to achieve the same objectives like paying college tuition. For instance, for a one-year-old child, a parent buys a variable life policy with an annual premium of ₹500 and expected annual net (of expenses) earnings of 10 percent. By the time the child reaches 18, this policy would most likely accumulate a cash value of approximately ₹13,200. If, however, the parent invests the same annual amount in a typical S&P 500 index fund which earns 10 percent a year, then that fund would accumulate ₹20,000 over the same period. Third, it can be argued that parents who can afford to pay these policy premiums should not need the financial protection offered by a juvenile insurance policy.

A careful consideration of all of the arguments presented above reveals that each side insists on taking an extreme position. As a general rule, people should not reject the idea of buying a juvenile policy merely because they erroneously believe that it adds no value. By the same token, people should not buy this type of policy simply because it appears to be inexpensive. In the final analysis, in this case, as elsewhere, the philosophy of buying insurance remains the same: One should purchase a child's insurance policy if the benefits of such a policy exceed its cost, and that too only after the insurance needs for breadwinners and other adults have been satisfied. While the cost of a juvenile policy can be easily handled because it is relatively inexpensive, only a parent can decide if the net benefits of such a policy exceed its associated costs.

Policy Replacement

A well-planned life insurance program requires an analysis of risk exposures, the examination of alternative strategies and products, and the development of an optimal solution. A careful planning goes into the selection process before an insurance policy is put into effect; hence, insurance policies should be treated as long-term purchases, designed to be held on a long-term basis. While this statement is generally true, there are circumstances which might call for switching of policies. Compelling reasons for replacing an existing policy include: (a) change in a family's needs, (b) concern for the financial stability of an insurer, (c) comparable policy pricing, and (d) features and benefits of the existing policy that have become inconsistent with a client's expectations.

Consider the case of temporary life insurance needs of two families that are now significantly changed. In one case, the existing policy will no longer be adequate if the duration of the risk exposure has been extended. In another case, a policy covering a spouse's life may no longer be necessary if the children are grown, and some of the carefully selected old riders may no longer be needed. Finally, in some cases, even the amount of coverage may have to be readjusted to suit a family's changing insurance needs.

A decline in the financial strength of an insurance company, or the downgrading of its credit or debt rating, would bring into question an insurer's ability to pay out his or her contractual obligations. That would certainly raise a "red flag" which would need to be addressed without delay. While there exist certain safeguards at the state level designed to protect policyholders against insurer insolvency (discussed in the next section), the insured can still lose portions of the invested premiums as well as a significant amount of the promised life benefits.

The steady decline in the cost of life insurance is another consideration that might justify switching policies. According to the new mortality table released by IRDA, in recent years the mortality rate has significantly declined. In fact, in India the life expectancy has dramatically improved from 70 to 75 years.[6] As a consequence, for many types of insurance contracts the premium rates have significantly dropped. For this reason alone, it pays to periodically investigate the advisability of switching older policies for new ones.

The relative attractiveness of UL and other, more flexible, types of policies relative to whole life policies constitutes another good reason for switching life insurance policies. The traditional whole life policies can be complex, inflexible, and costly. As mentioned, in 2010, IRDA changed UL products into VIPs and categorically stated that VIPs could be offered only under non-unit-linked platform.[7] Also, in a VIP policy the premium payments, death benefits, and the number of required payments remain fixed as long as the policy remains in force. The newer variable life policies are not only flexible with respect to both the death benefit and premium payments, but they also can generate more competitive rates of return.

[6] http://www.thehindubusinessline.com/industry-and-economy/banking/life-insurance-premiums-may-come-down-from-april-1/article4459275.ece (last accessed on October 6, 2014).

[7] https://www.irda.gov.in/ADMINCMS/cms/whatsNew_Layout.aspx?page=PageNo966&flag=1 (last accessed on October 6, 2014).

Switching of policies could also have several serious drawbacks, however. These include the following.

Commissions/surrender charge. The replacement of an existing policy with a new one would most likely incur a new sales load. Moreover, the old policy might still have a contingent deferred sales load associated with it which would become payable if it is switched for a new policy.

Two-year window. Most policies provide for a two-year period of contestability after which an insurer cannot refuse to pay the benefit for any reason except fraudulent misrepresentation, nonpayment of premium, and a two-year suicide clause. Both of these two-year contestability clocks start anew with a replacement policy.

Higher premiums. Because the new policy would be purchased at an older age and would generate new commissions or sales costs, premium payments for the new policy would most certainly be higher.

Insurability. Before considering a policy switch, it is vital that the issue of insurability be considered. The reason is that deteriorating health conditions and advancing age might make a client uninsurable.

Comparable benefits. The old policy may offer superior settlement options, disability provisions, suicide provisions, and other important benefits which might not be duplicated in a new policy. Also, as mentioned, when a whole life policy is switched to a UL policy, investment and mortality costs are shifted from the insurer to the insured, thereby creating a higher level of risk exposure for the insured.

It is noteworthy that since June, 2014, IRDA has required insurance companies to disclose full details of the related policies and a two-week due diligence period before allowing policyholders to switch policies. Equally important, insurance companies are now directed to advise customers not to surrender or make their existing policies paid up before switching to a new policy. These companies are also advised to warn their customers against withholding full or part of the surrender value and inform the new company of a customer's existing policies.[8]

It appears that the purpose of tightening the replacement norms is "to protect the long-term interests of life insurance policyholders and to discourage intermediaries persuading lapsing, surrendering, or making paid-up of an existing life insurance warning with the intent of canvassing or soliciting a new life insurance policy on the same life." It is hoped that this warning would encourage policyholders to retain their life insurance policies.[9] Clearly, the intent of the law is to ensure that insurance companies would offer to replace a life insurance policy only when it is in the best interest of a policyholder.

INSURANCE COMPANY SELECTION

Prior to choosing a life insurance company, a financial planner needs to critically examine a number of important selection criteria. These include: financial stability of the company, reputation for servicing policyholders and paying claims, underwriting standards, and comparative policy.

Financial Stability of the Company

For generations, life insurance companies have been a powerful force in our society, faithfully paying out death benefits, retirement income, and current income. People have always been led to believe that their policies are grounded in the bedrock of sound investments. For that reason, some years ago the

[8] http://www.business-standard.com/article/pf/replacing-your-life-insurance-policy-might-get-tougher-114062300842_1.html (last accessed on October 6, 2014).

[9] http://articles.economictimes.indiatimes.com/2014-06-18/news/50678704_1_life-insurance-policy-insurance-business-irda (last accessed on October 6, 2014).

financial woes of several giant insurance companies sent shockwaves throughout the financial services industry. Understandably, even today, high anxiety sweeps this country in the wake of occasional runs by policyholders and state takeovers of insurance companies.

An insurance industry does maintain guaranteed funds to safeguard the interests of its policyholders, but it operate by rules far different from those applied by IRDA. The state rules governing the insurance-financed guaranty funds considerably vary from one another. In fact, only a handful of state insurance funds cover guaranteed-insurance contracts (GICs). More importantly, for an insured to be able to collect funds, the insurance company must already be in liquidation (funds could not be collected when mutual benefit was in default but not in liquidation). In general, an insured is protected for only up to ₹100,000 in annuities and up to only ₹300,000 in cash values and death benefits. However, since these limits could vary, it is advisable to check the specifics with the insurance commissioner of the state in which the policyholder resides, because the present patchwork of state regulations of the insurance industry leaves some policyholders protected while others holding the bag.

Amid all the worries and confusion surrounding the soundness of individual insurance companies, policyholders tend to assess the financial stability of insurers by relying on the opinions of the rating agencies listed below, each of which can be conveniently accessed online.

1. ***Crisil.*** Founded in 1987, it is a full-service credit-rating organization providing ratings, research, and risk and policy advisory services. It rates insurance companies on a scale ranging from AAA down to D. The company refers to these as financial strength ratings.[10]

2. ***Icra.*** This rating agency was founded in 1991. It provides credit ratings, research and, financial markets analysis to the global market. The firm's ratings range from iAAA down to I C. The company refers to these as claim paying ability ratings.[11]

3. ***Care.*** Founded in April 1993, it is now the second-largest credit rating agency in India. Its ratings range from AAA down to D. The company refers to these as claim paying ability ratings.

4. ***Fitch India.*** Fitch India provides credit ratings, research, and financial markets analysis to the global market. The firm's ratings range from AAA (ind) down to C (ind). The company refers to these as financial strength ratings.[12]

Ratings by Crisil, Icra, Care, and Fitch India are presented in Table 4.5.

Table 4.5 *Ratings of Life Insurance Companies*

Crisil	Icra	Care	Fitch India
AAA	iAAA	CAREAAA (in)	AAA (ind)
AA	iAA	CAREAA (in)	AA (ind)
A		CAREA (in)	A
BBB			
BB	iA		
B			BBB (ind)
C			
D	iBBB	CARE BBB (in)	
		CARE BB (in)	
		CARE B (in)	
	iBB	CARE C (in)	BB (ind)
	iB	CARE D (in)	B (ind)
	iC		CCC/CC/C

[10] http://www.crisil.com (last accessed on February 24, 2015).
[11] http://www.icra.in/ (last accessed on February 24, 2015).
[12] http://www.fitchindia.com (last accessed on February 24, 2015).

Reputation for Servicing Policyholders and Paying Claims

It is vitally important to purchase a policy from an insurance company that has historically established an impressive track record of honoring insurance claims in a timely manner. It is equally important to ensure that the insurance company provides efficient and courteous service to its policyholders, both before and after claims are submitted.

Underwriting Standards

The underwriting standards of a company determine whether or not an applicant would be found insurable by that company. For example, a client with several driving-under-the-influence citations is likely to be found uninsurable by some insurance companies.

Comparative Policy Cost

Information on the true cost of buying a life insurance policy can be routinely obtained from insurance companies. But sometimes even that information might not be of much help, since uninformed buyers tend to focus directly on the actual premium payment without considering the overall cost-benefit profile. We have already discussed various provisions, options, and riders relating to an insurance policy, and it is advisable to critically review all of these factors before selecting a policy. It is worth repeating that an uncritical comparison of only the premium rates per ₹1,000 of coverage as routinely quoted by different companies constitutes is a highly inefficient method of shopping for a cost-effective insurance policy. For instance, a 21-year-old male shopping for a ₹100,000 policy coverage might receive the following quotes from different companies:

Policy	Year 1	Year 20
Five-year renewable term	₹6,000	₹5,500
Five-year renewable and convertible term	6,200	6,200
Whole life	7,000	6,500
Limited-pay life (paid up at the age of 65)	7,000	6,500

Clearly, these rates are not comparable (since in some cases they represent pure protection while others are based on cash value types of policies) but an unsuspecting client with little financial knowledge might completely miss that point.

When comparing an insurance policy (such as a ₹100,000 participating whole life policy) from more than one insurance company, insurance professionals focus on the concept of "net cost." Essentially, four factors determine the true cost of a policy: (a) premium payments, (b) dividends, (c) cash value, and (d) opportunity cost of investing in the policy (i.e., the rate of interest that a policyholder could earn by investing the funds elsewhere). The two most popular methods used for calculating the true cost of a policy are: the net-cost method and the interest-adjusted cost index.

Net-cost Method

The net cost, which is calculated for a given point in time during the life of the policy (say, at the end of the 10th year), is based on the following:

$$\text{Net Cost} = \text{Premiums Paid} - (\text{Accrued Dividends} + \text{Cash Value})$$

For instance, if Ashish has been paying an annual premium of ₹1,000 for 10 years in a participating policy, and the accrued dividend and cash values at the end of the 10th year are ₹5,000 and ₹15,000, respectively, then the net cost of the policy is: – ₹10,000 (₹10,000 – (₹5,000 + ₹15,000) = – ₹10,000). Of

Table 4.6 *Net Costs versus Interest-adjusted Cost Method*

{A} Net Cost Method	
1. Total premiums for 20 years (₹240/year)	₹4,800
2. Less dividends for 20 years (₹75/year)	–1500
3. Net premiums for 20 years (1–2)	₹3,300
4. Less cash value at end of 20 years (given)	–3,600
5. Insurance cost (3–4)	–₹300
6. Average cost per year (1/20)	–₹15
7. Cost per year per ₹1,000 of insurance divided by number of thousands of face amount of policy (10 in this case)	–₹1.50
{B} Interest-adjusted Cost Method	
1. Total premiums for 20 years, each accumulated at 4%	₹7,147[a]
2. Less dividends for 20 years, each accumulated at 4%	–₹2,233[b]
3. Net premiums for 20 years (1–2)	₹4,914
4. Less cash value at the end of 20 years (given)	–₹3,600
5. Insurance cost (3–4)	₹1,314
6. Amount to which ₹1 deposited annually will accumulate in 20 years at 4%	₹31[c]
7. Interest-adjusted cost per year: divide ₹1,314 by	₹42
8. Cost per year per ₹1,000 (1/10): divide ₹42 by 10	₹4.20[d]

Notes: The illustration is based on a ₹10,000 policy bought at 35 years of age. The policy is assumed to have been cashed in after 20 years. Cash value at the end of 20 years equals ₹3,600.

[a]PMT=₹240, n=20, i=4, FV=7,147

[b]PMT=₹75, n=20, i=4, FV=2,233

[c]PMT=₹1 (beginning of year, or annuity due), n=20, i=4, FV=31

[d]This figure is rounded off. The exact cost is ₹4.24 as shown here:

Line Number of Interest-adjusted Cost Method	Amount (2 decimals)
1	₹7,146.74
2	2,233.36
3	4,913.38
4	3,600.00
5	1,313.38
6	30.97
7	42.41
8	4.24

course, a negative net cost by no means implies that the company was actually paying the insured for the insurance. The reason for arriving at a negative value is that the net-cost method totally ignores the time value of money by not taking into account the opportunity cost of making premium payments in excess of the amount necessary to buy pure life insurance. For this reason, a better measure of the net cost is the interest-adjusted cost index.

Interest-adjusted Cost Index

The method for calculating the interest-adjusted cost index is demonstrated in Table 4.6. Not surprisingly, the table shows that for a 35-year-old the true cost of a ₹1,000 participating whole life insurance policy is ₹4.20 per thousand, and not –₹1.50, as calculated by the net-cost method. However, all is not totally lost with the net-cost method. While the participating policy costs are based on estimated dividends, and the cash surrender value depends on the number of years a policy has been in force, the net-cost method can still be used to compare the relative costs of two competing policies.

Interest-adjusted Cost Method

This method is technically superior to the net-cost method since it does take into account the time value of money. Nevertheless, it too has some shortcomings. For one thing, the choice of a specific period for comparison, such as 10 or 20 years, is purely arbitrary, and some companies might look better or worse when different time periods are chosen. For another, this method ignores mortality and policy lapse rates (although these factors are taken into account in making dividend projections) factors that could be effectively used to produce a more sophisticated index. Still, because of state requirements and voluntary actions by responsible organizations, nationally recognized associations like Consumers Union routinely publish insurance costs based on the interest-adjusted cost method, thereby making it possible for prospective insurance buyers to compare costs of different insurance policies.

Benchmark Method

This method, developed by Professor Joseph M. Belth, compares the cost of a UL or a variable life policy with a selected benchmark. Under this method, the annual cost per ₹1,000 of protection is computed by dividing total policy charges by the amount of pure life insurance protection. These annual charges are calculated by analyzing changes in the cash value. Since at any point in time the cash value of a policy equals the accumulated premiums plus the interest less any charges, during a given year the cost of a policy can be calculated by analyzing changes in the cash value. Belth's formula for computing the cost per ₹1,000 of protection is given by:

$$\text{YPT} = \frac{(P+\text{CVP})(1+i)-(\text{CV}+\text{D})}{(\text{DB}-\text{CV})(0.001)}$$

where

YPT = The yearly price per ₹1,000 of protection
P = The annual premium
CVP = The cash value at the end of the preceding year
i = The assumed interest rate expressed as a decimal
CV = The cash value at the end of the year
D = The dividend for the year
DB = The death benefit at the end of the year.

For instance, assume the following information associated with a policy under review:

Annual premium = ₹370
Cash value at the end of previous year = ₹675
Cash value at the end of current policy year = ₹915
Annual dividend = none
Interest rate = 6 percent
Death benefit at the end of the year = ₹50,000.

The cost of this whole life policy per ₹1,000 of coverage is ₹3.93:

(₹370 + ₹675) (1 + .06) – ₹915 + 0) (₹50,000 – ₹915) (.001) = ₹3.93

The ₹3.93 cost of protection per ₹1,000 can now be compared with benchmark costs that are computed with normal assumptions to determine whether the cost of this policy is reasonable or excessive. In general, as compared to the benchmark price:

If the Policy Cost Is:	Then the Mortality and Loading Charges Are:
Same or lower	Small
Higher but less than 200 percent of the benchmark cost	Medium
Higher than 200 percent of the of the benchmark cost	High

Incidentally, a point often overlooked is that the true cost of an insurance policy can depend on additional factors. As an example, often smaller companies have higher expenses than their more mature counterparts, due in part to the higher overhead expenses associated with running a small organization as well as the lack of management inexperience. A higher percentage of new premium rupees allocated to attract new business can also be a cost generator. Finally, higher death rates among policyholders can significantly increase the policy costs for the surviving policyholders. If the mortality rate among the company's policyholders is steep, the increased cost of insurance is generally met by either reducing dividends on existing policies or by increasing the premium rates on future policies.

Section IV: Business Uses of Life Insurance

INTRODUCTION

There are several important business uses of life insurance. These include:

1. Facilitating transfer of business ownership.
2. Protecting a business against loss of key employees.
3. Replacing income value of illiquid business.
4. Creating opportunity for recruiting, retaining, retiring, or rewarding employees through employee benefits.

In this section we will elaborate on buy–sell agreements, key employee life insurance, and uses of life insurance in qualified and non-qualified employee benefit plans.

BUSINESS TRANSFER AND INCOME REPLACEMENT

Life insurance can be used in many creative ways to accomplish a variety of business transfer and income replacement objectives. Consistent with the limited scope of this text, we will undertake a brief discussion of implementation of only the key techniques.

Buy–Sell Agreements

The death of the principal owner of a business can create serious financial difficulties both for the business and the survivors of the deceased owner. Since interest in the business is frequently a dominant portion of the deceased's total estate, a forced sale of the business to outsiders in order to pay the resulting estate tax liability could jeopardize the interests of the surviving shareholders.

Such a problem can be avoided with the help of a buy–sell agreement, which provides for an orderly transfer of the deceased's business interest to surviving partners, stockholders, or key employees at a fair value determined in advance. The money from such an agreement can be used to dispose of an owner's business interest in the event of death, disability, or retirement, or upon the owner's withdrawal from the business. A buy–sell agreement can be between the: (a) business and the individual owners (either a corporate stock redemption or a partnership liquidation agreement), called an "entity" plan, (b) individual owners, known as a cross-purchase agreement, and (c) individual owners and keepers, family members, or outside individuals, called a "third-party" business buy-out agreement. Such an agreement could also be in the nature of a "wait and see" arrangement, or it could take the form of a combination of the above choices.

In the case of corporations, the most common types of buy–sell agreements are stock redemption plans, often called stock retirement plans, or shareholder cross-purchase plans. The distinguishing feature of the redemption agreement is that the corporation itself agrees to purchase or redeem the stock of the withdrawing or deceased shareholder. In this case, the corporation is the owner and the beneficiary of each policy. In a cross-purchase plan, individuals agree between or among themselves to purchase the interest of a withdrawing or deceased shareholder. They are the owners and beneficiaries of each other's policies.

Key Employee Life Insurance

Business owners routinely purchase commercial property insurance to indemnify possible loss of assets, operating facilities, and profits, caused by fire, theft, or other natural disaster; they also purchase commercial liability insurance to cover losses resulting from general business and product liability. Along the same lines, through life insurance, business owners can protect themselves against the loss of a partner, an executive, or other key employees. Typically, the company that owns the insurance policy is the sole beneficiary and receives the full proceeds in the event of the death of the key person. The insurance proceeds replace lost income due to the death of the "rainmaker," and these funds can then be used to find and train the replacement. These cash proceeds can also be used to fund additional retirement benefits for the key employee, should that employee decide to retire. However, unlike other types of insurance policies, the death benefit in a key employee/man policy is taxed as ordinary income.

Insurance for the Professional

The need of life insurance coverage for professionals and small business owners is significantly different than the key employee coverage. Usually a professional practice or a small business does not have much resale value except for the equipment and furnishings it owns. Even under the best of circumstances, as compared to the income needs of the professional family, the price at which the business or the practice can be sold is relatively modest.

The solution to this type of problem faced by a small business lies in purchasing a life insurance policy. In the event of an untimely death of a professional or a small business owner, life insurance proceeds can be effectively used to generate a monthly income sufficient to help the family maintain the desired standard of living. Also, unlike the corporate executive, generally the professionals or small business owners do not have access to a corporate-type qualified retirement plan. Consequently, they can create a balanced retirement plan by effectively supplementing their qualified plans with life insurance policies.

EMPLOYEE BENEFITS

It is commonplace that employee benefits are important for recruiting and retaining valued employees. A business may use life insurance as a means of offering an attractive and employee-benefit package.

Group Life Insurance

Group life insurance provides a means for insuring, under one policy, a group of people made up of employees or members of an organization. Benefits of a group policy include: (a) no evidence of insurability for individual employee or member, (b) underwriting based on the statistics of the group and not the individual, and (c) an agreement to allow the conversion of a group policy into an individual cash value policy when an employee or a member leaves the plan. Each insured employee receives a certificate stating the amount of insurance coverage, the name of the beneficiary selected, and a summary of the rights and benefits.

Three types of popular group life insurance policies are: term insurance, permanent insurance, or a combination of the two.

1. ***Group term insurance.*** Generally, a group life insurance is issued as a one-year term life policy. Typically, the benefit amount is equal to a multiple (e.g., two times) of the employee's annual salary. Often the entire premium is paid by the employer. The premium associated with the coverage is tax free for the employer, since for income tax purposes it is treated as a normal business expense. Also, premiums paid by an employer are not treated as the perquisite of the employee. Of course, death benefits are always tax exempt under Section 10 (10D) of the Income Tax Act.

   Sometimes, employers wish to share the cost of group insurance with their employees. In such cases, with their consent the employees' portion might be automatically deducted from their salaries, with the balance of the premium paid by the employer. If an employee leaves the company, the group insurance coverage would be lost. However, within 31 days following the termination, the law allows the employee to buy an individual permanent policy for at least the same coverage even when that employee had become uninsurable.

2. ***Group permanent life insurance.*** Although less common than group term, financial planners may work with clients who have group ordinary whole life or group variable life benefits (through group universal life policy or GULP). Premiums for these permanent policies are deductible by the employer as a business expense, although the entire premium is generally considered as an employee's gross income.

   In the real world, a large portion of a person's life insurance coverage is likely to be of the group life protection variety. That is why a financial planner must watch out for clients who are likely to lose their group insurance after quitting their job. If possible, these people should be encouraged to start building individual insurance protection early on to guard against the possible loss of their group life insurance protection.

3. ***Endorsement method.*** Under this structure, an employer owns the policy on employees. An endorsement is filed with the insurance company specifying the division of ownership of cash value and death proceeds between the employer and the employees. Also, the employer typically makes the entire premium payment and has control over this type of policy. The benefit arrangement allows the employer to recover all costs (premium payments excluding interest), and the employee (or the beneficiary) receives excess benefits paid upon death or excess cash values paid upon policy surrender.

4. ***Collateral assignment method.*** Under this structure an employee, or a third party, such as a spouse or an irrevocable trust, owns the policy. According to the terms, the employee files with the insurance company a document called collateral assignment and assigns a portion of the policy to the employer. The amount of the premium paid by the employer is considered a below-market-rate loan. Here again, the benefit arrangement typically allows the employer to recover all premiums paid, and the employee (or the beneficiary) receives excess benefits paid upon death or excess cash values distributed upon policy surrender.

Life Insurance in Qualified Plans

Employers sponsoring pension plans like NPS and others are required to comply with Insurance Regulatory and Development Authority of India (IRDA) standards. These standards address several important issues, including: eligibility standards, vesting requirements, participation and coverage by non-highly compensated employees, nondiscrimination between key employees and rank-and-file employees, limits on annual contributions, and withdrawal rules. The objectives of the IRDA rules are to ensure that the retirement plan serves a broad employee base and that assets are used for their intended purposes. We will revisit these issues in Chapter 13. The employer and employee contributions are eligible for income tax deductions up to 10 percent of the basic salary plus dearness allowance (DA) under Section 80CCD[5] of the Income Tax Act, subject to a maximum of ₹150,000. However, an employer can claim tax benefits by treating it as a business expense.

One of the benefits of placing an insurance policy in a pension plan is that it provides significant benefits to the beneficiaries of relatively young employees whose premature death would severely limit the growth in their qualified plans. Another advantage of this strategy is to offer insurance protection for key employees who are rated and can only obtain insurance by paying significantly higher premiums. Naturally, the premium payments for these policies by the employer are treated as tax-deductible contributions. The distributed cash value (retirement benefit payments) is taxable to the employee as ordinary income. If an employee dies prior to retirement, the death benefit is treated as a tax-free distribution.

There are four ways in which these plans can be funded with insurance: (a) individual life policies, (b) group permanent life insurance, (c) group annuities, and (d) deposit administration contracts. Of these, the first two are self-explanatory. The group annuity contract is a method of pension funding in which units of individual annuity contracts are accumulated each year and are fully paid for on a regular basis. In contrast, a deposit administration contract is a form of group annuity in which an employer makes the contribution to a deposit administration fund, which is a single fund for all employees in the group. When an employee reaches the retirement age, sufficient funds are withdrawn from that fund to provide the retiring employee with an annuity.

Gratuity Insurance Plan

Gratuity is a statutory benefit governed by Payments of Gratuity Act, 1972. Under the Act, upon retirement after at least five years of continuous service, an employer's statutory liability is to pay each employee an amount equal to 15 days of his or her salary (15/26 of a month's wages, taking the last drawn salary as the basis) for every completed year of service. This total amount of gratuity payment is subject to a statutory limit set by the Act. Life insurance companies offer employers gratuity insurance plan as a deposit administration type of gratuity liability. The contribution made by an employer continues to accumulate and at year-end the accumulated interest is credited to the gratuity plan account.[13]

According to the current tax rule, gratuity received by government employees is fully tax exempt. For nongovernment employees, the maximum exemption for gratuity payments is ₹10 lakh. This exemption applies even to gratuity payments received upon resignation from service. Gratuity payments received by the widow, children, or dependents of an employee who dies in active service are also exempt from income tax.

Life Insurance in Non-qualified Plans

By way of providing a powerful incentive, sometimes corporations offer a deferred compensation plan under which the company promises (but does not guaranty) to pay a predetermined amount of compensation to a key executive following retirement. This arrangement helps both parties, since the corporation does not incur salary expenditures until after retirement, and the executive does not pay taxes until the deferred compensation is actually received. For the corporation, a deferred compensation payment becomes the tax deductible at the time the payment is made.

[13] Institute of Chartered Accountants of India, *Practical Approach to General Insurance Management: A Handbook for Insurance Professionals* (New Delhi: The Institute of Chartered Accountants of India, 2010), 737–38.

A deferred compensation agreement is only as good as the financial arrangements supporting it. A corporation can promise benefits to an executive, but the ability to carry out the commitment depends on the company's financial strength when the payments become due. Another potential drawback of this arrangement is that deferred compensation becomes a part of the general assets of a corporation and, hence, becomes accessible to its creditors. These problems can be mostly avoided with the help of a life insurance policy, although the company's creditors could still access the cash value of the policy.

Insurance on the life of the potential recipient of deferred compensation can provide a reserve fund from which payments could be made when they become due. The company sets up a fund with the insurance company issuing the policy and deposits money in the fund on an installment basis. Subsequently, funds become available when an employee dies or chooses to retire.

Section V: Life Insurance Needs: A Real-World Example

We have learned that the capital needs analysis technique can be applied to determine the life insurance needs of a family. We will now illustrate this point by point using a real-world example.

Anil Sharma, 30, and Shraddha Sharma, 29, have two children. Ankit is 4 and Neha is two years old. The Sharma's family and financial data are presented in Table 4.8, while the technique for arriving at the new capital needed for Anil Sharma is demonstrated in Table 4.8. This technique is discussed next.

Step 1: **Final Expenses**. The final expenses are estimated to be ₹27,000. Since the Sharmas have ₹2,500 in liquid assets and an additional ₹255 is expected to be received from NPS, additional capital needed to meet the final expenses is ₹24,245 (Line A).

Step 2: **Housing**. The Sharma's have a ₹70,000 mortgage loan and they would want it to be paid off in case of Anil's death (Line B).

Step 3: **Education**. The Sharmas estimate that it would cost ₹32,000 to educate Ankit and Neha. It is assumed that educational funds would earn interest at an after-tax rate of 5 percent and the rate of inflation would be 3 percent; that is, the real rate of return (actual rate minus the inflation rate) would be 2 percent. Finally, the Sharmas decide that they would like to have ₹32,000 in approximately 14 years when Ankit will turn 18 and Neha will be 16 years old (Line C).

Using a financial calculator (see Chapter 3 for details), we find that the present value of ₹1 growing at 2 percent per year for 14 years is 0.7578754. Multiplying the present value interest factor (PVIF) by ₹32,000, we determine that the capital required today to educate the two children is ₹24,252 (₹32,000 × 0.7578754).

Table 4.7 *Family and Financial Data of Anil Sharma*

Family Data			
Anil Sharma		Age 30	
Shraddha Sharma		Age 29	
Ankit		Age 4	
Neha		Age 2	
Financial Data			
Assets		Liabilities	
Cash/Liquid assets	₹2,500	Home mortgage	₹70,000
Invested assets	0	Other liabilities	12,000
Other assets	20,000	Net worth	30,500
Home	90,000		
	₹112,500		₹112,500
Life insurance coverage	₹50,000		

Table 4.8 *Capital Needs Analysis of Anil Sharma*

Line	Income Needed	Years Income Needed	Amount Needed	Available Sources			Additional Needed	Capital Required
				NPS/Other Pension	Employment	Other Sources		
A.	Final expenses		₹27,000*	₹255	0	₹2,500	₹24,245	₹24,245
B.	Housing		70,000*	0	0	0	70,000	70,000
C.	Education		32,000*	0	0	0	32,000	24,252
Monthly Income for Shraddha Sharma								
D.	Until Ankit is 18	14	2,200	1,043	₹1,067	0	90	13,200
E.	Neha between 16 and 18	2	2,200	522	1,067	0	611	14,387
F.	Alone, age 45–65	20	1,550	0	1,067	0	483	95,636
G.	Alone, age 65–80	15	1,550	695	0	0	855	133,087

Assumptions:

1. Capital amounts needed for monthly expenses are assuming that the capital will be exhausted when Shraddha Sharma is 80 years old.
2. Capital funds are assumed to earn interest at an after-tax, inflation-adjusted rate of 2 percent.
3. Client is eligible for NPS/other pensions.
4. Client wishes to pay off the mortgage immediately.
5. Education fund is available as a lump sum when Ankit reaches the age of 18—that is, in 14 years.
6. Wife does not receive pension between ages 45 and 65 (20 years).
7. Wife's life expectancy is 80 (15 years since the age of 65).

Capital Required Calculations

Line A: Capital immediately required. No calculation necessary.
Line B: Capital immediately required. No calculation necessary.
Line C: FV (PVIF). PVIF ($n = 14$, $i = 2\%$) is 0.757875 ₹24,252 = 32,000 (0.757875)

	PMT (Begin Mode)	*I* (%/mo)	*N*	PV
Line D:	90	2/12	14 × 12	13,200
Line E:	611	2/12	2 × 12	14,387
Line F:	483	2/12	20 × 12	95,636
Line G:	855	2/12	15 × 12	133,087

Note: Figures are rounded off.
*Optional at the discretion of the surviving spouse.

Step 4: **Monthly Expenses for Shraddha Sharma**. If Anil Sharma were to die today, for the next 14 years until Ankit is 18, Shraddha Sharma will receive ₹1,043 per month from NPS and ₹1,067 in today's rupees from her place of employment (Table 4.7). However, the Sharmas have decided that the family needs a monthly income of ₹2,200 to raise the two children. The resultant shortfall of ₹90 per month (₹2,200 – ₹1,043 – ₹1,067) can be obtained by purchasing an annuity for ₹13,200. The calculation method is shown at the bottom of Table 4.8, Line D.

Using the same technique, we can calculate that Shraddha will receive a monthly income of ₹611 for two years after Ankit leaves home at 18 and Neha becomes 18 by annuitizing a lump sum of ₹14,387. Finally, Shraddha will receive ₹483 per month for 20 years until she is 65 by annuitizing a lump sum of ₹95,636; similarly, she will receive ₹855 per month for 15 years until the age of 80 (life expectancy assumed by her) from a lump sum of ₹133,087.

Adding all the family's needs together, the total capital need of the Sharma family equals ₹374,807. This fact is revealed in Table 4.9.

Table 4.9 *Total Capital Needs of Anil Sharma*

Needs		Particulars	Capital Required (₹)
Final Expenses		Immediate need	24,245
Housing		Liquidation of mortgage	70,000
Education		Lump sum available when Ankit is 18—in 14 years	24,252
Monthly income	#1	Monthly income until Ankit is 18	13,200
	#2	Monthly income when Neha is between 16 and 18	14,387
	#3	Monthly income when Shraddha is between 45 and 65	95,636
	#4	Monthly income when Shraddha is between 65 to 80**	133,087
		Total	374,807
		Less existing insurance	–50,000
		Additional insurance need	324,807

Note: Figures are rounded off.

**Because the starting of this income is 36 years away when Shraddha turns 65, it is assumed that ₹133,087 expected at age 65 is discounted back to the present at the after-tax, inflation-adjusted rate of 0 percent. Hence, the present value today of ₹133,087 needed at Shraddha's age is also ₹133,087. This assumption makes it a highly conservative estimate of Shraddha's income needs far into the future.

FURTHER SOPHISTICATION

In the preceding illustration, we made several simplified assumptions which can be refined to calculate a more accurate capital needs analysis. Here, are a few examples of assumptions which are different from those made in the previous example:

1. The Sharmas do not wish to invade the principal in generating the required income.
2. Appropriate education funds become available at the beginning of the age of 18 for Ankit and Neha.
3. The present value annuity due (PVAD) of monthly income is discounted by inflation-adjusted interest rate (Lines E, F, and G).
4. Capital funds earn interest at an after-tax rate of, say, 8 percent.
5. The inflation rate is a more realistic 5 percent.
6. Spouse's employment income keeps pace with inflation.
7. The true inflation-adjusted interest rate is 2.857 percent [(1.08/1.05 – 1) × 100], instead of 2 percent assumed.

We can also use the following nine-step formula on the HP-12C to come out with the same result:

Step 1: 1.08
Step 2: Enter
Step 3: 1.05
Step 4: Divide
Step 5: 1
Step 6: –
Step 7: 100
Step 8: Multiply
Step 9: Result = 2.857

If further sophistication is desired, varied assumptions can be made about different tax rates and more realistic annual rates of return, depending upon the sophistication of the surviving spouse. Fortunately, these and other assumptions can be incorporated with relative ease in the capital needs analysis by using the time value of money tool developed in Chapter 3. Also, once the insurance need is determined, other techniques used in this chapter can be used to complete the life insurance planning process.

Section VI: Miscellaneous Life Insurance Issues

CAPITAL MAXIMIZATION STRATEGY

Life insurance professionals encounter a number of challenges in the wealth transfer market. The lack of liquid assets to meet wealth transfer costs for the wealthy is one limitation that with proper planning can be avoided. The capital maximization strategy (CMS) plan is designed for use in wealth transfer cases where the need for life insurance has been established but the funds required to pay premium might necessitate the liquidation of estate assets (e.g., high-performing investment portfolios, business assets).

The CMS plan offers an alternative method for paying life insurance premiums. Rather than using or liquidating current assets, funds needed to pay the premiums can be borrowed, thereby allowing a client's investment portfolio or other assets to remain intact. This program is designed for high net worth individuals who need to fund large annual premium but do not wish to liquidate assets. Applicants must qualify both financially and medically, and the loan is typically secured by a personal guarantee. In addition to the personal guarantee, the policy's cash value is used as collateral for the loan. The debt can either be repaid as a lump sum or in the form of periodic interest payments with the remaining balance to be paid from death benefits. Potential advantages of the program include: lower net out-of-pocket costs, access to low-cost funds, and asset transfer (death benefit) without gift tax consequences.

Life Insurance in Irrevocable Trust

One of the key insurance planning ideas relates to the creation of an irrevocable life insurance trust. Such a trust transfers the ownership of the insurance to the trust, and the current owner, who is generally the insured, gives up all rights to change the beneficiary and other terms of the policy. The irrevocable life insurance is designed to reduce estate taxes by removing the insurance proceeds from the owner's estate. In the case of large estates this could ultimately result in significant tax savings for the beneficiaries. Figure 4.6 demonstrates how a life insurance trust works.

While the irrevocable life insurance trust is a valuable planning tool, it does have several drawbacks. First, creating such a trust is an irreversible decision, and it may prove to be costly if conditions subsequently change. Second, possible gift taxes might have to be paid when a policy is transferred to a trust. Third, in the event life insurance is transferred to a trust within three years of the transferor's death, the proceeds are brought back to the owner's gross estate for purposes of computing estate taxes. Fourth, if following the transfer of the policy to an irrevocable trust the previous owner is required to make a gift to help the trust make the premium payments, taxes would be imposed on gifts exceeding the annual gift tax exclusion. Fifth, an irrevocable trust can create a major problem if it becomes necessary to change the beneficiary or the face value. Despite these shortcomings, an irrevocable life insurance trust remains a valuable insurance planning tool.

Life Settlement Options

Assume that in a typical life settlement, the health of the owner (over the age of 65) of a ₹250,000 insurance policy has deteriorated (but is not terminally ill), and he cannot afford to maintain the policy. Unfortunately, this is not an isolated case.

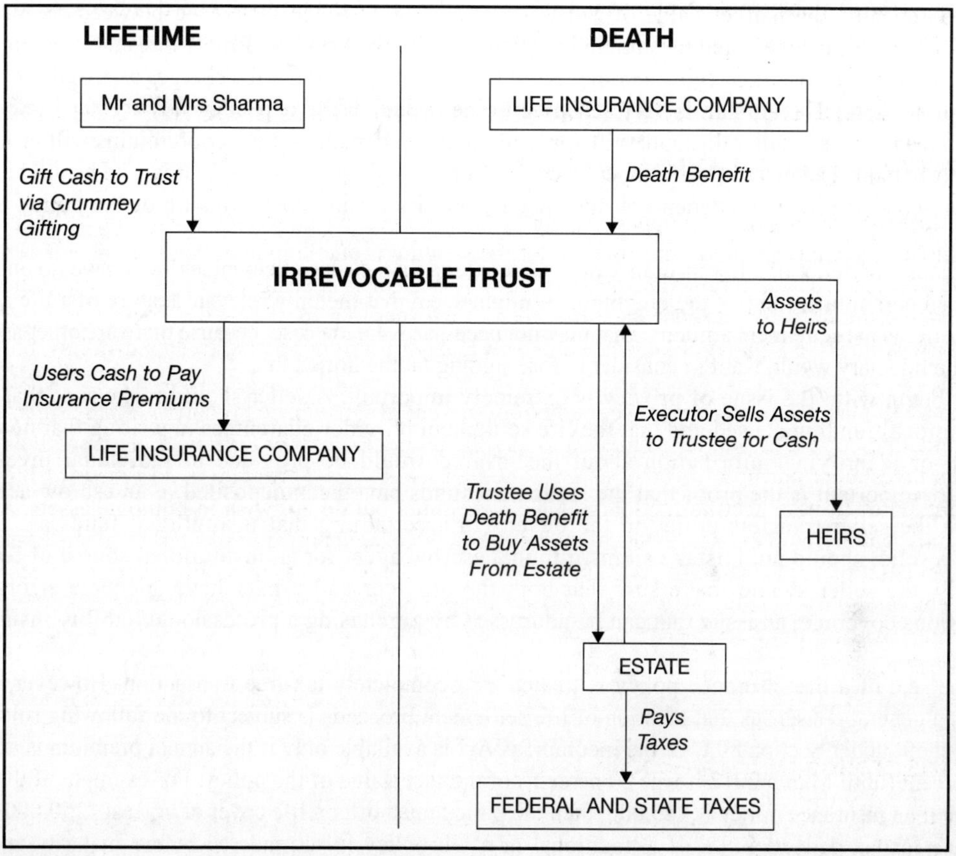

Figure 4.6 *How a Life Insurance Trust Works*

A life settlement of a life insurance policy can be a good option for a variety of reasons. These include: the risk covered by insurance no longer exists, the spouse has passed away, children have completed their education, business partnership has dissolved, or the insured, a key employee, has retired. And there are more. In some cases, investment projections used in generating the policy illustration turn out to be overly optimistic (in the current low-interest, average-market environment). In other cases, the expected "vanishing" premiums scenario has not materialized, and therefore, the financial plan built around that feature has collapsed. In such cases, the owner may wish to surrender the policy by investing the money in a different vehicle or by converting the existing policy to a more appropriate policy that better satisfy the current needs.

Clients interested in assessing a life settlement should have their policies appraised. Fortunately, obtaining a policy valuation is a relatively straightforward process. Generally, basic policy-related information, a policy illustration run until maturity, and health details (similar to those needed for a substandard insurance case without a medical exam), are submitted to a life settlement provider for valuation. The resulting valuation is the amount that the provider would likely pay to acquire the policy. Armed with this information, a policyholder can decide how best to use the life settlement value.

Theoretically, the market value of a life insurance policy is the difference between the present values of the death benefit and the anticipated premiums. (This simplification ignores the existing cash value and the real cost of carrying a policy is not the premiums paid but the charges assessed for insurance protection.) The amount is very sensitive to the insured's life expectancy. A shorter life expectancy means that a smaller discount will apply to the death benefit and fewer premiums will probably need to be paid. The insured's life expectancy depends on age, sex, smoking status, and health history. The anticipated premiums depend on the specific provisions and cost structure of the policy under review.

Because the seller of a life insurance policy receives a final cash settlement and will have no ongoing financial commitment to pay the premiums, it might seem that the only relevant feature of a life settlement offer is the settlement amount. That may not necessarily be the case, because there are other aspects that the fiduciary would want to consider before signing on the dotted line.

To begin with, the issue of privacy is extremely important. A seller should make sure that only institutional funding is used and that the life settlement provider guarantees in writing that no ownership or identifying information about the insured would be provided to individual investors. Equally important is the proof that the settlement funds have been deposited in an escrow account before the seller transfers policy to the buyer. (In ascertaining that institutional funds are being used, a seller should not mistake an institutional escrow agent for an institutional source of funds.) Finally, the seller should make sure that both the provider and broker have adequate errors and omissions coverage, an issue that can be addressed by purchasing a professional liability insurance policy.

The sale of a life insurance policy is treated as a completely tax-free transaction. However, there exists a general consensus that taxation of life settlement proceeds is subject to the following rules: (a) Tax benefit under Section 80 C of the Income Tax Act is available only if the annual premium is at least 10 percent (until March 2012 it was 20 percent) of the face value of the policy. For example, if the premium of an insurance policy is ₹25,000, then the policy must offer a life cover of at least ₹250,000 to be eligible for tax deduction. (b) If a traditional or a UL policy is surrendered before maturity and the insured has already paid at five premiums, then the proceeds will be exempted from taxes. If not, the surrender value will be fully taxed. (c) If an insured surrenders a pension policy before maturity, then all premium payments for which a deduction was originally claimed become fully taxable. In addition, the surrender value is also added the person's taxable income.

Living Death Benefits

Terminal illness or other life-limiting conditions produce devastating emotional and financial hardships both on the individual and the family. In order to ease this burden, many insurance companies allow a policyholder to use a portion of the death benefit if the insured is medically diagnosed with a condition limiting life expectancy to six months or less. Generally, the insured can receive any amount up to 75 percent of the proceeds that would be payable at death. Insurance companies do not impose restrictions on how these funds can be used by the insured.

The amount of living benefits paid to the insured acts as a lien against the policy, and it reduces the death benefit payable to the beneficiaries. This amount also reduces the cash value of the policy as well as the amount of money that can be withdrawn as loans. The following illustration demonstrates how living benefits works.

Harish is 55 years old and has been diagnosed with cancer. He is not expected to live longer than six months. He decides to submit a claim for living benefits offered by the ₹200,000 ABC whole life policy that he purchased at the age of 45. The current cash value in his policy, which also equals its loan value, is ₹50,000. Harish contacts his agent and finds that the maximum living benefits available to him is ₹150,000 (75 percent of ₹200,000). He requests half of this amount on his claim and receives a lump-sum payment of ₹75,000. Harish dies six months after filing his claim. His wife, as the beneficiary of his policy, receives ₹122,000. This amount is calculated as follows:

Before payment of "living benefits" Death benefit	₹200,000
Cash value and loan value	₹50,000
"Living benefits" payment maximum available (75 percent × amount requested ["Lien"])	₹200,000
	₹150,000
	₹75,000
After payment of "living benefits"	
Death benefit	₹125,000
(₹200,000–₹75,000)	
Six months later lien	₹75,000
Interest on lien*	₹3,000
Lien plus interest Death benefit	₹78,000
(₹200,000–₹78,000)	₹122,000

Source: ABC Life Assurance Society.
Note: *Interest at 8 percent for six months.

The lump sum required to generate a predetermined monthly income would depend upon whether the surviving spouse wishes to preserve the capital or deplete it over a predetermined period. In the former case, the monthly income generated would be far less than in the case of depleting capital where a part of the monthly income would represent a return of the principal. For instance, if a surviving wife wishing to preserve the capital invests ₹100,000 in a balanced fund generating 9 percent, she will receive ₹750 a month from this investment for, say, 10 years and the principal would be returned at the end of that period. If, however, ₹100,000 is annuitized over a 10-year period, the spouse may receive ₹1,270 per month but the principal would be exhausted in 10 years.

In purchasing life insurance one should recognize that the financial needs of a family change over time. For instance, group health insurance may expire sometime after retirement. The surviving spouse may not be able to work while the children are at home. Finally, annual investment returns, adjusted for inflation, can widely fluctuate, depending on the nature of investments and changing market conditions.

Policy Illustrations/Ready Reckoners

Policy illustrations are designed to help clients understand policy inflows and cash accumulations throughout the projected life of a policy. An illustration/ready reckoner offers a "guaranteed" projection, which is based on the worse-case scenario for policy interest rates based on an insurer's history and maximum mortality charges as contained in the Insurance Commission's standard mortality tables. Insurance companies can also generate one or more "current" or "non-guaranteed" projections, based on current interest rates and mortality charges.

Policy illustrations are created by actuaries. The premium, cash value, and death benefit numbers in the illustration/ready reckoner are driven by several factors: premium inflows, interest credit, mortality charges, insurer charges, and policy lapses. Assumptions regarding the investment performance of cash values, projected expenses, and policyholders' lifespan can significantly alter the illustrations, and aggressive inputs invariably skew projections, create an overly optimistic projection of future cash values, and recommend the amount of premium payments that ultimately will not support the policy. Clearly, differences in assumptions and projected performances make comparisons of policy illustrations difficult and unreliable.

While policy illustrations can be useful in helping a client understand how a policy works, it is important to emphasize that illustrations be viewed only as "what if" scenarios and not as guarantees. If a policy is in danger of lapsing because assumptions deviate from future realities, a policyholder would have to contribute a lump sum to the cash value account, pay higher premiums, reduce the death benefit, replace the policy, or, at the very least, seek some sort of modification.

Another item that might influence a policy illustration is dividend/premium payments. Participating policies return dividends back to a policyholder; hence, on principle, these payments can be incorporated into the policy illustration. However, the size of dividend payments depends heavily on the assumptions used (insurer expenses, future mortality rates, and so on). Aggressive assumptions would invariably result in magnifying the size of future dividend payments with predictable results. Projected dividends higher than historical norms result in projecting lower annual premium payments, which, in turn, increase the probability of a policy lapse.

In this chapter, we have presented the structures and concepts of various types of life insurance policies and discussed key life insurance planning strategies. Issues concerning other forms of insurance will be presented in Chapter 5.

5 Health, Homeowner's, Automobile, and Liability Insurance: Structure, Concepts, and Planning

Section I: General Principles

INTRODUCTION

Buying health insurance is a challenging undertaking. There are many reasons for this. (a) It takes special skills to accurately determine the amount of insurance needed. (b) Money spent on buying insurance is usually diverted from attractive investments. (c) When buying health insurance, one must avoid getting carried away by emotion. (d) Shopping for the least expensive yet comprehensive policy can become both time consuming and difficult. For these reasons, when buying insurance every individual should apply the basic principle followed by business professionals: obtain the best value for the premium payments.

In this chapter, we will present the structure, concepts, and planning strategies for health, disability, long-term care (LTC), auto, liability, and homeowner's insurance.

PRINCIPLES OF INDEMNITY AND LOSS SHARING

Let us begin by explaining the principle of *indemnity*. In the case of health, disability, and LTC insurance, an insurance company merely indemnifies an insured for the actual loss. Benefit payments *do not* generate a profit for the insured, since the payment of claim is intended to merely restore the individuals to the same position they were in prior to the loss. This principle of indemnity, however, does not apply in the case of life insurance, since it is impossible to adequately compensate for the loss of life. So, as the next best alternative, based on the assumption that everyone has an insurable interest in his or her own life, indemnification for the loss of life is linked to the loss of future economic value as a result of death. For example, an individual who is clearly positioned to earn ₹10 crore in future earnings would be insurable for a much higher death benefit than someone expected to earn only ₹1 crore in future earnings.

A second theme that is consistent throughout the following discussions can be characterized as *loss sharing*. Insurers generally require that in addition to making premium payments, policyholders also absorb some degree of loss. Such a loss sharing might take many forms, such as a deductible, co-pay, elimination or waiting period, coinsurance (up to the stop loss), and benefit cap. Loss sharing is, thus, an effective way of managing moral hazards associated with insurance.

INSURANCE AGAINST SIGNIFICANT RISKS

Insuring against relatively small potential losses consumes valuable resources that could be better spent on buying protection for larger risk exposures. Of course, only the insured can determine which losses are large, since the amount of loss one can afford to absorb depends primarily on the insured's financial resources and existing coverage. Therefore, the size of health insurance coverage should be based on how much risk an insured can comfortably afford to assume.

SHOPPING FOR INSURANCE

Insurance should be purchased with two cardinal rules in mind. (a) Insurance prices vary widely and considerable savings can be realized by shopping around. (b) Due diligence is required before selecting a policy, because many seemingly identical policies differ markedly on crucial points. For example, all disability policies provide income when an insured becomes disabled, but a particular illness or injury may not qualify as a disability under every company's definition. Thus, it is imperative to select a policy which is not only cost-effective but also provides *the desired coverage.*

LOSS CONTROL THROUGH PREVENTIVE MEASURES

The premium for an insurance contract is based on the size and number of claims resulting from accidents and other losses. Consequently, one can help reduce premium costs by reducing the hazards that cause the damage. For instance, health losses can be reduced by periodic physical check-ups, dietary control, regular exercise, and prompt attention to illnesses.

ORGANIZATION OF PERSONAL RECORDS

Record-keeping is an onerous chore. But in the areas of health insurance, it is essential to maintain up-to-date, accurate, and detailed records. This is especially true when submitting a claim because the extent of reimbursement by an insurance company largely depends on the ability of a policyholder to produce documents supporting the claims.

It is best to remember that accurate record-keeping helps expedite a health insurance claim. This is because the reimbursement of a health-related expense is directly dependent on the actual cost of sickness or injury covered by the policy.

Section II: Health Insurance

INTRODUCTION

Even though we live in a health-conscious society, everyday lots of people are afflicted with injuries and illnesses. However, according to Organisation for Economic Co-operation and Development (OECD) Health Statistics, 2014,[1] in 2012 the total health spending in India accounted for only 4.0 percent of the gross domestic product (GDP) as compared to the OECD average of 9.3 percent. Another source, Equentis Capital, estimated that during 2012, health care spending in India reached ₹78.6 billion (₹157 per capita based on purchasing power parity), and by 2017, it is expected to reach ₹158.2 billion. Interestingly, in 2012, 33 percent of health spending was funded by public sources (4.8 percent of the total government spending), while out-of pocket costs accounted for 60 percent of total health spending. The country's health insurance is dominated by the government-owned General Insurance Corporation (GIC) and its four subsidiaries (with about 60 percent market share). Private employers provide insurance for 40 percent of their employees. According to PricewaterhouseCoopers (PwC), health insurance in India, including government-supported schemes, covers less than 15 percent of the population.

[1] http://www.oecd.org/els/health-systems/Briefing-Note-INDIA-2014.pdf (last accessed on February 26, 2015).

A World Bank Study (2012),[2] estimates that by 2015 more than 630 million Indians will be covered by health insurance. During the last several years, the health insurance sector has been growing consistently with a compound annual growth rate (CAGR) of 30.05 percent. The total premium has dramatically increased from ₹2,221 crore in 2005–06 to ₹13,975 crore in 2012–13. The penetration of health insurance (health insurance premium divided by the total GDP of India) has also experienced a sharp growth. However, as compared to the total nonlife component, health insurance constitutes only 22.19 percent of insurance companies' business.[3]

The health insurance industry is dominated by four public sector companies, which cover 60 percent of the insured. These are: National Insurance Company Ltd, New India Assurance Company Ltd, Oriental Insurance Company Ltd, and United India Insurance Company Ltd. Private employers (17 companies) provide health insurance for the rest. Of these, the largest companies are: Start Health, Apollo Munich, Max Bupa, and Religare Health.[4]

Health insurance provides protection against financial losses caused by illness, injury, and disability. Interestingly, the concept of health insurance was not even established until 1912 when the first insurance act was passed. However, in 1947, the "Bhore Committee Report" made recommendations for improving health care services in India. Then, shortly after India gained independence, the central government introduced the Employees State Insurance Scheme (ESIS) for blue-collar workers employed in the private sector. Seven years later, in 1954, the Central Government Health Scheme (CGHS) was established covering central government employees and their families.

It took a little over three decades for the government to launch in 1986 the Mediclaim policy. Subsequently, in 2003, the government introduced health insurance for the informal sector (Universal Health

Table 5.1 *Evolution of Health Insurance*[5]

Time Period	Development
1912	Health insurance introduced when the first insurance act was passed.
1948	The central government introduced the ESIS for blue-collar workers employed in the private sector.
1954	The CGHS for central government employees and for their families was launched.
1973	GIC was set up as the controlling body with National Insurance Company Limited, New India Assurance Company Limited, Oriental Insurance Company Limited, and United India Insurance Company Limited as its subsidiaries.
Early 1980s	General insurance companies started individual health insurance products.
1986	Mediclaim or group medical insurance was introduced.
1990s	Limits in health policies were slowly removed.
1999	Insurance Regulatory Development Authority (IRDA) was set up. The insurance sector was opened to private and foreign participation.
2001	Introduction of Third-party Administrators (TPAs). Cashless option started.
2003	Introduction of UHIS-early attempts by the government to introduce health insurance for the informal sector.
2006	Star Health, the fist standalone health insurance company, was set up. Now there are five companies.
2008	Central government launched Rastriya Swasthya Bima Yojna (RSBY). This was followed by state government-sponsored insurance schemes.
2011	IRDA allowed portability of policies.

[2] http://www.business-standard.com/article/pf/over-630-mn-indians-to-have-health-insurance-coverage-by-2015-112101100272_1.html (last accessed on October 11, 2014).

[3] Annual Report, IRDA, 2012–13. https://www.irda.gov.in/ADMINCMS/cms/frmGeneral_NoYearList.aspx?DF=AR&mid=11.1 (accessed on March 8, 2015).

[4] http://zeenews.india.com/bbv/exclusive/health insurance-in-india-still-remains-an-untapped-market_877989.html (accessed on October 11, 2014).

[5] Cognizant 20-20 Insights and http://www.cognizant.com/InsightsWhitepapers/Healthcare-Insurance-Evolution-in-India-An-Opportunity-to-Expand-Access.pdf (accessed on March 8, 2015).

Insurance Scheme [UHIS]), a hospitalization indemnity product voluntarily purchased from a state-owned insurer at a heavily subsidized price (e.g., ₹165 a year).[6] These developments are presented in Table 5.1.

Health insurance represents one of the most complicated forms of insurance. These policies come in various sizes and forms and are difficult to analyze. Consequently, before selecting a health insurance company, individuals would be well advised to determine what type of protection will best satisfy their personal and financial needs.

HEALTH PLAN ORGANIZATIONS

There are several health benefit intermediaries from which one may obtain health care coverage. These are: commercial insurance companies, government health care insurance schemes (such as ESIS, CGHS, RSBY, and so on), and self-funded employee health benefits (for instance, Self-Employed Women's Association [SEWA] and Karuna Trust). Each serves the vital role of connecting an employer, the individual, or the government entity to the health care network. An overview of the health care sources is presented in Table 5.2.

Table 5.2 *Health Insurance in India*

Scheme	Particulars	Unit of Enrollment	Beneficiary Contribution	Subsidies	Average Premium Rates*
ESIS	ESIS provide services include sickness, maternity, temporary or permanent physical disablement, death due to employment injury resulting in loss of wages or earning capacity. It also guarantees reasonably good medical care to workers and their immediate dependents.	Family	Yes	95% centre	₹600–6,000
Central Government Health Scheme (CGHS)	CGHS provides comprehensive health care facilities for the Central Government employees and pensioners and their dependents residing in CGHS covered cities.	Family	Yes	12.5% by states	₹2,340–17,700
RSBY	RSBY provides health insurance coverage for families living below poverty line (BPL). It provides protection to BPL families from financial liabilities arising out of health shocks that involve hospitalization up to ₹30,000.	Family	No	100%, centre (75%) and states (25%)	₹440–750
Community Based Health Insurance (CBHI)	CBHI provides protection against the uncertain risk of catastrophic medical expenses individuals and families in exchange for regular payment of premiums.	Individual and families	Yes	No	₹175–1,000
Private Health Insurance	Both public and private insurance companies providing a variety of insurance products.	Individual	Yes	No	₹1,216

Source: Public Health Foundation Report, India, 2011.

[6] Cognizant 20-20 Insights, March 2015. http://www.cognizant.com/InsightsWhitepapers/Healthcare-Insurance-Evolution-in-India-An-Opportunity-to-Expand-Access.pdf (accessed on March 8, 2015).

Employee State Insurance Scheme

ESIS was introduced under the Employees State Insurance Act, 1948. This scheme provides for both cash and medical benefits to those blue-collar employees who are employed by those organizations that comply with registration requirements. In addition to providing OPD (Out Patient Department) and IPD (In Patient Department) services, the ESIS offers a variety of cash benefits to insured employees to cover certain contingencies and a loss of pay. The Act also guarantees medical care for workers and their immediate dependents.

The treatments, OPD and IPD, are provided at either government-owned or government-approved hospitals. ESIS provides cash benefits through the corporation (via its branch and pay offices), subject to certain limitations. This organization is financed by the beneficiaries (1.75 percent of salary), employers (4.75 percent of beneficiary's salary), and state governments (12.5 percent of medical care expenses under ESIS.

Central Government Health Scheme

As mentioned, in 1954, for central government employees the government introduced CGHS. Financed mostly by the central government (employees contribute only 5 percent), this scheme provides comprehensive health care, including OPD and IPD, in government and private hospitals.

Rashtriya Swasthya Bima Yojna

RSBY provides health insurance coverage for families living below the poverty line. This program protects these families from major health shocks resulting in hospitalization. Of the total, 75 percent of the Scheme's financing is provided by the central government; the rest comes from state governments.

Group Insurance Benefits

Traditionally, protection and cost control in health care services have meant providing conventionally insured group health care plans to employees as a part of fringe benefits. Today, under a novel alternative to group health care, the employer provides a unique plan design, claims management, and the monitoring of the utilization and provider performance.

In a partial Group Insurance Benefits (GIB) plan, an employer assumes the degree of risk (claims) that can be anticipated. Stop-loss insurance is then obtained to cover claims which exceed the actuarially predetermined level of risk. A specific stop-loss provision protects the plan against an individual catastrophic claim. An aggregate stop-loss provision provides coverage for claims exceeding a predetermined amount on the entire covered group, thus limiting overall costs of claims.

In a GIB plan, claim reserves are managed by the employer, which leads to greater financial control. Funds may be contributed to an employer-established account, which can be used to pay the approved claims. Excess funds remaining in the account earn interest. In addition, cost savings are realized because (a) in most cases premium tax, usually 2–6 percent, does not apply to self-funded claim funds, (b) the cost of self-operating the plan is generally lower, and (c) insurance carrier profits and risk charges are significantly reduced. Because of these benefits, many large corporations have adopted GIB plans.

Commercial Insurance Companies

Commercial insurance companies provide health insurance coverage for a large segment of the population. These companies increased their business swiftly in tier-1 and tier-2 cities with products centered on cashless payments and inpatient reimbursements. These companies, which include such household names as Apollo Munich, Religare Health Insurance, Star Health, and Max Bupa Health Insurance, enroll most of their participants through TV and radio advertisements. Under this arrangement, policyholders can receive medical care from any place of their choosing and they do not have to be treated by preassigned hospitals or doctors. However, with the emergence of other types of plans, its popularity has remained marginal at best.

TYPES OF HEALTH INSURANCE

Hospital Insurance

Hospital insurance covers the cost incurred during a hospital stay. Examples of expenses covered are: room and board charges, operating room charges, nursing services, and drugs. The majority of urban Indians have some sort of hospital protection; that is not true for people living in the rural areas.

Hospital insurance is divided into three categories: hospitalization insurance, hospital indemnity insurance, and hospital-service-incurred plans. These plans are described next.

1. ***Hospitalization insurance***. Hospitalization insurance covers, either partly or in full, the actual cost of the treatment in a hospital. This type of insurance is sold in two forms: expense reimbursement contracts and service contracts. The former are offered by commercial insurers who pay for hospital costs when an insured is confined to a hospital. The insurance company pays a flat daily rate up to a maximum amount, and the insured covers the expenses over that amount. By comparison, under the service contracts, the reimbursement amount equals the total expenses of the hospital stay less any deductible and coinsurance. Expenses covered under this policy are per diem hospital room fees, operating room fees, and costs of medical supplies. Frequently, restrictions are placed on hospital expenses, which include a daily maximum reimbursement, an overall per stay maximum, and a maximum number of days for which expenses are covered. These types of policies are available on an individual sum-insured basis, or on a family floater basis, where a single policy covers hospitalization expenses for the entire family.

2. ***Hospital indemnity insurance/Hospital daily cash benefit policy***. Hospital indemnity insurance offers a specific amount of cash payment for each day of hospitalization up to a stated maximum number of days. If the stated reimbursement does not cover the daily expenses, a policyholder must make up the difference. Of course, the policyholder can also keep the excess if the reverse is true. Hospital indemnity contracts often carry limited payout clauses, which can take the form of payments to cover only the costs resulting directly from an accident.

3. ***Hospital-service-incurred plans***. These plans pay hospitals directly for services provided and the policyholders make up the shortage. Except for this difference, these plans are similar to the hospitalization insurance plans. This type of plan provides actual hospital services to the insured for a set number of days at a rate pre-negotiated with the hospital.

While all hospital insurance policies cover the expenses associated with hospitalization, the total coverage, deductibles, coinsurance, and method of payment vary, depending on the types of coverage offered by various groups.

Surgical Insurance

Surgical insurance covers surgical procedures. One form of this coverage, known as *surgical expense insurance*, sets up a maximum amount for each procedure and reimburses patients directly (less deductibles) for many commonly performed operations. In addition, specific methods are used for figuring out the amount of reimbursement to be paid for procedures that are not listed. Another type of surgical insurance, called the *surgical-service-incurred plan*, directly pays the operation service providers. The reimbursement amount is calculated on the basis of the fees charged by most service providers for similar services in that geographic area.

Cashless Facility

Insurance companies have tie-up arrangements with several hospitals across the country as part of their network. Under the health insurance policy offering cashless facility, a policyholder can take treatment in any of the network hospitals without having to pay the hospital bills as the payment is made to the hospitals directly by a TPA on behalf of the insurance company. However, expenses beyond the limits or sub-limits allowed by the insurance policy, or expenses not covered under the policy, must be covered by the insured. Cashless facility is not available to the insured who is served by an out-of-network hospital.[7]

Medical Expense Insurance

Medical expense insurance pays for all medical services, excluding surgical procedures. These plans usually have a deductible clause, a coinsurance clause, and specified limits. In most cases, the deductible clause is written on a selected basis. This means that the insured is required to pay the charges incurred during the first few office visits, the number varying from one company to another. Medical expense insurance is another coverage which might be included on a service-incurred basis.

Major/Critical Medical Expense Insurance

Major medical expense insurance provides reimbursements for all-encompassing medical treatments. In general, this type of coverage is used as a supplement to hospital, surgical, and medical expense insurance and pays only the charges not covered by the other basic forms.

In this type of policy, the policy pays a fixed amount for the treatment of a specified illness or for covering the cost of a specified procedure. Such coverage can go a long way toward reducing the financial burden created by the exorbitant medical costs of treating a serious illness.

It is important to note that the policy coverage ends once a lump sum has been paid to the insured. However, the built-in coverage might differ between policies. One policy might cover accidental death and partial or total disability due to accidents; another policy might not offer a similar coverage.

Incidentally, many insurance companies now offer *cancer insurance*, which is generally treated as a covered medical expense under the major medical coverage. This development is the insurance industry's response to heavy medical expenses that go hand in hand with the graying of the general population. As people live longer, the odds are that many of them will become cancer victims and will have to pay for expensive cancer treatment. Cancer insurance pays for a significant portion of these expenses.

Comprehensive Health Insurance

A comprehensive health insurance plan combines hospital insurance, surgical insurance, medical expense insurance, and major medical expense insurance to one single package. This type of insurance coverage has coinsurance requirements of around 20 percent and deductibles; however, coinsurance and deductible amounts can vary between different plans. The high deductible and coinsurance feature of cost sharing helps insurance companies provide affordable and reasonable coverage. Comprehensive health

[7] Handbook on Health Insurance, Insurance Regulatory and Development Authority.

insurance plans are usually offered on a group basis by businesses willing to offer to their employees or members comprehensive health insurance protection.

Supplemental Health Insurance

Supplemental health insurance plans fill the void left by the basic insurance plans. These plans, advertised through the mail or on television, pay for surgery, hospital stay, treatment for accident, and so on, regardless of the existence of other medical coverage. In most instances, supplemental plans are not as attractive as they first appear to be. Premiums are exorbitant, and many restrictions are imposed on the coverage. Consequently, there is limited demand in the marketplace for supplemental health insurance plans.

Dental Expense Insurance

Dental expense insurance makes cash payments for dental care expenses. It is similar to other health insurance policies in that it defines covered procedures and exclusions, and includes deductibles, coinsurance requirements, and maximum limits. A unique aspect of dental insurance is that it includes defined classes of service. For example, all or most of the costs for diagnostic, preventive care, and X-rays are typically covered. On the other hand, the insured is required to bear higher cost sharing for major restoration and orthodontia care (e.g., braces and teeth alignment). The dental policy typically establishes coverage limits and defines the maximum number of annual visits. In most instances, dental expense insurance is offered by employers only on a group basis.

Vision/Eye Insurance

Eye care insurance provides protection from expenses connected with: routine eye exams, corrective lenses (contacts, prescription lenses, and frames), and possibly medical surgery (eye disease, laser surgery, and so on). The policy defines which procedures are covered or excluded and outlines the policy's provisions regarding deductibles, coinsurance requirements, maximum annual benefit limits, and number of visits. Eye care insurance, too, is generally offered by employers on a group basis.

HEALTH INSURANCE CONTRACT

The health insurance contract, including its amendments and riders, provides details regarding: who is covered, what services are covered or excluded (e.g., hospitalization, surgical, and medical expenses), what limitations apply, how the insured is required to participate in the sharing of losses, and what administrative procedures apply (e.g., grace period, reinstatement period, and so forth).

Covered Benefits, Exclusions, and Pre-existing Conditions

In the preceding subsections we discussed the types of health services typically associated with particular plans. However, it is still desirable for every insured person to carefully examine details of that coverage. Each policy carefully documents the services that are covered, and more importantly, the services that are specifically excluded. General *exclusions* might include: nonmedically necessary procedures (e.g., cosmetic surgery, contact lenses, and hearing aids), expenses that are covered under another plan (i.e., coordination of benefits), and injuries resulting from war, active duty, or self-infliction. Other procedures, such as maternity care or fertility procedures, might be specifically identified as either covered or excluded benefits.

The *pre-existing condition* clause, generally included in health contracts, reduces the insurance company's liability for paying future claims generated by a sickness or physical condition that a policyholder experienced prior to initiation of coverage. The Health Insurance Portability and Accountability Circular issued in September 2011 by Insurance Regulatory and Development Authority (IRDA) detailed the procedure of the use of the pre-existing condition by establishing the time-bound "look back" period for what constitutes a pre-existing condition. For group health insurance policies, individual members are given credit based on the number of years of continuous insurance cover, even when the previous policy contained pre-existing disease exclusions/time-bound exclusions.

Loss Sharing and Limits of Coverage

As previously noted, loss sharing is an effective way of managing moral hazard. Key loss-sharing mechanisms between health-insurance companies and covered persons or entities are: deductibles, fixed co-pay, coinsurance, and benefit caps.

Deductible and Fixed Co-pay

The "deductible" is an amount that an insured is required to pay before the insurance company considers a claim. For example, if a single insured person has a ₹500 annual deductible and the total amount of the first medical bill is ₹2,000, then the insurance company will assume that the submitted claim is only for ₹1,500 (₹2,000 less ₹500 deductible). Once the annual deductible is paid during an enrollment year, additional claims submitted during that year will no longer be subject to a deductible. That is, if the same insured has another ₹1,000 medical expense during the year, the entire amount of ₹1,000 will represent the total claim. However, family policies are typically governed by a "family deductible" arrangement, which waives future deductibles once a family's "deductible cap" is reached. In an event, each insurer has the right to define whether the deductible is applicable per year, per life, or per event, and also the specific deductible to be applied.

Another loss-sharing arrangement, "co-pay," is a fixed fee (e.g., ₹20) assessed each time an insured visits a doctor's office, hospital, or pharmacy. However, co-payment does *not* reduce the sum insured.

Coinsurance and Stop Loss

The term "coinsurance" refers to a sharing of medical expenses up to a certain rupee level (known as "stop loss"). A typical loss-sharing formula is 80/20. Under this arrangement, an insurance company pays 80 percent of the expenses not exceeding the stop-loss level, and an insured pays the 20 percent balance. After the stop-loss cap is reached, the insurance company pays all the expenses up to the policy maximum (if applicable).

Consider the following example: Ashish owns a health insurance policy which contains a ₹400 calendar-year deductible, an 80 percent coinsurance provision, and a ₹3,000 stop-loss cap. If a recent surgery (the first expense for the policy year) costs ₹20,000, how much will the insurance company pay?

1. ***Step 1*** (consider the deductible). Ashish must first pay the ₹400 deductible. The insurance company will then process a ₹19,600 claim.
2. ***Step 2*** (determine the coinsurance split). Ashish and the insurance company will share expenses until the insured incurs ₹3,000 of expenses (over and above the deductible). Since 20 percent of ₹19,600 equals ₹3,920, which is above the stop loss, Ashish will pay the deductible plus the ₹3,000 coinsurance component, and the insurance company will pay ₹16,600 [80 percent of ₹19,600 + ₹920 (₹3,930 less ₹3,000) of excess].

Contract Provisions

Unlike life insurance contracts, generally accident and sickness contracts are not standardized. Each health benefit intermediary has some discretion in developing its own health care contract. Policy provisions that are commonly included in health insurance contracts include: entire contract clause, grace period, reinstatement period, notice of claims, change of occupation, coordination of benefits, cancelation, illegal occupation, and intoxicants and narcotics.

GROUP AND INDIVIDUAL HEALTH INSURANCE

Most employers offer one or more types of group health and disability insurance. However, for relatively young employees who are nonsmokers and have no prior history of major sickness, an individual health insurance policy might provide a better option. This is because in a group policy the risk of insuring older employees and those with a medical history is spread across the board, thereby raising the insurance premiums for everyone, including the younger employees in good health.

Notwithstanding the argument just presented, a group policy still might turn out to be more attractive than an individual policy for a number of reasons. (a) A company issuing a group policy significantly reduces its expenses by writing one policy covering a large number of people. (b) By spreading the risks over a large number of diverse people, an insurance company might enjoy substantial cost savings, thereby enabling it to offer cheaper rates to the group members. (c) Group coverage is usually more comprehensive; as compared to individual policies, there are fewer exclusions and limitations in group policies. For instance, pre-existing conditions, exclusions, and waiting periods are less restrictive in a group policy (waiting periods for maternity coverage might be an exception). (d) In group policies, the insured is rarely required to take a physical or provide a detailed statement on existing physical conditions. (e) Nearly all accidents or illnesses, including heart conditions, are covered. Generally, the only eligibility requirement is that a person must be an active employee when the coverage begins. (f) Group insurance is generally cheaper than individual insurance. (g) Group health policy does not require medical check-up.

Group health insurance, however, has a major drawback: Leaving the place of employment automatically results in a loss of the group coverage. Of course, as a general rule, within 30 days the departing employee is permitted to convert the group health coverage to an individual policy with the same company. It is true that the coverage for the individual policy might not be as good as the group coverage, and the premium payments would most likely be higher. Another possible drawback might be that if a group insurance policy is terminated, the insurer might lose all the benefits accumulated in the policy.

Incidentally, all group plans are not alike, and not all of them turn out to be bargains. For instance, some group plans provide a major medical plan along with more basic coverage, while others do not. Also, many plans exclude maternity coverage, cover maternity costs inadequately, or provide only for problem pregnancies. Even the flat maximum payments for maternity in many group policies are often less than the full cost of pregnancy and childbirth. If the coverage is inadequate under a group plan, it is important for the insured to supplement that coverage to fill the existing gaps.

Important Developments

In this section, we will present several new developments in the area of group health insurance.

IRDA Health Insurance Guidelines, 2013. In order to improve the quality of health services, in 2013 the IRDA issued Health Insurance Guidelines to help the insureds to interact effectively with insurers, insurance companies, and TPAs. These guidelines elaborate on: critical illness, commonly used insurance terms, billing formats, discharge summary, standard contracts between TPA, insurers, and hospitals, and list of excluded items in hospitalization indemnity policies. These steps were taken to make the health insurance sector more efficient and useful to the end-users.

IRDA Health Insurance Portability Regulation. The Health Insurance Portability and Accountability Act, 2011, protects the insurability of an insured person. Under this Regulation, if a person has been insured for the past 12 months, a new insurance company cannot refuse to cover a person and cannot impose pre-existing conditions or a waiting period before providing coverage. For this purpose, medical conditions are considered pre-existing only if an individual receives medical care, treatment, consultation, or prescription drugs during the six-month period immediately preceding that individual's effective date of coverage. Also, a pre-existing condition waiting period cannot apply to pregnancy, newborn children, or newly adopted children. Finally, pre-existing conditions must be reduced by each month that an individual was continuously covered under creditable coverage prior to the date of enrollment.

MEDICLAIM POLICIES

Mediclaim represents health insurance products and policies issued mainly by nonlife insurance companies. Lately, however, even life insurance companies have started offering these products. This policy is available to institutions, corporations, and associations which satisfy the minimum-enrollment requirement.

Types of Mediclaim Coverage

Currently, Mediclaim is divided into the following categories: (a) Standard Mediclaim Group (policy), (b) Group Health plus Medical Expenses Policy, (c) Standard Mediclaim (individual) policy, (d) Floater Policy (family Plan), (e) Health plus Medical Expenses Policy, (f) Overseas Mediclaim Policy.

A Mediclaim policy covers the cost of hospitalization (minimum 24-hour required). Specifically, the policy covers: costs of medication, surgery, room, and ambulance. It also covers post-hospitalization costs of medication, tests, and doctor's fees for up to 60 days.

TAXATION OF HEALTH CARE BENEFITS

Benefits received from health insurance are generally tax free, regardless of who paid the premium (individual, employee, or employer). This is consistent with the tax concept that an injured or sick person is only restored to his or her original state. The benefit payments would be taxable, however, if the payments exceeded the medical expenses or if the payment was for a service that the Tax Department did not consider medically necessary.

The tax deductibility of the premium payment depends on who made the payment. If an employer provides the health care coverage as part of the company benefit package, then the amount of the premiums can be used as a business deduction. If an individual pays health insurance premiums, then the premiums can only be used as a deduction available under Section 80D of the Income Tax Act.

POLICY SELECTION: THE IDEAL HEALTH INSURANCE COMPANY

There is no magic formula by which one can unequivocally select the best and the most cost-effective health insurance company. Often big, financially strong, companies offer attractive premiums, good policies, and excellent service. But some of the small companies also meet these same criteria, so it is not possible to select a good company merely on the basis of size.

In selecting an insurance company, it is best to avoid those companies that have a poor financial record and have a history of fighting their customers' claims. Also, one should not buy insurance from a company that would not be able to withstand higher than expected losses or would consistently generate lower than anticipated investment income. So, one should select a company that is financially strong, offers liberal benefits, and charges reasonable premiums. Also, the company selected should be fair, efficient, and courteous in handling its claims.

An indication of the financial strength of insurance companies is the rating they receive from rating agencies. A high rating means that the company can withstand financial strains. One should try to avoid companies that do not receive either the *most substantial* or the *very substantial* rating from Best's. These ratings are available in most public libraries.

To conclude, in making the final selection of a health insurance company, it is desirable to obtain an affirmative answer to each of the following questions:

1. Is the company's loss ratio high? (The loss ratio is the percentage of premiums that a company pays back in benefits to its policyholders. A loss ratio of over 50 percent is desirable.)
2. Does the company receive one of the two highest ratings for financial stability from *rating agencies*?
3. Does the company offer efficient, fair, and courteous claim service?
4. Is the company prevented from canceling a policy?
5. Does the company have a policy of not raising premiums based on claims?

HEALTH INSURANCE PLANNING PROCESS

The task of picking an *ideal* health insurance plan is challenging for a number of reasons. (a) The employer may offer several plans such as a health maintenance organization (HMO), a preferred provider organization (PPO), Blue Cross, or some variant of these plans. (b) Each plan has both advantages and drawbacks, and it is often difficult to clearly sort them out before making the final selection. (c) If a family member suffers from a chronic illness, it might be necessary to select the plan that is best suited to handle that illness.

The following section presents a five-step process which might be followed for selecting the best plan, notwithstanding the various problems cited earlier.

Step 1: Select the appropriate plan. Select from the employer's list the plans that best suit the family. These include major medical care, preferred, and a number of other plans. By following our earlier discussion, it should be possible to identify the most suitable plan for the family.

Step 2: Analyze the coverage. Ensure that the coverage required by the family is being offered by the plan. In this context, each plan's annual and lifetime caps as well as restrictive caps on mental-health care should be carefully checked. Other restrictions, such as limits on outpatient visits for the year, should also be examined.

Step 3: Examine the costs. Total costs vary—sometimes considerably—between different types of plans. These costs include not only the premium costs but also additional costs which are passed on to the participants by the employers by means of co-pay, deductibles, drug coverage, and other expenses. It is best to choose a plan which has a reasonable cost structure and also offers the services most desired.

Step 4: Check the quality of plans. The National Committee for Quality Assurance, a nonprofit agency, issues report cards on insurers based on access to care, quality of service, and preventive programs. The quality of a plan can be checked by logging on to policybazar.com and apnapaisa.com.

Step 5: Convenience factor. Finally, it is important to check the location and easy accessibility of the medical facility which the family members would be required to use for medical care. In addition, if a policy requires the use of a specific hospital, then the quality and location of that hospital should also be checked.

To recapitulate, a time-tested approach is to select a good health insurance company which has consistently been stable in the health care market. Once such a company is selected, the limitations and exclusions in its policy should be carefully analyzed vis-à-vis its cost. If the company also passes the five selected criteria just presented, it would be a prime candidate for ultimate selection.

Section III: Disability Income Insurance

INTRODUCTION

Not all illnesses or injuries are curable or containable. Some may result in permanent or long-term disability. In fact, for most individuals, the probability of becoming disabled prior to retirement is assumed to be higher than the chance of death. Because long-term disability can be catastrophic to the wage earner and the family, strategies must be developed for covering the costs associated with disability. In fact, once disabled, the breadwinner may not be able to work again for a long time. To cope with such a situation, one must insure against the potential loss of income over a long period of time. There is no regular medical health program that offers income during periods of loss of income, and all conventional protections have limitations. Workers' compensation handles only work-related injuries. Company sickness or accident plans also have waiting periods. Finally, disability income riders on life insurance do not cover catastrophic illness or injury. The only safe way to be assured of adequate protection against a loss of income due to long or permanent illness is to purchase a disability income policy.

LOSS SHARING

As previously described, insurers need to mitigate the risk of moral hazard. Common loss-sharing arrangements in disability contracts include: waiting or elimination periods, limitation of benefit amounts, and coordination of benefits.

Waiting Period

The waiting period, or elimination period, is the number of days a disabled insured must wait before receiving disability benefits. This waiting period is like a deductible; the insured must bear all the expenses incurred during the elimination period. The following example illustrates the point:

Amount of loss	₹30,000
Less: Deductible	₹250
Expense over deductible	₹29,750
Insured pays 10% exp. over deductible (up to ₹10,000)	₹2,975
Insurer pays this amount (₹29,750 less ₹2,975)	₹26,775

Short-term disability insurance usually has a waiting period of 0–30 days. Long-term disability coverage typically has a waiting period of one, three, or six months, although some policies have a one-year or a six-month waiting period. As a general rule, the three-month waiting period buys the best value for the premium money paid for that type of policy.

Percentage of Pre-disability Income

Disability insurers usually limit benefits on short-term disability policies to approximately 60 percent of the insured's pre-disability gross income; the replacement ratio with long-term disability policies is typically around 70 percent. The intent of the provision is to compensate a policyholder with less-than-full, pre-disability income, so there would always be the financial incentive to return to work. The replacement percentage might be slightly increased by purchasing a second policy, although insurers tend to protect against this risk by including in their policies a coordination of benefits provision. It is interesting to note that the income-replacement limitation is comparable to the coinsurance concept in health insurance policies.

Cap on Monthly Benefits

Typically, insurers mitigate the moral hazard by putting a cap on the amount of monthly "rupee" benefit which impacts the higher-income employees. Here again, the monthly cap serves as an additional form of coinsurance.

Benefit Period

There are two types of disability policies. A short-term disability policy provides for a relatively short disability benefit period, such as 13 weeks, 26 weeks, or one year. Along-term disability policy provides for longer disability periods, such as five years, ending at the age of 60, or for life. Of the two, the long-term disability is more important, but it is also the one that is most often neglected. The benefit period serves the same risk-mitigation function as a "lifetime cap."

DISABILITY INSURANCE CONTRACT

As compared to health insurance policies, disability insurance contracts are not fully standardized. For this reason, it is important to carefully read the contract, its amendments, and its riders. These legal documents should clearly define: who is covered, the amount of benefit, the duration of that income benefit, loss-sharing provisions, covered and excluded perils, the definition of what qualifies as a disability, and the responsibilities of an insurer and an policyholder.

Covered Perils and Exclusions

As a general rule, all policies indemnify disabilities resulting from either sickness or accidental injury. General *exclusions* typically include disabilities relating to: pre-existing conditions (e.g., within the last two years), pregnancy, injuries resulting from war or active duty, injuries that were self-inflicted, and injuries caused by illegal occupation, narcotics, or intoxication. The underwriting of disability policies focuses on a number of factors, including the relative riskiness of the applicant's occupation. If a policyholder changes occupation to one that involves more risk, and if the contract so specifies, the benefits are generally reduced to a level that the current premium would provide based on the underwriting standards.

Definition of Disability

The definition of disability is the most important feature of a disability income policy. Most definitions of disability fall into two categories: the inability to perform any job and the inability to perform one's own occupation. Under the first definition, the company will pay full disability benefits only if the insured cannot perform *any job* that the person is qualified to perform based on training, experience, and education. Under the second definition, benefits will be paid if the insured is unable to perform "material duties" associated with his or her "own occupation." The latter definition is preferred by most people because it is easier to qualify for full disability when the trigger for benefits is focused on a clearly defined occupation. As expected, other things being equal, the premium for an own-occupation trigger is higher than that for the "any-job" trigger.

Some companies market disability policies by using a combination of both definitions. Typically, these policies provide the *own-occupation*-type benefits for two or three years after which the coverage switches to the *any job* definition.

Definition of Less-than-Total Disability

An important aspect of disability insurance relates to *partial disability*. Most companies pay total disability income even after the disabled person returns to work, but makes less than 50 percent of normal income. If the income earned is between 50 percent and 85 percent of the previous income, however, a proportionately reduced disability income is paid by the company. Another feature of disability insurance is *residual disability* which refers to the amount of income lost by the disabled person. In this case, benefits are paid on the basis of decreased earnings.

Options and Riders

Disability insurers typically provide various options and riders that enable policyholders to customize the coverage.

1. ***Guaranteed insurability option.*** Regardless of which definition of disability is used, it is often desirable to select the guaranteed insurability option. This option allows an insured to purchase additional amounts of disability insurance at stated intervals without the proof of insurability. However, higher benefits are available only if they are justified by higher income.
2. ***Guaranteed renewable option.*** Many disability policies are guaranteed renewable until the age of 60; however, if that is not the case, it is advisable to select a policy that does offer the choice of a guaranteed renewable option. This option provides a policyholder with the guaranteed right to renew the disability contract up to a certain age (typically up to the age of 60, although the age might be extended for those individuals who continue to work). While this right provides the policyholder with planning flexibility, it does permit an insurer to increase premiums on a class basis. The only exception is a noncancelable policy which allows renewal over a defined period with a guaranteed "no increase in premium" rate.
3. ***Cost-of-living adjustment rider.*** This rider ensures that the purchasing power of the disability benefit keeps up with inflation. For example, consider a situation in which a person is disabled for 10 years. A disability policy not adjusted for cost-of-living increases would still be based on the wages earned 10 years ago, not a very comforting situation.
4. ***Waiver of premium rider.*** This rider allows a policyholder to stop making premium payments during the disability period. Obviously, this right can be quite valuable if the disability continues for a prolonged period. The waiver typically begins after the policyholder has made premium payments during the elimination period. Once the waiting period is met and disability payments commence, the policyholder also receives a refund for the premiums paid during the elimination period.

Coordination of Benefits

When more than one policy is owned, the coordination of benefits contract defines which policy will pay the benefits to the insured and how the sharing of benefits between different policies would be managed. In addition, group or private policies are integrated with disability benefits. This means that the policy will pay a set benefit payments minus employees' provident fund (EPF) payments. For instance, suppose Shambhu has a disability policy which provides ₹3,000 in monthly benefits. Without the coordination of benefits provision Shambhu would receive ₹4,500 per month in disability benefits even if his EPF/other benefit pays him ₹1,500 a month. If the policy is integrated with EPF, however, Shelley would receive only ₹3,000 per month, because each rupee of EPF payments will directly offset the insurer's obligation to pay. Still, disability policies coordinated with EPF/other benefits could offer the best value for the money, although conditions for receiving disability payments under EPF/other benefits are so restrictive that it is advisable not to depend on that arrangement.

GROUP AND INDIVIDUAL DISABILITY INSURANCE

According to a recent government report, one in four workers entering the workplace in their early 20s will be disabled before retirement. This disturbing data underscores the need for buying work-related disability insurance. Employers are generally required to provide employees with Worker's Compensation Insurance. Additionally, although not required by law, they may offer supplemental employee benefits including sick leave, group short-term disability, and group long-term disability. Still, a comprehensive, individual long-term policy is generally a high priority need for everyone.

Workers' Compensation Insurance

Workers' compensation, popularly known as "Workers' Comp," is designed to indemnify work-related illness (i.e., occupational disease), injury, and death. This mandatory insurance program is controlled by the government and funded through employer contributions. The employer can generally maintain the required coverage by: (a) paying into a fund, (b) purchasing commercial insurance, or (c) qualifying for self-funding.

Workers' Comp, which pays for *health care expenses* related to "at-work" injuries and illnesses, has no rupees cap on related benefits. *Disability benefits* are based on statute, and the amount of disability benefit reflects: the type of disability (e.g., total, partial, total-permanent, or partial-permanent), the worker's salary, and possibly the number of dependents. If a worker dies while on the job, survivors are entitled to both a one-time payment and the ongoing survivor benefits. The amount and duration of the survivor benefit are specified by law.

Group and Individual Disability Policies

Group policies benefit from more lenient group underwriting standards, and these policies guarantee coverage for new employees. While it represents a valuable employee benefit, for the reason cited earlier, a group policy might not provide an optimal solution for everyone, and especially for younger employees. It might, therefore, be prudent to lay a carefully selected individual disability policy on top of a group plan. For example, if an employer provides only a short-term disability policy or the income replacement ratio on a long-term policy is only 60 percent, these shortcomings could be covered by purchasing an individual policy. It is also worth recalling that a group disability policy lasts only as long as an insured is employed.

Individual policies can be customized for every employee, so the features like definition of disability, income replacement, and waiting period can be carefully selected to serve each employee's needs. Of course, individual policy premiums could be higher than a group policy because these policies are tailored to individual needs and circumstances such as the insured's health, occupation, income, age, and avocations.

TAXATION OF DISABILITY BENEFITS

The taxation of disability benefits depends on who initially paid the premiums. Disability benefits are tax free if the premiums were paid by the individual or by the employee with after-tax rupees. Like the deductibility of health care premiums, disability premiums are treated as deductible expenses in the income tax return. In addition, deductions are allowed on the amount paid toward an insurance scheme for the maintenance of disabled dependent in case of his untimely death. However, if the disabled dependent dies, the policy amount is returned to a person and treated as taxable income.

Benefits received by employees from employer-provided disability benefits are generally taxed as gross income. The premiums paid by the employer are deductible to the employer as a business-related expense. If the employee pays part of the premium with after-tax rupees, then the benefits become partially taxable.

DISABILITY POLICY SELECTION

Features of a Good Policy

It is not always easy to select the best disability income policy because of the difficulties in determining how much disability income coverage is desirable, what the policy would cost, and which company is selling the best product. Before selecting disability insurance, every person should at least check the vital points listed in Table 5.3 to ensure that the policy fills the gaps in a regular health insurance plan. Of these, the "noncancelable and guaranteed renewable" clause is the most important clause.

Cost of Disability Policy

A typical long-term disability policy provides for either the payment of a stated percentage of a specified monthly salary or a specified amount per month. The cost of a policy depends on the amount of coverage, the duration of payment, and the additional riders selected.

Table 5.3 *Features of a Good Disablity Policy*

Key Questions	Suggested Recommendations
1. How does the policy define disability?	Select the policy that covers partial disability, not the one that specifies benefits only for total disability.
2. What job definition does the company use?	Select the company which uses the "your occupation" definition, not the "any job" definition.
3. Is the policy noncancelable and guaranteed renewable?	Choose a policy that guarantees that the policy will be renewed at the rates guaranteed in the policy up to the age specified (usually 65).
4. Does this policy cover disability resulting from both accident and illness?	Select the company that covers both forms of disability.
5. For what period of time will the policy pay?	Select the policy that covers at least through age 65.
6. How much will the policy pay?	Select the company which pays at least 60% of take-home pay at the time of accident or illness.
7. How long is the waiting period?	A three-month waiting period is preferable.
8. Does the company offer cost-of-living adjustments?	The basic benefit should rise automatically by a set percentage or in step with inflation.
9. Does the policy offer standard-of-living adjustments?	After a policy has been in force, the insured should be able to boost the monthly benefit by a certain amount at standard rates without a medical exam.

Disability insurance policies purchased on an individual basis can be fairly expensive; by comparison, larger groups get much lower rates. Consequently, whenever possible, disability insurance should be purchased on a group basis.

Filling Disability Benefit Gaps

In order to give insured individuals a financial incentive to return to work, disability insurers usually limit benefits to 60 percent of the insured's gross income. Some insurers offer extra features that can improve an insured's quality of life without putting incentive-killing cash in their bank accounts. Examples include funds to pay for children's education and make the claimant's retirement plan contributions. A number of companies also offer dependent education benefits together with comprehensive group long-term disability insurance.

PROCESS OF PLANNING FOR DISABILITY

Planning for disability risk is a multistep process. Financial planners need to understand the unique situation surrounding their clients, review their current disability risk-management policies (including employer and individual policies), assess their ability to fund the premiums, and/or absorb the loss of income. Once all that is accomplished, planners can help their clients choose the best disability policy.

Step 1: Know the client. The first step is to analyze a client's qualitative and quantitative data. What is the risk exposure? If married, are there two breadwinners or just one? How much emergency fund is available? What is the likelihood of disability based on job tasks and avocations? What are the client's goals regarding this coverage? These and other related issues should be carefully considered.

Step 2: Review the current risk-management plan. In order to assess the overall need in this area, the current resources should be analyzed. These include: sick days, worker's compensation insurance, and employer's short-term care and LTC policies. While receiving EPF payments always remains a possibility, it is prudent to ignore this source completely.

Step 3: Identify the gap. The difference between the projected monthly need and the projected monthly disability income from other sources is the gap that needs to be filled with a disability policy.

A simplified method for determining the disability income need is presented in Table 5.4. If Suraj, whose monthly salary is ₹4,000, becomes disabled today, his supplemental monthly income would be only ₹1,300 but his monthly expenses would continue to be ₹4,600, leaving a budgetary gap of ₹3,300. However, since his current monthly income is ₹4,000, he would be able to purchase disability coverage for only ₹2,400, equal to 60 percent of his salaried income. That would leave a shortfall of ₹900 per month in his budget, which would have to be met from other sources.

Step 4: Select the insurance company. In selecting a disability insurance company, a financial planner should consider the same variables as when selecting a health care company, namely the financial stability of the company, historical record for paying benefit claims, quality record for customer service, the availability of desired covered services and riders, and competitive pricing. Underwriting standards should also be considered to ensure that a client is insurable by this company for disability benefits.

Step 5: Select the policy. Once data have been collected on the insurance companies that make the cut for the final list, options provided by those companies offering comparable features (such as the same benefits, durations, elimination period, and riders) should be compared before undertaking the cost versus benefit analysis. That would ultimately lead to the selection of the best disability policy for a client.

Table 5.4 *Disability Insurance Need*

Current Monthly Income Available		
Group disability coverage	₹500	
Individual disability coverage	₹0	
Spouse/other family member income	₹700	
Investment income	₹100	
A. Total Monthly Income Available		₹1,300
Monthly Expenses		
Mortgage/rent	₹1750	
Insurance (life, health, home, auto, liability, and so on)	₹635	
Car payments/other loans	₹690	
Utilities	₹250	
Other (education, home maintenance)	₹475	
Savings/investments	₹800	
B. Total Monthly Expenses		₹4,600
C. Need for Additional Income Replacement due to Disability (A – B)		₹–3,300
Disability Coverage Available		
Salaried Income	₹4,000	
D. Maximum Disability Allowed: 60% (₹4,000)		₹2,400
Shortfall in Disability Coverage per Month (C – D)		₹900

Section IV: Long-term Care Insurance

INTRODUCTION

An Overview

As the Indian population ages, many families are bound to face the catastrophic expense of LTC. That includes, but is not limited to, skilled nursing, assisted-living facilities, life-care facilities, nursing homes, adult daycare, and home care. Indeed, projections for the growing needs for LTC are sobering. According to UN, by 2050 India's over-60 population will reach a staggering 323 million, higher than the total 2012 US population. Today, only 16 percent of the total population is 50 or above; by 2050 one out of three (34 percent) would belong to that category.[8] It is now easy to see why LTC coverage should be treated as an integral part of everyone's overall risk-management planning.

Cost of Care

LTC insurance provides a pool of funds to pay for ongoing daily and monthly medical or custodial care when the insured is no longer able to perform activities of daily living (ADLs). Having financial resources in place to cover these costs is important because the cost of nursing home care or home care can easily range anywhere from ₹10,000 to ₹50,000 per month or even more, and it is not typically covered by private medical insurance. The average monthly cost of nursing home stay will double in less than a decade if the current inflation rate continues unabated.

As noted, the basic Mediclaim policy excludes long-term custodial and nursing home care. And of course, the traditional health care insurance is not designed to pay for long-term care. And that makes the buying of an long-term care contract all the more important.

[8] http://www.thehindu.com/features/magazine/retire-without-hurt/article6862888.ece (last accessed on February 25, 2015).

LONG-TERM CARE CONTRACTS

LTC contracts are customized to reflect the insured's projected wants and needs; still, certain features are common to all contracts. These include: loss-sharing arrangements, description of covered services, and the benefit trigger.

Loss Sharing

Similar to the disability insurance contract, loss sharing is a fundamental arrangement in all LTC contracts. This arrangement includes: a waiting or elimination period, a limit on the amount of daily benefit, and a duration period. The elimination period effectively serves as a "deductible" for a policyholder because it specifies the length of time that must elapse before an insurer begins to make disability payments. The average waiting period is anywhere between 21 and 100 days, although a policy could have a waiting period of anywhere from 0 to 365 days. Generally, a 90-day waiting period is considered to be the most cost-effective, based on the value for the premium money paid. An insured can choose the benefit and duration amounts that are appropriate for the insured.

Covered Services

In customizing a policy, the applicant identifies the type of services desired, specifically the range of care activities and the intensity of care. Several types of care are presented next.

Skilled Nursing Care Coverage

Skilled nursing care is typically needed after hospitalization, and it tends to be short term in duration. Care by a licensed nurse is provided on a 24-hour schedule. Specialized services might include: intravenous therapy, feeding tubes, and respirators.

Intermediate Nursing Care Coverage

Intermediate care tends to be long term in nature. The duration of daily care ranges from a few hours a day to around-the-clock. Often intermediate care is designed to provide a patient with some ongoing help in daily health activities and therapies.

Custodial Care Coverage

A policy should provide coverage not only for skilled and intermediate care but also for custodial care which does not require the engagement of licensed medical professionals.

Home Care

LTC in an individual's home, rather than in a residential or nursing facility, can be an attractive alternative. Most policies offer this coverage only as a rider for an extra charge or as a percentage of the normal coverage.

Assisted Living

Assisted living is an arrangement in which customized help is provided to patients still capable of performing certain functions by themselves. Regular assistance might include: meals, administration of medications, help with personal grooming, and transportation to and from doctor visits or social activities.

Life-care Facilities

These facilities require residents to pay an entrance fee and monthly service fees for meals, housecleaning, and other related services. Residents unable to live independently are left with little choice but to move to the assisted living units, and ultimately to the skilled nursing facility.

Adult Day Care

This day-time care (typically during the weekdays) offers a reprieve for the caregiver who needs to work during the day or needs a break from the responsibilities of ongoing care. Adult day care center services range from social action to medical and mental care.

Pre-hospitalization

Some policies pay benefits only if the individual has been in a hospital before receiving LTC. However, since many individuals do not go to LTC facilities directly from a hospital, this requirement can result in a denial of benefits at a crucial time. Therefore, a good policy should not require the insured to be hospitalized before entering a nursing home care.

Alzheimer's Coverage

A good policy provides LTC coverage for the Alzheimer's disease, which is generally described in policy language as *organically based mental conditions*. If such language is not specifically included in the policy, probably Alzheimer's coverage is not provided by that policy.

Benefit Trigger (Activities of Daily Living)

The benefit for covered medical services typically becomes available when *all* the following conditions are met.

1. The policy owner is either: (a) unable to perform at least two of the six ADLs (*eating, bathing, dressing, toileting, continence, mobility*), or (b) suffers from cognitive impairment (e.g., dementia, Alzheimer's disease).
2. The policy owner's physician certifies that the inability to perform at least two of the ADLs or cognitive impairment exists.
3. This condition is expected to last for at least 90 days.

It is important to reiterate that a policy will require that all three conditions are met in order to trigger the release of benefits.

Options and Riders

LTC insurers typically provide a number of options and riders that enable policyholders to customize their coverage. These are discussed next.

Shared Cost

This rider links the policies of a husband and wife in terms of benefit duration. With this option either spouse can tap the unused long-term benefit period of the other spouse. This is particularly valuable if it is projected that one of the two will need LTC, although no one is certain who between the two would need such care.

Inflation Protection

This feature provides for the anticipated rise in the cost of LTC. A rider to offset inflationary increases can cause the premium to increase by as much as one-third; however, the catastrophic risk and the impact that inflation can have on future LTC costs make this a valuable rider. For this purpose, the use of a compounded, rather than a simple, inflation protection rider is recommended.

Waiver of Elimination Period for Home Health Care

This rider eliminates the waiting period for benefits when the care is provided at home. Assuming that most people wish to remain in their homes during sickness, this rider is recommended.

Waiver of Premium

In most policies it is common to find a waiver of premium provision. This provision waives future premium payments as long as the insured continues to receive benefits under the policy.

Guaranteed Renewability

The policy should be guaranteed renewable for life. This feature prevents an insurer from canceling the policy, except for the nonpayment of premiums. Note that all *qualified* LTC policies are guaranteed renewal by law and contain standard nonforfeiture options offering a policyholder the following three choices if the premium is raised.

1. ***Pay new premium.*** Paying the new, higher premium keeps the current policy and current benefits in place.
2. ***Pay prior premium.*** Continuing to pay the prior premium amount buys a reduced amount of benefits.
3. ***Nonforfeiture.*** Every *qualified* policy has a nonforfeiture option which provides a policyholder a paid-up policy equal to the total premiums paid should the policyholder decide to stop making payments. This right generally becomes available after the policy has been in force for at least three years.

Other policy features may include: clauses limiting coverage based on pre-existing conditions or medical history, premiums that remain level for life, and a grace period, giving a policyholder some protection against overlooking payment of a premium.

TAXATION OF BENEFITS

The Income Tax Act of 1961 specifies how premiums and benefits are taxed. The tax treatment of long-term care benefits is briefly discussed next.

Tax Treatment

Under the Income Tax Act, insurance benefits from *qualified* long-term "per diem" or indemnity contracts are tax free up to the daily benefit limit. However, benefits derived from an employer-funded policy in excess of the daily benefit limit are fully taxable. These rules apply to policies paid for by the individual, the employee, or the employer.

Employer premium payments are treated as a tax-deductible business expense and are not considered as taxable income to the employee. Individual policies are also accorded favorable tax treatment. Both the premiums paid for qualified LTC insurance and the consumer's out-of-pocket expenses for long-term medical care are eligible for medical expense deductions (under Section 80C and Section 10/10D). There are, however, limits based on a policyholder's age and for the total amount of LTC premiums that can be applied for deductions.

LONG-TERM CARE PLANNING PROCESS

LTC insurance is a hedge against uncertainty. While uncertainty for the future makes planning for LTC a challenge, it is this very uncertainty that makes planning for LTC needs a priority. In this connection, the key questions that need to be answered are as follows:

1. What is the likelihood that LTC will be needed, and if so, for how long?
2. How inflation will impact the future daily cost of health care or custodial care?
3. Given the existing financial resources, how effectively will the client be able to absorb the future health care costs?
4. In view of the ongoing and impressive medical advances, how would the client's life expectancy be extended?
5. What is the client's mindset concerning the depletion of the estate's assets?
6. Will there be any family caregivers in the picture?

The following section presents a five-step process for formulating a viable plan, notwithstanding the existence of various problems and uncertainties cited above.

***Step 1:* Understand Client's Objectives and Situation.** In preparation for quantifying LTC benefits that might be needed, the following factors should be explicitly taken into account: the client's current physical and mental health status, family physical and mental health history, current and projected future net worth, cash flows during retirement, risk tolerance, and the willingness to preserve or deplete the estate.

***Step 2:* Projecting the Benefit Needs.** Assumptions on which the benefit needs should be projected include the following:

1. ***Projected per diem cost of care.*** The average daily cost for nursing home in client's state, adjusted for the average inflationary growth rate for health insurance, can be used as a starting point for projecting the future per diem rates.

2. ***Suitable elimination period.*** A longer elimination period produces a lower premium (holding all other factors equal); however, not all clients can absorb the cost of a prolonged waiting period. As a general rule, it is advisable to purchase a policy with the maximum elimination period that the client can afford.

3. ***Length of benefit need.*** It is prudent to consider a minimum benefit period of five years, although a client's inability to fund ongoing premiums for a five-year period might make it necessary to reduce the benefit period.

4. ***Inflationary pressure on health care.*** Inflation can have a devastating impact on health care needs 20 or 30 years in the future. For example, the inflation rate relating to long-term health care costs has been approximately 10–15 percent; this rate doubles per diem health care costs every five to seven years. Therefore, purchasing a policy with inflation protection is recommended.

5. ***Home health care coverage.*** Based on most people's preference to remain in the family home, it is prudent to buy a policy that covers 100 percent of home health care.

6. ***Client's net worth and future cash flow situation.*** The availability of financial resources in the future (especially if held in illiquid form) and the client's mindset toward eroding the gross estate are important variables to consider when establishing the need for buying long term health care.

7. ***Project longevity.*** Since females outlive males, it is important to consider this fact of life in choosing the need for long-term health care for a male or a female client.

8. ***Existence of other health care coverage.*** A planner should take into account other long-term health care policies owned by the client.

Step 3: Assess the gap. Using the collected data a planner can calculate the existing asset-liability gap. First, he determines the annual cost of LTC in a client's state of residence. Next, from this cost amount other available sources of retirement income are subtracted. This potential gap, if any, can then be filled by purchasing a LTC policy.

Step 4: Identify best insurance companies. The first filter in finding an attractive LTC policy is the quality of an insurer. Here, the same features discussed in regards to the selection of health care companies apply, namely financial stability of the company, historical record for paying benefit claims, quality record for customer service, availability of desired covered services and riders, and competitive pricing. Another important filter to use is the *qualification* for tax purposes under the income tax rules.

Step 5: Select the best viable policy. Once data have been collected on the insurance companies that make the final list, services offered by those companies offering comparable features (such as the same benefits, durations, elimination period, and riders) can be compared before making the final selection.

A client's ability to fund ongoing premiums, costs that should be expected to increase over time, is an important issue to consider. If a policy selected by a planner appears to be too expensive for the client, then the planner would do well to manipulate certain benefits in an effort to lower the cost. This list of benefits include: the type of care selected, length of the elimination period, amount of daily benefit, duration of the benefits, and the selected riders. On the assumption that the client might not be able to use these services over a long period of time, it is recommended that the planner selects the best benefit package offered for a shorter duration of time, so long as the policy comes with a price tag that the client can afford.

WHO NEEDS LTC?

Considering the potential total cost of LTC and the range of uncontrollable risk variables associated with it, it is advisable for everyone over 50 to consider buying an LTC policy, assuming of course that the person has the capacity to make ongoing premium payments. In fact, most professionals advise buying such a policy around the age of 60. This is because at earlier ages, say at 40, it is difficult to forecast how much LTC coverage a person would need in life and what type of care would most likely be needed. On the other hand, waiting for too long (say, an age beyond 65) could make the policy cost prohibitive.

DISABILITY-TO-LTC CONVERSION POLICIES

Some of today's individual income protection policies are designed to address a variety of incomes and life stages. They do this in a hybrid design that provides income protection early in the client's career, is upgraded as income rises, and is finally converted to LTC protection during retirement. These contracts represent a new generation of income protection insurance called "conversion" policies, which evolve as people's needs change, and simultaneously address underserved segments of the disability income market.

These conversion policies should be of particular interest to younger people who are becoming increasingly aware of the need for LTC coverage, perhaps by witnessing parents or grandparents undergoing an LTC event. They realize that financing LTC can quickly erode the entire life savings, and

Table 5.5 *Health Insurance Worksheet*

	Current Coverage	Desirable Coverage
Hospital		
Expense: Amount per day	———	100% of semi-private room
Maximum number of days	———	365 days; thereafter 80%
Additional expenses	———	Reasonable
Diagnostic X-ray and lab work	———	
Deductible	———	
Surgical expense		
Highest surgical fee	———	100%
Regular medical rupees per day	———	100%
Number of days	———	30 days
Major medical coverage		
Major medical (deductible)	———	₹300 per illness
Maximum	———	₹10 lakh lifetime per family
Coinsurance Percentage		80% up to breakpoint, after which insurer pays 100%
Disability income Benefit:		
Short-term disability	———	60% of earned income
Long-term disability	———	60% of earned income
Disability benefit period:		
Short-term disability	———	1 year
Long-term disability	———	Until age 65
Waiting period		
Short-term disability	———	7 days, unless company provides sick pay
Long-term disability	———	90 days
Disability policy definition	———	Own occ.
Key features		
Noncancelable	———	(Yes/No)
Guaranteed renewable	———	(Yes/No)

become convinced that at retirement, what would matter most would be to preserve the assets rather than to protect a paycheck.

ASSESSING A FAMILY'S HEALTH NEEDS

It is always the best strategy to make sure that a family has adequate coverage for medical and hospital expenses, for loss of income caused by disability, and for LTC. Even more important, young families should buy adequate medical and disability coverage even if it that leads to a sacrifice of some portion of the life insurance coverage. This is because to a young family, in financial terms, a long-term disability is likely to be far more devastating than death. A convenient worksheet provided in Table 5.5 can be used to determine if individual levels of coverage match the desired levels of coverage.

Section V: The Homeowner's Policy

INTRODUCTION

A homeowner or renter is exposed to many types of risk. Damages may occur to the property and its structures due to fire or storm. Losses may be generated by injuries suffered on or off the premises. Personal property may also be lost because of theft or fire.The main elements of a homeowner's policy are coverage: (a) on the house, (b) for personal property, (c) against the homeowner's liability, and (d) for medical payments for bodily injury or property damage caused to other people or property. The standard homeowner's (HO) policy is a *package deal* containing all four types of coverage. The standard renter's or condominium policy offers only the last three types of coverage. In this section, we will undertake a discussion of these elements in detail.

LOSS SHARING

Loss-sharing arrangements in homeowner contracts include: coinsurance, deductibles, and policy benefit limits.

Coinsurance

The *Rule of 80* specifies that in order to receive full payment for any partial damage to the house, the house must be insured for at least 80 percent of its full replacement value (not including the cost of the lot). For instance, if a ₹150,000 home is insured for at least ₹120,000 and fire destroys the recreation room, causing ₹20,000 in damage, the entire ₹20,000 less the deductible would be covered. However, if the home was insured for only ₹100,000, then only a percentage of ₹20,000 less the deductible would be covered. It should be noted that the home must be fully insured for 100 percent of the replacement value in order to fully recover from a total home loss.

Deductibles

Deductibles play a significant role in the homeowner's policy loss-sharing arrangement. In contrast to the health care policy arrangement in which the deductible is applied before the insurer considers the claim and assesses the coinsurance liability, the homeowner's ISO (Insurance Service Office) form stipulates that the deductible is applied once the recovery amount is calculated. Applying the deductible after the calculation increases a policyholder's out-of-pocket expense, as explained below.

Assume a client has insured her home for ₹350,000 with a ₹1,500 deductible. The replacement value of the residence is ₹500,000. A fire causes damage to the residence, and she incurs an actual loss of ₹100,000. The insured's liability is calculated as follows:

1. ***Step 1:*** Calculate the required coverage subject to the "Rule of 80"—80 percent of ₹500,000 equals ₹400,000.
2. ***Step 2:*** Calculate the recovery percentage. The coinsurance percentage is equal to the amount of coverage carried (₹350,000) divided by the amount of coverage required (₹400,000). In this example, the ratio is equal to 87.5 percent.
3. ***Step 3:*** Calculate the client's loss recovery. It is equal to the actual loss times the recovery percentage, reduced by the deductible. In this example, it is equal to ₹86,000 (₹100,000 × 0.875 – ₹1,500).

Two additional issues are important: The deductible (a) is an annual amount, and once reached is no longer applicable in that year and (b) applies only to property claims, and not to personal liability claims.

Insured Amount

Typically, most insurers set the maximum recovery amount at 120 percent of house value.

POLICY FORMS

As revealed in Table 5.6, a standardized homeowner's policy comes in two primary forms: broad and special. The *broad* form is the least expensive. It covers the homeowner against personal liability and damage or loss due to the most common risks. This form includes the perils from its predecessor

Table 5.6 *Forms of Homeowner's Policies*

	Broad Form	Special Form
COVERAGE FOR:		
Dwelling	Yes	Yes
Replacement cost of dwelling	Yes	Yes
Related private structures	Yes*	Yes*
Personal property on premises	Yes	Yes
Personal property away from premises	Yes	Yes
Improvements made by tenant	Yes	Yes
Lawns, plants, shrubs, trees	Yes–limited perils	Yes–limited perils
Rental value	Yes–either rental value or additional living expense*	Yes–either rental value or additional living expense*
Additional living expense	Yes–either rental value or additional living expense*	Yes–either rental value or additional living expense*
Contents removed to new principal residence	30 days coverage at both locations	30 days coverage at both locations
Jewelry and furs	Yes	Yes
PERILS COVERED:		
Fire and lightning	Yes	Yes
Windstorm	Yes	Yes
Outside antenna windstorm damage	Only by endorsement	Only by endorsement
Hail	Yes	Yes
Riot and civil commotion	Yes	Yes
Explosion other than steam boiler	Yes	Yes
Explosion of VWHDP boiler	Yes	Yes
Bursting of steam or hot water appliances and heating systems	Yes	Yes
Smoke–sudden and accidental damage:		
From industrial operations	No	Contents only
From fireplaces	No	Yes
From heating or cooking unit	Yes	Yes
Aircraft	Yes	Yes
Sonic boom	Yes	Yes
Vehicle damage by other than occupant of property to:		
Building	Yes	Yes
Personal property	Yes	Yes
Fences	Yes	Yes
Driveways	Yes	Yes
Walks	Yes	Yes
Lawns	Yes	Yes
Trees, shrubs, and plants	Yes	Yes
Vehicle damage to house or garage by dwelling occupant	Yes	Yes
Vandalism and malicious mischief	Yes	Yes
Water:		
Surface water or flood	No	No
Backing up of sewers or drains	No	No
Leakage from plumbing or heating systems	Yes	Yes
Rain through doors, windows, bad roof	No	Yes–building only
Freezing of plumbing, heating systems	Yes	Yes
Falling objects (from outside)	Yes	Yes
Weight of ice, snow, sleet	Yes	Yes

(Continued)

Table 5.6 (*Continued*)

	Bread Form	Special Form
Collapse of building	Yes	Yes
Landside	No	No
Earthquake	No, expect by endorsement	No, expect by endorsement
Residence glass breaking	Yes	Yes
Sudden and accidental damage from artificially generated electrical current	Yes	Yes
Burglary damage	Yes	Yes–including theft of part completed and occupied structure
Unspecified perils	No	Yes ("all risk" coverage)

*This is an additional amount of insurance.

**Extended Coverage perils and Vandalism and Malicious Mischief are optional under DP-1.

Source: Compiled from homeowner's policies of various insurance companies.

dwelling policy of fire and lightning, plus risks covered by the acronym WHARVES (windstorm, hail, aircraft, riot or civil commotion, vehicles, explosion, and smoke, which were originally part of a policy known as the *basic* policy). In addition, it includes falling objects, weight of ice, snow or sleet, accidental discharge or overflow of water and steam, air conditioning systems and appliances, damage from artificially generated electricity, and volcanic eruption. The *special* form, which can be expensive, includes all perils except those specifically excluded, such as damage due to earthquake or flood.

Insurance companies offer several types of homeowner's policies: HO-2 (broad form), HO-3 (special form), HO-4, (broad form, which is also referred to as renter's insurance), HO-5, (comprehensive form), and HO-6 (coverage for condominium owners). The salient features of several of these forms are presented in Table 5.7. Two other forms, not shown in Table 5.7, are HO-1 and HO-8. HO-1 is a basic form that provides limited coverage; generally it does not provide appropriate protection for the average homeowner. HO-8, referred to as the modified form, is designed for older homes for which the fair market value has dropped below the replacement cost.

It should be noted that the householders' package policy generally does not cover loss or damage to the insured property due to willful destruction of property. Additionally, it does not cover loss and damage caused by war and nuclear explosive equipment.

In most forms of homeowner's policies, the insured is entitled to indemnification for a loss caused by a specifically named peril. HO-3 provides *all-risk* coverage for the dwelling (i.e., open perils) but not the personal property (i.e., named perils). However, if one desires to purchase an *all-risk* policy covering all personal property losses, except those that are specifically excluded, then the HO-5 comprehensive policy should be purchased. The HO-5 covers the dwelling, other structures, and personal property on an "open perils" basis. Incidentally, HO-5 is designed to provide replacement cost on contents coverage.

In order to get full coverage, the insured cannot buy less than the amounts of minimally specified insurance. If the coverage for a particular category of claims (e.g., personal property and loss of use) is calculated as a percentage of the insurance on the house, then the coverage can usually be increased for an additional premium without raising the overall coverage amount for the dwelling. In the event the home is damaged by fire or other disaster and the owner has to rent living quarters while it is being repaired, the policy covers the living expenses as well.

HO-1, HO-2, HO-3, HO-5, and HO-8 may be written for the owner-occupant of a dwelling that is used exclusively as a private residence. Special exceptions for persons doing business in the home can be added through endorsements. The dwelling may not accommodate two families.

There are two sections to the homeowner's policy (see Table 5.7). Section 1 contains four levels of coverage—A, B, C, and D—while Section 2 contains only two levels of coverage, E and F.

Table 5.7 *Homeowner Coverage*

Coverage	HO-2 (Broad Form)	HO-3 (Special Form)	HO-5 (Comprehensive Form)	HO-4 (Contents Broad Form)	HO-6 (Unit Owner's Form)
	Section 1 Coverage			*Section 1 Coverage*	
A. Dwelling	Named perils	Open perils	Open perils	Not applicable	Not applicable
B. Other structures	Named perils (10% of A)	Open perils (10% of A)	Open perils (10% of A)	Not applicable	Not applicable
C. Personal property	Named perils (50% of A)	Named perils (50% of A)	Open perils (50% of A)	₹6,000	₹6,000
D. Loss of use	Named perils (30% of A)	Open perils (30% of A)	Open perils (30% of A)	minimum 30% of A	minimum 40% of A
Covered perils	Fire or lightning Windstorm or hail Explosion Riot or civil commotion Aircraft Vehicles Smoke Vandalism or malicious mischief Theft Breakage of glass or safety glazing material Falling objects Weight of ice, snow, or sleet Accidental discharge or overflow of water or steam Sudden and accidental tearing, cracking, burning or bulging of a steam, hot water, air conditioning or automatic fire protective sprinkler system or appliance for heating water Freezing Sudden and accidental damage from artificially generated electrical current Volcanic eruption	Dwelling and other structures covered against risks of direct physical loss to property except losses specifically excluded Personal property covered by same perils as HO-2 plus damage by glass or safety glazing material, which is part of a building, storm door or storm window	Same perils as HO-3 except that personal property is based on open perils, rather than named	Same perils as HO-2 for personal property	Same perils as HO-2 for personal property
E. Personal liability	₹1,000,000	₹100,000	₹1,000,000	₹1,000,000	₹1,000,000
F. Medical payments to others	₹50,000 per person	₹50,000 per person	₹50,000 per person	₹50,000 per person	₹50,000 per person

Coverage A. This part of the policy insures the dwelling (including one under construction), attached structures, and materials and supplies located on or adjacent to the premises, such as those used in construction, alteration, and repair of the dwelling.

Coverage B. This coverage relates to structures completely separated from the building by a clear space. Examples include a detached garage and a detached fence. However, detached garages rented to other persons for a fee are excluded from coverage. The amount of loss protection under Coverage B is typically equal to 10 percent of coverage provided under Coverage A.

Coverage C. This coverage generally insures personal property for 50–70 percent of the Schedule A coverage. The insured's property is covered anywhere in the world. Property maintained in a secondary residence would also be covered by that policy. The coverage may vary, depending on the type of property, although the coverage can be increased through the purchase of endorsements. Certain types of property are excluded from coverage under homeowner's insurance, and special limits of liability exist on other types of property. Items that are generally excluded from coverage under Coverage C of the homeowner's policy include: property insured elsewhere, motorized land vehicles designed for street usage, aircraft, property that is rented out, property owned by renters or boarders, animals, birds, fish, and business data.

The following rupee sub-limits of coverage generally apply to Schedule C coverage: ₹2 crore on fire and allied perils, ₹10 lakh on furniture, ₹300,000 on electronic equipment breakdown, and ₹300,000 on electrical appliances breakdown. It is important to check the policy's sub-limits because not all policies contain identical rupee limits. Other limits are also imposed on this type of coverage. Stamps are classified with securities, evidence of debts, deeds, and tickets. Other valuables and collectors' items, such as fine art, antiques, cameras, and musical instruments, can be claimed up to their insured cash value, provided a sales receipt can be produced.

Coverage D. This part insures the loss of use and provides protection against losses involving both the premises occupied by the insured and those rented to others. If the premises are occupied by the insured, the company pays for the additional living expenses incurred by the family to maintain its normal standard of living. However, if the property is rented to others, coverage is limited to the fair rental value of the property. The amount of loss protection under Coverage D is typically equal to 30 percent of the coverage provided under Coverage A, although this percentage can be increased.

Coverage E. This coverage makes all payments, up to the limit of liability, that become the insured's legal obligation because of bodily injury or property damage falling within the scope of the coverage. Coverage E does contain certain exclusions, including: liabilities from motor vehicle and watercraft events, business and professional liabilities, and liability resulting from the use of illegal drugs. Personal liability protection means that if someone outside of the family is injured in an accident on the property, or in an accident (but not an auto accident) off the premises that is caused by a member of the family, the homeowner's policy covers the insured against a lawsuit.

Coverage F. This part of the policy relates to medical payments to anyone (other than the insured's family) who are injured while on the premises with the permission of the insured, or who are injured away from the premises if the injury results from an activity of the insured's family.

The insurance company covers medical expenses for people hurt by a member of the owner's family, or the pets, on or away from the home, even when they are not legally responsible for the injury. It also pays for damage to the property of others, even if the owner is not legally at fault. However, the insured does not personally receive any money for personal liability and damage to property of others and medical payments. The compensation is for injury to people other than family members living with the homeowner, and the money is paid directly to the injured person(s).

MAJOR HOMEOWNER POLICY PROVISIONS

The Home

Definition of Insured

The policy clearly defines the coverage as follows: the insured person and the family members permanently residing with the insured.

Insured Locations

The policy defines the locations that are insured under the homeowner's policy. Typically, the definition includes: the resident premises, other parts of the premise's grounds, the insured's temporary living space, vacant land, and a cemetery plot. In addition, personal property owned the insured anywhere else in the world is also covered.

Unscheduled Personal Property

Market Value

This coverage refers to personal household contents not specifically listed by name and value in the policy. The homeowner's policy typically provides insurance on these items equal to 50 percent of the amount of insurance on the house, although some insurers do offer a higher percentage of personal property coverage. When property is destroyed, in order to estimate the value of the damage, the company asks for proof of ownership and an estimate of the depreciated value of such property. For this reason, it is advisable to maintain a complete video or an updated itemized inventory of personal property.

Actual versus Replacement Cost

A policy covering the *actual cash value* of a property (i.e., the replacement cost less depreciation) leaves a great deal to be desired. For one thing, such a method requires the owner to maintain detailed records of the date of purchase, purchase price, estimated percentage depreciation on the date of loss, and other related bookkeeping records. For another, the reimbursement amount is likely to cover only a fraction of the replacement cost of the article. For these reasons, several years ago insurance companies started to offer *replacement cost* coverage. Under this provision, for an additional premium representing 5–15 percent of the policy's total premium, a homeowner can receive the actual replacement cost of a destroyed or stolen item. However, for best results, it is wise to maintain a detailed inventory of personal effects and video tapes of all the contents (both front and back) located inside the house.

Unfortunately, today insurance companies are covering themselves first and shifting more of the final burden to homeowners. Many insurers are phasing out *guaranteed replacement cost* policies that require companies to pay whatever it took to restore structures to their original condition. Some companies are also changing rupee-based deductibles to percent-based deductibles, which typically require consumers to pay more money when catastrophe strikes.

There are special discounts available for new or updated utilities. Also, a special coverage pays for damage by water backing up from sewers and drains. Building ordinance and law coverage protects homeowners against code changes. As a result of these changes in home replacement cost policies, homeowners are advised to reexamine their coverage and consider insuring their homes closer to their full value.

Endorsements

Inflation Guard

In view of the ever-increasing cost of replacing a home, it is advisable to purchase coverage for the actual replacement value of the house (excluding the lot). This is accomplished by keeping the insurance updated through an inflation-guard endorsement, so the home will always remain adequately insured. Every year this provision increases the amount of the coverage sufficiently to keep pace with inflation. The cost of endorsement does vary, depending on the type of coverage and variations in the cost-of-living index.

Personal Property Replacement Cost

After taking an inventory of personal valuables, a homeowner feeling the need for additional coverage may choose between two options. (a) The basic homeowner's coverage can be raised, which would automatically raise the unscheduled personal property protection (subject to sub-limits). (b) Valuables like furs, jewelry, fine art, silverware, cameras, stamps, coins, and sports and hobby gear can be listed individually in special endorsements or *floaters*. The personal property replacement cost rider is designed to recover losses based on replacement rather than the actual cost. Unfortunately, this rider does not apply to antiques or rare items like fine art, antiques, rare coins, stamps, and musical instruments.

Scheduled Personal Property Floater

In situations where personal properties are valued in excess of the coverage or limitations offered by a typical homeowner's policy, two types of floater policies are available. The *personal articles floater* provides all-risk protection for each article specified in the policy. By contrast, *personal property floater* offers protection on all articles on a worldwide basis. Because these policies can be expensive, it is best to cover only those articles that warrant special coverage, such as original paintings, authentic artifacts, jewelry, furs, and boats, although the insurance company may require the homeowner to have these items appraised before insuring them. When buying floaters, it is advisable to get the inflation-guard endorsement to have protection against rising replacement values. Although it may vary from one company to another, for 5 percent of the regular premium, the amount of coverage can be adjusted upward on a regular basis.

Additional Living Expense Coverage

This endorsement increases the payment for "Part D." Considering the time required to build a home after a major loss, the additional living expense coverage ensures that the family's normal standard of living will be maintained for a prolonged period of time during which the new home is built.

Other Endorsements

Other items that might be considered as endorsements to the homeowner's policy are: backup of sewer or drain, identification of restoration coverage, home business coverage, and building ordinance and law coverage.

Specialty Forms of Insurance

Flood Insurance

Most home insurance contracts provide protection against loss caused by overflowing of water within the house. However, in order to cover the damages caused by the natural disaster of flooding, a special flood insurance scheme is available to homeowners at rates subsidized by the government. To qualify for this program, the property must be located in areas declared as susceptible to floods.

Earthquake Insurance

Homeowner policies typically do not cover earthquake damage. The cost of earthquake insurance has escalated in certain parts of the country due to the actual loss experiences. For example, the cost for earthquake insurance might cost a bundle plus a deductible stated as a percentage (e.g., 10–20 percent) of the replacement cost.

Private Mortgage Insurance

Home buyers who make a down payment of less than 20 percent of the purchase price are required to buy a private mortgage insurance (PMI). At a cost of ₹50–100 for every ₹100,000 borrowed, this insurance protects the lender against the potential default on the mortgage. While the cost of this insurance appears to be insignificant when compared with the monthly mortgage for an expensive home, PMI does add up, simply because it can take years to reach that magic 20 percent equity threshold when it is no longer required.

Home Office Protection

Most home office equipment, such as computers, fax, and copy machines are generally excluded from conventional homeowner's policies. Homeowner's and renter's policies typically provide cap coverage for business property at ₹2,500. A typical policy provides no liability coverage for business-related claims either.

In order to buy additional coverage, a homeowner may wish to obtain separate insurance. This additional insurance becomes particularly important if the owner sees clients in the home office. For a low-risk home business, a rider that increases business-property and liability coverage to the same amounts as stated in the homeowner's policy costs only a few hundred rupees per year.

Other Specialty Insurance

Other specialty insurance useful in risk management planning include: insurance on watercraft, wind exposure or hurricane insurance, title insurance, and crime insurance.

TAXATION OF BENEFITS

Indemnification for property losses is not a taxable item. The income tax department maintains that the cash proceeds are designed to put the insured back in the original position. Premium payments for the homeowner's policy are not considered a deductible expense, however.

PLANNING PROCESS

The planning process for homeowner coverage is similar to planning for health risks. It involves understanding the client's objectives, assessing the strengths and weaknesses of the current plan, and filling the gap with a viable, customized policy.

Step 1: Understand client objectives and situation. The first step is always to understand the goals of the client. This includes understanding how does a client feel about being exposed to risk and is he in a position to absorb additional risk? Understanding the client's circumstances helps a planner determine what needs to be protected and the amount of cash flow available to support the premium payments associated with the purchase of adequate coverage.

Step 2: Assess the current risk management plan. A financial planner can assess the current risk by asking: (a) how the current homeowner's insurance policy looks like? (b) are all the major risk exposures covered? and (c) are there catastrophic *gaps* or serious *weaknesses* that need to be covered?

Gaps in homeowner's policies. A homeowner may wish to buy special riders for the following items which are not generally covered by a typical homeowner's policy:

1. Expensive items such as big-screen TVs and extra-fancy stereo equipment which are often excluded from most policies or inadequately covered. The same goes for antiques, collectibles, expensive jewelry, and furs.
2. A backed-up sewer can send waste spewing into the house.
3. Most people who live near a river or coastline know that homeowner's policies do not cover flood damage; they can buy flood insurance through the National Flood Insurance Program.
4. Homeowner's policies typically contain low sub-limits for theft of jewelry, and they offer no protection in case of a mysterious disappearance such as a ring falling down the drain. Additionally, if jewelry is not stolen and there is no police report, it may not be covered. The homeowner can buy a rider to cover such losses and tie the coverage level to the jewelry's appraised value. The cost is assessed on a "per-thousand-rupee" scale.
5. Some policies are called *all risk*, which means they cover damages caused by almost any situation except those specifically excluded in the policy. But others are named perils policies, which cover only damages caused by particular situations—such as fire, theft, a plane crashing into the house, and more than a dozen other circumstances. The laundry list seems to include everything, but inevitably leaves out some scenarios. In this case, getting an all-perils rider typically adds about 20 percent to the annual premium.

Step 3: Assess the alternatives and recommend a solution. A house is likely to be the single biggest investment most of us make. The general rule of thumb with homeowner's insurance is not to skimp on the adequate coverage of the home.

Steps 4 and 5: Identify possible insurance companies and select an appropriate policy. The final two steps involve implementing the plan, which is consistent with the planning process in the preceding sections.

Policy details. Here are several items a homeowner should look for in selecting a policy. (a) As previously mentioned, most insurers cap coverage at 120 percent of the value of the house. It is important to purchase extra coverage if the appraisal is low, or if the home has handcrafted cabinetry or other expensive features. (b) It can take months or even years to rebuild or repair a home. A loss-of-use clause covers living expenses over and above the normal costs. This insurance is usually capped at 20 percent of the home's coverage, but some insurance companies do allow homeowners to purchase more. (c) If the homeowner works from home, a home-business endorsement should be purchased to cover the business equipment and liability. (d) There are several ways in which premium costs could be pared down, include the following: alarm systems simple safety devices. Also, multipolicy discounts with the same insurer can lower the cost by 5 percent or more.

The Cost Issue

Managing the premium. The client's ability to fund higher premiums is often an issue that planners need to address through integrative planning. Of all the proven strategies for reducing the cost of a homeowner's policy, selecting the most economical policy from a group of alternative quotations for identical coverage tops the list. Another strategy for cost reduction is to increase the deductible which can

Table 5.8 *Homeowner's/Renters Insurance Worksheet*

	Current Coverage	Desirable coverage
Home replacement value		80% of replacement cost
Type of coverage	HO-2, HO-3	HO-3
Renter's/Condo insurance	HO-4, HO-6	HO-4, HO-6
Personal Property:		50% of face amount
Financial documents	Rupee limit	Increase limits to suit personal needs
Jewelry and furs	Rupee limit	Increase limits to suit personal needs
Silverware and gold	Rupee limit	Increase limits to suit personal needs
Musical instruments	Rupee limit	Increase limits to suit personal needs
Fine art	Rupee limit	Increase limits to suit personal needs
Other		Increase limits to suit personal needs
Liability insurance		Umbrella policy

significantly cut annual premiums. In general, small losses significantly increase administrative costs, thereby jeopardizing the renewal of a policy.

High-cost homes. Most large insurance companies use some form of an estimator for determining the estimated replacement cost of homes of higher quality than those considered by the replacement cost calculator. While homes such as these may have unique or unusual features, more of them will also have multiple levels, ornate staircases, top quality windows and doors, and many other features which are extra in homes of less value. Most of the typical additional features such as air conditioning, intercom, porches, and similar items are included in the base cost for each of these classes of high valued dwellings. Only a few extra features are listed for such features as garages, fireplaces, and so on.

Self-Analysis

For financial planning purposes, the best strategy for carrying a satisfactory homeowner's policy is to make sure that the family has adequate coverage against all major risks associated with owning a home. A convenient worksheet is presented in Table 5.8 which can be used to determine if individual coverage matches the desired levels of coverage.

Annual Check-up

In addition to self-analysis, it is advisable to have an annual check-up of the homeowner's policy by an insurance professional. We will briefly review here the annual check-up process for the family of Ratna and Sadhana Singh. We will review only the homeowner's policy here. Auto and liability policies will be examined in subsequent sections.

Recently, the Singhs received the following letter from their insurance agent.

June 15, 2014

Ratna and Sadhana Singh
BHU, Varanasi, 221005

Dear Mr. and Mrs. Singh:

As part of my continuing service to you, I review your file from time to time. Presently you have the following policies with me:

AUTO	2005 Scorpio, 2010 Maruti SX4
FIRE	HOMEOWNER'S (HO-5), PERSONAL LIABILITY
LIFE	None
HEALTH	None

I feel a thorough review of all your present policies would be very beneficial at this time. We call this review the Free Family Insurance Check-up service. To set up a convenient time for us to get together, give me a call at (248) 643-1234, or stop by to set up an appointment soon.

Remember, our company offers economical protection for all your insurance needs—car, home, health, life, boat, and even your business. I am attaching the following for your review:

Form	A:	Family Insurance Check-up Check List
	B:	HO Policy Status
	C:	Auto Policy Status
	D:	Umbrella Policy Status

Thank you for allowing me to serve you.

Sincerely,
Anish Dubey
Friendly Insurance Agent

FORM A

You should consider
Replacement cost on dwelling:
Replacement cost on contents:
Higher liability limits:
Higher deductibles:
Mortgage disability/life:
Umbrella coverage:

Do you have?
Other buildings on premises:
Improvements since insured:
Photo inventory:
Coins/gold/silver:
Cameras:
Stamp collections/collectibles:
Trailer (not boat):
Watercraft:
Oriental rugs/personal computer:
Jewelry/furs/fine arts/silverware:
Sports equipment/musical instruments:
Tools/equipment/goods for sale:
Pets:
Smoke alarms/extinguishers:
Dead bots/security systems:
Firearms:
Woodburning stove/kerosene heater:
Roomers/resident employees:
A need for professional liability:
Office/business:
Childcare in the home:
Sewer/drain/sump pump problems:
Earthquake/flood:
Other homes/rental properly/farms:

FORM B: HOMEOWNER'S POLICY STATUS

Date	January 2, 2012
Address	1234 Gross Street, Minneapolis, MN
Type	40-5
Premium	₹554 Deductible ₹1,000
Renewal date	January 2, 2013
Mortgage	Interfirst, Federal Savings
Policy Number	82-ET 5000-1 Z

Description of home	(1) Year built: 1990; (2) Number of stories: 2; (3) Construction: Masonry; (4) Ground floor sq ft: 2,292; (5) No. of corners: 4
No. of families	One
Special features	(1) Bedrooms adjoining a bathroom or sitting room; (2) Masonry fireplaces; (3) Brick or stone exterior walls; (4) Hardwood floors; (5) Stained/varnished woodwork
Other features	1) Deck; (2) Masonry chimney; (3) Kitchen package; (4) Central air; (5) Fireplace hearth; (6) Three-car attached garage
Policy discounts	(1) Sprinkler: 10%; (2) Home alert 10%; (3) home/auto discount: yes
Value covered	₹190,900
Special coverage	(1) Building ordinance: 10%; (2) silver/gold ware: ₹2,500; (3) firearms: ₹2,500; (4) Jewelry/furs: ₹2,500/₹5,000; (5) home computer: ₹5,000; (6) Personal property amount: ₹143,175; (7) Deductible: ₹500; (8) Liability: ₹500,000; (9) Medical payment: ₹1,000
Endorsements	(1) Back-up of sewer: ₹10,000; (2) Jewelry/furs: ₹1,000; (3) Personal injury; (4) Nurses professional liability; (5) Theft; (6) Rented personal property

Cost of Policy Coverage

	Limit	Annual Premium
Dwelling	₹190,900	₹528.00
Dwelling extension	19,090	
Personal property	143,175	
Liability	500,000	25.00
Medical payment	1,000	
Deductibles	500	
Credit: Home alert		(11.00)
Credit: Home/auto		(26.00)
Credit: Homeowners 369		(37.00)
Total		**₹554.00**

The Singhs met with Anish Dubey to review their homeowner's policy covering their home located at House No 5, Sector 46, Gurgaon, Haryana (see Form B). After some discussion the Singhs agreed to make the following changes in their policy in order to bring the coverage to a comfortable level.

1. Personal property coverage was increased to ₹200,000
2. Optional coverage was increased on:

   (a) Jewelry and furs: ₹5,000/₹10,000
   (b) Silverware/Gold ware: ₹5,000
   (c) Home computers and equipment: ₹10,000
   (d) Property used in business: ₹5,000
   (e) Face value of coverage: ₹300,000
   (f) Liability: ₹2 million

3. Art and other highly valued items were reviewed, and floater policies ere purchased.

Section VI: Automobile Insurance Policy

INTRODUCTION

Every year Indians set a new record for the number of automobile accidents, as well as the number of injuries and deaths they cause. These accidents result in economic losses amounting to crores of rupees, and these losses relentlessly continue their upward journey with no end in sight. These statistics should

Table 5.9 *Summary of Basic Automobiles Insurance Coverage*

Coverages	Policyholder	Other Persons
Bodily Injury		
Bodily injury liability	No	Yes
Medical payments	Yes	Yes
Protections against uninsured motorists	Yes	Yes
	Policyholder's Automobile	**Property of Others**
Property Damage		
Property damage liability	No	Yes
Comprehensive physical damage	Yes	No
Collision	Yes	No

be borne in mind as we discuss the need for having basic automobile insurance coverage. Additional coverage—such as collision, comprehensive, uninsured and underinsured motorists, and medical payments—is equally important.Determining the *basic* coverage of an automobile insurance policy, known as personal auto policy (PAP), is not that easy, for there is more to choosing the right policy than meets the eye. As can be seen from Table 5.9, there are two types of damages that could result from an auto accident: (a) property damage (including damage to the automobile), and (b) bodily injury (including death). These damages could be the result of the driver's negligence or that of *the other driver*. Accidents also happen due to circumstances beyond the control of the drivers involved. Add to these complications other factors such as: the *other driver* happens to be an uninsured motorist, or the motorist, is encouraged by a lawyer to build up a claim because he or she perceives the driver to be wealthy. That gives a fairly good idea of what is involved in selecting a good automobile insurance policy.

The selection task can begin with the minimum coverage. This coverage then can be expanded in various directions, depending on the family's special needs and budget constraints.

BASIC COVERAGE OF PERSONAL AUTO POLICY

Automobile policies are classified into two categories:

1. Liability only policy, which covers third-party liability for bodily injury liability and/or death and property damage where personal accident cover for owner-driver is also included. This type of policy includes death or bodily injury to a third person and damage to third-party property. In the case of injury or property damage, the liability coverage is as follows: ₹7.5 lakh for commercial and private vehicles, and ₹1 lakh for scooters and motor cycles.
2. Package policy, covering loss, or damage to the insured vehicle and its accessories. This policy also pays for towing charges from the place of accident to the workshop up to ₹300 for scooters/motorcycles and ₹1,500 for cars and commercial vehicles. The insured can purchase additional coverage for covering fire and theft (not available for vehicles ratable under Class D, Tariff for Miscellaneous and special types of vehicles).[9]

Details of these policies are discussed below.

Part A: Liability Coverage (Liability to Others)

Under the PAP, the following persons are covered: (a) the named insured, (b) the spouse living in the principal household, (c) the relatives of the first person named in the declaration, (d) any other person who obtained the consent of the insured or the spouse, and (e) any other person or organization liable for

[9] http://newindia.co.in/Content.aspx?pageid=59 (last accessed on February 25, 2015).

the use of such a car by one of the previously mentioned insureds. The coverage is not extended to automobiles used in any business or occupation or to persons working in any car business.

A significant feature of PAP is the *single limit* coverage for both bodily injury and property damage. The limit of liability included in the policy is the maximum limit of liability for bodily injury and property damage resulting from any one accident. Each of the two liabilities is discussed next.

Bodily Injury Liability/Third-party Liability under Motor Vehicles Act, 1988

In buying auto insurance the major concern should be to protect against others' claims arising from bodily injury or death caused by the members or employees of the family. When a policy is purchased that includes liability, the insurance company promises to honor the claims of the aggrieved party or parties up to the financial limits stipulated in the policy. These limits are often expressed as a split limit, such as 25/50, which means that the insurance company is liable for up to ₹25,000 for any one person injured and up to ₹50,000 for all persons injured in the same accident. However, as a bare minimum, one should carry at least a 100/300 coverage, which means ₹100,000 coverage for one person and up to ₹300,000 for all persons per accident. A financial planner should analyze the net worth and annual income of a family in order to determine the satisfactory level of liability insurance that family should carry. Liability is covered for an unlimited amount in respect of death or injury for all classes of vehicle.

Property Damage Liability

This coverage applies when the insured's car damages the property of others. The property may be the car of the other person or it may be other properties, such as lamp posts, buildings, or telephone poles. Property damage liability coverage provides protection in the form of legal defense and indemnification through the payment of damages for which a driver is legally liable. Liability is covered in respect of damage to third-party property for ₹7.5 lakh for commercial and private vehicles and ₹1 lakh for scooters/motor cycles. However, for damages to the property of the third party, the limit is ₹6,000.

Part B: Medical Payments Coverage

Unlike homeowner's insurance which provides coverage for medical payments to others, in the auto policy medical payments cover the cost of medical services provided for the insured, the relatives, and anyone else in the insured's car. This coverage, however, does not apply to other pedestrians or to occupants of the other vehicle. In addition to carrying liability insurance, the main benefit of having the automobile medical payments coverage is that the payment is prompt, since no time is wasted in determining liability. For Part B, the amount of coverage is low, typically ₹25,000–50,000 per person, but this amount can be raised by endorsement. Part B also covers the insured and the insured's family if they are injured by another vehicle while walking as a pedestrian or riding on a bicycle.

Part C: Uninsured Motorists

Under this coverage the insurance company protects the driver against losses inflicted by someone who: (a) has no insurance, (b) has insurance with an insolvent carrier, or (c) is a "hit-and-run" driver. However, in order to collect on a claim under this provision, the other driver must be at fault. Incidentally, this coverage applies only to bodily injuries, and the payment for injury by the insurance company is limited to the stated maximum liability amount.

A variation of this feature protects against underinsured motorists. In this situation the other driver is at fault but does not have sufficient insurance to cover the losses. A planner must make sure that the contract covers "underinsured motorists" are covered as part of the "uninsured motorist" coverage. If not, an appropriate policy endorsement should be purchased.

Part D: Coverage for Damage to Insured's Auto

There are two elements to Part D: collision and "other-than-collision."

Collision/Overturn

If a car is damaged by a person other than the driver, it should be possible to get the car repaired or replaced at the cost of the person at fault, provided the guilty person has coverage. If not, the insurance company representing the driver at fault may also delay paying for the damages, in which case the driver is left with little choice but to absorb the auto repair cost. Of course, the situation becomes more complicated if the insured causes damage to the car by colliding with another car (own fault), another object (e.g., a tree or a street sign), or by overturning the vehicle. To cover such contingencies, it is desirable to purchase collision insurance, which obligates the insurance company to pay for any damage to the car regardless of who is at fault.

The insured risks losing the amount of the deductible if the car is damaged, but the premium savings resulting from using that strategy are substantial. Another sensible strategy is to skip the collision coverage altogether if the car is old with a small "book value." This decision can easily be made by comparing the market value of the car with the collision premium charged.

Other-than-collision

Other-than-collision insurance (also called *comprehensive physical damage*) protects the car against various perils, including: theft, vandalism, falling objects, windstorm, glass breakage, fire, lightening, impact with animals, hail, water, flood, and earthquake. However, this coverage does not apply to cars damaged in a collision with another car or object, or to cars which lose value because of normal wear and tear. The extent of the coverage is specified in the policy, and the amount of deductible varies from one policy to another. A number of comprehensive fire and theft policies also reimburse the policyholder for a rental car during repair or until a new car can be purchased.

Part E: Duties after Accident or Loss

In case of a claim, a policyholder must: (a) inform the insurance company immediately and provide the insurance company accident-related paperwork duly filled out with pictures, (b) authorize the insurance company to obtain medical and other pertinent records, (c) submit proof of loss, and (d) cooperate with the insurance company in settling the claim.

Part F: General Provisions

The key provisions of a PAP are listed as follows:

1. The terms of a policy may be changed or waived only by an endorsement signed by the company.
2. The policyholder does not have a right of action against the company until all the terms of the policy have been met, and under the liability coverage, until the damage amount an insured is legally liable to pay has been determined.

The policyholder may cancel the policy by notifying the company in writing of the date of cancelation, signing a lost policy release, or returning the policy.

FACTORS AFFECTING PREMIUMS

The cost of auto insurance depends in part on whether the insured is an accident-prone individual. The minimum premium for vehicles designed for the use of physically handicapped persons is ₹25 (₹100 for vehicle). Factors considered by insurers when categorizing drivers and determining premiums include age, gender, and marital status. Individuals over the age of 25 are less likely to be involved in an accident than younger drivers. Women have fewer accidents than men, and married drivers have fewer accidents than single drivers. Insurers also consider:

1. ***Personal driving record.*** Drivers with a history of accidents and/or traffic violations (especially driving under the influence of alcohol) are more likely to incur losses than those with clean records. Some insurers give discounts for completing defensive driver or driver education courses.
2. ***Type of vehicle.*** High-performance vehicles and sports cars carry higher accident risk. Insurers may offer preferential rates for vehicles that have certain safety features (e.g., anti-lock brakes and air bags).
3. ***Cost to repair vehicle.*** Repair expenses can vary widely, even among vehicles that have comparable original purchase prices.
4. ***Vehicle use and location.*** Daily commuters in densely populated urban areas pose a higher risk than occasional drivers in rural areas.
5. ***Multipolicy discounts.*** Individuals who purchase their homeowner's and auto policies through the same company generally receive preferred rates on both policies.

MISCELLANEOUS CONSIDERATIONS

Cost of Auto Insurance

The law requires that drivers have some sort of automobile insurance in place or financial capacity to withstand losses incurred due to auto accident. And even if someone does not, it would be madness to drive without some form of protection, because a single accident could bankrupt the driver.

For many people, the auto policy can be quite expensive. The biggest bite of auto insurance comes from liability protection, which is effectively divided into bodily injury protection and property protection. This is one element of auto insurance no driver can afford to shortchange. However, to reduce the cost, one should consider raising the deductibles, which is the portion of the expense the driver has to pay before coverage kicks in. Pushing up deductibles to ₹500 or even higher can significantly cut the premiums. Another way to reduce the premium is to eliminate collision coverage if the car is old.

Other ways of cutting cost include: (a) a good safety record, because drivers with good records get better rates, (b) insuring every car with the same company, since multicar packages often mean lower premiums, (c) avoiding smoking, because smokers reportedly have more accidents than nonsmokers, and (d) college study, because if the driver is in college and getting good grades, the insurance company is likely to reduce the premiums.

Loopholes in Auto Insurance

Generally, when someone drives a person's car with the owner's permission, the insurance company covers that driver. However, if the driver lives in the same house but is not listed on the policy, then that general rule may not apply. Therefore, it is important to get this issue resolved by the insurance company. Experts recommend that the children should be included in the policy of the owner even if they are away to school. Also the insurance company should be informed if a nanny or a housekeeper will be using the car regularly.

One area of contention is when the car is used for business, since the insurance company may not cover the car for accidents that occur during business use. Another area of concern is when a traveler casually rejects insurance coverage by a car rental company on the assumption that his or her own policy will automatically cover it.

NO-FAULT INSURANCE

In no-fault insurance, an insurance company reimburses the policyholder for damages only if the insured is at fault. However, in an auto accident, determination as to who is really at fault may require legal negotiations, leading ultimately to a possible lawsuit. This problem is further exacerbated when neither motorist is at fault, or when both parties are at fault. For this reason, states have adopted no-fault insurance laws.

There are four essential elements in the basic no-fault plan. (a) An accident victim's losses should be paid for by his or her insurance company, making court action unnecessary to determine liability. (b) The right to sue for additional compensation is significantly limited. (c) No-fault insurance is mandatory, which insures quick payment to all accident victims without recourse to courts. (d) Insurance companies are required to provide safeguards against cancelation or nonrenewal of auto insurance policies following auto accidents.

The original idea of pure no-fault insurance was to eliminate lawsuits by having victims getting reimbursed by their own insurance companies for medical expenses but without any reimbursement for *pain and suffering*. This eliminated the *fault* concept associated with an accident and allowed immediate reimbursement for bodily injuries. However, no state has adopted this version of no-fault.

Coverage limits and deductibles vary from one company to another. This represents the amount the injured person must pay before making a no-fault claim. Coverage for personal injuries may range anywhere from ₹20,000 to ₹50,000.

A SUMMARY

The most common form of property insurance purchased by Indians is a personal automobile policy. Certain basic coverage is mandatory, but insurance companies offer options that extend protection beyond the legal minimum levels. In general, insurers offer the following types of auto insurance:

Types of Insurance	Items/Events Covered
Liability	Injuries to others and damage to their property
Medical payments	Medical and/or funeral expenses incurred because of an auto accident, regardless of who is at fault
Uninsured and underinsured motorist	Expenses (liability and/or physical damage) incurred when the insured is the victim of an accident involving an uninsured vehicle, or a vehicle that has insufficient coverage
Physical damage	Damage to the insured vehicle from an accident (collision) or causes such as theft, fire, or vandalism (comprehensive)

Other options are available as endorsements or "add-ons." These include: underinsured motorist coverage, road-service or towing assistance, collision transportation benefit (temporary replacement vehicle), and all-terrain-vehicle coverage.

TAX CONSEQUENCE OF SETTLEMENTS RECEIVED

Compensatory damages received for physical damages are tax free. Similarly, claims paid for auto repair work are not considered taxable income. However, punitive damage awards, awards for emotional distress and reimbursement for lost wages are taxable.

PLANNING PROCESS

Step 1: Understand client's objectives and needs. The first step in this planning process is to understand the client's goals, financial capacity to absorb the financial loss and pay the premiums. Some people wish to carry the minimum liability coverage allowed by law. However, considering the daily risk exposure, most motorists prefer to have auto liability coverage far in excess of these state-mandated minimums. The amount of liability coverage needed to take care of the other person's car might also be impacted by the geographic area in which the motorist does most of the driving.

Step 2: Review the current risk management plan. Before making a recommendation for buying the best auto insurance policy, the planner is advised to review the following items:

1. Available coverage (for gaps in current coverage).
2. Current coverage (for excess or overlapping coverage).
3. Maximum limits on current coverage (for appropriateness).
4. Drivers covered under the policy (for additions or deletions).
5. Vehicles covered under the policy (for additions or deletions).
6. Need for collision and/or comprehensive coverage.
7. Appropriateness of increasing deductibles for physical damage coverage.
8. Factors that affect premiums.

Step 3: Recommend improvements. Based on weaknesses and gaps in the current plan, a planner should recommend improvement in coverage. If the premium cost is a factor, then the planner can try to lower the premium by increasing the deductible or eliminating the Part D coverage for old vehicles (i.e., low book value). Of course, the planner should prioritize and tailor the recommended PAP based on the severity of the risk exposure.

Steps 4 and 5: Select insurance company and policy or modify the existing policy. The final two steps involve implementing the plan, and many of the factors discussed in the previous sections apply. It is important to recognize that multipolicy discounts are available when the coverage is provided by the same insurer. Moreover, some insurers provide other incentives for maintaining coverage over a number of years (e.g., discounts, disappearing deductibles, free road side assistance, auto loans, and so on).

Self-Analysis

Planning for adequate auto insurance coverage involves making sure that the existing coverage compare favorably with the desired limits.

Annual Check-up

It is necessary to have the auto policy revised annually by an insurance professional. We refer to Anish Upadhyay's letter to the Singhs presented earlier to which he attached the family insurance check-up list (Form A) and the automobile policy status (Form C).

The Singh family met with Anish to discuss their auto policy. Following the meeting, a number of changes were made, as listed next:

1. The bodily injury liability and the property damage liability on the 2002 Scorpio were increased from 100/300/50 to 100/300/100 to make them consistent with the coverage on the other cars.
2. Limited property damage coverage (Y) was increased for the Scorpio which had a lower coverage.
3. Comprehensive coverage on the 2012 Maruti SX4 car was increased because it was a "fancy" car.

The Singhs also discussed the advisability of purchasing a 2013 Mercedes 380 SE. However, when they discovered that it would cost ₹2,400 a year to insure this car, the idea was quickly dropped.

Form A: Auto	
How many cars are in the household:	Uninsured 100/300
Are cars driven to work/used for business:	Death, dismemberment, loss of sight: None
One car	Loss of earnings: Full coverage to state
Which children drive/which cars:	Maximum
Other regular drivers: H/W	Other coverage:
Annual mileage: Under 7,500 each	Nonowned auto coverage:
You should consider	***Do you have?***
High liability limits:	Motorcyles/scooters:
Higher medical/no-fault coverage:	Trucks/SUVs/motorhomes/campers:
Higher deductibles comp./collision:	Other vehicles/trailers:
Emergency road service:	Cellular phone/CB/cassette radios:
Rental/travel expense coverage:	Plans to purchase new car:

Form C: Auto Policy Status, January 1, 2015

	Honda, 2015	**Scorpio, 2002**	**Maruti SX4, 2010**
Policy number	0139849	0298379	0391365
Class	6A	6C	6B
Total premium	584.08	522.88	719.86
Covered date	8-1-12	8-1-12	8-1-12
Birth date	2-14-45	5-13-40	5-13-40
Bodily injury liability (A)	100/300/100	100/300/50	100/300/100
Limited property damage B	500 limit	100 limit	500 limit
Comprehensive deductible	100	100	100
Collision regular deductible	500	500	500
Uninsured motorist	100/300	100/300	100/300
Personal injury protection	Active	Active	Active
Property protection	Active	Active	Active
Catastrophic claim	Active	Active	Active

Application discounts: (1) multicar discount, (2) multiple line discount, (3) accident-free discount, (4) vehicle safety, (5) anti-theft, and (6) safety belt discount.

Section VII: Liability Coverage

INTRODUCTION

We live in a litigious society where lawsuits are filed every single day. Under property-casualty insurance policies, there are recommended liability and property damage coverage limits. These limits are designed to provide adequate protection for claims made against a policyholder resulting from the loss of property or personal injury. Unfortunately, the liability coverage provided by these policies may still turn out to be insufficient for reimbursing the aggrieved parties, particularly when a high net worth policy owner is involved. Because of the catastrophic nature of liability judgments, every person should consider buying a suitable umbrella liability policy.

GENERAL CHARACTERISTICS

Stacks on Underlying Liability Coverage

An *umbrella or comprehensive policy* is designed to stack on top of an underlying liability policy. It supplements, but does not replace, an insured's homeowner's, auto, boat, aircraft, and other non-business policies. Typically, umbrella coverage policies are underwritten for amounts up to the limits specified in the policy, and the premium costs of even large amounts of coverage are also very reasonable. Basic coverage under an umbrella policy generally extends to bodily injury, mental anguish, shock, sickness, disease, disability, false arrest, false imprisonment, wrongful eviction, detention, defamation of character, and invasion of privacy. A typical non-business umbrella policy excludes the insured's obligation for worker's compensation and disability benefits, damage to property of the insured, and product failure.

As a general rule, the perils covered in the underlying policy extend over to the umbrella. For example, if the underlying coverage protects the individual from liability claims due to negligence, then the umbrella extends that coverage. However, there are limitations to an umbrella policy. Many auto and homeowner policies do not protect against libel and slander liability judgments without endorsement. If the underlying policy does not cover slander, then a liability judgment for slander might not be covered by the umbrella policy. Since the umbrella stacks on top of existing coverage, it is important to carefully read the policy or speak with the insurance agent to assess the coverage of an umbrella policy.

Benefits of Coverage

The insurance company issuing the umbrella policy *promises to defend* a policyholder during the lawsuit proceedings. Costs associated with legal defense, which can be quite high, are provided over-and-above the liability protection. The company also promises to pay for *liability judgments* against the policyholder up to the limit of the coverage (e.g., ₹5 crore); this protection is on a per-claim basis.

The umbrella coverage is activated when the coverage under the homeowner's or the auto policy has been exhausted. Consider the following examples. An insured is sued for ₹10 lakh and owns ₹100,000 personal liability coverage under the homeowner's policy and a ₹10 lakh umbrella policy. The insurance company will pay ₹100,000 under the homeowner's policy and ₹900,000 under the umbrella policy.

As in the case of the homeowner's policy, an umbrella policy supplements the coverage provided by an auto policy. If an insured person carrying a 100/300 auto policy and a ₹10 lakh umbrella policy is sued for ₹750,000 in an auto accident, the insurance company will cover ₹100,000 per person under the auto policy and ₹650,000 under the umbrella policy. Without this umbrella coverage, the driver would have to pay that amount out of personal funds, which could financially cripple the insured.

As previously discussed in the auto insurance section, there are no deductibles for liability claims; however, because the umbrella begins when the liability protection offered by the underlying policy is exhausted, there might be a "self-retention deductible" if the underlying policy does not cover the cause of the judgment. It is imperative that liability limits and perils covered under the homeowner's and automobile policies be coordinated with the underlying deductible of the umbrella policy.

For example, assume an insured has a ₹100,000 limit under both the homeowner's and auto policies and a ₹300,000 underlying deductible under the umbrella policy. If this insured files a claim, the first ₹100,000 would be covered under either the homeowner's or the auto coverage, and amounts over ₹300,000 would be covered under the umbrella policy, thereby leaving a significant gap or self-retention deductible of ₹200,000. Similarly, if an insured has a ₹100,000 liability limit with the homeowner's policy and a ₹10 lakh umbrella, but the homeowner's policy does not cover slander, then in case of a slander liability claim the insured would have to pay a huge amount out of personal resources until the umbrella policy kicks in (assuming the umbrella covers slander). As a result, it is recommended that all property and casualty insurance, such as homeowner's, automobile, and umbrella policies, be purchased through one insurance company in order to minimize the possibility of any gaps in coverage.

DIRECTOR'S LIABILITY INSURANCE

This type of insurance is used to protect officers and directors of business entities from claims of wrongful acts, such as error, neglect, or omission, while performing their duties. In today's litigious society, almost routinely, directors are provided this coverage by corporations, banks, and other institutions. Board members of condo associations, subdivision associations, and charitable organizations should also be routinely covered by this type of insurance. A large deductible for the director's liability policy is the only way to keep the premium at an affordable level.

PROFESSIONAL LIABILITY INSURANCE

Today, many professionals like doctors, lawyers, chartered accountants (CAs), and financial planners are exposed to malpractice suits and other associated risks, and they need protection against these risks. Incorporating a professional business does not provide the needed protection simply because the corporate status does not shelter the corporate officer from malpractice suits. Most professional liability policies are written on a claim-made basis, which means that an insurance company is only responsible for claims made during the policy period. Costs of professional liability insurance policies are fairly high. Consequently, professionals shopping around for these policies should thoroughly investigate various options, including those offered by their respective professional associations, before selecting the right policy.

RISK MANAGEMENT PROCESS

Step 1: Understand client's risk exposures to determine need. Several factors are relevant when assessing a client's risk exposure and insurance needs for covering such exposure. These include: the net worth, economic value of individual based on earnings potential, geographic location, family composition, vocation, form of entity for any businesses owned (e.g., S Corporation), and avocation. A careful review of these factors can help a planner determine how much liability insurance is needed to protect each person.

Step 2: Review current liability plan. A careful analysis of the risk exposure and needs assessment enables a planner to calculate the existing gap. In this approach, the planner subtracts the current liability protection from a client's overall need, thereby arriving at the potential gap that needs to be filled. It is important to remember that typically liability umbrella coverage begins at ₹1 lakh and is raised in increments of 1 crore.

Step 3: Recommend improvements. Although the gap analysis helps a planner arrive at the rupee amount of exposure, it is always prudent to err on the side of conservatism by recommending liability protection that exceeds the potential gap. This idea makes sense especially with liability coverage because of the catastrophic nature and the variability of liability judgments and also because the cost of 1 crore increments in coverage is relatively small.

Step 4: Add the coverage. As previously discussed, for cost-effectiveness it is best for a client to buy homeowner, auto, and liability policies all from the same insurer. Adding the liability coverage to the other existing policies can usually involve making a simple phone call, although the underwriter would probably have the final say on how much liability coverage the company would be willing to offer.

Self-Analysis

The adequacy of the personal liability umbrella coverage should be checked at the time of the annual review of homeowner's and auto policy. A ₹10 lakh policy is an absolute minimum; however, depending on the circumstances, the possibility of increasing the coverage should also be explored. Individuals should also make sure that they carry proper insurance for household help, outdoor help, and babysitters.

Annual Check-up

Ratna and Sadhana Singh received the accompanying personal liability umbrella policy details (Form D) from Anish Upadhyay, their insurance agent. After a brief discussion, Ratna Singh decided to increase the policy coverage to ₹20 lakh, since this amount of insurance could be purchased at an additional cost of only ₹52 per year.

Form D: Personal Liability Umbrella

Term	Continuous	Date paid: 2-26-2015
Renewal date	2-26-2016	Amount paid: ₹196
Premium	₹196	
Bill to	Insured	
Present liability	₹1,000,000	
Self-insurance	₹500	
Rate class	II	
CL	Y	

In this chapter, planning issues relating to health, homeowner's, automobile, and liability insurance were discussed. However, because of space limitations, not all issues relating to these types of insurance were fully covered. In the next chapter, issues relating to cash and debt management will be undertaken.

PART 3

CASH MANAGEMENT AND EDUCATIONAL PLANNING

Chapter 6

Cash Management, Savings, Credit, and Debt Planning

Chapter 7

Educational Planning

6 Cash Management, Savings, Credit, and Debt Planning

INTRODUCTION

In the last four decades, financial planning has come of age. And yet, most of us have only a vague idea of how we stack up financially. Given the constant barrage of bad financial news in the media, most Indians worry about inflation, rising health care expenses, exploding education costs, volatile investment environment, and slow economic growth. Equally important, consumers generally feel that their net worth is not increasing as rapidly as it should. In fact, many feel—and rightly so—that if things do not significantly change for the better, they will certainly outlive the funds earmarked for retirement. So to put it bluntly, for many people, the highly acclaimed dream of a comfortable retired life is rapidly turning into a bad dream.

This pervasive sense of financial uneasiness explains why an average person takes a haphazard approach to money management. Some find even filing out income tax returns overwhelming, let alone constructing net worth statements to track their financial progress. Others confuse the documentation of every expense item with budget planning. Clearly, the problem is that most people do not handle their personal affairs as a business and, hence, do not enjoy the benefits that come from analyzing an annual income statement and a balance sheet.

In this chapter, we will discuss issues relating to cash management, savings, credit, and debt planning. In the first section, we will analyze the techniques of net worth and cash management planning. Systematic savings planning techniques will be presented in the next section. Finally, in the last section, we will discuss the issues relating to credit and debt planning.

Section I: Net Worth and Cash Management Planning

Effective cash management has two primary objectives: (a) Maintain a cash reserve sufficient to meet emergency needs, such as physical illness, injury or death, or loss of employment. (b) Systematically create and maintain a cash balance earmarked for capital investment. The three primary components of cash management are: budgeting, cash flow analysis, and planning. These components are prerequisites to the development of a comprehensive personal financial plan.

NET WORTH PLANNING

Basic Concept

Net worth planning involves calculating current net worth, setting a realistic net worth goal for the fol lowing year and developing strategies for meeting that goal. The main reasons for undertaking net worth planning are to: (a) establish a financial discipline, (b) organize a financial life around a future target, (c) measure the financial progress on a regular basis, and (d) feel financially secure about the future.

The starting point of net worth planning is clearly the calculation of net worth. This topic has been discussed next.

Calculation of Net Worth

Net worth is the total fair market value of all assets owned, such as a home, stocks, bonds, and real estate investments, minus all outstanding liabilities, such as mortgage and revolving-credit loans. That is, net worth is the amount by which assets exceed liabilities at a specific point in time.

The process of calculating net worth begins with pulling together the relevant financial records. These include the latest tax records, bank statements, canceled checks, credit card information, other itemized living expenses, brokerage accounts and mutual fund records, mortgage payments, real estate closing records, insurance policies, pension account records, and loan repayment schedules. Gathering all this information may seem daunting, but it is an integral part of net worth planning. Also, these records not only help us accurately calculate the net worth but also provide valuable data needed to analyze other planning areas.

The statement of net worth, presented in Table 6.1, has four important features: (a) assets are classified as liquid, investment, or personal assets, (b) investment assets are divided between as a short-term and long-term, (c) long-term assets are classified as equity, debt, or miscellaneous assets, and (d) liabilities are identified as either a short or a long term. Subtracting total liabilities from total assets provides the value of net worth as of a given date.

Planning Strategy

The net worth figure just derived provides the basis for developing an appropriate planning strategy. If the net worth is negative—a distinct possibility—that does not necessarily imply that the family is bankrupt. It does mean, however, that aggressive strategies must be developed that would lead to debt reduction, higher investment returns, and a more realistic goal setting.

Incidentally, surprising though it might seem, a positive net worth does not always mean that all is well. In fact, even if the annual rate of growth in net worth meets the prespecified target, it is still desirable to devise strategies for improving that rate. If the growth rate, however, falls short of the selected target, an effort should be made to either develop new strategies to correct the situation or set a more realistic goal.

There is little benefit to calculate the net worth unless it is done on an annual basis because only then can one determine if the savings, credit, investment, and other related targets measure up to the family's short- and long-term financial objectives.

CASH MANAGEMENT PLANNING

Basic Concept

The net worth statement determines the value of assets and liabilities at a given *point* in time, whereas a cash flow statement paints a picture of the cash *flow* over a period of time. The net worth grows only when the annual cash inflow exceeds the annual cash outflow. That, in fact, is the basis for using cash management planning as a dynamic financial planning tool.

If during the year, total savings fall short of the amount necessary to achieve the targeted growth in the net worth, then corrective actions must be taken to rectify the situation. Such actions can take the form of reduction of expenses, increase in income, or a combination of both. If, however, these strategies

Table 6.1 *Statement of Net Worth*

Assets			Liabilities		
Items	**Current Value**	**%**	**Items**	**Current Value**	**%**
I. Liquid Assets			I. SHORT-TERM		
1. Cash and checking accounts	___		1. Current Bills	___	
2. Savings accounts	___		2. Credit Cards	___	
3. Credit union	___		3. Installment Loans	___	
4. Memory market funds	___		4. Other	___	
5. Total (1–4)	___	___	5. TOTAL (1–4)	___	___
II. Investment Assets			II. LONG-TERM		
A. Short-term			1. Mortgage	___	
1. CDs	___		2. Life Insurance Loans	___	
2. Treasury bills	___		3. Browsing from Qualified Plans	___	
3. Cash value-life insurance	___		4. Loans to Purchase Investment	___	
4. Other	___		5. Other	___	
5. Total (A1–4)	___	___	6. TOTAL (1–5)	___	___
B. Long-term			III. NET WORTH		
(i) *Equity*			(Total Assets minus Total Liabilities)		
1. Common/Preferred stock	___				
2. Mutual funds—stock	___				
3. IRA-stock	___				
4. Pension/Profit sharing-stock	___				
5. Other	___				
6 Total (B-i–1-5)	___	___			
(ii) *Debt*					
1. CDs long term	___				
2. Corporate/Government/Muni. bonds	___				
3. IRA bonds	___				
4. Pension/Profit sharing bonds	___				
5. Other	___				
6. Total (B-ii–1-5)	___	___			
(iii) *Miscellaneous*					
1. Limited partnerships	___				
2. Tangible assets	___				
3. Business ownership	___				
4. Real estate (e.g. Residence)	___				
5. Other	___				
6. Total (B-iii–1-5)	___	___			

(*Continued*)

Table 6.1 (*Continued*)

Assets				Liabilities		
Items	**Current Value**		**%**	**Items**	**Current Value**	**%**
III. Personal Assets						
1. Residence/Vacation home	____					
2. Automobiles	____					
3. Personal property	____					
4. Others	____					
5. Total (1–4)		____	____			
Total assets	____	100		Total Liabilities & Net Worth	____	100

fail to generate additional savings necessary to meet the goal, then the family may have to reevaluate its net worth goal target. And, even in those cases where adequate savings are being generated, cash management planning can help a family reach a faster rate of growth of the net worth by generating larger savings.

The premise of financial planning is built on cash flow management. It is through the generation of surplus funds that clients will have sufficient funds to: (a) conduct ongoing family operations, (b) accumulate adequate emergency funds to meet unforeseen contingencies, (c) acquire productive assets, (d) prevent illiquidity from becoming a problem, and (e) set aside adequate funds for funding children's education, retirement, and other long-term goals.

Cash flow management also helps clients achieve financial independence by converting positive cash flows into productive investments. If, however, the net cash flow is negative, then the net worth would shrink, and it would be impossible to realize the financial independence goal.

Financial planners can take certain steps to assist their clients reposition their cash flow so that their financial planning goals can be achieved with greater efficiency. These include the following: (a) Underscoring the importance of exercising greater control over cash management. It is the lack of control over cash flows, rather than inadequate income, unwise investments, and catastrophic changes in circumstances that is at the root of most financial problems. (b) Setting up a cash flow strategy that would help generate the desired level of savings needed to achieve various financial goals. Of course, if the modified cash flow budget proves inadequate, a planner should help revise the clients' objectives to make the savings and revised financial goals mutually consistent.

The process of cash management consists of budgeting, cash flow analysis, and cash flow management. Each of these processes is discussed next.

Budgeting

The budgeting process consists of projecting cash flows, documenting actual receipts and disbursements, and monitoring expenditures and savings. This process identifies discrepancies between actual expenditures and the corresponding budgeted items. For this purpose, data relating to income and expenditures can be retrieved from tax returns, home improvement records, financial statements, insurance policies, retirement, and pension benefits, credit card records, investment data, and checkbook records.

Generally, living within one's means requires critically evaluating various expenditures. When that creates a problem, a financial planner can help identify those expenditures that can be eliminated or reduced. Also, since budgeting is a dynamic process, a planner should encourage a periodic review and readjustment of the existing budget. However, in the event that in the past a client has had only a marginal success in controlling budget expenditures, it is recommended that a planner consult a counseling service for guidance.

Cash Flow Analysis

Once a planner has helped develop a functional budget, it is time to perform a cash flow analysis. This involves: (a) gathering information on cash inflow and outflow, (b) developing a cash flow statement, and (c) calculating the net cash flow. And since most clients are oblivious to their net cash flow position, this exercise can constitute a valuable learning experience.

In situations where the net cash flow is negative, a planner would need to develop more realistic estimates of expected income and expenses. However, if even after that the desired target cannot be met, a planner would be left with little choice but to develop a more stringent strategy for helping a client achieve a positive cash flow position.

Steps in Cash Flow Analysis

There are three steps to undertaking the cash flow analysis: (a) gather current cash flow data, (b) estimate future income and expenses, and (c) create a comprehensive cash flow statement. Each step is discussed next.

Step 1: Gather data relating to current cash inflows and outflows. That would help develop an understanding of various sources of cash flows, leading a client to set short-term spending priorities consistent with carefully crafted long-term strategies.

When gathering income data, a planner should take into account all possible income sources, check them against tax returns, and include them in a cash flow statement. Also, in collecting expense data, a checkbook, charge cards, and petty cash statements can be examined to establish the basic spending pattern. Finally, tax-deductible and nontax-deductible expenses should be clearly identified so that the information could be used for tax planning.

Step 2: Estimate future income and expenses. As a start, differentiate between fixed and variable expenses. The former represent the expenses which are difficult to cut. Examples include: rent, mortgage, food, clothing, auto payments, insurance, utilities, taxes, loans, and charge accounts. By contrast, variable expenses represent items over which a client has some degree of control. If needed, many of these expenses could be modified, or even indefinitely postponed.

The data just collected can be used to make three-to-five-year expense projections. In doing so, expected future changes in inflation rates, tax rates, salary income, and other possible areas can be examined. Also, changes in living expenses may include possible care for aging parents, future college expenses, additions to the family, purchase of a new car or a home, and other desired expenses. These projections should then be analyzed against the client's preestablished long-term goals.

When projecting future expenses, it is important to take into account contingency plans involving emergency fund and adequate insurance coverage. The former is needed for meeting expenses such as unexpected repairs, costly maintenance, or loss of employment—all of which by design are excluded from the family budget. The emergency fund, which should equal at least six months of expenses, can be placed in highly liquid investments such as money market securities or savings account.

Step 3. Construct a cash flow statement by using Table 6.2. It identifies the net change in cash inflows and outflows. For this purpose, expenditures and income data should be condensed into general categories. Examples of inflows on the cash flow statement include: salary or self-employment income, interest, dividends, net rental income, and income tax refunds. Outflows include: housing, food, clothing, transportation, insurance, taxes, savings, and investments. Analyzing a cash flow statement helps clients better understand their spending habits over time. A cash flow statement records changes over time; by contrast, a balance sheet presents a snapshot or a picture at a given point in time.

Cash Flow Planning

This process involves three steps: (a) Implementing strategies to maximize the discretionary income and minimize expenditures. (b) Revising client's goals if Step (a) falls short of the desired goal. (c) Monitoring cash flow plan to ensure that the client is staying on track.

Step 1. Various strategies can be employed to maximize the discretionary income or minimize the expenditures. These include: (a) debt restructuring, (b) asset reallocation, (c) qualified plan options, (d) employee benefit plans, (e) incorporation of children's assets, (f) income tax planning, and (g) expenditure control. Each strategy is discussed next.

1. ***Debt restructuring.*** Pay off all outstanding credit card balances by (a) refinancing the personal residence in order to consolidate all the debts into one low personal line of credit, (b) discontinuing the use of credit cards, and (c) deferring major purchases on credit as long as practical.

Table 6.2 *Statement of Cash Flow*

Inflow	Amount	Outflow	Amount
I. Source, before Tax		I. Fixed Expenses	
1. Salary-Husband		A. Family Needs	
2. Salary-Wife		1. Food	
3. Self-employment		2. Clothing	
4. Divided/Interest		3. Auto	
5. Capital Gains/Losses		4. Other	
6. Rents/Annuities/Pension		5. Total (1–4)	
7. Bonus/Gift/Misc. income		B. Home	
8. Alimony/Child support		1. Mortgage	
9. Total (1–8)		2. Insurance	
II. Taxes		3. Utilities	
1. Central		4. Tax	
2. State		5. Total (1–4)	
3. Local		C. Insurance Premiums	
4. Social sec./Disability		1. Life	
5. Total (1–4)		2. Disability	
III. Inflow after Tax (I minus II)		3. Health	
		4. Auto	
		5. Liability	
		6. Total (1–5)	
		D. Other Debts	
		1. Installment Loans	
		2. Charge Accounts	
		3. Others	
		4. Total (1–3)	
		II. Flexible Expenses	
		A. Family Needs	
		1. Vacation	
		2. Entertainment	
		3. Gifts	
		4. Other	
		5. Total (1–4)	
		B. Education	
		1. Tuition	
		2. Other Expenses	
		3. Total (1–2)	
		C. Major Appliances & Expenditures	
		1. Appliances	
		2. Other	
		3. Total (1–2)	
		D. Miscellaneous	
		1. Charity	
		2. Other	
		3. TOTAL (1–2)	
		III. Total Savings (Total Inflow minus Total Outflow)	
Total Inflow		Total Outflow & Savings	

2. ***Asset reallocation.*** Switch underperforming assets into more productive investment assets. In addition, consider switching growth and taxable investments into income producing and tax-exempt investments.
3. ***Qualified plan options.*** Utilize qualified plans to a greater degree. This can be achieved by encouraging a client to contribute the maximum allowable amounts into an Employees' Provident Fund (EPF), pension, deferred compensation, and nonqualified savings plan. Self-employed clients can also benefit from participating in a simplified employer-sponsored plan, if one is offered to them.
4. ***Employee benefit plans.*** Encourage a client to use benefit plans for paying expenses with before-tax (as opposed to after-tax) rupees. Examples include using EPF, Public Provident Fund (PPF) or Flexible Spending Account through an employer for paying allowable child care or medical expenses.
5. ***Incorporation of Children's Assets.*** The technique involves saving for a child in either a custodial account or a trust). The marginal tax bracket applicable to the taxable investment earnings (in the custodial account or the trust) is likely to be lower than the parent's tax bracket.
6. ***Income tax planning.*** The objective here is to take advantage of the strategies available to reduce the tax burden, wherever feasible.
7. ***Expenditure control.*** Encourage a client to make a good faith effort to reduce consumption expenses. A planner can do so by emphasizing the role savings can play in building wealth over the long run.

Step 2. Help a client reprioritize the stated goals so that all the important goals can be successfully achieved. Examples include: eliminating negative cash flows, reducing income taxes, obtaining comprehensive insurance coverage, repositioning investment portfolio, and accumulating funds for a major purchase or target—be it a child's education, an early retirement, or wealth transfer upon death.

Step 3. Monitor the plan regularly to ensure that the cash flow plan is functioning properly. Variances from the original targets should be investigated, and if appropriate, corrected. The results of the plan should be measured against a client's objectives to ensure that the client is satisfied with the way the plan is operating.

The primary motivation for undertaking cash management planning is to determine the adequacy of savings to meet the desired net worth growth target. This target can be further refined by setting up more focused investment, educational, and retirement goals. An integral part of achieving these financial goals is to have adequate resources available to fund them, and cash management planning can help them provide the necessary funds for that purpose in a systematic and efficient manner.

Cash management planning can also be used as an important diagnostic tool. For instance, if negative savings are currently being generated, a close scrutiny of fixed and variable expenses can determine how the current trend can be reversed. This tool can also be used to identify areas of excessive spending so that the spending patterns can be restructured to reduce the cash outflow to the desirable level.

To recapitulate, cash flow management is crucial for the long-term success of a comprehensive financial plan. Laying a solid foundation for cash flow planning can go a long way toward accomplishing a client's financial short- and long-term objectives.

Section II: Systematic Savings Planning

As a general rule, people maintaining a monthly budget consider savings to be their primary target. Of course, a monthly budget is only a means of achieving a much broader, and a more valuable, objective—that is, the development of a systematic savings planning strategy. This strategy refers to the creation of specific plans to generate the required savings, and to direct them to achieve the targeted financial goals.

STARTING POINT

Systematic savings planning begins with net worth planning. This is because the desired annual rate of growth of net worth determines the rate at which these savings must be generated. This point is elaborated in the following illustration.

Assume Ashish Singh wishes his net worth of ₹750,000 to grow annually at a predetermined rate. As revealed by Table 6.3, he can achieve his objective only if his savings increase at an accelerated pace. For instance, if Ashish wants his ₹750,000 net worth to grow by 10 percent a year, he would have to generate a saving of ₹75,000 during the first year alone—a formidable target indeed. Even worse, during the fifth year his savings must equal a whopping ₹109,000 to meet his 10 percent growth target. And even if his net worth were at a much lower level of, say, ₹400,000, it would still require additional savings of ₹40,000 during the first year and larger amounts in the subsequent years—indeed a formidable challenge for him. This simple illustration demonstrates why it is so important for people to set a realistic net worth growth target.

GOAL SETTING

At the *macro* level, the systematic savings planning process begins with the setting of the overall savings target. However, it is in fact the setting of *micro*-level goals that is much more challenging.

Savings can be used to increase the level of net worth in one of the three ways: by increasing assets, decreasing liabilities, or a combination of both. A family should set appropriate goals for the first two areas. A goal-setting worksheet presented in Table 6.4 specifies not only the amount of savings needed to finance each of the stated objectives, but also commits future savings to achieve these goals.

The first step is to calculate the amount of savings required to achieve each of the specific goals and record them in the last column. This can be accomplished by using the time value of money concept described in Chapter 3.

Assume that the objective is to save ₹50,000 by the end of 10 years to finance a child's education. If net of inflation and taxes 3 percent compound interest can be earned on monthly educational savings, and if money is saved at the end of every month, then by using HP-12C calculator we can calculate that ₹357.80 (Table 6.5) of monthly savings would be needed to achieve this objective. The same technique can be used to determine the savings required for meeting other financial goals listed in Table 6.4.

The total *annual* savings required to meet all the stated objectives (total monthly savings required × 12 in Table 6.4) can now be compared with the total annual savings available (Item III of Outflow column in Table 6.2). If the available savings are greater than, or equal to, the savings required, one might simply do nothing or consider further improving the current savings target. If, however, the available savings fall short of the required target, specific steps must be taken to correct the potential problem.

Table 6.3 *Net Worth Planning Example*

	Target: Annual Growth: 5% ('000) Projected					
	Current	**Year 1**	**Year 2**	**Year 3**	**Year 4**	**Year 5**
Net worth (₹)	750	787.5	826.9	868.2	911.6	957.2
Additional savings required	–	+37.5	+39.4	+41.3	+43.4	+45.6
	Target: Annual Growth: 5%					
Net worth (₹)	750	825	907	998	1,098	1,207
Additional savings required	–	+75	+82	+91	+100	+109

Table 6.4 *Goal-setting Worksheet*

Goal	Annual Needed (₹)	Savings Period: Months	Expected after-tax Return (%)	Monthly Savings Required (₹)
I. Home	______	______	______	______
II. Appliance	______	______	______	______
III. Major Purchases	______	______	______	______
1.	______	______	______	______
2.	______	______	______	______
3.	______	______	______	______
4.	______	______	______	______
IV. Vacation	______	______	______	______
V. Education	______	______	______	______
1.	______	______	______	______
2.	______	______	______	______
3.	______	______	______	______
VI. Retirement	______	______	______	______
VII. Charity	______	______	______	______
VIII. Other ______	______	______	______	______
Other ______	______	______	______	______
Other ______	______	______	______	______
TOTAL:	₹			₹

Table 6.5 *Determining Monthly Savings*

Step 1: Identify known variables	
Future value:	₹50,000
Interest rate:	3%/12 months
Number of periods:	10 years × 12 months
Step 2: Clear calculator [f] [CLX]	
Step 3: Enter data	
Press	
[5] [0] [0] [0] [0] [FV]	
[3] [g] [*i*]	
[1] [0] [g] [*n*]	
[PMT]	
Answer: ₹357.80	

Adequate Savings Scenario

Even when the current savings are sufficient for meeting both short- and long-term financial goals and net worth growth targets, refinements in savings plans can still be made to further improve the situation. Here is a novel strategy to accomplish that objective.

We seldom think of *paying ourselves first* in the form of savings in order to ensure our own financial security. That is why we normally live up to our means and go into debt whenever we need replacement of big ticket items or have to meet a major financial crisis. A better strategy might just be to treat *savings as a fixed expense* and not as a residual amount after all other needs have been met. This strategy can help generate additional savings and, if properly channeled, can accelerate the rate of growth of net worth.

Inadequate Savings Scenario

If savings are inadequate to meet the stated goals, steps need to be taken to bring savings up to the desired level. For convenience, these steps are divided into several broad categories (see Table 6.5).

Expense reduction. It is best to begin by analyzing the current expenses, and especially the *flexible* expenses, which in most instances can be scaled back. These generally represent personal expenses such as clothing, personal care, and entertainment; but flexible expenses might also include big ticket items such as home remodeling and expensive vacations. Of course, it is also possible to reduce some fixed expenses. For instance, one can reduce fixed expenses by moving to a smaller home or by giving up a few amenities.

A practical expense reduction strategy is to make a monthly estimate for each major expense category and then compare the estimate with the actual expense in each category. If the *actual* expense for a given category consistently exceeds the *estimated* expense, then a conscious effort should be made to either reduce the actual expense or, if justifiable, increase the level of the estimated expense. A convenient worksheet is presented in Table 6.6 which can be used to develop a meaningful expense reduction strategy.

Increase in income. Families generally assume that the income flow will remain relatively stable, especially if the breadwinners earn salaried income. This is not always a valid assumption. In the following section, we will discuss how income can be augmented even for salaried employees.

Incomes for most people can be increased by taking a number of steps, including the following: (a) Select investments offering higher interest rates or returns but with an acceptable risk level. (b) Reduce the checking account balance to the minimum and shift the rest of the liquid funds into higher yielding money market funds and short-term government securities. (c) Reorganize the investment portfolio (discussed in Chapter 10). Here are several strategies that can help a person achieve the desired results.

First, in the investment world, risk and reward are positively related. This means that an investor can obtain higher returns by moving the funds from low-risk to higher risk investments. The success of this strategy, of course, depends on an accurate determination of the investor's risk tolerance level. A sensible strategy is to move the funds into those investments that are in the highest risk categories acceptable to an investor.

Second, it is important to become yield conscious. For instance, yields on special certificates of deposit (CDs) could be much higher than those offered by local banks.

Third, concentrate on tax savings. Assume that an AAA-rated, 10-year corporate bond is currently yielding 5.0 percent. Switching the money to a tax-exempt bond of similar quality and maturity and yielding 4.0 percent would increase the yield from 5 percent to 5.33 percent, assuming a 25 percent tax bracket.

Fourth, convert a growth-oriented stock portfolio into an income-oriented stock portfolio or a bond portfolio. Typically, growth-oriented stock portfolios have low dividend yields. By converting such a portfolio into an income-oriented portfolio an investor can increase the current cash flow.

Fifth, switch non-income-producing investments, such as gold, coins, and antiques, into income-producing assets. The former might be inappropriate for people with cash flow problems, and substitution of income-producing assets such as bonds and utility stocks for the nonproducing assets can generate much-needed additional income.

EFFECTIVE SAVINGS STRATEGIES

Several *common sense* strategies can help increase the flow of personal savings. These are discussed next.

Goal Setting

Unrealistic goal setting is perhaps the most important reason for savings strategies to fail. A planner can assist a client in setting realistic savings goals. For example, setting a 20 percent annual savings goal

Table 6.6 *Expense Reduction Worksheet*

Expenses	Jan.		Feb.		Mar.		Apr.		May.		Jun.		Jul.		Aug.		Sept.		Oct.		Nov.		Dec.		Annual		
	B	A	B	A	B	A	B	A	B	A	B	A	B	A	B	A	B	A	B	A	B	A	B	A	B	A	S/D
I. Fixed expenses																											
A . Family needs																											
1. Food																											
2. Clothing																											
3. Auto																											
4. Other																											
5. TOTAL (1–4)																											
B. Home																											
1. Mortgage																											
2. Insurance																											
3. Utilities																											
4. Tax																											
5. TOTAL (1–4)																											
C. Insurance premiums																											
1. Life																											
2. Disability																											
3. Health																											
4. Auto																											
5. Liability																											
6. TOTAL (1–5)																											
D. Other debts																											
1. Installment loans																											
2. Charge accounts																											
3. Other																											
4. TOTAL (1–3)																											

II. Flexible expenses														
A. Family needs*														
1. Vacation														
2. Entertainment														
3. Gifts														
4. Others														
5. TOTAL (1–4)														
B. Education**														
1. Tuition														
2. Other expenses														
3. TOTAL (1–2)														
C. Major appliances & exp.														
1. Appliances														
2. Other														
3. TOTAL (1–2)														
D. Miscellaneous														
1. Charity														
2. Other														
3. TOTAL (1–2)														

Notes: S/D: Surplus or Deficit. *A: Annual. **B: Budget.

for a family that can barely make both ends meet is a prescription for failure. For this family, a better alternative would be to set a savings goal that can be achieved with a concerted effort by every member of the family.

Self-rewarding Plan

Saving for college education, retirement, vacation, or for purchasing a big ticket item, presents a challenging undertaking. Consequently, if a family succeeds in exceeding its savings target, it may reward itself by spending part of the extra savings. This practice could well provide this family an added incentive to meet, and even beat, its savings target.

Savings-first Approach

In our consumption-oriented society, it is easy to buy consumer goods on credit. But few of us realize that over time our savings would significantly increase if we made cash purchases. The reason is that by saving first and then making purchases by paying cash we would not only avoid paying interest charges on loans but also earn interest by investing these savings.

Automatic Savings Plans

A relatively painless way of saving is to have the money deducted directly from the paycheck and invest it in an appropriate vehicle. Money saved this way has a tendency to grow uninterrupted, producing dramatic results.

Several vehicles are available for implementing automatic savings plans. Tax-free government bonds offer one such vehicle. Contribution to company qualified plans is the second method of initiating an automatic savings plan. A qualified plan can take the form of a pension, profit sharing, thrift, or a PPF plan. Many plans allow participants to choose among various investments, including stocks, bonds, and mutual funds, company shares, and guaranteed investment contracts. Earnings in qualified investments grow tax deferred, and coupled with the power of compounding, they can make a significant difference in the way savings grow over time.

A third technique is to reap the benefits of rupee cost averaging by directing the bank to switch each month a predetermined amount from the savings account into designated mutual funds. This strategy not only helps the net worth grow faster, but also dramatically improves the odds for achieving long-term financial goals.

EMERGENCY FUNDING STRATEGIES

Occasionally, even the best-structured family budget plans face temporary difficulties due to circumstances beyond one's control. Unfortunately, in many such situations, the liquid funds saved for a rainy day get exhausted. That is why it pays to become familiar with additional sources of emergency funds. Here are four valuable sources of funds that can come in handy.

First, **a loan against residential property**, since such a loan is always cheaper than a personal loan. Once the loan is approved, the homeowner can borrow up to 70 percent of the property's value.

Second, **accumulated cash value in a life insurance policy**. Loans from insurance policies are tax free, and most insurance companies charge low interest rates on these loans. Also, loans against cash values in policies are still cheaper than personal or credit card loans.

Third, **company savings plans**. Many companies allow their employees to borrow against their vested profit sharing, EPF, or company stock plan assets up to a certain limit.

Fourth, **the money earmarked as PPF investment**. No loan interest is charged on this money. Also, there is no tax liability triggered by this withdrawal.

CRITERIA FOR SAVINGS MEDIA SELECTION

The primary reasons for saving are: (a) accumulating funds for meeting emergencies, (b) having funds available for purchasing consumer items, and (c) increasing the net worth, often referred to as capital formation. Savings strategies designed to achieve the first two objectives are significantly different from those associated with capital formation. This is because the major emphasis for saving for the first two reasons is on popular liquid assets, whereas the main emphasis for capital formation savings is long-term growth, for which the more traditional long-term investment vehicles are used.

There are six criteria for determining where savings should be parked. These are: safety, liquidity, return on savings, simplicity and minimum balance requirements, special service features, and tax considerations. Each of the six criteria is discussed next.

Safety

All nationalized banks, private banks including foreign banks, and cooperative banks are members of the Deposit Insurance and Credit Guarantee Corporation (DICGC). This implies that, for each account holder, checking, savings, and CD accounts maintained at these banks are insured against bank failure for up to ₹100,000. In addition, savings placed in various types of government bonds are completely safe. However, money market accounts at various brokerage firms and other financial institutions are neither insured nor completely safe.

Safety concerns were foremost on the minds of the Indian public when in the past widespread failures of savings and loans chit fund companies were reported by the media. For that reason, the confidence of Indians in general, and people living in rural areas in particular, is placed squarely on government banks and related institutions.

Liquidity

If one desires to quickly convert savings into cash without losing the principal, checking and savings accounts in banks and credit unions as well as money market accounts provide the highest degree of liquidity. In contrast, CDs provide higher interest rates but restrict withdrawal privileges. Similarly, various types of government bonds lack complete liquidity in that an early conversion may result in a partial loss of return.

Return on Savings

An important criterion in selecting a savings institution is the return it offers. Actually, the *true return* on savings depends not only on the advertised rate, but also on other considerations, including the type of account used for accumulating savings. This point requires elaboration.

Bank Savings Accounts

The most traditional of all bank savings accounts, which were previously called passbook accounts, form the backbone of bank savings. Until the interest rate ceiling was removed in October 2011, the maximum legally allowable rate on regular savings in banks was 3.5 percent. With the legal ceiling removed, most banks started paying 5–7 percent (and sometimes even more) on savings accounts. However, in the low interest environment following the global recession and slowdown of the Indian economy, the interest rate paid on fixed deposits in banks has subsequently declined to 4–10 percent, depending on the period of deposit.

Bank Current Accounts

Unlike bank savings accounts, no interest is earned on current accounts. In fact, each month banks actually charge a nominal amount to maintain and service a *regular current* account. These accounts are basically used for convenience and not for accumulating savings or investment. Current accounts are highly liquid and no restrictions are placed on how frequently or extensively they can be used on a daily basis. As of February 2014, the variation in rates offered and conditions imposed—the negotiable order of withdrawal (NOW) account rate—have ranged from 4 to 7 percent. Minimum monthly average balance for key private sector banks such as HDFC, Axis Bank, and ICICI Bank, is fixed at ₹10,000; public sector banks do not impose this requirement.

Incidentally, money market deposit accounts (MMGAs) are not full-fledged checking accounts because they limit the depositors not only to six checks and six preauthorized transfers during a statement cycle, but they also require a minimum balance of ₹2,500–10,000. However, these accounts pay the highest rates of any bank account on which checks can be written.

For those with ₹200,000 in cash and securities, or employees with a net salary credit of ₹100,000 each, all-in-one accounts (AIOAs) provide the best alternative. These consist of a package covering automated cash management, preferential personal treatment, and certain investment services provided by the bank or its representatives. On the cash management side, a bank covers each check written by a depositor by transferring a matching amount from money market to current account. On the investment side, a depositor is permitted to use the bank facilities not only for trading in securities but also for financial planning, real estate investment management, and trust and estate planning. Even more important, dividends, interest, and proceeds from the sale of securities are deposited directly into the interest-bearing money market account.

Real Yield

One of the most difficult tasks that savers face is to figure out the real yield on their savings. The reason is not hard to find. Fierce competition for available savings often prompts financial institutions to make exaggerated claims which must be decoded to identify the real yields.

Simple versus Compound Interest

A common practice among financial institutions is to advertise a high interest rate on multiyear accounts, referring only to simple, and not compound, interest. This practice can be utterly misleading to the neophyte and the unsuspecting saver. For instance, if ABC bank pays 5¾ percent simple interest on its five-year CD, and XYZ bank pays only 5 percent interest on its CD compounded annually over the same period, to the uninitiated the former bank looks more attractive. But based on what we have learned in Chapter 3, for the long haul it is the XYZ bank which offers a better deal.

Delayed Deposit Credit

The *real* yield on a deposit partly depends on the number of days money is allowed to earn interest. Some banks wait several days before crediting the account with the new deposit. This practice can significantly cut the real yield for the deposit.

Minimum Monthly Balance Requirement

There are six methods of paying interest: (a) low quarterly balance, (b) low monthly balance, (c) pro rata balance—first in, first out (FIFO), (d) pro rata balance—last in, first out (LIFO), (e) day-of-deposit to day-of-withdrawal balance, and (f) average daily balance. For instance, assume a ₹10,000 deposit is made on January 1 at 5¼ percent, and no additional deposits or withdrawals are made for a year. If interest is compounded and paid quarterly, under each of the preceding six methods the annual interest would be ₹535.42. Differences among these methods, however, result from deposits or withdrawals of funds during the interest period and their effect on the final amount of interest paid, depending on which method of calculation is used.

The best savings method for depositors is the average-daily-balance method, in which a bank calculates the ending balance for each day, and then computes the average balance for the period to get the amount for which it is paying interest. The worst of course is the low-balance method, in which a bank pays interest based on the lowest daily balance on deposit each day.

Grace Period Allowance

Grace days are also important in determining how much interest an account will earn. A grace period for deposits allows savings institutions to pay the interest from the first calendar day of the month and also on deposits withdrawn during the month's last three business days (called dead days). When a bank allows a grace period, it automatically boosts the real yield.

Other Factors

Other factors that affect the real yield include charges for excess withdrawals, penalties for premature account closing, and other assorted charges. The impact of these charges and penalties on the real yield can vary greatly depending on individual policies adopted by financial institutions.

Money Market Mutual Funds

A money market fund is a mutual fund that invests only in short-term money market instruments. Investors purchase and redeem these shares without paying a sales charge. In most cases, the minimum initial investments vary between ₹100 and ₹5,000. Shares can also be redeemed from most money market funds by telephone or wire request, in which case the money is either mailed to the investor or is wire transferred to the investor's bank account.

Money market mutual fund rates are generally higher than those offered by banks on their savings accounts. However, unlike bank accounts, these funds are not insured by DICGC. Interest-earned money market mutual funds vary depending on the type of short-term securities held by the fund. The best rates offered are generally in the vicinity of short-term interest rates.

Certificates of Deposit

CDs significantly differ from savings accounts in that the former must remain on deposit for a specified period of time. Consequently, investors earn a higher return on CDs than they do on savings. The difference in the rates depends on a CD's amount and the length of maturity. However, a substantial interest penalty is imposed on a CD's early withdrawal, and in certain instances early withdrawal may even result in partial loss of the principal.

Minimum amount required to own a CD is ₹100,000; additional CD investments can be made in multiples of that amount. The maturity period of CDs issued by banks varies between seven days and one year. However, the financial institutions issue CDs for a period ranging from one year to three years.

Treasury Bills

Treasury bills are the shortest term marketable obligations offered and, by law, cannot exceed one year to maturity. The most frequent and most popular Treasury bill issues are three-month and six-month maturities which are offered on a weekly basis. Bids (tenders) for both issues are usually invited approximately one week prior to the auction. At that time, the amount offered and the terms of the offering are announced, with the terms for the two issues being similar. Treasury bills are sold on a discount basis. This means that investors pay a discount price for a bill but receive the face value upon maturity. The difference between the discount and maturity prices, or the additional cash received, as a ratio of that investment is the return on a Treasury bill. Incidentally, the minimum denomination of a Treasury bill is ₹25,000, and these bills are sold in multiples of ₹25,000. It should also be noted that although Treasury bills are perfectly liquid and absolutely safe, an investor selling them before maturity could incur a loss.

Simplicity and Minimum Balance Requirements

It is simple to deal with all of the various institutions under consideration. In most instances, a depositor need only provide the account information to a teller, have an account number put on a withdrawal/deposit slip, call a broker who deals in Treasury bills, or fill out a simple application to open a money market account with check writing privileges.

Regarding minimum-balance requirements, banks and credit unions require a small minimum balance to open an account and a reasonable balance to maintain it. Government bonds can be purchased for amounts ranging from a low of ₹10,000 (government bonds) to ₹25,000 for Treasury bills. Finally, money market accounts generally require a minimum of ₹100, although the minimum may be as high as ₹5,000 with some funds.

Special Service Features

No other institution can match the special services offered by commercial banks, or what are frequently called full-service banks. In addition to the traditional banking services, most banks offer special services that add to their quality. These include 24-hour banking through automatic teller machines (ATMs), good deals on loans, traveler's checks, income tax preparation services, investment management services, and even travel advice and airline tickets. Of course, many non-bank institutions provide similar types of services as well.

Tax Considerations

Of all the savings alternatives just discussed, only interest income received on a *tax-exempt* money market fund is exempt from income taxes. The simplest way to decide the relative attractiveness of a tax-exempt money market fund is to convert it into a fully taxable equivalent. This can be easily done by using the following equation:

$$\text{Equivalent Fully Taxable Yield} = \frac{\text{Tax Excempt Yield}}{1 - \text{Marginal Federal Tax Rate}}$$

Thus, if the yield on a tax-exempt money market fund is 4.5 percent and an investor is in the 25 percent tax bracket, the equivalent fully taxable yield is 6 percent: [4.5%/(1–0.25)]. It is also easy to calculate the after-tax equivalent yield from a fully taxable investment. For instance, suppose the taxable yield on a money market fund is 6 percent. Therefore, for an investor in, say, the 25 percent tax bracket, the after-tax yield will be 4.5 percent: [6% × (1–0.25)].

Table 6.7 *Selection of Savings Media*

	Safety	Liquidity	Simplicity	Special Services	Rate of Return	Minimum Required	Tax Advantage
Commercial bank	A	A	A	A	C	A	C
Mutual savings bank	A	A	A	B	A	A	C
Savings and loan	A	A	A	B	A	A	C
Credit union	A	A	A	B	A	A	C
Bonds*	A	C	B	C	C	B	B
Treasury bonds*	A	C	C	C	C	C	C
Municipal bonds*	A	C	C	C	C	C	A

Notes: Differences have been ranked on an A, B, or C scale, with A denoting the highest and C the lowest degree of characteristic.

*These investments are not discussed in the text and are included here merely for comparison.

Summing Up

Deregulation of financial institutions has brought about widespread changes in the financial services industry. Today's financial institutions provide a wide variety of choices and their services are superior to what they were even a few years ago. An overview of the popular liquid assets available today is presented in Table 6.7.

Record-keeping

Accurate record-keeping assists a client in achieving long-term goals and objectives. A planner should provide guidance and checklists to assist the client in establishing an effective record-keeping system. Good record-keeping can help the planner recognize the hidden problems, retrieve important information, and assist the client in tax preparation.

Record-keeping, which can be linked to budgeting, should be done on a monthly basis. Use of computer programs, such as Quicken, can help the client analyze all existing information and determine what percentages of funds are spent on various expenses.

Section III: Credit and Debt Planning

Shakespeare's Polonius was adamant on the subject of credit. "Neither a borrower nor a lender be," he cautioned his son. And many parents today believe that is still a good advice for their children. Unfortunately, such advice on credit is no longer sound. In our society, credit provides a valuable financial planning tool that should be used judiciously to maximize our welfare.

Credit, whether it is buying now and paying later or borrowing money to pay for it, allows us to have *what* we want and *when* we want it. Our primary objective, then, should be to weigh the cost of borrowing money against the benefit to be derived from it and obtain credit when the benefits exceed the cost of borrowing money. We should also protect our credit rating in order to maintain the highest level of creditworthiness at all times.

DEBT OR CREDIT?

A convenient way of stretching income is to borrow, commonly known as consumer credit or debt. Since there exists a great deal of confusion about the real distinction between debt and credit, we shall begin by defining both terms.

Formerly, debt was a taboo, and no one liked to be in debt. Today, old attitudes have changed. Most people now believe that debt allows families to raise their living standards and increase their productive capacities. In fact, debt has become such an integral part of our lives that it is not even considered cynical to ask: Remember when people worried about how much it took to buy something instead of how long?

While debt has generally contributed to growth and prosperity, it has also created financial difficulties. We have all noticed the disastrous consequences of excessive debt accumulation by a person or business. Most families filing for bankruptcy are generally overextended. Their debts accumulate to the point where they cannot pay them back without resorting to the court system. Thus, debt appears to be both good and bad—a paradox that must be resolved before debt can be used as a financial planning tool.

In our society, people who borrow are often looked upon as lacking thrift and a sense of responsibility, while those who are creditworthy are viewed with respect. Yet such perceptions are really two sides of the same coin: To incur credit is to incur debt. It is now easy to see why debt is inherently neither good nor bad. What is important is the relationship between debt and one's ability to adequately service it and ultimately liquidate it with assets.

Of all the different types of debts that exist today, consumer debt, or *consumer credit,* is of special interest, because it refers to the use of credit by individuals for personal needs, in contrast to credit used by a business or government. We will now undertake a discussion of consumer credit.

SOURCES OF CONSUMER CREDIT

Commercial Banks

The term *bank* refers to commercial banks and mutual savings banks. These are full-service institutions offering a variety of loans—secured, unsecured, installment, and noninstallment—to consumers and businesses. Many banks allow their depositors to use passbook savings accounts as collateral for loans, and consequently charge a lower interest rate. Most banks also make automatic overdraft loans, which permit depositors to write checks in amounts larger than the funds available in their accounts. Typically, banks tend to make loans to their own customers, although loans are also made to others who are good financial risks.

Consumer Finance Companies

These are lending institutions specializing in small loans, and they make secured and unsecured loans on an installment basis. There are limits on the maximum amount that can be charged. Interest rate charged on a consumer loan can be as high as 25 percent, although 15–20 percent is fairly typical depending on the amount of borrowing.

Credit Unions

Another important source of credit is credit unions, which are cooperative thrift and loan associations limiting their loans to their own members. The annual percentage rate charged by the credit unions is determined by the prevailing interest rates. In general, charges by credit unions are lower than those charged by commercial banks and finance companies.

Savings and Loan Associations

Savings and loan associations make mortgage loans, although they are also permitted to make other types of loans. In addition, using passbook savings as collateral, these institutions make home improvement and mobile home loans, as well as personal and education loans. Typically, saving and loan rates on consumer loans are similar to those charged by credit unions, depending on the prevailing market rates, the borrower's creditworthiness, and the terms of repayment.

Life Insurance Companies

Whole life insurance policies can serve as excellent collateral for inexpensive loans. Most insurance companies let their policyholders borrow most or all of the accumulated cash value at an interest rate of 5 or 6 percent. These loans are easy to obtain, and technically they do not even have to be repaid. However, life insurance protection is reduced by the loan amount, and that reduces the attractiveness of loans against insurance policies.

Auto Dealers

Loans from auto dealers are easily obtainable for financing automobiles. The formalities for obtaining these loans are kept at a bare minimum. However, auto loans are frequently expensive, and they may run as much as two percentage points higher than a typical bank installment loan used to finance new cars. Incidentally, new car dealerships frequently advertise low financing rates for certain dealer-selected models, and these loans can be quite attractive.

Summing Up

Clearly, no one source of credit is best for every occasion. Individual family situations vary considerably, and each of the sources presented above satisfies a specific family situation. For instance, credit unions lend to their members only, while banks grant loans only to those who qualify. Persons with poor credit ratings and in desperate need for money are left with little choice but to borrow from pawnbrokers or loan sharks, and families with limited payment capacity in need of small loans often find it more convenient to borrow from small loan companies.

CREDIT HISTORY

Importance of Credit History

Sooner or later everyone uses credit to acquire both consumer goods and capital assets. Even the few consumers who usually pay cash eventually make installment purchases. If these credit-conscious consumers do not establish a respectable credit rating in a timely fashion, it might become difficult for them to borrow money when they wish to buy on credit.

Opening that first charge account or getting that first charge card is not always easy. Factors such as age, income, address, and employment stability are important to credit managers. And even though existing laws prohibit them, noticeable biases do exist against young single or married adults of either sex, divorced women, ADC (aid to dependent children) mothers, and persons with legal problems. For this reason, in our credit-oriented society, establishing a good credit rating early in life is essential for *everyone*.

Factors Influencing Credit History

Consumer credit is based on faith in the consumer's good intentions and ability to repay. In this sense, each prospective debtor is judged in terms of "the four Cs of credit." These are:

1. ***Character*** as judged by honesty, reliability, responsibility, and record of financial responsibility.
2. ***Capacity*** as measured by the financial ability to meet obligations; that is, capacity is based on the present and future earning power.

Table 6.8 *Credit Rating Standards*

	Favorable	Unfavorable
Employment	With good firm two years or more. Job involves skill, education.	Shifts jobs frequently. Employed in seasonal industry such as construction work. Unskilled labor.
Income	Steady; meets all normal needs.	Earnings fluctuate, depend on commissions, tips, one-shot deals. Amount barely covers requirements.
Residence	Owns own home or rents for long periods in good neighborhoods.	Lives in furnished rooms in poor neighborhoods. Changes address frequently.
Financial structure	Has savings account and checking account that requires minimum balance. Owns property, investments, life insurance.	No bank accounts. Few, if any, assets.
Debt record	Pays bills promptly. Usually makes large down payment. Borrows infrequently and for constructive purposes.	Slow payer. Tries to put as much on credit as possible. Frequent loans for increasing amounts.
Litigation	No suits by creditors.	Record of suits and other legal action for nonpayment. Bankruptcy.
Personal characteristics	Family man. Not many dependents relative to income. Mature.	Large number of dependents. Marital difficulties. Young, impulsive.
Application behavior	Seeks loan from bank with which he regularly deals. Answers all questions fully and truthfully.	Applies for loan at banking office far removed from his residence or place of business. Makes misstatements on application. In great hurry to obtain cash.

Source: Constructed from various banking and credit union publications.

3. ***Capital*** as judged by the financial resources that can serve as collateral or security for the loan.
4. ***Credit*** rating as judged by the overall capacity to repay the loans.

The credit rating standards (recommended for use by bankers) constructed from various banking and credit union publications are presented in Table 6.8.

Protection of Credit History

Denial of credit by a finance company may hurt a consumer, especially if it is based on an incorrect credit report. The Consumer Protection Act, 2002, directs the credit company denying a loan to inform a consumer that the loan application was rejected on the basis of information contained in a credit report. The applicant is then free to contact the local consumer forum for further details. The Reserve Bank oversees the consumer protection regime for credit products and periodically issues guidelines relating to various aspects of consumer protection. In fact, a consumer can approach the Office of the Ombudsman created by the Reserve Bank to enquire about the credit report that is not directly available from the bank denying the loan.

TYPES OF CREDIT

Basic Issue

In our emerging credit-oriented society, we frequently find it desirable or even necessary to borrow. Hence, it is important to understand the nature of credit and learn the art of using it judiciously. This involves learning about the *true* cost of credit and selecting the credit that is least expensive and most suitable for the family.

Incidentally, it is best to recognize at the outset that the *single cost of credit* is a misnomer. Costs of credit do vary—sometimes considerably—due to a host of factors: types and sources of credit, the prevailing prime interest rate, the duration of loans, the credit rating of the borrower, and the value and type of collateral offered. In fact, depending on special circumstances, credit may even be available at no cost to the borrower. We will now discuss various categories of credit available and the principal ways in which credit costs are calculated and expressed.

Categories of Credit

All consumer credit transactions fall into two broad categories: *sales credit* and *cash credit*. Sales credit is granted by department stores, automobile dealerships, repair shops, and other types of businesses in connection with the purchase of goods or services. In contrast, cash credit is extended to individuals by lending agencies in the form of cash.

Cross-dimensionally, sales and cash credits could be classified as *noninstallment credit* and *installment credit*. The former is single-payment credit and is used for charge accounts, utility bills, bills for professional services, and single-payment cash loans. By contrast, installment credit is used for paying off loans over time, granted for buying durable goods, and for paying off major expenditures. A variant of installment credit is the *check credit plan*, under which the credit user is authorized to write checks against the credit limit as long as the amount for which checks are written does not exceed the approved limit.

Within these major categories, depending on borrowers' preferences, credit-granting institutions offer one of the three types of sales credit discussed as follows.

Thirty-day or regular charge accounts. Most new generation of Indians uses credit routinely as a convenience, especially when they are not charged for the use of such credit. A universal built-in feature of all regular charge accounts is that the seller of goods or services promises to deliver these products on credit without immediate payment, provided their customers pay for them within a stated grace period. This arrangement obviates the need for carrying cash and also helps consumers consolidate their payments at regular intervals. This credit for convenience is an excellent idea, although one must never lose sight of the fact that the credit users are charged a very high rate of interest (18 percent or more) on the unpaid balance of the loan if payments are not made by the due date.

Revolving and optional charge accounts. Revolving accounts revolutionized our major stores. These accounts not only boosted sales but also changed the budget styles of consumers. Under this arrangement, businesses allow their customers to make repeated purchases as long as the total does not exceed the limit established when the account was opened. Equally important, there is no finance charge if the payment is made within a stated grace period. But if a customer chooses not to pay for the purchases either partly or in full within the grace period, then a finance charge is imposed on the unpaid balance. Charges computed at 1, 1½, or 2 percent monthly are equivalent to the annual rates of 12, 18, or 24 percent, respectively.

Installment purchases or time-payment plans. The most popular demand for credit, of course, stems from the use of installment credit for buying durable goods. A sharp rise in personal expectations and demands for durable consumer goods, coupled with the inability of most buyers to pay cash for them, has been instrumental in the phenomenal growth of installment credit. In all cases installment credit or buying on time—as it is popularly called—is payable in several predetermined installments, hopefully, but not necessarily, spread out over the useful life of the durable goods being financed.

As mentioned, there are two methods of financing installment credit: buying on time directly from the seller and borrowing money from a credit institution. In either case there is a cost involved in incurring a debt. This cost, which has several names—simple interest, add-on interest, interest discounted, monthly interest, finance charges, and points—is not a uniform charge.

Regardless of which payment method is selected, the consumer will probably have to go through sales finance agencies to make the specific choice. Most retailers and other businesses find it uneconomical to extend their customers credit by tying down their working capital, and hence, they transfer their loan business to sales finance agencies. If an account is transferred to a finance company, the consumer will become responsible to that company for the repayment of the loan.

An important alternative to paying directly to sales finance companies is the credit card, the issuer of which honors the customer's creditworthiness. There are several advantages to using credit cards, chief among them being convenience, creation of instant credit, flexibility, ease of payment, and emergency use. Not all credit cards are cost free, however. Travel and entertainment cards charge an annual fee but no interest on the loan. There is also a fee for cards issued by banks; in addition, there is an interest charge if payment is not made within a specified time. Typically, this ranges from 1 to 1½ percent per month—a 12–18 percent annual rate. The same is true of most retail store cards.

A planner can assist his or her client in learning credit management techniques. This would include ensuring that credit is used wisely, reviewing the current debt structure, establishing banking relationships, projecting borrowing needs, advising on borrowing sources, and helping with financial emergencies.

EFFECTIVE INTEREST RATE

Anish and Ankita Upadhyay recently shopped around for a quality stereo system. The information they gathered about the cost of credit is summarized in Table 6.9. They learned that if they took out a two-year simple interest loan from a credit union at a 12 percent interest rate, the ₹1,000 stereo would ultimately cost them ₹1,125. The same stereo would cost them ₹1,131.15 at an interest rate of 12.59 percent, ₹1,190.63 at 18.3 percent, and ₹1,256.25 at 24.6 percent. The Upadhyays also discovered that the longer the repayment period, the higher is the cost. For instance, the finance charge on a 12 percent, ₹1,000 loan for one year was ₹65; if the time period was extended to three years, the finance charges almost tripled. Understandably, the Upadhyays got confused by all of this gobbledygook and could not decide which method of financing the stereo was best for them.

Like the Upadhyays, millions of consumers are unable to cope with such decisions. Unfortunately, to make an intelligent buying decision there is no substitute for identifying *effective* or *real* interest rates under various types of loan provisions.

Interest represents the price borrowers pay to lenders for credit over the life of the loan. The amount of interest paid depends on a number of factors: the amount of money lent or borrowed, the length of time involved in the transaction, the stated or nominal annual rate of interest, the repayment schedule, and the method used to calculate interest.

Table 6.9 *Cost of Borrowing ₹1,000*

I: High Interest Rates Raise Total Cost of Credit					
Total amount borrowed (₹)	1,000	1,000	1,000	1,000	1,000
Interest rate (annual, %)	12	12.59	18.3	24.6	40
Finance charge (₹)	125.00	131.15	190.63	256.25	416.67
Total payment (principal and interest) (₹)	1,125.00	1,131.15	1,190.63	1,256.25	1,416.67

Note: A two-year simple interest loan is used in this illustration.

II: Longer Time Payments Raise the Total Cost of Credit			
Total borrowed amount (₹)	1,000	1,000	1,000
Interest rate (annual, %)	12	12	12
Financed over (years)	1	2	3
Finance charges (₹)	65.00	125.00	185.00
Total payment (principal and interest) (₹)	1,065.00	1,125.00	1,185.00

Note: Finance charges are calculated by using a complex system consisting of: (a) declining-balance method, (b) a point system, and (c) a varied loan payment method.

BURDEN OF DEBT

An Overview

We have learned that consumer credit is a powerful financial planning tool. However, used unwisely or irresponsibly, it can create a nightmare for the family. Therefore, every family should limit their debt to the level they can efficiently handle. Unfortunately, no simple formula or all-purpose table is available that can accurately determine how much debt is safe for a family. Therefore, people must establish their own credit capacity, based on their psychological make-up, financial resources, values, goals, and willingness to maintain a disciplined approach to debt creation.

Guidance from Business World

One way to determine how much debt a family can afford is to borrow from the corporate model. A business reaches its debt limit when its debt reaches its level of equity. In other words, financial lenders consider businesses with a debt/equity ratio equal to or greater than one to be non-creditworthy and hesitate to grant them additional loans. Consumers may also regard their personal debt/equity ratio, calculated from their net worth statement, as a yardstick for determining their credit capacity. Note, however, that in this calculation the value of home (an asset) and its mortgage (a liability) should be excluded, since financing a home falls into a category separate from other types of borrowing.

Rule of Thumb Approach

Another approach to sizing up the debt limit involves setting the consumer installment debt limit as a fixed percentage of monthly income. Experts say the debt payment should be no more than 10–15 percent of the net monthly income. These payments should include all items (except home mortgages) purchased on credit. Net monthly income can be calculated by subtracting all taxes, EPF contributions, and contributions to pension and other plans. A debt limit calculation worksheet is presented in Table 6.10 which can be used to determine the maximum amount of debt that is safe for a family. As the table suggests, if debt to equity ratio exceeds, say, 44 percent, then immediate action should be taken to correct the situation and the assistance of a professional should be sought.

BANKRUPTCY

Modern Interpretation

Formerly, a debt was supposed to be honored by all means, and bankruptcy was a taboo. That is how the maxim was interpreted by Mark Twain, the world famous author of the immortal *Adventures of Huckleberry Finn,* often called "the Great American Novel." To his utter disbelief, in 1894 due to his overextended credit situation, he was forced into bankruptcy. His creditors were happy to come to a compromise with him, but he promised to return *100 cents on the dollar*, and at the age of 59, despite uncertain health, he embarked on a 13-month foreign lecture tour to earn the necessary money. He did not return to the USA until after he had fulfilled his vow to return "100 cents on the dollar," not even when he learned of the illness and subsequent death of his beloved daughter.

Today, the legendary Mark Twain would probably be regarded as a nut. The stigma once attached to taking a financial bath no longer seems to be an important consideration for many modern-day debtors. Indian courts are filled with bankruptcy petitions from real estate agents, contractors, schoolteachers, journalists, stockbrokers, architects, engineers, and financial planners. In fact, even wealthy movie stars, professional athletes, and prominent business people have declared—and others like them continue to declare—bankruptcy.

Table 6.10 *Debt Limit Calculation Worksheet*

1. Monthly mortgage/rent	₹______	Debt to income ratio
2. Monthly credit card payments (average)	₹______	Line 5/Line 12: ______
3. Monthly auto lease or loan payments	₹______	
4. Monthly "other" obligations	₹______	Less than 35%: Excellent
5. Monthly debt payments (lines 1+2+3+4)	₹______	35–44%: Okay
6. Annual gross salary	₹______	45–49%: Poor. Take immediate action.
7. Bonus	₹______	
8. Overtime	₹______	Over 50%: Danger zone.
9. "Other" income	₹______	Seek professional help.
10. Alimony received	₹______	
11. Total income (lines 6+7+8+9+10)	₹______	
12. Monthly income (line 11/12)	₹______	

While bankruptcy is no longer a taboo, it still *must be avoided.* In the following section, we will address this issue.

Avoiding Bankruptcy

Road to recovery. There is an old cliché in the financial world which states that people cannot correct dangerous behavior unless they recognize that it is harmful. One simple way to find out if a person has a debt problem is to determine if sufficient money is available to pay off all the monthly expenses plus the minimum credit card and other debt obligations.

Clearly, not all financial difficulties result in bankruptcies. Financial problems may arise when expenses and obligations consistently exceed income, and the ability to make payments becomes a major issue. Such a situation may be created by either mismanagement of finances or a set of circumstances totally beyond one's control. Whatever the reason, an individual can avoid a lot of grief by knowing some basic facts about the alternatives available to people who experience financial difficulties.

Repayment account. If money can be saved from cutting back on unnecessary expenditures, then the extra savings can be deposited in a separate bank account. Instead of using this account to pay off monthly bills, it should be used to pay more than the minimum required payment on credit cards and boost the emergency fund balance.

Be a banker. Many savings accounts, such as PPF and EPF accounts allow participants to borrow against them. Naturally, the borrowers would have to repay the loan with after-tax rupees. But it is still a good deal because retirement funds typically charge loan rates of 8–9 percent, far lower than those charged by credit card companies. Besides, in this case, borrowers would be paying interest to themselves, rather than to a bank.

Adopt creative measures. One way to reduce the burden of heavy debt is to switch to a less expensive home or a more modest car and use the funds to reduce debt. Another idea is to prioritize debts and start paying off the debts which charge exorbitant rates of interest (such as credit card debt). A third debt reduction idea is to freeze the credit cards so they could not be used on an impulse.

The objective approach. It is impossible to solve a financial crisis merely by juggling books or making random payments to some creditors. These creditors are professional people who can easily outwit debtors when it comes to confronting such delinquent payers with legal claims. The best thing, then, is to make a statement showing the money that can be spared for loan payments and the total monthly payments that must be made. This statement clearly reveals where a consumer stands with respect to outstanding debts.

Informal arrangements with creditors. When financial difficulties can no longer be handled by a consumer, an informal arrangement can still be made with the creditors to settle out of court. If the necessary goodwill is shown by working with creditors rather than avoiding them, they may be willing to defer payments or refinance the debt to reduce the size of monthly payments. To reduce the debt, these creditors may also permit the return of some of the merchandise bought on credit.

If the informal arrangements fail to resolve the overextended debt problem, it may be possible to find a lending agency that could arrange for lower monthly payments extended over a longer period of time.

Credit counseling. If the first two steps fail, it is advisable to seek the help of a credit counseling service which provides expert, confidential guidance for little or no charge. It can be located through a banker or a lawyer. Incidentally, there are two Acts that govern bankruptcy in India: (a) Presidency Towns Insolvency Act, 1909 (PTIA), which is applicable in Kolkata, Mumbai, and Chennai. (b) Provincial Insolvency Act, 1920 (PIA) which is applicable to the rest of the country. People under severe financial stress should become familiar with these Acts.

Credit counseling services operate at two levels. First, through recasting the budget at a more modest level, the service may be able to help one keep the spending plan at a realistic level, thereby enhancing one's ability to meet the financial obligations. Second, if expenses far exceed the income and there is no way to bring the two closer, the counseling service may try to arrange new repayment schedules with the creditors. If this is possible, a debtor may be asked to give the service a predetermined amount every month. According to an established plan acceptable to the creditors, the service will then distribute the amount to creditors.

Bankruptcy Abuse Prevention and Consumer Protection Act of 2005

Major provisions of this Act include the establishment of a means test that determines whether a debtor is eligible for Chapter 7 relief, which generally discharges all unsecured debts, or must file under Chapter 13, which requires debtors to repay certain creditors in installments over three to five years. The intent of the new law is to compel debtors who are able to pay at least a portion of their debts to do so. In general, a Chapter 7 case will be converted to Chapter 13 if the debtor can pay a lesser of ₹10,000, or a greater of either (a) 25 percent of unsecured, non-priority debt or (b) ₹6,000. A debtor has the option to rebut the means test by demonstrating that in this case "special circumstances" and certain "safe harbor" exemptions apply.

In a nutshell, the 2005 Act has made it much more difficult to resort to bankruptcy declaration as a means of solving an inconvenient financial problem.

In this chapter, we presented issues relating to budgeting, credit management, and debt planning. In Chapter 7, we will discuss planning for funding education costs.

7 Educational Planning

INTRODUCTION

Indians consider college education extremely important, and understandably it is so. It broadens the students' perspective of the world, widens their appreciation of all that it offers, and enhances their self-esteem. Besides, college graduates with a bachelor's degree earn much more during their career than high school graduates. That difference jumps to many lakhs of rupees for those earning a professional or a master's degree. While there is debate regarding the difference between escalating costs of education and challenging job markets, there is no doubt that higher education does offer real long-term benefits. According to a study by Associated Chambers of Commerce and Industry of India (ASSOCHAM), parents spend nearly ₹18–20 lakh in raising children by the time they graduate from high school.[1]

Unfortunately, financing education appears to defy the laws of physics. When it comes to even pre-college costs, "what goes up just keeps going up." In India, in the last decade or so, costs of sending children to school have risen by 160 percent. And yet, over the same period, the average annual income of fairly well-off parents has not even increased by more than 30 percent.[2] The fee at structure schools (other than government) is around ₹80,000 at the entry level (grade below class V) and ₹150,000 at the diploma level (classes XI and XII). In addition, higher education fees continue to climb unabated. And that is not all. Specialized courses in the areas of medical and management fields involve even higher fees escalation. Assuming an annual increase of 5 percent in cost, by 2030–31, parents will have to spend ₹3,000,000 and ₹4,000,000 for college tuition and living expenses leading to, respectively, graduation and postgraduation degrees. If the baby is destined for an international ivy-league degree from, say, Harvard or Massachusetts Institute of Technology (MIT), the parent could be looking at a four-year bill of over ₹5 crore. This expense, of course, is just for one child. That college cost, multiplied by the number of children in the family, is sufficiently scary to make most parents throw up their hands in despair.

Fortunately, the bleak picture just painted need not lead one to desperation and inaction. It is of course true that school and college education is the second largest expense many Indian families will undertake, next to the purchase of a home. Given the astounding costs involved, funding the school and four years of college for a child frequently represents a formidable financial goal. With careful planning, however, it can be prevented from becoming an overwhelming financial burden.

So, the clear message about education funding is simply this: Whether a family will need to meet school and college costs in the next decade or within a few short years, the best way to pursue this goal

[1] http://www.tflguide.com/2012/10/cost-of-higher-education-in-india-calculator-infographics.html (last accessed on November 22, 2014).

[2] http://www.fpguru.com/cms/index.php?option=com_content&view=article&id=155:start-your-childs-education-planning-now&catid=54:articles&Itemid=54 (last accessed on November 22, 2014).

is to start the planning process *today*. The reason is that the sooner the planning process begins, the closer the family will move toward the goal of accumulating the necessary funds for financing school and college education. And this is a goal worth pursuing, because college education is one of the greatest gifts a child will ever receive.

EDUCATION COSTS

According to the Ministry of Statistics and Programme Implementation (MOSPI), school expenses today are nearly five times higher than they were 10 years ago (from 2004 to 2013). For instance, based on the ASSOCHAM Survey (2011), the average school fee in rural India increased from ₹49 in 2004 to ₹260 in 2013, a whopping increase of 530 percent. This works out to be an annual increase of 18 percent, as compared to an annual inflation rate of 6.5 percent.

Interestingly, higher education costs appear to be escalating at even a faster rate. The cost of an engineering course, for instance, is expected to rise from ₹5.5 lakh in 2014 to nearly ₹10 lakh in the next five years and around ₹18 lakh in 10 years. Five years from 2014, the tuition fee for an MBA course, currently around ₹14.5 lakh, would be nearly ₹30 lakh; in 10 years, it is likely to be over ₹60 lakh.[3] No matter what estimate is used, every parent should make a concerted effort to ensure that funds are available for financing the institution of choice when the child is ready to enter school and college.

It should now be clear that in the future, school and college costs will continue to rise dramatically and parents will continue to be shocked by the price tags attached to educating their children. Consequently, a financial planner would be wise not to start a discussion on educational planning by showing parents what it is going to cost them and how difficult it would be for them to reach their educational goals. Instead, it is recommended that they adopt an alternative approach as described next.

First, planners should emphasize that parents who have time on their side should capitalize on the magic of compounding. Second, they need to explain that parents do not have to *save it all*. In fact, saving is only one of the several ways to pay for college. The others are: pay as you go, funding college out of earned income, financial aid, merit scholarships, borrowing, grant money, work study, and, finally, letting someone like the grandparents pay the bills.

In the next section, the use of power of compounding in educational planning will be discussed. Alternative methods of paying for college will be addressed later in this chapter.

MAGIC OF COMPOUNDING

In educational planning, as in every other segment of financial planning, it is *time in*, and not *timing*, that makes all the difference. The illustration in Figure 7.1 demonstrates this concept.

Consider the case where an investor Shweta just gave birth to a son. At the beginning of every month she plans to save for his college education by investing ₹100 in a mutual fund. If she continues to set aside the same amount every month for 18 years, she will have invested a total of ₹21,600 (₹100 × 12 × 18). Assuming an annual, after-tax reinvestment rate of 6 percent, the total value of the portfolio at her son's college age would be ₹38,929 (set calculator to "begin" mode; calculator inputs: N=216, I=0.50 (6/12), PV=0 and PMT=100, solve for FV).

Now consider the case of Suraj who just became a proud father of a cute girl. Suraj does want to save for her college, but due to his other commitments he plans to begin investing after 10 years. Fortunately, Suraj is able to invest ₹225 at the beginning of each month (instead of Shweta's ₹100 per month) for the

[3] http://articles.economictimes.indiatimes.com/2011-09-19/news/30175826_1_education-costs-higher-education-school-fees (last accessed on November 23, 2014).

next eight years, that is a total investment of ₹21,600, the same amount that Shweta invests in her mutual fund. However, to Suraj's great surprise, even though his investment also generated the same annual, after-tax return of 6 percent, the total value of his investment amounts to only ₹27,775 when his daughter is ready to go to college (set calculator to "begin" mode; calculator inputs: $N=96$, $I=0.50$, PV=0, PMT=225, solve for FV). At the end of 18 years, Suraj's portfolio is almost 29 percent less than Shweta's portfolio.

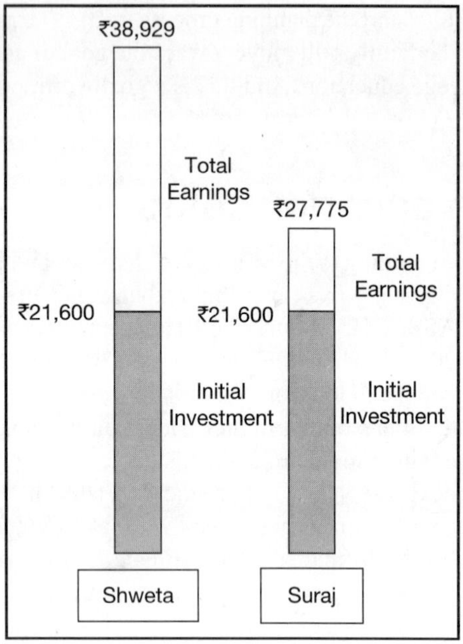

Figure 7.1 *Investing for a College Education*

These illustrations clearly demonstrate that since Shweta started early, time was on her side, and she was able to capitalize on the magic of compounding. What this implies is that since Shweta reinvests the earnings in her account along with her original principal, the investment gains build up over time, not only on the money she originally invested but also on the gains she made in previous years.

The power of compounding over time can be demonstrated both in terms of the number of years of investing *and* the amount of periodic investment. Table 7.1 reveals that an individual would have accumulated ₹38,929 if a beginning-of-the-month monthly investment of ₹100 was made for 18 years and compounded at an after-tax 6 percent annual return. If that individual would like to have a slightly higher amount (₹43,036) in nine years, then the amount of monthly investment would have to be increased to ₹300, or three times the monthly investment in the previous example.

SAVING FOR COLLEGE COST

Assume that we wish to know the amount of savings that would be required to pay for the full projected costs of college education. For this analysis, it is necessary to determine the four-year public or private education costs, which will be assumed to increase at 5 percent per year.

Table 7.2 presents the framework for determining for the Sharma family how much monthly savings are necessary to meet the shortfall in their child's educational funding cost. Their son, Rohit, is expected to be a public school, in-state resident in nine years. The Sharmas have already saved up ₹25,000 for Rohit's college and expect this fund to earn a before-tax annual return of 8 percent. Based on these assumptions, an educational funding calculation (Table 7.2) shows that the Sharmas would have to invest ₹171 every month to reach their educational funding goal (i.e., annual need divided by 12).

Table 7.1 *Growth of Investments over Time* (Amount in ₹)*

Monthly Investment	3 Years	6 Years	9 Years	12 Years	15 Years	18 Years
100	3,953	8,684	14,345	21,120	29,227	38,929
200	7,907	17,386	28,691	42,240	58,455	77,858
300	11,860	26,052	43,036	63,360	87,682	116,787
400	15,813	34,736	57,381	84,480	116,909	155,716
500	19,766	43,420	71,727	105,600	146,136	194,645

Note: *Assuming an after-tax return of 6 percent and the beginning of the month contributions.

Table 7.2 *Education Funding Cost Calculation*

I. Cost of Education in Nine Years		
1.	Current cost in public institution	₹50,000
2.	Number of years until college	9
3.	College inflation rate	5 percent
4.	College cost in nine years	₹77,566
II. Value of Savings in Nine Years		
5.	Current value of savings	₹25,000
6.	Before-tax rate of return	8 percent
7.	Number of years until college	9 years
8.	Future value of savings	₹49,975
III. Additional Savings Required		
9.	College cost in nine years (line 4)	₹77,566
10.	Value of savings in nine years (line 8)	₹49,975
11.	Savings shortfall (line 9 – 10)	₹27,591
12.	Annual savings required (assume $i=8\%$, $n=9$)	₹2,046
13.	Monthly savings required (line 12/12)	₹171

EDUCATION SAVINGS

Numerous long-term savings vehicles are available to families to save for education. The popular forms of savings plans are: Public Provident Fund (PPF), fixed deposit for children, insurance policies, mutual funds, gold, and stocks. These instruments will be discussed in detail in Chapter 8.

Tuition payments are tax deductible (Section 80C) up to ₹150,000. This is allowed on the payment made toward a child's education in any school, college or university. Coaching for various competitive exams is also considered as the tuition cost. However, in order to qualify, the fees must represent the actual tuition fees paid and only for a maximum of two dependent children.

The interest paid on loans taken to finance educational costs for self and members of the family is tax deductible (Section 80E). The deduction is allowed for eight years or until full interest is repaid, whichever comes earlier. This loan, solely to fund a regular or a vocational course, can be taken from a recognized financial institution by the borrower, the parent or the spouse of the student.

ASSET ALLOCATION STRATEGY

Investing in a growth asset is not without risk. There is, of course, no magic formula for investing school and college funds, but there is an eternal truth: Higher returns are generally associated with higher risks. Because school and college costs must be paid when due, caution should be exercised in assuming above average risks when investing college funds. In this section, a brief review of several investment options will be undertaken.

Numerous studies have demonstrated that, in the long run, stocks handsomely beat all other forms of investment. But these studies also reveal that stocks are far more volatile than bonds and money market securities. One of the keys to sound investing for college funding is to have an intelligent investment strategy that aims at maximizing returns for the level of risk acceptable to the family. Generally, this involves diversification across three different asset classes—stocks, bonds, and money market securities. This point requires elaboration.

As mentioned, history has shown that while the highest growth potential is in stocks, they are also the riskiest of the three asset classes. In contrast, money market securities carry no market risk, but they also generate the lowest return. In fact, money market returns and interest on bank deposits are substantially below the current inflation rate applicable to college expenses (2011–12). Consequently, a rational strategy would be to put more weight on stocks when a child is relatively young. As the child grows older, however, the proportion of stocks should gradually drop, the share of bonds and money market securities should gradually increase.

Incidentally, people saving for college generally prefer mutual funds over individual stocks and bonds. This is because mutual funds offer diversity, permit investment of relatively small amounts at desired intervals, and, if invested in a family of funds, provide an easy way to rebalance the portfolio over time. Also, as a child gets closer to college, with relative ease, the parent can shift from a growth mutual fund to an income mutual fund.

INSTRUMENTS OF EDUCATIONAL INVESTMENT ALTERNATIVES

There are many financial products available to the family seeking to save for future college costs. A number of other investment choices are also available for financing education. The key investment alternatives available to a family for this purpose are discussed next.

Zero-Coupon Option

An option with an iron-clad guarantee consists of investing in zero-coupon government bonds, with maturity dates corresponding to the child's years of school and college. That is because by doing so the durations of an asset and a liability are perfectly matched.

For example, assume that a father who prefers safe investment buys four government zeros for his new-born daughter. These bonds will deliver to the daughter approximately ₹45,000 a year during her four years in college. While the market value of the zero-coupon government bonds will rise and fall during the intervening years due to fluctuations in interest rates (as is true of all bonds prices), these fluctuations can be safely ignored because the bond's face value will be unaffected at maturity.

Savings Bonds

Tax-saving bonds are generally issued by a government in the form of Reserve Bank of India bonds or by private banks such as ICICI, IDBI, and HDFC to allow investors to save on taxes. Interest on these bonds is compounded every six months and the bonds mature in five years. The benefit of investing in these bonds is that the interest which an investor receives is tax free. These tax-free bonds with a face value of ₹1,000 or multiples thereof are not subject to maximum investment limits.

Inflation Indexed Bonds

The Union Budget of 2013–14 introduced a new type of international instrument known as inflation-linked securities. These securities were designed to help protect investors against the inflation risk of owning bonds, and are particularly suited for saving for college. These securities pay a fixed rate of interest on a principal amount that is continuously adjusted for inflation. The Reserve Bank expects these securities to help investors diversify their fixed income portfolios and reduce the government's own borrowing. For retail investors, the distribution/sale of linkers is through commercial banks. The interest rate on these securities is linked to the consumer price index (CPI [Base: 2010 = 100]). The minimum and maximum investments per annum are ₹5,000 and ₹5 lakh, respectively.

Inflation-indexed securities are issued with fixed maturities of 10 years. As mentioned, these securities are sold in minimum and maximum (in multiples of ₹5,000) denominations of ₹5,000 and ₹500,000 respectively, and the timely payment of interest and principal is guaranteed by the full faith and credit of the government. However, unlike traditional government securities, the inflation-indexed securities are structured to help interest and principal payments keep pace with inflation.

Interest on inflation-indexed securities, like the interest on all government securities, is exempt from state and local income taxes. For income tax purposes, semiannual interest payments are taxable by the national government in the year they are received. However, the greatest drawback of this investment is that the inflation adjustments to the principal amount are taxed like interest in the year in which the adjustments occur, even though these principal adjustments will not be paid until maturity. Because of this adverse tax treatment, Treasury Inflation Protected Securities (TIPS) are more appropriate for tax-deferred accounts.

In the case of TIPS, tax is levied on the interest as per the investor's tax bracket in the same way as bank fixed deposit accounts are treated. For this reason, this product is more suitable for those in the lower tax bracket (10–20 percent). Another disadvantage is that these bonds are not tradable in the secondary market. Finally, redemptions are allowed only after one year for senior citizens (65 and over) and three years for the rest, subject to a 50 percent penalty for early redemption.[4]

Low-load/No-load Insurance

Another choice available, especially to older parents needing insurance, is the low-load/no-load cash value life policy. While there are drawbacks to investing educational funds in cash value policies, the following illustration demonstrates how it might work in certain cases.

Assume Nitin Rai is a healthy, 40-year-old man, and he needs a ₹500,000 life insurance policy. Nitin buys a low-load universal life policy with ₹500,000 as death benefits. Next, he puts maximum allowable cash into the policy.

In this situation, Nitin would have to follow a complicated payment schedule: ₹19,277 per year for the first four years, ₹3,275 in the fifth year, nothing for the years six to seven, ₹1,921 in the twelfth year, and then ₹6,859 for the remaining eight years. At the end of 10 years, the cash value should approximate ₹130,000; after 20 years, it would be ₹310,000. Nitin can pay the school and college costs by borrowing against, or withdrawing tax free, the policy's cash value. *A buy term and invest the difference* strategy would provide Nitin with the same amount if he earned an after-tax annual return of 4.7 percent for 20 years. However, in that case, at the age of 60, his term insurance would start costing him ₹4,550 a year, and at the age of 65 it would become prohibitively expensive. So, in Nitin's case, a low-load insurance policy would be preferable, because that would provide him both the desired protection and the vehicle for funding college costs.

Another benefit of this strategy is that, if and when a child applies for college aid, the life insurance asset would be *excluded* from the parent's assets. As previously mentioned, parents' assets are taken into consideration in determining the "expected family contribution" toward college expenses.

Minor's Trust

Minor's trust is a gift tax tool that enables a grantor to make an irrevocable gift to a minor in trust and still obtain the annual gift tax exclusion. This trust is used when a person wishes to make a gift to a minor child, and when a grantor's income tax bracket is higher than the recipient's tax bracket. It is also used when a grantor owns an asset that is likely to appreciate over time but he does not want the appreciation to be included in his gross estate.

The tax implications of the minor's trust are enormous. If the income of the trust is distributed each year, it is taxable to the recipient who by definition is in a lower tax bracket. If the income is accumulated, it is taxed to the trust. Gifts to the trust constitute a "present interest." Therefore, the annual gift tax

[4] http://www.moneylife.in/article/inflation-index-bonds/35765.html (last accessed on November 23, 2014).

exclusion of ₹50,000 (2014) applies as long as the necessary conditions are met. Finally, appreciation on property from the date it is placed in the trust is removed from the grantor's estate.

Trust assets are managed by a trustee for the benefit of the beneficiary, and the property can be used for the benefit of the beneficiary before the child reaches the age of 18 (e.g., college tuition and fees). If the beneficiary dies before distribution, these assets become part of the beneficiary's estate.

As a general rule, a child will have the right to the assets at the age of 18.

FINANCIAL ASSISTANCE

By far the best policy for financing education costs is to commit to a long-term savings plan. Systematic investing, leveraged by the power of compounding, can certainly move the family toward goal achievement. However, families who unsuccessfully plan, and certainly those who fail to plan, will find it necessary to look for alternative sources of funding. In many instances, families with other, more-pressing commitments are unable to save the necessary funds in a timely fashion and, hence, must fall back on other means of support for financing their children's education.

Financial aid from central and state governments is available to almost all students who meet established eligibility standards. In fact, each year crores of rupees of aid are awarded to students as financial need.

FORMS OF FINANCIAL AID

Various forms of central, state and university financial aid in the form of grants, scholarships, work study, and student loans are available. These are investigated next.

Scholarships

Scholarships represent "free money" to the students because the proceeds do not have to be repaid. The central and state governments, universities, and private and public organizations offer a massive amount of scholarships for students who want to study in India or abroad. University Grants Commission (UGC), All India Council for Technical Education (AICTE), Ministry of Human Resource Development, universities, trusts, and colleges often award merit-based scholarships and grants. For example, students who fall within the top 10–15 percent of the incoming class or exceed a certain NET/GATE score level, automatically qualify for UGCs/CSIR/ICAR/ICSSR scholarships. In addition, several international organizations such as Fulbright, DAAD, and Commonwealth also provide scholarships for higher education. Schools competing for a student frequently offer financial aid, often in the form of scholarships. For these reasons, when considering a good college match for the students, it is important to investigate all available financial resources. It is also worthwhile to scrutinize state scholarship programs, private and community scholarships, and industry scholarships and grants. Academic scholarships are also available at nearly all institutions of higher learning.

Student Loans

Student loans constitute a substantial source of college, institutes, and university funding. In fact, between 2004 and 2012 student loans increased more than 35 percent annually. However, during the same period, banks expanded the overall credit by only 23 percent.[5] Along with housing loans, student loans constitute a part of the priority lending category, and bank student loans are subsidized. This means that a student does not have to start paying back the loan until some period after graduation (e.g., one

[5] http://www.business-standard.com/article/pf/tax-benefits-for-children-113032300349_1.html (last accessed on November 27, 2014).

year after the end of studies or six months after getting a job, whichever is earlier). Although education loans have tenure of five–seven years, in special cases the repayment period can be extended to 10–15 years.

Home Equity Loan

A parent may wish to consider taking out a home equity loan because interest payments on these loans are tax deductible. These loans are generally available through commercial lenders.

Other Sources of Funds

Other sources of funds for education are also available. The more important ones are discussed as follows.

1. ***Loans from qualified plans (Employees' Provident Fund [EPF]).*** Funds can be borrowed from a qualified retirement fund, but this option should be exercised only as a last resort because it is not the intended purpose of the funds. It is good to remember that funds can normally be borrowed for education (with some tax advantages), whereas it is difficult to borrow funds for retirement.

2. ***Withdrawal from PPF.*** Early withdrawals (before maturity) from PPF are permitted once a year, starting from the seventh year. However, such premature withdrawals should not exceed the lower of (a) 50 percent of the balance at the end of the fourth year and (b) 50 percent of the balance at the end of the immediate preceding year. Between the third and the sixth year a loan against the PPF deposit can also be obtained up to a maximum of 25 percent. However, the interest charged on the loan must be 2 percent higher than the PPF interest rate.

3. ***Loans from cash value life insurance.*** Another source of funds is a loan against the cash value of life insurance. This is a preferred option because the cash value of permanent life insurance does not factor into the expected family contribution calculation. Of course, funds borrowed from life insurance policies do reduce the death benefit until repaid.

REPAYMENT OF STUDENT LOANS

Obtaining a student loan is no easy task. But the repayment of a student loan can be even more challenging, since the amount could run as much as ₹1,000,000 for those graduating from a law or a business school, and ₹2,000,000 or more for those graduating from a medical school.

Student loans are, of course, granted on the assumption that every recipient would make a good faith effort to repay the loan in a timely fashion. However, in today's uncertain economic environment, many graduates are unable to repay the loan either because they do not have a job or because they do not earn enough to make the loan payments. For these people, other options are available.

Deferment

Unlike mortgages, which never have cancellation or postponement of payment options, student loans do accommodate the borrowers' special financial needs. If a graduate does not have a job, he or she might be eligible for a deferment of the regularly scheduled student payments. This means that a graduate does not have to immediately start making payments, and in most cases the interest on the loan would be deferred. The government grants deferments on its loans for about a dozen reasons, including returning to school, being pregnant if recently out of school, being temporarily disabled, or serving in the military.

Forbearance

People who cannot make ends meet, but still do not qualify for a deferment, may be able to get the forbearance. This arrangement suspends principal and interest payments. However, unlike the deferment arrangement, in this case, the interest continues to accrue during the forbearance. The student can either elect to pay the interest charge or have it added onto the principal.

Discharge

Some borrowers actually get their loans forgiven if they meet certain criteria, such as poor income, medical problem, and so on. Sometimes, the government waives off the interest on student loans to provide relief to students who cannot get jobs because of poor economic conditions.

Graduated Payment

Graduated payments, featuring low monthly payments that gradually increase, may also be an option. For instance, a ₹5,000 loan at 8 percent would normally carry a monthly payment of ₹60.67. In contrast, a new college graduate opting for a graduated repayment would pay only ₹35.50 a month at first and end up with a final payment of ₹101.92 after 10 years.

Direct Consolidation Loan

One of the major problems of managing student loans is that most students put together a portfolio of loans and each month end up writing several checks to satisfy a variety of terms and conditions. That is one reason why some graduates choose to consolidate their student loans.

A direct consolidation loan allows the borrower to combine multiple loans into one; as such, one monthly payment is needed rather than several to service these loans. The consolidation might result in lower monthly payments if the interest rate is lower than the original loan rates or if the term of the loan is longer. Extending the term of the loan offers a good compromise for people who cannot cover their current monthly payments. However, consolidation does have a cost.

The Loan Counseling Task Force provides the following example: A person with ₹23,000 in school loans from three different programs pays ₹84.42 less a month by consolidating and extending payments for 20 years. But over the life of the loan, that person also pays ₹14,336 as additional interest charges.

When deciding on loan consolidation, it is important to consider all the features of the existing loans. Are there any benefits with the current loans that might be lost? Are any of the existing interest rates lower? Are there any principal rebates that might be lost? Comparing all the pros and cons will lead to a cost-effective decision, avoiding a decision solely based on convenience.

EDUCATIONAL TAX INCENTIVES

The Income Tax Department made changes in tax laws that affected educational funding. Several of these changes have already been introduced in previous discussions. Important educational tax incentives available are discussed further in the text.

Employer-provided Educational Assistance

Employer-paid educational expenses up to ₹1,000 (Section 80C of the Income Tax Act) are generally deductible by the employer and are excludable from the employee's income. However, the deduction is available only for tuition paid for two children. Education allowance of ₹100 per month for each child (maximum of two children) is also treated as tax exempt.

Student Loan Interest Deduction

The interest paid (not the principal amount) on an education loan is tax deductible for up to eight continuous years, starting from the year in which the interest becomes payable. This can be claimed by either the child (if the loan is in the child's name) or by the parent.[6]

Summary of Education-related Tax Benefits

As described throughout this chapter, the Income Tax Law provides a variety of tax breaks to promote the social objective of education. These benefits fall into several categories:

1. ***Exclusions from gross income.*** Scholarships and grants used for education, tax-free cancellation of student loans (for specified occupations), and student loan repayment assistance.
2. ***Tax deductions.*** Student loan deduction under Section 80E and miscellaneous deductions.
3. ***Employee benefits.*** These include employee education assistance, employer tax deduction under Section 80C.
4. ***Gift tax exclusion.*** Direct tuition and fee payments made to an accredited educational institution are exempt from gift and generation skipping taxes. There is no limit to the amount of the direct payment.

PLANNING PROCESS

When planning for education many important issues need to be considered. Of course, a financial planner's involvement might focus specifically on helping a client fund the educational needs. If focused on saving for the educational need, a planner would need to know the specific school/university or type of school (public or private, in-state or out-of-state) selected, the intended starting date, and the costs that would be included in the planning assumption (e.g., paying 50 percent of the total tuition over four years for room and board, etc.). Based on the client's objectives and the planner's assumptions of reinvestment rates and annual growth rate in educational expenses, the financial planner can develop a recommended systematic savings plan and also help implement and monitor it.

Some planners offer extensive counseling for funding education. As a specialist in educational funding, a planner could assist his or her client in: establishing reasonable expectations, identifying a "good-match" school, exploring financial aid or merit-based aid, positioning the client so as to optimize the access to financial aid, and planning for the efficient use of available cash flows. At this level of planning engagement, it makes sense to include the child in the conversations. This value-added process involves the following planning steps.

Step 1: *Understand a client's objectives and situation.* The family's financial situation is an important issue. However, that does not constitute the primary concern at the beginning of the discovery process. The reason is that there exist numerous sources of financial aid, including "free money." Matching a student to the right school is generally the first priority. Students who excel in college, particularly during the first year, are positioned for future success.

The discovery process starts by asking a set of pointed questions. What is the child looking for in a school, and what type of career is being considered? A planner would need to understand a child's preferences regarding: school enrollment, location and setting, school culture and mission, learning philosophy, academic programs, graduation rates, extracurricular activities, sports programs, and campus safety. He or she would also need to explore what opportunities are important to the child and parents,

[6] http://www.business-standard.com/article/pf/tax-benefits-for-children-113032300349_1.html (last accessed on November 27, 2014).

including: study abroad programs, internship opportunities, job placement, and alumni networks. As all this information is being collected, a planner would need to clarify which are the "non-negotiables"—those school attributes and student opportunities that must be there, as opposed to merely "nice to have."

Step 2: *Research schools that match student's preference.* There are several online, quantitative search engines, and reference guides that can help identify possible matches.

Step 3: *Consider admission requirements.* Once a manageable subset of schools that matches a student's preferences is identified, it is time to consider the admission requirements. How does a student's grade point average (GPA)/test score and standardized test scores measure as compared to the school's statistics? A useful resource for finding out statistical data is the about.com college admissions webpage.

While the GPA and scores are important, it is good to remember that a school's admission officer generally considers other variables as well. The intent of every school is to admit well-rounded (e.g., leadership and service) students and add to the diversity and quality of the overall student body. Realizing this, a student should not eliminate a school solely on the premise that his or her test score or GPA is below the median.

Step 4: *Research short list of schools.* Now that the vast universe of possible schools has been reduced to a manageable subset, it is time to research each school in detail. A planner needs to check out colleges' websites. Call the admissions offices. Review the schools' histories of awarding financial aid. Research the academic curriculum, student life services, facilities, financial aid statistics, and other pertinent information. Are the images of a school consistent with the look and feel of the university that a student prefers?

Step 5: *Submit applications and receive admittance letters.* The final set of applications should span a number of schools—some of which are near certainties, some highly probable, and others that are "reaches."

Step 6: *Submit application.* After a student is accepted at a college, a financial aid officer sends an aid package describing school grants, loans, and campus work-study programs. At this point, a student needs to submit an application so that the financial need is documented. Schools do not have access to this information until after accepting a student.

Step 7: *Consider all admittance letters and offers of financial assistance.* At this point, the student and family can review all the admissions and offers of financial assistance. After that families can negotiate with the aid officer to substitute grants and work-study programs for loans.

REDUCTION OF COLLEGE DEBTS

While there may be no alternative to incur college debt, as described below, there are several debt-cutting tools available to families.

Two Years at Lower Cost School

Many families consider the option of having their child enrolled for two years at a central school/government college or lower priced school before applying to the higher priced school of choice. This strategy can be very cost-effective.

Tuition at Freshman Rate

With tuition costs escalating at more than 10 percent per year, a tuition freeze could save a family thousands of rupees. Guaranteed tuition plans come in two forms. At some schools, the freshman rate can be fixed through senior year for a fee, but tuition is still paid annually. Other schools allow payment for four years up front, in which case a student locks in the freshman rate.

Tuition Discounts

It is generally a mistake to assume that unless someone has a direct influence on the financial aid officer, an aid application will automatically be rejected. Many schools offer tuition discounts of one form or another. Even families with high income sometimes qualify for low-cost loans and grants.

EDUCATIONAL PLANNING: A REAL-WORLD EXAMPLE

In this section we will present an educational funding plan for the Srivastava family. Anil and Abha Srivastava have two children, Manoj, aged 4, and Sana, aged 1. Recently, the Srivastavas had a discussion with their financial planner, Ramesh Sahu, regarding the steps they should take now to plan for their children's education. Results of this discussion and the plan that followed are presented below.

The process started with the Srivastavas filling out a confidential education funding worksheet (Table 7.3). On the basis of this data, Ramesh developed an education funding plan which is presented in Table 7.4. Since the Srivastavas have already saved ₹5,000 toward Manoj's education, his four-year education would be adequately financed if the Srivastavas invest ₹5,924 per year in an investment portfolio earning an after-tax annual return of 6.2 percent. Ramesh also pointed out (not shown in the table) that the Srivastavas could achieve their goal by making a one-time deposit today of ₹57,764, or making monthly contributions of ₹500 until Manoj enters college. Since for Sana there is no money already on deposit, her education funding would require an annual investment of ₹5,626, or a one-time investment of ₹61,706.

Many advisors use a financial planning software to develop education funding plans. These tools allow planners to quickly assess new scenarios, incorporate new assumptions, and generate user-friendly client reports.

Consider for example, the following scenario. After reviewing the previous work, Anil and Abha hope that Manoj would be accepted at a well-recognized private/public school. They wonder how much savings would be required assuming: a monthly systematic savings discipline, annual current costs of ₹38,500 at a private institution, a college-expense inflation rate of 5 percent, and a more aggressive reinvestment rate of 8 percent. Ramesh could run the manual calculations and engage in the conversation at the next meeting or he could efficiently generate the requested information with the comprehensive software. The following "education savings report" was generated from the education savings calculator in NaviPlan® Premium, a software from Zywave, Inc. This report only took a couple minutes to produce.

Table 7.3 *Confidential Education Funding Worksheet*

Name: Anil and Abha Srivastava

	Manoj	**Sana**
Age	4	1
Age when starting college	18	18
Years of college funding	4	4
Percentage of costs	100% tuition, fees, room and board	100% tuition, fees, room and board
Projected school	In-govt. public university	In-govt. public university
Current annual costs (today)	₹17,131	₹17,131
Inflation assumption	5.6%	5.6%
Current education savings	₹5,000	0
Reinvestment rate assumption	6.2%	6.2%
Contribution strategy	Level payments	Level payment

Table 7.4 *Education Funding Plan (in ₹)*

Manoj				Sana			
Age	**Deposit**	**Tuition**	**Balance**	**Age**	**Deposit**	**Tuition**	**Balance**
			5,000	1	5,626		0
4	5,924		11,602	2	5,626		5,975
5	5,924		18,613	3	5,626		12,320
6	5,924		26,059	4	5,626		19,058
7	5,924		33,966	5	5,626		26,214
8	5,924		42,364	6	5,626		33,814
9	5,924		51,282	7	5,626		41,885
10	5,924		60,753	8	5,626		50,456
11	5,924		70,811	9	5,626		59,559
12	5,924		81,494	10	5,626		69,226
13	5,924		92,838	11	5,626		79,493
14	5,924		104,886	12	5,626		90,396
15	5,924		117,680	13	5,626		101,272
16	5,924		131,268	14	5,626		127,332
17	5,924		145,699	15	5,626		141,201
18		(36,734.79)	115,719	16	5,626		155,930
19		(38,791.94)	81,697	17	5,626		171,572
20		(40,964.29)	43,258	18		(43,258.29)	136,269
21		(43,258.29)	0	19		(45,680.75)	96,205
				20		(48,238.87)	50,940
				21		(50,940.25)	0

EDUCATION SAVINGS REPORT[7]

Objectives

You want to accumulate sufficient assets to fund an education goal of four years at a total cost of ₹38,500 per year, in today's rupees,[8] beginning in the year 2026.

Analysis

Based on our assessment, it appears that you do not have sufficient savings strategies in place to meet your goal.

On the basis of your assumptions, in order to meet your goal beginning in 2012, you need to start saving ₹1,112 per month (indexed at 0.00% annually).

The following graph (Figure 7.2) indicates the total savings required to finance the education goal using a non-qualified savings plan.

Assumption	
Initial Investment	₹5,000
Savings Required (indexed)	₹1,112/month
Return Rate	8.00%
Average Tax Rate	25.00%
Savings Index Rate	0.00%
Education Cost Index Rate	5.00%

[7] This report was produced in NaviPlan® Premium software from Zywave, Inc., presented with permission.

[8] Education costs of ₹38,500 per year for four years (indexed at 5.00% annually) would be equal to a total education cost of ₹328,549.

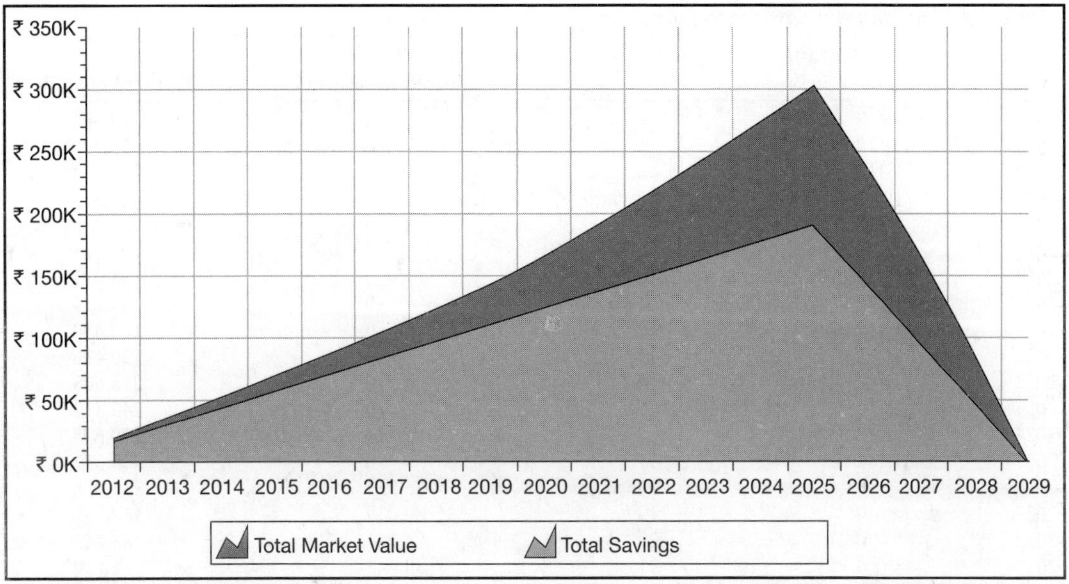

Figure 7.2 *The Total Savings Required to Finance the Education Goal Using a Non-qualified Savings Plan*

Consider the Following

1. Determine realistic values for tuition and related college expenses. Factor in the effects of inflation. College costs have historically increased at a significantly higher rate than inflation.
2. Invest regularly for your children's education, starting as early as possible.
3. Where possible, take advantage of educational savings vehicles.

Education Savings

Table 7.5 shows the monthly savings required for an education goal in 14 years. The monthly savings amount is indexed by 0.00% annually for the entire savings period. The education costs have been indexed by 5.00% annually throughout the entire education goal (including the education withdrawal period).

Case Summary

The education funding plan presented above is only the beginning. Decisions must still be made regarding the selection of investment products, management of educational portfolios, and adjustment of planning parameters as conditions change. Regardless of which method is used, however, there is no substitute for a careful analysis and starting the funding process when the children are relatively young.

Table 7.5 *The Monthly Savings Required for an Education Goal in 14 Years*

Year	Monthly Savings for Student (in ₹)	Student's Age	Total Education Cost (in ₹)	Year End Market Value (in ₹)
2012	1,112	4	0	19,067
2013	1,112	5	0	33,978
2014	1,112	6	0	49,784
2015	1,112	7	0	66,538
2016	1,112	8	0	84,298
2017	1,112	9	0	103,123
2018	1,112	10	0	123,077
2019	1,112	11	0	144,229
2020	1,112	12	0	166,650
2021	1,112	13	0	190,416
2022	1,112	14	0	215,608
2023	1,112	15	0	242,312
2024	1,112	16	0	270,618
2025	1,112	17	0	300,622
2026	0	18	76,227	237,858
2027	0	19	80,039	167,289
2028	0	20	84,041	88,243
2029	0	21	88,243	0

In this chapter, we discussed the key issues relating to educational planning. Over the next three chapters, investments planning will be discussed.

PART 4

INVESTMENT PLANNING

8 Investment Products and Markets: An Introduction

INTRODUCTION

Investment products are issued by the government (central, state, and local), corporations, and other statutory bodies. There are two major types of investment products: equities and fixed-income securities.

In this chapter we undertake a broad review of the basic investment products, the security markets, and the key market indices. In the next chapter we will have a detailed discussion of investment theories and concepts.

Section I: Fixed-income Investments, Preferred Stocks, and Common Stock Investments

FIXED-INCOME INVESTMENTS

Fixed-income investments have a fixed maturity and a fixed payment schedule. Although the legal strength of the promise may vary, sometimes, considerably, bond investors are promised specific payments at predetermined times. The salient features of the key forms of fixed-income investments are presented below.

Savings Accounts

Passbook savings accounts are the most obvious example of fixed-income investments. These accounts (*negotiable order of withdrawal*) are *interest-paying checking* or *check accounts* that restrict the number of check transactions similar to conventional savings accounts and are insured by the Deposit Insurance and Credit Guarantee Corporation (DICGC) up to ₹100,000. A variation of the savings account is the savings flexi account in which the balance in excess of a pre-fixed limit is treated as a fixed deposit.

Post Office Savings Account

Post office savings account is similar to a bank savings account. Interest earned (up to ₹10,000) from this account is tax exempt both for single accounts and joint accounts (if the first holder is the same single account holder). There is no limit to how much can be invested in this account.

Public Provident Fund Scheme

The Public Provident Fund (PPF) Scheme is offered by the government through the post office and selected banks. An individual can open a PPF account with a minimum deposit of ₹500 at the post office or at selected banks. The maximum annual deposit allowed is limited to ₹100,000. The original term of a PPF account is 15 years. After that, the effective period can be extended up to 40 years by way of five-year increments. Deposits in a PPF account are deductible from the taxable income. Currently (2014), a PPF account earns a tax-exempt compound annual interest of 8.7 percent. Interest, however, accumulates inside a PPF account and not paid annually to a subscriber. The accumulation in the PPF account is fully exempt from wealth tax as well. Starting with year six, and terminating in year 15, a PPF account holder is permitted to make one withdrawal every year. Interest earned on a PPF account is totally tax exempt.

National Savings Certificate

National Savings Certificate (NSC) is a government savings scheme issued at the post offices in denominations of ₹100, ₹500, ₹1,000, ₹5,000, and ₹10,000, each with a term of five years. There is no upper contribution limit established for this saving scheme. NSC contributions are deductible from taxable income. In 2011, a new saving instrument titled 10-year National Certificate was issued, effective December 1, 2011. Investment in this certificate can earn 8.4 percent annual interest (compounded semiannually). An investment of up to ₹100,000 made in this vehicle is deductible from taxable income.

Certificates of Deposit

Certificates of Deposit (CDs), a part of the call money market, are available from banks, and savings and loan associations. It requires a minimum deposit of ₹1 lakh and for specified time periods, typically from seven days to three years. The maturity period of a CD issued by a bank is typically from seven days to one year; however, financial institutions can issue CDs with maturities of 1–3 years. The promised rate of interest on a CD is higher than for passbook savings, and the rate increases with the CD's length of maturity. Physical CDs are freely transferable by endorsement and delivery; however, *demated* CDs can be transferred as per the rules applicable to other demat securities.

Incidentally, savers can buy *brokered* CDs from brokerage firms. These CDs are insured by banks or savings and loan associations. These are sold through middlemen, known as brokers, and they receive commissions paid by the issuing institution. Brokered CDs are insured when the issuing bank has the central deposit insurance coverage. Incidentally, post offices also offer Recurring Deposit Accounts which require a monthly investment of a fixed amount. Currently, these Accounts pay an annual interest of 8.5 percent.

Monthly Income Scheme

Quite popular in India, this Scheme carries an annual interest of 8.4 percent and typically has a maturity of five years. This Scheme allows premature payments after the completion of a three-year period.

Time deposit. Post offices offer time deposits with a maturity of one–five years and carry an annual interest of 8 percent.

Fixed deposit with banks. Another popular investment product is the fixed deposit with banks. Its popularity among the savers also rests on the fact that up to 75 percent of the balance can be withdrawn in the form of a loan.

Marketable Government Issues

Marketable issues, which make up more than three-quarters (81.2 percent at the end of March 2013) of the government debt, can be purchased through a dealer, a broker, without bidding for interest rates or through the Reserve Bank of India with bidding. Marketable government securities differ mainly in the length of time to maturity.

Treasury bills. Treasury bills (T-bills) are short-term securities which mature in 91 days (13 weeks), 182 days, and 364 days (52 weeks) from the date of issue. Bills are sold on a discount basis, that is, an investor pays a price lower than the face value and, upon maturity, receives the face value. T-bills are sold in a minimum increment of ₹25,000, in multiples of ₹25,000 available above the minimum, and are auctioned to the highest bidder. Consequently, the T-bill interest rates vary, depending on the amount of bid received for each issue. In both initial offerings and in secondary market trading, T-bills' yields are quoted on a true annualized yield basis. Participating bidders can be either competitive or noncompetitive, the latter submitting only one bid. If not fully subscribed, bids are accepted at the weighted average of the successful bids.

Cash management bills. Cash Management Bills (CMBs) are issued to meet the temporary mismatches in the cash flow of the government. The CMBs have the generic character of T-bills but are issued for maturities of less than 91 days. Like T-bills, they are also issued at a discount and redeemed at the face value at maturity. The settlement of the auction is on T+1 basis.[1] However, these instruments are tradable and qualify for ready forward facility. For statutory liquidity ratio (SLR) purposes, banks also treat investment in CMBs as an eligible investment in government securities.

Certificates of indebtedness. A Certificate of Indebtedness with a term of one year and issued at par value pays a fixed interest, or coupon, rate; the interest rate is printed on the bond and it never changes. The investor collects this interest by cashing in coupons at a bank, post office, or another central office.

Treasury notes and bonds. Treasury notes and bonds are sold at par as long-term investments. Both notes and bonds may be purchased through commercial banks, brokerage firms, or the Reserve Bank of India. Bills, notes, and bonds are liquid investments. Notes are government coupon obligations with an original maturity of 1–10 years; they carry fixed interest rates which are paid semiannually. Bonds are long-term issues with an original maturity of more than 10 years, but no longer than 30 years. Treasury bonds are used to finance the government debt.

Agency issues. Agency issues represent bonds issued by government agencies or public sector undertakings (PSUs) wherein the interest and principal are guaranteed by the central government or one of the state governments. The former includes, among others, the Export-Import Bank, the National Housing Development Corporation, India Infrastructure Finance Corporation of India (IIFCL), National Bank for Agricultural and Rural Development (NABARD), Rural Electrification Corporation (REC), Indian Renewable Energy Development Agency (IREDA), and so on. Government agencies cover a wide spectrum of activities, ranging from financing agricultural industry to providing the funds necessary to satisfy the country's need for homes, develop the nation's infrastructure, and so on. Debt securities issued by the latter agencies, which include banks, financial institutions, and public sector companies and cooperatives, are guaranteed by the government. Most of the activities of these agencies are concentrated in the area of farm credit and housing.

[1] Refers to the settlement date of security transactions and denote that the settlement occurs on a transaction date plus one day.

Nonmarketable Government Issues

The principal and interest on government securities, also known as gilt-edged securities, are guaranteed by the government. These securities can be held as stock certificates, promissory notes, or bearer bonds.

Dated Government Securities

Dated government securities, also known as G-sec, are long-term fixed coupon securities and carry a fixed or floating coupon (interest rate). Based on the face value, interest is paid at fixed time periods (usually semiannually). The term of dated securities can be from 2 to 30 years. The Reserve Bank of India acts as the registry/depository of government securities and deals with the issue and the interest payments as well as repayment of the principal at maturity. Through the medium of auctions, dated securities of both the Government of India and state governments are issued by Reserve Bank of India.

1. ***Floating rate bonds.*** Floating rate bonds are securities which do not have a fixed coupon rate. The coupon is reset at preannounced intervals (say, every six months or one year) by adding a spread over a base rate. In the case of most floating rate bonds issued by the Government of India, the base rate is the weighted average cutoff yield of the last three 364-day T-bill auctions preceding the coupon reset date. The spread is decided through the auction.

2. ***Zero-coupon bonds.*** Zero-coupon bonds are bonds with no coupon (interest) payments. Like T-bills, these are issued at discounted face value.

3. ***Bonds with call/put options.*** Bonds can also be issued with features of optionality. This means that, during the life of the bond, an issuer has the option to buy it back (call option) from an investor, while the investor has the option to sell it (put option) to the issuer.

Special Securities

In addition to T-bills and dated securities issued by the Government of India under the market borrowing program, as a substitute for making compensation payments in cash, the Government of India issues special securities to entities such as Oil Marketing Companies, Fertilizer Companies, and the Food Corporation of India. These are usually long-dated securities, carrying coupons with a spread of about 20–25 basis points over the yield of the dated securities of comparable maturity.

State Development Loans

State Development Loans (SDLs) are debt securities issued by the state governments. SDLs are dated securities issued through an auction similar to the ones conducted for dated securities issued by the central government. The Interest Scheme is serviced at half-yearly intervals and the principal is repaid on the maturity date. Like dated securities issued by the central government, SDLs issued by the state governments qualify for SLR. They are also eligible as collateral both for borrowing through market repo and borrowing by eligible entities from the Reserve Bank under the liquidity adjustment facility (LAF).

Inflation-protection Securities

Inflation-protection securities are primarily issued to protect against a decline in the currency value due to inflation. The value of these securities is linked to a benchmark index, fluctuations in which will cause the security value to fluctuate.

Capital-indexed Bonds

As a hedge against inflation, principals of these bonds are linked to an accepted inflation index. All bonds, and especially long-term bonds, can lose a substantial portion of the purchasing power due to inflation, and capital-indexed bonds provide a viable solution for the inflation risk problem.

The inflation protection is provided by adjusting the principal amount of the security according to variations in the inflation rate, and the semiannual interest payment is calculated based on the adjusted principal amount. The inflation-adjusted principal amount is paid at maturity.

Like interest income from other direct obligations of the government, interest income from Inflation Indexed Bonds (IIBs), called Treasury Inflation-protected Securities (TIPS) in the US; is taxed by the central government, but is generally exempt from state and local taxes.

A unique characteristic of these types of securities is that any adjustment of the principal amount is considered currently taxable "interest" income. For instance, if the bondholder has ₹30 of taxable interest income from the bond for the first year and receives ₹20 of interest in cash, then the difference of ₹10 is treated as inflation adjustment to the principal amount.

Municipal Bonds

Municipal bonds are issued by state or political subdivisions, such as municipalities, airports authorities, port trust, school districts, cities, towns, and villages, and also by state agencies. In general, interest paid on municipal bonds is exempt from both central and local income taxes within the state of issue. Principal and interest payments on these bonds are guaranteed by the issuing authority. Municipal bonds can be grouped into two broad categories: *general obligation* and *revenue* bonds.

General obligation bonds. General obligation bonds are backed by full faith, credit, and taxing power of the issuing government unit. An investor can buy state issues backed by the state government, city bonds backed by the municipality, or various other bonds backed by local government entities.

Revenue bonds. Revenue bonds are strictly dependent on the revenue from the project being financed to make the interest and principal payments. These include sewer and water bonds as well as bonds sold to finance bridges, tunnels, toll roads, airports, and hospitals.

Investors can also invest in other types of revenue bonds. For instance, *special tax bonds* are payable from the proceeds of a special tax, such as tax on gasoline, liquor, or tobacco. Local school bonds are another good example. When these issues are backed by full faith, credit, and taxing power of the issuing authority, they become general obligation bonds.

Public Sector Undertaking Bonds

PSU bonds are mainly of two types: taxable bonds and tax-free bonds. Tax-free bonds are issued with the approval of the Ministry of Finance, Government of India. PSU tax-free bonds are transferable by mere endorsement and delivery, and on transfer, stamp duty is not applicable. These bonds are traded on the stock exchanges.

Other bonds. Sometimes local governments issue bonds for financing development projects or meet similar goals. Industrial development bonds, for example, fund facilities for private businesses expected to spur development in economically challenged areas. Also, some states issue baccalaureate bonds, which are zero-coupon bonds sold at a discount to help people save money to pay for their children's in-state college education.

Corporate Bonds

Corporate bonds are issued by public limited companies and are either listed or unlisted. These are loan obligations of the issuing companies, and each bond carries a fixed interest for the life of the bond. Payment of interest, treated by the bond issuer as a tax-deductible expenditure, is guaranteed even when the company reports a loss.

Debenture is a type of debt instrument that is not secured by physical assets or collaterals. These bonds are backed only by the general creditworthiness and reputation of an issuer. A debenture can be convertible, partly convertible, or nonconvertible.

At regular intervals, creditors and corporate bondholders receive interest payments from the issuing firm (even when the firm reports a loss) and the repayment of the principal upon maturity. Also, in the case of business failure or liquidation, bondholders must be repaid before equity holders can receive any payment.

Types of Corporate Bonds

Some corporate bonds carry special features and privileges, while others are distinguishable by the type of security pledged against bond repayment. Bonds can be *secured* or *unsecured*. With a secured bond, an issuer reinforces its promise to pay to the bondholders the interest and principal by pledging specific property as collateral. In the case of an unsecured bond, no such collateral is pledged and the issuer merely promises to pay the stated interest and principal. There are several types of secured and unsecured bonds.

1. ***Debentures.*** A debenture is an unsecured bond, backed only by the faith and general credit of an issuing company. The only difference between *subordinated* or *junior* debentures and regular debentures is that the former holders are paid after regular debenture holders have received their payment.

2. ***Guaranteed bonds.*** A guaranteed bond has its interest, principal, or both guaranteed by a company other than an issuer. The railroad industry uses this type of bond when larger railroads, leasing sections of track owned by small railroads, guarantee the bonds of the smaller railroads.

3. ***Mortgage bonds.*** A mortgage bond is a debt obligation secured by a mortgage on property. The value of the property may or may not equal the value of the mortgage bond issued against it. Because these securities are usually issued by giant utility companies, they make up a major segment of the corporate bond market.

4. ***Convertible bonds.*** These debt instruments may be exchanged by the owner for common stock or another security—usually of the same company—in accordance with the terms and exchange ratios for the issue identified in the original issue. Any of the previously listed types of bonds could be convertible, although most convertible bonds are either debentures or subordinated debentures.

5. ***Callable bonds.*** A callable bond has a set maturity date, but it can be redeemed by an issuer at specified periods after sufficient notice has been given to the bondholders. The call feature is stated in the original offering prospectus. The callability feature of this type of bond is likely to be exercised when current market rates drop below the coupon rate.

Junk Bonds

Corporate bonds rated below BB+ by Cooperative for Assistance and Relief Everywhere (CARE), BB or below by Credit Rating Information Services of India Limited (CRISIL) are classified as *junk bonds*, compared to the higher rated bonds known as investment quality bonds. The connotation *junk* comes from the investment community's belief that, under unfavorable economic conditions, market prices of such bonds will significantly drop, producing at least a paper loss.

Junk bonds should not be confused with deep discount bonds. The latter sell at discount prices because they carry a low coupon rate. By contrast, junk bonds sell well below par because they carry substantial default risk. Clearly, junk bonds offer a higher yield, reflecting the degree of default risk they carry.

Zero-coupon Bonds

These bonds offer no periodic interest payments, are sold at a discount from their face value, and gradually increase in value representing interest income as they approach maturity. Yield to maturity is based solely on the difference between the initial investment and the amount received upon sale or maturity. These bonds do not pay interest on a semiannual basis. However, a bondholder is required to pay taxes on the imputed annual interest as if the payments were actually received.

Bond Ratings

The three Indian key bond-rating agencies are CRISIL, ICRA, and CARE. In addition, there is also a foreign rating agency known as Fitch (Dull and Phelps). The highest quality bonds are rated AAA, while the lowest grade bonds have the rating of D. The higher is the rating of a bond, the lower is its default risk, and the lower is the default risk premium associated with it.

As a general rule, in rating bonds, the agencies take into consideration five major factors: (a) the level and trend of fixed charge coverage, (b) company's long-term debt-to-equity ratio, (c) company's liquidity position, (d) significance of the company in the industry, and (e) nature (secured versus unsecured) of the specific debt issue.

Warrants and Rights

Warrants and rights are related to both stocks and bonds. These represent neither the ownership nor the debt of the issuing company. Warrants and rights only represent the privilege of purchasing a specified corporate security at a particular price within a specified time. However, the ownership of these instruments is of temporary, rather than of continuous, interest.

Warrants

Warrants allow a holder to purchase a corporate security—usually common stock—at a given price within a specific period of time, which may be finite or indefinite. A company may issue warrants to shareholders or creditors as an inducement to purchase these securities when a new stock or bond issue is released. Generally, warrants begin trading on stock exchanges after the security has been issued.

Rights

Unlike warrants, rights have very short expiration dates, generally extending between 2 and 10 weeks. Rights to purchase a common stock are often given to shareholders when additional stock is issued. Shareholders are then entitled to purchase more stock in proportion to their current holdings in order to maintain their existing percentage equity in the firm.

Secured Premium Notes

A relatively new comer to the Indian capital market is nonconvertible debentures bonds (NCD) with an attached warrant. Each warrant holder has the right to buy for cash one equity share for ₹100 per share. This right must be exercised during the period of 1–1½ years from the right's date of issue. After 1½ years, the secured premium notes (SPN) is fully paid up.

Commercial Paper

A commercial paper is a short-term unsecured money market instrument issued by corporations, primary dealers, and financial institutions according to the guidelines set by the Reserve Bank of India. Maturity of commercial papers varies from seven days to one year. This paper is generally issued at a discount and is redeemed at par.

Any corporation is authorized to issue a commercial paper if it meets the following criteria: (a) the tangible net worth of the company is at least ₹4 crore, (b) the company meets the working capital requirements applicable to financial institutions, and (c) the borrower account of the company is classified as *standard asset* by financing bank institutions.

PREFERRED STOCK

Preferred stock (or preference share) mirrors a fixed-income security because the yearly payment in the form of dividend is stipulated either as a coupon (e.g., 5 percent of the face value) or as a stated rupee amount. However, this type of security is junior, or subordinate, to all bonds issued by the company. Preferred stockholders do not generally participate in company management, and they have no voting rights like those enjoyed by common stockholders (equity shareholders). It should be noted that the payment of dividend is not mandatory even if the company makes a profit. The dividend is always paid as part of the paid-up capital.

There are different types of preferred stock available in the market. If the stock is *cumulative*, the claim to dividends may be carried over from one year to the next; if the company falls behind in dividend payments, it must make these delinquent dividend payments before paying dividends to the common stockholders. Another variety, called *convertible preferred stock*, carries a contractual clause entitling the holder to exchange it for shares of common stock of the same company within a specified period. A third type is called *participating preferred stock*. Unlike typical preferred stockholders, a participating preferred stockholder not only receives dividends, but also shares additional earnings with the common stockholders. Finally, many preferred stocks are *callable*, and the issuing company has the right to redeem them at a prespecified "call price" within a specific number of years after they are issued.

COMMON STOCK

Key Features

Common stockholders (or equity shareholders) have equity in the corporation, and they are usually the only group who can participate in the increased earnings via an increase in the stock value. Equity shareholders are first to contribute toward the capital of the company and the last to receive income in the form of dividend. The main reason for investing in equities is to have the privilege of participating in the price appreciation of the underlying stock. These stockholders are not personally liable for debts incurred by the corporation, but in the event of business failure or liquidation, they are the last group entitled to receive any payment from the company. They do, however, retain residual rights to any assets that may remain after all the creditors have been paid. Owners of common stock are entitled to participate in the management of the enterprise by way of voting to elect directors and approving specified changes in the company's charter.

Types of Stock

Generally, investors divide common stocks into a set of traditional classifications, namely blue chips, growth stocks, value stocks, income stocks, and so on. These are discussed next.

1. ***Blue chips.*** Blue chip stocks are high-grade investment quality stocks issued by major companies which have long unbroken record of earnings and dividend payments. Usually, these companies hold important, if not leading, positions in their industries, and can weather economic downturns and post strong earnings gains during upturns since they have the resources to capitalize on a recovery.
2. ***Non-blue chip.*** These stocks include all stocks not classified as blue chips. In some cases, stocks may be issued by established companies with impressive earnings records and excellent future prospects. However, the company may lack the size, corporate resources, or industry position that many consider necessary to qualify the stock as a blue chip.

   Under these broad general categories that divide thousands of stocks, equities can be further classified according to other investment features. None of these classifications are mutually exclusive; it is, therefore, possible for some stocks to fall under one or more of the following types.
3. ***Growth company stocks.*** Growth company stocks are shares in companies that exhibit above-average and accelerated growth of earnings. These companies typically pay only a small portion of earning in dividends, because they can maintain or accelerate their growth by reinvesting earnings in the business.
4. ***Value stocks.*** These stocks are shares that are assumed to be selling below their true worth, given their existing operations, future growth prospects, or current assets. There are several measures of value: these stocks trade at a below-market multiple to earnings, sales, cash flow, or book value. Investing in value stocks was popularized by Graham–Dodd in the 1940s, and more recently by Warren Buffett.
5. ***Large-cap, mid-cap and small-cap stocks.*** Another popular category is based on the size of the issuing company, usually measured by its market capitalization, that is, the total value of all outstanding shares of the company's common stock. Based on size, stocks are divided into three categories: large cap, mid cap, and small cap. While there is no exact definition of large cap, the term usually refers to companies with market capitalization exceeding ₹20,000 crore. These are the biggest companies in the investment universe and are usually household names. Large-cap stocks are shares of large companies whose common stock is widely owned by many individuals and institutions, such as the stocks included in the extensively used Standard & Poor's Bombay Stock Exchange (S&P BSE) Index. Mid-cap stocks are shares of companies that fall between large-cap and small-cap companies, with a market capitalization between ₹5,000 crore and ₹20,000 crore. Small-cap stocks are shares of smaller companies with a market capitalization between ₹1,000 crore and ₹5,000 crore.
6. ***Cyclical company stocks.*** Cyclical company stocks are shares of companies whose earnings are accentuated by business cycles. When a certain industry prospers, earnings of the cyclical companies associated with that industry also register significant growth. Likewise, when the course of that industry changes direction, the associated cyclical companies suffer earnings setbacks and adversities.
7. ***Defensive stocks.*** On the other end of the spectrum are the recession-resistant stocks, commonly known as defensive stocks. These companies sell products and services the demand for which does not materially fluctuate with the business cycle. Familiar examples of recession-resistant industries are those involved with health care, food, utilities, and cosmetics.
8. ***Income stocks.*** Income stocks are characteristic of those firms that pay a high dividend relative to their stock prices. The dividend yields on these securities are above average for stocks and frequently are competitive with the returns on debt instruments. People invest in income stocks like utility stocks primarily for their current yield, and not for their potential for price appreciation.
9. ***Speculative stocks.*** Investors in speculative stocks assume a high degree of risk in the hope of realizing significant returns on this investment. To be sure, all stocks, including blue chips, have

the potential for generating a short-term profit. However, speculative stocks generally refer to electronics, biotech, and other types of technological stocks that can widely fluctuate on a short-term basis and that are perceived to have a much greater potential for delivering short-term profits.

10. ***Unlisted stocks.*** Unlisted equities are common stocks and other securities that are not listed on organized (Bombay Stock and National Stock) exchanges. Instead, these securities are traded *over-the-counter* (OTC). Sometimes they are referred to as *pink-sheet stocks* referring to the time when their listings were printed on pink paper. These stocks are far more difficult to analyze and trade than other stocks, and hence are regarded as high-risk investments.

11. ***Penny stocks.*** Penny stocks are high-risk stocks, selling for less than ₹10 per share. These stocks generally represent shares of young companies with short histories or companies that for various reasons are experiencing difficult times. Frequently, penny stocks are considered illiquid investments.

12. ***Miscellaneous stocks.*** In recent years a number of new instruments have been added to the capital market, each satisfying a special need of the progressively more sophisticated investing public. Here is a list of these instruments: (a) nonvoting shares, (b) detachable equity warrants, (c) participating debentures, (d) participating preference shares, (e) convertible debentures with options, (f) debt–equity swaps, and (g) Dutch Auction Notes. It is beyond our scope to discuss these instruments in detail in this text. However, information on these instruments can be obtained from any standard investment textbooks.

Section II: Mutual Funds

INTRODUCTION

A mutual fund is a corpus created by the contribution of individual investors. Mutual funds are designed to attract funds from a variety of investors and use them for financing many productive investments. In recent years, mutual funds have been sponsored by many organizations, including banks, insurance companies, private sector financial institutions, and individuals. Mutual funds operate within the framework of Securities and Exchange Board of India (SEBI) regulations which prescribe the mechanism for getting a mutual fund registered, laying out its constitution and duties, and specifying its duties and responsibilities. The Association of Mutual Funds in India is a self-regulatory organization that sets the standards of governance cf mutual fund players.

Mutual funds are companies through which investors pool their assets. It is a fast, and easy way for investors to create comprehensive investment portfolios. These funds sell their own shares to the public and invest the proceeds into a variety of investment securities.

A mutual fund manages its shareholders' investments with a view to achieve a stated objective. Specific objectives include: stocks for capital appreciation, bonds for regular income, and a mixture of stocks and bonds for both growth and income. In sharp contrast to individual money management firms, the universe of mutual funds is open to anyone with money to invest. Typically, the price of admission to a mutual fund is ₹5,000.

CLOSED-END VERSUS OPEN-END FUNDS

Most mutual funds are open-end type, since they create additional shares whenever people want to invest in them. Each afternoon, these funds calculate the total value of their investments and determine the price of a share—called the net asset value (NAV)—by dividing the total investment value by the number of fund shares outstanding. Investors can buy shares from the fund at NAV and sell them back to the fund at NAV as well. In sharp contrast, a closed-end mutual fund issues a fixed number of shares, which like typical stocks are traded through a broker on the stock exchange. So, the market price of a closed-end fund share could conceivably be higher or lower than the fund's NAV, depending on the relative demand and supply for that stock. A closed-end fund stock purchased for less than its NAV is said to be selling at "a discount;" if a higher price is paid, then it is said to be selling at "a premium." Closed-end funds do not have to buy back their shares from investors the way open-end funds do; hence, these funds can pursue their long-term investment strategies with greater efficiency.

ADVANTAGES OF FUND INVESTMENT

Every mutual fund, regardless of its objective, offers investors at least three advantages, as follows:

1. ***Diversification.*** Each rupee invested in a mutual fund buys an interest in its entire portfolio. That portfolio usually contains the stocks or bonds of a large number of companies.
2. ***Professional portfolio management.*** The fund's manager, supported by a staff of investment analysts, professionally manages the investment portfolio, making continuous buy-sell-hold decisions, taking into account the market's behavior and always in keeping with the fund's objective.
3. ***Liquidity.*** Majority of mutual funds issue new shares and redeem existing shares on demand. The share price of a load mutual fund is the NAV (the current market value of the fund's investments divided by the number of shares outstanding) plus sales charges. Funds with no sales or redemption charges are called *no-load* funds.

TYPES OF FUNDS

Funds of all shapes, sizes, and colors abound; however, the main categories consist of equity funds, fixed-income funds, balanced funds, and money market funds. Most equity funds lean toward one of two basic styles of investing: Value funds favor buying stocks trading at bargain prices and selling them when the prices have risen to their intrinsic value. By contrast, rather than focusing on prices, growth funds like to invest in companies whose earnings are experiencing significant growth, even when these stocks have already risen in value. As their name implies, fixed-income funds buy interest-paying bonds issued by both private companies, and federal and state governments. Balanced funds invest in a combination of both stocks and bonds. Finally, similar to savings accounts in banks, money market funds are essentially parking places for cash.

Within these broad categories, mutual funds can be differentiated on the basis of their investment objectives and potential for volatility. These are described next.

Aggressive Growth Funds

Aggressive growth funds invest mostly in small company stocks that provide low current income (because they reinvest their profits in their businesses) but have the potential for rapid growth and capital appreciation. However, the downside is that these funds provide low stability of the principal since the stocks in which they invest generally experience wide price swings.

Aggressive growth funds generally carry higher risks because they make a concerted effort to secure more pronounced growth of the principal. Hence, these funds are not suitable for *risk-averse* investors or those who need their investment to produce current income.

Growth Funds

Growth funds invest in more matured, established companies to achieve long-term growth; hence, they are assumed to be more conservative than aggressive growth funds. Also, these funds do not invest in less stable, smaller companies, which provide substantial gains over the short term but also carry with them the risk of significant declines. Growth funds are not suitable for investors who are unable to assume market risks or are dependent on investment income.

International/Global Funds

International funds strive to realize significant investment growth through investments in companies outside India. By contrast, global funds invest in securities around the world, including India. Both types provide investors with an opportunity to further diversify their mutual fund portfolio, especially since foreign markets do not always move in tandem with the Indian market. While these two types of funds offer opportunities for growth and diversification, they also carry currency and other related risks, and are, therefore, not suitable for risk-averse investors.

Growth and Income Funds

Growth and income funds seek both long-term growth of capital and current income. At one end of the spectrum, some of these funds invest in a combination of growth stocks, stocks paying high dividends, preferred stocks, corporate bonds, and money market instruments. At the other end are those that invest in growth stocks and generate current income by selling options. These funds are suitable for investors who can assume some risk but also want a moderate level of current income.

Fixed-income (Bond) Funds

The goal of fixed-income (bond) funds is to provide high current income while at the same time preserving the capital. For the sake of safety, bond funds invest primarily in government and corporate bonds, and preferred stocks. However, since bond prices do fluctuate with changing interest rates, these funds do carry interest rate risk.

As compared to money market funds, fixed-income funds offer a higher level of current income but a lower stability of principal. Within the fixed-income category, funds vary greatly both in terms of stability of the principal and in their ability to generate current income. High yield funds, which seek to maximize income by investing in lower-rated, or junk, bonds of longer maturities, entail less stability of principal than fixed-income funds which invest in higher-grade bonds but offer lower coupon rates.

Balanced/Equity Income Funds

The main objective of balanced/equity income funds is to generate current income by investing primarily in stocks paying large dividends. Since stocks are generally more volatile than bonds, these funds are less stable than fixed-income funds. Balanced and equity income funds are suitable for conservative investors who want current income with limited growth of principal.

Specialty/Sector Funds

Specialty/sector funds invest in securities of specific industries or sectors such as health care, high technology, leisure, utilities, and precious metals. Since each specialty fund invests primarily in one sector, these funds do not protect investors from risk the way regular mutual funds do. However, sector funds do provide the opportunity to diversify among several companies within an industry, such as the computer industry or the service industry.

Asset Allocation Funds

Asset allocation funds allocate their funds between stocks, bonds, and cash in predetermined proportions. Often included in this category are the new life-cycle funds, which do a much better job of providing one-stop shopping than traditional balanced funds.

It is apropos to add a word of caution. A number of the "so-called" asset allocation funds are either market timers or market timers in drag, and for that reason are unsuitable for serious long-term investors. However, the legitimate asset allocation funds do tend to move funds between stock, bond, and money market instruments in response to the fund managers' view of the relative market prospect. These funds are, therefore, suitable for investors who can tolerate some risk, are seeking capital appreciation, and are not seeking high levels of income.

Money Market Funds

For a cautious investor, money market funds provide a very high stability of principal while seeking a moderate to high current income. They invest in highly liquid, virtually risk-free, short-term debt securities of agencies of the government, banks, corporations, and T-bills. These funds have no potential for capital appreciation.

Index Funds

Long ignored or disparaged, index funds are the investment community's ugly ducklings. These funds buy and hold groups of stocks that mimic the performance of a noted market yardstick like the S&P BSE 500-Stock Index. While that is not a prescription for excitement, index funds do hold their course regardless of the currents that send high-flying funds soaring or diving. Also, advantages of investing in these funds include both low operating costs and lower annual taxes because their holdings are not traded so frequently.

READING A MUTUAL FUND PROSPECTUS

Before making an investment decision, every investor should examine the fund's goals and objectives and the ability of its management to carry them out. Additionally, one must evaluate the services provided by the fund and the costs of such services.

A wealth of information is contained in the fund's prospectus which, by law, must be furnished to all potential investors before a purchase application can be accepted by the fund. In the following paragraphs, we will discuss statements of investment objectives and policies, risk factors, investment restrictions, costs and fees, and other miscellaneous information contained in a mutual fund prospectus.

Investment Objectives and Policies

Mutual funds can be classified into various categories according to their objectives.

1. ***Capital gains or growth funds.*** These cater to the needs of those investors who prefer future long-term capital gains over immediate dividend income. Their investments are largely made in established companies that have demonstrated the ability to expand faster than the nation's economy.

2. ***Income funds.*** These basically favor securities with above-average, current income potential, although growth possibilities are not completely ruled out. Since their objective is to select stocks

with high and stable dividend payments, income funds offer greater price stability than capital gains and growth funds.

3. ***Growth and income funds.*** These invest to realize a combination of capital gains and current income. However, some funds seek income as their primary objective and growth as a secondary aim, while others seek to maintain an even balance between the two. Funds seeking both growth and income generally invest in a more broadly diversified group of securities than those that concentrate on generating current income.
4. ***Index funds.*** These are designed to match the performance of a key stock market index. These funds operate under the notion that matching the selected market average will produce better long-term results than would be the efforts of money managers who try to beat the market. An example of an index fund relates to the situation where the portfolio manager attempts to match the S&P BSE 500 Index.
5. ***Balanced funds.*** These hold bonds and preferred stocks in addition to common stocks in order to minimize market risk.

The important characteristics of objectives for various types of mutual funds are presented in the accompanying boxed insert.

Risk Factors

An important section contained in every prospectus deals with the risks fund managers plan to assume. For instance, one prospectus may specify that in seeking capital appreciation it will purchase stocks of small companies trading on OTC Exchange of India market which have a history of greater price volatility than the stocks of more mature companies. Another prospectus may declare: "We expect to be fully invested in stocks under most market conditions." A third prospectus may caution that the fund deals in call and put options. These statements should be taken into account in determining the riskiness of the fund.

Investment Restrictions

Besides determining the riskiness of a fund, it is also important to note the investment restrictions imposed on the fund as well. Of course, every prospectus contains the usual investment restrictions imposed by the SEBI (mutual funds) Regulations, 1996. But in addition, it may also impose other restrictions on the portfolio managers. A list of typical restrictions includes the following.

1. The fund will not indulge in short selling.
2. It will not purchase securities on margin.
3. Its assets will be diversified so no more than 7.5 percent of the total is invested in a single industry group.
4. It will not borrow more than 3 percent of the total assets for meeting emergencies.

It is worth noting that many funds have left these restrictions wide open.

Past Performance

Mutual funds generally compare their five-year track record with S&P BSE 500 Index or the Industrial Average. In addition, the prospectus reveals such important data as the ratio of expenses to average net assets and the portfolio turnover rate. While past performance does not guarantee future performance, a good track record is certainly an attractive feature of any fund. Also, a low ratio of expenses to average net assets of up to 1 percent and a moderate portfolio turnover rate (say, 30–40 percent) might demonstrate that the fund is being efficiently run.

CHARACTERISTICS OF SELECTED MUTUAL FUNDS

Type		Characteristics
Aggressive growth	Key strength:	Growth potential in rising sectors and markets
	Main weakness:	High vulnerability to slumps
	Investor profile:	Risk takers who won't need cash for at least three years
Growth	Key strength:	Long-term growth
	Main weakness:	Slight protection from market drops
	Investor profile:	Long-term investors who want capital growth with roughly market level risk
Value	Key strength:	Buy out-of-favor stocks not widely followed or recommended by analysts
	Main weakness:	Upturns in performance may not occur and may take considerable time for the market to recognize value, because they may be temporarily out-of-favor with investors
	Investor profile:	Contrarians, investors who desire low P/E, low price-to-book value
Total return	Key strength:	Comparatively steady gains in variety of market conditions
	Main weakness:	Tepid results in high times
	Investor profile:	Risk averse investors looking for capital growth and moderate income
International	Key strength:	Can outpace Indian stocks
	Main weakness:	Vulnerable to currency fluctuations
	Investor profile:	Growth investors who want diversity
Gold	Key strength:	Gains not dependent on Indian stock market
	Main weakness:	More ups and downs, government policy
	Investor profile:	Investors who want to hedge against inflation
Bond fixed income	Key strength:	Dependable monthly income
	Main weakness:	Rising interest rates can zap principal
	Investor profile:	Income seekers and equity investors looking for diversity

MUTUAL FUND FEES AND EXPENSES

Understanding mutual fund fees and its impact on investment decisions is the key to successful investing in mutual funds. Table 8.1 presents details of mutual fund fees and charges. It should be added, however, that fund charges are but one of several variables that should be considered in making mutual fund investment decisions. Other factors to be considered include: the fund's long-term performance, its investment style, the strength of the management team, its risk volatility profile, and additional features and services offered by a fund.

Load or Sales Charges

All load mutual funds charge a load in the form of a fee or sales commission on the sale of their shares. There are two kinds of loads: front-end load and back-end load. As the names imply, the front-end load charge is an up-front fee whereas a back-end load is charged when the shares are sold. No-load funds do not charge either the front-end or the back-end load. The front-end load (entry load) can be up to 2.5 percent, whereas the back-end load (exit load) is usually much lower, ranging from 0 to 3 percent.

Table 8.1 *Mutual Fund Charges*

Front-end load. An initial sales expense (up to 2.5 percent) that is charged before the shares are purchased. Some of this money goes to managing the fund but most of it goes to paying sales commission.	**Exit fee.** A charge to cash in any shares of the fund. It is usually a flat rate or one to two percent of the proceeds.
Back-end load. A deduction taken from the proceeds of the sale of shares. The percentage charged usually decreases as the length of time over which shares are held increases.	**Managing fee.** Used to cover costs like salaries, expense, and so on.
Re-load. A charge to reinvest the gain and/or cash dividends.	**52 (4) and 52 (6).** Used to cover advertising, commission, and other costs.
	Transfer fee. A charge to switch from one fund in the company to another. It is usually 0.5–1 percent.

Most investors naively assume that, based on cost considerations, no-load funds are always more preferable to load funds. That is not a valid assumption. If after deducting the load, a load fund consistently delivers superior returns, it makes perfect sense to consider paying that load.

Management Fees and Operating Expenses

All mutual funds—both load and no-load—charge management fees and operating expenses. These expenses represent compensation to portfolio managers for managing fund portfolios and to others for providing administrative services, such as maintaining shareholder records and furnishing shareholder statements and reports. These fees are reflected in fund's share prices and are not charged directly to shareholders. The fees charged by an asset management company area are as follows: 1.25 percent of net assets up to ₹100 crore and 1 percent of net assets above ₹100 crore. However, in the case of no-load funds, an asset management company is also entitled to charge, during each financial year up to 1 percent of the average weekly outstanding net assets. The annual management fees and operating expenses relating to average weekly net asset are as follows:

1. Up to ₹100 crore : 2.50 percent
2. From ₹101 crore to ₹300 crore : 2.25 percent
3. From ₹301 crore to ₹500 crore : 2.00 percent
4. Above ₹500 crore : 1.75 percent

52 (4) and 52 (6) Fees

The SEBI allows mutual funds to charge additional fees to help them recover the cost of promoting and selling fund shares. Most load funds (and a few no-load funds) charge an annual fee of up to 0.75 percent to recover their sales costs. Mutual funds can also tack on an additional 0.25 percent to cover the cost of shareholder assistance and account maintenance.

Redemption Fees

Some funds charge a fee even when shares of one fund are exchanged for shares of another from the same company. Other funds may charge a fee only when fund shares are liquidated and the proceeds are mailed to an investor. That is, at redemption, the investor may be charged a redemption or exchange fee, or may have to pay a back-end sales charge known as contingent deferred sales charge (CDSC). The difference between the two is important.

A redemption or exchange fee is often returned to the fund itself, rather than to the management company. This arrangement benefits long-term investors in the fund because they are not paying the transaction costs attributable to investors who are getting in and out of the fund on a trading basis. By contrast, a CDSC goes to the management company to pay sales commission. An asset management company is entitled to levy a CDSC not exceeding 4 percent of the redemption proceeds during the first year, 3 percent in the second year, 2 percent in the third year, and finally 1 percent in the fourth year and becomes zero upon the completion of four years from the date of investment.

Trustee Fees

Every mutual fund is governed by an independent board. In order to find out how advisors are compensated, one should consult the prospectus supplement—the Statement of Additional Information—which breaks down the costs that make up the *other* expenses.

EXPENSE RATIO

Mutual funds express their fees in the form of expense ratios. This ratio is calculated by dividing the fund's total operating expenses (salaries, research expenses, telecommunications, shareholder statements, check processing, tax reporting, and other costs of keeping the fund running) by total money under management. Thus, a fund with ₹1 crore in assets and ₹120,000 in operating expenses will have an expense ratio of 1.2 percent (₹120,000/₹10,000,000). A fund publishes its net return in the financial press after netting out these expenses. So a fund with a 1.2 percent expense ratio must earn 11.2 percent (10 percent + 1.2 percent) in order to deliver a 10 percent net return. By contrast, a fund with an expense ratio of 0.5 percent would need to earn only 10.5 percent to generate the same 10 percent net return. This means that the higher the ratio, the better the fund manager has to perform to generate a stated return.

Lock-in Period

Lock-in period refers to the time period during which an investment made in a scheme cannot be withdrawn. For mutual funds, a lock-in period of three years applies to the equity-linked savings schemes.

FEE REDUCTION STRATEGIES

There are a number of systematic ways of reducing mutual fund fees and expenses. These are discussed next.

Select Right Asset Class

An investor should select the share class that charges the lowest fees for the expected holding period. For example, if Class B shares of ABC Mutual Fund have a back load of 6 percent, which disappears after five years, and the investor plans to hold this fund at least for five years, the back load can be avoided altogether by investing in B shares.

Take Advantage of Fund Break

Load mutual funds generally offer significant break points for large purchases of shares. For instance, a typical load mutual fund may offer the following breaks (Table 8.2):

Table 8.2 *Breaks that a Load Mutual Fund May Offer*

Investment	Load
Less than ₹50,000	5.5%
Between ₹50,000 and less than ₹100,000	5.0%
Between ₹100,000 and less than ₹250,000	3.5%
Between ₹250,000 and less than ₹500,000	2.5%
Between ₹500,000 and less than ₹1,000,000	2.0%
Over ₹1,000,000	None

So, it pays to pool the available resources to take advantage of the break-point reduction in loads.

Sign Letter of Intent

If an investor plans to invest ₹100,000 over time but the initial investment amount is limited to ₹60,000, a *letter of intent* can be signed that promises to invest the balance over the next 12 months. On the strength of that letter, the fund would charge a lower load of 3.5 percent on the entire investment. However, in the event the investor is unable to invest additional money (₹40,000) during the expected time period, the mutual fund would merely recalculate a load of 5 percent on the initial ₹60,000 investment.

Time Liquidation

If an investor originally purchased a fund that had a back load, it may pay to hold that fund until the back load disappears, or is drastically reduced. Of course, the risk of holding the fund too long should be weighed against the benefit of reducing or eliminating the back-end load.

Invest Fund Distributions

Most mutual funds permit the reinvestment of dividend and capital gain distributions without charging a load or investment fees. This reinvestment of distributions on a no-load basis can significantly add to the value of the portfolio.

Consolidate Investments

Sometimes mutual funds offer break points based upon *all the purchases* of funds in the family. If a person wishes to invest ₹10 lakh inheritance among four of ABC Fund's load funds, then a load of 3 percent per fund would have to be paid. However, if the fund accepts it as a single ₹10 lakh investment, this investment would qualify for a no-load status, saving a huge sum of money.

Utilize Group Discounts

Participants in a corporate Central Provident Fund (CPF) plan are sometimes allowed to apply the company discount to their own retirement account or taxable account. A fund may also allow a discount if the person belongs to a company retirement plan, church, or an investment club. Finally, where *flesh* and *blood* discounts are permitted, the fund may add up investments of all the family members in order to give everyone the break-point advantage.

Find a Seller

If an investor can find a seller of a load fund, then the shares could be directly purchased from the seller without paying the normal load.

Fund Information

Several financial information services help investors track fund information concerning fund performance characteristics and portfolio investment. These include: moneycontrol.com, Value Research, and Funds India. Information contained in these publications allows investors to identify particular funds that meet their own objectives and helps them make better informed decisions. However, since past performance is an unreliable predictor of future performance, overuse of rankings and ratings generated by these fund information services can lead to poor decisions. During certain periods, the winners are the highly volatile funds which often do not repeat their short-term successes. Finally, over the long run, different types of funds tend to enter into the winner's circle. For these reasons, in making fund selection it is best to take both a short-term and a long-term view of fund performance.

Costs and Fees

The SEBI requires every fund to include a table of all fees toward the front of the prospectus, followed by a hypothetical total of all fees for several years. A pure no-load fund usually indicates this fact on the cover, while front-load, low-load, and back-load funds disclose their costs inside the prospectus. Notwithstanding these mandated disclosures, it is advisable for every investor to be creative in identifying additional costs that are not self-evident. For instance, instead of stating that all dividends are subject to the usual full front-end load, one prospectus puts this in a roundabout way: "Dividends will be reinvested in additional full and fractional shares at the public offering price (the NAV plus a sales charge)."

Miscellaneous Information

The back pages of the prospectus contain valuable information on additional services available through the fund. These include, among other items, share purchases, sales and exchange privileges, transfers between funds within a family, participation in systematic withdrawal plan, dividend distribution, reinvestment, and automatic deposit and withdrawal plans. Information is also provided on telephone switches, check writing privileges, and other related services provided by the fund.

MUTUAL FUND RATING SERVICES

Mutual fund ratings and other fund performance evaluations provide investors with important tools to compare the past performance of their funds vis-à-vis other funds. We will now present the major rating services available in the marketplace.

Morningstar India

This is the industry's best resource for comprehensive, unbiased, and accurate mutual fund information. It publishes several key reports, including Morningstar Principia Pro for Mutual Funds, Morningstar Principia Pro for Stocks, and Morningstar Principia Pro for Variable Annuities/Life. It also publishes guides to help tracking the funds, and also provides a platform to interact with experts.

As an example, the Pro for Mutual Funds Report tracks 13,000 mutual funds. It provides complete securities holdings for each fund and identifies all funds that hold a particular security. The Multi-Asset Portfolio Developer lets a user construct and analyze real-world portfolios containing mutual funds. Most important of all, this Report publishes style boxes, risk-adjusted star ratings, and category ratings of various mutual funds so that their relative performance could be determined with considerable accuracy.

Lipper India

Lipper, a leading global mutual fund information company, analyzes fund companies and financial intermediaries. The firm tracks 47,000 funds worldwide with assets in excess of ₹1,000,000 lakh crore. The analysis of Lipper is unmatched for its quality, reliability, and level of precision. It integrates comprehensive fund research, fund performance, asset growth, portfolio composition, and expense information. It also uses customized approach which allows the user to measure and compare performance with other peer groups.

Value Research

Value Research, a leading global mutual fund information company, analyzes fund companies and financial intermediaries. The firm tracks the universe of Indian mutual funds. It is an independent provider of investment information. It has emerged as the most trusted provider of mutual fund information in India. It publishes several key reports, including Mutual Fund Insight, Wealth Insight, and Mutual Fund Year Book.

Standard & Poor's

S&P's is one of the most widely accepted financial rating organizations around the globe, setting the standard in the financial markets. This gives them the ability to provide fund sponsors, intermediaries, and money managers—the information they need to stay ahead of the competition—and to provide investors the information they need to make more informed decisions.

S&P's conducts institutional quality research and analysis on over 1,500 funds, covered by their 400 professionals in 13 countries. In addition, they provide the industry's most comprehensive database of funds with nearly 60,000 institutional, pension, insurance, and mutual funds worldwide.

CRISIL

For mutual fund rankings in India, CRISIL has developed methodology based on global best practices. Over the past 10 years, it has gained high acceptance among investors, intermediaries, and asset management companies. Its performance criteria cover not only risk-adjusted returns, but also portfolio characteristics such as industry concentration, company concentration, and liquidity, which make the analysis forward looking.

In addition to the above, CRISIL publishes customized *Mutual Fund Rankings* which are made available to wealth management, private banking, and advisory firms. The benchmarking of Indian mutual fund schemes is based on a combination of qualitative and quantitative parameters. The customized rankings are based on the fund houses and fund categories shortlisted by investors. Monthly or quarterly mutual fund rankings are provided to clients based on mutually defined methodology and criteria.

Thomson Financial

Thomson Financial is a global provider of data, analysis, and information tools. It offers the most comprehensive range of indispensable, market-leading services, and customizable solutions to help investors make better decisions, be more proactive, and make better mutual fund selections to achieve superior financial results.

Section III: Traditional Index Funds

AN OVERVIEW

Traditionally, investors selected their stocks with the objective of holding them for long periods of time. Next appeared on the scene the mutual fund boom, and investors started engaging mutual fund managers to make stock selections on their behalf and manage their portfolios. Finally, when without any significant declines the longest bull market in history continued through 1999, many investors decided that they no longer needed to hire astute money managers; instead, they started investing in a group of mutual funds whose sole purpose was to mimic the performance of the stock market. And with that, a new category of mutual funds known as *index funds* was born. These funds became popular as investors, exuberant over the winning performance of the stock market, became convinced that in order to make money in the stock market all they had to do was to be *in the market*.

Simply stated, index funds hold shares in all the companies that make up one of the key market indices: S&P BSE 500, CNX 500, S&P 500, DJ Wilshire 5000, Russell 2000, and Morgan Stanley Capital International Europe, Australia and the Far East (EAFE) Index. In essence, these funds run on autopilot, not only giving up the chance to do better than the selected market average but also promising that, except for the cost of running a fund, they will do no worse.

It is true that index funds operate in a routine fashion. That is their glamor. They do not provide investors the opportunity to beat the stock market by a dazzling 20 percent. But neither do they let their fund lag S&P BSE 500 by 10 percent.

Index funds owe a great deal of their recent success to their investment style and to the rapid rise of the stock market in the 1990s. The major advantages of investing in index funds are discussed next.

FEWER CAPITAL GAINS

Unlike other stock funds, whose managers are constantly buying and selling securities in an effort to maximize returns or minimize losses, index funds are managed very conservatively. Managers buy and hold stocks longer, selling or buying only those securities which drop out of, or are added to, the index.

It is of course true that both index funds and actively managed funds lose money when the market is down. But on April 16 investors in actively managed funds wonder how they could simultaneously lose money and still generate massive tax bills via capital gains distributions. Index fund shareholders rarely experience that problem because these funds do not trade frequently, generating capital gains. That constitutes an important benefit of investing in index funds.

Keeping Pace with S&P BSE 500

Most stock mutual funds reportedly underperform the S&P BSE 500, partly because they have to sell stocks to cover net withdrawals. For instance, from 1992 to 2013, the majority of stock funds failed to beat the S&P BSE 500.

An S&P BSE 500 index fund virtually guarantees that the investor will do as well as the index. The risk, of course, is that the fund will do poorly when the S&P BSE 500 underperforms, such as in a bear market. But over time, the index fund will likely approximate the long-term market average.

Painless Strategy

Index fund investors have neither the time nor the ability to ferret out the few exceptional fund managers who regularly beat the market averages. It also makes sense to choose the largest indices, since they include companies that are followed by Wall Street and the financial press. For that reason, it is best to buy an index fund that invests in large, well-known, and well-researched companies, such as those that make up the S&P BSE 500 group.

LOWER COST

The cost of investing in an index fund could be as low as 0.18 percent a year, significantly lower than the comparable cost of 0.75–1.25 percent or more for investing in a managed fund. This implies that investors of actively managed funds rack up huge investment costs as they attempt to discover superior investment managers.

The advantage of investing in index funds was best summarized by a young investor: "I am 32. I think it would be hard to find an actively managed fund that does better than the index for the next 35 years—or even 25 or 20. In that sense, indexing is a more conservative option."

Names of the popular index funds can be obtained from any brokerage firm. They are also available online.

PITFALLS OF INDEX FUNDS

Downside Risk

Statistics reveal that the majority of index funds have cropped up since 1995. During most of the period covering 1995–2001, the major stock market indices have never fallen more than 10 percent. When the overall stock market significantly declines, an index fund will decline as much as the market. This is because, unlike a general stock fund, an index fund cannot hold cash or bonds which often cushion a market fall.

The impact of a significant fall in any fund, including the index fund, is more severe than is usually recognized. For instance, if a fund were to fall 50 percent, then it would take a 100 percent increase in its value just to break even.

Skewed Weighting Systems

Similar to the S&P BSE 500 Index, index funds are weighted by a company's market value. Therefore, movements in the prices of the biggest stocks, such as ICICI, HDFC, Reliance, TATA, and LIC Nomura, have a magnifying effect on the performance of the index. In recent years it is these big stocks that have contributed to the largest advances in the S&P BSE 500 Index.

Divergence between Index Funds

Contrary to commonly held belief, index funds do not always mirror the market index. In fact, over time, because of redemptions and other administrative factors, some index funds fail to keep up with the index they are supposed to match. When that happens, many planners come up with *new versions* of indexing that inject more human judgment into the formulas. This human analysis and personal analytical opinion contradict the philosophy that is the cornerstone of managing index funds.

Tax Ramifications

One reason why index funds can operate with such low costs is that they almost never sell their stocks—so investors rarely have to pay taxes on stock gains. But when nervous investors—even those who profess to be in the market for the long haul—begin redeeming their shares at the first sign of the faltering of the market, index funds are compelled to sell their shares. When that happens, taxable index fund investors are required to pay taxes, which hurt their after-tax returns.

A Narrow Focus

Historically, small-cap stocks have handsomely beaten the large-cap ones. Also, numerous studies have demonstrated that international stocks and bonds can increase the return and lower the risk of individual portfolios. Unfortunately, these choices, as well as the choice of holding cash, are out of bounds for index funds.

Value Added by Money Managers

Selected actively managed mutual funds do beat the market on a consistent basis, even allowing for the fact that in the past 10 years the broad market has outperformed its very long-term average of around 11 percent. In addition, few neophyte investors recall a period like the five years that ended in 1998, when more than 80 percent of actively managed portfolios beat the S&P BSE 500 Index. On this basis, a strong case can be made for active management by those money managers who have established long-term venerable track records.

Increased Volatility

S&P BSE 500 Index funds, which approximate 500 in number, are more volatile than the majority of actively managed stock funds, most of which hold around 5–10 percent cash all the time. Index funds are fully invested, with very close to 100 percent of their assets invested in stocks. Managed funds also cut volatility by owning foreign stocks and a variety of fixed-income securities, which index funds cannot do.

So, the question, "Are index funds right for investors?" can only be answered after taking into account all of the advantages and pitfalls of investing in these funds, and the special needs and limitations of every investor.

NEW HORIZON IN INDEX FUNDS

Several years ago, index funds became popular because many research studies showed that, after costs, the majority of money managers could not beat the markets in which they operated. Today, however, there exists more than one way of indexing. Investors now have the choice of buying traditional *index funds* or index stocks that trade on a stock exchange. Salient features of a variety of index stocks are presented next.

iShares

iShares are different from index funds that trade like stocks. Each share represents a portfolio of stocks or bonds designed to closely track one specific index. iShares behave like stocks in that investors can buy and sell them the same way they trade stocks of individual companies. iShares consist of stocks or bonds that represent the underlying index tracked by the fund. These shares may use futures to simulate full investment in the respective underlying index to facilitate trading, or to reduce transaction costs.

iShares offer two distinct benefits for investors concerned with reducing taxes. First, they are engineered to minimize portfolio turnover, which can reduce capital gains distributions. Second, investors in these iShares, like those in common stocks, pay taxes on the investment's appreciation only at the time of sale.

In dealing with iShares, investors can make adjustments at any time without short-term restrictions or redemption fees, although a brokerage commission is charged on every transaction. Also, if investors margin these iShares, the standard margin rules apply.

Redemption of iShares is handled differently from redemption of mutual fund shares. iShares funds aim at minimizing portfolio turnovers and potential capital gains tax consequences by restricting the creation and redemption of these iShares to large transactions carried out by institutional investors designated as "authorized participants." Individual investors seeking to liquidate iShares positions simply place orders through their brokerage accounts for execution on the exchange.

International Index Investing with iShares Nifty Fifty Funds

iShares index funds extend the concept of index investing to the international level. Each share of this fund is designed to expose investors to specific international equity markets when they purchase a diversified portfolio of stocks trading in that country. The S&P India Nifty Fifty Index is a universally recognized benchmark against which international money managers are measured. The index measures the performance of 50 large-cap Indian stocks.

Exchange-traded Index Funds

Exchange-traded index funds (ETF Index Funds) are hybrid securities that combine the advantages of the traditional index mutual funds with many of the features of listed equity products. ETFs are baskets of stocks that allow an investor to buy or sell a portfolio of securities through a single share. However, unlike mutual funds, ETFs can be bought and sold at intraday prices, typically based on S&P CNX Nifty or BSE Sensex. The ETF's trading value is based on the NAV of the underlying stocks that it represents. It is a mutual fund which an investor can buy and sell in real-time and at a price that changes throughout the day. ETFs are comparable to index funds, but they do have several special advantages.

1. An investor can buy a single share of an ETF for as low as 1/10th of the index value. However, the premium and the discount also tends to be higher in the futures segment than in ETFs.
2. Index funds may be famous for their low expenses, but ETFs beat even these funds, with an average annual expense ratio of just about 0.59 percent, as compared to the average stock index fund expense ratio of 1.50 percent.
3. ETFs are highly tax efficient. It is true that traditional index funds are relatively tax efficient, since the fund managers do not make many trades. But if the market dives and a lot of shareholders redeem their shares, the manager is left with little choice but to sell stocks and pass on the taxable capital gains to the shareholders. ETFs also refrain from trading, but redemption is not an option for ETF investors. If ETF shareholders want to cash out, they would have to sell their shares in the open market.
4. Unlike mutual funds, which place limits on the frequency and size of trades, an investor can trade ETFs as often as desired. Active traders might move in and out of an ETF several times in a single day—just as they do with individual stocks. But unlike mutual funds, an investor can place an order to buy or sell an ETF at a special price.
5. The most important tax efficiency of ETF comes from what is known as *redemption in kind*. It is commonplace that traditional mutual funds trade at the NAV. Occasionally, a gap opens up between the NAV and the price at which ETF is traded, and that creates a unique opportunity for ETF investors to cash in on this opportunity.

Assume that such a gap has opened, and Nova Tech is trading at a *slight discount*—may be one paisa per Nova—to NAV. An institutional investor will jump on that opportunity, buying up 25,000 shares of Nova at the discounted price and turning them over to the ETF company. In exchange, instead of cash, an ETF company will give the investor a basket of stocks, the same stocks that make up the EFT's index. The investor will immediately sell these stocks in the market, benefiting from the discrepancy between the price that was paid for the Nova shares and the slightly higher price for which the newly exchanged shares can be sold.

The benefits derived from this transaction should be clear. Although the institutional investor effectively redeemed the shares, the fund manager did not have to sell any stocks in order to cash him out. And because the stocks were simply traded, the transaction did not generate any capital gains on which shareholders would owe taxes. Even more important, the manager can pick the shares that would be handed over to the institutional investor, giving up the shares of TATA, for instance, for which the least amount was paid. Over time, such a transaction plan can significantly reduce the EFT's capital gains exposure.

Section IV: Annuity and Life Investment Products

The term annuity simply means a regular periodic payment to individuals or their dependents over a number of years in return for money paid either in a lump sum or in installments. There are broadly two types of annuities.

1. ***Immediate annuity.*** It is purchased with a single premium called purchase price and is also known as fixed annuity. These products are called immediate annuity plans because they start making annuity payments as soon as the lump sum payment is received.
2. ***Variable annuity.*** The main difference between a fixed annuity and a variable annuity (VA) is that while the former can invest only in fixed-income products, the latter can invest in equities as well. Hence, by its very nature, VAs can distribute only a variable rate of return. At present, premiums accumulated within a VA are invested only in debt securities like unit-linked insurance plans (ULIPs) and its fund value is known.

   VAs have become a juggernaut in the financial services industry operating outside India.

Buoyed by the spectacular growth, life insurance companies have introduced several variants of the traditional VA contract. Since these products directly compete for the funds earmarked for stocks, bonds, and mutual funds, in this section we will present a brief description of each of the VA products.

DEFERRED ANNUITY

An annuity is a contract between an investor and an insurance company. A deferred annuity allows investment of money in one lump sum—a single-premium annuity—or in gradual increments over a number of years. Deferred annuities are mostly sold as pension plans and tax-saving devices as a means of maintaining long-term financial health of the participating companies.

There are two types of deferred annuities: fixed and variable. The former guarantees a fixed rupee amount when the fixed term expires. The premiums paid are exempt under Section 80CCC of Income Tax Act. VAs, however, allow investors to choose from a variety of investment products, such as stocks, bonds, and managed accounts, and they offer a broad spectrum of options, including global investments and capital preservation accounts. In essence, a VA in the USA is a mutual fund wrapped inside an insurance contract that allows the earnings to compound on a tax-deferred basis.

At present, insurance companies in India are not allowed to sell VA products. However, the Insurance Regulatory and Development Authority (IRDA) has set up a committee to examine the viability of VA products in India.

EQUITY-INDEXED ANNUITY

An equity-indexed annuity (EIA) grows either at an annual, guaranteed minimum rate of return (typically, 11 percent) or the net (of certain expenses and formulas) return from a stock market index such as the S&P BSE 500, whichever is higher. If the selected index rises beyond the guaranteed minimum during a given period, the market's return is credited to the contract owner's account for that period. But if the stock market index registers a modest gain or declines, the value of the policy increases only by the minimum guaranteed amount. So at a very minimum, the owner is guaranteed to receive the entire principal plus the minimum guaranteed growth, if an EIA contract is held for a minimum period of time, known as the "penalty period."

While the concept of EIA is based on the simple notion of a limited upside and a guaranteed safety of the principal, its execution is complicated. This is because EIAs invest in a mix of zero-coupon bonds and index options, and the terms, guarantees, payouts, and fees are all over the map. That makes shopping for EIAs tricky. EIAs have fixed terms, ranging from 1 to 10 years, and they typically impose steep "surrender charges" for cashing out early.

Key to an EIA selection is the *participation rate*, which is the portion of the index's gain received by the annuity owner. The calculation of that percentage is also important. Some EIAs use a "point-to-point" method, which gives a flat percentage for the total return achieved by the index during the lifetime of the contract. By contrast, the "annual ratchet" method calculates the value of the return on an annual basis. The difference between the two methods can produce significantly different results.

Assume a person invested in an EIA that uses the annual ratchet method. The S&P BSE 500 was at 1,400 when the contract was issued. On the first anniversary date, had the index declined to 1,100, the policy value would have remained unchanged and the starting point for the second year would have been 1,100. In that situation, an investor would benefit when the index rose above 1,100. However, had the insurance company used the point-to-point method to realize any gain, the investor would have to wait until after the index crossed 1,400.

Fees and annual charges also vary—sometimes considerably—between insurance companies marketing EIAs. Also, some companies replace these charges with *performance caps*.

VARIABLE LIFE INSURANCE

In the case of a variable life insurance policy, known in India as a nonlinked products in India, from each premium payment the company first deducts its normal expenses and mortality charges. It then permits the policy owner to allocate a portion of each *net* premium payment to one or more investment options, placed in separate sub-accounts. Variable life insurance policy combines investment and insurance similar to ULIPs. The benefit illustrations are required to assume gross investment returns between 4 and 8 percent per annum. In addition, the illustrations must use the annual rates specified by IRDA or the Life Insurance Council (6 percent and 10 percent, respectively).

The death benefit and cash value of a variable life policy increase or decrease based on the performance of the selected investment options. The death benefit, however, never drops below an initial guaranteed amount, unless policy premiums are not paid, or if loans or other withdrawals are taken from the policy. Even so, the ultimate death benefit always remains subject to the claim-paying ability of the insurer.

The investment options available inside a variable life policy usually involve securities; hence, the IRDA requires this type of policy to be accompanied by a prospectus. It provides detailed information on how the policy works, its risks, and all expenses or charges involved. The IRDA also requires individuals selling variable life policies to be licensed to sell securities. There are two types of variable life insurance policies—participating and nonparticipating. While the former offers guaranteed return, the latter offers yearly bonus at the end of each financial year in addition to guaranteed returns. For entry at the age below 45 years, the guaranteed minimum amount is ₹50,000, or 10 times the annualized premium, whichever is higher. Beyond that age, the minimum guarantee is the higher of ₹50,000 or seven times the annualized premium. Top-up or higher premium is allowed throughout the term. However, if the insured decides to increase the contribution through a onetime top-up, in the form of charges, the company is permitted to deduct no more than 3 percent from the top-up. The product also provides for loan of up to 60 percent of the balance at a specified rate of interest.

Another notable feature of this plan is that it is not automatically canceled even if the insured fails to pay the premiums. This is because the rules allow the insurance coverage to continue until all the previously collected premiums have been totally exhausted.

One of the major disadvantages of this form of life insurance is the high cost of premiums. As per the recent IRDA guidelines, the maximum expenses are capped at 35 percent of the first-year premium.

For the second- and third-year premiums, the cap is set at 7.5 percent and 5 percent, respectively; the last rate continues for subsequent years. The plan offers less flexibility on three counts: (a) it allows no changes in the annual premium payment, (b) no partial withdrawal is allowed, (c) the plan does not permit the addition of any rider.

In essence, the factors specified above take away the main benefit of variability from variable insurance plans. Equally important, the guaranteed rate of return is not sufficient to compensate for assuming the inflationary risk.

VARIABLE UNIVERSAL LIFE

A variable universal life insurance policy combines features of both a universal life policy and a variable life policy. Similar to a variable life policy, a variable universal contract permits a policy owner to allocate a portion of each premium payment to one or more investment options, placed in separate accounts, after deductions for expense and mortality charges. The annual statement detailing the expenses, charges, and credits allows a policy owner to track over time the investment performance of the policy.

Like universal life policies, within certain guidelines, a variable universal contract permits a policy owner to modify the death benefit and to change the amount and timing of premium payments to meet changing circumstances. Of course, the ultimate death benefit always remains dependent on the claim-paying ability of the insurer.

There are two primary types of variable universal life policies, based on the level of death benefits. Type I variable universal life policies, also known as "Option A," pay a fixed, level death benefit, which is usually the face amount of the policy. Type II variable universal life policies, also known as "Option B," generally pay the face amount of the policy *plus* the accumulated cash values. Consequently, as the cash value grows, so does the potential death benefit.

UNIT-LINKED PRODUCTS

ULIPs, unlike traditional insurance products, are long-term investment instruments combined with protection plans that offer the opportunity to avail both market-linked returns and life insurance protection. Based on the need to assume risk, an insured has the option to choose from a host of funds with varying degrees of risk associated with them.

Flexibility and transparency are additional features that make ULIPs attractive. Insurers provide details of annual charges and expected benefits for each policy year, using each of the two interest rates, namely 6 percent and 10 percent. In these illustrations, the premium is assumed to remain unchanged.

Incidentally, excluding single premium products, all limited-premium-paying term-unit-linked insurance products require premium payments for at least five years. Also, all unit-linked products (excluding pension and annuity products) enjoy a mortality or health cover. For of insurance Products, any additional payment is treated as a single premium. Reflecting the long-term protection benefit of the policy, the lock-in period is fixed at five years.

Systematic investment plans (rupee cost average investment plans) are in practice instruments which one part of the investment is for investment in securities (shares and debentures) and the other part for risk coverage through insurance policy.

Section V: Sophisticated Investment Products

REAL ESTATE INVESTMENT TRUSTS

The passage of SEBI Securities and Exchange Board of India Regulations, 2013, revived interest in group real estate investments known as *real estate investment trusts*, or REITs. These institutions are exempt from taxation if they (a) have 75 percent of their assets in real estate, mortgages, cash, or government securities at the end of each quarter; (b) derive 75 percent of their gross income from real estate and receive no more than 25 percent of their income from capital appreciation (to discourage investing in highly speculative projects); (c) distribute at least 90 percent of their income to shareholders (officially known as beneficiaries); and (d) have at least 100 shareholders, no five of whom can control more than half of the shares. In exempting the REITs from taxation, the lawmakers intended that these institutions be publicly held and that they be instrumental in diverting public funds primarily into the real estate industry.

There are two major types of REITs in the market: *mortgage trusts* and *equity trusts*. Mortgage trusts provide short-term financing for construction loans or for permanent mortgage loans for large projects. Equity trusts buy or build their own real estate property and hire management firms to run them.

REITs offer the investor an opportunity to invest in real estate without committing a large amount of money. Shares of REITs are generally readily marketable, especially those listed on exchanges or traded OTC. Because a REIT is, in effect, a closed-end investment company, its price is determined in the open market. The price of REIT shares may be above or below the actual book value of the real estate holdings.

The SEBI Act contains a number of conditions which a trust must meet in order to qualify as a REIT, including the requirement that an REIT pays out at least 90 percent of its taxable income. If an REIT meets these conditions, the income paid to the shareholders is not taxed twice (as it would be in a regular corporation), but is taxed only once in the hands of the shareholders. That is, income from sources such as rents and mortgage interest received is only taxed to the shareholder as ordinary income. Also, capital gains from the profitable sale of real estate investments are treated as long-term gains, regardless of the length of time an individual has owned the shares in the REIT. Of course, if a shareholder sells the shares in an REIT, the gain or loss is treated as long or short term, depending on how long the shares were owned.

INVESTMENT DERIVATIVES

In Saul Bellow's 1956 novella, *Seize the Day*, the hero uses his last $700 to buy lard futures on the advice of a close friend. To the hero's dismay, he watches lard prices plummet, and a shocked broker closes out his account. This scenario is enough to scare a reader away from such markets for life.

But derivatives—financial instruments that, like futures, are derived from an underlying transaction of goods, currencies, stocks, bonds, or money itself—are quite popular. Originally invented for commodities providers as a hedge against price fluctuations, futures and options also provided speculators with the chance to make a fortune or lose everything. Now, financial engineers design derivatives that ideally meet specific investment needs.

It is difficult to summarize the arcane world of derivatives in the short space available. Consequently, as an alternative, a short description of the key derivatives is presented below.

1. ***Options.*** Options are a standardized contract between a party and one of the exchanges, or a custom contract between two parties. This contract gives a buyer the right, but not the obligation, to exercise an option to buy or sell at a predetermined price on or before a specified date. A *call option* gives the holder the right to *buy* the underlying asset by a certain date at a certain price. A *put option* gives the holder the right to *sell* the underlying asset by a certain date at a certain price. Mutual funds buy calls to take advantage of a potential price increase in an underlying asset without risking more than the premium paid for the option. Puts are used to protect against price declines. Losses are limited to the premium that a fund manager pays for the option, while the profits are potentially unlimited. Seller's profits are limited to the premiums they receive, but they have unlimited loss potential if a buyer chooses to exercise an option. Standardized options are widely traded on exchanges, but there is also a universe of customized option contracts traded OTC.

2. ***Option spreads.*** An infinite variety of option spreads exists today. This includes yield curve spreads, money market spreads, spreads on LIBOR (London Interbank Offered Rate), T-bill and Eurodollar futures, and spreads on mortgage, swap, commodity, currency, hybrid equity, and bond markets. For example, a fund manager expecting the US bond market to outperform the Indian bond market in terms of yield can buy an inter-governmental bond option spread. Managers with exposure to spreads can buy option spreads to hedge their bets.

3. ***Straddle, strip, strap, and strangle.*** These are a combination of option trading strategies which involve taking a position in both calls and puts on the same stock. Of these, straddle is the most common strategy; it involves buying equal amounts of puts and calls with the same strike price, the same underlying asset, index, or currency, and the same expiration date.

4. ***Futures.*** Exchange-traded futures are standardized contracts between two financial institutions or a financial institution and a corporate client that obligates one party to buy and the other to sell a specific underlying asset at a specified date and price in the future. The right to offset, or cancel, an existing future position (by acquiring an equal but opposite position, leaving participants with zero exposure), allows buyers, sellers, and clearing houses to cut their losses or take profits without negotiating with counterparties.

5. ***Eurodollar futures.*** Managers buy these exchange-traded contracts based on the rate of three-month Eurodollar time deposit funds as a way of pricing Eurodollar-based financial instruments such as swaps and forward rate agreements.

6. ***Swaps.*** A plain vanilla interest-rate swap is when one party, B, agrees to pay another party, A, a cash flow equal to the interest at a predetermined fixed rate on a common principal amount for a number of years. At the same time, party A agrees to pay party B cash flows equal to the interest at a floating rate on a common principal for the same period of time. The currencies of the two sets of cash flows are the same and the life of the swap can range from 2 to 15 years. There are currency, option, future, commodity, and municipal swaps. By obtaining financing from one market and then swapping all or part of the cash flows for the desired currency denominations and/or rate indices, fund managers can diversify their activities in global markets, hedge their holdings, and increase their liquidity. Because they are tailored to a manager's projections, swaps can be a gamble if interest or currency rates widely fluctuate.

SHORT SELLING

Short selling is the reverse of the usual market transaction. Instead of buying a stock in the hope that it can be sold later at a higher price, a short trader *first sells stock* and later *buys it back* at what the seller hopes will be a lower price; that is, the short seller attempts to first sell high and then buy low. Short traders borrow stock to sell short from their brokers, who acquire stocks so that they can lend them from the margin accounts. At a subsequent time period, the short seller purchases the stock to cover the sale. At that point, the short seller realizes either a profit or a loss, depending on the purchase and sale price of the stock. When the transaction is completed, the borrowed stocks are returned to a broker.

MONEY CONTROL

Traditionally, mutual funds have been subjected to two major criticisms. First, when it comes to taxes, they are managed inefficiently, since funds can generate capital gains even when they are losing money. Second, they charge an ongoing management fee. For these compelling reasons, investors have been tempted to abandon the mutual funds in favor of individually managed portfolios of stocks. But for the most part, their desire has remained a wishful thinking, since only wealthy investors with ₹10 lakh or more can afford to engage professional money managers.

All that is changed now. Investors with as little as ₹5,000 can now afford individually managed accounts through moneycontrol.com, mprofit.in, fundsindia.com, and so on. These providers allow investors to choose from a list of top-ranking money management firms that focus on large-cap growth stocks, small-cap value, or other investment styles. Investors can also establish their individual preferences. For instance, investors who have accumulated capital gains elsewhere can request the manager to begin generating capital losses to offset those gains.

Another advantage of dealing with these firms is to gain, on a daily basis, access to the composition of the portfolio. It is commonplace that mutual fund companies are required to provide progress reports to their shareholders only twice a year.

Goldman Sachs Nifty Exchange-traded Scheme (GS Nifty BeES)

GS Nifty BeES is an open-ended index scheme, traded on BSE and National Stock Exchange (NSE), in the form of an exchange-traded fund (ETF). The objective of GS Nifty BeES is to provide investment returns that, before expenses, closely correspond to the total returns of the securities as represented by the CNX Nifty Index. However, the performance of the scheme may differ from that of the underlying index due to tracking error. The initial price of GS Nifty BeES represents one-tenth of the value of CNX Nifty Index. For example, if the CNX Nifty is trading at 6,000, GS Nifty BeES will trade at about 600, where a 10-point move in Nifty will mean a 1-point move in Nifty BeES. The maximum expense ratio, as mentioned in the Scheme Information Document, is 0.80 percent on an annualized basis.

Goldman Sachs Liquid Exchange-traded Scheme (GS Liquid BeES)

GS Liquid BeES is an open-ended liquid scheme, traded on BSE and NSE, in the form of an exchange-traded fund (ETF), with daily dividend and compulsory reinvestment of the dividend. The investment objective of the GS Liquid BeES is to provide current income, consistent with relatively low-risk products while providing a high level of liquidity primarily through a portfolio of T-bills, government securities, call money, collateralized lending and borrowing obligation (CBLO)/similar instruments, repos and reverse repos, and other money market instruments. The maximum expense ratio, as mentioned in the Scheme Information Document, is 1.10 percent on an annualized basis.

Goldman Sachs Gold Exchange-traded Scheme (GS Gold BeES)

GS Gold BeES is an open-ended scheme, traded on BSE and NSE, in the form of an ETF investing in physical gold. The investment objective of the GS Gold BeES is to provide returns that, before expenses, closely correspond with that of the domestic price of physical gold. As specified by the Scheme Information Document, the maximum expense ratio is fixed at 1.50 percent on an annualized basis.

EXCHANGE-TRADED INDEX INVESTING

Exchange-traded funds (ETFs) continue to gain popularity among individual and institutional investors alike, and the growing demand has produced a wide range of investment products. ETFs now cover virtually every equity asset class, while tracking the most popular and widely followed indices. ETFs are hybrid securities that combine the advantages of the traditional open-end index mutual funds, while offering many trading features of listed equity products. Exchange-traded fund is a security that tracks an index, a commodity, or a sector such as an index fund or a sectoral fund but trades like a stock on an exchange. It is similar to a close-end mutual fund listed on stock exchanges. ETFs experience price changes throughout the day as they are bought and sold.

Exchange-traded funds (ETFs) have been in existence in India for quite some time. But thus far ETFs have not enjoyed the kind of popularity conventional mutual funds enjoy. One reason for the absence of enthusiasm could be the lack of understanding of the concept of ETF. But a more compelling reason might be that since ETFs track only a narrow set of indices (such as, S&P BSE SENSEX and the BANKEX), the returns one expects to earn from ETFs would be limited to the rise in that index. And since India is the home of a growing market offering huge opportunities lurking within the non-index shares as well, that is sufficient to dampen the incentive in ETFs. The result is obvious: ETFs (and by association index funds) have comparatively negligible asset under management (AUM).

Two things could change the situation, however. First, as the market becomes appropriately valued or slightly overvalued, it will become progressively more difficult for money managers to beat the index. When that happens, it is highly likely that index-based funds (both conventional mutual funds and ETFs) will offer a better option than actively managed funds. It is apropos to add that since gold ETFs and real estate ETFs have no comparable products in the conventional mutual fund sector, investors have little option but to invest in these products through the mutual fund route. In fact, as the majority of managers continue to underperform the market index they are paid to beat, investors have already begun to embrace the strategy that moves away from professional management and aims toward duplicating market returns. The growing popularity of this investment philosophy has helped fuel the demand for ETF products worldwide.

Following are some of the recognized benefits of ETFs.

1. Trading flexibility, such as continuous pricing, intraday liquidity, margin purchases, stop and limit orders, and the ability to sell short—even on a downtick.
2. Tax efficiency.
3. Low operating costs.
4. Convenient access to targeted market sectors and countries.
5. Accurate tracking of underlying benchmark indexes, with dividends from stock holdings passed along to the investor.
6. Broad diversification within specific industries.

Trading flexibility. The trading flexibility of ETFs sets them apart from traditional open-end mutual funds. Unlike open-end mutual funds, which are bought and sold throughout the day at a price that is equal to the fund's NAV (determined at the end of the day), ETFs trade more like stocks? ETFs are continuously priced throughout the trading day and can be bought and sold by investors at intraday market prices. Investors can also place stop and limit orders to specify the prices at which they wish to trade. ETFs can be purchased on margin, and unlike stocks, they can be sold short even on a downtick. ETFs trade just like any other normal listed security on the BSE, and settlement is just like any other stock. In case an investor has purchased ETF from the market, he or she has to pay the broker before the pay-in on T+2, and in the case of sale, an investor has to transfer ETF units from his or her demat account[2] to his or her brokers account before the settlement on T+2.

Tax efficiency. ETFs are tax efficient in that they are designed to track an index, which normally results in lower portfolio turnover and taxable gains when compared to actively managed funds. The fact that ETFs trade on an exchange also contributes to their tax efficiency. When an open-end mutual fund experiences large redemptions from investors for cash, the need to meet investor redemptions usually forces the fund to liquidate securities, which may create capital gains tax liabilities. This tax burden is then passed on to the investors who remain in the fund. Because ETFs trade on exchanges, investors simply sell their shares to other investors. This exchange-trading feature eliminates the need for the fund to liquidate their holding, thereby possibly generating capital gains. Because ETF shares are created and redeemed as an "in kind" transaction, the creation/redemption process is also treated as a nontaxable transaction.

Low operating costs. ETFs are designed to closely approximate the returns of well-known indices and are passively managed. Passively managed funds are generally less likely to demand high management fees and ETFs are among the lowest cost products available. ETFs have a lower expense ratio than comparable securities. Costs are also minimized, since ETF shares trade on an exchange, thereby eliminating the expenses associated with buying and selling portfolio securities. There are no minimum investment amounts (one can buy a single ETF share), loads, short-term restrictions, or redemption fees associated with ETFs. Instead, investors pay a standard brokerage commission for all transactions.

Targeted investing. These are exchange-traded funds that follow almost every widely followed index, allowing investors to easily move in and out of entire sectors of the economy with minimum trading costs. For example, investors can maintain a core holding of the US market with an investment in SPDR® S&P 500® Exchange Traded Fund (SPY), while overweighting the energy sector with the Energy Select Sector SPDR if they so prefer. Investors are also able to tap into the international markets by using either broad-based international indices such as the iShares EAFE Index Fund or one of the many country-specific funds, such as the iShares MSCI Hong Kong Index Fund. In addition, ETFs can be used to temporarily equitize cash in a portfolio, since there is no minimum holding period. By temporarily investing cash in a broad market ETF, such as the Vanguard Total Stock Index Viper, investors can remain fully invested in the market while planning their next investment move.

Accurate index tracking. ETFs consist of a basket of stocks in specific weights, designed to closely track the performance of a benchmark index. ETFs can either hold substantially all of the underlying securities maintaining their appropriate weightings, or these can use a representative sampling technique to approximate the returns of the underlying index. ETFs structured as a unit investment trust, such as SPY, Midcap SPDRs, Nasdaq Index Tracking Stock, and DIAMONDS, hold dividends paid from constituent stocks in a noninterest bearing account and pass them along to the shareholders on a quarterly basis. DIAMONDS distribute dividends on a monthly basis. Reinvestment of dividends paid from stocks within the portfolio is not available for trusts with this structure. The ETFs structured as open-end funds

[2] Demat account is a account where shares and securities are held electronically in a account rather than the physical possession of certificates.

(iShares, streetTRACKS, and Vipers) normally distribute dividends, less expenses, to the investors on a quarterly basis. These funds have the ability to reinvest dividends paid from stock holdings in the fund on a daily basis.

Diversification. Diversification is an important means of reducing the risk of one or more underperformers having a large impact on an investor's portfolio. Using ETFs, investors can easily construct well-diversified portfolios within specific sectors of the market, with lower trading costs than building a diversified portfolio of individually selected stocks. By owning a larger basket of stocks within a specific sector, instead of taking on the increased risk of overweighting a single loser in a smaller, more volatile portfolio of stocks, investors can successfully capture the average return of the sector. However, some ETFs are narrower in scope and may experience greater volatility than the broad-based ETFs.

EXCHANGE-TRADED FUNDS COMPARED TO CLOSED-END FUNDS

Exchange-traded funds should not be confused with closed-end funds. ETF shares are continuously created and redeemed, and a prospectus must accompany all sales. This efficient creation/redemption process allows for arbitrage opportunities, and as a result, discounts and premiums that commonly exist with closed-end funds are typically not associated with ETFs. These funds share a number of similar features with closed-end funds; however, they still are distinctively different. Like closed-end funds, ETFs are listed on an exchange and have an underlying NAV and market price. Both of these trade like stocks, offering continuous pricing, intraday liquidity, margin capability, and the ability to be sold short. However, closed end fund shares are created in an initial public offering, following which the number of shares remains fixed. Investors who wish to buy shares after the initial public offering (IPO) must do so by buying them from other investors on an exchange and at a price determined by supply and demand. Closed-end funds can issue new shares in a rights offering and redeem shares in a tender offer, but they do not do so on a continuous basis. Since closed-end fund shares are not redeemable directly through the fund company, they often trade at significant discounts or premiums relative to their underlying NAV.

ETFs differ from closed-end funds in that ETF shares are continuously created and redeemed in large blocks, directly with the fund company. The creation/redemption feature of exchange-traded funds is a self-regulating mechanism that generally avoids the creation of discount or premium situations. The creation/redemption feature allows ETFs to grow when investor demand is high and shrink when demand wanes. Liquidity can become an issue with closed-end funds that have low trading volume, where a sizable order can considerably move the price of an illiquid fund. Liquidity is generally not an issue with ETFs because of the existence of creation/redemption mechanism.

In this chapter, we presented various investment products available in the marketplace. In Chapter 9, investment theories and concepts will be presented.

Appendix: Market Benchmarks

CNX NIFTY

The CNX Nifty is a well-diversified 50 Stock Index, accounting for 22 sectors of the economy. It is used for a variety of purposes such as benchmarking fund portfolios, index-based derivatives, and index funds.

CNX Nifty is owned and managed by India Index Services and Products Ltd. (IISL). IISL is India's first specialized company focused upon the index as a core product. The CNX Nifty Index represents about 70.14 percent of the free-float market capitalization of the stocks listed on NSE as on March 31, 2014.

The total traded value for the last six months ending March 2014 of all index constituents is approximately 55.67 percent of the traded value of all stocks on the NSE. Impact cost of the CNX Nifty for a portfolio size of ₹50 lakh is 0.06 percent for the month March 2014.

CNX Nifty is professionally maintained and is ideal for derivatives' trading. From June 26, 2009, CNX Nifty is computed based on free-float methodology.

CNX NIFTY JUNIOR

The next rung of liquid securities after CNX Nifty is the CNX Nifty Junior. It might be useful to think of the CNX Nifty and the CNX Nifty Junior as making up the 100 most liquid stocks in India.

As with the CNX Nifty, stocks in the CNX Nifty Junior are filtered for liquidity, so that they are the most liquid of the stocks excluded from the CNX Nifty. The maintenance of the CNX Nifty and the CNX Nifty Junior are synchronized so that the two indices will always be disjoint sets; that is, a stock will never simultaneously appear in both indices. Hence, it is always meaningful to pool the CNX Nifty and the CNX Nifty Junior into a composite 100 Stock Index.

As of March 2014, the CNX Nifty Junior Index represented about 11.42 percent of the free-float market capitalization of the stocks listed on NSE.

For the last six months ending in March 2014 the total traded value of all index constituents was approximately 16.01 percent of the traded value of all stocks on NSE. In March 2014, the impact cost of CNX Nifty Junior for a portfolio size of ₹25 lakh was 0.09 percent. Computation of CNX Nifty Junior is based on free-float methodology.

LIX 15

LIX 15 Index is designed to provide exposure to the liquid stocks while making the index easily replicable and tradable. In order to achieve that objective, in selecting the stocks criteria such as minimum turnover ratio and free-float market capitalization are applied. The index constitutes only 15 stocks with maximum weight of single stock being capped at 15 percent.

As on March 31, 2014, the index comprised stocks from nine different industries. For the last six months ending in March 2014, the total traded value of all index constituents was approximately 21.75 percent of the traded value of all stocks in the cash segment and 25.76 percent of all the stocks in futures and options segment (F&O) segment of the NSE.

CNX 100

CNX 100 is a diversified 100 Stock Index accounting for 38 sectors of the economy. It is owned and managed by IISL which is India's first specialized company focused on the index as a core product.

In March 2014, the CNX 100 Index represented about 81.57 percent of the free-float market capitalization of the stocks listed on NSE. Also, during the six months ending in March 2014, the total traded value of all index constituents was approximately 72.53 percent of the traded value of all stocks of the NSE. Finally, in March 2014, the impact cost of CNX 100 for a portfolio size of ₹50 lakh was 0.08 percent.

CNX 200

The CNX 200 Index is designed to reflect the behavior and performance of the top 200 companies measured by free-float market capitalization. The index comprises 200 companies listed on the NSE.

The CNX 200 Index represents about 90.22 percent of the free-float market capitalization of the stocks listed on the NSE as on March 31, 2014. During the last six months ending in March 2014, the total traded value of all index constituents was approximately 88.26 percent of the traded value of all stocks of NSE.

CNX 500

The CNX 500 is India's first broad-based benchmark of the Indian capital market. This Index represents about 97.00 percent of the free-float market capitalization of the stocks listed on the NSE as on March 31, 2014. During the last six months ending in March 2014, the total traded value of the constituents was approximately 97.08 percent of the traded value of all stocks of the NSE.

The CNX 500 companies are disaggregated into72 industry indices. For instance, if the banking sector has a 5 percent weightage in the universe of stocks traded on the NSE, then banking stocks in the index would also have an approx representation of 5 percent in the index.

NIFTY MID-CAP 50

The medium capitalized segment of the stock market is being increasingly perceived as an attractive investment segment with high growth potential. The primary objective of the Nifty Mid-cap 50 Index is to capture the movement of the mid-cap segment of the market. It can also be used for index-based derivatives' trading.

The Nifty Mid-cap 50 Index represents about 6.47 percent of the free-float market capitalization of the stocks listed on the NSE. During the six month period ending in March 2014, all index constituents were approximately 14.38 percent of the traded value of all stocks of the NSE.

CNX MID-CAP INDEX

The medium capitalized segment of the stock market is being increasingly perceived as an attractive investment segment with high growth potential. The primary objective of the CNX Mid-cap Index is to capture the movement and be a benchmark of the mid-cap segment of the market.

In March 2014, the CNX Mid-cap Index represented 12.89 percent of the free-float market capitalization of the stocks listed on the NSE as on March 31, 2014. Also, during the last six months ending in March 2014, the total traded value of all index constituents was approximately 19.28 percent of the traded value of all stocks of the NSE.

CNX SMALL-CAP INDEX

The CNX Small-cap Index is designed to reflect the behavior and performance of the small capitalized segment of the financial market. The CNX Small-cap Index comprises of 100 tradable companies listed on the exchange.

The Index is calculated using free-float market capitalization methodology with a base date of January 1, 2004, indexed to a base value of 1,000.

S&P BSE SENSEX

The S&P BSE SENSEX (S&P BSE Sensitive Index), also called the BSE30, or merely the SENSEX, is a free-float market-weighted stock market index of 30 well-established and financially sound companies listed on the BSE. The 30 component companies which represent the largest and most actively traded stocks are representative of various industrial sectors of the Indian economy. Published since January 1, 1986, the S&P BSE SENSEX is regarded as the pulse of the domestic stock markets in India.

On April 1, 1979, the base value of the S&P BSE SENSEX was fixed at 100 with 1978–79 being selected as its base year. On July 25, 2001, BSE launched DOLLEX-30, a dollar-linked version of S&P BSE SENSEX. As of April 2011, the market capitalization of S&P BSE SENSEX was about ₹29,733 billion (US$497 billion representing 47.68 percent of market capitalization for the BSE, while its free float market capitalization was ₹15,690 billion (US$262 billion).

During 2008–12, SENSEX 30 Index share of the BSE market capitalization declined from 49 percent to 25 percent due to the rise of sectoral indices such as the BSE PSU, Bankex, BSE-Teck, and so on.

S&P BSE 100

Ace Equity Not Sure If the Two Should Be on the Same Line??

S&P BSE 100 Index is broad based. The base year of this Index has been set as 1983–84 when it was launched in 1989. In line with the shift of the S&P BSE Indices to the globally accepted free float methodology, S&P BSE 100 was shifted to free float methodology effective April 5, 2004. The method of computation of free float index and the determination of the free float factors is similar to the methodology for S&P BSE SENSEX.

The S&P BSE 100 represents about 75 percent of the total market capitalization of the stocks listed on the BSE as on December 31, 2013.

S&P BSE 200

Ace Equity

Over the years, the number of companies listed on the BSE continued to register a phenomenal increase, namely, from 992 to over 3,200 companies by March 1994, with combined market capitalization rising from ₹5,421 crore to ₹398,432 crore.

It is true that the S&P BSE SENSEX (1978–79 = 100) was faithfully reflecting the stock price fluctuations. Still, the rapid market growth created the need for creating a new broad-based index series to effectively capture market fluctuations and more fully recognize the growing stock market as well as the diverse industry groups. Consequently, in May 1994, the BSE created two new index series, namely S&P BSE 200 and S&P Dollex 200.

Once launched, based on the current market capitalization of the listed scripts, equity shares of 200 selected companies from the specified and nonspecified lists of BSE were included in the sample for S&P BSE 200. In addition, the market activity of the companies as reflected by the volumes of turnover and certain fundamental factors were considered in making the final selection of the 200 companies.

S&P BSE 500

In August 1999, the BSE Limited constructed a new index titled S&P BSE 500. It consisted of 500 scrips. The changing pattern of the economy and that of the market were taken into account while constructing this Index.

S&P BSE 500 Index represents nearly 93 percent of the total market capitalization on the BSE. It covers all 20 major industries of the economy. In line with other S&P BSE indices, effective August 16, 2005, calculation methodology was shifted to the free-float methodology.

S&P BSE MID-CAP INDEX

Ace Equity

Companies with large market capitalization biased the movement of the S&P BSE 500 Index. This necessitated the construction of a separate indicator to capture the trend in companies with lower market capitalization.

Consequently, the BSE introduced the new index series called "S&P BSE MID-cap" Index and "S&P BSE Small-cap" Index to track the performance of companies with relatively smaller market capitalization. Over the years, the S&P BSE Mid-cap and S&P BSE Small-cap indices have proven to be of significant value to the investing community.

S&P BSE SMALL-CAP INDEX

Ace Equity

The S&P BSE Small-cap Index is designed to reflect the behavior and performance of the small capitalized segment of the financial market. The S&P BSE Small-cap Index represents about 5 percent of the total market capitalization of the stocks listed on the BSE as on December 31, 2013.

9 Investment Management: Concepts and Strategies

INTRODUCTION

In this chapter, we will present the key elements of investment concepts applicable to individual securities and efficient portfolios constructed primarily with mutual funds. We will begin this chapter with a discussion of the concepts and strategies associated with individual securities. However, we will devote the majority of this chapter to the theory of portfolio construction and the time-tested strategies of managing investment portfolios consisting solely of mutual funds.

Investment can be defined as the commitment of a given sum of money today with expectations for receiving a larger sum in the future. This definition underscores two important points. First, the process of investment involves the trade-off of *present* income for *future* income. Second, the objective of the investment is to receive a *larger* flow of funds in the future. It must be recognized, however, that there is a significant difference between investment and speculation. Essentially, speculators concentrate on returns expected to be received over relatively short periods of time. In contrast, investors seek to derive benefits from their investments over a longer time horizon. Another important difference between the two is that speculators act quickly on the available information *not yet analyzed or acted upon by the general public*, whereas investors generally base their action on the results of careful investment analysis, even though such action might result in making short- or long-term investment decisions.

Section I: Fixed-income Securities

FIXED-INCOME SECURITY RETURN

As a general rule, risk and return are positively related. Consequently, the higher the risk of a fixed-income security, the higher is the return that investors demand to entice them to invest in that security. The return on a bond is a combination of the coupon payments and the profit or loss realized if the bond is sold before maturity or if the issue defaults on coupon or principal payments. For instance, if an investor purchases a 30-year bond with a coupon of 8 percent and holds it until maturity, then the annual return on that bond, known as yield to maturity (YTM), is 8 percent. If, however, an issuer defaults on the coupon payments or the principal, then the annual return would be less than 8 percent, depending on the nature and the timing of default.

FIXED-INCOME SECURITY RISK

The concept of bond risk is more complex than bond return. In Chapter 8, we presented a description of various types of fixed-income securities. We will now learn that bonds are much more than mere legal

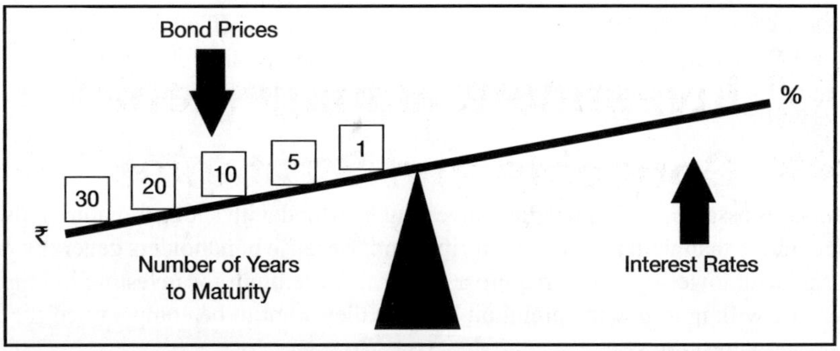

Figure 9.1 *Relationship of Interest Rates to Bonds*

documents. Investing in bonds involves making decision about their associated risk and return, or more appropriately, about the income and capital appreciation that an investor expects to receive by investing in them. It is, of course, true that many investors do not like to assume risks. But they also realize that all investments have some degree of risk associated with them. Consequently, every serious investor needs to learn how to deal with risks associated with fixed-income securities.

Any discussion of bond risk must begin with the realization that even bonds with identical maturities and yield to maturity can have varying degrees of risk associated with them. Equally important, several types of risks have major impact on bond prices, as discussed below.

Key Fixed-income Risks

Interest Rate Risk

Interest rate risk refers to the variations in bond prices as a result of fluctuations in market interest rates. Bond prices and interest rates are inversely related. When market interest rates rise, bond prices decline, and the opposite is true when market rates drop. The reason is that when the interest rate rises, bonds with lower coupon rates fall out of favor and their prices decline. Figure 9.1 demonstrates this relationship. This figure also shows that the longer the maturity of a bond, the higher is the impact of a change in interest rates on bond prices.

The interest rate–bond price relationship conceals an important fact. Even in the case of a perfectly safe, noncallable Treasury bond, the impact of the rise in interest rates can be significant. For instance, Figure 9.2 reveals that a mere 2 percent increase in the interest rate would slash the price of a 30-year, 7.5 percent Treasury bond by 18 percent. Of course, the reverse is also true. In 1991, for instance, because of steadily declining interest rates, long-term US Treasury bonds racked up total returns of 19.3 percent—a stunning performance not likely to be repeated any time in the near future.

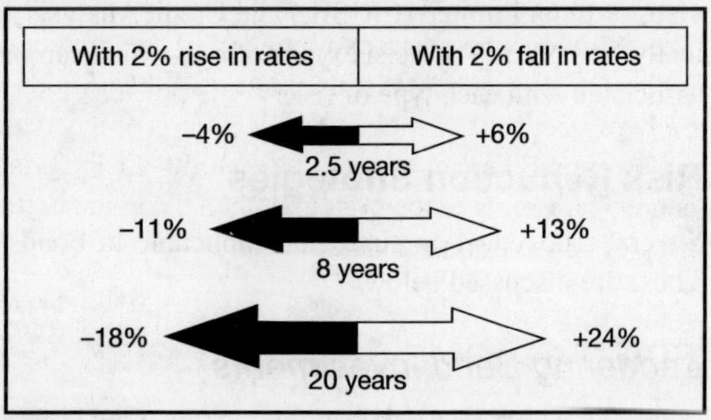

Figure 9.2 *Bond Price Volatility (based on 7.5% coupon)*

Inflation Risk

Inflation risk is the impact of inflation on coupon payments and return of the principal. If an investor holding a 10-percent bond receives an interest payment of 10 percent or ₹100 at the end of one year, and during that year the price level rises by, say, 6 percent, then the *real interest rate* (the *nominal* interest rate adjusted for inflation) would be only 9.4 percent. So, assuming that the principal is received after one year, the buying power of ₹1,000 would drop to ₹943.40 in real rupees, a loss of 5.66 percent.

Maturity Risk

Because the future is assumed to be uncertain, investing in a bond with a longer maturity always involves a higher degree of risk than with a shorter-maturity bond. Because bondholders generally prefer shorter-term investments with lower risk, they require a higher risk premium for investing in long-term securities. Borrowers are willing to pay the premium because they want to be compensated for the impact of future increases in interest rates.

Default Risk

A bond yield reflects a borrower's credit quality. Lower quality or non-investment grade bonds—those rated BB or below—generally offer higher yields than better quality issues, but they have more potential for price volatility. The higher yield compensates an investor for lending money to a company that is considered more likely to default in terms of interest and principal payments. Thus, a rising yield (or falling price) on a bond may reflect a company's deteriorating financial situation rather than any overall rise in market interest rates. Similarly, when a company's financial situation improves, generally the yields on its obligations decline.

Callability Risk

Callability risk refers to the possibility that the bond is being called before maturity due to falling interest rates, in which case a bondholder would be compelled to invest the proceeds at a lower interest rate. Typically, if a bond is called, a premium over the maturity price is paid by the issuer to the bondholder; this premium often varies directly with the remaining years to maturity. A common premium for a corporate bond called at the end of the call protection period would be one year's interest.

Liquidity Risk

A bond may also be subject to liquidity risk. This risk refers to the price concession that one must grant in order to quickly convert the bond into cash and receive the original investment. In general, the less liquid a security, the higher is its liquidity risk.

Table 9.1 presents a list of categories used by ICRA Limited (ICRA), Credit Rating Information Services of India Limited (CRISIL) and Credit Analysis and Research Limited (CARE) to rate bonds. Typically, bonds carry these six types of risk which can be broadly measured in terms of the risk premiums associated with each type of risk.

Risk Reduction Strategies

Several risk reduction strategies applicable to bonds are available that have worked well over time. These are discussed below.

Laddering Bond Investments

Laddering bond investments is a commonly recommended strategy for bond investors, whether they wish to hold individual bonds or shares in funds. Laddering refers to the technique of buying bonds

Table 9.1 *Investors' Services Rating Classification*

General Description	ICRA	CRISIL	CARE
Highest safety	LAAA	AAA	CARE AAA
High safety	LAA	AA	CARE AA
Adequate safety	LA	A	CARE A
Moderate safety	LBBB	BBB	CARE BBB
Moderate risk	LBB	BB	CARE BB
High risk	LB	B	CARE B
Very high risk	LC	C	CARE C
Default	LD	D	CARE D

maturing at different times. This technique works best if investors buy bonds with maturities of 10 years or less. That way, every other year or so, as bonds representing 20 percent of their portfolio comes due, new bonds are purchased at the prevailing rates. With this approach, investors can systematically purchase bonds at prevailing market rates, which over time can help smooth out the overall volatility of their bond portfolio.

Diversifying with International Bonds

When foreign countries are still in a recession, or are beginning to recover from a recession, higher interest rates are generally offered by international bonds. However, investors going overseas for bonds should not let the relatively high returns tempt them into committing a disproportionate portion of the bond portfolio to these potentially volatile foreign bonds. As a general rule, 10–15 percent of the total funds invested in fixed-income securities should be sufficient to increase the foreign exposure measurably and achieve the diversification needed to help mitigate price and interest rate risks on domestic holdings. Of course, in investing in international bonds, currency risk and current regulations should always be taken into account.

Investing in Tax-exempt Bonds

Yields of tax-exempt bonds could provide an attractive investment vehicle, especially for investors who pay top tax rates. And in a high-tax environment, increased demand for tax-exempt funds can help provide some support for municipal bond prices.

Adopting Rupee Cost Averaging Strategy

Rupee cost averaging (RCA)—regularly investing a fixed amount in bonds—can be an attractive strategy for long-term investment. This strategy can be particularly effective when reinvesting bonds came due, or when investments need to be shifted to reflect changing goals and needs. With RCA, investors buy more bonds or shares when prices are lower, and buy fewer when they are higher. Of course, RCA does not protect against a loss in declining markets or ensure a profit in rising markets, and when selling their bonds, investors could wind up with a gain or loss.

Buying a Bond

As a general rule (with the exception of government bonds which are always presumed to be appropriately priced), it is advisable to purchase an undervalued bond. However, since bonds are long-term obligations to pay a fixed amount of money at maturity, several special factors should be taken into account when purchasing a bond.

Bond Yield

The critical variable in bond investment is its yield: Given a fixed coupon rate, the lower the price of a bond, the higher is its yield. Although there are many exceptions, when the stock market is up, at least in theory, the bond market weakens and vice versa. Consequently, the stock market bears careful watching when selecting a bond.

Two important caveats of bond yields deserve special mention. First, during periods of restrictive monetary policy, interest rates generally rise, thereby depressing bond prices and pushing up bond yields. Second, when short-term interest rates decline, investors start investing in long-term securities, which ultimately leads to a decline in the long-term rates as well. These factors should help an investor determine the appropriate time for investing in bonds.

Bond Ratings

Bond ratings regularly published by ICRA, CRISIL, and CARE facilitate the task of selecting attractive bonds. The ratings range from AAA for the safest bonds to D for highly speculative bonds which may even be in default. The ratings of A or better are given to investment grade bonds, while speculative bonds are rated lower than BB.

Current Yield and Yield to Maturity

The *current yield* on a bond is the ratio of the current coupon payments to the current market price of that bond. The YTM is the interest rate at which the *present value* (PV) of all future coupon payments and the *face value* (the principal amount paid at maturity) of the bond equals its current market price. The YTM is the true interest rate underlying any bond. The current yield provides a good approximation for the YTM for longer maturity bonds.

Assume, for example, that a 10-year maturity, ₹1,000 face value bond which carried an 8 percent coupon (₹80 in interest payment each year) was issued one year ago. Naturally, at the time of issue, the bond price was ₹1,000 (equal to the value of 10 ₹80 coupon payments and the principal payment of ₹1,000 in the 10th year discounted at 8 percent interest rate), and both the YTM and current yield ([₹80/₹1,000] × 100) are equal to 8 percent. Now assume that because of an increase in the market interest rate the bond price has fallen to ₹884.82.The current yield of the bond (₹80/₹884.82) is 9.04 percent and the YTM is 10 percent (which is also the market interest rate). That is, ₹884.82 is the PV of nine ₹80 coupon payments (since one year has elapsed when the bond was issued), and ₹1,000 face value to be paid in the 9th year (now the maturity date) discounted at a 10 percent interest rate. In technical jargon, this bond with 8 percent coupon is priced to yield 10 percent at ₹884.82. The PV concept that underlies the determination of the bond price was presented in detail in Chapter 3.

Selling a Bond

Selling a bond is a complex process which requires a different discipline than that required for buying a bond. This can become a challenging task, and it is best to check the following points before making the final decision.

Underperformance

This is the most challenging task faced by an investor. First, what time period should be selected for checking the performance: six months, five years, or something in between? While there are no set rules to follow, prudence dictates that the shortest period to be selected is 12 months but the longest period should be no more than three years.

Change in Company Position

If the financial condition of a bond issuer has changed significantly, resulting in the downgrading of the bond's rating, then serious consideration should be given to liquidating the holding.

Extent of Loss

It is important to accurately calculate the extent of the loss, since the *real loss* in the bond holding could very well be less or more than what appears on the surface.

Tax Consequences

Whether the sale of the bond results in a gain or loss, it is best to assess every situation carefully, so that a bondholder can fully utilize either the resultant gain or loss to minimize the overall tax burden.

Incidentally, when a financial market is volatile, investment in a bond is preferred by investors not willing to assume the market risk. However, the fact that in India currently there is no active bond market for subsequent trading in bonds should also be taken into account in making the final decision.

Section II: Equity Securities

EQUITY RETURN

As explained in Chapter 8, equities are a very different type of investment instrument from fixed-income securities. In these securities, there are no promised coupon payments and return of principal upon maturity. Instead, the annual return on a stock over time is based primarily on the increase in the sale price of the security; dividend payments are neither guaranteed nor promised, although dividends can be declared even when a company does not generate a profit.

It is best to explain the method of calculating a common stock return with the help of a series of examples. Assume an investor paid ₹60 per share for ABC mutual fund and sold it for ₹72 per share. Assuming that the investor received no dividends, the percentage gain is 20 percent ([gain/original pric e] × 100 = [12/60] × 100 = 20 percent).

Here is another example. Three years ago an investor bought a stock for ₹5,000 and in subsequent years reinvested all dividends and capital gains. The stock is worth ₹7,604 today. As demonstrated in the following in-text table, the compounded annual rate of return is 15 percent.

Line	Items	Stock Return
1.	Original investment	₹5,000
2.	Current market value (including reinvested cash flow (dividends plus capital gains)	₹7,604
3.	Number of years held	3 years
4.	Total return:	
	(a) Subtract line l from line 2	
	(b) Divide (a) by line 1	
	(c) Multiply (b) by 100	52.08%
5.	Compound annual return:	
	Use a calculator to find the rate	
	(see Table 3.11)	15%

We will now turn to another illustration that is more involved than the previous ones just presented. Assume an investor had an investment worth ₹10,000 at the beginning of the quarter and added a net ₹1,500 during the quarter. At the end of the quarter, the value of the investment was ₹12,000. Capital gains and dividends were reinvested. As demonstrated in the following in-text table, the annual rate of return was 19.7 percent.

I. Rate of Return during the Quarter

Line	Items	Stock Return
1.	Value of investment at the beginning of quarter	₹10,000
2.	Value of investment at the end of quarter	₹12,000
3.	Net addition or withdrawal during the quarter (withdrawal will be a negative number)	₹1,500
4.	Multiply line 3 by 0.5	₹750
5.	Subtract line 4 from line 2	₹11,250
6.	Add line 4 to line 1	₹10,750
7.	Divide line 5 by line 6	1.046
8.	Subtract 1 from line 7	0.046
9.	**Return during the quarter: Multiply line 8 by 100**	**4.6%**
	II. Return for the Whole Year	
10.	Multiply line 7 by itself three times (e.g., in sample case, it is 1.046 × 1.046 × 1.046)	1.197
11.	Subtract 1 from line 10	0.197
12.	**Annual return: Multiply line 11 by 100**	**19.7%**

In the previous illustration, it was assumed that the quarterly returns remained unchanged. If these returns did change, the annual return would be calculated in the manner presented in the following in-text table.

III. Compound Annual Rate of Return

Line	Items	Stock Return
13.	Return during the first quarter	4.6%
14.	Return during the second quarter	–2.5%
15.	Return during the third quarter	3.5%
16.	Return during the fourth quarter	4.0%
17.	Divide line 13 by 100. Add 1 to the amount.	1.046
18.	Divide line 14 by 100. Add l to the amount	0.975
19.	Divide line 15 by 100. Add 1 to the amount	1.035
20.	Divide line 16 by 100. Add 1 to the amount	1.040
21.	Multiply line 17 by lines 18, 19 and 20	1.097
22.	Subtract 1 from line 21	0.097
23.	**Compound Annual Return: Multiply line 22 by 100**	**9.7%**

The final illustration presents a *simplified* method of calculating a portfolio return during the preceding year, because this is precisely the type of calculation in which most investors are interested. However, for a more accurate return calculation, it is best to use *Quicken Deluxe* or portfolio trackers available online.

To start the calculation process, all that is needed is the value of investments at the beginning and the end of 2014, and the total amount of money added or withdrawn during the year. All purchases are treated as additions. Withdrawals include proceeds from sales but not dividends, interest, or capital gains distributions. If those were distributed in cash, they should be added to the year-end total. If they were reinvested, then they should not be counted separately because they will be reflected in the year-end balance. As demonstrated by the following in-text table, the total return for the year 2014 was 17.78 percent.

Steps		Stock Return
1.	Enter the value of portfolio at the start of 2013.	₹50,000
2.	Enter the value of portfolio at the end of 2013.	₹62,000
3.	Add to line 2 any dividends, interest or capital gains distributions that was taken in cash. The total is the ending balance.	₹62,000+₹500=₹62,500
4.	Enter the net total of any additions or withdrawals made during the year.	₹2,500
5.	Subtract line 1 from line 3.	₹62,500−₹50,000=₹12,500
	Divide the result in half and then add that figure to line 1.	₹12,500/2=₹6,250
	The result is the average monthly balance.	₹50,000+₹6,250=₹56,250
6.	Add line 1 to line 4. Subtract that total from line 3.	₹50,000+₹2,500=₹52,000
	The result is the total gain for 2013.	₹62,500−₹52,500=₹10,000
7.	Divide line 6 by line 5. Multiply by 100.	₹10,000/₹56,250=0.1777
	This is the 2013 total return percentage, before taxes.	0.1777 × 100=17.78%
	Total return for the year	**17.78%**

EQUITY RISK

When investing in a stock, an investor assumes the risk of realizing less than the expected return. Closer scrutiny reveals that this risk has two important components: (a) risk that the variability in return would be caused by factors that affect the prices of all stocks, called market or *undiversifiable risk* and (b) variability in return that can also be caused by factors that are unique to a firm or an industry, known as nonmarket or *diversifiable risk*.

Market or undiversifiable risk refers to both the economic and the market risk. The former refers to the risk that slower economic growth will cause investments in stock to decline. Recessions can adversely affect shares of growth companies, cyclical companies, and other types of companies. In addition, market risk refers to risks associated with political developments, tax law changes, investor psychology, foreign domination of the Indian investment market, leveraged buyouts, and insider trading fiascos. In contrast to the undiversifiable risk, diversifiable risk refers to that portion of the variability of a stock's return that is the result of unexpected events or developments within the company or the related industry.

It is important to note that different strategies are needed to deal with the two types of risk just identified. Investors deal with undiversifiable risks by using a strategy, known as the risk–return trade-off, which refers to the higher returns demanded by investors as compensation for assuming a higher level of risk. In contrast, investors reduce—even eliminate—diversifiable risk by constructing efficiently diversified portfolios. A risk–return pyramid, which demonstrates the risk–return trade-off between various types of investments, is presented in Figure 9.3.

Risk is the most important word in the lexicon of every serious investor. And yet, because it dampens the enthusiasm of even the most upbeat investor, few investors discuss it—and that to rarely with any clarity or understanding.

Here is a typical scenario. Without exception, before buying a major fund most serious investors examine the fund's 1-, 3-, 5-, and (if available) 10-year returns. All financial magazines (such as *Money Magazine*, *Business World*, *Mutual Fund*, *Outlook Money*, and *Business Standard*) diligently publish these returns on a regular basis. And yet, few investors pay attention to the sections that identify risks associated with these returns. Unfortunately, looking at returns without adjusting for risk is fraught with danger and can spell disaster.

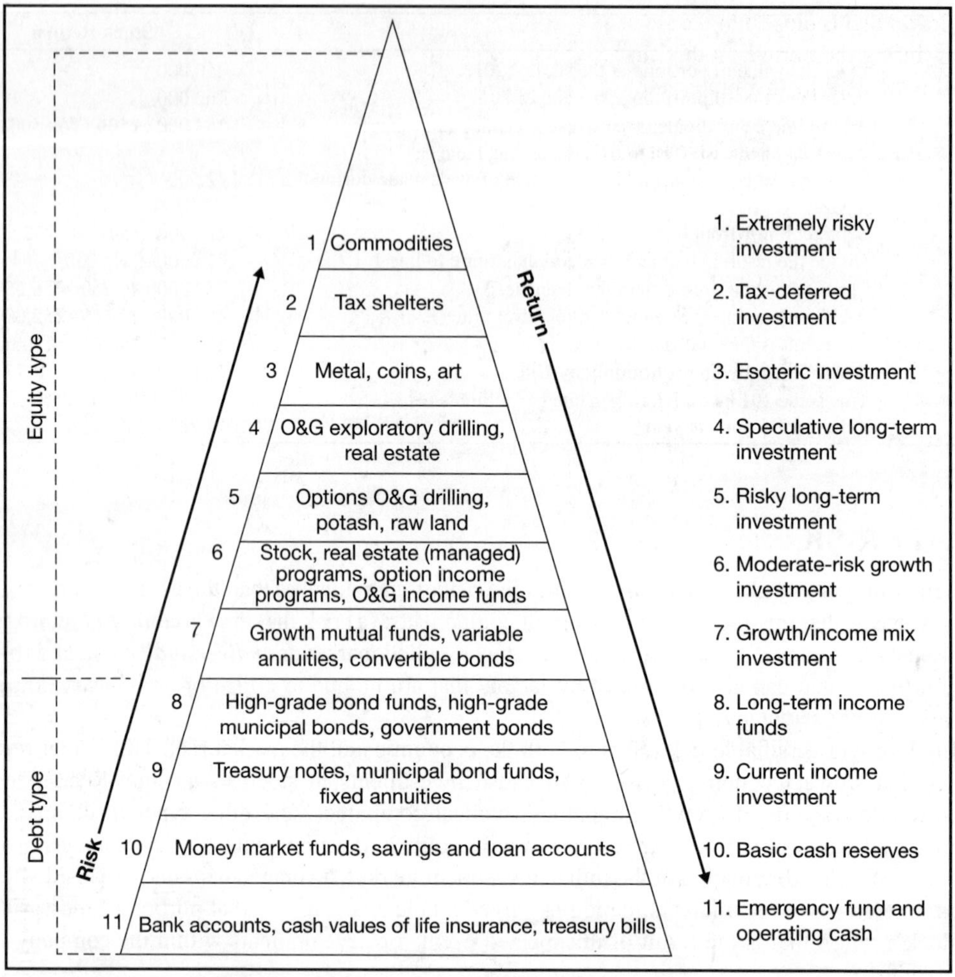

Figure 9.3 *Risk–Return Pyramid*

Risk is a more complicated concept than return, simply because the former does not lend itself to an easily understandable measure. However, every serious investor must objectively deal with risk. The following are the three measures of risk with which every investor should become familiar.

Key Measures of Risk

Beta

We begin with a simple equation for a straight line: $Y = a + bX$, where X and Y can be any two variables [Figure 9.4(A)]. Here, the "a" represents the value of Y when X is zero, while "b" measures how fast Y changes in response to a given change in X. Now let us turn to Figure 9.4(B), where Y and X have been replaced by, respectively, the XYZ stock and the Standard & Poor's Bombay Stock Exchange 500 (S&P BSE500) Index, which represent the market. Fluctuations in the stock's return vis-à-vis S&P 500BSE return have been plotted for five years (not shown) and the AB line (a least-squares line) has been drawn that is closest to the stock's returns during the period. In this chart, the value of beta [b in Figure 9.4(A)] represents the average percentage change in the XYZ stock's return in response to a percentage change in S&P BSE500 return. That is, beta measures the riskiness of the XYZ stock relative to the volatility, or risk, associated with S&P BSE 500. Beta of 1 implies that the stock is as volatile as the market, whereas a beta of higher or lower than 1 implies that the stock is, respectively, more or less volatile than the market.[1]

In this context, beta indicates how much the stock will likely rise or fall in relation to changes in the market index. Implicitly, the market has a beta of 1 because the market index chosen is the measure of the market's movement. In Figure 9.4(A), the stock has a beta of 0.6. This means that on average the stock moves up or down by a factor of 0.6 in the market index. Consequently, a beta of less than 1 results in lower *highs* and *lows* than the market. The opposite is true for a stock which has a beta of greater than 1.

But that is not a guarantee, only a tendency. In fact, stocks seldom perform precisely according to their beta.

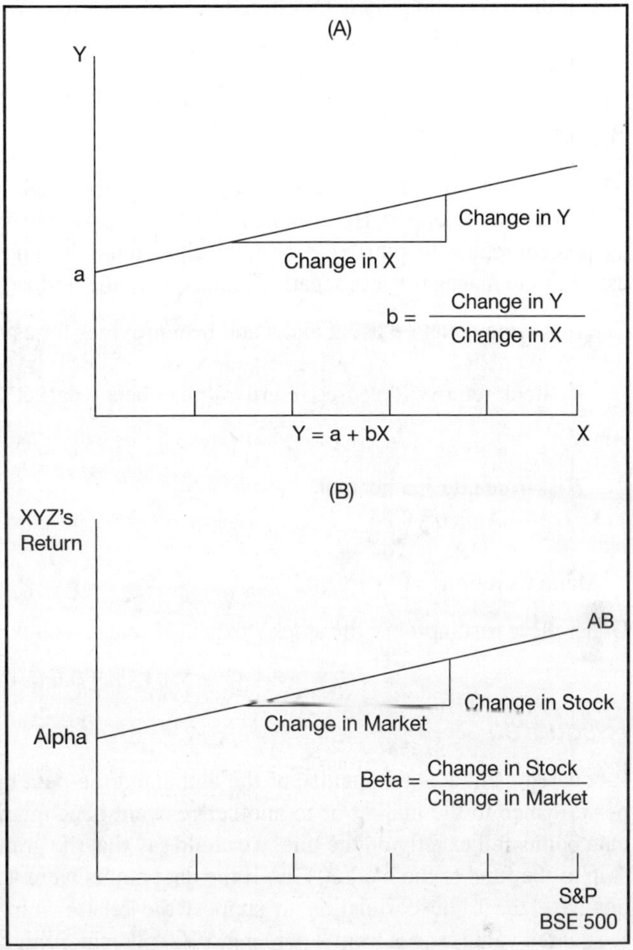

Figure 9.4 *Key Measures: Alpha and Beta*

[1] For the pros, the formula for beta is as follows:

$$\beta = \frac{\sum_{i=1}^{n}(x_i - \bar{X})(y_i - \bar{Y})}{\sum_{i=1}^{n}(x_i - \bar{X})^2}$$

where:

Σ = the mean of the sum of subsequent equation, from month 1 through month n
n = the number of months
x_i = each x observation (the excess monthly return of the bookmark index over the 90-day T-bill)
$\bar{X}$ = the average of all x observations
y_i = each y observation (the excess monthly return of the fund over the 90-day T bill)
$\bar{Y}$ = the average of all y observations

One of the risks of high-beta investing is that stocks do not always produce as high returns as their betas suggest they would. That is, beta defines an *inexact relationship* with the market that works more on the law of averages than the law of physics.

Alpha

Alpha is a measure of the value added by the manager's luck or skill.[2] In Figure 9.4(B), alpha [a in Figure 9.4(A)] is, say, 4 percent. Here, alpha indicates the expected return of the stock when the market provides a 0 percent return. In a different case, the alpha might be a negative number in which case it would indicate that the manager has a negative impact upon the performance of the stock.

The following equation using alpha and beta provides for estimating a stock's return:

$$\text{Stock return} = \text{Risk-free return} + \text{alpha} + \text{beta (Market's expected return} - \text{Risk-free return)}$$

where

$$\begin{aligned} \text{Risk-free rate} &= 5 \text{ percent} \\ \text{Alpha} &= 0.04 \\ \text{Beta} &= 0.6 \\ \text{Market's return} &= 14 \text{ percent.} \end{aligned}$$

Under these assumptions, the stock's expected return would be:

$$14.4\% = 5\% + 4\% + 0.6\ (14\% - 5\%).$$

R-squared

R-squared estimates the quality of the alpha and the beta by correlating the relationship of a stock's performance to the market or to another relevant benchmark. Referring back to Figure 9.4(B), if the data points fell exactly on the line, we could say that the graph shows a high correlation in the relationship of the fund to the market. But, if the data points were widely distributed about the line, we would not have the same correlation to support the relationship between the stock and the market. The R-squared value ranges from 0 percent to 100 percent. A high concentration of the data points about the line gives an R-squared value close to 100 percent and strengthens confidence in the relationship of a stock to the market. Conversely, the lack of concentration of data points close to the line yields an R-squared value close to 0 percent and, therefore, reduces confidence in the relationship of the stock to the market.

In conclusion, it should be stated that often alpha, beta, and R-squared are used improperly with the result that they give out misleading signals. The most common error is to compare a stock to an index that has no relevance to it. For example, it is of little use to compare a portfolio of small-cap international stocks and corporate bonds to S&P 500 BSF Index because the R-squared value would be closer to zero. Also, alpha does not give insight as to whether the value added was due to the skill of the manager or pure luck. When used with care, however, these measures can assist planners in making better investment choices for their clients.

[2] In technical lingo, alpha is a measure of the difference between a fund's actual returns and its expected performance. A positive alpha figure indicates the fund has performed better than expected. In contrast, a negative alpha indicates the fund's underperformance, given the expectations. All modern portfolio theory (MPT) statistics (alpha, beta, and R-squared) are based on a least-squared regression of the fund's return over Treasury bills (called excess return) and the excess returns of the fund's benchmark index.

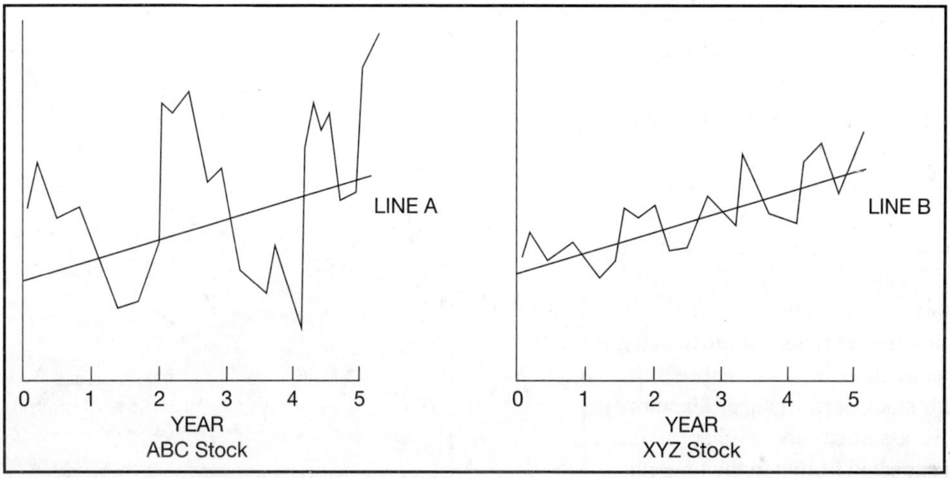

Figure 9.5 *Stock Prices over a Five-year Period*

Standard Deviation

Risk, or variability, of the stock's or mutual fund's return is measured by standard deviation.[3] Figure 9.5 presents the prices of the ABC and XYZ stocks over a five-year period. When line A (called least-squares line) is drawn that minimizes the total vertical distance between individual points that make up the curve and the line, and the exercise is repeated to complete line B, two important facts emerge: (a) the slopes (or elevation) of both lines are identical and (b) the ABC stock has fluctuated much more than the XYZ stock; therefore, the standard deviation (roughly, a kind of average distance between the line and

[3] For the pros, two equations make up the current standard deviation calculation. The first part calculates the fund's monthly standard deviation. The second part annualizes the monthly number to put it in a one-year context. The formula for monthly standard is shown as follows:

$$\text{Monthly Standard Deviation } (\sigma) = \sqrt{\frac{(x_1-\bar{x})^2+(x_2-\bar{x})^2+\cdots+(x_n-\bar{x})^2}{n}}$$

where:

X_1 = return for first month
X_i = return for the ith month (each month between the first and last month)
X_n = return for the last month
n = the total number of returns being used, in this case 36.
$\bar{X}$ = The average monthly total return during the 36-month period, also called the arithmetic mean. This number is arrived at by together adding all 36 monthly returns for the fund and dividing by 36. The formula for calculating $\bar{X}$ is as follows:

$$\bar{X} = \frac{X_1 + X_2 + \cdots + X_n}{n}$$

In the second equation, we annualize the monthly standard deviation to put the number in more useful one-year terms. The equation is as follows:

$$\text{Annualized Standard Deviation} = \sqrt{[\sigma^2 + (1+\bar{x})^2]^{12} - (1+\bar{x})^{2^{12}}}$$

where:

σ = monthly standard deviation, from the first part of the calculation.
$\bar{X}$ = the average monthly total return, or arithmetic mean, from above.

individual points) of ABC is much higher than that of XYZ. This implies that ABC investors have taken a bumpier ride than their XYZ counterparts to get to the same place. So, since the slopes of lines A and B are identical, which implies that both stocks generated the same average return, it can be concluded that ABC investors were not rewarded for assuming higher risks. Put differently, risk can be thought of as the price one pays for stock performance. The more of it is assumed, the higher is the return expected from it in the long run.

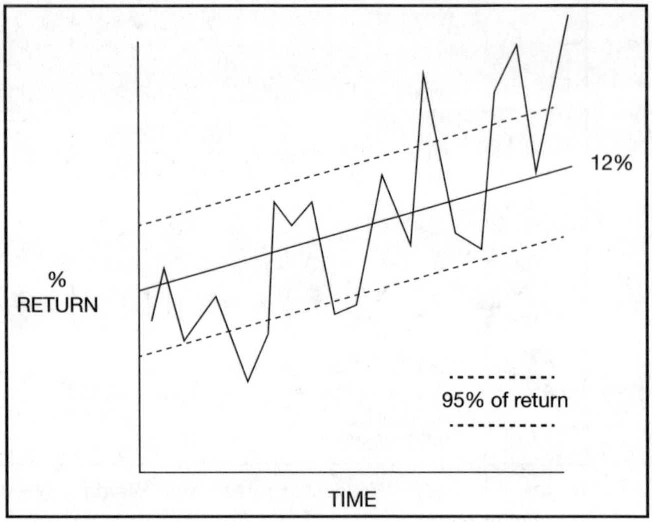

Figure 9.6 *Standard Deviation of Stocks*

Incidentally, standard deviation has another interpretive quality: assuming a normal distribution, 95 percent of the stock's return is expected to fall between the average return plus/minus two standard deviations (Figure 9.6). So, if the stock's average return is 12 percent and its standard deviation is 2 percent, then over time the stock is likely to return 12 percent plus/minus two standard deviations (i.e., between 8 and 16 percent). This information can come in handy in making investment decisions. It should be recognized, however, that the past history may not be repeated in the future.

Figure 9.7 demonstrates how standard deviation can be used as a decision-making tool in the real world.

Sharpe Ratio

Standard deviation is not without its flaws. It can be misleading because it penalizes upward moves as much as downward moves. A stock or a fund whose performance is consistently mediocre can score higher than one with a lot of upside volatility. Similarly, downside risk also can make a mediocre stock look better than one that had a few big disappointments but still soared over time.

A measure called the Sharpe ratio, named after Nobel Laureate William Sharpe, attempts to address this problem by adding performance data to the formula. This ratio is calculated by recording the difference over time between a stock's investment return and the yield of short-term Treasury bills. The

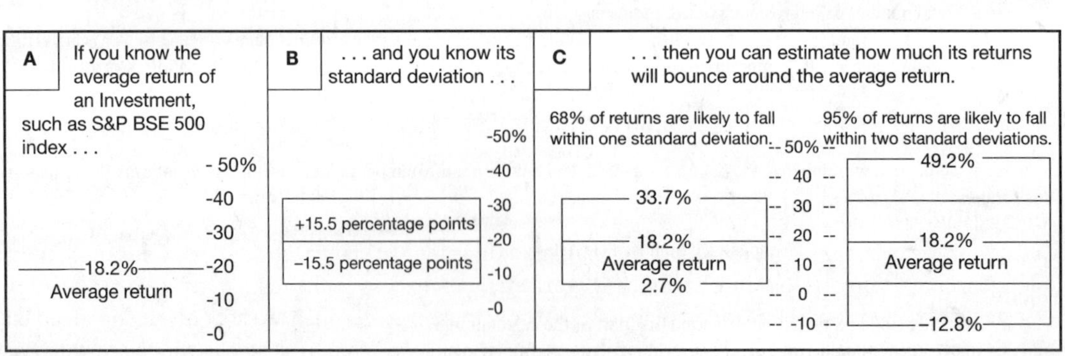

Figure 9.7 *Standard Deviation*

average of these measures is then divided by their standard deviation. Another way of explaining this ratio is to say that it is calculated by using standard deviation and excess return to determine reward per unit of risk. The higher the Sharpe ratio, the better is the stock's historical risk-adjusted performance.

The original Sharpe ratio has some of the same drawbacks as standard deviation, because standard deviation is part of the equation. To remedy that problem, Sharpe developed what he calls the *selection ratio* to measure risk-adjusted returns relative to a benchmark or index. This more recent version of the Sharpe ratio effectively puts all funds or stocks on an even playing field, assuming that benchmarks are correct.

Morningstar India Risk-adjusted Rating for Mutual Funds

Popularly known as Star Rating, this System rates performance vis-à-vis the associated risk. To determine a fund's star rating for a given time period (3, 5, or 10 years), its Morningstar Risk Score is subtracted from its Morningstar Return Score. For each time period, the result is then plotted on a bell curve to determine the fund's rating for each time period. If the fund scores in the top 10 percent of its broad asset class (domestic stock, international stock, taxable bond, or municipal bond), it receives a five star rating (highest); its placement in the next 22.5 percent category earns it a four star rating (above average); its place in the next 35 percent earns three stars (neutral); those in the next 22.5 percent slot receive two stars (below average); and the bottom 10 percent earn only a one star rating (lowest).

To be sure, Morningstar recognizes that no rating system can take into account all the factors that one must consider before investing in a mutual fund. For that reason, it is best to use this Rating as a means of identifying those mutual funds that have maximized returns relative to the risk they have assumed in producing these returns. Investors should, therefore, recognize that while it serves as an initial screen, the rating is only the first step toward a more comprehensive evaluation of each fund's performance.

TRADING IN EQUITIES

Buying a Stock

The key to successful stock market investment is the ability to size up a stock in order to determine whether or not it should be purchased. The time-tested strategy is to invest in an undervalued stock because, over time, the market price of a stock tends to gravitate toward its PV. That is, an investor should invest in a stock which is fundamentally strong and offers good value, but is currently selling below its present or intrinsic value.

It may be of some value to present here the techniques of fundamental analysis. The single most important variable in fundamental analysis is the projection of future earnings. With that in mind, the first order of business is to construct a comprehensive company profile. This profile would provide the basis for the analysis of the price/earnings ratio, the dividend yield, the growth of future earnings, and, finally, the analysis of the expected price appreciation. The company's position in the industry, the prevailing economic conditions, and the investor's risk tolerance level would help the investor calculate the discount rate with which the future earnings should be discounted to determine the PV of the stock. The final step in this analytical process is to select the stock whose PV exceeds its current market price.

While the identification of a fundamentally strong stock is the basis for stock market investment, the timing issue is equally important. The market does not always spot an attractive stock and frequently undervalued stocks perform poorly in a given market. Investing in such a stock at that time might mean a longer than anticipated holding period and even a temporary loss in the market value of the holding. Consequently, investors should attempt to invest in only those stocks which are not only undervalued but also exhibit technical strength. These securities are commonly referred to as stocks which are both *fundamentally* and *technically* strong.

Selling a Stock

The first law of successful stock investing is: Buy a stock which is both fundamentally and technically strong. The buying part may be relatively easy. Without a strict investment discipline, however, determining the right time to sell a stock might be extremely difficult. For one thing, when prices fall, it appears reasonable to postpone selling in hopes of a recovery. And when prices rise, greed can get in the way of taking profits. Notwithstanding the difficulties associated with the sale of a security, for good investment results, the task must be successfully performed. The reason is that, in the final analysis, in investing the potential gain is of little value unless it is actually realized. Several key selling strategies provide broad guidelines for selling a stock.

Theory of Undervalued Security

A good test of the attractiveness of a security at a given time is whether or not it is still an undervalued security. That is, if a stock which was undervalued when it was first selected and if it is still undervalued, then it makes sense to hold it until it becomes appropriately valued. If not, then it is a prime candidate for sale, regardless of how well it is performing at this time. This rule keeps emotions of greed out of the decision process.

Realization of Goals

After a stock has met an investor's goals, unless there are overriding considerations, it should be sold. For instance, suppose an investor purchases a stock at ₹25 because its book value is ₹40 and it generally sells at 85 percent of its book value. There is no law that says stocks have to be sold at the book value. But if the company is fundamentally sound, there is a good reason to believe the stock will return to near its historic price/book value ratio of 85 percent. So, if the price approaches ₹34 (85 percent of the book value of ₹40), an investor should consider selling the stock.

Change of Conditions

It is also appropriate to sell a stock if the reason for which the stock was purchased is no longer valid. Suppose an investor purchases the stock of a drug company which introduced a miracle drug in the market. If the product fizzles, it is best to face the new facts and sell the stock.

Speculator Success Syndrome

Quite often a spectacular price increase signals trouble for a stock.

Myth of Break-even Strategy

One myth that never seems to die is that a depressed stock should be held until the current losses are recouped. In order to appreciate the fallacy of this thinking, one needs to only consider the following in-text table:

Current Loss (%)	% Gain Required to Recoup the Loss
10	11
15	18
20	25
30	43
40	67
50	100
75	300

Note that if a stock loses 75 percent of its value, which was the case in 2008–10 for many stocks, then the stock must appreciate 300 percent merely to recoup the past losses. A more sensible and practical strategy would be to determine the PV of a security and sell it when the price exceeds the PV.

In this context, a mention should be made of the use of *stop loss orders* which are designed to minimize an investor's exposure to loss. When a stock is purchased, or at any time thereafter, the investor can instruct the broker to sell the stock if the price falls to a certain level, such as 5 or 10 percent below the purchase price. This would generally protect the investor against an extended drop, although the broker cannot guarantee a sale at the specified price. In the event of panic selling, such as that which occurred on the infamous Black Monday in the USA in 1987, there might not be any buyers. To avoid such a contingency, the investor could also place a *stop limit order*, authorizing the broker to sell at a specified price. Of course, such an order does not unconditionally guarantee that the order would be filled.

Tax Considerations

While as a general rule tax considerations should not be allowed to influence a decision to sell a stock, sometimes it is desirable to resort to tax selling at an opportune time. Basically, selling at a gain or a loss is a taxable event. Consequently, if a decision has been made to sell a security on fundamental grounds, selling it at a given time (for instance, before the year-end) could produce favorable tax outcomes.

LIMITING THE RISK

Weathering the market's ups and downs is a key concern for most investors, regardless of their risk tolerance level, age, tax bracket, or net worth. While the risk associated with stocks, bonds, and other investment vehicles cannot be eliminated, there are ways in which investors can reduce risk to manageable levels. Some of the better known techniques of weathering the market's fluctuations are discussed next.

Rupee Cost Averaging

RCA is a systematic program of investing equal sums of money at regular intervals, regardless of the price of shares. Clearly, RCA cannot guarantee a profit or prevent a loss. However, it does reduce the effects of market fluctuations over the long term. The reason is that instead of timing the market, an individual invests a predetermined amount of money regardless of whether the share price is high, low, or in between. Hence, he or she buys more shares when the price is low and fewer when it is high, thereby avoiding the common mistake that investors usually make of buying high and selling low.

The key advantage of RCA is that, in the long run, it has the potential of making the average share cost less than the average share price. Two illustrations, covering a weak market and a strong market, demonstrate this strategy. Each illustration assumes an investment of ₹100 per month.

A RCA program during a period of declining market is presented in Table 9.2. After four months and a total investment of ₹400, the average price of this investment is ₹7.00 while the average cost is ₹6.23.

Table 9.2 *Rupee Cost Averaging in a Declining Market*

Investment (₹)	Total Invested (₹)	Market Price (₹)	Shares Bought	Total Shares	Average Price/ Share (₹)	Average Cost/ Share (₹)
100	100	10	10.0	10.0	10.0	10.00
100	200	8	12.5	22.5	9.00	8.89
100	300	6	16.7	39.2	8.00	7.65
100	400	4	25.0	64.2	7.00	6.23

Table 9.3 *Rupee Cost Averaging in an Advancing Market*

Investment (₹)	Total Invested (₹)	Market Price (₹)	Shares Bought	Total Shares	Average Price/ Share (₹)	Average Cost/ Share (₹)
100	100	10	10.0	10.0	10.0	10.00
100	200	12	8.33	18.33	11.00	10.91
100	300	14	7.14	25.47	12.00	11.78
100	400	16	6.25	31.72	13.00	12.61

This situation is the result of purchasing progressively larger number of shares for ₹100 as the market price consistently declines, assuming that the stock continues to be undervalued and fundamentally strong. The second illustration, presented in Table 9.3, relates to an advancing market. In this case, the average cost of the investment is ₹12.61, but the average price is slightly higher (₹13.00) than the average cost. This is the result of an appreciation in the stock price in a rising market.

A word of caution should be added here. While both illustrations demonstrate their power as an investment tool, RCA is not an appropriate technique for short-term investments and, as mentioned, cannot guarantee a profit or prevent a loss. However, it does provide investors with the benefit of a disciplined investment program that eliminates the need for market timing and helps alleviate the effects of a fluctuating market.

Incidentally, investors who use the RCA strategy may find that market volatility particularly useful. The proof is in Table 9.4. In this table, the low-volatility case, presented on the left side, is contrasted with the high-volatility case, presented on the right side. Clearly, if the prices swing widely, by investing ₹12,000 over a 12-month period, then the investor is able to acquire 1,587 shares at an average cost of ₹7.56 per share. When the market swings are tempered, however, the same ₹12,000 buys only 1,484 shares at an average cost of ₹8.09 per share.

Constant Ratio Plan

The *constant ratio plan* (CRP) is a variation of RCA in which the monthly contribution is equally divided between a stock fund and a money market fund. Subsequently, if an increase in the share price makes the equity portion worth, considerably, more than the value of the money fund, then part of the equity fund

Table 9.4 *Market Volatility and Rupee Cost Averaging (Example: ₹1,000 Systematic Investment per Period)*

Low-volatility Case		High-volatility Case	
Price (₹)	Number of Shares	Price (₹)	Number of Shares
10	100	10	100
8	125	7	143
6	167	5	200
8	125	9	111
10	100	11	91
12	83	13	77
10	100	9	111
8	125	7	143
6	167	5	200
6	167	5	200
8	125	9	111
10	100	10	100
Total shares purchased	1,484		1,587
Average cost per share	₹8.09		₹7.56

would be liquidated and the proceeds transferred to the money fund. The reverse action would be taken if equity prices drop, thereby making the money fund worth more than the equity fund.

A 55/45 ratio limit is generally applied to the CRP, although other ratios would work equally well. This means that whenever the value of either fund exceeds 55 percent of the total value of the portfolio, an automatic readjustment plan is put into motion to make the ratio equal (50 percent). For instance, if the value of the stock fund rises to 55 percent, an investor shifts cash from the partially liquidated equity fund into the money fund to make them of equal value. Likewise, if the equity fund drops to 45 percent of the portfolio, the investor quickly shifts funds from the money fund into the equity fund to make them of equal value. The advantage of this strategy is that the investor automatically buys low and sells high.

Variable Installment Plan

A refined approach to investing in stocks is known as the *variable installment plan* (VIP), which begins with an equal investment in both stock and money funds, but shifts the emphasis on stock investment when the fund's share price declines. A simple rule is for the investor to direct the entire monthly contribution to the stock fund whenever its share price falls by a predetermined (e.g., 10 percent) percentage. Similarly, the investor would skip the monthly stock fund investment if its share price rises by 10 percent and invest the entire monthly contribution into the money fund.

A more sophisticated VIP strategy requires the investor to keep track of the average cost of the stock fund shares, including those purchased with reinvestment dividend and capital gains distributions. When the fund's current share price is higher than the average cost, the investor invests less in the stock fund. Conversely, when the share price is lower, more is invested in the stock fund.

A simple rule, which can be devised to determine how much of a contribution should be made to the stock fund, is described here:

$$\text{Amount of Contribution} = \frac{\text{Average Cost of Shares}}{\text{Current Price}} \times \text{Original Contribution}$$

For example, suppose an investor started investing ₹1,000 a month in a stock fund when the share price was ₹10.00. If, after a month, the price jumps to ₹12.00, the contribution for the second month would be ₹833.00 [(₹10/₹12) × ₹1,000]. The difference (₹167) would be invested in the money market fund.

Incidentally, investors can use other, more sophisticated, variations of the VIP just described. One such variation is known as the *leveraged variable investment plan* (LVIP), which requires the calculation of a leverage factor to minimize the average cost of a stock fund. In fact, an imaginative and sophisticated investor can design a variety of complex plans to suit his or her investment objectives.

Strategy of Covered Calls

The market risk can also be reduced by the sale of covered call options. A call option gives the buyer the right to purchase a stock at the *strike* or set price within the call option period. The option is covered by the stock the investor owns at the time of the option sale. A covered call option reduces the investor's risk exposure, although it simultaneously reduces the potential for profit as well. An illustration should make this strategy clear.

Let us assume Susan owns 100 shares of ABC stock, trading at ₹30 per share. Susan sells a contract giving the buyer the option to buy these shares for ₹30 within the next six months; in return she receives a premium of ₹3 per share, or a total of ₹300. If ABC's price drops to, say, ₹28 per share in the next six months and the option is not exercised, Susan's investment drops to ₹2,800 (100 shares × ₹28). However, the loss is more than compensated by the ₹300 option price, so that she ends up with a profit. Clearly, a stockholder can always continue to write options to generate additional investment income. This strategy works best in a stable market.

But what if the stock price rises to ₹35 and the option is exercised? In that case, Susan must surrender the stock at ₹30 per share. The result will be that she will end up with ₹3,300 (₹3,000 from the stock sale plus ₹300 option price) instead of ₹3,500 which she would have received from the sale of the stock had she not sold the option. It is now easy to see why a covered call option reduces the risk exposure but also simultaneously reduces the potential for profit.

Call Option with Stock Sale

A reverse strategy is to lock in profits by selling an appreciated stock and simultaneously buying call options on the same stock. As mentioned, a call option gives a buyer the right to buy 100 shares of the stock at a certain price for a fixed time period.

This strategy works in the following manner. Suppose Roshan owns 100 shares of XYZ in which currently he has a ₹1,200 profit. Roshan thinks the stock is overpriced and will eventually plunge. However, he notices that XYZ is hot and thinks it might still make one or two upward moves before taking a nose dive. Consequently, Roshan sells XYZ at ₹40, thereby locking in the ₹1,200 profit and buys a six-month call option on the stock for ₹300. If the stock does rise, Roshan will exercise the option and realize additional profit. If not, all Roshan would lose would be the ₹300 option price, but he would have locked in the ₹1,200 capital gain on that stock.

Mutual Fund Returns

The main purpose for investing in a mutual fund, as it is for any investment, is to realize an acceptable return. It is, therefore, important to learn how to determine mutual fund returns.

A typical mutual fund statement received by Shweta on December 30, 2014, is presented in Table 9.5. Based on the data presented in this table, Shweta's rate of return on her sensible mutual fund investment can be determined in the manner presented in Table 9.6.

SALE OF MUTUAL FUNDS

Basic Issue

Buying mutual fund shares completes only half the transaction. The other half consists of the decision one faces to sell it at the most appropriate time—unquestionably the toughest decision one faces as a mutual fund investor. Unfortunately, matching the PV of a fund's share to its market price is not a viable approach. The reason is that the mutual fund is a portfolio of stocks, bonds, and other related securities, and at any given moment a portfolio is likely to contain both undervalued and overvalued securities. Consequently, different strategies must be developed to decide when to sell mutual fund shares. In the following paragraphs, we will present several of these strategies.

Change of Investment Objective

Buying into a mutual fund, of course, is just the beginning of an investment process. A change in the stock or bond market or in an investor's risk preference, or because of a change of the fund manager, could necessitate switching, or liquidating investment in mutual fund shares. Each fund is committed to a particular investment philosophy which dictates the types of securities it will hold. Although its managers may alter the holdings on a regular basis, they cannot completely change direction to capitalize on basic changes in investment conditions. In fact, by the terms specified in the prospectus, many funds are required to invest only in certain types or grades of securities. For example, an income fund may replace certain stocks with others, but even the new stocks must be income stocks. Consequently, an income

Table 9.5 *Sensible Mutual Fund Account*

Confirmation date: December 30, 2013
Page 1 of 1
2012–13 Statement
Shweta
DLF Tower
Sector 43, Gurgaon
Account number : 0000213944

Statement Date	Transaction Date	Transaction Detail Description	Amount of Transaction	Share Price	Shares This Transaction	Total Shares Owned
		Beginning balance	₹5000.00			164.870
06/01/2012	06/01/2012	Investment	5000.00	₹26.92	185.735	350.605
18/04/2012	07/04/2012	Income reinv. at. .250	87.65	28.50	3.075	353.680
18/04/2012	07/04/2012	Short-ter, cap.gain at .450	157.77	–	–	353.680
02/06/2012	02/06/2012	Investment	1000.00	30.34	32.955	386.635
18/07/2012	05/07/2012	Income reinv. at. .250	96.66	31.30	3.09	389.725
25/10/2012	11/10/2012	Income reinv. at. .250	97.43	35.80	2.72	392.445
04/01/2013	04/01/2013	Redemption	1000.00	37.90	–26.39	366.055
27/01/2013	18/01/2013	Income reinv. at. .200	73.21	37.92	1.93	367.985
27/01/2013	03/01/2013	Short-ter, cap.gain at .500	183.03	–	–	367.985
27/04/2013	04/04/2013	Income reinv. at. .300	110.40	38.02	2.90	370.885
19/07/2013	05/07/2013	Income reinv. at. .250	92.72	37.50	2.47	373.355

Table 9.6 *Rate of Return*

Line	Result
A. Average Cost	
1. The number of months (maximum 24 months) over which the return is calculated	19
2. Value of investment at the beginning of the period: 350.605 shares × ₹26.92	₹9,468
3. Value of investment at the end of the period 373.355 shares × ₹37.50	₹14,000
4. Dividend income and capital gains distributions paid out in cash and not reinvested	₹341
5. Net redemptions or investments, excluding reinvested distributions and initial investment: ₹1,000 (investment on 02/06/2006)-₹1,000 (redemption)	₹0
6. Add Line 2 to half of Line 5	₹9,468
7. Add Lines 3 and 4, then subtract half of Line 5 amount	₹14,341
8. Divide Line 7 by Line 6	₹1.519
9. Subtract 1 from Line 8, then multiply by 100	51.9%
10. For annualized return, divide 12 by the number of Line 1. Multiply the result by Line 9	32.7%
B. Average Cost	

$$\frac{₹\,10{,}000 + 87.65 + 96.66 + 97.43 + 73.21 + 110.40 + 92.72}{373.355}$$

$$= \frac{₹\,10{,}558.07}{373.355}$$

$$= ₹\,28.28$$

fund investor unwilling to hold income stocks has little choice but to move the money to another type of fund with a different goal or method of operation.

Consistent Poor Performance

Mutual fund investment is for the long term, and one or two bad quarters should not be the compelling reason for liquidating the shares. However, if for several quarters the fund's performance ranks in the bottom fourth or fifth of funds of its type, consideration should be given to liquidating the fund. Of course, in making this decision the back-end load charges, if applicable, and tax consequences of the sale, must be taken into account.

Fund Size

The general maxim for mutual fund investment in stocks is: *smaller is better*. The critical size for a mutual fund appears to be assets of around ₹10–12,000 crore, as portfolio managers face increasingly difficult investment choices as the assets exceed ₹10,000 crore. Clearly, investing large amounts of money makes it more difficult to accumulate meaningful positions in individual stock issues, especially if these issues are relatively small. There are exceptions, of course, as is evidenced by the extraordinary success of the US mutual funds, Fidelity Magellan and Vanguard, which manage billions of dollars. But these exceptions are rare, and investors would be well advised to get out when their fund gets too big for their taste. This small size criterion does not apply to bond mutual funds, however, since the more bonds a fund holds, the slimmer are the chances of its being badly hurt should some of its bond issuers default.

Miscellaneous Changes

If a fund portfolio manager responsible for the fund's admirable record quits the fund, and the new manager does not have a respectable track record, it would be wise to carefully watch the fund's future performance under the new manager. Investors should also be leery of spectacular performance for several consecutive months. Such performance is usually the result of the manager's taking unusually high risks with investors' money. Finally, a change in economic conditions might warrant a shift from a stock or bond fund into a money market fund.

MUTUAL FUNDS AND TAXES

At tax time, every mutual fund shareholder is faced with a dual task: reporting fund distributions (dividend income and capital gain distribution) and calculating capital gains and losses as a result of the sale (redemption) or exchange of fund shares.

Fund Distributions

At the beginning of every year, every mutual fund sends its investors a form for each of the regular, nonqualified accounts. This form lists the taxable dividend and capital gains distributions that the fund declared during the previous year and paid by March 31 of the current year. All dividend and capital gains distributions listed on this form are considered taxable even if they were reinvested in the fund, unless it is a municipal bond fund in which case dividends are treated as tax-free distributions. Currently, short-term capital gains (STCGs) are taxed at the same rate as dividend distributions.

If an investor holds for less than 365 days the investments in a mutual fund scheme, then that investment is treated as a short-term investment; hence, any gains resulting from the sale of that investment would be treated as STCGs. By contrast, gains resulting from the sale of an investment held for more than a year would be treated as long-term capital gains (LTCGs). Dividends received by mutual fund holders are classified as dividend payout, dividend reinvestment and dividend growth, depending on the type of mutual fund declaring the dividend.

Let us now discuss the taxation aspects (capital gains tax and dividend distribution tax [DDT]) in case of "mutual fund investments" from the perspective of "investors."

Taxation of Equity Mutual Funds

Equity mutual funds have at least a 65 percent share of equity in the entire portfolio.

1. ***Short-term capital gains tax (as per Section 111A).*** Investors realizing STCGs are subject to a tax rate of 15 percent.

   Assume Niraj bought units of equity mutual funds for ₹1 lakh. He redeems his mutual fund units within six months (instead of a year) and gains ₹25,000. In this case, he has made a STCG and has to pay the STCG tax. For the 2013–14 fiscal year, the STCG tax on mutual fund schemes is 15 percent. Hence, in this case, the tax amounts to ₹3,750 (₹25,000 × 15% = ₹3,750).

2. ***Long-term capital gains tax (exempt from tax U/s 10[38]).*** There is no tax applicable to investors realizing LTCGs.

   In the previous example, had Niraj sold these units after 12 months for ₹1.25 lakh, he would have realized an LTCG of ₹25,000. And since for equity funds LTCGs are tax free, Niraj would have paid no taxes on this gain. Incidentally, for securities held in equity funds for more than a year, at the time of sale or switching to other units, securities transaction tax is automatically deducted from the sale proceeds.

3. ***Dividend distribution tax.*** There is no tax applicable to investors on dividends realized on the mutual fund scheme.

Debt Mutual Funds

For the fiscal year 2014, Table 9.7 summarizes information on short-term and long-term capital gains tax, dividend income tax and dividend distribution tax.

1. ***Short-term capital gains tax.*** Investors realizing STCGs are subject to a tax rate equal to their individual tax slab applicable under Income Tax Act (ITA), 1961.

2. ***Long-term capital gains tax.*** In contrast to STCGs, LTCGs are subject to LTCGs tax of 10 percent in case of no indexation and 20 percent for the rest plus applicable cess/surcharge.

3. ***Dividend distribution tax.*** DDT (25 percent plus surcharge plus cess) is payable by mutual fund companies on dividends received by debt mutual fund scheme holders and the same also gets adjusted in the net asset value (NAV) of the scheme. In other words, dividend received by an investor is not taxable, however, the mutual fund company/fund manager pays a DDT and this correspondingly reduces investors fund NAV. Fund managers do not pay your dividend taxes from their income; instead investors pay these taxes indirectly.

Calculating Capital Gains/Losses on Fund Sales

In order to calculate the taxable gain or loss on mutual fund shares sold, the investor has to determine the sale price and the true cost of those shares, known as the cost basis. The former is easy to determine; the

Table 9.7 *Capital Gains and Dividend Tax for Debt Mutual Funds for FY2014*

Tax	Tax Rate for Individuals and Hindu Undivided Families (HUFs)
Long-term capital gain tax	10% without indexation or 20% with indexation whichever is lower
Short-term capital gain tax	30% (assuming the investor falls in the highest tax bracket)
Dividend income	Exempt or nil
DDT	25% (applicable from 1 June 2013)

latter is more complex. Under the Indian ITA, 1961, gain or loss derived from the sale/redemption of debt mutual fund units held as investments is characterized as capital gains. However, the capital assets are classified into short-term capital assets and long-term capital assets depending on the period of holding of investments. Long-term capital assets are the assets held for more than 12 months from the date of purchase. Assets held for less than 12 months after the date of purchase are short-term capital assets. However, in case of equity mutual funds, LTCGs are tax exempt. A 15 percent tax is applicable to STCGs.

Though for the purpose of computing the capital gains and determining the period of holding first-in-first-out (FIFO) method is allowed in India, there are various ways to determine the cost basis. These are discussed next.

Specific identification method (applicable in the USA). When a capital gain is reported on a mutual fund sale, the Indian Revenue Service (IRS) allows an investor to identify the sale of those shares for which originally the highest price was paid. Obviously, this constitutes the best strategy, since that would automatically minimize the gain and the tax liability.

First-in, first-out method. When a capital gain is reported on a mutual fund sale, the income tax law allows an investor to identify the sale of those shares that were acquired first, known as the FIFO approach. This method may maximize the tax bill, since as a general rule, the shares bought first are likely to have the lowest cost.

Long-term capital gains/losses (LTCG/L). Gains/losses arising from sale/redemption of long-term capital asset are termed as LTCG/L. LTCG is taxed at a concessional rate of 10 percent without indexation or at 20 percent with indexation (subject to the total income including LTCG exceeding the basic exemption limit). Indexation means inflating the investment cost using the cost inflation index (CII) table published periodically by the government. An investor can choose to pay tax based on the lower of the two sums, whichever is beneficial. For instance, if the tax computed using the rate of 10 percent (plus applicable surcharge and education cess, and secondary and higher education cess) without indexation is lower than the tax computed using 20 percent (plus applicable surcharge and education cess, and secondary and higher education cess) with indexation, the investor pays the lower amount of tax. The losses arising from sale/redemption of long-term capital asset may be offset against gains arising from the transfer of other long-term capital asset during the same assessment year. In case long-term capital losses cannot be offset against LTCG during the same year, it can be carried forward and offset against LTCG arising in future assessment years. Such losses are permitted to be carried forward up to eight assessment years.

Short-term capital gains/losses (STCG/L). Gains/losses derived from the sale/redemption of short-term capital assets are termed as STCG/L. STCG are included in the total income of an investor and are taxed at the slab rates applicable to the investor (subject to the total income, including STCG exceeds the basic exemption limit). The losses arising from the sale/redemption of short-term capital asset may be offset against gains arising from the transfer of other short-term capital asset or long-term capital asset for the same assessment year. In case short-term capital loss cannot be set off against the income under same head in the same year, it can be carried forward and set off against STCG and LTCG arising in future assessment years. Such losses are permitted to be carried forward up to eight assessment years.

An investor acquired/subscribed 1,000 units of a debt fund in the financial year 2004 at the rate of ₹10 An investor acquired/subscribed 1,000 per unit. In the financial year 2014, the investor sells/redeems the units at a price of ₹45 per unit. The indicative computation of the LTCG is shown in Table 9.8.[4]

[4] http://www.hdfcfund.com/InvestorEducation/ContentDisplay.aspx?ReportID=3756BBC5-8EB6-4E73-9905-B955A2C99523 (last accessed on June 1, 2014).

Table 9.8 *Mutual Fund Tax Calculation (Long-term Capital Gains/Losses)*

Particulars	Tax with Indexation	Tax without Indexation (% of the Net Assets)
Nature of gain/loss	Since units are held as investments for over a year, gain are taxable as LTCG.	
Sale value (1,000 units × 45 per unit)	₹45,000	₹45,000
Actual cost (1,000 units × 10 per unit)	₹10,000	₹10,000
Indexed cost	₹18,402	–
Profit	₹26,598	₹35,000
Tax rate	20%	10%
Tax amount	₹5,320	₹3,500

Applying the beneficial rate, tax on capital gains could be ₹3,500 (plus applicable surcharge and education cess and secondary and higher education cess), subject to the total income including LTCG exceeding the basic exemption limit.

The indexed cost of acquisition. To arrive at the indexed cost of acquisition, the formula is:

Indexed Cost = Cost Price multiplied by CII of the current year divided by CII of the year of purchase

Financial year of purchase: 2004
Financial year of sale: 2014
Purchase CII (2004–05): 463
Sale CII (2013–14): 852 (As prescribed by the CBDT periodically on financial year basis)

Hence, indexed cost = 10,000 × 852/463
Indexed cost: ₹18,402

Short-term capital gains/losses of STCG. In the above illustration, had the investor acquired/subscribed 1,000 units of a debt fund in the year 2013 at the rate of ₹10 per unit and sold/redeemed the units in 2013 at a price of ₹45 per unit in the same financial year holding the investment for less than 12 months, the gains of ₹35,000 would have been taxed as STCG as per the slab rates applicable to the investors (subject to the total income including STCG exceeding the basic exemption limit).

Individual investors can also claim the benefit of deduction against the LTCG arising from sale/redemption of mutual funds by making investments in specified bonds under Section 54EC of the ITA or by making investment in residential house property under Section 54F of the ITA. The said deductions are subject to fulfillment of other conditions specified by law.

Dividend payout option. Dividend received from debt scheme of mutual funds under dividend payout option is tax exempt in the hands of investors. For instance, if an investor receives a dividend of ₹1,250 from a debt scheme under this option, it will not be treated as taxable income. Instead the mutual fund would be liable to pay the DDT at the rate of 28.325 percent on the dividend payout to resident individual.

Dividend reinvestment option. Under this option, dividends declared by a mutual fund are reinvested at NAV at the time of declaration of the dividends. This results in the investor receiving additional units of mutual fund. For instance, if a mutual fund declares a dividend of ₹1,250 to an investor, it will be reinvested at the then prevalent NAV (₹15) in the scheme on behalf of the investor. In this illustration, the investor will be entitled to receive additional 83.33 units (₹1,250 divided by ₹15) based on the dividends reinvested in the scheme. The mutual fund is liable to pay DDT at the rate of 28.325 percent on the dividend declared and reinvested. The investor is liable to pay capital gains tax at the time of sale or redemption of the units at applicable rates.[5]

Average cost method (applicable in the USA). A better alternative might be to use the average cost approach, which requires calculating the average per-share price for all the shares of the fund. This may generate a lower tax liability than with the FIFO approach.

Section III: Theory of Portfolio Construction

INTRODUCTION

The market can be a lot like the weather: One day, everything feels hot. The next day, cold winds start to blow. Trying to predict the direction of the market from one day to the next is even harder than predicting the weather. Steep declines or huge gains in the market in quick succession are the reason for developing a sensible investment portfolio strategy that could serve investors over the long horizon.

Experts say that, contrary to the popular belief, real investment success is not always due to the ability to select the best investments at the most opportune times. Instead, most effective strategies are based on diversification and asset allocation—strategically spreading the investments across broad asset classes such as stocks, bonds, and cash to achieve the investment goals. In fact, a landmark study found that over 90 percent of the variability in total portfolio return was determined by long-term asset allocation, while less than 5 percent of *variability* in return was the result of specific investment selection. In this section, we will present the use of the concepts of diversification and asset allocation in the construction of an efficient portfolio. Also, for pedagogical reasons, we will use only mutual funds in demonstrating the technique of portfolio construction.

THEORY OF EFFICIENT PORTFOLIO

In 1952, Harry Markowitz developed a novel approach to stock investment, which virtually revolutionized the thinking of the academic community. In fact, the basic elements of MPT are based on a series of propositions concerning rational investor behavior which were first developed by Markowitz.

The basis of Markowitz's approach was the use of fluctuations or variability of investment returns as an approximation of the risk of investment. If Stock A is expected to yield 8 percent +/–2 percent (i.e., between 6 and 10 percent) and Stock B is expected to yield 8 percent +/–4 percent (i.e., between 4 and 12 percent), then both stocks have the expected return of 8 percent. But because Stock B's return can fluctuate more widely than A's, B is more risky and, hence, less desirable than A. First, Markowitz sought to formalize this concept of risk by using the statistical concept of variance. Then he developed the portfolio theory by demonstrating that once the level of risk the investor is willing to assume is established, a computerized theoretical model could be used for selecting the optimum portfolio that would maximize the rate of return.

Once the basis for measuring risk and return of a single stock was established, the academic community formally addressed the risk problem that was created by putting all the eggs in the same basket. Ultimately, diversification became as hypnotic a mantra for investors as location is for real estate buyers. Professionals universally agreed that investors should spread their investment bets among different types of investments to reduce the overall volatility of their portfolio. If one investment sinks, the other may hold up or even take off.

[5] http://www.hdfcfund.com/beginners-guide-to-debt-mutual-funds-details/BB882842-2DC7-4E53-9991-7456AE072EA1 (last accessed on March 23, 2015).

While the concept of diversification revolutionized the investment world, it was driven by an amazing discovery with two counterparts. First, it was established that the expected return of a portfolio is simply the *weighted average of each of the individual assets making up the portfolio.* Second, it was discovered that if the assets in a portfolio are not perfectly correlated, the risk of that portfolio will be *less than the weighted average of the risks of the individual assets* in the portfolio. So, by properly diversifying a portfolio with assets that do not move in tandem, an investor can *reduce the overall risk of the portfolio without sacrificing the average return*. This is the essence of the MPT.

CAPITAL ASSET PRICING MODEL

The Markowitz Model was theoretically sound. However, its serious limitation was that it related each security to every other security in the portfolio, demanding the sophistication and volume of work well beyond the capacity of all but a few analysts. Then surfaced the *beta revolution* launched by William Sharpe, who subsequently became the Nobel Laureate for his path breaking work. Sharpe assumed that the return on a security could be regarded as being related to a single index like the market index. This index should consist of all the securities trading on the market, and could be represented by a popular average like the S&P 500 Index. This new relationship was identified as the Market Model.

The Market Model provided the conceptual foundation for the Capital Asset Pricing Model (CAPM), which is at the heart of the MPT. Under the CAPM, the attention was shifted from variance between numerous securities in the market to beta, which measures nondiversifiable risk. Also, to complete the beta revolution, the relationship between risky and risk-free returns was carefully established around beta as the key variable of the model.

The finding of the CAPM with beta measuring the risk of risky securities, and the inclusion of risk-free securities in a portfolio is extremely powerful. It claims that the expected return on a portfolio is equal to the risk-free rate plus a risk premium that is proportional to the risk measure, beta. Based on this relationship, we arrive at three powerful conclusions:

1. An astute investor expecting to beat the market without assuming additional risk must generate a rate of return that exceeds the expected return of this portfolio.
2. If an investor assumes a higher level of risk than is associated with this efficient portfolio, then a higher level of return must be realized to compensate for the additional risk assumed.
3. If the return of a portfolio with similar risk is less than the expected return of the efficient portfolio, then the investor is failed to construct an efficient portfolio.

The basic assumptions of CAPM can now be summarized.

1. Investors are generally risk-averse. They expect to be rewarded for risk.
2. Investors behave in a rational manner. They choose only efficient portfolios that maximize return for a given level of risk, or minimize risk for a given level of return.
3. Investors want to maximize their returns. They optimize their portfolio combinations by efficient diversification.

POWER OF DIVERSIFICATION

Basic Observations

By now, we have clearly established the importance of diversification: Investors must make sure that their investment portfolios are suitably diversified, and that they are familiar with an array of mutual funds, since investing in funds is a good way to spread their risk and extend their opportunities.

Few of us have the time or the knowledge to diversify our holdings effectively by picking individual stocks. As a result, we wind up being either under-diversified or, its somewhat less evil twin, over-diversified. Since both are likely to result in an unfavorable outcome, it is important to fully recognize the power of proper diversification.

One of the key elements of the CAPM is that the market portfolio is the optimum portfolio. However, this portfolio consists of hundreds of securities, which makes it virtually impossible (except through an index fund) for anyone to invest in it. This difficulty must be viewed against the twin facts that diversification reduces diversifiable risk, and that only the fully diversified market portfolio succeeds in completely eliminating this risk. Therefore, the critical question becomes: What is the minimum number of securities that an investor must buy to eliminate *most* of the diversifiable risk. Research studies have clearly demonstrated that, at the properly selected 15-stock level, almost 95 percent of the portfolio's diversifiable risk can be virtually eliminated.

Mutual fund investors enjoy a built-in head start on diversification, since most equity funds hold anywhere from several dozen to a few hundred stocks. However, that creates another potential problem. Individual funds often concentrate on a narrow slice of the market, such as putting most of their money in technology companies or focusing on just small-cap or large-cap issues. This means that investors are more vulnerable to price shifts than might be assumed, based on the number of stocks these funds own.

And that leads to a different question: "How many mutual funds should an investor carry within a given investment class?" Or to put it differently, how many growth funds does an investor need before the benefits of diversification diminish? How many balanced or international funds? In short, how many funds are enough, and how much is too much?

A research study completed some time ago covered four equity categories—growth, growth and income, international, and balanced funds—and compared the results against the benchmark indices. The study found that best results are obtained when for each category more than one, and no more than three, mutual funds are selected. By the time four funds are included, the category is highly correlated with the benchmark, so that little benefit is derived from the last addition. Of course, in adding funds to mitigate risk and optimize performance, it is important to choose funds that are unrelated to one another. The story is much the same when overseas funds are considered. If one could select the single international fund with the smallest relationship to Morgan Stanley Capital International's EAFE (Europe, Australasia and Far East) stock index, the portfolio would still be at the 75 percent correlation mark. Adding a second fund would make the portfolio move in lockstep with the market.

Investors can consult BSE Morningstar's *Value Line Mutual Fund Survey*, or a fund's annual report to see how various funds are correlated with each other, and with the relevant benchmark. In the final analysis, the best chance to beat the market is to invest in funds that bear little statistical relationship to a benchmark index.

At this point, it is important to add a caveat. In trying to accurately determine how many mutual funds should be selected for an efficient portfolio, investors should not lose sight of their investment objectives, tolerance for risk, and sense of whether the market is headed up or down. After all, the objective of an efficient portfolio is not only to deliver the highest return for the level of risk acceptable to an investor, but also to provide the comfort level that every investor needs to stay the course.

Global Diversification

Thus far, the discussion has centered on the benefits of diversification without making a distinction between domestic and international funds. Academic studies have clearly demonstrated that foreign securities represent additional asset classes that can be blended with domestic stocks, bonds, and cash to form a *balanced* portfolio. Even more important, over the long-term the right combination of funds enables investors to earn higher returns while actually reducing risk of the overall portfolio.

The reasons for focusing our attention on global investment can now be spelled out. More than three-fourth of the world's stock market values are outside India. Also, investing in foreign markets may reduce risk if overseas markets are not correlated with the Indian market. For that reason, they are likely to hold up when the Indian stock market sinks, smoothing out year-to-year returns for the overall portfolio. That is, markets do not move in lockstep, and blending international stocks with domestic issues can bring more stability to a portfolio.

THE EFFICIENT FRONTIER

The final step in building an *efficient* portfolio through diversification is to place this portfolio on the *efficient frontier*. This concept is discussed next.

The concept of diversification can be used to construct numerous portfolios with different combination of stocks, bonds, and cash. These portfolios will differ from each other not only with regard to the individual securities they contain, but with regard to the relative weights of individual securities as well. Assume that A, B, and C have been identified (see Figure 9.8) as model portfolios. Clearly, B is preferable to A, because both offer the same expected return, but B is less risky than the latter. Similarly, C is preferable to A, because it offers higher expected return, even though it is in the same risk class as A. However, portfolio B *may not* be preferable to portfolio C, because it not only offers lower expected return but also has smaller risk. An aggressive investor might prefer C, but a conservative investor would probably choose B.

From the foregoing discussion, a clear theme emerges. All portfolios below the EBCD curve are inefficient portfolios because, compared to the portfolios on the curve, they either offer lower returns or assume higher risks. By the same logic, all portfolios *on the curve* are efficient in that each portfolio offers *the highest expected return for its risk class*. For this reason, the EBCD curve is known as the Efficient Frontier.

The power of the Efficient Frontier can be gleaned from the real-world global portfolios presented in Figure 9.9(A and B). This chart underscores two important facts. First, once the risk level acceptable to an investor has been determined, it is important to create a portfolio that will lie on the efficient frontier for that level of risk. Second, diversification between stocks, bonds, and cash [Figure 9.9(A)], and between domestic and global diversification [Figure 9.9(B)] can increase return while reducing risk (a journey to the northwest).

The twin concepts of diversification and efficient frontier led to the establishment of Asset Allocation Model (AAM) as the foundation for diversifying a portfolio. This model is discussed next.

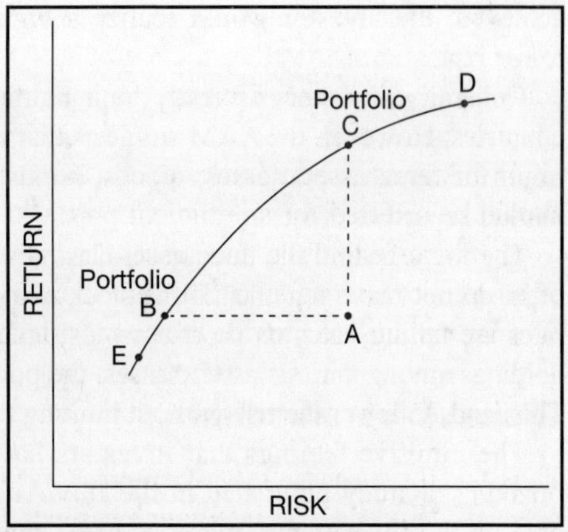

Figure 9.8 *Model Portofolios*

ASSET ALLOCATION MODEL

One of the hottest buzzwords in financial planning—the AAM—is no passing fad. Formally introduced into the finance literature more than three decades ago as MPT, AAM provides the foundation for diversifying a portfolio.

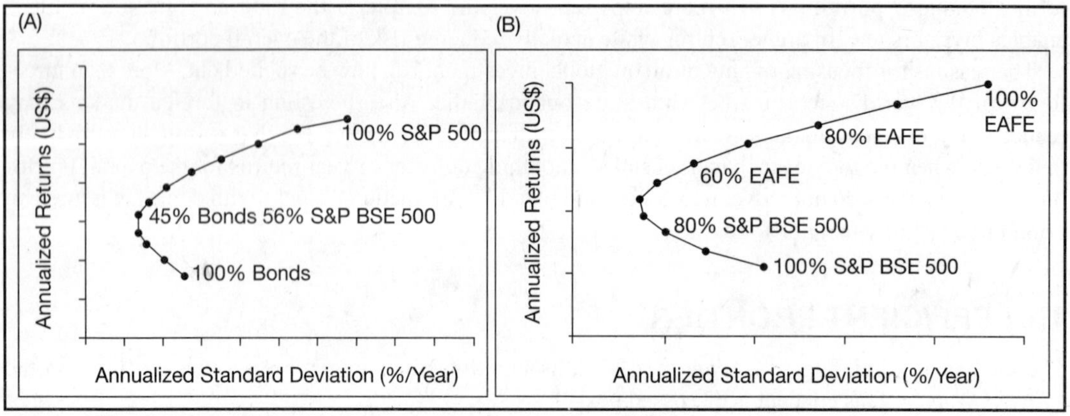

Figure 9.9 *Portfolio Diversification Benefits (A) and Portfolio Return and Risk (B)*
Source: Acadamic Annual Management.

Every investment portfolio can be plotted on Figure 9.10, which measures the returns obtained by various portfolios at different levels of risk. Each portfolio has a risk and a reward element. An investment counselor assembles a mix of assets to offer the highest return consistent with the client's risk level.

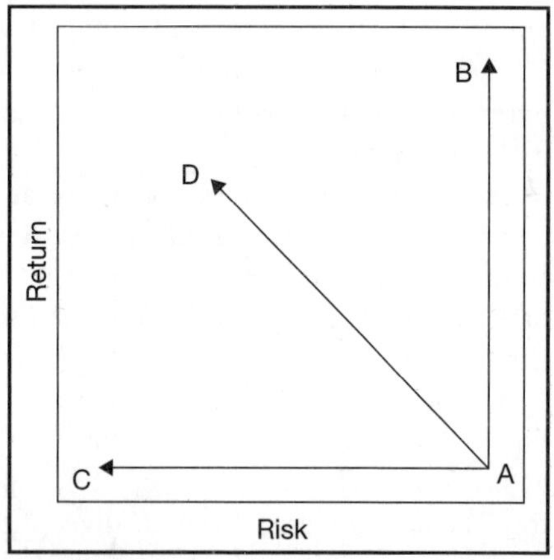

Figure 9.10 *Risk-Return Relationship*

Assume an investor currently owns a portfolio positioned at point A. The initial objective of the portfolio manager is to systematically alter the current mix so that the portfolio will move from point A to point C which represents less risk without sacrificing return, or from A to B which represents higher return without assuming higher risk. The ultimate aim of using the AAM is to move portfolio A northwest and terminate the journey at, say, point D. if this could be achieved, the investor would realize a *higher return at a lower risk.*

Generally, investors diversify their holdings by spreading assets among companies, industries, and countries. However, the AAM suggests that investors should also diversify their securities across a minimum of three asset classes: stocks, bonds, and liquid instruments such as Treasury bills or money market securities.

The logic behind the three-asset-class diversification strategy is simple: The stock and bond markets often do not move together. If the stock market is down, bonds could go up. Or if the long-term interest rates are falling, rates on short-term instruments could be increasing. So if an investor can diversify the holdings among various asset classes, the portfolio's exposure to any single investment arena is reduced. This tends to lower the risk without limiting the return.

The intuitive feelings that investors have toward the benefits of diversification were first legitimized by a study published in the July/August 1986 issue of *The Financial Analyst Journal*. Using data on the investment strategies of 91 major pension funds of the USA over a 10-year period, the results showed that more than 90 percent of the variability in an individual portfolio's performance can be attributed to asset allocation policy, with market timing and the selection of securities playing only a minor role. Put differently, spreading assets across stocks, bonds, and short-term instruments can affect the variability in a portfolio's performance more than trying to pick the right stocks at the right time.

Risk–Reward Connection

In order to fully appreciate the power of AAM, we must establish the risk/reward connection by identifying the many types of risk that can influence a portfolio's returns. Market or systematic risk refers to that portion of total variability of stock's return caused by factors which simultaneously affect the average return of all marketable securities. That is, market risk refers to the possibility that individual investments could lose values because of a general weakness in the market.

Besides market risk there are other risks that affect the values of individual stocks and bonds in a portfolio. For instance, inflation risk is the probability that the value of the return on an investment would be eroded by inflation. Another risk particularly inherent in every investment in fixed-income securities is interest rate risk, which suggests that an increase in the interest rate would lower the value of interest-sensitive instruments like bonds. However, the total impact of interest rate fluctuations on fixed-income securities may be confusing. For instance, higher interest rates may increase the interest rate of short-term instruments like money market accounts while lowering bond prices. In contrast, a decline in interest rates, which lowers the income from money market instruments, might increase the demand, and, hence, the value, of existing bonds carrying higher coupon rates.

Indeed, there are still more risks that can influence a portfolio's return. Nevertheless, when holdings are spread across various asset classes, the *decline* in value of one class due to these risk factors is likely to be accompanied by a simultaneous *gain* by another class. As a result, the portfolio's risk level would most likely be reduced when return increases.

In Figure 9.11, which presents the long-term historical return of various portfolios, two portfolios are of special interest. As expected, portfolio A, which consists of only fixed-income securities, has the lowest return and a low level of risk. However, portfolio C, which combines equities and fixed-income securities, has a *higher* return and *lower* risk. This northwest journey is made possible by the application of the AAM.

Over a period of 10 years ending in 2013, a balanced, moderate-risk portfolio with 35 percent in stocks, 35 percent in 10-year Treasury bonds, and 30 percent in Treasury bills gained substantially more than the investment in Treasury bills, but it was worth much less than an all-stock portfolio. To earn the higher returns as compared to a Treasury bill investor, however, the diversified portfolio investor encountered more volatility in annual returns. But these fluctuations were considerably less than those of the all-stock investor.

Interestingly, a diversified approach can mitigate the degree of loss in any one year. Even in 1993, when the S&P BSE Stock Index lost a whopping 46.78 percent, the diversified portfolio lost less than 2 percent.

An Essential Tool

In an AAM strategy, investments are typically distributed among three broad asset classes—stocks, bonds, and cash equivalents like money market securities. Each asset class offers specific advantages, as described below:

1. ***Stocks.*** Historically, stocks have constituted the best-performing asset class over the long term and also the best hedge against inflation.

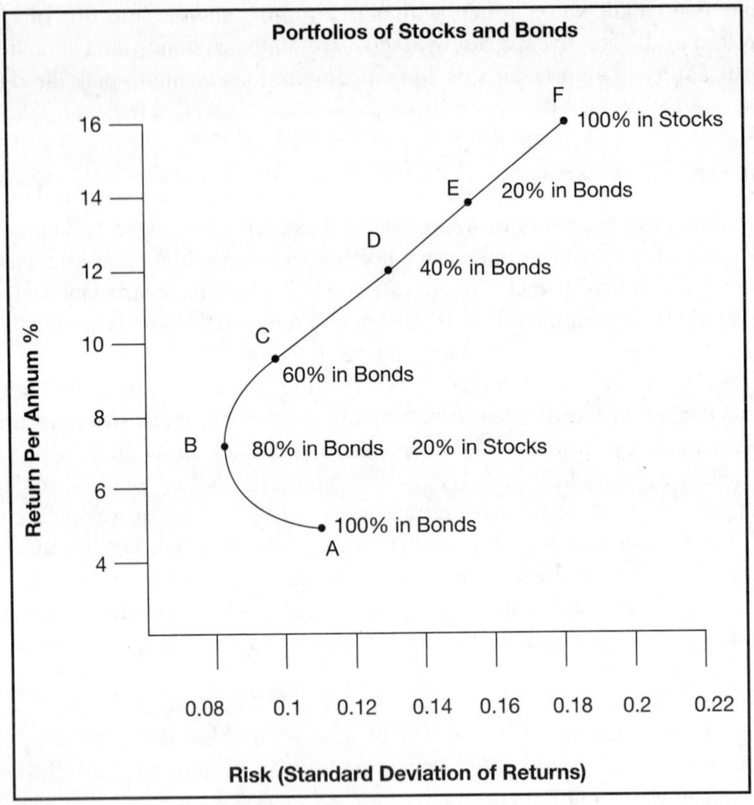

Figure 9.11 *Return/Risk Trade-off*

2. ***Bonds.*** Bonds can provide a regular stream of income and, historically, have offered greater stability than stocks.

3. ***Money market instruments.*** Money market instruments such as Treasury bills and high-quality money market instruments provide liquidity and income and offer the surest means of preserving capital.

Allocating assets appropriately among stocks, bonds, and cash equivalents can help investors achieve their long-term goals by managing risk. As demonstrated by several studies, individual investors often fail to match the long-term returns of the stock market, or even of the funds they own, because of a tendency to change strategies midstream. By attempting to provide a more stable, predictable return, the AAM may provide investors with the confidence they need to stay the course for the long term. Therefore, given the fact that most investors are expected to behave as though their time horizons were short, allocation of available funds among various asset classes may well represent the most important investment decision that investors can make. In fact, as stated earlier, an important study in the USA concluded that 92 percent of the variability in the performance of a diversified portfolio was based upon the appropriate asset allocation policy, while security selection and market timing represented only 6 percent and 2 percent, respectively, of the variability in the portfolio's performance. Consequently, a realization of this power of the AAM to deliver attractive portfolio returns while minimizing risk may well be what investors need to stay the course and act as long-term investors.

To recapitulate, asset allocation works because of two important financial facts:

1. ***Not all asset classes are adversely affected at the same time.*** For instance, in 1992 when the stock market started its free fall, the debt market, beaten down through much of the year, began a strong two-year rally. Subsequently, in 1998, the pattern repeated itself; a bond rally gathered steam as the stock market lost 46.78 percent.
2. ***Assets rise and fall in value, but eventually the overall gains far exceed the losses.*** For example, despite the violent market fluctuations that were recorded between 1992 and 1998, bonds and stocks ended up with the overall gains of 32 percent and 41.57 percent, respectively. Another important statistic: between April 5, 1990 and March 31, 1998, there were 1,751 trading days. The days of up and down markets were, respectively, 899 and 852. And yet, during this time period, the market increased by a whopping 390 percent.

Asset Allocation Model Steps

The AAM involves a four-step process, which is presented in Table 9.9.

Step 1. Determine the type of portfolio that matches the investor's risk tolerance level and can help him or her achieve his or her return objectives. Asset allocation portfolios are marketed as aggressive growth, growth, growth and income, balanced, and fixed-income portfolios. Of these, aggressive growth portfolios offer the highest return but also have the highest risk. Both the return and the risk decline as we move from aggressive growth to growth, growth and income, balanced, and fixed-income portfolios.

Step 2. Analyze the prevailing market and financial conditions. Results of this analysis form the basis for determining the percentage allocation of investable funds among the three major asset classes, namely equity, fixed income, and money market instruments.

Step 3. Select different types of investment products in each asset class. For the equity class, the following types of stocks might be selected: international large and small cap, domestic large, mid-cap and small-cap, value and growth stocks, and aggressive and conservative stocks. The fixed-income class might include: government and corporate long-, intermediate-, and short-term bonds, international bonds, and municipal bonds.

Step 4. Select the best mutual funds or individual securities that match the selections made in Step 3. This is a major undertaking, and it requires professional analytical skills as well as extensive knowledge of various investment products to complete this step.

A sample asset allocation portfolio format is presented in Figure 9.12 to demonstrate how the asset allocation process is pressed into action.

Risk Tolerance Guidelines

Asset allocation programs typically classify portfolio risk into three categories of investment portfolios because of their adherence to strict risk tolerance guidelines. These categories are popularly known as conservative, moderate, and aggressive portfolios. Guidelines of these programs are designed with the objective of limiting the maximum decline in portfolio value under *adverse* market conditions to 0–10 percent, 10–20 percent, and 20–40 percent, respectively. Adverse market conditions are defined as a substantial increase in the interest rate accompanied by a similarly substantial decline in one or more commonly followed stock market indices over a 12-month period. The structured discipline helps protect an investor from exposure to unacceptable levels of market decline and allows the portfolio to seek the highest possible total return consistent with an acceptable level of risk tolerance.

Table 9.9 *Asset Allocation Process*

Asset allocation strategy involves the following four-step process. A sample four-step process is presented below.

Step one Determine the type of portfolio that meets the investor's needs and goals

Aggressive Growth
Growth
Fixed Income
Growth and Income
Balanced

Step two Determine percentage distribution of Asset Allocation classes
Based on portfolio type (Step one)

% Equity
% Fixed Income
% Money Market

Step three Select appropriate investment types

Stocks	Bonds	Money Market
International	Government	Taxable
Domestic	Corporate	Tax Exempt
Large Cap	Domestic	
Small Cap	International	
Value	Municipal	
Growth	Long-term	
Income	Short-term	
Aggressive		
Conservative		

Step four Selection of appropriate mutual funds/securities

Fund 1	Fund 4	Fund 7
Fund 2	Fund 5	Fund 8
Fund 3	Fund 6	Fund 9
Security #1	Security #2	Security #3

It is important to recognize, however, that risk reduction is generally associated with a reduction in the total return. That is, the more conservative the asset allocation strategy adopted, the greater is the potential reduction in the expected return generated by that portfolio. However, a professional asset allocation strategist can succeed in significantly reducing the risk while sacrificing only a relatively small amount in returns. That is, when an effective asset allocation strategy is used, the benefits associated with a reduction in risk can far outweigh its cost measured in terms of reduction in return.

In this context, it is important to establish a direct relationship between the three risk categories (conservative, moderate, and aggressive) and five categories under which asset allocation portfolios are

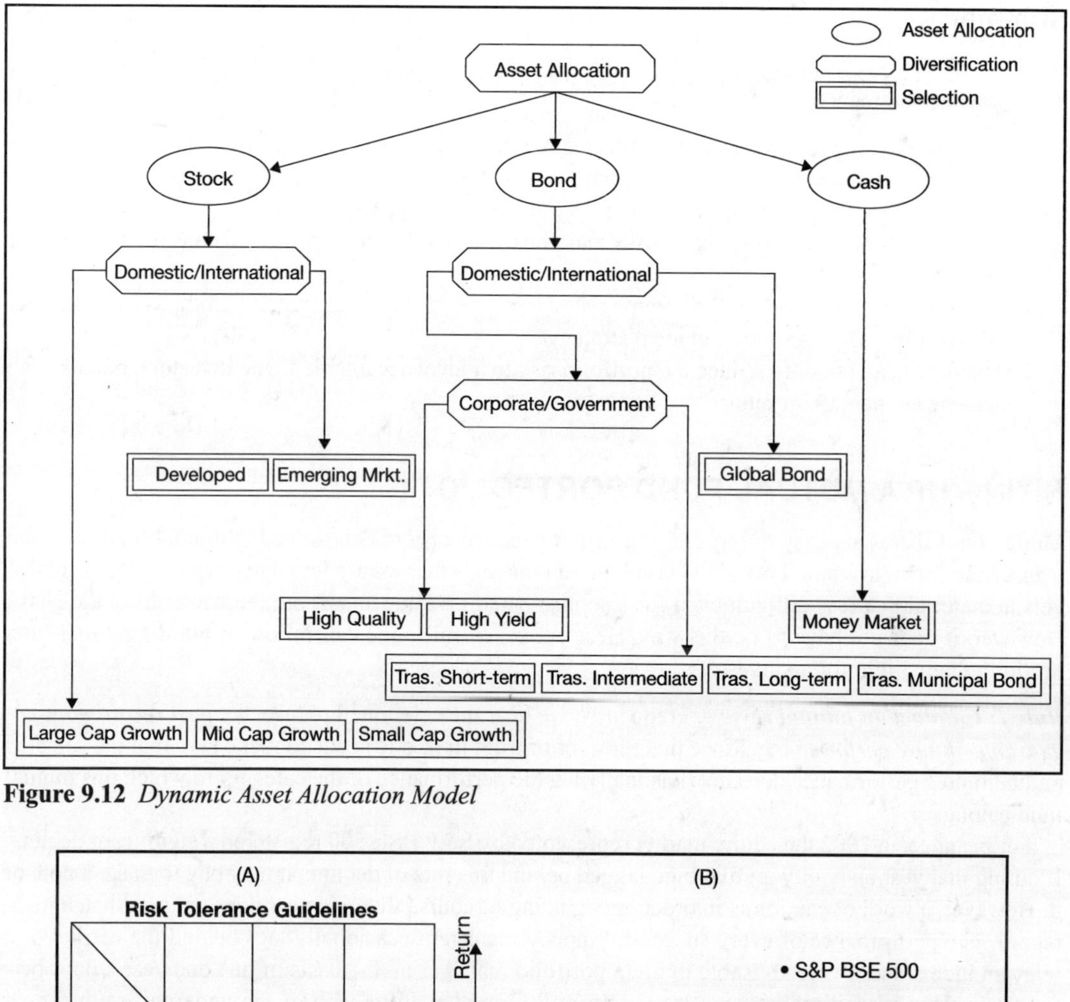

Figure 9.12 *Dynamic Asset Allocation Model*

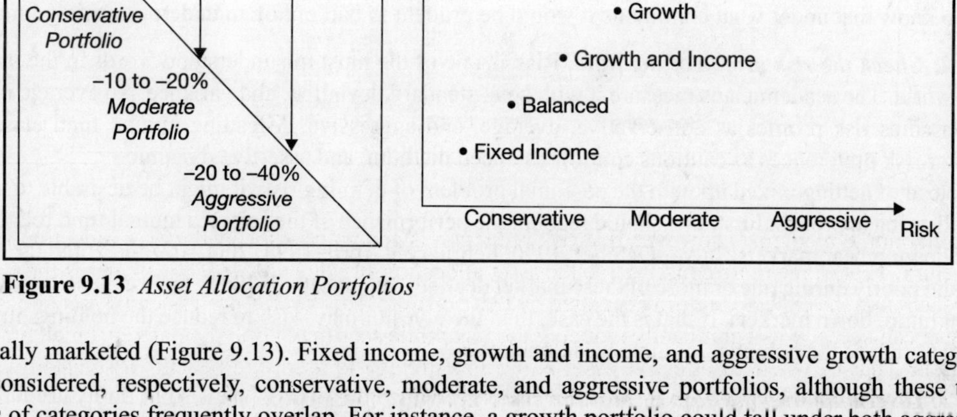

Figure 9.13 *Asset Allocation Portfolios*

typically marketed (Figure 9.13). Fixed income, growth and income, and aggressive growth categories are considered, respectively, conservative, moderate, and aggressive portfolios, although these three types of categories frequently overlap. For instance, a growth portfolio could tall under both aggressive and moderate risk categories. Similarly, a growth and income portfolio could be classified under both moderate and conservative risk categories.

Summary

Based partly on the preceding discussions, and drawing upon the results of other studies, we can make the following statements:

1. The majority of people, regardless of their time horizon, are risk-averse investors.
2. Because of the many faces of stock market risk and the peculiarities of the market, even the long-term investors are likely to behave as if they are short-term traders.
3. Most investors do not stay the course and consequently fail to earn respectable returns on their investments.
4. For short-term or uncertain time-frame risk-averse investor classes, which encompass the majority of investors, AAM provides an ideal strategy.
5. The AAM can not only reduce the portfolio risk to a level acceptable to the investors, but also can achieve an increase in return.

SIZING UP A MUTUAL FUND PORTFOLIO

Mutual fund shares are easy to buy and sell. But it is not so easy to determine if a mutual fund portfolio is just right for an investor. Part of the problem, of course, is that we are inundated with so much controversial material that it is difficult even for a sophisticated investor to sort out the wheat from the chaff. However, it does not have to be this way. Here are seven rules one can follow to build a mutual fund portfolio that is right for an investor.

Rule 1: Conduct an annual review. Frequently, we hear the celebrated phrase, the *past record does not guarantee future performance*. Since there is a lot of truth in it, one needs to make sure that the selected mutual fund's performance does not drastically lag the performance of the category to which this mutual fund belongs.

For instance, in 2002 the equity market represented by S&P BSE 500 registered a significant decline. If during that year an equity mutual fund lagged behind this rate of decline, it may pay to make a note of it. However, a word of caution is in order, recognizing of course that one year does not establish a track record. The performance of every successful money manager occasionally lags behind the market or a relevant index, and it is inadvisable to fire a portfolio manager on the basis of just one year's poor performance. However, it makes sense to get more information from each of the underperforming fund managers in order to determine if switching the manager is advisable. In any event, it is always a good idea to know that under what conditions it would be prudent to bail out of an underperforming fund.

Rule 2: Check the risk profile of the fund. Risk is one of the most misunderstood words in the investment world. The academicians measure it with beta, standard deviation, and variance. An average investor classifies risk profiles as conservative, average, and aggressive. A leading mutual fund classifies investor risk preferences as cautious control, balanced medium, and assertive dynamic.

Instead of getting mixed up with the perennial problem of defining risk, it might be desirable to adopt the following approach. First, one should recount the performance of the selected mutual fund relative to the following bear markets: July—October, 1990, February—April, 1994, 2000–02, and 2008–09. If the fund did poorly during one or more of these market declines, an investor is likely to be exposed to serious risk in future down markets. If that is the case, then the investor may wish to reduce the holdings in such a fund to reduce the potential loss in a weak market.

Rule 3: Determine who the boss is. Most investors recognize their funds' names but rarely are familiar with the respective portfolio managers. This can be a costly mistake for two reasons. First, if the performance of the mutual fund is tied to a specific manager, and that manager leaves the fund, the investor may be surprised when the new manager's record card shows up. Second, if in the past a portfolio manager has been successful in following certain investment policy, but chooses to change that policy, that change may not even be recognized. This can prove to be troublesome in the long run.

It is, therefore, important for investors to become familiar with the names of their portfolio managers, basic philosophies, and track records. Fortunately, a growing number of mutual funds are recognizing the importance of exposing their fund managers directly to investors and, in fact, express an interest in exposing them even more. Unfortunately, most shareholder representatives have limited training, and strict limitations are imposed on what they are allowed to say to callers. Therefore, to fill that information gap, some fund companies have inaugurated hot lines on which managers discuss their holdings and market outlook.

Rule 4: Tighten the portfolio. People are usually attracted to what is hot, and frequently wind up buying multiple funds with similar concentrations. For instance, until the fiasco with Mexico, Japan, and Asia, huge amount of money were pouring into international funds. Similarly, because of the unmanageable flow of funds, at one point many funds specializing in stocks of small companies stopped accepting new money. So, an investor holding several top-performing funds could have ended up with several funds with similar holdings. It is, therefore, advisable to correct the situation and tighten the portfolio by weeding out funds that duplicate the types and investment philosophies that an investor wishes to retain in the portfolio.

Rule 5: Eliminate unnecessary funds. Investors frequently make the mistake of owning several mutual funds to achieve similar objectives, such as retirement, financing college education, or making large purchases. This is not only unnecessary but can be counterproductive, since it is both expensive and difficult to track a large number of mutual funds. Investors would, therefore, be better off streamlining their portfolios and having only a limited number of funds for each goal.

Rule 6: Beware of the emerging markets. Financial magazines are replete with exciting stories about emerging markets. These markets are growing rapidly, often generating annual returns in excess of 30–40 percent, and sometimes even higher. It is, therefore, wise to allocate at least a portion of the portfolio to mutual funds specifically dealing with emerging markets. However, risk-averse investors, or those close to retirement should invest no more than 5–10 percent of their portfolio in emerging markets.

Rule 7: Diversify the portfolio. Various types of investments can be included in a diversified portfolio. Generally, performance of a portfolio can be improved if it is broadly diversified between stocks, bonds, and money market securities, as well as between domestic and international markets.

Rebalancing a Portfolio

In the 1990s, and especially since the beginning of 1995 and until 2000, there was a surge in stock prices. Subsequently, during 2000–02, all the market indices suffered significant declines but they rose again in 2003 and 2004. Because of the market's strong advance in the 1990s, and subsequent declines and advances since the beginning of 2000, it is likely that the equity portion of investors' portfolios has significantly changed, throwing off the original asset allocation distribution.

One effective way of guarding against *risk creep* and maintaining a consistent investment strategy is to regularly rebalance the portfolio. This involves periodically shifting funds among various asset classes to keep the portfolio diversification in line with the desired asset allocation strategy.

The strategy of rebalancing a portfolio can not only protect investors from gradually taking on more risk than desired, but it can also improve the portfolio's performance. This is because occasional rebalancing forces investors to shift money from an asset that has performed well (sell high) into one that has lagged (buy low). For example, if stocks have been in a slump, an investor using a rebalancing approach would shift money from bonds and money market securities into stocks, taking advantage of the lower stock prices. By the same token, if this strategy is followed, after a period of rising stock prices, funds would be shifted from stocks to bonds or money markets.

Let there be no misunderstanding, however. Asset rebalancing is not a market timing strategy, in which an investor attempts to *outguess* the vagaries of the financial markets. Rather, it is a systematic approach to maintain a relatively consistent risk profile. The strategy is most appropriate for tax-deferred retirement plans, since gains realized on the sale of securities are not subject to taxation until the funds are withdrawn. This strategy could also be used for regular accounts, but frequent rebalancing could cause complicated tax reporting headaches.

Rebalancing in Practice

The following example demonstrates the use of a periodic rebalancing strategy. Consider the results of a ₹10,000 investment made in December, 1979, in two different tax-deferred plans with a diversified mix of 60 percent stocks, 30 percent bonds, and 10 percent cash. One portfolio is rebalanced each quarter so that the original investment mix is maintained. In other words, if the percentage invested in stocks rises above the 60 percent guideline as a result of market appreciation, money is shifted from stocks to bonds and cash to bring the portfolio back in line with the investor's original strategy.

With the second portfolio, the investment mix is not rebalanced, so it changes over time reflecting the actual performance of stocks, bonds, and cash. In this case, the equity rose from 60 percent of assets at the beginning of December, 1981, to 84 percent by September, 1995, substantially raising the investor's risk exposure.

In this example, asset rebalancing helped mitigate losses during stock market downturns in 1980–82, 1987, 1990, and 1995. Furthermore, the investor took advantage of the lower equity prices by shifting money into stocks during these periods.

It is also interesting to note that over the entire period the rebalanced portfolio modestly outperformed the unbalanced one, even though the latter took on a higher risk profile as its equity position increased over time. By September, 1995, the value of the more conservative, rebalanced portfolio was ₹145,000, compared with about ₹141,000 for the unbalanced one.

The results reflect the long-term impact of the 1989–90 bear market on the performance of these two portfolios. The steep decline in equity prices reduced the equity allocation of the unbalanced portfolio to 49 percent while the rebalanced portfolio maintained its 60 percent equity position by buying stocks at bargain prices. The rebalanced account benefited from the market's recovery after the bear market, and it maintained its advantage every year after that.

While the unbalanced portfolio succeeded in closing the gap during strong bull markets, its gains were not sufficiently strong to overtake the rebalanced portfolio. In effect, the rebalanced portfolio reduced an investor's loss during severe market downturns, but over time provided a competitive return relative to a more aggressive portfolio.

Naturally, the relative performance of portfolios can vary, depending on the time period measured. Also, there is no guarantee that the story just presented will be repeated in the future or that a rebalancing strategy will always be effective. Still, periodically rebalancing a portfolio appears to be a conceptually sound strategy.

PORTFOLIO MANAGEMENT AND MONETARY POLICY

The basic rule of using the rebalancing strategy is that it be used at regular intervals, say, every quarter or every six months. However, another rule, which often supersedes the rebalancing rule, concerns a change in monetary policy, which may require immediate attention. Since these two rules appear to contradict each other, a brief explanation is necessary to clarify the issue.

The official goal of the Reserve Bank of India (RBI) is to formulate monetary policy in order "…to regulate the issue of Bank Notes and keeping of reserves with a view to securing monetary stability in India and generally to operate the currency and credit system of the country to its advantage." Since these can be, and often are, conflicting goals, the RBI must try to simultaneously weigh several issues while striking a balance between the short-run and the long-run economic goals.

The RBI's monetary policy works through its effect on the interest rates. Increases in interest rates raise the cost of borrowing and lead to reductions in business investment spending and household purchases of durable goods such as homes and autos. These declines in spending reduce the aggregate demand for the economy's output, leading firms to cut back on production and employment. By contrast, interest rate declines stimulate aggregate spending and lead to increases in production and employment.

In recent years, there has been a major shift in the way investors perceive the intent of the RBI to pursue either a tight or an easy monetary policy. This shift has become so pervasive that today's market sharply reacts to every *anticipated move* by the RBI, which exacerbates the volatility of the market experienced in normal times. This point requires elaboration.

Banks are legally required to hold a specified percentage of deposits in reserves, which they hold as vault cash or deposits with the RBI. When banks need additional reserves in the short term, they can borrow directly from the RBI at the discount rate. The discount rate is directly set by the RBI in response to economic conditions, raising rates to slow borrowing and lowering rates to stimulate the economy. While banks can borrow directly from the RBI, the RBI discourages the excessive use of the discount window.

In reality, however, the discount rate is virtually a defunct instrument. At present, member banks have only a relatively small amount (in lakh) of borrowing from the RBI. And yet, on February 21, 2014, total member bank reserves consisting of vault cash and deposits at the RBI were ₹312,018 crore. This clearly demonstrates that borrowings at the discount rate are miniscule.

Given RBI's bias against banks' excessive borrowings from the central bank, when short-term needs for cash arise, typically banks borrow from the RBI at a rate popularly known as the repo (repurchase) rate. The RBI also lends money to other banks at a rate called the bank rate. The bank rate signals the central bank's long-term outlook on interest rates. If the bank rate moves up, long-term interest rates also tend to move up, and vice versa. It is also called the RBI's *target rate*. And therein lays the problem. What does it mean when the RBI announces that it is going to target a rate that is determined in a market—interbank loans—in which the RBI is not a participant? And yet, the stock market reacts sharply every time the RBI changes its "target funds rate." This is the backdrop against which investment portfolios must be managed. While there is no question that, as a general rule, short-term fluctuations should not be allowed to unduly influence long-term objectives, due to the enormous effect that RBI's decisions have on the stock market, it is important for investors to watch the RBI's moves closely and adjust their portfolios to protect them from being unduly influenced by short-term moves on the part of the RBI.

Appendix: Fundamental and Technical Analysis

FUNDAMENTAL ANALYSIS

An Overview

A time-tested analytical method used by many financial planners is to identify, and eventually recommend, the purchase of undervalued securities. This strategy is based on the assumption that the price of an individual security always gravitates toward its intrinsic value, or in technical jargon, its PV. This method, called fundamental analysis, examines general economic conditions, such as economic growth, financial conditions, such as interest rates, and a host of related fundamental factors. This approach also requires the analysis of the industry conditions and projected industry growth. Finally, fundamental analysis involves the examination of a firm's economic performance and its potential earnings growth.

Ratios, financial data, and analytical savvy are the cornerstones of fundamental analysis. As mentioned, the ultimate objective of fundamental analysis is to calculate the PV of a security so that it could be compared with its current market price to determine whether or not it is an undervalued security and, therefore, offers an attractive investment opportunity.

Forecasting Earnings

Essentially, a dependable earnings forecast is the key to the calculation of the PV of a security. Consequently, forecasting earnings growth is at the heart of fundamental analysis. Accurate prediction of earnings growth, in turn, depends on a careful examination of the general economic conditions prevailing in the country, the industry conditions, and the overall growth of the company whose earnings are under analysis.

The Economy

In a nutshell, earnings of a company largely depend on prevailing economic conditions. Similarly, forecasting of earnings depends upon the forecasting of economic conditions. A study of two groups of variables covering the economy and company earnings is helpful in predicting the future of the economy. Another measure of value is the dividend yield. Historically, a dividend yield of below 3 percent of all stocks taken as a group has signaled the end of a growing economy and a bull market.

A third measure of prevailing economic conditions is the existing liquidity situation. Stock prices increase to artificially high levels when an ever-expanding supply of money starts chasing a dwindling supply of stocks.

Analysis of the nation's general economic conditions is important because there is a direct relationship between the economy and the performance of an individual firm, of which earning power is a key measure. In general, growth in the real gross domestic product (GDP) reflecting the nation's economic health, and changes in earning power representing the performance of individual firms, are positively related.

The Industry

Variations in earnings of individual companies are closely related to variations in earnings of related industries. This can be inferred from the fact that a significant portion of the price variations of an individual stock is the result of average price variations of all the companies within related industries.

The key industry fundamentals are presented in Table A9.1. Analysis of these fundamentals can help an investor identify those industries that are likely to record superior performance.

Published Reports

An investor need not depend totally on the annual report published by the company. Both Value Line and S&P's publish extensive data on stocks that are most actively traded. In addition, the publication entitled BSE *Morning Star Mutual Funds* publishes extensive data on the mutual funds.

Earnings per Share Model

The annual report and the published reports just discussed provide a basis for predicting a company's future earnings. The techniques for estimating future earnings are based on a detailed examination, and eventual prediction, of several financial ratios.

The construction of the earnings per share (EPS) model for XYZ company is presented in Figure A9.1. It shows that, for the EPS to increase, one or more of the key variables (production efficiency, coverage ratio, leverage ratio, and so on) must also increase. For instance, the company can increase its EPS from

Table A9.1 *Key Industry Fundamentals*

Indicator	Description
Historical Performance Industry Life Cycle	Three distinct phases. Pioneering Stage—Rapid sales and earnings growth. Investment Maturity Stage—Consolidate market positions and begin to encroach on competitors' market share by broadening capital base and establishing earnings and dividend policy. Stabilization—Unit costs become stable and market becomes saturated.
Performance during a Business Cycle	Cyclical or countercyclical performance of a company during an economic cycle.
Economic Structure	Degree of competition which prevails within the industry.
Capital Investment	Highly capital intensive industries usually make effective long-term plans for capital investment, are generally technologically more advanced than less capital intensive industries, and have a much larger growth potential than labor intensive industries.
Government Regulations	Some industries are subject to continual government intervention. Others may be subject to antitrust suits or attacks from environmental groups.
Labor Conditions	History of labor negotiations and impact of previous labor strikes can help determine the risks associated with certain industries.
Miscellaneous Factors	Price and income elasticities of demand for products, changes in consumer tastes, foreign competition, and the availability and cost of raw materials.

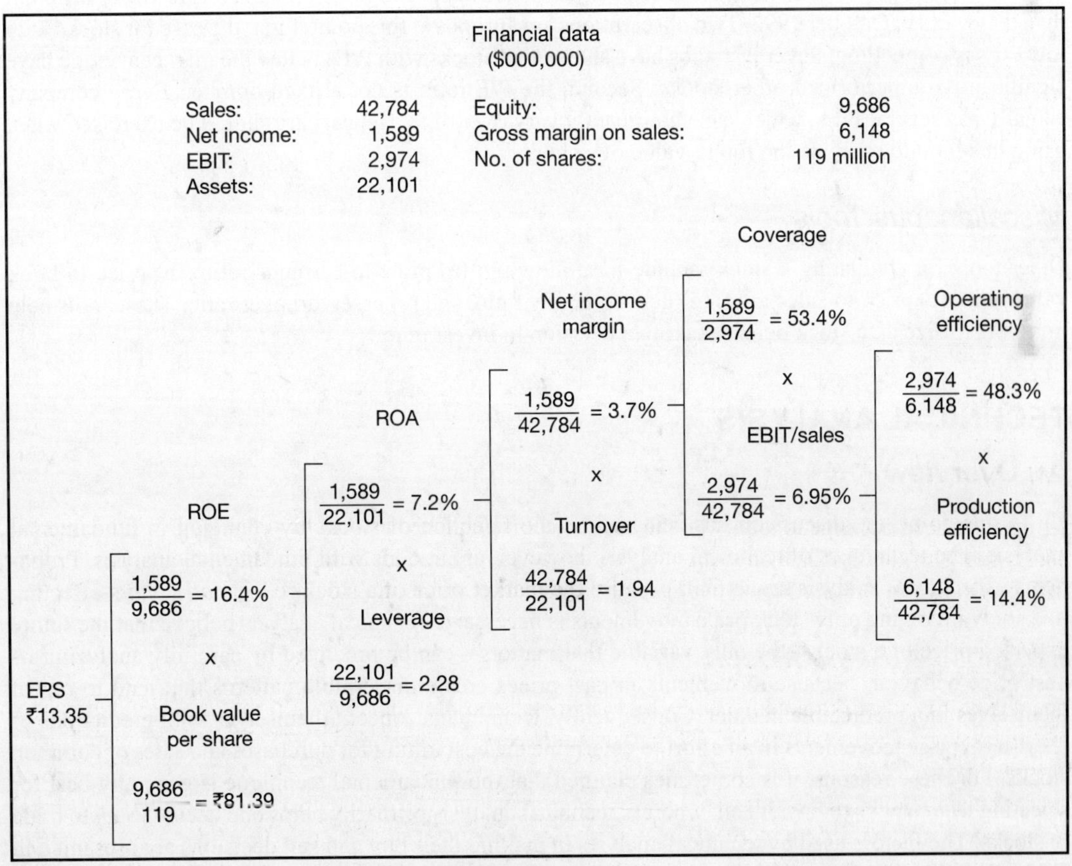

Figure A9.1 *EPS Derviation Model for the XYZ Company*

its current level of ₹13.35 by improving its production efficiency ratio of 14.4 percent, turnover ratio of 1.94, leverage ratio of 2.28, and so on.

Price–Earnings Ratio

The main purpose of undertaking fundamental analysis is to calculate the PV of a stock. It can then be compared with the current price to determine whether or not it is undervalued. A time-tested yet simple method is to estimate the PV by multiplying the projected future earnings by its price–earnings (P/E) ratio.

Essentially, the P/E ratio is the price that multiple investors are willing to pay for each rupee of a company's earnings. Literally, it is the price of a company's stock divided by its annual earnings. If a stock sells for ₹50 per share and the company's next year's expected earnings are ₹5, it carries a P/E ratio of 10. It should be pointed out that the P/E ratio of a company with negative or negligible earnings is meaningless. However, the vast majority of stocks have meaningful P/E ratios as do most popular stock indices.

The P/E ratio can be used to estimate the attractiveness of a stock. Consider first the big picture. The S&P's traditional P/E was 13–15 during a bull market and 8–10 in a declining, or bear, market. So, when the S&P's BSE P/E ratio shot up to 36.11 in April 1992 and then increased again to touch 45 in March 1994, there was definite cause for alarm. In the fall of 1996, the S&P's BSE P/E ratio fell to 10.5, just one-fourth of the level touched in 1994. It is worth nothing, however, that in 2000 the P/E ratio of S&P 500 was hovering around 30, but the fundamental factors supporting this P/E level were vastly different than they were in October 1992. Two observations are apropos at this point. First, the case for stocks with low P/Es is compelling. Several studies have shown that stocks with P/Es below the market average have significantly outperformed other stocks. Second, the P/E ratio is not a fixed number. Every company actually has several P/Es, which can significantly vary over time. Hence, care should be exercised when using this ratio to estimate the future value of a stock.

Miscellaneous Tools

Other tools for evaluating a stock include the following: (a) price-to-earnings ratio, (b) price to book value ratio, (c) price-to-sales ratio, (d) debt-to-equity ratio, and (e) asset turnover ratio. These tools help investors to size up a stock before making a decision to invest in it.

TECHNICAL ANALYSIS

An Overview

Up to this point, the discussion has centered on the selection of stocks by engaging in fundamental analysis. The techniques of technical analysis, however, are at odds with fundamental analysis. Proponents of technical analysis argue that, because the market price of a stock reflects *all* factors affecting it, a study involving only stock price movements is necessary. Technical analysts believe that the future expected price of a stock—the only variable that matters—can be predicted by carefully analyzing its past price behavior, because movements in past prices create discernible patterns that tend to repeat themselves in a predictable manner. Consequently, technicians concern themselves with predictions of short-term price movements in an effort to determine the best timing for purchases and sales of common stocks. For these reasons, it is sometimes claimed that the fundamental technique is generally best for selecting *what* stocks to buy or sell, whereas technical analysis primarily helps one decide *when* to trade in stocks. The factors used by technical analysts in making their buy and sell decisions are presented in Table A9.2.

Table A9.2 *Factors Used in Technical Analysis*

	Description	Claim by Technical Analysts
ACTIVITY FACTORS		
High-Low Index	Average number of NYSE stocks making new highs (surpassing their previous highest price levels for preceding 52 weeks) minus the number making new lows.	During a rising market an increasing number of stocks reach new highs and a decreasing number reach new lows (market technically strong). The reverse is true in a declining market (market is technically weak).
Advances-Declines Index	Ratio of the number of issues that advanced to the number that declined.	Changes in the ratio predict short-term market trends.
Most Active Stocks	*Wall Street Journal* listing of most activity traded stocks. Their high, low, and closing prices on the New York and American stock exchange.	Because of degree of risk involved in holding low quality stocks, market is generally more vulnerable when low quality stocks become popular.
Lo/Price Activity Ratio	Compares activity in speculative socks to that in quality issues. Represents the weekly ratio of volumes in Barron's Lo/Price Stock Index to volume in DJIA.	High speculative activity usually occurs at the top of the market, whereas low speculative activity occurs at the bottom.
Dow Jones Momentum Ratio	Measures spread between the DJIA and its 30-day moving average.	Assumed to pinpoint turning points in the market. In bull market, difference of 30 to 40 points indicates the markets has reached the top; −30 to −50 suggests the market has reached the bottom. In a bear market, a spread of 20 to 30 singles a market top, whereas −50 to −70 signals a market bottom.
MARKET STRENGTH FACTORS		
Breadth Index	Computed by subtracting the number of advances from the number of declines every week and dividing the result by the number of stocks that remain unchanged during that week. Index for the week is added to the previous week's figure.	When plotted on a graph, the trend in the market is determined from the direction of movement in the breadth index.
Relative Strength Index	Ratio of the price of a stock to the DJIA.	As long as the ratio continues to rise, that stock price is rising at a faster rate than the market and vice versa.
Volume of Trading	The volume of stocks changing hands daily.	Rise or decline in stock prices on high volume signals a continuation of the existing price trend; whereas a low volume points to an impending reversal of price trend.
Large Block Transactions	Financial journals regularly publish data concerning large transactions (25.000 shares or more) in specified stocks and prices at which these transactions were made.	Large blocks of shares traded on a downtick indicate a weak market. Conversely, large transactions on upticks suggest a strong bull market.
DIRECTIONAL FACTORS		
Daily Trading Barometer	A weighted composite of three oscillating factors: 1. Last seven days of advances and declines on the NYSE; 2. Algebraic sum of the last 20 days of plus and minus volumes on the NYSE: and 3. Ratio of the closing value of the DJ1A to the average closing price for the last 28 days.	Proponents argue that it is a reliable indicator of overbought and undersold market conditions.

(*Continued*)

Table A9.2 (*Continued*)

	Description	Claim by Technical Analysts
Directional Moves	Directional moves of the various Dow Jones Indicators While divergence is not unusual, it is assumed that this divergence is not likely to persist for long.	Movements in weaker segment of the market (transportation) precede movements in the stronger counterparts (industrials and utilities).
CONTRARY OPINION FACTORS		
Short Interest	Measure of short sales. An investor is selling short when, without first owning a stock, he/she sells it at a certain price in the hope of later being able to buy it at a lower price and realizing a profit.	Two interpretations: 1. Large short interest indicates widespread expectation of a price decline and is bearish. 2. Indicates a strong potential demand for stock and is, therefore, bullish.
Odd-Lot Index and Odd-Lot Sales Index	Ratio of odd-lot sales to odd-lot purchases (less than 100 share units).	Small investors are ill-informed and can be counted on to make the wrong moves at critical moments. If odd-lotters are net-buyers, "smart money" will get out of the market.
NYSE Specialists Short Sales Ratio	Ratio of specialists short sales to total NYSE short sales.	Measures extremes of sentiment of NYSE specialists who sell short most heavily at market tops when nonmember enthusiasm for buying is greatest and less heavily at bottoms when public selling is accelerated.
Advisory Service Sentiment	Weekly index of the percentage of leading bearish advisory services.	When the advisory service becomes overly one-sided, technical analysts view it as a contrary indicator because services follow trends rather than anticipate changes.
CONFIDENCE FACTORS		
Barron's Confidence Index (CI)	Ratio of high grade to low grade bond yields. High quality bond yields are always lower than low quality bond yields because investors have more confidence in them.	In a rising market, the CI rises. When the CI slides downward, the market is believed to be getting ready for a downturn because investors are reluctant to place confidence in lower quality bonds.

Charting

Technical analysis of individual stocks involves the interpretation of important chart patterns known by such esoteric names as head and shoulders, necklines, triangles, double top, double bottom, wedges, flags, and saucers. Each pattern signals to technical analysts a major or minor upward or downward movement in the stock. Several popular chart patterns are discussed next.

Support and Resistance Levels

One of the most important aspects of chart analysis is the identification of support and resistance levels, as shown in Figure A9.2. A support level is a barrier to a price decline; a resistance level is a barrier to price advancement. Although the barrier is an obstruction, it is by no means impassable. Stock prices do break support and resistance barriers.

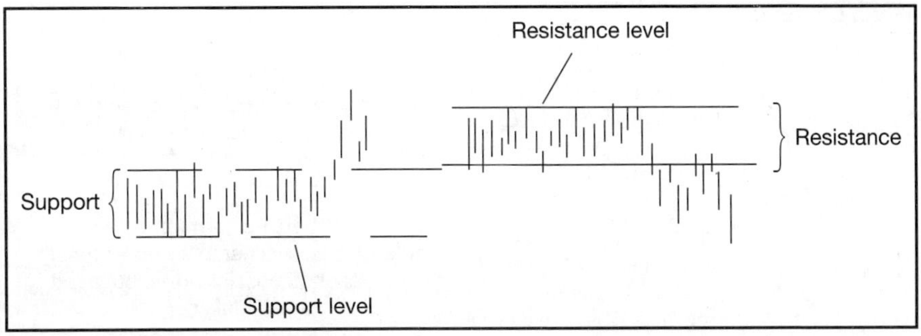

Figure A9.2 *Support and Resistances Lavels*

Head and Shoulders Configurations

Basic reversal patterns help analysts identify the turning points so that they can decide when to buy or sell stock. The key reversal pattern is popularly known as the head and shoulders configuration. This configuration, shown in Figure A9.3, is merely another name for an uptrend or a downtrend in a stock; neckline is the familiar resistance or support level.

A head and shoulders formation should be analyzed against the background of volume trend. As the head and shoulders top is formed, resistance to further price increases dampens investor enthusiasm; therefore, the volume decreases on each of the rally phases within the top formation. The reverse is true when the head and shoulders bottom is under formation. It should be emphasized that the completion of a head and shoulders top or bottom is not considered final until the penetration of the neckline is apparent.

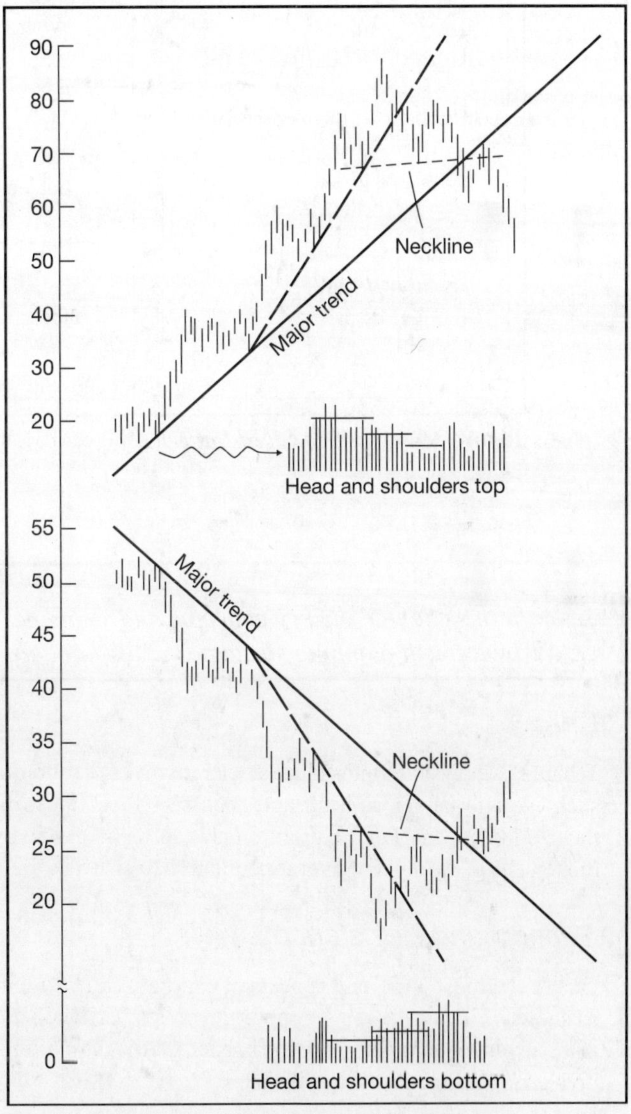

Figure A9.3 *Head and Shoulders Configuration*

Five Broad Patterns

It is worth noting that of all the many chart patterns and techniques just discussed, five broadly classified patterns are claimed to best describe the price behavior of most stocks. These patterns, shown in Figure A9.4, should be self-explanatory.

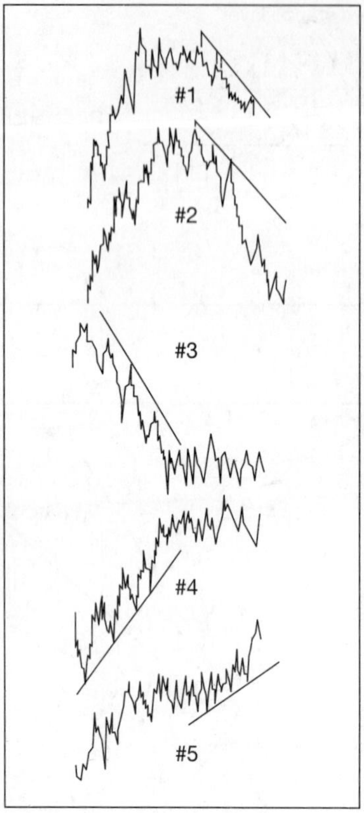

Chart Pattern #1	Stocks with vulnerable trends and/or possible downside potential
Chart Pattern #2	Stocks with less vulnerability that appear to have reached possible lows, but need consolidation.
Chart Pattern #3	Stocks that have declined and experienced consolidation, and could do well in a favorable market.
Chart Pattern #4	Stocks that have performed relatively well but are currently in "neutral" trends.
Chart Pattern #5	Stocks in established uptrends and/or with possible upside potential

Figure A9.4 *Various Chart Patterns*

In this chapter, the key concepts and strategies of investment management were presented. Investment planning strategies will be undertaken in Chapter 10.

10 Investment Planning Strategies

INTRODUCTION

Investment planning is a complex and often an overwhelming task. But the basic definition of investment planning is relatively simple: The development and implementation of an investment portfolio is designed to achieve an investor's short- and long-run investment objectives. This definition suggests that, for the investment planning process to be successful, a financial planner must not only understand the investor but also play a crucial role in achieving a delicate *balance* between risk and return, concentration and diversification, current income and growth, taxable and tax-advantaged products, and liquid and nonliquid investments. An overview of the concept of investment planning is presented in Figure 10.1.

This chapter is divided into three sections. In Section I, we will analyze in detail the investment planning process. In Section II, the key investment planning strategies will be discussed. In Section III, we will present a real world investment plan developed by using the investment planning process presented in the first section of this chapter.

Section I: Investment Planning Process

INTRODUCTION

The investment planning process involves taking five major steps: (a) identification of a client's goals, (b) determination of the client's risk tolerance level, (c) articulation of the client's investment preferences, (d) analysis of the current investment portfolio, and (e) reorganization of the current investment portfolio. In discussing these steps, we will draw upon the investment models, theories, and concepts developed in Chapter 9 and make extensive use of the basic investment alternatives presented in Chapter 8. A set of forms and questionnaires will also be used to determine a client's goals, the risk tolerance level, and investment preferences.

GOAL SETTING

An Overview

The investment planning process begins with the identification of a client's goals. This is easier said than done for the following reasons: (a) Investment goals are likely to change as the client passes through the different stages of life cycle. (b) Investment planning objectives are harder to verbalize than other (education, risk management, and so on) planning goals. For instance, it is often difficult for clients to articulate their needs for liquidity and current income, and their expectation of investment returns. (c) Few

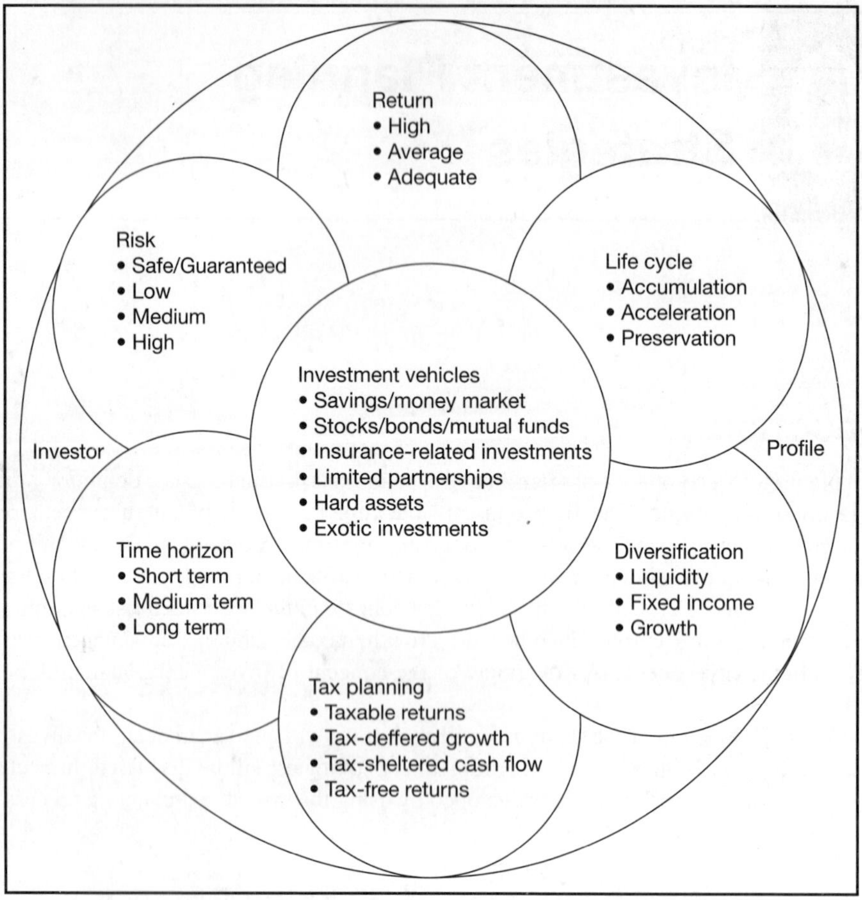

Figure 10.1 *Concepts of Investment Planning*

clients appreciate the power of diversification and the value of using the asset allocation model (AAM) in constructing an investment portfolio. (d) Following the passage of the Tax Reform Act of 1986 which removed most of the effects of tax considerations in investment planning, many clients naively assume that tax saving strategies no longer need to play an important role in investment goal setting. (e) Clients seldom realize that their time horizon often determines the appropriateness of various investment products. For instance, the investment selected to fund a child's education may well depend on the number of years remaining before the withdrawal begins. (f) An unrealistic expectation of investment returns can frustrate the achievement of the desired goals. Development of strategies for dealing with these and other related issues will provide the framework for articulating investment goals.

Life Cycle

The starting point is the recognition of the stages of a person's financial life cycle. Although an investor passes through many stages of life cycles, for practical reasons, we will classify them as accumulation, acceleration, and preservation cycles.

The *accumulation* cycle begins at the start of an investor's financial life. During this stage, an investor is preoccupied with: (a) protecting the growing family from a potential financial disaster due to death

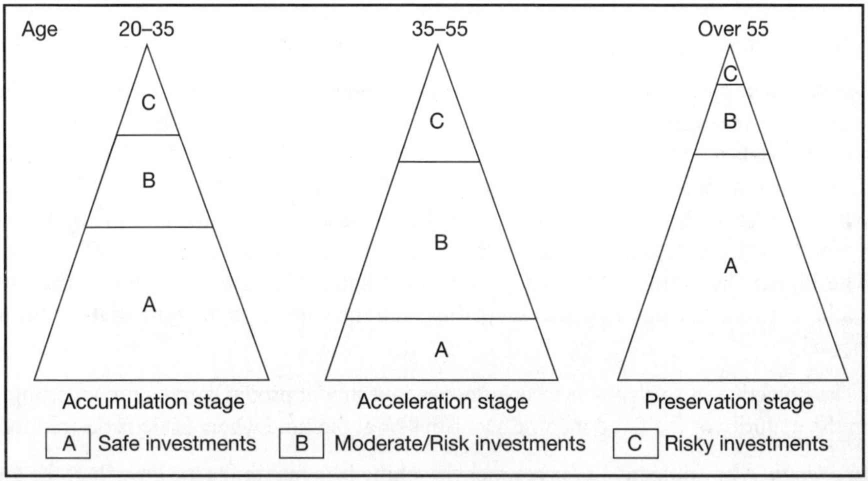

Figure 10.2 *Life Cycle Stages and Distribution of Investment*

or disability, (b) providing for children's education, (c) accumulating basic assets such as home and furnishings, and (d) building cash reserves and emergency funds to meet unexpected contingencies. An investment portfolio suited for this stage invariably consists of a large percentage of cash reserves and a variety of safe and low-risk investments designed to help the investor's savings grow at a slow but steady rate.

The *acceleration* cycle is ushered in when an investor enters the peak earning years and feels secure about having taken care of the family's basic needs and emergency situations. During this cycle, the investor usually changes from being a risk-averse person to being a risk taker, since now the investor has the time and the resources to recover from potential investment losses. So during the acceleration cycle, the portfolio deliberately turns riskier as higher risk investments are added for potentially realizing a higher return.

The third stage, known as the *preservation* cycle, begins when an investor starts preparing for retirement. Gone are the peak earning years and the capacity to bounce back from significant investment losses resulting from taking high risks. During this cycle, the major objective is the preservation of capital accumulated during the previous cycles, so that the maximum amount of capital would be available for generating current income as regular sources of earned income disappear. Once again, the portfolio is reverted to a relatively risk-free status that was appropriate for the accumulation cycle, although the major emphasis now shifts from low-risk, slow-growing investments to income-producing investments.

The concept of shifting investment goals as an investor passes through the three cycles of life is presented in Figure 10.2.

Basic Investment Objectives

The second consideration in goal setting is the establishment of basic investment objectives which, in turn, leads to the determination of other, broad-based objectives like a proper balance between risk and investment return. The four basic investment objectives are liquidity, current income, solvency, and investment growth.

Liquidity. An essential component of a well-designed investment portfolio is the percentage allocated for cash reserves. An investor's liquidity needs can be classified into three categories: operating funds, emergency funds, and funds earmarked for capitalizing on future investment opportunities. The cash reserves portion of an investment portfolio satisfies all three of these liquidity needs.

Current income. The types and amounts of fixed income securities and annuities to be considered for inclusion in an investment portfolio are determined by two factors. First, the total of all the income sources—salary, pension, current investment income, bonus, and so on—should be compared with the current income needed to maintain the desired standard of living. The excess (if any) of income needs over the total income sources is the amount of additional income that must be generated by new investments. Second, an investor needs to recognize the trade-off involved in this process: The higher the amount invested in securities generating current income, the lower is the amount available for investing in growth securities, and the smaller is the potential for future growth of the principal.

Solvency. The objective of solvency is to ensure that investment products remain convertible into cash either upon the maturity of the fixed income securities or at the time when a sale is desired for equities.

Investment growth. A key objective of investment planning is to maximize the growth of the total investment portfolio. A number of considerations determine the amount of investable funds to be allocated to growth investments and the types of investment products that should be selected to achieve this objective. These considerations include the returns desired, the investor's risk tolerance level, and the investor's future income needs and time horizon.

Diversification and Asset Allocation Model (AAM)

The third element in the goal setting process is the realization of the benefits of using the AAM. It is of course true that one of the most celebrated investment advices was offered by Andrew Carnegie: "Put all your eggs in the same basket and watch it carefully." However, such an advice is impractical for most investors, for rarely do they have the time or the expertise to select the *right investments* and liquidate them at the *right time* when they are no longer attractive. Consequently, for most investors the use of the AAM becomes essential in investment planning.

It was explained in Chapter 9 that in order to optimize the portfolio return for a given level of risk, the AAM provides a system for diversifying a portfolio among three asset classes. This diversification is the process of reducing risk within a particular asset class by spreading individual issues of stocks, bonds, or other investments within a broad range. While the value of diversification is universally recognized, appreciation for the effective use of AAM largely depends on an investor's level of sophistication. For instance, a sophisticated investor may use the AAM for (a) maximizing the portfolio return, (b) achieving a delicate balance between risk and return, and (c) striking the perfect mix between liquid, fixed, growth, and nonliquid funds. In contrast, a not-so-savvy investor may simply be content with a much more modest asset allocation objective of a safe portfolio with a relatively modest but reasonable return.

There is one aspect of diversification that deserves special mention, namely the difference between *growth* and *value* investing in the area of large-cap investments. A brief description of growth- versus value-style investing is presented next.

Most investors have a common goal: The growth of investments over time. This goal may be achieved by investing in stocks, bonds, real estate, or any combination of these instruments. While investors can use both individual securities and mutual funds to achieve their goals, because of the complexity of dealing with individual stocks and bonds, in most instances sticking with mutual funds may produce the most efficient results.

Investment styles refer to the techniques used by fund managers to select securities and construct portfolios. It is possible for investors to have similar investment objectives of capital appreciation, but by using different criteria they may select totally different mutual funds to achieve this goal. Two major styles of stock selection consist of growth and value investing.

Even though the names may not directly reflect it, the primary focus of both styles is on capital appreciation—buying a stock today for less than it is expected to be worth in the future. However, the two styles significantly differ in how they define what constitutes a *good buy*. Growth stock managers look for companies with rapid and expanding growth, while value stock managers are attracted to stocks of companies whose prices appear to be cheap relative to their earnings, assets, or dividends.

The growth-based investment style is generally concerned with selecting stocks expected to produce above-average and accelerated growth in earnings. Here, the manager identifies the industries and companies that are in the aggressive growth stages of their life cycle—a period associated with rapid and increasing growth rates in sales and earnings associated with reasonable profit margins.

Minimally, growth companies maintain a growth rate above the rate of increase in gross domestic product (GDP). Some experts consider the benchmark for classifying a growth stock as 20 percent annual growth rate in earnings per share (EPS). Growth rates of this magnitude generally require significant amounts of capital spending so that the impressive growth pattern of the EPS could be maintained.

By contrast, value investing represents the selection of stocks that are priced low relative to their levels of earnings, sales, assets, and equity. Common measures of value include: low price–earnings ratios, low price-to-book ratios, and high dividend yields. Of course, that does not imply that all firms with low price–earnings ratios or high dividend yields offer good values. In fact, some stocks with low price–earnings ratios may have little future potential and deserve their low prices. Consequently, selecting good-value stocks requires special skills and experience.

Markets often move on emotions and overreact to both good and bad news. Value-investing managers seek to identify stocks that are undervalued because they are either neglected or currently out of favor primarily for psychological reasons. That is why value managers are sometimes called contrarian investors.

It is important to underscore some of the similarities and differences between growth and value investing. The diversification potential of holding investments representing both styles can be rewarding, because these two management styles are vastly different in the short run.

Tax Considerations

At the heart of comprehensive investment planning is the tax ramifications of managing an investment portfolio. The reason is that the most meaningful number representing investment performance is the *net,* after-tax return. The tax issues relating to various investments are discussed at length in Chapter 12 and need not be repeated here. Returns on various investment products can be classified as taxable, tax deferred, tax sheltered, and tax free. Municipal bonds are tax free. Many limited partnerships generate tax-sheltered cash flows. Insurance-related investments, such as annuities and single premium whole life, as well as all qualified plan investments, generate tax-deferred returns. Finally, returns on all other investments are fully taxable. Other things being equal, investment portfolios should be managed to maximize their after-tax returns. This is especially true in India where tax consideration plays a crucial role in general, and for investments in life insurance products, post office products, mutual funds, and infrastructure bonds, in particular.

Time Horizon

Selection of investment products is frequently shaped by the amount of time remaining for an investor to reach financial goals. Classification of various investments into short-, medium-, and long-term, and the trade-offs associated with investments in different time categories, are presented in Table 10.1.

Table 10.1 *Terms of Investment*

Investment Examples	Advantages	Drawbacks
Short (less than two years)		
Money market funds Short-term certificates of deposit (CDs) Short-term bonds Treasury notes	Low volatility—price changes slightly or not at all Moderate yields Regular income Ready access to funds	Lower overall returns Frequent reinvestment decisions
Medium (3–5 years)		
Intermediate-term bonds Flexible-rate CDs High-income conservative stocks	Moderately high yields Price moves in narrow range Regular income	Less safe than short-term investments Can be vulnerable to inflation Income can vary
Long (more than five years)		
Long-term bonds Long-term CDs Real estate Growth stocks (if held) Gold and silver	Highest yields or capital growth potential Returns usually outpace inflation	Most volatility Less liquid Principal can be vulnerable to inflation

Investment Return

The cornerstone of investment planning is that risk and return are positively related, that is, the higher the return of an investment, the higher is the risk it carries. In constructing a *target investment portfolio* (TIP), given an investor's risk tolerance, a financial planner selects those products that tend to optimize the portfolio's returns for the level of risk acceptable to that investor.

An important dimension of the problem of maximizing investment return is revealed by asking the question: What is the reasonable return an investor can expect from a given security or portfolio? It is difficult to find a straight answer to this important question, primarily because it is highly influenced by a great deal of both myth and misunderstanding.

Statistics on long-term returns on common stocks for the period 1979–2014 reveal the following: (a) On a year-to-year basis, at one extreme, common stocks have yielded an annual return of as much as 266.88 percent, but during certain years these have also annually lost as much as 46.78 percent. Interpreted slightly differently, an investor expecting to double the value of a common stock investment portfolio every two years could also suffer a massive decline in its value. (b) The longer an investor's time horizon, the smaller is the risk of losing the principal; however, that also reduces the potential for higher return. (c) The average long-term annual return on large-cap common stocks (S&P 500) on a one-year basis is around 20 percent (2013–14). This means that, following the Rule of 72, an investment earning a 10 percent annual return can be expected to double every 3.6 years (72/20=3.6).

Prioritizing Goals

It is important for financial planners to learn about the priorities their clients place on various investment goals. The worksheet, presented in Table 10.2, helps to underscore how strongly investors feel about different investment goals; it also brings to the surface some of the important goals they routinely miss to identify. Equally important, a rating of 1 or 2 selected for a specific goal clearly suggests that an investor does not consider that goal to be significant.

Summing Up

The success of an investment planning process largely depends on the ability of financial planners to help their clients clearly define their investment planning goals. Some investors prefer to state their

Table 10.2 *Prioritizing Investment Goals*

	Weak				Strong
Diversification	1	2	3	4	5
Liquidity	1	2	3	4	5
Safety of principal	1	2	3	4	5
Capital appreciation	1	2	3	4	5
Current income	1	2	3	4	5
Inflation protection	1	2	3	4	5
Future income	1	2	3	4	5
Tax reduction/deferral	1	2	3	4	5
Earn of management	1	2	3	4	5

investment goals in broader terms, such as diversification, a reasonable mix of liquid and nonliquid investments, and a balance between investment risk and return. Others wish to achieve specific investment goals such as an after-tax investment return of 5 percent and a monthly cash flow of ₹1,000. While both are acceptable forms of stated goals, a written set of clearly specified goals helps a planner appreciate more fully the client's risk and investing preferences, fears, and level of sophistication.

SECTION II: Key Investment Planning Strategies

RISK TOLERANCE

Risk versus Return

In Chapter 9, it was explained that risk is associated with the variability of expected returns. It was also pointed out that risk and return are positively related, that is, investments offering higher returns generally carry higher degrees of risks.

The concept of the positive risk–return relationship vis-à-vis investment product selection underscores two important facts. (a) Debt securities generally carry lower risks but offer lower returns, whereas equity-type securities offer higher returns but also carry higher risks. (b) As an investor climbs the risk–return pyramid, both risk and return increase; the reverse is true when a move is made in the opposite direction.

It is necessary to recognize that fixed income securities suffer a loss during inflationary periods when interest rates rise; but they also offer an assurance of return of the principal upon maturity. In contrast, equity-type investments offer a much greater potential for growth, but they carry an increasing risk of losing the principal. Finally, the highly risky investments, such as tax shelters, commodities, and hard assets, have the best potential for highest returns over time. However, they are also illiquid investments and carry the maximum risk of losing the principal. And that is not all. Some of these investments may lose the current tax benefits if *phantom income* is received, or the income tax department retroactively denies some of the previously realized tax benefits.

Risk Tolerance Level

There exists no universally established technique for determining an investor's risk tolerance level. Although in certain instances measuring risk tolerance can be objective, for most part it is a *subjective* measure of an investor's emotional and financial strength to withstand investment losses. Even more important, an investor's risk tolerance may rise with an increase in the net worth, income, investment knowledge, and sophistication, but it could also decline as he or she approaches retirement. Regardless, as part of the investment planning process, financial planners have little choice but to make a concerted effort to determine the risk tolerance level of every client.

For this purpose, investors can be classified as high, medium, low, and zero risk takers. The most effective way of making this determination is to subject an investor to take a well-designed test. A *sample* test, presented in the box entitled "Do You Take Risks?" is designed to determine an investor's risk tolerance level. Another questionnaire, entitled "Measuring Attitude Toward Risk," helps record an investor's general attitude toward risk.

DO YOU TAKE RISKS? A QUIZ

1. An investment loses 15% of its value in a market correction a month after you but it. Assuming none of the fundamentals have changed, do you:

   (a) Sit tight and wait for its journey back up?
   (b) Sell it and rid yourself of further sleepless nights if it continues to decline?
   (c) Buy more, if it looked good at the original price, it looks even better now?

2. A month after you purchase it, the value of your investment suddenly skyrockets by 40%. Assuming you cannot find any further information, what do you do?

   (a) Sell it.
   (b) Hold it on the expectation of further gain.
   (c) Buy more, it will probably go higher.

3. Which would you have rather done:

   (a) Invested in an aggressive-growth fund that appreciated very little in six months.
   (b) Invested in a money market fund only to see the aggressive-growth fund you were thinking about double in value in six months.

4. Would you feel better if:

   (a) You doubled your money in an equity investment.
   (b) Your money market fund investment saved you from losing half your money in a market slide.

5. Which would make you happiest?

   (a) You win ₹1 crore in a publisher's contest.
   (b) You inherit ₹1 crore from a rich relative.
   (c) You earn ₹1 crore by risking ₹200,000 in the option market.
   (d) Any of the above, you are happy with the ₹1 crore, no matter how it ended up in your wallet.

6. The apartment building you live is being converted to condominiums. You can either buy your unit for ₹80 lakh or sell the option for ₹20 lakh. The market value of the condo is ₹1.20 crore. You know that if you buy the condo it might take six months to sell, the monthly carrying cost is ₹120,000, and you would have to borrow the down payment for a mortgage. You do not want to live in the building. What do you do?

   (a) Take the ₹20 lakh.
   (b) Buy the unit and then sell it.

7. You inherit your uncle's ₹1 crore house, free of any mortgage. Although the house is in a fashionable neighborhood and can be expected to appreciate at a rate faster than inflation, it has

deteriorated badly. It would net ₹1 lakh monthly if rented as is, or ₹1.5 lakh per month if renovated. The renovations could be financed by a mortgage on the property. You would:

(a) Sell the house.
(b) Rent it as is.
(c) Make the necessary renovations, and then rent it.

8. You work for a small but thriving privately held electronics company. The company is raising money by selling stock to its employees. Management plans to take the company public, but not for four or more years. If you buy stock, you will not be allowed to sell until shares are traded publicly. In the meantime, the stock will pay no dividends. But when the company goes public, the shares could trade for 10–20 times what you paid. How much of an investment would you make?

(a) None at all.
(b) One month's salary.
(c) Three months' salary.
(d) Six months' salary.

9. Your long-time neighbor, an experienced petroleum geologist, is assembling a group of investors (of which he is one) to fund an exploratory oil well, which could pay back 50–100 times its investment. If the well is dry, the entire investment is worthless. You friend estimates the chances of success at only 20%. What would you invest?

(a) Nothing at all.
(b) One month's salary.
(c) Three months' salary.
(d) Six months' salary.

10. You learn that several commercial building developers are seriously looking at underdeveloped land in a certain location. You are offered an option to buy a choice parcel of that land. The cost is about two months' salary and you calculate the gain to equal 10 months' salary:

(a) Purchase the option.
(b) Let it slide, it is not for you.

11. You are on a TV game show and can choose one of the following. Which would you take?

(a) ₹10,000 in cash.
(b) A 50% chance at ₹40,000.
(c) A 20% chance at ₹1 lakh.
(d) A 5% chance at ₹10 lakh.

12. It is 2011, and inflation is returning. Hard assets such as precious metals, collectibles, and real estate are expected to keep pace with inflation. Your assets are now all in long-term bonds. What would you do?

(a) Hold the bonds.
(b) Sell the bonds, put half the proceeds into money funds and the other half into hard assets.
(c) Sell the bonds and put the total proceeds into hard assets.
(d) Sell the bonds, put all the money into hard assets and borrow additional money to buy more.

13. You have lost ₹25,000 at the blackjack table in Atlantic City. How much more are you prepared to lose to win the ₹25,000 back?

    (a) Nothing. You quit now.
    (b) ₹5,000.
    (c) ₹12,500.
    (d) ₹25,000.
    (e) More than ₹25,000.

SCORING

Total your score, using the point system, listed below for each answer you gave

1. (a) 3 (b) 1 (c) 4
2. (a) 1 (b) 3 (c) 4
3. (a) 1 (b) 3
4. (a) 2 (b) 1
5. (a) 2 (b) 1 (c) 4 (d) 1
6. (a) 1 (b) 2
7. (a) 1 (b) 2 (c) 3
8. (a) 1 (b) 2 (c) 4 (d) 6
9. (a) 1 (b) 3 (c) 6 (d) 9
10. (a) 3 (b) 1
11. (a) 1 (b) 3 (c) 5 (d) 9
12. (a) 1 (b) 2 (c) 3 (d) 4
13. (a) 1 (b) 2 (c) 4 (d) 6 (e) 8

Below 21: You are a conservative investor who's allergic to risk. Stick with the sober, conservative investments until you develop the confidence or desire on take on more risk.

21–35: You are an active investor who's willing to take calculated, prudent risks to achieve greater financial gain. Your investment universe is more diverse.

36 and over: You are a venturesome, assertive investor. The choices that are available to you promise dynamic opportunities. Remember, though the search for more return carries an extra measure of risk.

MEASURING ATTITUDE TOWARD RISK

For each statement, choose the answer that most resembles your attitude toward investing over the next five years. Remember: There are no right or wrong answers.

	True	False	Not Applicable
1. I cannot afford any loss of principal regardless of potential return.	____	____	____
2. I cannot afford any *significant* loss of principal but I wait the best return I can get.	____	____	____
3. Since I can get high yields from bonds. I don't wish to suffer through market ups and downs by investing in stocks.	____	____	____
4. I want both income for current needs and reasonable growth of my portfolio.	____	____	____
5. Since the economy changes rapidly, frequent rebalancing of my portfolio is essential to realize satisfactory results.	____	____	____

6. Risk means major ups and downs in my portfolio even if the overall portfolio value continues to go up.	____	____	____
7. I know investments generating higher returns have higher risks, but I must earn higher returns at any cost.	____	____	____
8. I like to *play* the stock market, and long-term investment is not for me.	____	____	____
9. There is no way to successfully compete with big investors, so I should concentrate on safe, guaranteed investment products.	____	____	____
10. I like my portfolio to show superior results and I believe I need a professional to help me achieve my goal.	____	____	____

Summing Up

We have just touched upon the many issues relating to the development of an investor's risk profile. Clearly, additional issues, such as the state of an investor's financial life, degree of affluence, and a host of other factors, should be analyzed before an accurate risk profile can be compiled. However, because of space constraints we present in the box entitled "Strategic Investment Planning Worksheet," a simple worksheet which can assist a financial planner in developing a functional risk profile for an investor.

STRATEGIC INVESTMENT PLANNING WORKSHEET

A. Time Horizon

In order for historic rates of return and risk measurements to be a meaningful basis for investment planning, the investment time horizon is ought to be at least five years. For most individuals and qualified plans this will be the case. While the plan will be reviewed and possibly revised on a regular basis, allocations should be based on long-term expectations.

1. Is your time horizon in fact five years or more?
   Yes__________No__________
2. Do you foresee any specific need to withdraw principal during that time?
   Yes__________No__________
3. What is a comfortable emergency reserve to meet unanticipated needs?
   ₹______________________________

B. Rate of Return Objectives

Prior to considering the rate of return, it is necessary to define the total amount of funds to be invested. Liquid investable assets refer to those assets which are earmarked for long-term investment in financial instruments (stocks, bonds, Treasury bills, and so on). For individuals, this means liquid net worth and less emergency cash reserve. Do not include illiquid funds targeted for real estate, metals, and other tangible assets. For qualified plans, liquid investable assets refer to total plan assets less any required reserve.

₹________________ – ₹________________
Liquid net worth   Cash reserve

= ______________________________
Total liquid investable assets

Following are the three different ways to quantify return objectives (I–III). If only one is meaningful, fill out only the applicable section. If more than one, please prioritize. While hopefully a plan can be presented to meet all parameters, it may be necessary to make trade-offs, and thus to know which set of objectives is most important to you.

I. Absolute Returns:

1. To what rupee amount would you like to see your assets grow in 5 years? ₹______
   In 10 years? ₹____________
2. Alternatively, what compound annual rate of return would you like to achieve on your entire investment portfolio?
   __________________%
3. Do you look for these assets to provide you an income at some point in the future?
   Yes ____________ No_____________
   If so, what amount (in today's rupees)?
   ₹______________When__________?

Some facts to help you answer the above:

II. Inflation Adjusted (Real Returns)
Would you prefer to confine the analysis to rupee returns or are goals more meaningful to you when restated to reflect purchasing power?
Rupee returns ______ Purchasing power ____________ (if rupee returns, proceed to Section III).

(a) In today's rupees, to what amount would you like to see your assets grow in five years?
(b) What real rate of return (after inflation) would you like to realize over the long term?
_____________%

III. Relative Return:
Most people like to set standards by which the long-term performance of their equity managers is to be measured. Which standard is most relevant to you?
__________Outperform BSE
__________Outperform NSE by ___________%.

C. Risk
Most individuals and fiduciaries have a strong concern for "safety" or "preservation of capital." Yet most investments carry some risk of fluctuation in principal value. In fact, it is because one assumes the risk that higher returns are expected. Risk can be quantified by the response to the following two questions concerning the overall portfolio.

1. Is a risk of loss once every three years tolerable to you? One in 10? 20? Never? Indicate one of the following:
   ________one out of ____years
   ___________never
2. Is a risk of extreme loss (greater than 15%) tolerable to you once every 10 years? 20? Never? Indicate one of the following:
   ________one out of ____years
   ___________never

To aid you in answering the above questions, the long-term rate of equity return mentioned earlier (10.4%) was achieved with approximately three loss years every 10. Moreover, extreme losses were suffered about one out of every 11 years while producing this return.

Source: Adapted from the questionnaire developed by Investment Advisory Services (IAS), a division of Raymond James & Associates, Inc., St. Petersburg, Florida.
IAS utilizes the answers to this questionnaire to help clients allocate their assets in concert with their individual time horizon and risk tolerance.

INVESTOR PREFERENCE

Investor preference refers to an investor's predisposition toward or away from specific investment products. As a result of past experiences, and based on previous training, most investors seem to have firm opinions about various investment products. A financial planner should not only recognize these preformed opinions but also should gauge the depth of these feelings. A simple questionnaire presented in the box entitled "Attitudes Toward Investment Products" is designed to help a planner determine an investor's predisposition toward specific investments. It is important to add that an investor's preference is also influenced by social needs and family commitments.

ATTITUDES TOWARD INVESTMENT PRODUCTS

1	2	3	4	5	6	7
Can't Sleep at Night	Jittery	No Feeling Either Way	Comfortable	Extremely Comfortable	Don't Know	Don't Care

________ Savings account	________ Treasury bills
________ Commodities futures	________ AAA Corporate bonds
________ Hedge funds	________ Blue chip common stocks
________ Private placement: real estate	________ Utility stocks
________ Zero coupon bonds	________ Money market acct (uninsured)
________ Growth mutual funds	________ Municipal bond funds
________ Gold coins	________ High yield mutual funds
________ Diamonds	________ call options
________ Universal life insurance	________ Variable life insurance
________ High yield bond funds	________ High grade bond funds
________ Government bond funds	________ Speculative stocks
________ High quality stock funds	________ International mutual funds
________ Single prem, whole life	________ Aggressive stock funds
________ ETF shares	________ Single prem. deferred annuity
________ iShares	________ Single prem. immediate annuity
________ ADRs	________ Equity index annuity
________ Real estate investment trust	________ Variable annuity
	________ Equity index funds

INVESTMENT PORTFOLIO

The objective of constructing a TIP is to bring about a synthesis between the various competing investment objectives just discussed. This goal is achieved by including the right combination of investments in the portfolio. In Chapter 8, we presented the key investment products. We will now discuss the placement of these investment products in a real world portfolio.

Cash Reserves and Emergency Funds

The starting point is to determine the percentage allocation for cash reserves and emergency funds. In a family's financial life there will occur unforeseen contingencies which must be successfully met to avoid catastrophic consequences. In addition, cash reserves provide liquidity needed to capitalize on emerging investment opportunities. The primary considerations in selecting these assets are safety and liquidity with the clear understanding that the trade-off is a low investment return. Investments listed in Table 10.3 under "Cash Reserves and Emergency Funds" fall in this category.

Table 10.3 *Investment Vehicles and Their Objectives*

Objective	Type	Investment Vehicles
Cans reserves and emergency funds	Cash reserve	Cash Money market funds Savings and loan accounts Checking accounts Short-term CDs Cash value of life insurance Treasury bills
Income flow	Fixed income	Corporate bonds Government (Treasury) bonds Municipal bonds Bond mutual funds Fixed annuities Convertible bonds Real estate investment trusts Utility stocks
Growth	Equity	Common stocks Variable annuities Stock mutual funds Real estate (managed) programs Option income programs Oil and gas income funds
Long-term growth and tax advantages	Real estate tax shelters hard assets miscellaneous	Real estate Oil and gas drilling programs, equipment leasing programs hard assets (gold, coins, art), and commodities

Income Flow

Another investment planning consideration is the income flow. A portfolio should be required to generate income to help maintain the desired lifestyle. Income-oriented investments emphasize current income but as a trade-off sacrifice growth of the principal. Most, though not all, fixed income investments have a fixed maturity date. These securities appreciate in value during periods of falling interest rates and lose their value during periods of rising interest rates.

Let us add an important caveat here. The view that bonds are the primary vehicle for generating current income is too parochial. There exist a number of other income generating investment products, such as utility stocks, high-yield stocks, mortgage-backed securities, fixed annuities, master-limited partnerships, and real estate investment trusts. Each of these has distinct investment characteristics and provides a valuable income planning tool. Table 10.3 lists the investments satisfying the income flow objective.

Growth

Equity investments offer a potential for appreciation in value but generate relatively limited amounts of cash flow. These investments are subject to market as well as industry- and company-related risks, and can result in sizeable losses if an investor is compelled to sell them under adverse market conditions. Investments listed in Table 10.3 under the category "Growth" are examples of products that satisfy an investor's growth objective.

Long-term Growth and Tax Advantages

The objectives of long-term growth and tax savings are achieved through investments in a variety of vehicles listed in Table 10.3. The main categories of these investments are discussed next.

Real estate investments. There are various ways in which an investor can participate in real estate investments. These include real estate partnerships, real estate investment trusts, investment in apartment complexes and shopping centers, and investment in undeveloped lands. Each has a different degree of risk associated with it, and great care should be exercised in making sure that the risk of a real estate investment is consistent with the risk tolerance level acceptable to an investor.

In general, real estate investments perform well during periods of economic growth and moderate inflation. However, history suggests that high interest rates are generally disastrous for these investments and real estate markets could be depressed for long periods of time. Also, these investments are illiquid, and in an emergency they can rarely be converted quickly into liquid funds.

Tax-sheltered investments. As a general rule, tax-sheltered investments generate cash flows that are sheltered from income taxes. This is accomplished by deducting depreciation, loan interest, and other deductible expenses against the cash flow. Tax shelters include investments in equipment leasing, breeding and cattle feeding programs, real estate, and gas and oil companies. A number of tax shelters are available on the marketplace such as retirement plan, cash flow through limited partnerships, financing arrangements, offshore companies, etc.

Hard assets. Generally, investments in gold, silver, rare coins, stamps, and precious metals, popularly known as hard assets, become attractive during periods of actual or anticipated high inflation and are, therefore, called inflation hedges. Investments in hard assets are appropriate only for risk takers who are able to sustain large losses and are not affected by their total illiquidity.

Miscellaneous investments. We have not yet discussed other exotic investment products, such as commodities, exploratory oil and gas programs, and race horses, the list of which is indeed very long. Since such investments fall outside our purview, it suffices to say that these exotic investments are inappropriate for all but a chosen few who are highly sophisticated, affluent, and resourceful investors.

Target Investment Portfolio

Let us analyze the current investment portfolio of the Shahi family. The family consists of Alok, aged 38, Shweta, 35, Rudransh, 10, and Rumi, 7. The family's gross annual income is ₹850,000. The Shahi family's investment portfolio is presented in Table 10.4 (Columns 1 and 2). The portfolio reveals that the Shahis: (a) favor equity investments over fixed income investments (60 percent and 6 percent, respectively), (b) have a low level of cash reserves (1 percent), and (c) have disproportionately high investments in real estate (14 percent) and tax shelters (16 percent). However, the construction of a TIP by using the portfolio repositioning technique requires a great deal more *analysis* than just a superficial review of the current portfolio, as we shall now observe.

Table 10.4 *Alok and Shweta, Investment Portfolio, March 31, 2014*

Type (1)	Current Amount (2)	Distribution (3)	Target Distribution (4)	Recommended Action
Cash reserve	₹125,000	1%	10%	₹787,500
Fixed income	50,000	6	33	2,511,250
Equity	5,500,000	60	33	–2,488,750
Real estate	1,250,000	14	16	210,000
Tax shelters	1,500,000	16	5	–1,043,750
Hard assets	250,000	3	3	23,750
Miscellaneous	0	0	0	0
Total	9,125,000	100%	100%	₹0

PORTFOLIO REORGANIZATION

Basic Steps

A financial planner can systematically reorganize an existing portfolio by completing the following four steps:

Step 1: Reallocate the percentage distribution of various classes of investments based on changes in the economic conditions.

Step 2: Change investment strategy as a result of changes in a client's life cycle, investment needs, time frame, and tax considerations.

Step 3: Change in product selection due to readjustment of a client's risk tolerance.

Step 4: Change in strategy to accommodate a client's special needs.

Effective Strategy

In our discussion, we will assume that the Shahis: (a) are risk averse, (b) need to generate additional current income to maintain their desired standard of living, and (c) recognize the need for increasing their cash reserve. Based on these assumptions, and the desired percentage distribution of assets generated by the AAM, we have generated a *target investment distribution* plan, presented in Table 10.4 (Column 4). In this case, our recommended actions (Column 5) include the following: (a) increasing cash reserves by ₹15,750, (b) investing ₹50,225 in fixed income securities to generate additional current income, and (c) purchasing additional real estate (₹4,200) and hard assets (₹475). Funds for these new investments are expected to be generated by sale of equities (₹49,775) and tax shelters (₹20,875).

The target distribution plan just presented is based on the AAM, taking into account the Shahis' risk tolerance level, current income needs, and desire for growth. However, it did not take into account the fact that at this time it might not be possible for the Shahis to implement this plan. Reasons include: (a) the inability to sell the illiquid tax shelters, (b) the prevailing weak market conditions that might dictate postponing the sale of equity securities, (c) possible conflict between the implementation of TIP recommendations and other financial goals, (d) the lack of availability of recommended investments at a reasonable price, and (e) the unfavorable tax consequences of liquidating various investment products that might require a reexamination of the suggested plan.

Despite these compelling reasons for not implementing the plan, a financial planner, who more than likely is also a registered investment advisor authorized to sell securities, has the responsibility for cautiously acting on these recommendations. Of course, the responsibility for selecting specific products could also be shifted to other investment professionals or advisors. Regardless of who makes the product selections, a financial planner should make sure that: (a) appropriate due diligence is performed on each product, (b) recommended products are appropriate for a client's portfolio, and (c) the client fully understands and accepts the benefits and drawbacks of each recommended product.

Section III: A Real World Investment Plan

Thus far we have presented the basic investment planning process and key investment planning strategies. We will now apply these concepts to an efficiently constructed investment portfolio. Assume the clients are P.K. Rai, aged 50, and Anju Rai, aged 48. This couple has requested their financial planner, R.P. Singh, to construct an efficient investment portfolio for them. In the following section, Singh presents his recommendations directly to P.K. and Anju Rai.

PORTFOLIO PRESENTATION TO THE RAIs

P.K. and Anju Rai, several weeks ago you requested us to develop a plan for investing an economic windfall you have just received. P.K. Rai during our initial interview you informed us that you are a 50-year-old scientist with a Ph.D. in mechanical engineering, and are currently employed as a senior manager with a progressive engineering firm. At present you participate in a defined benefit plan. Starting at the age of 65, this plan will provide you with a lifetime of income equivalent to 70 percent of your salary at that age. In addition, upon your death, this plan will pay your spouse during her lifetime an amount equivalent to 50 percent of your salary at the age of 65. It is our understanding that your wife is a homemaker, receiving no outside income and not participating in a retirement plan.

The lump sum you have received is from the death of Anju's great aunt. This sum represents the net amount distributed to you after all applicable expenses and taxes.

GOAL SETTING

P.K. Rai during our initial interview you informed us that you wish to retire at the age of 65, and that you want us to structure your investment portfolio in a way that it would help you achieve the following competing objectives.

1. Your investments should generate sufficient income to help finance your desired lifestyle following retirement.
2. You want part of your investments to be liquid so you could face any emergency situation with relative ease.
3. You prefer that we avoid investing in tax-deferred, retirement vehicles which are illiquid by nature.
4. You wish us to use the asset allocation strategy, which would help us create a portfolio that would maintain a proper balance between safety, liquidity, and growth.
5. You are interested in learning about the investment products we select for you.

RISK TOLERANCE LEVEL

An analysis of your risk tolerance questionnaire reveals that you are a risk-averse person. However, we feel you did not fully realize that the loss of principal represents only one of many faces of risk and that it is vitally important for you to appreciate other forms of risk. For instance, you erroneously believed that there is no market risk associated with a *safe* government bond mutual fund. Fortunately, after an extensive discussion of the many faces of investment risk, and a study of the volumes of published information we provided on investment products, we believe you have acquired a good working knowledge of this topic.

P.K. and Anju Rai, it is gratifying to note that even though you are basically a risk–averse family, you do wish to assume *some* risk by investing a small portion of your funds in one or more relatively high-risk products. We will certainly take this fact into account while structuring your portfolio.

TARGET INVESTMENT PORTFOLIO

We have made an extensive analysis of the AAM, your risk-tolerance level, and your need for current income and growth. On the basis of this analysis, we have developed for you a TIP. However, before making a formal presentation, we wish to emphasize the intermediate steps we have taken in arriving at our final recommendation. (a) Initially, we developed a *preliminary* TIP by applying our current AAM.

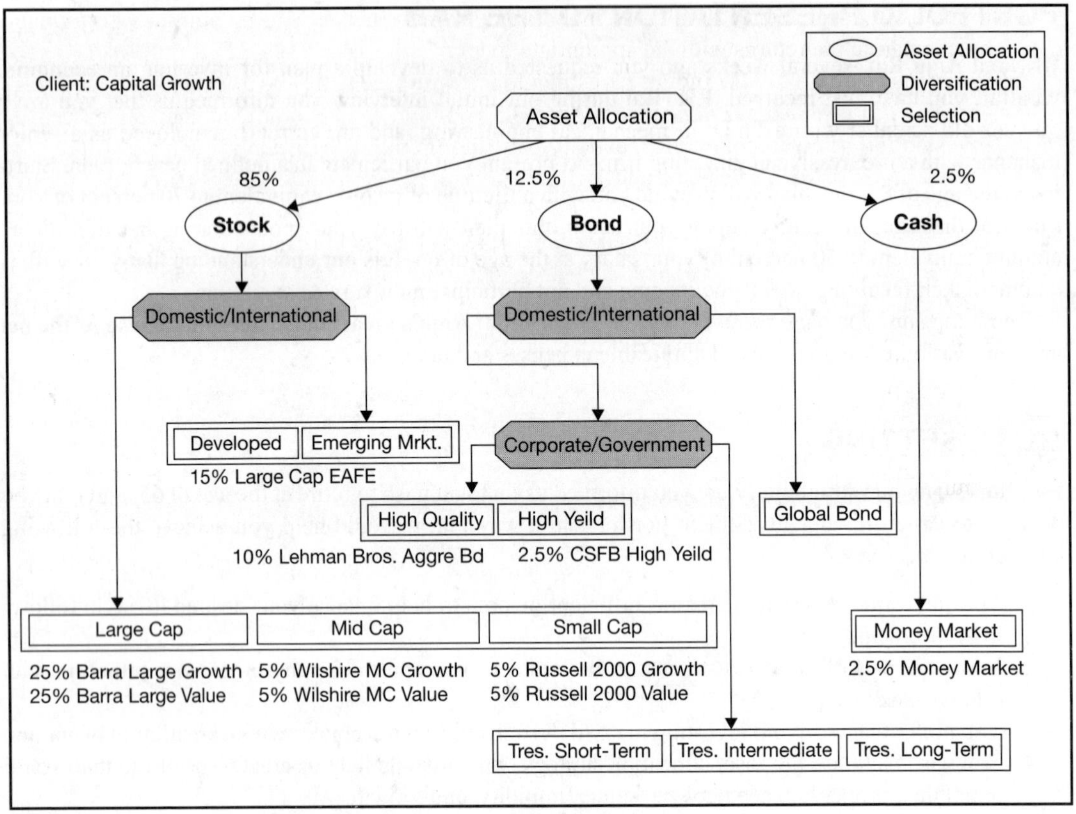

Figure 10.3 *Dynamic Asset Allocation Model—Captital Growth*

In developing this model, we analyzed the current business cycle, prevailing financial market conditions, inflationary expectations, interest rate predictions, and other ancillary factors. (b) On the basis of our interview, we developed a realistic risk profile for you. (c) We carefully analyzed your current financial situation and considered your special requests before finalizing your TIP.

P.K. and Anju Rai, your TIP, which represents a 15-year capital growth portfolio, is presented in Figure 10.3. On the basis of this portfolio, we wish to make the following recommendations:

1. Since your TIP is a long-term growth-oriented portfolio, we recommend that the majority of the funds be invested in equity securities. History of long-term market performance has demonstrated that, among all the various investment vehicles available, equity securities have provided by far the best returns.
2. Since the performance of various types of investments varies—sometimes greatly—over different economic cycles, in order to provide stability to the TIP, we recommend that a relatively small percentage of the portfolio be invested in fixed income securities and money market instruments.
3. We recommend selecting those bond mutual funds which specialize in high-quality corporate bonds and attempt to beat the performance of the Aggregate Bond Index. A small percentage of funds should also be placed in mutual funds investing in high-yield corporate bonds and seeking to beat the CS First Boston High Yield Bond Index.
4. Since we live in a global economy, many excellent opportunities can be located beyond our borders. We, therefore, recommend that a percentage of your funds earmarked for equities be directed

to mutual funds investing in international developed markets. We will monitor their performance by comparing the returns with the appropriate Index.

5. We recommend that your Indian investments in equity securities be allocated between large-cap, mid-cap, and small-cap mutual funds. Of these, we recommend that 80 percent be invested in large-cap companies, equally splitting the funds between growth and value companies. Performance of these funds will be measured against S&P BSE Large Cap Growth Index.
6. We further recommend that the remaining 20 percent of the funds be divided equally between the more aggressive mid-cap and small-cap companies, with proportionate divisions between growth and value companies. The performance of mid-cap funds will be judged against the Mid-cap Index; for the small-cap funds, as a guide, we will use the Index.

Currently, we are in the process of finalizing your TIP. Once constructed, we will present it to you for your consideration and approval. After you have approved the recommended portfolio (or some variation of it, if needed), we will promptly implement it.

One final point: We live in a dynamic world in which market conditions change, sometimes with a lightning speed. We will, therefore, monitor on a regular basis the performance of your portfolio and update it when necessary. Also, as part of our responsibility as your financial planner, periodically we will rebalance your portfolio so that it always reflects your goals, your short- and long-term expectations, and your dynamic financial situation.

GOLDEN RETIREMENT YEARS

P.K. and Anju Rai, your main objective in engaging our planning services is to make sure that your retirement years do in fact turn out to be the golden years. In order to give you a kaleidoscopic view of your retirement years, we will now fast-forward the remaining 15 years of your working life. So, for this exercise let us assume that P.K. Rai just turned 65 and both of you are currently reviewing the preretirement investment plan.

The 15-year Record

Thanks to our engaging superior fund managers to manage your portfolio and our continuous monitoring of their progress, your portfolio has enjoyed a sustained, annual after-tax growth of 10 percent, an impressive track record by any standard. Currently, the value of your portfolio is around ₹1,020,000.

P.K. Rai, during the last five years, you were the senior vice president of engineering of Atlas Corp., and last year you earned an annual salary of ₹250,000. Now that you are about to retire, starting immediately, your defined benefit plan promises to pay you for life an annual income of ₹175,000 (70 percent of ₹250,000).

P.K. and Anju Rai, you wish to receive an annual retirement income of ₹250,000 in order to be able to maintain your desired lifestyle during retirement. This means that your investment portfolio needs to generate an annual return of 6.3 percent, which would translate into an annual cash flow of ₹75,000. This amount, added to the defined benefit plan payment of ₹175,000 per year, should provide you with the desired retirement income. While we can structure with relative ease your portfolio to generate an annual cash flow of ₹75,000, in the absence of a creative management strategy, this portfolio would experience no future growth, certainly not a comforting thought by any means. So, in this case, our main challenge is to develop a *different* portfolio which will continue to grow while generating the cash flow you definitely need.

Investment Vehicles

A variety of investment products can be effectively used to produce the desired results. These are listed below.

Fixed annuity. At the currently prevailing interest rates, it is possible to select a fixed annuity that will guarantee an annual rate of 6.3 percent. However, annuities generally do not allow for the growth of capital, and frequently a fixed rate is offered for a limited period.

Split annuity. In a split annuity, you invest a portion of the money in a fixed annuity which generates the prespecified monthly income. The rest of the money can be invested in equities, so eventually it would equal the original amount.

Bond funds. Funds may be invested in a combination of high-quality and high-yield bond funds to generate the required income.

Retirement Plan

P.K. and Anju Rai, we congratulate you for reaching your golden years on schedule. We also take great pleasure in noting that we have succeeded in efficiently managing your investment portfolio, helping it to grow from ₹300,000 to a whopping ₹1,020,000. But, of course, that was not always a safe journey. Over the past 15 years, we have seen the portfolio grow handsomely for a couple of years only to see it plunge to much lower levels. Fortunately, because of our faith in our long-term investment strategy based on the time-tested AAM, we did not waver and, as a result, ultimately assisted you in reaching your retirement goal.

So, it is time to present for consideration your retirement TIP (Figure 10.4). Based on your risk tolerance and current expectations, we have concluded that for best results it would be wise to have four years of income available to you at all times. This money, which represents 25 percent of your portfolio, would be invested in money market instruments and short-term government bonds. The remaining 75 percent of the funds would be invested in equity securities, designed to realize long-term growth.

We realize, of course, that this new portfolio needs to generate an annual cash flow of ₹75,000, equivalent to a return of 6.3 percent on your current portfolio. But we are also mindful of the fact that your portfolio should generate more than 6.3 percent, so it would continue to grow while simultaneously generating the cash flow you seek.

After a careful consideration of alternative strategies, we have finally devised what we call the *moving money to the right* strategy. This strategy requires us to periodically liquidate a portion of equity and fixed income securities (located in the left and middle columns of Figure 10.4) and to shift these funds to money market and short-term securities (located in the right column of Figure 10.4). In addition, our plan would require us to carefully monitor the performance of your portfolio on a regular basis so that we could rebalance it, whenever warranted, to achieve our dual objectives of liquidity and growth.

FINAL THOUGHTS

P.K. and Anju Rai, the TIP we have just presented is indeed comprehensive. In developing it we have taken the following investment planning principles into account (A through F), some of which might not be self-evident.

A. *After-tax return:* Maximize, subject to income needs and risk tolerance level.
B. *Balanced approach:* Maintain a balance among liquidity, current income, and growth.
C. *Client's risk:* Match investment diversification with investor's risk tolerance level.
D. *Diversify:* (a) In terms of investment vehicles, (b) within a class or type of investment, and (c) through different maturities and time horizons.

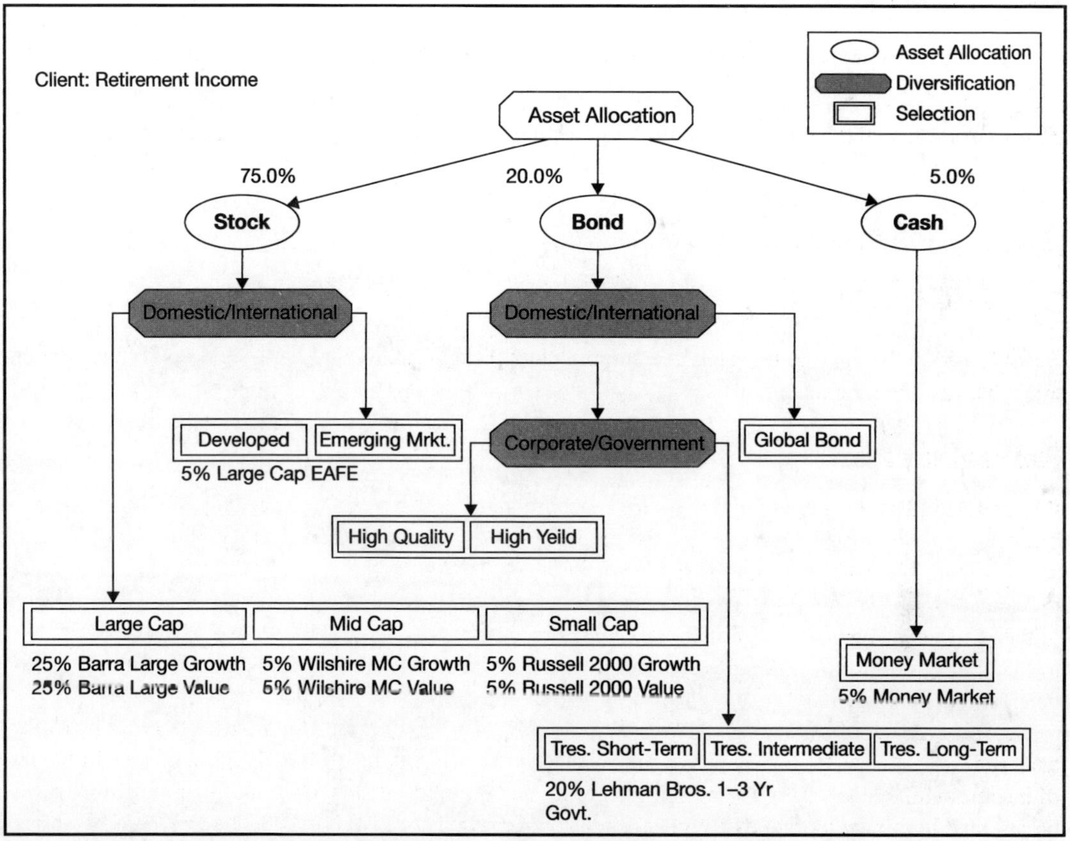

Figure 10.4 *Dynamic Asset Allocation Model—Retirement Income*

E. *Eliminate the tax on wealth:* Use investment techniques to reduce or eliminate taxes.
F. *Focus on growth over time:* Use the time-honored time value of money concept to maximize the growth of investable funds.

Naturally, we have made sure that the TIP is consistent with your risk tolerance, liquidity needs, desired investment returns, and the overall financial goals. It is important to emphasize, however, that because of the uncertainties we constantly face, this portfolio might not always function as smoothly as we would like it to. But there is no reason to despair. If we maintain our vigilance and do not waver, in the end we will surely succeed.

The trip tick we have developed for you represents a practical plan designed to maximize the benefits generated by an efficient investment portfolio we have created for you. We are ready to assist you in expeditiously implementing this plan. In addition, as stated frequently, we will continually monitor your progress and provide investment counseling to you for a long time.

In this chapter, we discussed investment planning concepts and strategies. The basic federal income tax structure will be presented in Chapter 11.

PART 5

TAX PLANNING

11 Basic Income Tax Structure

Section I: The Basic Tax Structure

INTRODUCTION

The sweeping changes brought about by the tax laws in India enacted during the past 15 years have successfully refined income tax rates for taxpayers. In fact, the highest income tax bracket is only 33.99 including surcharge percent (2014), down from 56 percent in 1993. Since problems that central and state governments face today are increasing, and taxes are the major source of income for these governments, tax rates could increase sometime in the future, taking an ever-increasing bite out of individual income. A basic understanding of tax law and the method of tax computation can help each taxpayer: (a) utilize all allowable deductions to reduce taxes, (b) develop tax planning strategies to minimize long-term tax liability, (c) avoid violating tax limits or rules that could result in sizable tax penalties, and (d) make improved financial decisions, with full consideration of tax implications.

There are many types of taxes paid by individuals: central, state, city, and so on. However, in this chapter we will concentrate only on central income taxes because, for most individuals, this is the largest and most complex component of their tax liability.

COMPUTATION OF TAXABLE INCOME

Before embarking on a discussion of the calculation of taxable income, it is useful to review the basic income tax structure, presented in Figure 11.1. This figure reveals that the first step toward arriving at total tax liability is the calculation of *gross income*. From this figure, standard or itemized deductions and exemptions are subtracted to arrive at the *taxable income*. This income is the basis for computing the tentative income tax. From this tentative figure, *tax credits* allowed by law for certain conditions are deducted. Based on Figure 11.1, Tax Form 16 is reproduced in Appendix 11.1 for easy reference. It is helpful to be fully comfortable with all lines and items included in this Form.

Having briefly reviewed the basic income tax structure, we now proceed to a discussion of the procedures for calculating gross income.

Calculation of Gross Income

Calculation of tax liability begins with the computation of total gross income. Unless specifically excluded from the law, this income comprises all income received in the form of money, property, and services. For joint returns, incomes of both spouses must be reported. Also, based on the source, income must be divided into several major categories, discussed in detail in the following section.

Active income. Active income of employees is reported annually in Form 16 entitled "Wages and Tax Statement" or in Form ITR for self-employed individuals. While salary, commissions, fees, and business profits are the most common forms of earned income, there are additional types of income directly related to gainful employment. An example of this type of income is self-employment income which as stated is reported in Form ITR. Because active income depends on some form of personal activity and remuneration for that activity, losses generally cannot be deducted against this form of income. The only exception is that ordinary and necessary business expenses may be deducted even if that results in a business loss.

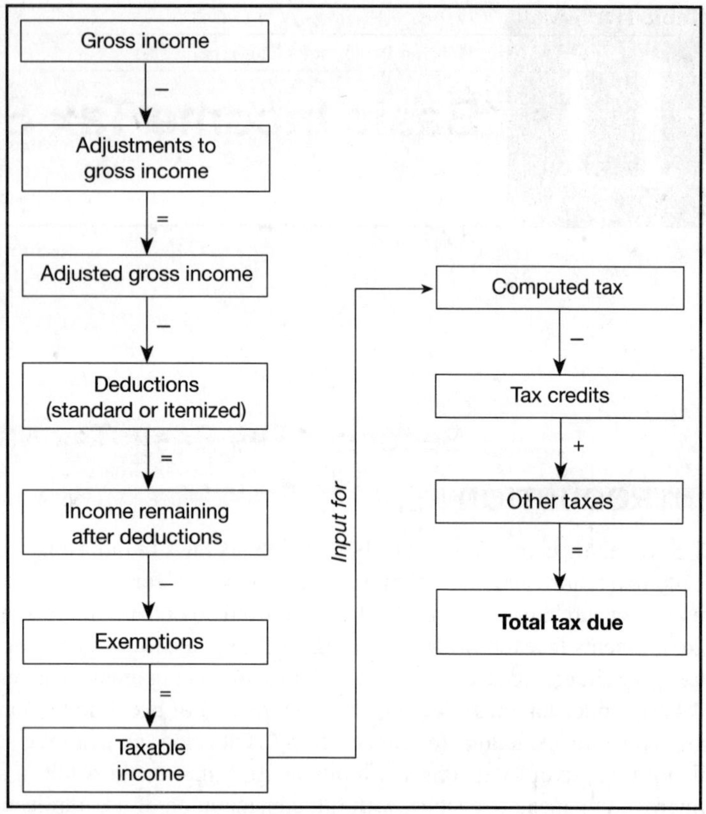

Figure 11.1 *Basic Income Tax Structure*

Portfolio income. Portfolio income, which is generated directly from investment activity, consists of interest, dividend income, and capital gains. The current tax law has specific rules governing the reporting of portfolio income and the deduction of losses against this income.

Interest. Interest income includes interest from accounts with banks, credit unions, savings and loan associations, money market funds, and mutual funds. Interest from the following sources must also be reported as income: (a) personal notes, (b) loans and mortgages, (c) corporate bonds and debentures, (d) government bills and bonds, (e) certain taxable municipal bonds, and (f) maturing or annual liquidation of government savings bonds. Generally, a payer sends each income recipient a Form ITR for this income. If the total interest exceeds ₹10,000 in a savings account, these sources of interest must be reported on the tax return.

Dividends. Dividend income results from the distribution of earnings and profits which corporations or mutual funds pay to shareholders. Generally, a payer sends the income recipient a Form ITR reporting dividend income. Unlike interest income, the total dividend income is tax free but it must be detailed in Form ITR of the tax return. All dividends are treated as tax-exempt income of the recipients; however, the companies paying these dividends are required to pay dividend distribution tax.

Mutual fund dividends that pass through to shareholders are also not taxable. However, debt-oriented mutual funds are liable for paying income distribution taxes of 14.16 percent in general and 22.66 percent on the distribution of incomes to individual/Hindu Undivided Fund and other persons in particular.

Table 11.1 *Holding Periods for Long-term Gains*

Asset	Min. Holding Period for Long-term Gains		Taxation*
Equity	1 year		Zero
Debt	1 year		Whichever is beneficial: 10% without indexation 20% with indexation benefit
Real estate	3-year		20% with indexation benefit
Gold	3-year	Physical Gold, e-Gold	20% with indexation benefit
	1 year	Gold ETF Gold MF	Whichever is beneficial: 10% without indexation 20% with indexation benefit
Bonds/ NCDS	1 year		10% without any indexation benefit

*Education cess of 3 percent is applicable to all tax rates.

Dividends received from a mutual insurance company are treated as a nontaxable return of excess premium payment. However, if a company reports capital gains as dividend income, then this income is included in Form ITR.

Capital Gains[1]

Since taxation of capital gains from various types of assets is highly complex, at the outset it is appropriate to undertake an in-depth discussion of this topic. Gains from trading in equity, debt, gold and real estate are treated as capital gains and differing tax rules apply to them.

Capital gains from these asset classes are classified as either long term or short term, based on the holding period of each investment. For instance, a real estate property, gold, or debt held for at least three years is treated as a long-term investment. By contrast, equities need to be held only for one year to qualify as a long-term investment.

In general, as compared to short-term gains, long-term capital gains (LTCGs) are taxed at a lower rate so as to encourage entrepreneurship and investment in the economy. The following example should make these complex rules clear.

Long-term Capital Gains

LTCG is realized when an asset is held for at least a prespecified period. As mentioned, this period ranges from one year to three years across different asset classes. Table 11.1 shows the holding period needed for generating long-term gains in various asset classes and the applicable tax rates for each asset class:

Clearly, LTCGs from equity sales conducted on a stock exchange and subjected to the securities transaction tax (STT) are no longer subjected to capital gain taxes. Gains from real estate and physical gold investment are, however, taxed at a flat rate. Finally, bonds are taxed at 10 percent and are not accorded the privilege of indexation benefits.

Incidentally, specific income tax provisions can be used to reduce LTCGs through indexation or to save on LTCG taxes by investing the gain in specified investments. Put differently, in addition to reducing the tax liability by utilizing indexation benefits, taxes on LTCGs could be further reduced by investing these gains in specified securities for a prespecified time period.

[1] "How to compute long and short term capital gain," EconomicTimes.com (December 27, 2013). Retrieved from http://economictimes.indiatimes.com/wealth/savings-centre/analysis/how-to-compute-long-short-term-capital-gains/articleshow_opt/28009081.cms (last accessed on December 6, 2014).

Here is how indexation benefit works. Since over time inflation can erode the value of the rupee, to counter that decline the law permits an inflationary adjustment of the capital gains by using an inflation adjustment factor. The following illustration (Table 11.2) demonstrates the use of this strategy.

Table 11.2 *How Indexation Works*

Purchase price of property in April 2007:	₹3,500,000
Sale price of property in May 2011:	₹5,000,000
Inflation index:	2007–08: 551; 2011–12: 785
Indexed purchase price:	₹3,500,000 × 785/551 = ₹4,986,388
Long-term capital gains:	₹5,000,000 – 49,86,388 = ₹13,612*
Tax on LTCG:	13,612 × 20% = ₹2,722
Education Cess:	2722 × 3% = ₹82
Total Tax on LTCG:	***₹2,804***

Note: *The non-indexed gain would have been ₹15 lakh.

Short-term Capital Gains

Profits from investment in any asset class, if held for less than the minimally specified holding period, are taxed as short-term capital gains. Except for investment in equities, short-term capital gains generated by sales of other forms of assets are treated as ordinary income and taxed as per the currently prevailing slab rate. Table 11.3 presents details of taxability of short-term capital gains.

Table 11.3 *Taxability of Short-term Capital Gains*

Asset	Holding Period for Short-term Gains	Tax Rate*
Equity	Less than 1 year	15%
Debt	Less than 1 year	Added to income
Gold	Physical/e-Gold – Below 3-year ETF/Gold MF – Below 1 year	Added to income
Real Estate	Below 3-year	Added to income
Bonds/NCD	Less than 1 year	Added to income

Note: *Education cess of 3 percent is applicable to all tax rates.

The following example demonstrates the calculation of short-term capital gains generated by the sale of mutual funds.

Cost of investing in equity mutual fund in 2011:	₹100,000
Sale proceeds from equity investment after six months:	₹120,000
Short-term capital gains:	₹20,000
Total taxes on gain (₹20,000 × 15%):	₹3,000
Education cess (₹3,000 × 3%):	₹90
Total tax payable:	***₹3,090***

Capital Losses[2]

As is the case with capital gains, capital losses generated by dealing in equity, debt, gold, and real estate are classified as either long term or short term, based on the holding period of each investment. For instance, a real estate held for at least three years is treated as a long-term investment. By contrast,

[2] "How to compute long and short-term capital gain," EconomicTimes.com (December 27, 2013). Retrieved from http://economictimes.indiatimes.com/wealth/savings-centre/analysis/how-to-compute-long-short-term-capital-gains/articleshow_opt/28009081.cms (last accessed on December 6, 2014).

investment in equities held only for one year is qualified as a long-term investment. The Income Tax Act lays down various rules applicable to use capital losses for reducing capital gains and for carrying them forward for future use.

A short-term capital loss can be used to reduce both short-term capital gain and LTCG. However, a long-term capital loss can be used only to reduce LTCG. Any long-term capital loss which cannot be used during a given year can be carried forward for future use over the next eight years.

Incidentally, long-term capital losses on security transactions subject to STT cannot be used to reduce any taxable income and carried forward to set off against any future gains. That is, these losses can be used only against short-term capital gains and LTCGs from non-equity assets such as real estate, jewelry, debt mutual funds, and gold exchange-traded funds.

It is important to note that short-term capital losses must be used first to reduce short-term capital gains and after that to reduce LTCGs on transactions not subject to STT. Equally important, a short-term capital gain on which STT has not been paid (i.e., it was taxed at 20 percent) can be reduced by short-term capital loss on which STT was paid (i.e., taxable at 10 percent). Furthermore, since LTCG on shares where STT is paid is totally exempt from income tax, long-term capital loss from shares where STT is paid cannot be used against any short-term capital gain or LTCG from any source. Also, this loss cannot be carried forward to the next year.

Computation of Capital Gains and Losses

Tax rules on capital gains and losses can be best articulated by presenting the following steps required for reporting gains and losses:

Step 1. Calculate the cost or tax basis of the capital asset. The *basis* is the purchase price of the asset, plus expenses incurred in improving the asset, minus depreciation (if applicable).

Step 2. Determine whether based on the holding period each transaction should be treated as a short-term capital gain or an LTCG or a long-term capital loss. Once that decision is made, calculate the *net* LTCG or short-term capital gain or loss associated with each transaction. The formula is:

$$\text{Net gain/Loss} = \text{Amount realized} - \text{Adjusted basis}$$

Step 3. Subtract short-term losses from short-term gains, thereby arriving at the *net* short-term capital gain or loss.

Step 4. Subtract long-term losses from long-term gains, thereby arriving at the net LTCG or long-term capital loss.

Step 5. Determine the *net* capital gains amount by combining Steps 3 and 4.

The results of these computations are used to calculate the taxable income. The capital gain or loss reporting rules are summarized in Figure 11.2.

Capital Gains and Sale of Residence

If a homeowner is considering the sale of the principal residence, and the home has appreciated in value since it was purchased, or the homeowner has accumulated a lot of deferred profit from previous sales, the current tax law could be of a significant value. But the law is still no more sympathetic than in previous years to homeowners who wind up *selling at a loss*.

Here are the salient features of the relevant provisions of the current law. Any profit realized after holding the property for three years is treated as a long-term gain. The calculation is similar for short-term gain, except that in the former case the cost of acquisition and the improvement of the property can

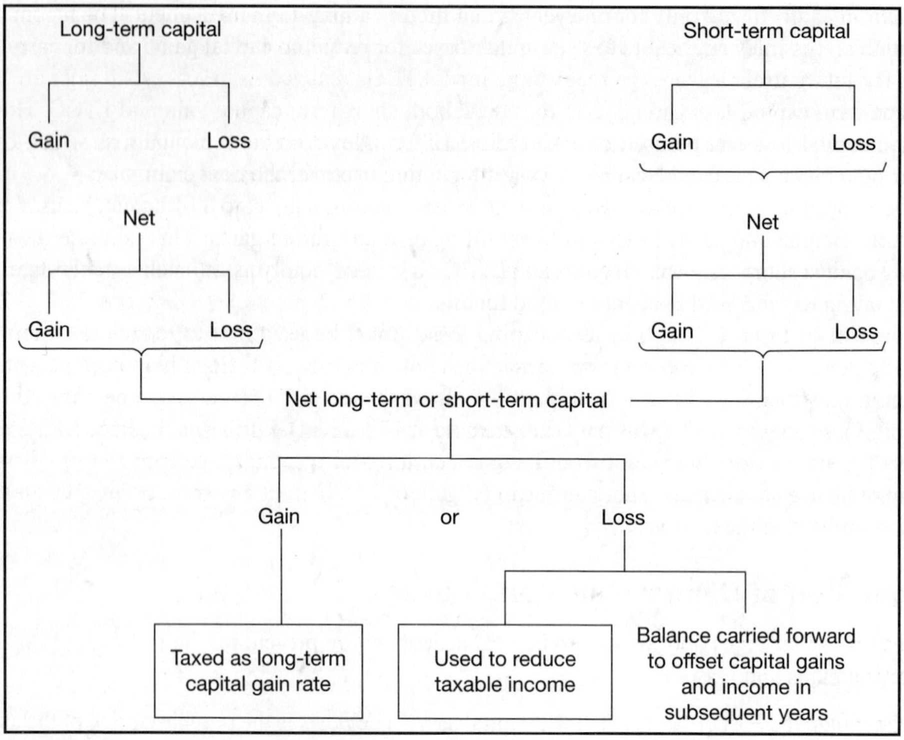

Figure 11.2 *Capital Gain Tax Calculation*

Table 11.4 *Benefit of Indexation*

Cost of purchasing a property in April 2009	₹3,500,000
Cost of selling the property in May 2014	₹5,000,000
Inflation index	**2008–09: 551; 2014–15: 785**
Indexed purchase cost	₹3,500,000 × 785/551 = ₹49,86,388
Long-term capital gains	₹5,000,000 – ₹4,986,388 = ₹13,612
Tax on LTCG	₹13,612 × 20% = ₹2,722
Education cess	₹2,722 × 3% = ₹82
Total Tax on LTCG	₹2,804

be adjusted for inflation, a process known as *indexation*. This technique can be used to adjust income payments with the help of a price index so as to maintain the purchasing power of the income flow. A practical example presented in Table 11.4 should make the benefit of indexation clear.

House for Sale

Under the current law, if the property is sold at profit within three years of purchase, it is considered as a short-term capital gain. Short-term capital gain is calculated by deducting from the sale price the cost of acquisition, the money spent on improving the property, and the transfer cost. The gain is included in the taxable income for the year the money is received and taxed according to the person's tax slab.

As expected, profit realized after three years of buying a property is treated as a long-term gain. The calculation is the same as that for short-term gain, except that the cost of acquisition and improvement is adjusted by indexation, a process already explained. LTCGs realized from real estate sales are taxed at a 20 percent tax rate.

Incidentally, a possible complication can arise if after indexation the actual gain turns out to be lower than the cost. Such a case can best be explained with the help of a practical example.

Assume Ravi, aged 50, buys a property for ₹30 lakh, sells it after five years for ₹40 lakh and realizes a profit of ₹10 lakh. Applying indexation to this case, the LTCG then turns into a long-term capital loss. In such a case, regular tax deductions against LTCGs cannot be claimed; instead, taxes on such gains must be computed separately. If Ravi's total income is below the tax exemption threshold (₹2 lakh for individuals who are not senior citizens), only that part of the LTCG that is above the exemption limit will be taxed at the applicable rate. It is important to reiterate that, unlike short-term gains, long-term capital losses can be used to reduce only LTCGs.

There is a special tax break the law allows to the recipients of LTCGs generated by real estate sales. The Income Tax Act exempts capital gains from the sale of a home if a taxpayer invests the gains in a residential property (not a commercial property) within two years from the date of sale or constructs another home within three years from the date of sale.

A taxpayer gets yet another tax break if the gain is invested in capital gain bonds issued by National Highways Authority oflndia (NHIA) and Rural Electrification Corporation Limited (REC). This transaction has a lock-in period of three years and the maximum limit for investing in such an instrument is ₹50 lakh. Money invested in this bond can be withdrawn after three years without paying any taxes.

Income

The tax law classifies income in five categories, namely salary, income from house property, profits and gains from business or profession, capital gains, and income from other sources. Of these, as the following table illustrates, the definition of salary includes both fully and partially taxable items.

Fully Taxable	Partially Taxable
Basic salary	House rent allowance
Dearness allowances (DA)	Leave travel allowance (LTA)
Special allowance	Vehicle maintenance
Bonus	Medical reimbursement up to ₹25,000 exempted in a year
Band pay	Transport allowance up to ₹1600 per month exempted
Overtime	Uniform allowance—amount up to ₹24,000 per annum is tax free
Arrears	Children education allowance (₹100 per month per child and ₹300 for hostel expenditure) maximum for two children
Personal pay	Telephone allowance
Shift allowance	Meal coupons
Food allowance	Newspaper/journal allowance—up to ₹12,000 per annum is tax free
Furniture allowance	

Losses from passive activities, such as tax shelters, in which an individual does not materially participate, may be used only to offset income from such activities. That is, the *passive activity losses* may not be used to offset income from compensation, interest, dividends, non-business capital gains, or from active business. However, passive activity losses can be carried forward and applied against income from passive activities in future years. These losses may also be deducted in the year in which the passive activity is entirely liquidated.

Clubbing of Minor's Income

The income of a child is added to parent's higher income as long as the child remains a minor, that is, below 18 years. However, only up to ₹1,500 of a minor's income can be claimed by the parent as a deduction. In addition, if a recurring/fixed deposit with a bank or a post office is in a child's name, then the interest on that deposit is also added to the parent's income.

Tax-exempt Income: Municipal Bonds

Municipal bonds are qualifying tax-free bonds issued by municipalities (such as states, cities, and institutions) to raise funds for financing local projects. Interest income from municipal bonds is completely exempt from income tax. The reason for this exemption is to make it easier for municipalities to sell bonds and obtain financing for community improvement by making the municipal bond interest rate more attractive than the interest rates on comparable corporate bonds, and net of central government and state taxes.

Tax-exempt municipal bonds provide investors with an alternative to invest in taxable corporate bonds and government instruments. The key question, therefore, becomes: Which of the three types of bonds offers the highest after-tax rate of return? The answer, of course, depends on the marginal tax bracket of an investor. Consider, for example, an investor in the 30 percent income tax bracket who wishes to purchase either a municipal bond paying 8 percent or a corporate bond of equal riskiness, currently yielding 10 percent. The municipal bond pays 8 percent after-tax, whereas the corporate bond pays only 7.2 percent on an after-tax basis, as calculated here:

$$\begin{bmatrix}\text{Before tax}\\ \text{interest rate,}\\ 10\% = .10\end{bmatrix} \times \left[1 - \begin{bmatrix}\text{Investor's}\\ \text{income tax}\\ \text{rate,}\\ 30\% = .30\end{bmatrix}\right] = \begin{bmatrix}\text{After-tax}\\ \text{interest rate,}\\ 7.0\% = .070\end{bmatrix}$$

In this case, the investor in the 30 percent tax bracket will find the municipal bond to be more attractive than the corporate bond. A comparison of tax-exempt with taxable yields for several interest levels is presented in Table 11.5. It can be seen from this table that a taxpayer in the 30 percent tax bracket would prefer a fully taxable corporate bond over a municipal bond yielding 8.5 percent only if the taxable bond yielded over 12.31 percent.

Reverse Mortgage

Reverse mortgage is the opposite of taking a home loan at the time of purchase or construction of a house. The benefit of the reverse mortgage is that a house can be used for living for life and the owner need not repay the loan amount. The legal heir may get the house back after paying the outstanding loan amount. For example, one can buy a home through home loan for 20 years after retirement and to gets tax-free monthly cash flow from banks/housing finance companies to cover regular expenses.

Nontaxable Income

Several sources of income are treated as nontaxable income. These sources include: (a) inheritances, (b) interest on certain state and municipal bonds, government companies, and interest received from certain mutual funds that hold such bonds, (c) interest on Public Provident Fund/General Pension Fund/Employees' Provident Fund (PPF/GPF/EPF), (d) interest on RBI Relief bonds, (e) capital receipt from an insurance company, (f) amount received as gratuity or leave encashment, subject to limits, (g) house rent allowance or other specified allowances received from an employer, subject to limits (h) agricultural

Table 11.5 *Tax-exempt versus Taxable Yields*

Tax-exempt Yields (%)	Tax Brackets		
	10%	20%	30%
2	2.22	2.5	2.86
2.5	2.78	3.125	3.57
3	3.33	3.75	4.29
3.5	3.89	4.375	5.00
4	4.44	5	5.71
4.5	5.00	5.625	6.43
5	5.56	6.25	7.14
5.5	6.11	6.875	7.86
6	6.67	7.5	8.57
6.5	7.22	8.125	9.29
7	7.78	8.75	10.00
7.5	8.33	9.375	10.71
8	8.89	10	11.43
8.5	9.44	10.625	12.14
9	10.00	11.25	12.86
9.5	10.56	11.875	13.57
10	11.11	12.5	14.29
10.5	11.67	13.125	15.00
11	12.22	13.75	15.71
11.5	12.78	14.375	16.43
12	13.33	15	17.14
12.5	13.89	15.625	17.86
13	14.44	16.25	18.57
13.5	15.00	16.875	19.29
14	15.56	17.5	20.00
14.5	16.11	18.125	20.71
15	16.67	18.75	21.43

income returns of capital, (i) reimbursements received from an employer for business expenses, if properly reported, and (j) compensation for injury or sickness and certain disability payments.

Adjustments to Gross Income

Once all forms of income (and appropriate losses) are totaled, a select group of expenditures can be deducted from gross income to help reduce an individual's final tax liability to its minimum legal amount. These deductions are often referred to as "above-the-line" deductions, since they represent deductions included in the calculation of adjustments to adjusted gross income (AGI). So, in effect, AGI is a key element in determining an individual's taxes, given that a person's tax rate, and the ability to take various tax credits, is determined by the AGI. In fact, AGI even impacts other aspects of a person's financial life because banks, mortgage lenders, and college financial aid programs all routinely ask for a person's AGI. The above-the-line deductions are presented in Table 11.6.

Health/Medical Insurance Contributions

Health savings accounts (HSAs) are tax-deductible savings plans that allow a taxpayer to save pretax money for future health care expenses. For 2014, tax deductible contributions are limited to ₹20,000 for senior citizens and up to ₹15,000 for the rest of the taxpayers. For health/medical insurance of parents, an additional relief of ₹20,000 is available for parents under the senior citizen category and ₹15,000 for the rest with effect from for the assessment year 2014–15. Hence, under Section 80 of the Income Tax Act, the

Table 11.6 *Tax Deductions*

Sections	Tax Savings Available
80C	Principal payment on home loan, stamp duty, and the registration cost of the house, tuition fee of 2 children, EPF, PPF, NSC, SCSS, tax savings FD for five years, ULIPs, ELSS and life insurance premium, deferred annuity, and bonds issued by NABARD.
80CC	Pension schemes.
80CCD	NPS, ELSS, Central Govt. Employees Pension Schemes. Deduction is available up to ₹50,000.
	The maximum deduction combining all these investments/expenditures is ₹150,000
80CCC	Deductions and income in respect of contributions to certain pension funds by an individual assessee, pension plans of insurance companies, and payment of premium for annuity plan of LIC or any other insurer. Deduction is available up to a maximum of ₹100,000.
80D	Medical insurance premium paid for self, spouse, parents, and dependent children. Maximum deduction is ₹25,000 below 60 years of age and ₹30,000 above 60 years of age.
80DD	Maintenance and medical treatment of dependent disabled. The deduction allowed is ₹50,000 which goes up to ₹100,000 if the disabled person is a person with severe disability.
80DDB	Treatment of certain diseases/ailment such as AIDS, cancer and neurological diseases for self and dependents. The maximum deduction allowable under this section is ₹40,000 and ₹60,000 in case of senior citizens.
80U	A physically disabled assessee with problems such as blindness and low vision, leprosy cured, hearing impairment, locomotor disability, mental retardation and illness, Austin, cerebral palsy, and multiple disabilities is entitled to get deduction up to ₹50,000. In case of severe disability (80 percent), an assessee is entitled to get a deduction of ₹100,000.
80G	Donation to charitable organizations. The donations which are paid only in cash/checks are eligible for deduction. Some of the donations are exempted for 100% of the amount donated (national defense fund, PM's national relief fund, national sports fund, national cultural fund etc.), some for 50% of the amounts donated (Jawaharlal Nehru Memorial Fund, PM's Drought Relief Fund, National Children Fund, Indira Gandhi Memorial Trust, Rajiv Gandhi Foundation, World Vision India, etc.) while others for 10% of the adjusted gross total income.
80GGA	Donation to scientific research institutions or rural development. The deduction allowed under this section is 100% of the donation made in the following for scientific research: university, college, association/institution to be used in social science statistical research or undertaking scientific research, or undertaking rural development, etc.
80GGC	Donation to political partied. 100% deduction is allowed for donation to the political party registered under section 29A of the Representation of the People Act, 1951. However, the maximum deduction that an assessee can claim under this section is 10% of the total gross annual income.
80E	Educational loan for pursuing higher studies of individual, spouse, children of the individual or of the student of whom individual is a legal guardian. The deduction is only available on the interest paid not the payment of the principal amount of the loan.
80EE	Interest on home loan. Total deduction allowed under this section is ₹100,000. Terms included in this are: this should be an assessee's first house, the value of the house should not be more than ₹40 lakh, loan amount should not be more than ₹25 lakh, and loan amount should be sanctioned by a financial institution during 2013–14.
80GG	Deduction of house rent in case of no HRA. an assessee can claim deduction for the rent paid even if he does not get HRA. House rent deduction will be lower of the following three amounts: (a) ₹2,000 per month, (b) 25% of the annual income, and (c) rent paid less than 10% of the annual income.
80CCG	Rajiv Gandhi Equity Saving Scheme. This is in respect of an investment made under a notified equity saving scheme. The scheme has a lock-in period of three years. The amount of deduction is at 50% of the amount invested in equity shares. However, the amount of deduction under this provision cannot exceed ₹25,000.
80TTA	The deduction is restricted to ₹10,000 or the actual interest whichever is lower.
80RRB	Royalty income to the author of certain books other than textbooks. The maximum deduction is ₹300,000.
80QQB	Royalty income on patents. The maximum deduction is ₹300,000.

maximum deduction available for this purpose is ₹40,000. This relief is in addition to the maximum relief of ₹100,000 available for investments under Sections 80C, 80CCC, and 80CCD of the Income Tax Law.

Moving Expenses

Qualifying unreimbursed moving expenses incurred in moving to a new job location are deductible as an above-the-line deduction. As per Section 10(14) of the Income Tax Act, 1961, along with Rule 2BB of the Income Tax Rules, 1962, any allowance granted to meet the cost of travel on transfer (including packing and transportation of personal effect) or the ordinary daily charges incurred during the period of journey in connection with a transfer can be claimed as exempt from tax. For this purpose, only certain types of expenses are fully deductible, such as the cost of moving household goods and related travel costs. Other expenses, such as the costs of pre-move house hunting trips, or temporary quarters at the new job location, are not deductible.

Penalty on Early Withdrawal of Savings

If a taxpayer withdraws money from a certificate of deposit or other time-deposit savings account prior to its maturity date, it might be subjected to a penalty for early withdrawal. This penalty is charged by the bank and withheld directly from the proceeds of the certificate. The amount of any penalty is deductible from the income.

Contributions

Individuals can reduce their taxable income by contributing money to a traditional individual saving account such as PPF, EPF/Voluntary Provident Fund (VPF), National Savings Certificates (NSC), Senior Citizen Savings Scheme (SCSS), Bank Fixed Deposits (FDs), Post Office Time Deposits (POTDs), and National Housing Bank (NHB) Suvriddhi. Contributions to these schemes can be made as late as the first due date of a tax return (generally April 1) and still be considered retroactive to the previous tax year. For 2014, the annual rupee limit for contributions is ₹150,000. As will be discussed in detail in Chapter 13, contributions to a traditional savings schemes might be fully deductible, partially deductible, or entirely nondeductible, depending on factors as the taxpayer's age and total income, and also on whether the taxpayer and the spouse are covered by a retirement plan through their employer.

Contributions to Simple and Individual Pensions Plans by Self-employed Persons

A person with self-employment income can take a tax deduction for contributions to an NPS or other pension plans. For the purpose of this deduction, self-employment income means net profits from a sole proprietorship or a partnership. A taxpayer must set up and fund a qualified retirement plan by the required deadline. Each plan has a different deadline and funding limits (to be discussed in detail in Chapter 13).

Student Loan Interest Deduction

Individuals can deduct student loan interest on loans issued for their benefit, their spouses' benefit (if filing jointly), and for the benefit of dependents. The maximum deduction for interest paid is ₹2,500 (2014). If a taxpayer's income is between ₹60,000 and ₹75,000 (between ₹125,000 and ₹155,000 for married people filing jointly), the deduction is prorated. If a taxpayer's income is over ₹75,000 (₹155,000 for a married couple filing jointly), student loan interest is not deductible.

A deduction is available under Section 80E of the Income Tax Act for any amount paid in the previous year by an assessee out of his or her taxable income in the form of interest on a loan taken from a financial institution or an approved charitable institution for the purpose of pursuing higher education for self, spouse or children.

Employer-provided Educational Assistance

Employer-paid educational expenses are fully deductible by an employer and are excludable from the employee's income. Neither the *income tax credit* nor the *lifetime learning credit* may be claimed for a student in the same tax year in which his or her employer pays all the student's qualified tuition and related expenses.

Educational assistance benefits include payments made by an employer for tuition fees, books, supplies, and equipment. It does not include payments for meals, lodging, transportation, or tools.

Deductions

The next step in the process of calculating tax liability is to subtract all allowable deductions from the AGI. At this point, a taxpayer can take either the standard deduction or the itemized deductions.

Standard Deduction

The standard deduction is the amount that all taxpayers (except some dependents) are permitted to take when filing a tax return. The amount of the standard deduction is the rupee threshold for determining whether or not an individual may itemize deductions. The standard deductions for 2014 are presented in Table 11.7.

Age 60 to below 80

Taxpayers who are between ages 60 and below 80 and do not itemize their deductions may take a standard deduction of ₹50,000 (2014). If a husband and wife are both either 60 or over, they may claim an additional deduction of ₹50,000 on their return. Finally, taxpayers who are at least 80 years of age are permitted to take an additional deduction of ₹200,000.

Medical Expenses

Medical expenses for the treatment of certain diseases (neurological, Parkinson's, malignant cancer, AIDS, chronic renal failure, hemophilia, thalassemia, and so on) of up to ₹60,000 for seniors and ₹40,000

Table 11.7 *Standard Deductions*

Filing Status	2014 Standard Deduction
For Individuals below 60 Years	
Up to ₹250,000	Nil
₹250,001 to ₹500,000	10%
₹500,001 to ₹1,000,000	20%
Above ₹1,000,000	30%
For Individuals Who Are 60 Years or More but below 80 Years	
Up to ₹300,000	Nil
₹300,001 to ₹500,000	10%
₹500,001 to ₹1,000,000	20%
Above ₹1,000,000	30%
For Individuals Who Are 80 Years or More	
Up to ₹500,000	Nil
₹500,001 to ₹1,000,000	10%
Above ₹1,000,000	20%

for others can be deducted from the taxable income. For this purpose, qualifying expenses include: (a) the diagnosis, treatment, or prevention of disease; (b) payments to health care professionals and facilities; (c) prescription drugs; (d) transportation needed for receiving medical care; (e) insurance covering medical care; and (f) lodging while away from home primarily for medical care. Expenditure on the medical treatment (including nursing), training, and rehabilitation of a disabled dependent and the related insurance premiums are also eligible for deductions. The deduction allowed is ₹50,000; this amount is raised to a maximum of ₹100,000 if severe disability is involved.

And that is not all. Medical insurance premiums paid by families (husband, wife, children, and parents) also qualify for deduction from taxable income. For individuals below 60, the deductible amount is limited to ₹15,000. The deductible amount is raised to ₹20,000 for individuals who are 60 years old or older. An additional deduction of ₹15,000 can be claimed if health insurance is purchased to cover the parents (if either parent is a senior citizen the deduction is raised to ₹20,000), whether or not parents are dependent on the taxpayer.

Interest Expense

Tax rules applicable to the deductibility of various types of interest expenses are summarized in Table 11.8. This is followed by a brief discussion of interest expenses.

Qualified residence interest expense is tax deductible. Interest paid on first home loan is deductible for up to ₹2 lakh in case of a self-occupied house. In case the house is in the joint name of the spouse (joint loan), each one can claim ₹2 lakh as interest deduction. In case the house is under construction, interest deduction must be postponed. After the house is occupied, interest deduction is allowed in five equal installments, for the next five years, along with the interest of that financial year. The principal repayment component of a loan is also allowed as a deduction of up to ₹150,000 along with the expenses for LIC premium, NSC, EPF, Equity-linked Savings Scheme (ELSS), and so on. This last deduction, however, is not available if the loan is used to buy a second property. Incidentally, interest expense can be used to reduce the taxable income generated by the second home; such an expense can also be carried forward for up to eight years.

Turning now to investments: Interest on loans to acquire taxable investments or tax-exempt investments like municipal bonds is not tax deductible. By contrast, interest on loans taken to operate a business is fully deductible. A similar rule applies to the interest paid on loans assumed to finance higher educational studies; this interest cost is fully deductible. In passing, it should be mentioned that consumer interest expense is not deductible.

Table 11.8 *Deductibility of Interest Expense*

Interest Category	Its Nature	Deductibility Rules
Home loan interest expense	Interest on indebtedness secured by any property that is a qualified residence of a taxpayer.	Deductibility limits deductions of interest on acquisition loans up to ₹200,000.
Investment interest expense	Interest on debt incurred to carry property that is held for investment.	Not deductible.
Business interest expense	Interest on loans taken to operate a business.	All interest expenses are fully deductible.
Education loan	Interest expenses generated on the loan taken for higher education for self, spouse, or children.	All interest expenses are fully deductible. Deduction of interest for up to eight years from the start of the assessment year can be claimed.
Consumer/Personal interest expense	Interest on personal loans.	Not deductible.
Passive activity interest expense	Interest expense generated in carrying out passive activity in which a person does not materially participate.	Not deductible.

Charitable Contributions

Contributions to a qualified charity or a tax-exempt trust are fully deductible. Deductions for contributions to charitable organizations (such as, National Defense Fund, Prime Minister's National Relief Fund, National Sports Fund, NGOs, schools, and other qualifying nonprofit funds) are allowed up to 100 percent of AGI (although some limitations apply). Any *excess* deductions during a given tax year can be carried forward for the next five tax years.

Donations to scientific research institutions or rural development are also fully deductible. Contributions to a political party registered under Section 29A of the Representation of the People Act, 1951, are deductible as well.

For purposes of tax deduction, appreciation in gifts of tangible personal property, such as art, antiques, and collectibles, is disallowed entirely unless the gift is used for the charity's tax-exempt purposes. For instance, suppose a taxpayer donates to the local museum a painting that cost him or her ₹10,000 and is now worth ₹300,000. If the museum auctions off the painting instead of displaying it, a taxpayer will get a deduction of only ₹10,000.

Casualty or Theft Losses

Casualty or theft losses relating to personal-use property net of reimbursement by the insurance company and in excess of 10 percent of AGI are deductible. To be deductible, these must be personal losses attributable to theft or natural disasters, such as fire, storm, vandalism, flood, etc. Also, taxpayers may claim a deduction for decline in the value of the personal property stolen, damaged, or destroyed as a result of such occurrences. Finally, a different set of rules applies to disaster losses subsequently determined by the Government of India to warrant central assistance, and to bank deposit losses.

Business Use of a Home

More and more Indians are working out of their homes. However, just because the home is used as a convenient place of business, it does not give a taxpayer an automatic right to deduct certain expenses. The office must be used exclusively on a regular basis as the principal place of any business operated by the taxpayer, or as a place to meet patients, clients, or customers of the business. Furthermore, if a taxpayer is an employee, for the expenses to be deductible, the use of a home office must also be for the convenience of the taxpayer's employer.

Home office deductions are allowed for the space essential to the running of a venture, even if it is just for administration, provided that another such fixed location is not available.

At this point, a word of caution is in order. Deducting heat and electricity for one room, for example, may mean only a minor tax saving, and depreciation for the space must stretch over 39 years. Taking depreciation will also bar tax exclusion for some of the profit if the house is sold. But someone who conducts business from home—whether or not a deductible office is set aside—can deduct telephone calls, supplies, and equipment as business expenses.

Summing Up

Once the amount of the standard deduction or the itemized deduction has been determined, the greater of the two is subtracted from the AGI to arrive at the penultimate step in the process of taxable income calculations.

Exemptions

The final step necessary to determine taxable income is to compute exemptions, which represent the legally permitted deduction from a taxpayer's taxable income based on the number of persons supported by that income.

Number of Dependents

Generally, one exemption is allowed for each person claimed as a dependent. To claim a dependency exemption, the dependent must be a "qualifying child" or a "qualifying relative." The law requires that children (limit age 25) who can be claimed as dependents on parents' returns may not claim themselves on their own returns. Further changes in tax laws governing tax rates on the income of children under 18 will be discussed in Chapter 12 as they relate to the use of gifts as a form of tax planning.

Section II: Computation of Income Tax

TAX COMPUTATION

Basic Computation

For the 2014–15 financial year, there are three tax rates—10 percent, 20 percent, and 30 percent as specified below:

For Taxable Income of:	The Tax Is:
Over ₹0—₹250,000	Exempt from taxes
Over ₹250,000—₹500,000	₹0 + 10% of the excess over ₹250,000
Over ₹500,000—₹1,000,000	₹25,000 + 20% of the excess over ₹500,000
Over ₹1,000,000	₹125,000 + 30% of the excess over ₹1,000,000

2014 Income Tax Table

Individuals below 60 Years	
If taxable income is:	**The tax is:**
Not over ₹250,000	Nil
Over ₹250,000 but not over ₹500,000	₹0 plus 10% of the excess over ₹250,000; **less** (in case of resident individuals only): Tax credit U/s 87A—10% of taxable income up to a maximum of ₹2,000.
Over ₹500,000 but not over ₹1,000,000	₹25,000 plus 20% of the excess over ₹500,000.
Individuals above 60 Years but below 80 Years	
If taxable income is:	**The tax is:**
Not over ₹300,000	Nil
Over ₹300,000 but not over ₹500,000	₹0 plus 10% of the excess over ₹300,000; **less:** Tax Credit U/s 87A—10% of taxable income up to a maximum of ₹2,000.
Over ₹500,000 but not over ₹1,000,000	₹20,000 plus 20% of the excess over ₹500,000.
Over ₹1,000,000	₹120,000 plus 30% of the excess over ₹500,000.
Individual 80 Years and above	
If taxable income is:	**The tax is:**
Not over ₹500,000	Nil
Over ₹500,000 but not over ₹1,000,000	₹0 plus 10% of the excess over ₹500,000.
Over ₹1,000,000	₹100,000 plus 30% of the excess over ₹1,000,000.*

Note: ***Surcharge:** 10 percent of the income tax, where total taxable income is more than ₹1 crore (marginal relief in surcharge,[3] if applicable). **Education Cess:** 3 percent of the total of income tax and surcharge.

[3] Marginal relief is that the sum of the total amount payable as income tax and the surcharge shall not exceed the total amount payable as income tax on total income of ₹1 crore by more than the amount of income that exceeds ₹1 crore.

Marginal Tax Rate

An understanding of the difference between marginal and average tax rates is crucial to the tax planning process. The average, or effective, tax rate is merely the total tax payable divided by the taxable income. However, marginal tax rate is the rate applying to each additional ₹100 of income.

The marginal tax rate is used to describe the rate at which a taxpayer pays tax on the last rupees of income earned. Taxable income that falls within certain brackets or ranges is taxed at a specified percentage as set forth in the Income Tax Act.

Let us assume Ashish has a taxable income of ₹500,000 for the year 2014–15. The method of calculating marginal tax is presented in Table 11.9.

Tax Credits

After the tax liability is computed, tax credits may be used to reduce this liability rupee for rupee. Credits, which can be written off directly against tax, are worth much more than deductions. For example, a ₹600 credit saves a taxpayer ₹600 in tax. However, a ₹600 deduction only *reduces the taxable income* by ₹600. If the taxpayer in this example is in the 30 percent tax bracket, the tax savings would be just ₹180. Tax credits are available to persons for payment of foreign taxes and employment of special targeted groups in the form of job credits. Low-income elderly taxpayers may be allowed a tax credit while receiving taxable disability benefits. Other tax credits, applicable to certain taxpayers, are explained below.

Dependent care credit. The law grants a credit between ₹50,000 and ₹100,000 for covering a disabled dependent's medical and care expenses. In order to claim this credit, a taxpayer is obligated to demonstrate that this expense (for home upkeep, medical and general care expenses, and maintenance cost) was incurred because he or she was working or seeking work, or because the spouse was attending school on a full-time basis). The credit is limited to ₹50,000 but it can be raised up to a maximum of ₹100,000 due to severe disability. The above deductions are also available if a taxpayer himself or herself is disabled. For taxpayers with two or more qualifying dependents, the credit allowed is determined on the basis of the nature of disability.

TAXATION OF CORPORATIONS/FIRMS

Corporations/Firms

For the taxable year 2014–15, for domestic companies, the income tax rate applicable to companies is a flat 30 percent of the income generated by the company. A surcharge of 5 percent is applied to the base rate if the total income falls between ₹1 and 10 crore. Income of ₹10 crore and higher is subjected to a surcharge of 10 percent. For nondomestic companies, the respective surcharges are as follows: For income of ₹1–10 crore: 2 percent and for income of ₹10 crore and beyond: 5 percent. Currently, Indian corporate tax rate for a domestic company stands at 33.99 percent (where the net income exceeds ₹10 crore.

Table 11.9 *Calculation of Marginal Tax*

Tax on ₹250,000	**Tax Exempt**
Tax on (500,000 – 250,000 = ₹250,000) @10%:	₹25,000
Total gross tax:	₹25,000
Education cess (3% of ₹25,000):	₹750
Total tax liability	₹25,750
Tax on ₹500,000	**₹25,750**

Note: The average tax rate in this case is 5.15 percent whereas the marginal tax rate, including education cess, is 30.9 percent.

Table 11.10 *Taxable Income Using Tax Rate Schedule*

1. Enter taxable income	₹1,000,000
2. (a) Look for filing status	
(b) Look for the tax rate schedule taxable income range taxable income falls under	
(c) Enter the lower number from the tax range	₹500,000
3. Put difference here	₹500,000
4. Enter tax rate from tax range here	20%
5. Multiply lines 3 and 4	₹100,000
6. Enter the tax amount from tax range line here	₹25,000
7. Total Tax: lines 5 plus 6	**₹125,000**

REAL WORLD INCOME TAX CALCULATIONS

Now that the techniques of individual income tax calculations have been discussed in detail, we will present the complexity of calculating the income taxes of an upper-income family.

Anish and Arushi are 40 and 35 years old, respectively. Anish is a TATA employee and Arushi is a book-keeper at a local grocery store. In 2014, their gross wages and salaries were ₹1,000,000, and on that income they paid income taxes of ₹25,000. A summary of income tax calculations is presented in Table 11.11.

Table 11.11 *Anish and Arushi Singh's 2014 Income Tax Analysis*

	2014 Gross	2014 Net
Total gross wages and salaries	₹1,000,000	₹1,000,000
Net long-term gain (loss)	₹20,000	
Net short term gain (loss)	(₹3,000)	
Net taxable gain (loss)		0
Gross Taxable Income		**1,000,000**
Adjusted Gross Income (AGI)		**1,000,000**
Deductions/Exemptions		
80C	150,000	
Home loan interest	200,000	
Medical insurance premium	15,000	
Medical reimbursement Contributions	15,000	
HRA	120,000	500,000
Total allowable deductions		
Total deductions		500,000
Taxable Income		**500,000**
Total Income		**1,000,000**
Total Deductions/Exemptions		500,000
Taxable income		500,000
Income tax		25,000
Education cess (2%)		500
Secondary and higher education cess (1%)		250
Net Spendable Income after Taxes		474,250

In this chapter, we presented the basic income tax structure and demonstrated the technique for computing federal income tax. In Chapter 12, we will explore in detail various tax planning strategies.

APPENDIX: FORM NO. 16

[*See* rule 31(1)(*a*)]

Certificate under section 203 of the Income-tax Act, 1961 for tax deducted at source from income chargeable under the head "Salaries"

Name and address of the Employer		Name and designation of the Employee		
PAN No. of the Deductor	TAN No. of the Deductor	PAN No. of the Employee		
Acknowledgement Nos. of all quarterly statements of TDS under sub-section (3) of section 200 as provided by TIN Facilitation Centre or NSDL web-site		Period		Assessment year
Quarter	Acknowledgement No.	From	To	

DETAILS OF SALARY PAID AND ANY OTHER INCOME AND TAX DEDUCTED

1. Gross salary			
(a) Salary as per provisions contained in section 17(1)	Rs.		
(b) Value of perquisites u/s 17(2) (as per Form No. 12BA, wherever applicable)	Rs.		
(c) Profits in lieu of salary under section 17(3) (as per Form No. 12BA, wherever applicable)	Rs.		
(d) Total		Rs.	
2. *Less* : Allowance to the extent exempt under section 10 Allowance Rs.			
		Rs.	
		Rs.	
3. Balance (1 – 2)			
4. Deductions :			
(a) Entertainment allowance	Rs.		
(b) Tax on Employment	Rs.		
5. Aggregate of 4(a) and (b)		Rs.	
6. Income chargeable under the head 'Salaries' (3 - 5)			Rs.
7. *Add* : Any other income reported by the employee			

Rs.			
8. Gross total income (6 + 7)			Rs.
9. Deductions under Chapter VI-A			Rs.
(A) sections 80C, 80CCC and 80CCD			
		Gross amount	Deductible amount
(a) section 80C			
(i)	Rs.		
(ii)	Rs.		
(iii)	Rs.		
(iv)	Rs.		
(v)	Rs.		
(vi)	Rs.	Rs.	Rs.
(b) section 80CCC		Rs.	Rs.
(c) section 80CCD		Rs.	Rs.

Notes : 1. Aggregate amount deductible under section 80C shall not exceed one lakh rupees.

2. Aggregate amount deductible under the three sections, *i.e.*, 80C, 80CCC and 80CCD, shall not exceed one lakh rupees.

(B) other sections (*e.g.*, 80E, 80G etc.) under Chapter VI-A	Gross amount	Qualifying amount	Deductible amount
(a) section	Rs.	Rs.	Rs.
(b) section	Rs.	Rs.	Rs.
(c) section	Rs.	Rs.	Rs.
(d) section	Rs.	Rs.	Rs.
(e) section	Rs.	Rs.	Rs.
10. Aggregate of deductible amount under Chapter VI-A			Rs.
11. Total income (8-10)	Rs.		Rs.
12. Tax on total income	Rs.		Rs.
13. Surcharge (on tax computed at S. No. 12)	Rs.		Rs.
14. Education Cess @2% (on tax at S. No. 12 *plus* surcharge at S. No. 13)			Rs.
15. Tax payable (12+13+14)			Rs.
16. Relief under section 89 (attach details)	Rs.		Rs.
17. Tax payable (15-16) Rs.	Rs.		Rs.
18. *Less* : (a) Tax deducted at source u/s 192(1)		Rs.	Rs.
(b) Tax paid by the employer on behalf of the employee u/s 192(1A) on perquisites u/s 17(2)		Rs.	Rs.
19. Tax payable/refundable (17-18)		Rs.	Rs.

DETAILS OF TAX DEDUCTED AND DEPOSITED INTO CENTRAL GOVERNMENT ACCOUNT

(The Employer is to provide payment-wise details of tax deducted and deposited)

No.	TDS Rs.	Surcharge Rs.	Education Cess Rs.	Total tax deposited Rs.	Cheque/DD No. (if any)	BSR Code of Bank branch	Date on which tax deposited (dd/mm/yy)	Transfer voucher/Challan Identification No.
1.								
2.								
3.								
4.								
5.								
6.								
7.								
8.								
9.								
10.								

I, ______________, son/daughter of ______________ working in the capacity of ______________ (designation) do hereby certify that a sum of Rs. ______________ [Rupees ______________ (in words)] has been deducted at source and paid to the credit of the Central Government. I further certify that the information given above is true and correct based on the books of account, documents and other available records.

Place

Date

____

Signature of the person responsible for deduction of tax

Full Name ______________________________

Designation ______________________________

12 Tax Planning: Concepts and Strategies

INTRODUCTION

Tax planning is primarily concerned with the *timing* and *method* by which income is reported and deductions and credits claimed. Tax law permits every taxpayer to select among various options in reporting income and claiming deductions and credits. Every taxpayer has the right to decide which of these options would minimize his or her overall tax burden.

A good place to identify financial planning needs is the Income Tax Return Form. A planner can examine various line items on the tax return to identify potential financial risks that a client faces and can help develop the tax planning strategies to reduce these risks and improve the financial well-being of the client.

In the first section, we will discuss tax planning ideas for individual taxpayers. Then we will briefly review the key tax planning ideas to help various types of business organizations.

Section I: The Individual Taxpayer

There are many ways in which individual taxpayers can minimize their tax burden. These myriad tax reduction techniques can be conveniently grouped into five major categories, which we prefer to call the *five* "Ds." These categories will be discussed in the following pages.

DEDUCTION

In Chapter 11, we presented in detail the deductions allowed under current tax laws. In this section, we will explore some of the important planning ideas pertaining to tax deductions.

Let us begin with miscellaneous deductions which offer a valuable opportunity for tax reduction. For instance, the cost of membership dues, financial planning fees, investment-related expenses, accounting fees, and unreimbursed business expenses are examples of often overlooked miscellaneous expenses.

Other itemized deductions often ignored by taxpayers involve charitable contributions and state and local income taxes. Also, deductible are expenses such as phone calls and travel expenses for charity work. A ticket to a fund raiser is deductible to the extent that its price exceeds the normal admission cost. By not accepting the ticket or returning it for resale, a taxpayer can in fact deduct the entire cost.

Moving Expenses

The tax treatment of moving expenses is different from the treatment of most employee business expenses in that this deduction is not subject to other miscellaneous deductions. The moving expenses and company reimbursements must be accounted for separately on tax returns. All company reimbursements for personal moving expenses are considered taxable. However, these expenses may be deductible, subject to limitations, as an above-the-line deduction if the move is related to beginning full-time employment in a new location beyond certain minimum distances from the previous place of residence. Deductible moving expenses include, with certain limitations, moving personal effects, traveling, lodging, and incidental expenses.

Tax-deductible Interest

Consumer interest cannot be treated as a deductible expense. Therefore, an interesting tax planning idea is to completely pay off all outstanding consumer loans. Money for paying off the consumer debt can be raised in several ways, each of which constitutes an important tax planning idea. Here is a partial list of tax-wise borrowing methods:

1. A taxpayer can take out a home equity loan. Interest on this loan up to ₹200,000 is fully tax deductible.
2. If a taxpayer has accumulated cash value in a life insurance policy, it might be borrowed at a reasonable interest. This interest cost on this loan would be much lower than the cost of a conventional consumer loan.
3. If circumstances permit, a taxpayer can sell an investment and use the proceeds to pay off a consumer debt. Later, he or she could borrow on margin to make a similar investment. The interest on the second loan can be fully deducted against investment income.

A novel way to increase interest deductions is to shift debt on the second home (if it is used as rental property), thereby moving interest out of the lineup of expenses on the second home. Incidentally, the ₹200,000 interest cap that typically applies to a home equity loan does not apply to the *second home*. This means that even an interest amount of ₹3 lakh on a loan pertaining to a second home is fully deductible, even when the second home is neither being used nor rented out.

Still, owning a loan on a second home might not always turn out to be beneficial to a taxpayer. For one thing, if the home loan on the second home has already been fully paid-up, then there would be no deductible interest available. For another, if the interest cost plus the standard deduction is less than the annual value of the permissible amount, then a taxpayer does not receive any tax benefits from holding an outstanding loan on the second home.

Prepayment Strategy

When a taxpayer's deductions are over the minimum tax slab, prepaying certain expenses can not only lower the overall tax liability, but it can also be useful if the tax rates were to decrease in the future. Two deductible items that can be prepaid are home mortgage and education loans. This prepayment strategy allows a taxpayer to reduce the loan burden, thereby reducing the current tax liability.

Here is an example. Taxpayer Anirban owns a self-occupied property. Since the interest deduction is capped at ₹200,000, and Anirban is maxed out, he receives no tax deduction for interest payment on this loan. For that reason he may wish to pre-pay the loan without impacting his tax savings. Alternatively, Anirban can consider switching to another lender willing to charge a lower interest rate on the loan.

Educational loan is another item which raises a trade-off issue for Anirban. Normally, interest paid on an education loan is eligible for deduction under Section 80E of the Income Tax Act. However, in case of pre-payment of this loan, this benefit would be eliminated. Therefore, Anirban would need to calculate the trade-off between (a) continuing to hold the loan (enjoying the associated tax benefits) and investing the money and (b) paying off the loan and saving on interest cost associated with the loan.

Other Deductions

Business expenses. If a taxpayer reports self-employment income on tax return, many of the same expenses, which are then treated as business expenses, become fully deductible. Examples of these expenses include accounting fees, interest expense, professional licenses, subscriptions for publications, auto expense, rent, cost of resale products, and salaries to employees.

Real estate losses. If a property is sold for profit within three years of the date of purchase, it is treated as a short-term gain, subject to the highest tax rate applicable to the current income. This gain is calculated by deducting from the sale price the cost of acquisition, the cost of improvement, and the transfer cost. The gain is then included in the taxable income for the year the money is received and taxed according to a person's tax slab. However, there exists an important exception. Capital gain from the sale of a long-term asset can be claimed as tax exempt (under Section 54EC of the Income Tax Act) provided the gain is invested within six months in notified bonds. Tax rules relating to capital gains and losses have already been discussed in chapter 11.

Rental expense. Any property not self-occupied is treated as a rental property. Rental income from this property (or a higher rental amount generated by a comparable property in the neighborhood) is taxed at an appropriate rate after deducting the following items from the rental income: (a) property taxes, (b) repair and maintenance charges up to the approved limit, and (c) interest on home loan.

An important caveat. Unless the second house is rented for more than 300 days a year, an additional 1 percent wealth tax is also imposed on a home if it is valued at more than ₹30 lakh.

In conclusion, it should be emphasized that every taxpayer should undertake as much tax planning as is necessary to enjoy all the tax deductions allowed by law. A list of major allowable deductions was presented in Chapter 11.

DIVERSION

The second strategy of tax reduction is diversion, which refers to the steps a taxpayer can take to channel investment returns into money that will (a) be taxed at lower rates, (b) offer higher deductions, or (c) completely avoid taxation.

Home Ownership

The most widely used tax planning strategy of diversion is home ownership, because both mortgage interest and interest on home equity loans are tax deductible. Even mortgage interest on a second home used for rental income is deductible. Real estate taxes are deductible. Points paid on securing a mortgage on a primary residence are also deductible.

The most significant benefit to home ownership as a tax avoidance strategy, of course, is the ability to minimize taxes on the gains realized in the sale of the principal residence. Under the current law, long-term capital gains in the sale of a residential property held at least for three years is subjected to a preferential tax rate of 20 percent. However, a homeowner can claim an exemption from taxes (Section 54/54F) if the sale proceeds are reinvested in (purchase or build) a residential property within the designated period.

Municipal Bonds

Interest on state and local obligations is not subject to income tax. It is also exempt from the tax of the state in which the obligations are issued. Tax law treats bonds as follows:

1. Public-purpose bonds issued to meet essential government functions and investment needs are tax exempt.
2. Bonds issued to finance housing and infrastructure needs are tax exempt for regular income tax purposes.

Taxpayers can also save on taxes by investing in municipal bond funds. Interest on these bonds is exempt from income taxes. This tax exemption feature is especially attractive for people placed in the high-income (say, ₹10 lakh) tax bracket.

Matching Incomes and Losses

The strategy of matching incomes and losses can also minimize the tax liability. The law specifies how and when losses and credits from other activities can be claimed by a taxpayer. Losses from other activities are deductible only against income from those or other passive activities. Unused losses can be carried forward indefinitely and can be used to offset passive income realized by a taxpayer in subsequent years.

The current law permits the carrying forward of current losses to the future, up to eight years. However, if a taxpayer has significant capital gains from a passive activity in one tax year and has a potential loss on an investment, then the overall tax liability can be reduced by selling the losing investment and realizing the loss in the same tax year as the capital gain to offset the gain and reduce tax liability.

Tax Shelters

Because passive losses may only offset passive income, the use of tax shelters as a tax-saving vehicle has been dramatically reduced. Historically, tax shelters represented investments designed to create *accounting losses* that could be used as deductions against taxable income from other sources. Investors did not materially participate in the management of these investments, hence the designation *passive activity*. Most shelters were set up to generate the largest deductions in the first few years so that investors could get their money back quickly in the form of tax reductions. If an investment went well, eventually the tax shelter turned profitable. However, most tax shelters never turned profitable partly because relatively few economic benefits were expected from them. Under the current law, the write offs generated by tax shelters are deductible only against income from a passive activity.

The change in tax law shifted the emphasis on tax shelter investments from tax write offs to economic profit motive. As a planning strategy, taxpayers use tax shelters to help them appropriately time or offset their passive gains and losses. While investors who currently have significant passive income still seek passive losses, most investors with existing tax shelter investments and passive losses should seek to generate additional passive income.

Limited Partnerships

Most tax shelters are structured as limited partnerships, or master limited partnerships. Limited partnerships make an investor liable only for the amount of money invested in them by that investor. Many of the real-estate-limited partnerships intend to buy office buildings, shopping malls, apartments, or other real estate properties that can pay investors immediate rental income. Other major interests of limited partnerships include oil and gas, equipment leasing, and research and development. The losses from these partnerships are carried forward and not allowed to be allocated to the partners. Current yield on limited partnerships is shielded by depreciation and other write offs. However, investments in limited partnerships may have significant risk, and, in addition, promised income streams may not materialize. Despite these risks, however, limited partnerships frequently offer tax benefits which could reduce an individual's overall tax liability.

Like-kind Exchanges

When a property held for productive use in a trade, business, or investment is exchanged for property of a "like-kind" used for a similar purpose, no tax-related gain or loss is recognized upon the exchange. Whether two properties are of a "like-kind" is generally determined on a case-by-case basis. For example, a swap of one real estate property for another is considered a like-kind exchange.

The tax law allows a lot of flexibility in this maneuver. The swapped properties do not have to be equal in value. In that case, tax rules allow cash, called "boot," to be paid to make up for the difference in the property values, although "boot" is taxable to the extent of the realized gain. Furthermore, properties do not have to fall into the same category. A vacant lot can be traded for a house, an office building can be exchanged for an apartment building, and a condominium is considered a like-kind exchange for a beach home, so long as each is an investment and not a personal real estate property.

Often, the best time to consider a "like-kind" exchange is when a property has significantly increased in value. A swap lets a taxpayer secure the profit and plough back a larger untaxed fund into another underdeveloped property or a turnaround situation.

Charitable Donations

The tax law allows a taxpayer to receive tax benefits for making charitable donations. The law classifies charity funds into several categories, each allowing the donor a different kind of tax rebate, and each donation subject to a prespecified limit.

Charitable donations are divided into four categories: (a) 100 percent deduction without any qualifying limit (e.g., Prime Minister's National Relief Fund), (b) 50 percent deduction without any qualifying limit (e.g., Indira Gandhi Memorial Trust), (c) 100 percent deduction subject to qualifying limit (e.g., an approved institution for promoting family planning), and (d) 50 percent deduction subject to qualifying limit (e.g., an approved institution for charitable purpose other than promoting family planning). While there is no maximum limit for the deduction which can be claimed for charitable donations, in certain cases the deduction might be limited to a maximum of 10 percent of a taxpayer's adjusted gross income. Most charitable organizations routinely inform the donors whether or not they represent 100 percent limit organizations. For charitable contributions made to organizations that are not 100 percent limit organizations, the deductions cannot be more than 10 percent of a donor's adjusted gross income (AGI) for the year.

Tax-free Retirement/Pension Benefits

Under the current law, for individuals aged 60–80 with an annual income of less than ₹300,000 and for very senior citizens with an annual income of less than ₹500,000, retirement/pension income is not taxable. For the rest, a viable tax planning strategy is to reduce the modified income to the ₹300,000 (₹500,000 for very senior citizens) level so that all income would become nontaxable. This is accomplished by a thorough review of currently existing investments and, if appropriate, shifting part of the investments into assets that generate non-reportable income. An example of such an asset is a single premium deferred annuity. The income from this annuity is tax deferred and, therefore, is not reported as current income for the purposes of tax calculation. Furthermore, when annuity payments are received, a portion of each payment is treated as a return of the original principal and is, therefore, not taxed. The remainder of the payment represents the prior deferred income and is fully taxed.

DEFERRAL

The third strategy of tax reduction is deferral, which refers to the action taken to defer taxes to future years. There are two main types of tax deferral: deferral with pretax rupees and deferral with after-tax rupees.

Deferral with Pretax Rupees

Employer-sponsored qualified plans (Employees' Provident Fund [EPF] and New Pension System [NPS]). Employer-sponsored qualified pension and profit-sharing plans are essentially saving plans that offer two tax incentives for participating employees: (a) money contributed to these plans by employees is deductible from gross income and, therefore, it reduces their annual taxable income and (b) interest income, earned in these plans, is not taxable unless a participant withdraws the funds before completing five years of service.

Qualified plans for self-employed individuals (NPS). Self-employed individuals who make contributions to NPS retirement plans also benefit from the two tax deferral benefits described above for employer-sponsored plans.

Individual plans. A tax-deferral option available to all taxpayers is a Public Provident Fund (PPF). Individuals are allowed to contribute to a PPF fund up to a maximum of ₹100,000 per year. These accounts provide all PPF holders with the second tax advantage described above for employer-sponsored plans, that is, tax deferral on the earnings that accumulate within the account. However, whether or not a PPF owner will benefit from the first tax deferral advantage (reduction of gross income) depends on the individual's tax filing status, level of income, and participation in an employer-sponsored plan.

Deferral with After-tax Money

Insurance Contracts. Insurance contracts purchased with after-tax rupees provide an excellent vehicle for after-tax accumulation of earnings as long as these earnings accumulate within the policy contract. The types of insurance contracts which qualify for tax deferral include single premium deferred annuity, single premium whole life, single premium universal life, and variable life and annuities. These investments have already been discussed in Chapter 4. At the time of withdrawal, that part of the annuity payment which represents the cost of the initial investment is treated as a nontaxable return of principal; the balance of the withdrawal is taxed as ordinary income.

Gold. Gold can be bought either in physical form or in the form of shares of exchange traded funds (ETFs); the latter are easier to buy, hold, and trade. Investment in gold is tax efficient. Since gold does not generate current income during the holding period, no tax liability is incurred. Gold can also act as collateral for borrowing money at a reasonable interest rate. However, because of the logistics involved in trading in gold, generally gold ETFs provide a better option.

DEFLECTION

The fourth tax reduction strategy is deflection, which involves shifting taxable income to someone in a lower tax bracket. There are several ways of accomplishing this objective.

Kiddie Tax

The first deflection technique of reducing taxable income is to shift part of the income to a child. However, careful planning is required to take advantage of this technique due to a "kiddie tax" that is imposed on investment income earned by children.

A person of course can claim deduction for children's education for which no planning is required. Apart from that, if the intent is to lower the overall tax burden by gifting to a child, then that cannot be accomplished merely by investing the money in the child's name. That is so because the tax rule requires that the child's investment income *be clubbed* with that of the parent's income so that nothing of substance is gained by this manipulation. Thus, an alternate strategy is to invest the child's gift money in tax-free instruments such as PPF, mutual fund, or unit linked insurance plans (ULIPs). For instance, if a minor PPF account is opened in the child's name, then that income will not be subject to *clubbing*. The only limitation for this strategy is that the total contribution to the PPF account (both parent and child combined) cannot exceed ₹1 lakh per year.

Other attractive options are also available to benefit from using this strategy. These include: buying a child's plan from an insurance company and investing in a mutual fund. A private trust can also be created for the child to save on taxes.

Finally, taxes can also be reduced by gifting an amount to an adult child who is not required to pay any gift tax. Income earned on this gifted amount is then taxed at the adult child's lower tax rates, while the gift simultaneously reduces the taxable income of the parent.

Gifts

An attractive way of shifting income for an individual with a high marginal tax bracket is to give a gift to a child in a low tax bracket. A gift of cash would benefit the taxpayer if the after-tax return received by the child works out to be higher than the taxpayer's after-tax return. A gift of appreciated property, such as common stock or income-producing property, can bring even higher tax benefits. For instance, the appreciated stock could be liquidated and reinvested to generate a greater after-tax return for the child than it would for the taxpayer. Although the gift is not deductible by the parent, it is not treated as income to the child.

The following example demonstrates the use of gifts as a way of reducing the tax liability. Assume Raj wishes to create a college fund for his son Rudra and has ₹10,000 in a fixed deposit with a bank earning 5 percent interest. Assuming a 30 percent tax bracket, Raj currently pays a tax of ₹150 per year (30 percent of ₹500). If he gifts the fund to Rudra, who has no other source of income, Raj immediately gains ₹150 because he would not owe this tax to the government.

An individual is allowed to gift up to ₹50,000 (2014) annually to any number of individuals without incurring gift tax. Thus, parents in a high tax bracket may deflect tax by gifting up to ₹50,000 (2014) in cash or other investment assets to each of their children who is in a lower tax bracket. However, in gifting to adult children interest-free loans should be used to reap the maximum tax benefit from that arrangement.

Parents

Taxes can also be saved by gifting to parents and parent-in-laws. That way, future taxes on these gifted funds are automatically shifted to the gift receivers, thereby reducing the overall tax burden of the gift giver. An example should make this clear.

Assume both parents of Pramod are senior citizens, which entitles them to receive an annual tax-free income of ₹30 lakh. In order to reduce his tax burden Pramod gifts ₹15 lakh to each parent, or a total of ₹30 lakh. Pramod's father, in turn, invests ₹15 lakh in a senior citizens savings scheme earning a 10 percent return on the money. Simultaneously, his mother places her ₹15 lakh in the State Bank of India's eight-year fixed deposit account earning 8.5 percent interest. In this scenario, the parents will earn an annual interest of ₹5.8 lakh, all of which will be earned as tax-free income (₹3 lakh tax-free limit per person). A similar planning strategy can be created involving the parent-in-laws as well.

Spouse

An often-overlooked option involves gifting to a nonearning spouse who can invest the funds in a tax-free instrument. There is no gift tax applied to a spousal gift, regardless of the size of the gift involved. Of course, investing the funds in a taxable vehicle would automatically trigger the clubbing of the income rule. That is why only the tax-free investment vehicles such as the PPF scheme or the equity linked savings scheme (ELSS) should be considered.

Child Employment

A taxpayer can shelter income by putting a child on a summer payroll. Although the child's income would be added to the parent's income until the child turns 18, the parent will get a deduction of ₹1,500 from the child's income. Also, to avoid clubbing of income, the child can be encouraged to invest the earnings in tax-free instruments.

DIMINUTION

In this concluding section, we will briefly mention a number of additional tax-saving ideas which were not discussed in the previous sections.

Income Deferral

The deferral of income from the current year to the following year will defer payment of income tax until March 31 of the year following the next tax year. Deferral of income may be accomplished by the following: (a) timely negotiation of bonus or salary payment into the subsequent calendar year ("timely" in general requires negotiation prior to rendition of services); (b) accelerating the payment of business expenses, or delaying the mailing of bills or invoices, thus forestalling the collection of income; (c) investment in government securities, short-term certificates of deposit or similar investments where income will not be recognized until the following year; (d) delaying retirement benefit payouts (in some cases including lump-sum distributions) until the following year or later; (e) investing in government securities or bonds, since interest may be subject to tax when the bond matures or is redeemed; (f) deferring the exercise of stock options that result in the recognition of income as well as the sale of ordinary or capital gain assets.

Income Acceleration

Taxpayers who expect their tax rate to be the same or lower in the following year would want to utilize the deferral strategies described above. Conversely, taxpayers who expect their marginal tax rates to be higher in the following year would want to accelerate some of the following year's income into the current year. This may be accomplished by taking the following steps:

1. Accelerate bonus payments.
2. For cash basis taxpayer, accelerate mailing invoices and delay the payment of business expenses.
3. Invest in obligations which bear interest daily.
4. Redeem government saving bonds.
5. Take qualified plan distributions.
6. Sell appreciated securities.

Charitable Contributions

Anyone planning additional charitable contributions should consider accelerating or deferring those payments. Prepayments of two, three, or more years of contributions to any charity could provide tax savings. Taxpayers should be aware that there are general limitations—100 percent, 50 percent, or 10 percent of the AGI—which restrict the deduction for contributions based on AGI and the type of donee organization.

Donations of used clothing, furniture, etc. to charitable organizations are deductible, in general, to the extent of their fair market value. An organization receiving donation should provide a taxpayer with a receipt.

Contributions of Appreciated Property

In lieu of cash, a taxpayer should consider contributing property that has appreciated in value, and if sold, would have generated a capital gain. A deduction may be claimed for the full fair market value (within limitations based on the taxpayer's AGI), and, in most cases, no income is reportable for the increase in value. In order to meet the tax definition of "qualified," an appraisal cannot be prepared by a donee organization; an appraiser must possess verifiable education and experience in valuing the type of property subject to the appraisal.

Accelerating Interest Deductions

Generally, a deduction for prepayment of interest, including interest and principal on home mortgages, is permitted. If the owner of a house has an option of paying off the loan over a shorter period, then that option should be actively considered.

Interest offset accounts. Interest offset accounts can deliver attractive savings. Banks provide interest offset accounts to home loan borrowers. No interest is paid on the funds in the interest offset account; however the home loan is reduced by an amount equal to the nominal interest earned. This is a tax-effective way of paying off the loan, since a borrower does not pay taxes on interest earnings being used to pay off the loan. An added feature of this strategy is that the funds in the offset account are readily accessible.

Personal and Qualified Residence Interest

Consumer loans. Interest paid on consumer loans, credit card loans, and other similar items, is not deductible. Consequently, a taxpayer should hasten to pay off all personal loans, where possible, since interest on these loans is no longer deductible.

Employee Business Expenses

Home office expense. The cost of maintaining an office in a taxpayer's home is available as a deduction only if the home office is used exclusively on a regular basis as the principal place of business operated by the taxpayer or as a place to meet with patients, clients, or customers of the business. If the taxpayer is an employee, the use of a home office must be for the convenience of the taxpayer's employer. Thus, if an employer routinely provides adequate office space for its workforce, then an employee who chooses to work during evenings and on weekends at her or his personal residence is precluded from claiming a home office deduction.

Use of personal automobile for business. An employee may deduct transportation expenses as a miscellaneous deduction (if the expenses are paid in connection with services performed as an employee and they are not reimbursed by the employer). Transportation expenses include the expenses of traveling from one place of business to another in the course of employment (and, therefore, not commuting) when the employee is not traveling away from home.

Business meals, entertainment and travel. Business meals, entertainment, and travel expenses must be substantiated by a taxpayer in order to be deductible. The current law provides that deductions for meals and certain entertainment expenditures are based on the amount paid.

Club dues. Currently, no business expense deduction is allowed for club dues. All types of clubs are covered, including business, social, athletic, sporting, airline, and hotel clubs. Specific business expenses, such as meals, green fees, etc., incurred at a club may still be deductible as long as such expenses meet the standard travel and entertainment deduction rules.

Income Shifting

If a lower marginal income tax rate is expected in the future, one can postpone income to lower the tax liability. Certain tax payments can be postponed by delaying some investments or other earnings. For instance, if a taxpayer defers nonwage income, which is not subject to withholding, then the money could be received early in 2014. But taxes on this income will not be due until the 2014 tax return is filed in April 2015. Of course, a taxpayer still would have the obligation of prepaying 90 percent of all (wage and nonwage) income taxes to avoid underpayment penalties.

Expense Shifting

The reverse strategy works with respect to expenses. Since expenses reduce taxable income, accelerating deductions during the year may prove to be an attractive strategy. Prepayment of charitable contributions and professional dues, and the realization of losses by selling property are examples of expense shifting.

Second Home

The income tax law allows a taxpayer to deduct many of the costs associated with a second home. Consequently, rental income and tax deductions generated by a second home can be an important part of a tax reduction strategy.

Section II: The Business Organization

INTRODUCTION

Once a decision has been made to establish a business, an entrepreneur must decide on the most appropriate form of that entity. There are tax considerations that will enter into this decision process. Normally, a business is conducted as a sole proprietorship, partnership, limited liability company (LLC), or a corporation.

For a sole proprietorship, partnership, or LLC, the business itself does not pay any income taxes. The sole proprietor, partners, or members include the profits or losses on their individual income tax returns. A sole proprietorship is the simplest form of a business organization. The business has no existence apart from the owner. Its liabilities are the proprietor's personal liabilities, and the proprietary interest ends when the owner dies.

A partnership is a relationship existing between two or more persons who joined together to carry on a trade or business. Each person contributes money, property, labor, or skill and expects to share in the profits and losses of the business. A partnership is not a taxable entity, except for certain state taxes. However, it must compute its profit or loss and file a return.

An LLC is a form of unincorporated business organization allowed by statue in most states. An LLC is best viewed as a partnership or sole proprietorship surrounded by a limited liability shield. Properly structured, an LLC could be treated as a partnership or sole proprietorship for federal income tax purposes. It allows organizers to coordinate the benefits of taxation as a partnership or sole proprietorship with the limited liability profits of a corporation.

Corporations include associations, joint stock companies, insurance companies, and trusts that operate as corporations. Corporate profits normally are taxed to a corporation. When the profits are distributed as dividends, the dividends are taxed to the shareholders but are not deductible to the corporation.

It is beyond the scope of this book to discuss in detail the tax considerations of the various types of business entities just presented. It may nevertheless be useful to briefly present some tax planning ideas relating to these business entities.

SOLE PROPRIETORS

As mentioned, a sole proprietorship is the simplest form of business organization. The business has no existence apart from the owner. Its liabilities are the owner's personal liabilities, and the proprietary interest ends when the owner dies. When the taxable income is calculated for the year, the owner must add in any profit, or subtract out any loss, from the sole proprietorship. Also, in this type of a business set up, the owner has an unlimited liability, which means that all the assets owned by the owner are *at risk*.

EXECUTIVES

The primary tax planning objective for most corporate executives is to reduce, defer, or eliminate the tax liability associated with salary income. There are pay benefits that are not taxable, such as certain fringe benefits, disability pensions, health and accidental death benefits, and certain housing costs while working abroad. Other tax-saving plans may be instituted through pension and profit-sharing plans, stock options, and deferred pay plans.

The major objective of a deferred pay plan is to defer the receipt of salary income to a future time period when the income will hopefully be taxed at a lower tax rate. Incentive bonus plans provide another example of compensation that assists the executive in the deferral of income. These plans include stock option grants and cash bonuses that are payable based on increases in the company's stock price. The tax deferral features related to pension and profit-sharing plans will be discussed in Chapter 14.

Certain fringe benefits, such as employer-paid insurance protection (life, accident, and health) result in tax savings due to the fact that they represent a form of compensation that is tax free to executives.

PROFESSIONALS

Many professionals prefer to form a limited liability corporation or a corporation, both of which were covered in the previous section. For others who prefer to be sole proprietors, or partnerships, many of the planning ideas have been rendered obsolete under the current law. There is, however, an important strategy that is still applicable to doctors, lawyers, architects, professional financial planners, and other professionals who are in business for themselves

Under the present law, passive losses can offset only passive income that is earned from passive activities. However, the law allows professionals who retain personal ownership of their offices and equipment to rent their office and equipment to their business. The rent they receive from the corporation is passive income. Then they can shelter that income from taxes by offsetting it with passive losses from investments. The rent payments may leave the firm with less cash to compensate the professionals, but they can come out ahead, since the rental income offset by passive losses is not taxed as income but the compensation is taxed as ordinary income.

LIMITED LIABILITY COMPANIES

LLCs are unincorporated entities that offer investors limited liability for debts incurred by the business. From an income tax standpoint, LLCs tend to resemble partnerships and proprietorships rather than corporations because income or loss generated from the LLC is taxed directly to investors based on their proportionate ownership. One danger inherent in using LLCs is that there have been relatively few litigations concerning the liability protection afforded by LLCs. While there is a large body of case law concerning the liability protection afforded by corporations and limited partnerships, it is still not clear that under what circumstances the courts would permit a litigant to pierce the entity structure and reach individual members of an LLC.

AMENDMENT OF TAX RETURN

The tax law allows taxpayers to amend their previously filed tax returns, if they discover that an error has been made in tax calculation.

Revising a tax return can boost the refund a taxpayer originally claimed or cut the taxes initially owed. It is also a way to correct an underpayment situation, thereby possibly reducing the payment of penalty and interest. Taxpayers should also bear in mind that amending a return will not, by itself, trigger an audit.

An overpayment of taxes can be rectified by filing a refund claim. This would be the case if a taxpayer failed to take allowable deductions or credits, overstated income, or wished to take advantage of a retroactive change in the law.

The most important part of a refund claim is the detailed statement that a taxpayer must provide. A general claim simply noting an overpayment, without supporting facts and grounds, is not sufficient. A taxpayer must make a claim showing all the facts that support the claim, and the grounds for the claim.

TAX AUDIT

One of the most harrowing experiences for a taxpayer is to receive the following letter from the income tax department: "Dear taxpayer, we selected your income tax return for the years shown below to examine the items checked at the end of this letter. We have scheduled an appointment for you … ."

"Prevention is better than the cure" is the maxim that best applies to all audit situations. Tax experts across the country point out that currently there are several areas that are carefully scrutinized by the income tax department: (a) interest expense deductions, (b) mortgage points, (c) home office deductions, (d) Schedule C (self-employed income), (e) passive income/losses, (f) tax shelter losses, and (g) suspicion that all income is not being reported.

If an audit letter is received from the income tax department, it does not mean that a taxpayer must panic. It could be a routine query that is easily satisfied. In some easily resolved cases, the income tax department merely conducts a mail audit. In other cases, however, a face-to-face meeting may be demanded.

In a personal audit, the best defense is consistency, cooperation, and confidence in handling the situation in a professional manner. In more complex cases, or in those cases where a taxpayer needs more support, it is often a good idea to take a financial planner, a chartered accountant (CA), or an attorney licensed to practice before the income tax department to the meeting. Most issues are resolved satisfactorily by following these guidelines. If the impasse still persists, then the taxpayer can take the income tax department to court. However, the process can be complex, time-consuming, and possibly more costly than if it had never been initiated.

In this chapter, various tax planning concepts and strategies were presented. A discussion of the basic structure of retirement income is undertaken in Chapter 13.

PART 6

RETIREMENT PLANNING

13 Basic Structure of Retirement Income

INTRODUCTION

Of all the many strategies which might be developed to meet different financial objectives, none are more difficult than those relating to financial independence and retirement planning. This is because, for most people, financial independence or retirement seems far away, and in these uncertain times planning for the distant future is extremely difficult. However, in most cases, the days of employment pass by rather quickly and suddenly people are faced with decisions affecting the retired life. For this reason, planning for retirement is essential for peace of mind and financial independence in old age.

In India, until about the beginning of the 21st century retirement planning had been of passive interest. But even so, retirement planning has not yet come of age. For instance, for government employees, retirement planning has generally been confined to pension, gratuity, leave encashment of earned leave, and contractual savings such as insurance and provident fund (PF) (primarily for tax saving). The situation is slowly improving, however. The government has recently introduced the National Pension Scheme (NPS), and other options could well be under consideration.

In addition to the government, the private sector has also become more active in the area of retirement planning. As an example, a number of mutual funds and insurance companies have initiated retirement income plans. Examples include: retirement benefits plan launched by the UTI Mutual Fund, the Franklin Templeton Pension Plan, the Principal Mutual Fund Pension Plan, the LIC Pension Plan, and the Post Office Senior Citizen Pension Plan. These plans, of course, are in addition to Public Provident Fund (PPF), General Provident Fund (GPF), Contributory Provident Fund (CPF), and Systematic Investment Plan (SIP).

Regardless of how many of these plans have now not become available to retirees, and no matter how far away retirement age seems to be at the moment, we should prepare for the day *now*. There is nothing worse than discovering on the day of retirement that, given the existing financial position, it is impossible to maintain the desired standard of living during retirement.

The argument for planning early for retirement is indeed compelling. According to a 2011 survey conducted by HSBC (a joint venture partner of Canara HSBC Oriental Bank of Commerce Life Insurance),[1] Indians are perceived to be so financially unprepared for retirement that it has virtually become a crisis. Not surprisingly, this survey finds that Indians are progressively becoming more concerned about retirement as the economic downturn continues to stymie income growth, wreak havoc on investments, and dramatically reduce home values.

In terms of specifics, the report finds that among the middle-class Indians 33 percent view retirement as a new phase of life earmarked for rest and relaxation, while only 22 percent of those in the

[1] http://www.banknetindia.com/banking/90823.htm (last accessed on June 12, 2014).

middle-class category (mainly older respondents) expect to face financial hardship past retirement. Only one out of 10 plans to continue working past retirement age to provide income for the family.

There is yet another finding of the survey that gives planners a pause. Currently in India, formal pension arrangements cover only 13 percent of the workforce. As a result, Pension Fund assets constitute only 5 percent of the country's gross domestic product (GDP), a matter of serious concern to financial planners.

While it may be difficult for a 30 or 40 year old to visualize life after another 25 or 30 years, it is imperative that planning for the future begins without delay. This is because financing the lifestyle a person hopes to lead during retirement will have a dramatic impact on the rate of accumulation of retirement savings. For instance, assume a 30 year old hopes to retire at the age of 65 with an annual retirement income of ₹500,000 at today's value. Assuming a 6 percent inflation rate, a life expectancy to the age of 85, and an inflation-adjusted reinvestment rate on investments of 5.3 percent, this person would need to amass savings of ₹4.67 crore at the time of retirement. Calculations are shown next:

Step 1. Inflate ₹500,000 (today's currency) to the first day of retirement

PV = ₹500,000
PMT = 0
n = 35
i = 6
Solve *for* FV = ₹3,843,043.40

Step 2. Calculate the lump sum needed for retirement (at day one of retirement)

Set calculator to the BEGIN mode
PMT = ₹140,693
FV = 0 (assuming not legacy wishes)
n = 20
i = 5.3
PV = ₹46,697,638 *or* ₹4.67 crore

This gloomy picture dims even further when we add to this scenario the fact that pensions are not likely to provide adequate cushion for retirement. On the expenses side, a key concern is the health care cost during retirement, which has been increasing above the rate of inflation. Many of the costs of long-term care, such as those required for Alzheimer's disease or nursing care are not covered by health insurance policies. When we put it all together, we begin to realize how important it is to develop and implement an effective retirement plan at the earliest possible opportunity.

Planning for retirement involves taking four major steps: (a) preretirement expenses should be estimated. (b) On the basis of Step (a), monthly or annual retirement expenses needed to maintain the desired standard of living should be determined. (c) The total expected income during retirement from all sources, including corporate retirement plans, personal retirement plans, personal savings, and employment should be estimated. (d) If the expected income falls short of the expected expenditure needs, appropriate steps should be taken *now* to alleviate the anticipated retirement income deficit problem. This concept of planning for retirement is presented in Figure 13.1.

This chapter will be devoted to a discussion of the major sources of retirement income. The techniques of estimating capital needs during retirement, taxation of a distribution from qualified plans, and the key retirement planning techniques will be discussed in Chapter 14.

The key sources of income available upon retirement can be conveniently classified into the following categories: (a) government-sponsored plans, (b) corporate and small-business retirement plans, (c)

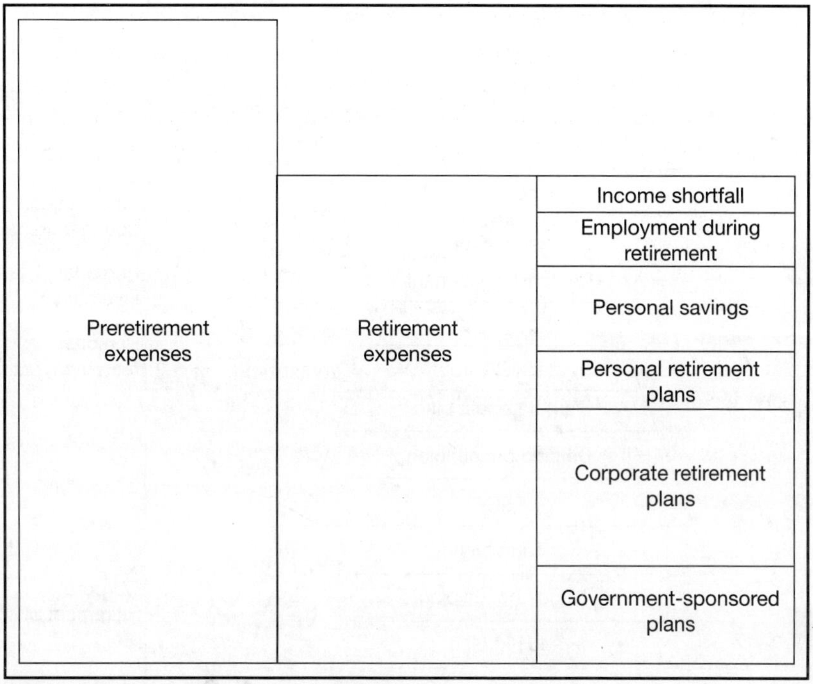

Figure 13.1 *Planning for Retirement*

personal retirement plans, (d) personal investment, and (e) employment during retirement. These sources are listed in Figure 13.2. Of these, the personal investment strategies have been fully discussed in Chapters 8, 9, and 10, while employment during retirement needs no further consideration. Consequently, we will now analyze the first three sources of income just listed.

Section I: Government Sponsored Plans

NEW PENSION SYSTEM[2]

Basics

In April 2004, as a defined contribution pension plan the government launched the New Pension Scheme (NPS), designed to be regulated by Pension Fund Regulatory and Development Authority (PFRDA). The purpose of launching this plan was to provide all citizens with not only pension benefits to ensure retirement income security but also the assurance that every citizen receives retirement and related benefits in a timely fashion. The social and ideological objective of this plan, of course, is to initiate pension reforms and to instill in all citizens the healthy habit of systematically saving for retirement. Under this plan, each participant will be permitted to invest every month a predefined sum in a pre-selected fund. Then, upon retirement, depending on how the selected fund performed over the long term, each participant will have a lump sum ready to be used during retirement years.

To be sure, NPS significantly differs from the earlier defined benefit system under which government employees received a monthly pension for life (occasionally adjusted upward representing inflationary

[2] This has also been referred to in the media as National Pension Scheme, New Pension System, and New Pension System. Available online at http://india.gov.in/spotlight/national-pension-system-retirement-plan-all (last accessed on March 12, 2014).

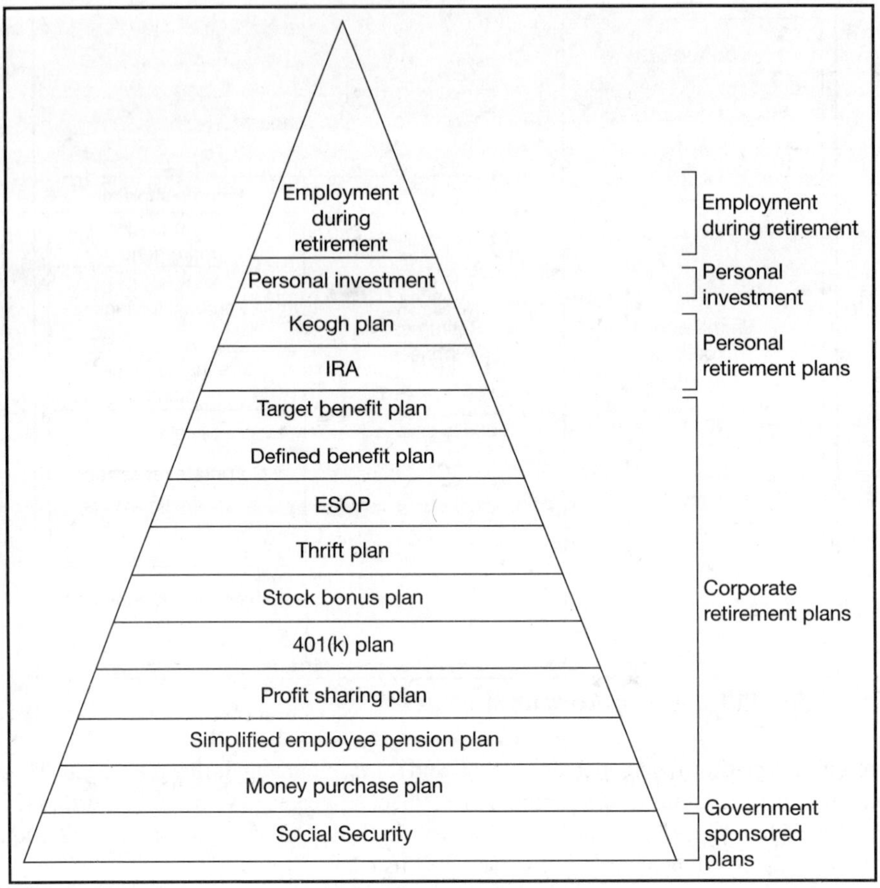

Figure 13.2 *Retirement Earnings Tree*

adjustment). Under NPS, however, the size of the monthly retirement payments will depend solely on the size of the lump sum payment received upon retirement.

Incidentally, when NPS was launched in 2004, it was made available only to government employees. Subsequently, in May 2009, the plan was extended to private employees as well. Additionally, by way of encouraging workers from the unorganized sector to save for retirement, the central government simultaneously launched a co-contributory pension scheme.

Plan Eligibility

Central Government Employees

NPS offers two important features that positively help a subscriber better manage the retirement account. (a) Each subscriber is allotted a specific Permanent Retirement Account Number (PRAN). The number assigned to a subscriber, guaranteed to remain unchanged for life, can be conveniently used from any location in India. (b) In order to make its operation smoother and more efficient, PRAN provides access to two personal accounts: *Tier I* account, a non-withdrawable account allocated for retirement, and *Tier II* account, a regular savings account with no tax benefits. This account can be tapped freely.

Eligibility. All Indian citizens (both residents and nonresidents) between the ages of 18–60 years are eligible to join the NPS. In order to complete the eligibility process each person must submit an application to Point of Presence (POP)/Point of Presence-Service Provider (POP-SP) and subsequently receive a letter of acceptance.

NPS is available to all employees of central government services (except armed forces) and central autonomous bodies joining government services effective January 1, 2004. Any other government employee not automatically covered by NPS can also subscribe to NPS under the "All Citizen's Model" through a POP-SP.

Contribution to NPS. Central government employees are required to make their contributions to the NPS through their nodal office. Each monthly contribution represents 10 percent of a participant's base (i.e., the basic salary plus the dearness allowance). Each employee's contribution is automatically matched by government's contribution.

Withdrawal Policy. NPS rules permit subscribers to withdraw their retirement funds upon retirement, resignation from service, or death. However, rules of disbursement of these funds do vary, depending on the primary reason for the withdrawal.

In case of retirement, a subscriber is required to spend a minimum of 40 percent of accumulated savings in purchasing a life annuity from PFRDA. However, if the subscriber resigns, at least 80 percent of the accumulated funds must be annuitized. Finally, upon the death of the subscriber, the entire balance is transferred to the legal heir.

State Government Employees

For state government employees, rules governing contributions to NPS are virtually identical to those for central government employees. The only difference is that state employees contact the Drawing And Disbursing Officer who, in turn, forwards the request to the respective Pay and Accounts Office/District Treasury Officer for final registration.

Corporate Subscribers

For all of its employees, a corporation can make investment choices either at the subscriber level or at the corporate level. At the operational level, either the corporation or the subscriber can choose any one of the listed Pension Fund managers (PFMs). The person making the selection is also permitted to select specific funds as well as determine the allocation of funds among various asset classes.

A corporation can extend NPS to its employees by connecting through any of the approved PoPs through MOUs (Memorandum of Understanding). An eligible corporate entity is free to negotiate charges with PoPs where POP-SP (an authorized branch of POP for NPS) undertakes the task of uploading the entire data vis-à-vis the All Citizen's Model.

As is the case with other entities, at the end of the registration process, the Central Record-keeping Agency assigns specific registration numbers to various subscribers which remain permanently fixed. Rules governing withdrawals upon retirement, termination of service, and death are the same as with other entities.

Individual Subscribers

As already mentioned, all Indian citizens between the ages of 18–60 are eligible to join the NPS. For these people, all rules specific to other categories of subscribers generally apply.

Subscription. Any individual can open a Permanent Retirement Account (Tier I and/or Tier II) with NPS. Rules governing Tier I account are identical to the rules for other entities. For Tier II account, an individual with an active Tier I account is required to submit to the associated POP-SP a copy of the PRAN Card along with UOS-S10 form (Tier II activation form). At the completion of all formalities, the POP-SP issues a registration number to the subscriber.

Contribution. A subscriber is required to make the first contribution at the time of applying for registration (minimum contributions fixed at ₹500 for Tier I and ₹1,000 for Tier II). Minimum contribution amounts are set at the following levels: (a) minimum amount at opening: ₹500, (b) minimum amount per contribution: ₹500, (c) minimum contribution per year: ₹6,000, and (d) minimum number of contributions per year: 1. No maximum limits have been set for Tier II.

Withdrawal. Rules governing the withdrawal of funds from Tier I account are virtually identical to the withdrawal rules for all other entities. For Tier II, a subscriber can withdraw any amount; units are redeemed based on the NAV (net asset value) of the account at the time of withdrawal.

Unorganized Sector Workers—Swavalamban Yojna

Anyone between 18 and 60 years of age and belonging to the unorganized sector (that is, anyone not in a regular employment of the central or a state government or an autonomous body/public sector undertaking (PSU) of the central or state government) can open an NPS-Swavalamban account. The prospective subscriber applies to the aggregator who ultimately issues a PRAN, thereby completing the registration process.

Withdrawal. All the rules governing the withdrawal of funds from the NPS-Swavalamban account are identical to those presented above, with only two exceptions. Early withdrawal before the age of 60 is permitted if certain preconditions are met. In that case, a subscriber must use a minimum of 80 percent of accumulated savings to purchase an annuity (the balance of 20 percent can be withdrawn). If the annuity amount that a subscriber is required to purchase with 40 percent of accumulated savings turns out to be below ₹1,000, a higher (than 40) percentage might be used to bring the amount up to the ₹1,000 level. Table 13.1 summarizes the key features of the National Pension System— age restrictions, eligibility and vesting rules.

Table 13.1 *Retirement Plans—NPS*

General Characteristics	Who Is Eligible?	Vesting Rules
Starting at the earliest age of 60, upon application, payments begin. Monthly income is based on several factors. No age restrictions apply for payments due to disability or death.	Everyone is eligible for NPS benefits. Spouse and dependents are eligible for receiving 100% of NPS pension wealth in a lump sum. However, nominees wishing to continue must subscribe to NPS individually, consistent with Know Your Customer (KYC) procedures.	Before attaining the age of 60, a subscriber must invest at least 80% of the pension wealth to purchase a life annuity from an Insurance Regulatory and Development Authority (IRDA) regulated life insurance company. The rest can be withdrawn as a lump sum. Between ages 60 and 70, at least 40% of total pension value (higher value is permitted) must be used to purchase a life annuity from any IRDA-regulated insurance company. At subscriber's option, the remaining pension wealth can be withdrawn either as a lump sum on attaining the age of 60, or in a phased manner between age 60 and 70, at the option of the subscriber.

TYPES OF BENEFITS

Benefits

NPS offers two types of benefits: (a) monthly checks to retirees, to their families, or to the families of deceased workers and (b) tax benefits to retirees and their families.

Investment Choices

Subscribers are offered two choices: active choice of individual funds (Asset Class E, Asset Class C, and Asset Class G) and auto-choice life-cycle fund.

Active Choice Individual Funds

These comprise three asset classes, as described below.

Asset Class E. Funds in this asset class are invested in an index mimicking a specific index, such as BSE Sensitive Index or the NSE Nifty 50 Index. Funds are invested in securities with the same weights as those in the selected index.

Asset Class G. This asset class represents investments in central and state government bonds.

Asset Class C. Funds in this asset class are invested in the following fixed income securities, excluding government securities. These include:

1. Liquid funds of asset management companies (AMCs) regulated by Securities and Exchange Board of India (SEBI) with the following filters: (a) AMCs are SEBI regulated, with average total assets under management of a minimum of ₹5,000 crore and (b) all assets are accepted by SEBI for investment into liquid funds.
2. Other fixed income securities such as fixed deposits of scheduled commercial banks with the following filters: (a) net worth of at least ₹500 crore and a track record of profitability in the last three years, (b) capital adequacy ratio of not less than 9 percent in the last three years, and (c) net NPS of below 5 percent as a percentage of net advances in the last year.
3. Debt securities with a maturity of not less than three years tenure issued by Corporate Bodies including scheduled commercial banks and public financial institutions as defined in Section 4 (A) of the Companies Act with the following filter. At least 75 percent of investment is placed in instruments with an investment-grade rating by Credit Rated Public Financial Institution/PSU Bonds or Credit Rated Municipal Bonds/Infrastructure Bonds.

An individual is permitted to invest in either G or C asset classes, subject to the following limits: (a) a maximum of 50 percent of the pension wealth and (b) a maximum of 50 percent in equities (Asset Class E). An investor can also freely choose between E, G, and C asset classes. However, if the investor wishes to play an active role in selecting investment options, then the choices must be limited to the Pension Funds selected from the following list of funds selected by PFRDA: (a) ICICI Prudential Pension Funds Management Company Limited, (b) IDFC Pension Fund Management Company Limited, (c) Kotak Mahindra Pension Fund Limited, (d) Reliance Capital Pension Fund Limited, (e) SBI Pension Funds Private Limited, and (f) UTI Retirement Solutions Limited.

Auto-choice Life-cycle Fund

For those who lack the skills or the expertise to make their own investment selections, NPS offers a convenient option known as "auto-choice option." Even so, an investor is required to select the PFM who would be entrusted to manage the funds. However, if an individual fails to make this selection, then the *present service provider* will be authorized to make the selection.

In this option, funds are invested in a life-cycle fund. The fraction of funds to be invested across three asset classes is determined by a predefined portfolio. Table 13.2 is a convenient table that lays out the percentage distributions for each asset class at various ages and shows the ratio of investments applicable to a life-cycle fund.

Table 13.2 *Life-cycle Fund Allocations among Asset Classes*

Age (Years)	Asset Class E (%)	Asset Class C (%)	Asset Class G (%)
Up to 35	50	30	20
36	48	29	23
37	46	28	26
38	44	27	29
39	42	26	32
40	40	25	35
41	38	24	38
42	36	23	41
43	34	22	44
44	32	21	47
45	30	20	50
46	28	19	53
47	26	18	56
48	24	17	59
49	22	16	62
50	20	15	65
51	18	14	68
52	16	13	71
53	14	12	74
54	12	11	77
55	10	10	80

Incidentally, the NAV for each fund is published regularly so that informed judgments could be made regarding their relative attractiveness. Also, it is best to remember that returns are never guaranteed for any of these funds.

Investment Cost

Pension Funds regularly charge a management fee of 0.9 percent per annum In addition, as specified under the contract, service tax, and other related charges are added to the management fee. Details of charges and method of deduction are presented in Table 3.3.

Taxation of National Pension Scheme Benefits

In general terms, the NPS states that "tax benefits would be applicable as per Income Tax Act, 1961, as amended from time to time." In practical terms, withdrawals from NPS are taxed under the EET (exempt, exempt, taxable) system. This implies that while contributions and returns to the NPS are exempt up to the prespecified amount, withdrawals are fully taxed as regular income. However, employers contributing to the NPS on behalf of their employees do receive tax benefits from the government.

Contributions made by individuals to the NPS (Tier I scheme) are deductible from the total income (Section 80CCD of the Income Tax Act). Contributions made by an employer on behalf of an employee are also deductible (Section 80CCD). However, the aggregate deduction (Sections 80C, 80CCC, and 80CCD) is fixed at ₹1.5 lakh. The total *eligible* deduction for a subscriber (Sections 80C, 80CCC, and 80CCD), such as PPF, bank, LIC premium, National Savings Certificate (NSC) deposits, Equity Linked Savings Scheme (ELSS) and NPS, is also pegged at ₹1.5 lakh.

There is, however, an exception. The Finance Act, 2011 (amended Section 80CCE), provides that the contributions to the pension scheme made by the central government or other employers (Section 80CCD) would not be subject to the ₹1.5 lakh limitation (Section 80CCE). In essence, this clause makes employers' contributions to NPS on behalf of their employees totally exempt from taxation.

Table 13.3 *Fund Charges and Method of Deduction*

Intermediary	Charge Head	Service Charges	Method of Deduction
Central Record-keeping Agency (CRA)	PRA opening charges	₹50	Through cancellation of units
	Annual PRA maintenance cost per account	₹350[3]	
	Charge per transaction	₹10[4]	
POP	Initial subscriber registration and contribution upload	₹40	To be collected upfront
(maximum permissible charge for each subscriber)	Any subsequent transactions[5]	₹20	
	Per transaction emanating from a RBI location	Zero	Through NAV deduction
Trustee bank	Per transaction emanating from a non-RBI location[6]	₹15	
Custodian[7] (on asset value in custody)	Asset servicing charges	0.0075% p.a. for Electronic segment and 0.05% p.a. for Physical segment	Through NAV deduction
PFM charges	Investment management fee[8]	0.0009% p.a.	Through NAV deduction

Income Tax Concession to Employers under NPS

The law also provides (Section 36) that as an employer, contributions made to the NPS by an employee, up to 10 percent of the employee's salary, can be treated as a deduction when calculating profits and gains of business or profession. This law became effective in April 2012.

Benefit Reductions for Excess Earned Income

At present, the amount contributed is entitled for deduction from gross total income up to ₹1 lakh along with other prescribed investments (as per Section 80C of the Income Tax Act, 1961). The initial investment in the annuity and the subsequent growth are not taxable. Only the amount withdrawn by a subscriber after 60 years of age is taxable.

[3] When the number of accounts in CRA reaches 10 lakh, the service charges, exclusive of service tax and other taxes as applicable, are reduced to ₹280 for annual PRA maintenance per account and ₹6 for charges per transaction. Further, when the number of accounts in CRA reaches 30 lakh, the service charges, exclusive of service tax and other taxes as applicable, are reduced further to ₹250 for the annual PRA maintenance per account and ₹4 for charges per transaction. CRAs charge for the maintenance of the permanent retirement includes charges for the maintenance of electronic information of the balances in the PRA, for incorporating changes to PRA details received by the CRA in electronic form, for sending annual account information once a year in printed form, etc.

[4] See note 3.

[5] These include—regular subscriber's contribution, change in subscriber details, change of investment scheme/fund manager, processing of withdrawal request, processing of request for subscriber shifting, issuance of printed account statements, and any other subscriber services as may be prescribed by PFRDA.

[6] Trustee bank charges are not charged to the subscriber directly. Transaction refers to the entire chain of activities starting from the receipt of electronic instructions/receipt of physical instrument to transfer of funds to the designated PFMs, on the outflow side; it would include all activities leading to credit of a beneficiary account.

[7] Charges of demat/remat, receipt of shares and the SEBI charges are extra.

[8] The investment management fee is inclusive of all transaction related charges such as transaction, brokerage cost, etc., except custodian charges and taxes. The fee is calculated on the average monthly assets managed by the pension fund.

Section II: Employees' Provident Fund

GENERAL DISCUSSION

The Employees' Provident Fund (EPF), a creation of the Labour Welfare Legislation, is a form of fund designed for employees' benefit. During the period of active service, both the employee and the employer make monthly contributions to a PF. Accumulations in this Fund, in turn, serve as a key element of retirement income. Currently, the law offers the following choices: (a) CPF, (b) pension benefits to the employees/family members, (c) insurance coverage for members of the PF.

PF provides an excellent means of accumulating wealth on a tax-deferred basis. In addition, the distribution of this wealth can be timed in a way so that the owner could maximize the after-tax income during retirement. Finally, distributions under the plan might be accorded favorable for tax treatment.

PF offers tax advantages both to the employer and the employee. The company gets a current tax deduction for amounts contributed to the plan, while the employees are not taxed on their contributions to the plan at the time contributions are made. Also, the plan is not taxed on its earnings, resulting in a tax-deferred buildup of retirement benefits. Incidentally, under different situations, appropriate tax rates would apply.

Applicability

Companies with 20 or more employees are required to be registered with the PF Department. That number includes contract employees such as housekeeping as well as security or other contractual workers in the business. Establishments which do not have the prescribed number of employees but are willing to register themselves to provide the benefits of PF to their employees can register voluntarily with the Regional Provident Fund Office. Registration must be completed within the specified time to avoid a penalty.

Eligibility

All employees with a starting annual wage of at least ₹6,500 are required to become a member of the PF. For this purpose, the definition of wages includes basic wages, dearness allowances, cash value of food concessions, and retaining allowances.

Fund Contributions

Employee contribution. Employees earning up to ₹6,500 must contribute 12 percent of their wages to the PF. However, the law does allow employees to make voluntary contributions in excess of the statutory minimum.

Voluntary contribution. By selecting Voluntary Provident Fund (VPF) employees can voluntarily contribute to the PF an amount up of to 100 percent of their wages. However, the contribution to VPF must be a percentage of wages, and not a fixed amount. Regardless of the choice made by the employee, the employer is not obligated to make any additional contributions beyond their statutory obligation.

Employer contribution. An employer is required to contribute 12 percent of an employee's wages to the PF. Of this amount, 3.67 percent is allocated to the PF and the balance of 8.33 percent is transferred to the Pension Fund.

Specific Requirements

The EPF is a compulsory retirement plan. It provides retirement benefits for employees through efficient management of their savings. EPF is governed by the Employees' Provident Funds & Miscellaneous Provisions Act, 1952 (EPFMPA) and is valid everywhere in India (except Jammu and Kashmir). For all employees in the organized sector, EPFMPA administers a CPF, a pension scheme and an insurance scheme. Incidentally, in terms of client base and the volume of financial transactions undertaken, it is one of the largest organizations of its kind in the world.

The current requirements under EPFMPA are presented in Table 13.3. The board operates three schemes which are also presented in Table 13.4.

Participating Requirements

EPFMPA extends to 187 classes of establishment. Any establishment falling into any of the specified categories and employing 20 or more people is automatically covered under this Act.

EPFMPA is a compulsory program for all employees. The Act defines an employee as:

> [A] person who is an employee for wages in any kind of work manual or otherwise, in or in connection with the work of an establishment and who gets wages directly or indirectly from the employer, and includes any person employed by or through a contractor in or in connection with the work of the establishment. (Section 2[f], EPF & MP Act, 1988)

This definition includes all employees (including, part time, casual. daily wages contract, and so on). The only exceptions relate to those employees (a) who have withdrawn their full accumulated amount upon retirement at the age of 55 or (b) whose monthly pay exceeds ₹5,000 and are entitled to become a member of the Fund. The term, basic wages, is defined to include all contractual emoluments earned by an employee and paid or payable in cash. However, it does not include food concessions, dearness and overtime allowances, house rent, and bonus, commission, or other allowances.

Contribution rates (percentage of wages) for financing and administering the benefits under the EPFMPA are presented in Table 13.4.

Table 13.4 *EPEMP Contribution Rates and Administration Accounts*[9]

	Contribution Accounts			Administrative Accounts		Total
	EPF	**EPS**	**EDLI**	**EPF**	**EDLI**	
Employee	12	0	0	0	0	12
Employer	3.67	8.33	0.5	1.10	0.01	13.61
Total	**15.67**	**8.33**	**0.5**	**1.10**	**0.01**	**25.61**

Source: Employees' Provident Fund Organization

Incidentally, for certain categories of establishment the contribution rate is only 10 percent. These are:

1. Any establishment in which less than 20 employees are employed.
2. Any sick industrial company and which has been declared as such by the board for Industrial and Financial Reconstruction.
3. Any establishment which has at the end of any financial year accumulated losses equal to or exceeding its entire net worth.
4. Any establishment in following industries: jute, beedi, brick, coir, and guar gum factories.

[9] http://www.epfindia.com/epfbrief.html (last accessed on March 12, 2014).

The contributions are statutorily payable up to a prescribed wage ceiling of ₹6,500. Contributions are invested according to the prescribed pattern of investment. Members' Provident Fund Balances earn interest declared annually by the government.

TYPES OF BENEFITS

Basically, there are three types of benefits offered by the PF: (a) Employee Provident Fund Organization (EPFO) provides funds upon retirement or death, (b) Provident Fund Organization provides monthly checks to retirees, to their families, or to the families of deceased workers, and (c) the Trust provides insurance coverage to PF members.

Retirement Benefits

Provident fund benefits. Benefits fall under the following categories: (a) employers contribute 12 percent (10 percent in certain cases) to the employees' PF Fund, (b) EPFO guarantees employer contributions and accumulating interest at government-specified rates, (c) participants are allowed to withdraw from this Fund to meet financial exigencies, and (d) upon resigning from employment, a participant receives the entire balance in the registered account.

Pension benefits. Pension benefits are paid to members or to their families in case of death. If a member, not yet 58 years old, quits the job, a Scheme Certificate is issued that records the employment history. This Certificate must be swapped for a new one when the member rejoins another firm. After attaining the age of 50, a member can apply for pension, provided service has been completed for a period of at least 10 years. This is a better choice than withdrawal benefits, since family members of an individual holding a Scheme Certificate at death will receive a pension.

Withdrawal benefits. A member ineligible for pension can still withdraw the accumulated amount in the pension account. The pension amount is calculated on the last average salary and service. Incidentally, no amount is collected from the member; the size of the pension amount is based solely on the contributions made by the employer (8.33 percent) and the government (1.16 percent).

In passing, it should be mentioned that EPFO guarantees that pension payments would be made to a member even if the employer had failed to make contributions to the Pension Fund.

Death benefits. Upon the death of an employee, either the entire PF amount or a monthly pension is paid out to the family or the nominee of the deceased. Likewise, the amount of insurance from Employees' Deposit Linked Insurance [EDLI] is also distributed to the family or the nominee of the deceased. Other, more involved rules, concerning the distribution of the death benefits also apply.

Advances/withdrawals. Advances and withdrawals from the Pension Fund are permitted to fulfill certain needs. These include, but are not limited to: (a) marriage, (b) medical treatment, (c) construction or remodeling of a home, or paying off a home loan, (d) payment due to permanent disability. Various rules apply to each of these and other situations, and details can be obtained from the Pension Fund or the employer.

In order to receive payment from the Fund, a member has to resign or retire from the company and follow the settlement rules. Following the termination of employment and receipt of Pension Funds, an employee not yet 55 is prohibited from joining another firm for a period of 60 days. In case of death, however, standard procedure can be followed by the beneficiaries to receive the payment.

Employees' Provident Fund, India[10]

EPFMPA, 1952, which covers all of India (except Jammu and Kashmir), was passed to establish PFs for people employed by factories and other establishments. Its administrative arm consists of the Central Board of Trustees Employees' Provident Fund and includes all parties represented by the government, the employer, and the employee.

The Board administers a CPF, a pension scheme, and an insurance scheme for the benefit of the workforce engaged in the organized sector. It is one of the world's largest organizations in terms of clientele and the volume of financial transactions undertaken by it. The organization has a well-equipped training set up for its officers and employees.

The Board operates three schemes: (a) EPF Scheme 1952—it is a mandatory saving scheme for old age/contingencies; (b) pension payments to members and other individuals nominated by the employee; and (c) EDLI Scheme 1976. This entity provides insurance benefits to beneficiaries of deceased members who died while in service. Benefits admissible and method of financing under each of these three schemes are presented in Table 13.5.

Provident Fund versus Pension

The following illustration underscores the importance of the time value of money concept, discussed in Chapter 3. It, thus, provides a justification for choosing a PF over a monthly pension.

Mr Anish works in an organization covered under the EPF Act, 1952. His basic salary is ₹20,000. He contributes 12 percent of his basic salary to the PF, which is matched by his employer. Mr Anish is 30 years old. What would be the total value of this fund when he turns 60? The average annual rate of return on the PF is 9 percent.

As can be seen from Table 13.6, when Anish turns 60, the value of the fund would be a whopping ₹2.62 crore.

Thus, by putting aside each month only ₹4,800 (12% of ₹20,000=₹2,400+2,400, or ₹4,800 representing employer and employee contributions), in 30 years the total amount grows to a whopping ₹2.62 crore. Even more surprising, this amount does not even take into account the annual salary increases.

Pension Plans of Insurance Companies[11]

Insurance company pension plans are the reverse of life insurance plans. In a pension plan a person routinely declares a vesting age, the desired age when regular pension payments should begin. The subscriber commits to make regular monthly contributions to the Pension Fund until reaching the vesting age.

Insurance companies offer two types of pension plans, namely Unit Linked Plan (ULIP) and Endowment Plan. The former invests in fixed income securities which are less risky (as compared to stocks) but also generates a lower rate of return; the latter invests solely in the stock market. In both plans contributions can be discontinued after 10 years. In a ULIP, the insurance company invests the money in one of the options selected by the policyholder, namely all fixed income securities, a mixture of debt and equity securities, or all equities.

All pension products represent the defined assured benefits available at death, when surrendered, or on vesting, which is declared at the time of sale. The assured benefit is calculated on the vesting date, at the time of surrender, or upon death. An employer maintains a superannuation fund, lumping all group pension products together. This implies that the assured benefit is applicable to the entire superannuation fund. Subsequently, claims generated due to death, retirement or termination of service are honored based on the existing superannuation scheme rules.

[10] http://www.epfindia.com/epfbrief.html (last accessed on July 12, 2014).

[11] IRDA, Circular, November 8, 2011.

Table 13.5 *Benefits and Financing under Various Schemes*

	Employees' Provident Fund Scheme, 1952	Employees' Pension Scheme, 1995	Employees' Deposit Linked Insurance, 1976
Benefits:	Accumulation plus interest upon retirement, resignation, or death. Partial withdrawals allowed for specific expenses such as house construction, higher education, marriage, and illness.	Monthly benefits for superannuation/retirement, disability, survivor spouse, and children. Amount of pension based on average salary during the preceding 12 months from the date of exit and total years of employment. Minimum pension upon disability. Past service benefit to participants of Family Pension Scheme, 1971.	Benefits provided upon death of a member employee. Family receives 20 times the average wages of the last 12 months. Maximum benefits are ₹1.3 lakh, as the wage ceiling, up to which contribution can be paid is ₹6,500.
Declaration:	Any person joining an establishment, to which the EPFMA applies, must submit a declaration to the employer, whether or not already a member of PF (Form 11). This will ensure continuity of service and subsequent benefits.		
Nomination:	Same form (Form 2R) applies to all three schemes. Nominations for the EPF Scheme are also applicable to the EDLI Scheme.	Member must give names of spouse and all children in the prescribed form.	
	Member with a family can nominate any one or more of the family members as defined under Para 2(f) of the EPF Scheme, 1952.	In case the member has no family, one person can be nominated.	
	Member without a family member can nominate another person; however, the nomination will be voided if the member acquires a family.	However, such nomination will become invalid once the member acquires a family.	The nomination under the EPF Scheme will be applicable for the EDLI Scheme also.
Claim forms:	For final settlement by member: **Form 19**. For transfer of old account to the new one: **Form 13**. For withdrawal in certain cases: **Form 31**. For financing LIC Policy: **Form 14**. For final settlement in favor of the nominee/beneficiary of a deceased member: **Form 20**.	For monthly pension: Form 10D. For withdrawal benefit and Scheme Certificate: Form 10C.	For claiming insurance benefit by a nominee/beneficiary in case of the member's death while in service: Form A

Source: Employees' Provident Fund Organization.

Incidentally, pension products offered by an insurer are always protected by an insurance cover or offer riders. The sum of all rider premiums attached to the pension product is limited to no more than 15 percent of the paid premium. The rider premium is separately accounted for; hence, it is not included in the assured benefit available at the time of death, surrender, or vesting.

Vesting. At the time of vesting, an annuity is provided to the subscriber by the insurance company.

Table 13.6 *Compound Value of Monthly Payments*

Year	Amount Deposited Every Year	Rate Factor (%)	No. of Years	Future Value (₹)
1	57,600.00	9	30	764,218.28
2	63,360.00	9	29	771,229.46
3	69,696.00	9	28	778,304.96
4	76,665.60	9	27	785,445.37
5	84,332.20	9	26	792,651.29
6	92,765.40	9	25	799,923.32
7	102,042.00	9	24	807,262.07
8	112,246.00	9	23	814,668.14
9	123,471.00	9	22	822,142.16
10	135,818.00	9	21	829,684.75
11	149,400.00	9	20	837,296.53
12	164,340.00	9	19	844,978.15
13	180,773.00	9	18	852,730.25
14	198,851.00	9	17	860,553.46
15	218,736.00	9	16	868,448.45
16	240,609.00	9	15	876,415.86
17	264,670.00	9	14	884,456.38
18	291,137.00	9	13	892,570.65
19	320,251.00	9	12	900,759.38
20	352,276.00	9	11	909,023.22
21	387,504.00	9	10	917,362.89
22	426,254.00	9	9	925,779.06
23	468,880.00	9	8	934,272.45
24	515,768.00	9	7	942,843.75
25	567,345.00	9	6	951,493.70
26	624,079.00	9	5	960,223.00
27	686,487.00	9	4	969,032.38
28	755,136.00	9	3	977,922.59
29	830,649.00	9	2	986,894.35
30	913,714.00	9	1	995,948.43
				26,254,534.70

Surrender. At the time of surrender, a policyholder can choose from the following options: (a) convert the full amount into an immediate annuity, guaranteed for life, (b) convert the entire proceeds to purchase a single premium deferred pension product, and (c) if below 55, the subscriber is permitted to extend the accumulation period/deferment period in the same policy.

Death. In the event if a policyholder dies during the deferment period, the nominee is entitled to either convert the entire proceeds into an annuity or withdraw the full amount accumulated in the policy.

To conclude, on a regular basis the insurance policy is obligated to send each subscriber details of the policy which include the following: the current balance, accumulated balance expected on the date of vesting, and expected annuity amount based on the then-prevailing annuity rates.

SBI SARAL PENSION

This is an individual, participating, non-linked, traditional pension plan. It offers a choice of investing retirement funds in vehicles sheltered from stock market fluctuations. Key features of this plan are presented below.

Table 13.7 *Product Snapshot*

Age at Entry*	Min: 18 years	Max: For single premium: 65 years, For regular premium: 60 years
Age at Vesting*	Min: 40 years	Max: 70 years
Policy Term	Min: For single premium: 5 years For regular premium: 10 years	Max: 40 years
Sum Assured**	Min: ₹100,000	Max: No limit
Premium Frequency	Single/Yearly/Half-yearly/Monthly# The premiums for various modes as percentage of annual premium are given below: • Monthly premium—8.4% of annual premium • Half-yearly premium—50.2% of annual premium	
Premium	Min: ₹7,500 p.a.	Max: No limit

Notes: *All the references to age are age as on the last birthday.

**Sum assured is always greater than or equal to the total premiums paid and accumulated at an interest rate of 0.25 percent compounded annually.

#Three months premium is to be paid in advance and renewal premium payment through Electronic Clearing System (ECS) or Standing Instructions (where payment is made either by direct debit of bank account or credit card). For Monthly Salary Saving Scheme (SSS), two months premium is to be paid in advance and renewal premium payment is allowed only through salary deduction.

Guaranteed bonus. This option offers simple reversionary bonuses for the first five years. For the first three years an interest rate of 2.5 percent is applied to the guaranteed amount; the rate is raised to 2.75 percent for the next two years. Guaranteed bonuses are applied only to in-force policies.

Vesting (maturity) benefit. This item represents the assured sum plus the vested simple reversionary bonuses including terminal bonus, if any. The sum assured carries an implicit guaranteed annual interest rate of at least 0.25 percent applied to the total premium payment.

Death benefit. This item consists of the *higher of* (a) total premiums paid, compounded at 0.25 percent per year plus the vested reversionary bonuses including terminal bonus and (b) an amount equal to 105 percent of the total premiums paid.

Life cover. This option refers to additional life coverage through SBI Life-Preferred Term Rider (UIN: 111B014V02).

Incidentally, the recipient is given the option to buy immediate annuity with the entire sum, or to commute up to one-third of the lump sum, and to buy an annuity with the available balance. Another important option available is that the recipient can extend either the vesting date until reaching the age of 70 or the accumulation/deferment period if at the vesting age of below 55.

Ability to buy life immediate annuity. On vesting, the recipient is given the option to buy immediate annuity with the entire sum, or to commute up to one-third of the lump sum, and to buy an annuity with the available balance.

Flexibility. Another important option available is that the recipient can extend either the vesting date until reaching the age of 70 or the accumulation/deferment period if at the vesting age of below 55.

Table 13.7 provides a product snapshot of SBI Saral Pension.

Benefits of Saral Pension offered by the state Bank of India are briefly described as follows:

Vesting benefits. At the vesting age, vesting benefit proceeds equal the assured sum plus the vested simple reversionary bonus including terminal bonus. This amount can be used to: (a) purchase immediate annuity, (b) purchase immediate annuity with an option to commute up to one-third of the policy proceeds as per current Income Tax rules, (c) purchase a single premium deferred pension product, or (d) if below 55, extend the accumulation period or defer the vesting date—the maximum extended period will be up to the age of 70 years.

Death benefit. Upon death, the total amount available for distribution equals the higher of (a) the total premiums paid, compounded at an annual interest rate of 0.25 percent plus vested reversionary bonus, including terminal bonus and (b) an amount equal to 105 percent of total premiums paid. The nominee can choose between the following options for final distribution: (a) receive entire proceeds as a lump sum or (b) utilize all or part of the proceeds to purchase an annuity from SBI Life.

Tax benefits. Premiums paid for this policy are tax deductible (U/s 80CCC of the Income Tax Act). On vesting, a policyholder can commute up to one-third of the policy proceeds. This amount is distributed tax free (Income Tax Act, 1961). This commuted value is exempted from tax under Section 10(10A) (iii) of the Income Tax Act 1961. The noncommuted pension amount taken in the form of immediate annuity is currently taxable.

SBI LIFE ANNUITY PLUS

This is a traditional, nonparticipating, immediate annuity plan. It offers a comprehensive range of annuity options and also has built-in flexibilities. Key features of this Plan include: (a) wide range of annuity options, (b) choice of beginning the payout period at the age of 40, (c) lifetime annuity payment for self and a family member, and (d) determination of the frequency of payouts in a year. It also offers higher annuity rates for large premium payments and an accidental death benefit rider.

Annuity Options

The Plan offers a wide variety of annuity options. These include the following:

Life annuity (single life). In this case, the annuity payments continue for as long as the annuitant is alive. A person can choose between (a) lifetime income, (b) lifetime income with capital refund, and (c) lifetime income with capital refund in parts.

Lifetime income with balance capital refund. Here, the annuity is payable at a fixed rate. Upon death, the remaining balance, if any, is fully distributed.

It provides lifetime income with an annual increase of 3 or 5 percent.

Lifetime income with period certain. In this option, annuity payments are made for the period chosen (5, 10, 15, 20 years, or for life).

Life annuity for joint lives. Here, the annuity payments continue upon the death of the first annuitant. Payments equal 50 or 100 percent of the income either with or without capital refund.

Benefits

There are many benefits for participating in this Plan. The annuitant has the freedom to choose the frequency and duration of payment. An accidental death benefit is also offered as a rider. The maximum age of maturity is fixed at 70. The minimum and maximum guaranteed amounts are, respectively, ₹25,000 and ₹50 lakh. There is an exclusion relating to the accidental death benefit rider.

In addition, this Plan also offers a major tax benefit. Funds inside the insurance company continue to grow tax deferred until withdrawn. Of course, as expected, all annuity payouts are taxed at ordinary tax rates.

In this chapter, we analyzed in detail the basic structure of retirement income. In Chapter 14, we will undertake a detailed review of the key concepts and strategies relating to retirement planning.

14 Retirement Planning: Concepts and Strategies

INTRODUCTION

For the past couple of generations, Indians have relied on the venerable two pillars to provide for their retirement Employees' Provident Fund (EPF) and personal savings. Government employees who joined before 2004 relied on family pension; however, those who joined after January 1, 2004, rely on national pension system which is now open to everyone.

Many factors currently threaten the stability of this stool. For instance, retirees of the 21st century will grow far older. When Contributory Provident Fund (CPF) was enacted in 1956 and retirement was set at 60, an average male could expect to live an additional 10–12 years in retirement. In 2004, he could live for 18 years in retirement, and by 2025, that period could be extended to 20 years or more. At the same time, the age at which full CPF and National Pension Scheme (NPS) benefits can be collected would rise to 62–65, and the portion of benefits that individuals sacrifice when they retire early would be greater.

Longer lives will require more financial support. Yet the ability of CPF and NPS to provide this expanded support appears questionable. In addition, the viability of many insurance plans is in doubt.

Clearly, anyone with a sizable retirement plan and/or Public Provident Fund (PPF) benefits should begin planning early in order to maximize the value of those benefits, by avoiding penalty taxes and taking advantage of beneficial tax treatments. In some cases, deferral of taxes on appreciation in employer stock may be appropriate, using the net unrealized appreciation opportunity. However, most individuals would achieve greater value by a tax-free rollover to another qualified plan or PPF. The rollover would further defer taxation on the amount rolled over, thereby permitting additional tax deferred earnings.

The distribution of rollover PPF account balances can be planned to maximize the total value received by an individual, his or her spouse, and their beneficiaries. In general, this planning entails delaying the start of distributions and stretching them out as long as possible.

Accordingly, if the money is not needed for living or other expenses, receipt of retirement benefits should be deferred as long as possible. Because retirement distribution rules are complex, professional assistance may be necessary to achieve the best results.

Retirement planning, or planning for financial independence after retirement, is one of the key areas of personal financial planning. We work all our lives, expecting to earn the privilege of maintaining a desired lifestyle upon retirement. It is conceivable, however, that without proper planning, this retirement dream could turn into a nightmare. For instance, without proper planning and systematic directive actions, a retiree might not have an adequate income upon retirement. An accumulated capital fund like EPF might not last as long as both spouses are alive. Retirees might not make the right decisions with regard to: (a) tax-wise distribution of retirement funds, (b) picking the right retirement age, and (c) selecting the appropriate strategies for investing retirement funds.

In retirement planning, individuals first define their goals for the quality of life after retirement. Next, they measure their ability to meet their goals and develop strategies for improving their performance. In the final analysis, success in retirement planning is assured only if an individual is able to retire at the desired retirement age with the expected level of income.

This chapter is divided into four parts. First, an in-depth analysis of retirement income needs is undertaken. Next, distribution requirements and tax implications of retirement fund distributions are explored. Following that, several methods of receiving retirement income are presented. Finally, several retirement planning strategies are discussed.

At this point, it is necessary to make an important assumption. Any sophisticated discussion on retirement planning should take into consideration the differences in individuals planning for retirement, such as: (a) a financially sophisticated person, (b) a dual-career couple, (c) a highly compensated executive, (d) an owner of a professional practice, (e) an owner of a closely held business, and (f) a salaried employee. However, since such sophistication is beyond the scope of this book, in our discussions on retirement planning *we will treat all individuals as part of a homogeneous group*. While that will inevitably create distortions, by so doing we will be able to focus our attention on the major issues relating to retirement planning.

Section I: Retirement Income Needs Analysis

RETIREMENT BUDGET

The retirement income needs analysis begins with the construction of a realistic retirement budget, which involves the estimation of income and expenses during retirement years. We will now turn to the construction of such a retirement budget for a hypothetical family.

Sanjay and Shweta Sharma are an average couple. Sanjay is a corporate employee and Shweta is a dental hygienist. Both participate in NPS. Sanjay is 40 and wishes to retire in 20 years. Shweta is 30 but intends to retire with Sanjay.

Retirement Expenditure Analysis

We will begin with Sanjay's current expenditures, which are presented in Table 14.1. These expenditures are strictly for the Sharma family and do not necessarily represent either a national average or an ideal expenditure pattern. In fact, in analyzing retirement budgets, it may be counterproductive for financial planners to make value judgments about their clients' expenditure patterns.

Once the current expenditures are recorded, our next task is to estimate the expenditures expected during retirement. There are, of course, no hard and fast rules for estimating these expenses. The accepted rule of thumb is that a retiree is likely to spend 60 or 70 percent of the preretirement expenditure level. This rule, however, appears too rigid and often misleading, because it does not specifically recognize the differences between (a) various categories of expenditures and (b) people who aspire to maintain different—and more specifically richer—lifestyles after retirement.

A better approach to estimate expenditures during retirement is to divide fixed and flexible expenditures into several key categories and encourage a client to estimate the retirement expenditure in each category. This approach provides individuals with an opportunity to fine tune their retirement income estimates. For instance, Table 14.1 reveals that the Sharmas plan to keep on making mortgage payments after retirement. Consequently, after retirement their housing expenditures will remain virtually unchanged. For another family expecting to own a home free and clear before retirement, these expenses would be drastically reduced after retirement. Another area of interest is entertainment expenditure. Some families may wish to drastically reduce their entertainment expenses after retirement, while others

Table 14.1 *Retirement Budget Estimate*

Income	Current Year (₹)	At Retirement (₹)
Current income	1,963,960	600,000*
Expenditures		
Housing		
Mortgage, property taxes, utilities (gas, oil, electricity, and water), telephone, home furnishings, household service, maintenance, and improvements	30,000	25,000
Clothing		
Purchase and cleaning	25,000	15,000
Food	200,000	150,000
Transportation		
Car repair and maintenance, installment payments, gas, commuting costs, etc.	50,000	50,000
Gifts	15,000	50,000
Contributions	480,000	200,000
Education, books, subscriptions	20,000	5,000
Insurance		
Life, medical, auto, property, liability	50,000	100,000
Medical and dental care		
Premiums, deductible and out-of-pocket costs	20,000	30,000
Loan-repayment costs	300,000	0
Personal care		
Grooming, health club, other	5,000	5,000
Entertainment		
Vacations, dining out, movies, plays, concert, sports events, cable TV, CD/VCD, entertaining, sports, hobbies, other	25,000	10,000
Domestic help	90,000	163,248
Savings and retirement		
Contribution to company plans	180,000	0
PPF, insurance, post office savings		
Taxes	333,106	0
Miscellaneous	25,000	50,000
Total expenditure	1,848,106	853,248
Surplus (+)/deficit (–)	115,854	–253,248

Note: *Expected income from EPF, PPF, other pension plans, and other sources.

may plan to spend a great deal more by undertaking world travels or developing other expensive hobbies such as golf or scuba diving.

Returning to the Sharma family, we find that after retirement the Sharmas expect to spend ₹853,248 per year (71,104 a month), which is 46.2 percent of their current expenditure.

Retirement Income

We now turn to an estimate of the retirement income for the Sharmas. The family expects to receive a monthly income of ₹50,000 from insurance and noninsurance qualified plans as well as from NPS, as shown next:

NPS	₹12,500
Pension/Profit sharing plans	₹4,200
Insurance plan	₹16,000
Other incomes	₹17,300
	₹50,000

NPS benefits can be calculated with the help of the NPS website[1]. Note that the NPS benefit assumption used in this example is conservative in order to account for the possibility that these benefits might be reduced in the future. This conservative estimate, in recognition of future uncertainties, offers a "margin of safety" in planning for the savings needs. A company's benefits department can estimate the income from pension and profit sharing plans. The annual income from EPF and PPF plans can be calculated by estimating the value of each plan upon retirement and acquiring from a life insurance company the lifetime annuity value for the accumulated amount.

To sum up, at retirement, the Sharmas expect to have annual expenses of ₹853,248, whereas their incomes from EPF, pension plans, NPS, and other sources are expected to be ₹600,000. The balance of ₹21,104 per month (₹253,248 per year) must come from personal investment to enable the family to meet its retirement goals.

Potential Shortfall

Now that we have learned that the Sharmas must receive ₹21,104 every month from personal investments in order to meet their retirement goal, we can determine if they can reasonably expect to meet this goal.

The analytical framework for calculating the savings required for retirement is presented in Table 14.2. In constructing this table, we have made the following assumptions: (a) Sharmas' current personal, nonqualified savings amount is ₹859,540; (b) the number of years to retirement is 20; (c) the number of years in retirement is 30; and (d) both qualified and personal savings will grow at an inflation-adjusted real rate of 3 percent. As depicted in line 3 of the table, the Sharma's must receive a monthly income of ₹21,104 from nonqualified investment sources.

Based on the assumptions that the Sharmas will retire in 20 years and live for 30 years in retirement, the first step is to determine how much needs to be saved by the beginning of year 21 in order to generate ₹21,104 a month, received at the *beginning* of each year, for 30 years. We calculate that amount to be ₹3,485,916:

Table 14.2 *Determination of Savings Required for Retirement (Amount in ₹)*

Line 1	Annual budget after retirement		853,248
Line 2	Annual distribution from:		
	1. NPS	150,000	
	2. Pension/profit sharing plans	50,400	
	3. Insurance plan	192,000	
	4. Other incomes	207,600	
	Total		600,000
Line 3	Annual income needed from personal savings (line 1 – line 2 total)		253,248
Line 4	Lump sum retirement need (in current ₹) n=30, i=3, PV=?, PMT=253,248, FV=0		
	Set a calculator to the "begin" mode and solve for PV		3,485,916
	Current personal savings		
Line 5	Value of current savings at retirement		859,540
	n=20, i=3, PV=859,540, PMT=0, FV=?		
Line 6	Set calculator to the "end" mode and solve for FV Savings shortfall (line 4 – line 6)		2,756,661
Line 7	Savings required for retirement		729,255
	n=20, i=3, PV=0, PMT=?, FV=729,255		
Line 8	Set calculator to the "end" mode and solve for PMT		19,825

[1] www.http://india.gov.in/spotlight/national-pension-system-retirement-plan-all (last accessed on March 12, 2015).

PMT=₹253,248
FV=₹0
i=6
n=30
Solve for PV=₹3,485,916

Next, we estimate the value of personal savings on the day of retirement. Currently, personal savings of the Sharma's are ₹859,540 (line 5). If these savings grow at an after-tax, inflation-adjusted rate of return of 6 percent, the value of the savings in 20 years will be ₹2,756,661:

PV=₹859,540
PMT=0
i=6
n=20
Solve for FV=₹2,756,661

We have determined that, at retirement, the Sharmas need a total personal savings of ₹3,485,916 (line 4), whereas their expected savings would be only ₹2,756,661 (line 6). That is, the expected shortfall of savings is ₹729,255 (line 7). This shortfall can be met if each year the Sharmas save an additional amount of ₹19,825 for 20 years (contribution made at the end of the year) and realize an after-tax, inflation-adjusted rate of return of 6 percent:

PV=0
FV=729,255
i-6
n=20
Solve for PMT=19,825

An oversimplified calculation of retirement income shortfall reveals that without additional savings the Sharmas would experience an annual shortfall of ₹19,825 when they retire in 20 years. While the family realizes that the additional annual savings of ₹19,825 required to meet their retirement goal can quickly change with a change in the key variables (e.g., inflation rate or family situation), this analysis does provide them with a basis for effective retirement planning.
Given the basic assumptions made in this example, the Sharmas have four distinct options:

Option 1. They can retire on time if they manage to save an additional ₹19,825 per year and make it grow at a 6 percent after-tax real rate of return.

Option 2. Even if the Sharmas cannot save additional funds, they still can conceivably meet their retirement goal if they succeed in having their savings grow at a rate faster than the 6 percent after-tax real rate assumed in the previous discussion.

Option 3. The Sharmas can lower their retirement income goal.

Option 4. Sanjay Sharma can extend his desired retirement age beyond the age of 60.

Recapping a potential shortfall in the retirement budget requires the development of specific strategies to solve the problem. These strategies can be conveniently divided into the following categories.

1. ***Tax-advantaged investment planning.*** This strategy requires that the family considers the possibility of making the maximum contribution to their qualified plans if that is not currently being done.
2. ***Savings planning.*** Increasing the amount of annual savings may entail a thorough examination, and eventual reduction, of current monthly expenses. A more austere budget may force the family to choose between nonessential current expenditures and a better standard of living at retirement.

3. ***Asset repositioning planning.*** A review of the existing investments may induce the family to shift the current portfolio into more aggressive investments if there are strong feelings about the desired level of retirement income. Of course, if these planning strategies do not produce the desired results, the family would be forced to lower the desired retirement income or advance the retirement age, neither of which might offer an attractive alternative.

Potential Surplus

Not every retirement plan has a potential shortfall. For instance, assume the Sharmas wish to have annual retirement expenses of ₹853,248 (Table 14.2), but at retirement expect to receive an income of ₹900,000 instead of ₹600,000. In that case, they will have a potential surplus in their retirement budget, and no further corrective action will be necessary on their part.

Section II: Distribution from Qualified Plans

INTRODUCTION

Qualified plans are subject to strict rules about when and how they can make distributions to participants. As a general rule, some deferral is required before employees can receive distributions. Also, employee contributions are generally subject to fewer restrictions than employer contributions. In addition to these general rules, however, there are specific rules which apply to different types of qualified plans. A description of various types of plans and the key distribution rules governing them is presented next.

PENSION PLANS

Pension plans are subjected to the most stringent distribution rules. Furthermore, within the pension plans, rules applying to defined benefit plans are stricter than those applicable to the defined contribution plans. As a general rule, the law allows distribution from a pension plan: (a) at retirement, (b) upon the attainment of normal retirement age, (c) upon the separation of service, (d) upon death, (e) in the event of permanent disability, or (f) upon the plan's termination.

PROFIT SHARING PLANS

The rules governing profit sharing plans are less restrictive than those governing pension plans. In general, distribution from a profit sharing plan is allowed: (a) upon the attainment of the age of 59½; (b) when certain specified events such as layoff, illness, disability, or termination of employment occur; or (c) after the passage of a prespecified time period.

OTHER QUALIFIED PLANS

Other types of qualified plans are subject to varying distribution rules. For instance, EPF plans cannot make distributions based on the passage of time, but they can make distributions at retirement, death, separation from service, or attainment of the age of 60. Also, because of hardship, these plans are allowed to distribute elective contributions, but not earnings on them. Other plans, such as employee stock ownership plans (ESOPs), profit sharing, and so on are governed by a slightly different set of rules.

Employee contributions to various types of plans are not subject to the same restrictions as those imposed on employer contributions. However, a waiting period is generally imposed before employee contributions can be distributed.

REQUIRED DISTRIBUTIONS

All qualified plans are required to make compulsory distributions to the participating employees when certain conditions are met. Chief among these conditions is the participants attaining age 60.

TAXATION OF PLAN BENEFITS

There is a provision in the law that permits the commutation of retirement benefits and receiving up to one-third of the value of total retirement benefits in the form of a lump sum. The remaining balance will then be paid in the form of monthly payments.

The tax consequence of a distribution from a pension plan depends upon the types of EPF. There are basically two types of EPFs—government-managed EPFs and employers-managed EPF. The government allows employers to manage their own provident fund schemes, subject to certain conditions. Though there are 31 conditions for setting up a private provident fund, the main conditions are that the employer's contribution should not be less than in the statutory schemes and the annual rate of interest should be at least what the government EPF pays to its subscribers. In case of the government EPF scheme, an employers' contribution is exempted from tax. The interest earned is also tax free. However, the rules are slightly different in case of private EPF schemes. An employer's contribution is tax exempt only up to 12 percent of the basic pay. Also, the interest earned up to the rate offered by the Employees' Provident Fund Organisation to its subscribers is tax free. Anything over and above that is taxed. The employees' contribution up to ₹150,000 is deducted from the taxable income under Section 80 (C) of the Income Tax Act. The details of the same are provided in Table 14.3.

Once the amount of distribution subject to taxation has been identified, the tax treatment of this amount would depend upon whether the distribution is taxed under the lump sum distribution rules or the annuity rules. The tax treatment under each method is discussed below.

Lump Sum Distribution

For the government EPF scheme, the distribution/repayment of sum on retirement, resignation, or termination is fully exempted from tax. However, in case of private EPF schemes, nothing is taxable subject to the following conditions: employee leaving the job after five years of service or where the period of service less than five years, the termination is due to ill health, discontinuance of the business of an employer or here on reemployment, the balance in EPF is transferred to EPF with a new employer. For the purpose of computing the five-year period, the period of service rendered with a previous employer

Table 14.3 *Tax Benefits on EPF*

Tax Benefit on EPF			Stay Invested	
Both Contribution and Interest Are Tax-exempt			Impact of Withdrawal before Five Year	
	Govt. EPF Scheme	Pvt. EPF Scheme		Taxability
Employer's contribution	Not taxable	Exempt up to 12% of basic salary	Employer's contribution	Taxable as salary
Employee's contribution	Deduction under Section 80C	Deduction under Section 80C	Employee's contribution	Taxable to the extent deduction claimed under Section 80C
Accrued interest	Not taxable	Exempt up to the rate fixed by the govt.	Accrued interest	Taxable as other income

Source: http://businesstoday.intoday.in/story/facts-about-employee-provident-fund-epf-impact-savings/1/192006.html (last accessed on December 6, 2014).

shall also be included. If none of the conditions mentioned above are satisfied then the amount not taxed earlier shall be taxed and any tax concessions availed by the person shall now be withdrawn.

Annuity Distribution

The second option available to plan participants is to receive the distribution as an annuity. Distributions received as an annuity, less the return of a participant's cost basis, are taxed as ordinary income. This cost basis represents the contributions made by the employees with after-tax money and any previously taxed employer contributions. Income tax consequences for annuities are discussed in a subsequent section.

TAXATION OF THE NATIONAL PENSION SCHEME

The benefit of NPS consists of the deduction that is available to individuals on their own contribution to the fund. If it is the case where they are contributing an amount and so is the employer, then they would need to see their own contribution and this should not exceed 10 percent of their salary. While the employee contribution up to 10 percent of the basic plus the dearness allowance, or DA, is eligible for deduction under Section 80CCD within the ₹100,000 limit, an employer's contribution up to 10 percent of the basic plus the DA is eligible for deduction under Section 80CCE over and above the ₹100,000 limit. This is a onetime benefit in the sense that if, say, ₹100,000 is invested, then subject to the other limits this amount would be allowed as a deduction for the individual. There is earning on this amount that will be present after the investment and which will be added to the account over the life of the investment but this is not to be taxed. This does not mean that the amount is tax free, because the way in which this will be taxed is at the time of receipt. When an individual actually gets a pension from the account, then the amount would be taken as income of the person and added to his or her income as required. Here, there is just deferment of the tax aspect till the amount is received; thus, NPS, like other pension products, is EET (exempt, exempt, taxed) which means it will be taxed later when an individual finally receives the money. The tax benefit from NPS is presented in Table 14.4.

Tax implications of NPS on an employer:

1. As per Section 36 (1) (iv a) of the Income Tax Act, 1961, an employer contributing to the NPS on behalf of an employee gets deduction from his income (i.e., employer's income) an amount equivalent to the amount contributed or 10 percent of basic salary plus the DA of the employee, whichever is less.
2. As per the Income Tax Act, 1961, an employer's contribution to NPS on behalf of an employee is treated as a perquisite in the hands of the employee, but is deductible to the extent of 10 percent of the basic salary. This deduction is over and above the limit of ₹100,000 under Section 80C of the Act. This will lessen the tax burden of an employee to the extent of amount deductible under Section 80CCD (2) of the Act.

Table 14.4 *The Tax Benefit from NPS*

Particulars	Without NPS	With NPS
CTC	2,500,000	2,500,000
Basic salary (40% of CTC)	1,000,000	1,000,000
NPS contribution (10% of the basic salary)	–	100,000
Less: Deductions under Section 80CCD	100,000	100,000
Less: NPS Deduction under Section 80CCE	–	100,000
Total taxable income	2,400,000	2,300,000
Total tax @30	720,000	690,000
Additional tax saving through NPS	0	30,000

3. Additional contribution by individual employee is eligible for deduction from income under Section 80CCD of the Income Tax Act 1961. However, investments under Section 80C plus the premium on pension products mentioned in Section 80CCC should not exceed ₹100,000 per assessment year to claim for the deduction.

Employees' Provident Fund versus National Pension Scheme

EPF is a mandatory retirement savings instrument in which an employee contributes 12 percent of the basic and DA every month and an employer makes a matching contribution. The employee's contribution is eligible for income tax deduction up to ₹100,000 a year. On the other hand, the NPS model (except government employees) is a voluntary retirement savings scheme in which an employee contributes at least ₹6,000 every year. There is no cap on investment. Similar to EPF, an employee's contribution is also eligible for income tax deduction up to ₹100,000 a year in NPS. In addition, NPS also offers additional tax deduction on the employer contribution up to 10 percent of the basic and DA. This is over and above the ₹100,000 limit of Section 80C.

The EPF money is not invested in equities. However, NPS allows up to 50 percent equity exposure. EPF, on the other hand, offers the option of premature withdrawal without foreclosure. It allows premature withdrawal for specific purposes such as house construction, marriage, and illness.

In NPS, any premature withdrawal will lead to the closure of the account. Only up to 20 percent of the funds can be withdrawn before an employee turns 60. The rest has to be used to buy an annuity.

TAXATION OF INSURANCE PLANS

Under Section 80CCC, an investor can avail of tax benefit of up to ₹100,000 on the premium paid toward a pension plan. On maturity, while the whole of the amount is treated as tax free in the hands of the individual in case of conventional insurance plans, only one-third of the maturity amount can be withdrawn and treated as tax free in case of pension funds. Monthly pension receipts from the remaining balance is treated as income in the hands of an assessee and taxed accordingly.

OTHER TAX CONSIDERATIONS

Premature Distributions

If an individual makes a withdrawal from an EPF account prior to five years, all tax benefits availed on it will be reversed. Of course, this penalty is waived if the distribution is triggered by: either ill health, death, or disability or discontinuance of an employer's business or any other reason which is not in the control of the employee.

However, if an EPF account is transferred to a new employer, then the previous service from which the account is transferred is also considered as a service period.

Section III: Retirement Income—The Ultimate Decision

INTRODUCTION

As retirement age draws near, every individual is faced with the dilemma: How can one make a rational decision on the most efficient means of distribution of qualified money? As revealed by Figure 14.1, the major sources of retirement income consist of income from: personal investment, corporate-sponsored plans and other tax-advantaged plans (pension and PPF), NPS plans for self-employed income earners, and individual NPS. Of these, personal investment income was discussed in detail in Chapters 8, 9, and 10. The

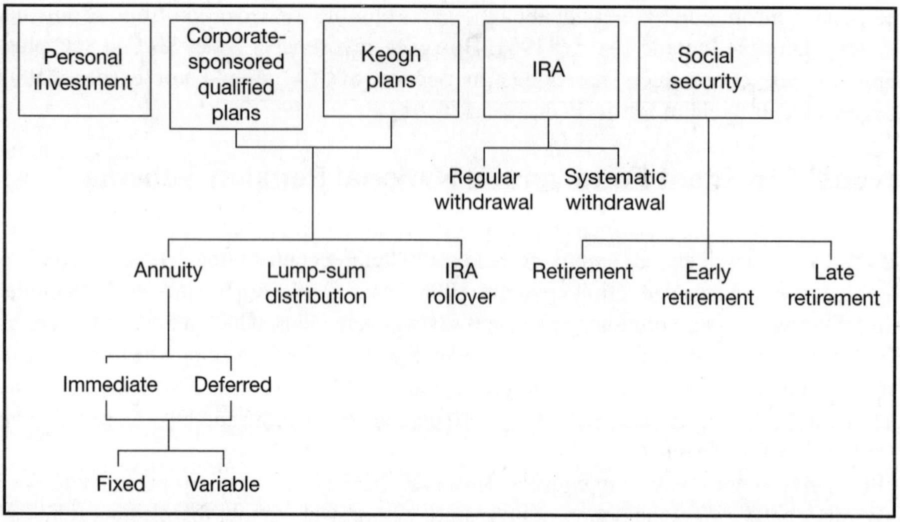

Figure 14.1 *Major Sources of Retirement Income*

Note: Some plans are available only in the U.S. These are included simply to emphasize that retirement may depend on many sources.

rest of the choices will be discussed in this section. Also, since there is little difference between corporate-sponsored plans and NPS plans insofar as distribution of retirement income is concerned, no distinction will be made between them.

Company-sponsored Plan and Insurance Plan

There are three principal ways in which an individual can withdraw retirement money: an annuity, lump sum distribution, or a rollover. At stake is the bulk of the retirement wealth. Furthermore, since the choices open to the retiree are almost always irrevocable, and the outcomes of the distribution decisions are vastly different, great care should be exercised in making this important decision. We will now discuss in detail each of the three key distribution choices available to a retiree.

Annuity

The Annuity Principle

Life insurance enables an individual to purchase a contract providing a definite sum of money at the time of death. Such contracts are possible because the mortality of a large group of individuals can be predicted with reasonable accuracy.

A different problem, however, faces the individual who has accumulated a sum of money and wants to determine how much can be safely spent each year during lifetime so that he or she will not run out of money. If the money is spent too rapidly, some day the funds will be exhausted—possibly with several years of life remaining. In contrast, if the funds are disbursed too slowly, at the time of death a portion of the funds will be left, money that could have been used to maintain a higher standard of living.

Confronted with this problem, no one person can be certain as to what sum can be *safely* spent each month. However, this uncertainty does not apply to a large group. Through the use of mortality tables, in return for the payment of a lump sum or a series of payments, insurance companies can make *guaranteed life-income payments* to various individuals, because the mortality rates of each group can be predicted with reasonable accuracy. Put differently, the greater total sums paid to those who live to unusually

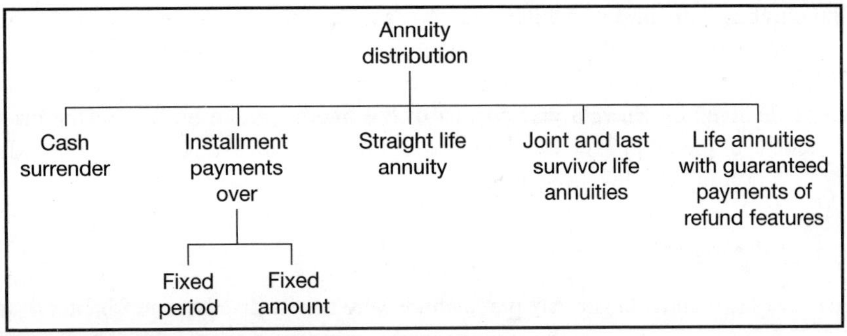

Figure 14.2 *Forms of Annuities*

advanced ages can be balanced by the smaller payments made to those who die relatively early. Such payments are called annuities.

The word *annuity* implies payments made by an insurance company at fixed intervals, such as monthly, quarterly, or yearly. When a life insurance policy is purchased, payments are made to the insurance company during a policyholder's lifetime, and the company pays a stipulated amount when the policyholder dies. With an annuity, an individual pays a given sum to the insurance company and in return receives an income according to various options (discussed later). An annuity contract, therefore, is essentially the reverse of a life insurance policy, although it is *not* an insurance policy.

Under the classic, or original, type of annuity, the income ceases with the death of the annuitant, and the insurance company is under no further obligation. Fortunately, many important variations of the original type are available in the marketplace today, as revealed in Figure 14.2. This figure reveals that annuity contracts vary according to how the payment for the annuity is made, how the proceeds are distributed, how earnings accrue, and when the benefits are received by the annuitant or beneficiary. Of these features, the disposition of proceeds is of special interest for an individual planning to retire.

It might be interesting to think of an annuity as a *liquidating* retirement payment plan, illustrated in Figure 14.3. Assume Shweta Sharma retires at the age of 60 with an after-tax lump sum distribution of

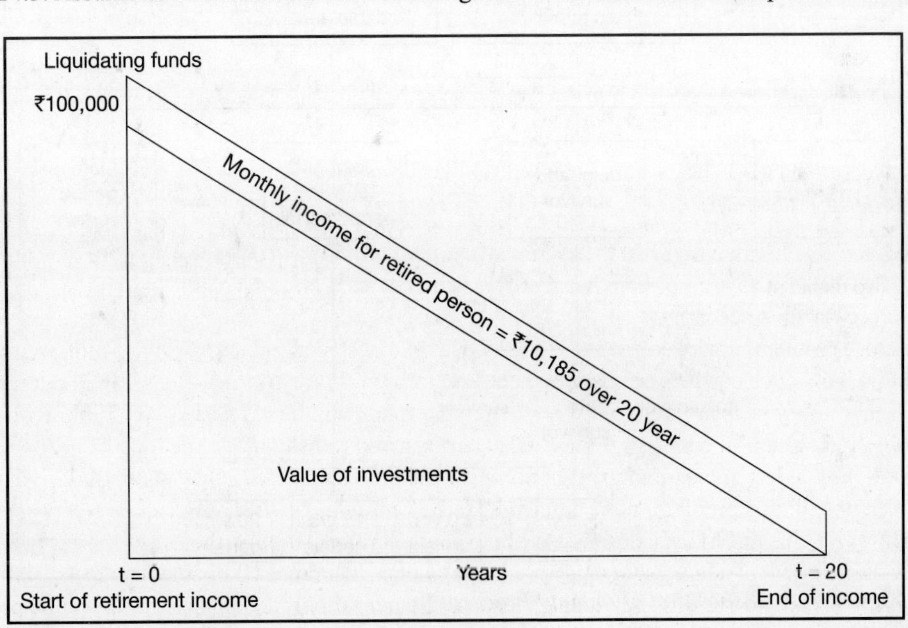

Figure 14.3 *Liquidating Retirement Payout Plan*

₹100,000. She purchases an annuity which guarantees an income for 20 years (20-year fixed period). During this 20-year period, in addition to receiving her principal of ₹100,000, Shweta will receive an additional ₹10,185 representing the return on the principal in the form of interest. Put differently, the monthly income received by Shweta will consist of the interest and a portion of the original investment. Consequently, at the end of the 20-year period, the entire investment will be liquidated and the company will owe nothing to Shweta Sharma.

Disposition of Proceeds

Various options available under an annuity plan, which were briefly discussed in Chapter 4, are presented in Figure 14.4. This figure reveals that the annuity can be either *fixed* or *variable*. The former refers to an annuity contract which promises a fixed return during the life of the contract and is, therefore, not dependent upon the results of the vehicle in which the money is invested. However, typically the payment is fixed on an annual basis (with a minimum guarantee of 2–4 percent) so that the fixed payment does not vary from year to year. In contrast, a variable annuity is a form of contract that is invested in one or several mutual fund portfolios. In this case, payments can vary in size, depending upon the rate of return on the portfolios selected. In both cases, the options available to the annuitant are identical, although generally the amount of the annuity payments will vary—sometimes greatly—between the two methods of payment. We will now discuss the key choices available to an annuitant.

1. ***Life-only option.*** It pays for the annuitant's lifetime and pays nothing to the surviving spouse or other heirs.
2. ***Joint and survivor option.*** It pays a reduced amount to the annuitant during his or her lifetime and then continues 100 percent or 50 percent of the original payment over the remaining lifetime of the

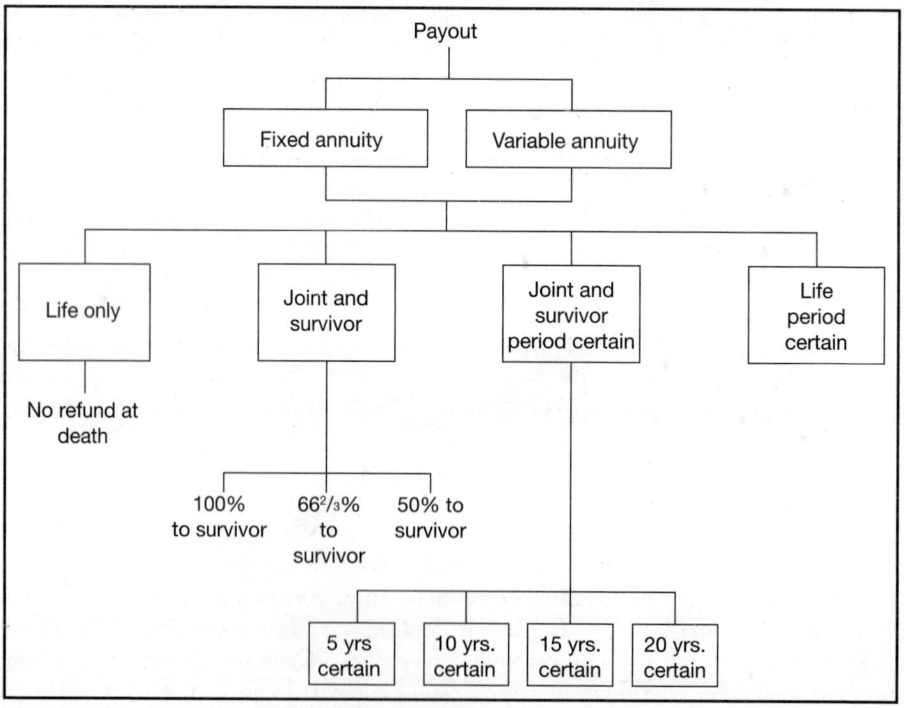

Figure 14.4 *Disposition of Annuity Proceeds*

Table 14.5 *Calculation of the Excludible Portion of Each Payment*

Age on Annuity Starting Date	Number of Anticipated Payments
Not more than 55	360
More than 55 but not more than 60	310
More than 60 but not more than 65	260
More than 65 but not more than 70	210
More than 70	160

surviving joint annuitant. Payments stop after the death of the annuitant *and* the joint annuitant, and the company owes nothing to the beneficiaries.

3. ***Joint and survivor annuity option.*** It pays 100 percent of the annuity payable to spouse during his or her lifetime on death of the annuitant. Pension is paid till the life assured is alive. On the death of the life insured, 100 percent of the pension continues to be payable to spouse as long as the spouse is alive. Incidentally, annuity payments might be made on a monthly, quarterly, semi-annual or annual basis. There is an incentive for the annuitant to purchase an annuity of ₹150,000 or more.
4. ***Payment option.*** Annuity may be paid monthly, quarterly, half-yearly, or yearly. There is an incentive for purchase of ₹150,000 of annuity or more.

Tax Treatment of Annuity Payments

Each annuity payment represents a combination of the return of principal and interest on the principal. Since the principal has not been taxed, it is taxed when the payment is received. In the event that after-tax contributions had been made to the qualified plan, Table 14.5 illustrates that the excludible portion of each payment is calculated as a recovery of the after-tax portion by dividing the cost basis by the number of anticipated payments.

Variable Annuity

Under the variable form of annuity payments, the monthly payments are made from a variable account which fluctuates on the basis of investment results. As such, the expected return cannot be accurately determined in advance. Therefore, it is assumed that the expected return is equal to the investment in the contract. The excludable portion of each payment is calculated by dividing the investment in the contract by the anticipated number of months times the monthly payout. Assume the monthly payout of a five-year variable annuity is ₹990.02 and the initial lump sum payment is ₹50,000. In this case, the ₹50,000 investment would be divided by the five years of payout (₹50,000/[₹990.02 × 12 × 5] = 84.17 percent), and 84.2 percent of each monthly payment of ₹990.02, or ₹833.30 would be excluded from gross income. Essentially, the tax treatment is the same for both fixed and variable annuities.

The Best Choice

Clearly, the best choice of an annuity option depends upon the objective of the annuitant and the total amount of retirement income expected to be received from other sources. Individuals who wish to receive a guaranteed income for life to supplement pension and other investment income should choose either the life-only or the joint and survivor option, possibly with a minimum period of guarantee of 10 years. However, those who have other sources of income and wish to use up the lump sum in a relatively short period of time may choose a guaranteed income for, say, 5 or 10 years.

Finally, if the retiree can assume the market risk, a variable annuity should be considered, because there is a potential for growth in this type of annuity.

Lump Sum Distribution

An Overview

One of the valuable options available to most retirees is to receive the nest egg in one lump sum instead of as an annuity. If a decision is made to receive the lump sum, then the retiree comes to the second crossroad: whether to pay the tax on the lump sum right away or to postpone the tax by rolling over the money into other investment instruments. Though there is no tax on the lump sum amount received from pension funds, income on the same is taxable. So if the latter decision is made, the money must be directly transferred or rolled over into to other investments and the employee must resort to a rather sophisticated tax planning strategy, as described next.

Rollover

The third distribution option is to directly transfer the funds or roll over the funds to a Senior Citizen Savings Scheme (SCSS) or other investments options after receiving the lump sum distribution. Individuals older than 60 years or those who are above 55 but less than 60 and have retired under a voluntary retirement scheme can invest in the scheme. A person can open more than one SCSS account, but the total investment cannot exceed ₹1,500,000. The tenure of the scheme is five years, extendable for three years. The interest is paid quarterly and is clubbed with income for taxation. If the total income is less than the income tax threshold of ₹250,000, an individual can avoid paying tax by submitting Form 15H. Retiree can also invest in post office term deposit (POTD), monthly income plans (fixed maturity plans [FMP]) in mutual funds, bank fixed deposits, etc. The advantage in choosing the option depends on the income and the saving of taxes.

ANNUITY, LUMP SUM OR ROLLOVER: A TAXING DECISION

The discussion undertaken in the previous section underscored an important point: To choose between an annuity, a lump sum distribution, a direct transfer, and a rollover is an income and taxing decision. There is no clear choice, and the best alternative depends on a variety of factors.

Systematic Withdrawal: Personal Investment

Let us take the case of Govind. At the age of 45, he started investing ₹2,000 at the beginning of every year into an PPF investment which grew at an annual rate of 8 percent. Now, 20 years later, the PPF investment has grown to ₹91,524 (set a calculator to the end mode, $n=20$, $i=8$, PV=0, PMT=2,000, and *solve for* FV). Now that Govind is retired he decides to start receiving ₹500 per month from his PPF investment. Also, since the long-term inflation rate is expected to be around 3 percent, Govind wants his initial monthly income of ₹500 to increase by 3 percent every year so that he could maintain the purchasing power of the monthly income at the current level. After some investigation, Govind has identified the ABC growth and income mutual fund which has consistently generated a long-term annual return of 8.5 percent. Satisfied with this record, Govind invests ₹91,524 into ABC stock mutual fund and simultaneously sets up a systematic withdrawal plan. Through this plan, Govind will achieve his retirement objective of receiving an inflation-adjusted monthly income of ₹500 (i.e., income increasing at three percent every year), and his PPF funds will hopefully last beyond Govind's 90th birthday.

PENSION ENHANCEMENT STRATEGY

We have learned that one of the distribution options of a retiree is to choose the joint and survivor annuity. This option continues to pay the spouse a stated percentage of the original monthly benefit (ranging from 50 to 100 percent) after the death of the annuitant. However, this option generates a lower monthly payment than the life-only option. An interesting alternative is to choose the life-only option and purchase an appropriate amount of permanent life insurance with the higher monthly payout. This strategy can duplicate the benefits of the joint and survival option.

An example should make this clear. Let us suppose Ashwin, aged 55, intends to retire at the age of 62. His wife, Asha, is aged 50. If upon Ashwin's retirement they select a joint and survival payout option that pays Asha 75 percent of their initial benefit at Ashwin's death, their annual retirement income while both are alive will be ₹26,671. If they select a life-only option their annual income will be ₹31,452—an increase of ₹4,781 per year.

We then estimate that ₹200,000 will replace Asha's survival pension benefit. This rounded-off figure is arrived at by taking 75 percent of the initial payout of ₹26,671, or ₹20,003, and capitalizing it at 10 percent (₹20,003/0.10). Ashwin and Asha could then compare the annual cost to purchase a ₹200,000 policy on Ashwin's life with the additional income received under the life-only pension option. If the annual cost of the policy is less than ₹4,781, the life-only option combined with the insurance purchase should be considered.

The pension enhancement plan presents an interesting retirement strategy. However, it does not provide a panacea for all annuity problems, since the outcome can change dramatically in other family situations.

FINANCIAL PLANNING FOLLOWING RETIREMENT

Retirement marks the end of an important chapter in life. It also signals the beginning of another chapter which requires careful planning around a whole set of new challenges. Currently, the once dependable interest on bank fixed deposits is no longer keeping pace with inflation. Tax rules applicable to various retirement investment options are complex and require professional advice. Aggressive use of retirement income might put the future retired life into jeopardy. An unwise or a hasty decision to invest a large sum representing provident fund distribution might spell disaster. Mixing of tax-exempt pension money with taxable income (rent, dividend, interest, and so on) might trigger unexpected tax consequences. The list goes on and on.

There is, of course, no one strategy that fits all retired families. Still, certain planning strategies fit nearly all newly retired individuals. These are listed as follows.

1. ***Beating inflation.*** A significant portion of the money received in the form of pension fund, provident fund, and other personal savings should be invested in products that are relatively safe and generate a positive inflation-adjusted return.

2. ***Current income.*** Since the normal employment income stops during retirement, it is desirable to place money in investment products that generate the desired (after-tax) monthly or quarterly income.

3. ***Medium-term investment products.*** After the need for immediate income is satisfied, retired individuals should concentrate on investing most of their surplus money in those products that mature in, say, three to five years.

4. ***Tax efficient products.*** For those who are forced into a higher income tax bracket because of their high income status, it is advisable to seek out investment products that are tax efficient. After all, the ultimate objective of investment planning is to optimize the after-tax return.

5. ***Equity exposure.*** Even risk-averse retirees should plan to invest a portion (10–25 percent) of retirement funds in equities, preferably through stock mutual funds. For one thing, it is hard to find an alternative product that can match the after-tax return on equities for the *long term*. For another, the risk exposure is considerably mitigated by holding stocks or stock mutual funds for the long run.
6. ***Other options.*** Other options for parking retirement money include: PPF and (for high income individuals) tax-free bonds.

EARLY RETIREMENT

Preparing for early retirement takes extensive time and planning. Not everyone, however, has such luxury. If an employer makes an early retirement offer, the employee may only have a few weeks to make the decision to accept or reject it. This is not as far-fetched as it may seem. Many companies have in recent years made such offers to their employees.

The early retirement question has two distinct dimensions: psychological and financial. Before accepting such an offer, or voluntarily deciding to retire early, one should frankly ask the following question: "Am I ready to retire?" If the answer is negative, or if there are lingering doubts, then the idea of early retirement should be abandoned.

Assuming that the psychological issue has been satisfactorily resolved, the financial dimension should be handled by undertaking a preliminary review of the following three key areas.

Pensions

The terms of pension payments should be explored. As a general rule, an early retirement offer should pay a pension equal to, or greater than, the amount that one would receive under normal retirement. In some cases, employers calculate the benefit by adding on three to five years to an employee's age or tenure. Both types of offers can increase the pension by as much as 30 percent over the expected normal pension income.

Health Insurance

The law requires employers with more than 20 employees to continue group health insurance coverage (excluding long-term care insurance) at the employee's expense (not to exceed 102 percent of the normal premium) for up to 18 months after normal termination or retirement, or up to 36 months for the surviving spouse of the employee, the divorced or legally separate spouse of the employee, or children who lost dependent status. It is important to determine the cost and availability (regarding the pre-existing conditions or the current health conditions) of buying individual health insurance after group coverage runs out. Generally, after the extension period, a conversion to an individual policy is available.

Life Insurance

An early retirement may require switching from a company's group life policy to an individual policy. The cost of such a policy may run around ₹400 a year per ₹10,000 of coverage. An employer may also offer a decreasing term policy; the benefit would shrink each year and virtually disappear at the age of 80. It is advisable to obtain documents from an employer to determine the specific provisions of the life insurance arrangements after retirement.

NONQUALIFIED DEFERRED COMPENSATION PLAN

Certain individuals can draw on payments from a nonqualified deferred compensation plan as an additional source of retirement income. This type of arrangement is nonqualified because the company chooses to benefit a selected group of employees without regard to the antidiscrimination rules of qualified plans. A deferred compensation plan is documented by an agreement between the company and the selected employee. The essence of the agreement is that the company promises to pay the employee for the currently performed services at some future date. This type of arrangement is attractive to highly compensated employees because considerable income tax savings could be realized by deferring the receipt of income to retirement years, when it might be taxed at lower rates.

Incidentally, deferred compensation can be tied to an insurance policy. If an employee dies before retirement, proceeds from the policy would be used by the company to pay the death benefit. If he or she reaches the retirement age, the company may wish to keep the policy in effect and make payments to the employee out of the accumulated cash value.

PLANNING FOR RETIREMENT: ADDITIONAL CONSIDERATIONS

Deferral of income taxes on retirement contributions and the earnings thereon is the major advantage of retirement plans. Accordingly, if the money is not needed for living or other expenses, receipt of retirement benefits should be deferred as long as possible. Also, because retirement distribution rules are complex, professional assistance may be necessary to achieve the best results.

Early Planning Needed

Anyone with a sizable retirement plan and/or tax benefits should begin planning early in order to maximize the value of those benefits. The early planning strategy should strive to avoid penalty taxes and take advantage of beneficial tax treatments. In some cases, the payment of current taxes using 10-year averaging or deferral of taxes on appreciation in employer stock may be appropriate. However, most individuals would achieve greater value by a tax-free rollover to another qualified plan, which would further defer taxation on the amount rolled over and permit additional tax-deferred earnings.

The distribution of rollover qualified account balances can be planned to maximize the total value received by an individual, his or her spouse, and their beneficiary. In general, this planning entails delaying the start of distributions and stretching them out as long as possible under the minimum distribution rules.

COMBO STRATEGY

Basic Structure

A creative strategy, called the Combo Strategy, exists in the area of retirement planning. This traditional strategy involving annuities provides a guaranteed income for life, but it suffers from three major drawbacks. First, the annuity is a fixed monthly payment, so that inflation erodes its purchasing power over time. Second, if death comes early, annuitants do not get their money's worth because annuity payments stop upon death. Third, annuities are designed to completely exhaust the capital at the completion of the annuity period, or in the case of a life time annuity, upon the death of the annuitant. Therefore, a better alternative is to use a Combo Strategy that uniquely combines the strengths of annuities and growth investments. This Strategy involves a six step process, as discussed next.

Step 1. Begin with an estimate of a client's monthly budget. The budget should include not only the client's fixed and flexible expenses but also an amount for emergencies and an allowance for "play money." Let us assume that the client's estimated monthly budget is ₹5,000.

Step 2. Call the appropriate government department to obtain the client's monthly pension income. It will vary from one family to another, depending upon the starting age, single or joint income, and so on. Assume the client's monthly EPF income will be ₹1,400.

Step 3. Instruct the client's employer to transfer the lump sum directly from the pension plan to a tax-deferred money-market mutual fund that can serve as a temporary shelter for the money until it is decided as to how to invest the funds. Requesting that the employer transfers the funds directly to a mutual fund, a trustee avoids the need to have 20 percent of the distribution amount withheld for taxes. Assume the lump sum due to the client is ₹1 million.

Step 4. Calculate the shortfall in budget by subtracting from the client's estimated budget expenses the Social Security income and any other guaranteed income (such as railroad or military pensions) that the client might have. Assuming no additional income, in this case the deficit is ₹3,600 (₹5,000 – ₹1,400).

Next, shop around for the highest monthly annuity income that the client can purchase from an insurance company that is rated at least A by two rating agencies. If shopping is done carefully, it might be possible to purchase a monthly annuity of ₹3,600 for, say, ₹600,000. That would leave the balance of ₹400,000 (₹1 million – ₹600,000) for growth investment.

Step 5. At this point, the assistance of an investment manager should be sought in setting up an investment portfolio that would be growth oriented and would carry the degree of risk acceptable to the client. This portfolio should coordinate the balance of the lump sum distribution with other retirement money, such as PPF, gratuity, and personal investment. If the portfolio is diversified by investing in national and international stocks, central government and corporate bonds, and liquid investments, and it is managed by a professional manager for a reasonable fee, then over a 5–15-year period the client might reasonably expect to earn an average annual return of 6–8 percent.

Step 6. The client should plan on withdrawing from this portfolio if and when funds are needed to keep up with inflation.

Concluding Remarks

The Combo Strategy just described is merely one of the many options available to a client. For instance, if the client does not need to receive a guaranteed monthly annuity income in order to be able to sleep well at night, the annuity route could be skipped altogether, and a financial counselor could start managing the investment portfolio so that the client could live off the income generated by that portfolio. That way the client can not only enjoy the desired standard of living but can also set the stage for a healthy growth of the estate that will eventually be passed on to the beneficiaries. It should be remembered, however, that the more the client is concerned about outliving the assets, the more he or she should lean toward purchasing a joint life annuity. Also, since the tax implications of annuity or lump sum distribution can be complex, it is always desirable to consult a tax attorney. In the final analysis, the retirement years cannot be enjoyable unless they are also free of financial worries.

In this chapter, we discussed retirement planning concepts and strategies. A discussion of estate planning will be undertaken in Chapter 15.

PART 7

ESTATE PLANNING

Chapter 15

Basic Structure of Estate Planning

15 Basic Structure of Estate Planning

INTRODUCTION[1]

As a general rule, the estate of a person consists of personal assets, real property, joint interests, qualified retirement plans, life insurance owned by the individual, life insurance policies gifted within three years of death, and any business interests. Upon death, the estate will pass by different means to other family members, friends, and designated entities. This estate can be likened to a funnel shown in Figure 15.1, through which all of the assets will pass. What emerges at the bottom of the funnel is the amount of the estate remaining to be distributed. The amount of property actually distributed can be significantly affected by the form of ownership and the means chosen by the decedent to effectuate the transfer.

The strategies developed for establishing various forms of ownership and legal titles are commonly referred to as *estate planning*. The objectives of estate planning include: (a) protecting the family, (b) providing for an efficient utilization of assets during lifetime, (c) ensuring that the estate property is adequate for family needs, (d) arranging for an orderly distribution of assets to the beneficiaries, and (e) taking steps to ensure that, upon death, the surviving family members would be able to obtain proper guidance and advice from trusted professionals.

UNAUTHORIZED PRACTICE OF LAW

The financial planners must avoid performing services for their clients that constitute an unauthorized practice of law. It is clear that the drafting of documents by someone other than an attorney is the unauthorized practice of law. The task for the planner, however, normally relates to the review of a will or a trust instrument and the advice rendered relative to the desirability of specific clauses. Generally, when a statute or legal interpretation applies to the specific situation, the planner should always take a conservative approach by consulting an attorney.

DEALING WITH DEATH: PSYCHOLOGICAL IMPLICATIONS

The estate planning process can help a client come to terms with the financial problems created by death. In many respects, the client must accept the fact that death is inevitable, and the estate planning process should begin *now*. A planner's role is to raise the issues associated with death and dying to help the client

[1] This chapter utilizes, with permission, the publication, *Wealth & Estate Planning: Indian & International Perspectives* by Nishith Desai Associates, August 2014. Available at http://www.nishithdesai.com/fileadmin/user_upload/pdfs/Research%20Papers/Wealth_Estate_Planning.pdf (last accessed on March 13, 2014). The firm advises Indian and international clients in wealth and estate planning matters. Those wishing to consult the firm should contact the firm at Nishith@nishithdesai.com

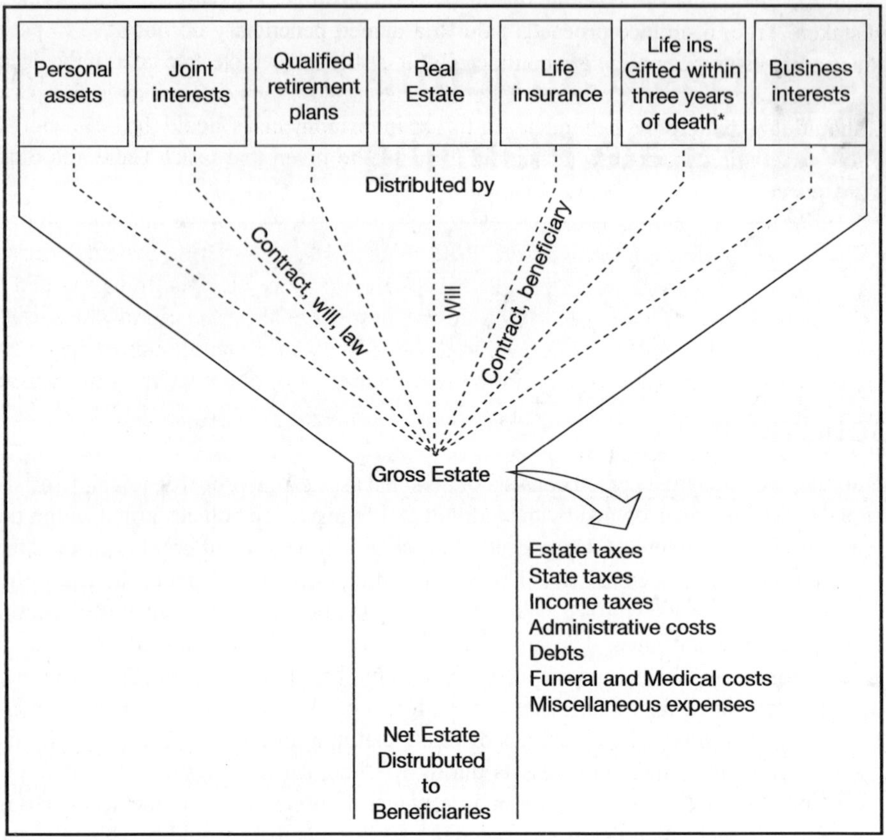

Figure 15.1 *Estate Distribution*

Note: *Title to the policy is, however, transferred outside the will.

come to personal realizations and conclusions. Reducing fear and anxiety about death can help the client fully enjoy the pleasures of life. A plan that structures the future and provides support for the survivors upon death can be psychologically satisfying to the client.

Section I: An Overview of Estate Planning

THE COMMON MISCONCEPTIONS

A popular myth that is widely prevalent is that estate planning makes sense only for wealthy people. That is simply not the case. In fact, even those people at lower financial levels need to plan for their estates. Besides, not every estate is as small as it might appear, since appreciated values of solely owned homes, stocks and bonds, life insurance proceeds, and the prorated portion of jointly held properties are included in every estate.

Those who believe that estate planning can be dispensed with if both husband and wife own everything jointly are also mistaken. In fact, when property is held by non-spouses as joint tenants with the rights of survivorship, upon the death of the first joint tenant the entire value of the joint property is included in the decedent's gross estate, unless the surviving joint tenant can prove that he or she contributed to the joint property. Property jointly owned by spouses is subject to federal estate tax at the surviving spouse's death.

Some people believe that purchasing life insurance constitutes a complete estate plan. They are grossly mistaken. True, insurance proceeds paid to a named beneficiary do not have to pass through probate, since a life insurance policy is a contract. But it is still subject to estate taxes if the deceased had incidents of ownership at the time of death. Choosing the right options on a policy is also part of estate planning. Should it be paid to the beneficiary in full or in installments? Should the beneficiary be solely responsible for managing the money, or should a trustee be given that task? These and other related questions are answered as part of estate planning.

Finally, a myth that never dies is that making a will completes the estate planning process. A will does not govern the distribution of all assets. Retirement and profit sharing benefits or assets transferred to a living trust, for example, are not subject to the manner of distribution provided for in the will. The fact is that a will documents an individual's wishes relating to certain assets, but by itself it is not an estate plan. The will does not cover all the aspects of estate planning, since some of the assets may pass outside the will or may not be coordinated with the transfer of other assets to the beneficiaries.

OBJECTIVES OF ESTATE PLANNING

The primary objective of a comprehensive estate plan is to make sure that the maximum value reaches the intended beneficiaries in a manner directed by the deceased. In order to accomplish this goal, it is necessary to carefully consider the impact of estate and transfer taxes so as to legally minimize the impact of current estate tax laws. Although, the Estate Duty Act, 1953, which provided for the payment of tax on transfer of assets consequent upon the death of the owner was abolished in 1985, provisions related to clubbing of income ensure that income tax continues to influence estate planning. The planning process can be both cumbersome and technical. It is, therefore, advisable to seek the help of a practicing estate planning attorney or a financial planner specializing in estate planning.

TOOLS OF ESTATE PLANNING

The word *estate* refers to everything solely or jointly owned by a living person. An effective estate plan lays the foundation for an orderly transfer of an estate upon death in accordance with the wishes of the deceased.

A person's estate comprises two types of property: one type passes through probate (probate estate), and the other type passes outside the probate estate. The former type consists of assets owned outright by a person. These assets can be disposed of by the person as desired. The latter type of assets includes, but is not limited to, life insurance policies, jointly owned property, retirement benefits payable to designated beneficiaries, and assets transferred to an inter vivos trust, commonly called a *living trust*, which designates how the property is to be treated upon death. Incidentally, those properties that pass outside probate could still be subject to federal estate tax.

The following are four basic tools of estate planning:

1. The will.
2. Joint ownership.
3. Trusts.
4. Lifetime gifts.

In addition, when creating an estate plan, a skillful estate lawyer can create other documents designed to save thousands of tax rupees and make the estate plan more efficient. For instance, there are a number of ways to avoid the payment of estate taxes at the time of the clubbing of income.

At this point, it is useful to make a distinction between estate planning practices in the USA and India. These practices are highly developed in the USA and financial planners should be well versed with them. Essentials of these practices can be found in the American version of our textbook.[2] However, since estate planning in India is still in its infancy, for practical reasons we will present here only those elements of estate planning that are currently pertinent for India. For material relevant to India, we have heavily relied on a well-researched publication of Nishith Desai Associates.[3]

Section II: Indian Law on Wills and Probate[4]

INTRODUCTION

If an individual desires to leave his property to certain persons/relations, he or she can do so by means of a will. A will gives effect to the wishes of the individual on his death, once the will is proved in a court of law in accordance with law.

If a person dies without leaving a will (i.e., intestate), this triggers rules under the laws of intestate succession under which the deceased's properties pass to relations specified under the laws. However, these default rules will not apply[5] with respect to the property bequeathed under a valid will.

A will has been defined under the Indian Succession Act, 1925 (ISA), as "the legal declaration of the intention of the testator, with respect to his property, which he desires to be carried into effect after his death." In other words, a will or a testament means a document made by a person whereby he or she disposes of his or her property (such individual is called a testator), but the disposal comes into effect only after his or her death. Persons to whom property is bequeathed under a will are called legatees.

In India, the law governing substantive rights in relation to wills is tied to the religion of the individual. Therefore, the respective personal law will apply based on the religion of the testator. Personal laws may be wholly codified (i.e., enacted into statutory law) or partly codified and partly customary. However, for wills made by Christians, Parsis, persons married under the Special Marriage Act, 1954, or under the Foreign Marriage Act, 1969, the provisions of the ISA 1925 will apply. Testamentary succession in respect of moveable properties is governed by the law of the domicile of the owner, while succession to immovable properties is governed by the law where the immovable property is situated.

Procedural aspects (such as probate) are governed by provisions of the ISA 1925 (with some exceptions in case of Muslims). We discuss below certain threshold considerations for drafting a will followed by the process governing probate and letters of administration (LoA).

WHO CAN MAKE A WILL?

Every individual who is major, of sound mind and with free consent, is capable of making a will. Under the Indian Majority Act, 1875, majority is attained at the age of 18 years (21 years, if a guardian is appointed by the court). Under Muslim personal law, majority is attained at the age of 15 years but the provisions of the Indian Majority Act will apply for the purpose of legal capacity to make a will.

Sound mind refers to such a mind and memory that would enable a person to understand the elements of which the will is composed and the disposition of his property in simple forms.[6] Courts have

[2] *Practicing Financial Planning for Professionals*, 11th Edition, by Sid Mittra, Anandi P. Sahu, and Harry Starn, Jr.

[3] See note 1.

[4] Starting with this section, the chapter utilizes the material from the publication, *Wealth & Estate Planning: Indian & International Perspectives*. See note 1.

[5] An exception to this principle is forced heirship. Forced heirship refers to laws which specify a share of property that mandatorily must pass on the deceased's heirs and cannot be disposed by free will of an individual.

[6] *Banks v. Goodfellow* 180 LR 5 QB 549, in *The Indian Succession Act*, ed. Subramani and Kannan, 9th edition (Lexisnexis Butterworths, New Delhi, 1995).

considered factors such as the history of mental illness, the testimony of medical witness, relations with family members, and the state of sobriety in determining whether a person could be said to be of sound mind. An ordinarily insane person can make a will during an interval in which he or she is of sound mind. A will made with fraud, coercion, or importunity is void.

WHO CAN INHERIT PROPERTY UNDER A WILL?

Under Muslim personal law, any person who is capable of holding property may be made a legatee. A bequest may be made for the benefit of an institution or for a charitable object. A bequest in favor of an unborn person is void, but if the child is born within six months (Sunni law) or 10 months (Shia law) of the date of making the will, then the bequest is valid.

For non-Muslim testators, a will can be made in favor of a person or a class of persons. It cannot be made in favor of an unborn (i.e., not born at the date of testator's death), subject to certain exceptions. A bequest in which the vesting of the property is delayed beyond the lifetime of one or more persons is not valid. However, charitable bequests are an exception to this rule.

WHAT PROPERTY MAY BE DISPOSED OF?

A Hindu may dispose of any property by will or other testamentary disposition (including his or her share in undivided coparcenary property), which is capable of being disposed of by him or her. Muslim law has forced heirship rules under which Muslims are permitted to dispose only one-third of their estate under a will. However, more than one-third may be bequeathed if all heirs agree to such disposal either before the testator's death (under Shia law) or after the testator's death (under Sunni and Shia law). Sharia compliant trusts may be used to sidestep the limitation on testamentary disposition unless the settlement is made in anticipation of death. India does not have forced heirship rules except under customary Muslim law and under Goan community law.

Regardless of the religion of the deceased, the Portuguese Civil Code of 1860 applies to the residents of Goa, which provides for forced heirship and community property. 50 percent of the intestate's estate devolves to the spouse automatically on death, while the other 50 percent devolves upon legal heirs. The rule of forced heirship in the Portuguese Civil Code is as follows:

1. Spouse only (one-half of the estate).
2. Descendants and spouse (two-thirds).
3. Descendants only (one-half or two-thirds, depending on the number of descendants).
4. Ascendants and spouse (two-thirds).
5. Parents only (one-half).
6. Other ascendants only (one-third).

The remainder is freely disposable.

WHAT ARE THE FORMALITIES FOR MAKING A WILL?

Formalities for making a will depend on the religion of the testator. Wills made by persons of all religions including those who marry under the Special Marriage Act, 1954 (except Muslims who marry under a customary law), must meet the conditions below:

1. The will must be in writing made by a person who is a major, of sound mind, and with free consent
2. The will must be signed by the testator or by some other person in the testator's presence and at his or her direction.

3. The will must be attested by two or more persons.
4. The document must be a declaration of intent of the testator with respect to his or her property.
5. The document must specify that his or her intent should be carried out after his or her death.
6. There must be a disposition of property under the document. The will should clearly set out the properties intended to be transferred and should also set out that the document has been executed without coercion or undue influence. Case law has held that where one of the natural heirs is to be disinherited, the testator must set out clear reasons as to why he or she wishes to disinherit the individual.

A will must be dated; otherwise proof of the day on which the will was executed is to be given at the time when the petition for probate is filed. Registration of a will is optional and no adverse inference can be drawn against the will in case of non-registration.

Registration of a will is optional under the provisions of the Indian Registration Act and no adverse inference can be drawn against the will in case of non-registration.[7]

PROCEDURAL ASPECTS

When a person dies, there must be somebody to deal with/administer the estate of the deceased, for example, sell property, collect debts, repay debts, and close bank accounts. Estate and succession laws provide for administrative procedures so that actions taken in relation to the matters of an individual after his or her death are legally effective. Legal systems broadly divide estate administration procedures into two situations:

1. Where a person has died leaving a will.
2. Where a person has died without leaving a will, that is, intestate.

A person named in the will to administer the estate is called an executor(s). An executor derives the authority to act from the will but this authority must be confirmed by a legal procedure called probate which establishes the genuineness of the will. Where a person has died intestate, the court (on an application by an interested party) appoints a person called the administrator. An administrator is also appointed (upon application) where the will is invalid or an executor is not named in the will or the executor is unable or unwilling to act. Unlike an executor, an administrator's authority to administer the estate is both conferred by and confirmed under the court-issued document called LoA. Executors or administrators are called personal representatives of the deceased. A third document important for estate administration is called the succession certificate and has limited application.

It approximately takes about 8–10 months to obtain a grant of probate from the court if it is uncontested or between six and nine years if it is contested. The time limit also depends on whether the matter is before the district court or the High Court. The process for obtaining an LoA or a succession certificate is estimated to take between six and nine months if it is uncontested. If it is contested, the number and location of other parties will also have to be considered. The process may then extend to between two and five years (or even more).

PROBATE

Probate is mandatory where the testator is a Hindu, Sikh, Jain, Buddhist, or Parsi and the will is: (a) executed in certain specified territories or (b) is executed outside those territories but relates to immovable property located within such territories. These territories are the cities of Calcutta, Chennai, and

[7] *MSP Rajesh v. MSP Raja* (1994) 1 Mad LJ 216.

Mumbai. Probate is not mandatory where the testator is a Muslim or Indian Christian even if conditions (a) and (b) stated above are satisfied.

Probate is essential because no right as an executor or legatee can be established in any court unless the relevant court has granted probate of the will under which the right is claimed.[8] However, a person who sets up a will which does not mandatorily have to be probated (as per the conditions above) can establish his right without obtaining a probate. In such a case, obtaining of probate is optional. But if a person applies for a grant of probate, then the court must determine the genuineness of the will. It cannot refuse to grant probate only on the ground that the will does not fall within the categories of wills that require to be mandatorily probated.[9]

To Whom Can a Probate Be Granted?

Probate can only be granted to an executor appointed by will either expressly or by implication. When there is more than one executor, probate must be granted to all those persons who have applied, unless those who do not apply renounce their right as an executor. Probate will not be granted to minors, persons of unsound mind, or to any association of individuals unless it is a company, which satisfies the rules prescribed by the state government to be an executor.

To obtain a grant of probate, the following procedure is prescribed but there may be some variations depending on the rules of the particular court which has jurisdiction over the matter.

Procedure to Apply for a Probate

An application/petition for probate must be filed in the court along with the original will in question. The application should be made before the district judge (or High Court depending on the property value and also on whether the High Court has original jurisdiction for testamentary matters) in whose jurisdiction the testator at the time of his death had fixed abode or had some property situated.

The application should contain the following facts:

1. The time of the testator's death.
2. A declaration that the will attached is the last will and testament.
3. A statement that the will was duly executed.
4. The value of assets which are likely to be inherited.
5. Title deeds pertaining to the immovable property mentioned in the will, if any.
6. Documents pertaining to movable property in the will, if any.
7. A statement that the executor making the application is named in the will.

On receipt of the application, the court issues notices to the next of kin of the deceased to file their objections, if any, to the grant of probate. A general public notice is also given in a newspaper. The executor is thereafter asked to establish the proof (a) of the death of the testator, (b) that the will has been validly executed by the testator, and (c) that the will is the last will and testament of the deceased. Proof of death is usually shown by submission of the original death certificate.

In order to assess whether the will has been validly executed and is a genuine document, it must be shown that the will was signed by the testator and that he or she had put his or her signatures to the testament of his or her own free will, that he or she was at the relevant time in a sound disposing state of mind and understood the nature and effect of the dispositions, and that the testator had signed it in the presence of two witnesses who attested it in his or her presence and in the presence of each other.[10]

[8] *Bhaiyaji v. Jageshwar Dayal Bajpai*, AIR 1978 All 268 and *Bhaiyalal v. Kashi Bai*, 2001(1)MPLJ429.

[9] *Vidhayaram v. Devlal*, MP High Court, 1981 JLJ 203.

[10] *Daulat Ram and Ors. v. Sodha and Ors.* (2005)1SCC40.

There may, however, be cases in which the execution of the will may be surrounded by suspicious circumstances. In such cases, the court would see that all legitimate suspicions are completely removed before the document is accepted as the last will of the testator. Case law[11] has identified some of these circumstances:

1. The alleged signature of the testator may be very shaky and doubtful, and evidence in support of the argument that the signature is of the testator himself or herself may not remove the doubt created by its appearance.
2. The condition of the testator's mind may appear to be very feeble and debilitated, and evidence adduced may not succeed in removing the legitimate doubt as to the mental capacity of the testator.
3. The dispositions made in the will may appear to be unnatural, improbable, or unfair in the light of the relevant circumstances.
4. The will may otherwise indicate that the dispositions may not be the result of the testator's free will and mind.

Revocation of a Probate

A person who is adversely affected by the grant of a probate has a right to avoid the grant by making an application to the court to revoke the probate. Probate once granted can be revoked by the court which has the jurisdiction to grant the probate. The grant of probate can be revoked or annulled for just cause. A just cause shall be deemed to exist where:

1. The proceedings to obtain the grant were defective in substance.
2. The grant was obtained fraudulently by making a false suggestion or by concealing from the court something material to the case.
3. The grant was obtained by means of an untrue allegation of a fact essential in point of law to justify the grant, though such allegation was made in ignorance or inadvertently.
4. The grant has become useless and inoperative through circumstances.
5. The person to whom the grant was made has willfully and without reasonable cause omitted to exhibit an inventory or account, or has exhibited an inventory or account which is untrue in a material respect.

PRACTICAL ISSUES TO KEEP IN MIND

An executor must within six months of the grant of probate or letter of administration exhibit inventory and accounts relating to and containing the full and true estimate of all the property in possession and all the credits related to it and also all debts that are owed to the executor in his or her character. The accounts exhibited must show the assets that have come under the executor's hands and must also depict the manner in which they have been applied or disposed of.

Keeping in mind the compliances that must be adhered to by an executor, it would be advisable if the executor was an Indian resident.

Probate being a court process at times requires the deposit of a portion of the property with the court. For this reason, individuals avail the remedy of creating a trust structure prior to their deaths in order to reduce the hassles relating to administration upon death and execution of the testament.

However, there is stamp duty cost for setting up a trust[12] and at times setting up a trust is not recommended especially when immovable property is involved. The income that is generated from a trust that

[11] *Surendra Pal and Ors. v. Dr (Mrs) Saraswati Arora and Anr.* (1975)1SCR687; *Smt. Guro v. Atma Singh and Ors* (1992)2SCR30; *Meenakshiammal (Dead) Through and Ors. v. Chandrasekaran and Anr.* AIR2005SC52.

[12] Article 64 of Schedule I of Indian Stamp Act, 1899.

is set up for charitable purpose is exempted from the computation of income tax from the total income of the person in receipt of such income,[13] and such a trust may be created through a testamentary disposition.

However, when the income from the property held under a trust is for (a) private religious purposes, which does not ensure the benefit of the public; (b) if the trust or institution has been created or established for the benefit of any particular religious community or caste; (c) if any part of the income ensures or any part of such income or any property of the trust or institution is used directly or indirectly for the benefit of any person, then such exclusion from computation of income does not apply[14] and, thus, the creation of a trust may not always be the best way to avoid administrative hassles.

LETTERS OF ADMINISTRATION

Where an individual governed by the ISA dies intestate, a person must be appointed to administer his or her estate. A person who has an interest in the property of the deceased must apply to the relevant court for the grant of LoA. The court would examine documents to determine the relationship between an applicant and the assets of the deceased. A grant of an LoA establishes the administrator as the legal representative of the deceased and does not decide any question of title, but it only decides the right to administer.

However, the above provisions are not mandatory where the deceased intestate is a Hindu. For such cases, the ISA contains an enabling provision providing for the grant of an LoA. In such a case, the applicant for an LoA may be a person who would be entitled to the whole or any part of the deceased's estate according to the rules applicable to the distribution of the deceased's estate. In the event there are other persons who also apply for an LoA. It is the court's discretion to grant the LoA to any one or more of the applicants. If no such person applies for an LoA, it may be granted to a creditor of the deceased (if those persons primarily entitled did not respond after notices/advertisements were issued).

Procedure to Apply for an Letters of Administration

A petition must be filed before the relevant court (depending on the value of the estate) in the format prescribed for such a petition. The relevant court is the court within whose jurisdiction the deceased ordinarily resided at the time of his or her death or within whose jurisdiction any part of the property of the deceased may be found.

The petition must state particulars about the deceased, his or her time of death, the petitioner's right to claim, and a statement of the value and location of assets. The petition must also state that to the best of the petitioner's belief no application has been made to any other court for LoA of the same estate or where such application has been made, the person has no knowledge of the persons by whom it was made and the proceedings thereon, if any.

The court would issue a public notice or place an advertisement in newspapers (in English and the local language, for a period of about 30–45 days) to which a person may respond if he or she has any objection to the grant of the LoA to the applicant. The court may refuse the grant of an LoA for any of the following reasons:

1. The applicant is not the right person to the grant.
2. The deceased had no property to which grant could be given.

[13] Section 11 of ITA, 1961.

[14] Section 13 of ITA, 1961.

3. The deceased did not reside or did not have property in the court's jurisdiction.
4. The estate has been fully administered and grant of an LoA will be nugatory.

Therefore, it would be advisable to support the petition with documents to address each of the possible grounds of opposition above. The applicant would be required to be present in person to be examined by the court.

If the LoA is granted to the petitioner, then he or she must furnish a bond to the court with one or more surety/sureties. The bond is to be given before the grant and not after. Any person above 18 years of age may act as surety. The bond is to be given for the amount as specified by the court for which a grant is received except where an insurance or other approved class of company is accepted as surety.

SUCCESSION CERTIFICATE

A succession certificate has limited effect. The certificate does not give any general powers of administration of the estate of the deceased. The certificate is limited to the collection of debts which were in existence at the lifetime of the deceased and enables the applicant to have shares transferred in his or her name if he or she is otherwise entitled to it.

Further, the grant of a certificate does not establish the title of the grantee as the heir of the deceased. It only confers on the grantee authority to collect debts and allows debtors to make payments to the grantee. That said, a succession certificate (together with the death certificate) is usually requested by authorities when a change in title records has to be carried out. Therefore, in terms of practical use, a succession certificate serves as a supporting document and would be a useful document to have. If the certificate granted is with respect to debt or securities for which previously an LoA has been granted and such grant is in force, the certificate granted after it shall be invalid.

Procedure to Apply for a Succession Certificate

A petitioner must file a petition before the relevant court (depending on the value of the estate) in the format prescribed for such a petition. The relevant court is the court within whose jurisdiction the deceased ordinarily resided at the time of his death, within whose jurisdiction any part of the property of the deceased may be found.

The petition must contain particulars such as the time of death of the deceased, ordinary residence of the deceased, right of the petitioner to claim, details of family and other relatives of the deceased, and debts and securities for which the certificate is being applied for.

Upon application, the judge may extend the certificate to any debt or security not specifically covered under the original application. The extension shall also cover any power to receive interest or dividends or negotiation of transfer. The judge may require additional bond or security to be furnished for such extension.

If the court is satisfied with the application it fixes a date of hearing of the application. The court would issue public notice or place an advertisement in newspapers (in English and the local language, for a period of about 30–45 days) to which a person may respond if he or she has any objection to the grant of certificate. If no one contests the petition, the applicant must lead evidence to support the relationship of the deceased and the applicant to the assets. After this examination, the court may order a succession certificate to be issued. If there is a person who raises any objection, an applicant will be given the opportunity to counteract the allegations of the person objecting. After the parties are examined, the court would then decide if the applicant has proved his or her case.

Section III: Trusts in India

HISTORICAL BACKDROP

Trusts originated at the end of the middle ages as a means of transferring wealth within the family and have remained the characteristic device employed for organizing intergenerational wealth transmission in situations where the transferor has substantial assets or complex family affairs.[15] Modern-day private trusts are used to carry out this function in India. Public trusts, on the other hand, may be used to contribute property toward religious and charitable purposes.

The first attempt to regulate the management and administration of trusts was made by the British Government in 1810 by passing a regulation, followed by many such regulations. Currently, the legislations governing trusts in India are, among others, The Indian Trusts Act, 1882 ("Trusts Act"), The Charitable and Religious Trusts Act, 1920, The Religious Endowments Act, 1863, The Charitable Endowments Act, 1890, and The Societies Registration Act, 1860.[16]

REASONS FOR SETTING UP A TRUST

The reasons that clarify why setting up a trust is important include:

1. Providing for family and protecting, in particular, the interests of very young children and adults with special needs.
2. Attaching certain conditions to gifts.
3. Bypassing the probate process while ensuring succession from one generation to another.
4. Giving children the benefits of family wealth without losing control over key assets.
5. Creating a single relatively large pool of investment funds, which has more scope to perform well than a series of smaller pools.
6. Creating a legal framework and a tax-effective structure for the family assets which will last for a long time.
7. Protecting these assets against actual and potential creditors.
8. Allowing administrative, investment, and record-keeping functions and possibly also property management functions to be centralized and handled more efficiently and at a lower cost.
9. Managing tax risks that may arise on the devolution of the trust property.

THE INDIAN TRUSTS ACT

Trusts in India are governed by the provisions of the Trusts Act, 1882. A trust as per the Trusts Act is "an obligation annexed to the ownership of property, and arising out of a confidence reposed in and accepted by the owner, or declared and accepted by him for the benefit of another, or of another and the owner."

The person who reposes or declares the confidence is called the "author of the trust" (commonly referred to as a "settlor"). The person who accepts the confidence is called the "trustee." The person for whose benefit the confidence is accepted is called the "beneficiary." The subject matter of the trust is called "trust property." The "beneficial interest" or "interest" of the beneficiary is the right against the

[15] John H. Langbein, "The Contractarian Basis of tire Law of Trusts," 105 YALE L.J 625. 632-43 (1995) cited in John H. Langbein, "Secret Life of the Trust: The Trust as an Instrument of Commerce," Available at http://www.law.yale.edu/documents/pdf/Faculty/Langbein_Secret_Life_of_Trust.pdf (last accessed on March 16, 2015).
[16] Indian Trusts Act, 1882, and Commentary by H.C. Johari.

trustee as the owner of the trust property. The instrument, if any, by which the trust is declared is called the "instrument of trust" (commonly known as the "trust deed" or "indenture of trust").

The property in case of a trust is not transferred directly to the transferee but is put in control of the trustee for the benefit of the transferee. Depending upon the nature of the trust, a trustee either transfers the property or its earnings to the transferee at the happening of certain events or applies the property and/or its gains for the benefit of such a transferee.

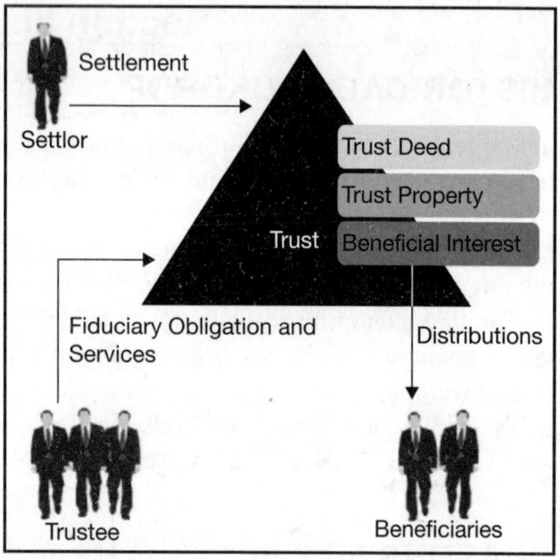

HOW TO CREATE A TRUST

Four essential conditions are necessary to bring into being a valid trust.[17]

1. A person who creates a trust (settlor) should make an unequivocal declaration of an intention on his or her part to create a trust. In order to create a trust, the settlor must properly manifest his or her intention by an external expression of it (by written or spoken words or by conduct) as opposed to an undisclosed intention.
2. The settlor must clearly define and specify the purpose. Since the purpose has to be accomplished by a trustee, who may not always be the author himself; it is necessary that the purpose is clearly declared so that the trustee can faithfully accomplish the author's purpose, for which the author has reposed confidence in the trustee.
3. The settlor must specify the beneficiaries. Where there is no transfer of ownership, there is no trust.[18] The settlor gives up the ownership of the property, thus, resulting in the transfer of legal ownership of the property to the trustee and transfer of beneficial ownership to the beneficiaries of the trust.

   The concept of ownership in the case of a trust is different under Indian and English laws. India does not recognize duality of ownership in the case of a trust, that is, it recognizes only legal ownership and not equitable ownership as is provided for under English law which recognizes the duality of ownership, that is, legal and equitable. Under the Indian law, the trustee is both the legal and beneficial owner of trust property.
4. The settlor must transfer identifiable property under an irrevocable arrangement and totally divest himself or herself of the ownership and the beneficial enjoyment of the income from the property.

TYPES OF TRUSTS

As discussed, trust may be private or public:

Private Trust

A private trust is created for the benefit of specific individuals, that is, individuals who are defined and ascertained individuals or who within a definite time can be definitely ascertained.

[17] Section 5 of Indian Trust Act, 1882.
[18] *Nadir Shaw v. Times of India*, AIR 1931 Bom 300.

A private trust does not work in perpetuity and essentially gets terminated at the expiry of the purpose of the trust or happening of an event or, at any rate, 18 years after the death of the last transferee living at the time of the creation of the trust.

Private trusts are governed by the Trusts Act. This Act is applicable to the whole of India except the State of Jammu and Kashmir and the Andaman and Nicobar Islands. That apart, the Trusts Act is not applicable to the following:

1. Waqf.
2. Property of a Hindu undivided family (HUF).
3. Public or private religious and charitable endowments.

A person can be a settlor of a private trust if he or she has attained majority (i.e., has completed 18 years of age or in case of a minor, for whom a guardian is appointed by the court or of whose property the superintendence has been assumed by the court of wards the age of majority is 21 years), is of sound mind, and is not disqualified by any law.

But a trust can also be created by or on behalf of a minor with the permission of a principal civil court of original jurisdiction. Apart from an individual, a company, firm, society, or association of persons is also capable of creating a trust.

A family trust set up to benefit the members of a family is the most common purpose for a private trust. The purpose of the family trust is for the settlor to progressively transfer his assets to the trust, so that legally the settlor owns no assets himself or herself, but through the trust, beneficiaries get the benefit of these assets. A family trust can be set up either while one is still alive (by a declaration of trust contained in a trust deed) or upon death, in terms of a will.

The Foreign Exchange Management Act, 1999 ("FEMA"), of India has granted general permission to a person resident in India to hold, own, transfer, or invest in foreign currency, foreign security, or any immovable property situated outside India if such "foreign currency assets" had been acquired, held, or owned by such a person when he or she was a resident outside India or when it is inherited from a person who was a resident outside India. Such a person may set up a trust in such jurisdiction or any other jurisdiction to which he or she could contribute the foreign currency assets.

However, a trust receiving foreign contribution in India would need approval under the Foreign Contributions Regulations Act 1976, which is administered by the Ministry of Home Affairs in India. However, such trust can only be a trust, the objects of which are dedicated to cultural, economic, educational, religious, or social purposes.

Family (private) trusts may be set up either *inter vivos* (i.e., during a person's lifetime) or under a will (i.e., testamentary trust) or either orally or under a written instrument; however, when the subject matter of the trust is an immovable property, the trust would need to be declared by a registered written instrument.

Private trusts may also be used as collective pooling vehicles for individual retail investors.

Mutual funds. All mutual funds in India are set up in the form of trusts which are registered under the Securities and Exchange Board of India (mutual fund) Regulations. Mutual funds are portfolios of stock market shares and other financial instruments built with funds collected from usually small investors whose primary concern is the security of investment. These funds are run by government trusts, banks, and now private financial institutions as well. These funds can be open ended or close ended.

Real estate investment trusts. A real estate investment trust (REIT) is an entity which pools in money and invests in real estate assets. It provides a similar structure for investment in real estate as mutual funds provide for investment in stocks. An REIT can be publicly or privately held and is generally listed on a stock exchange. Assets of such a trust are managed by a fund manager. Further to the 2014 Budget, REITs are eligible for a pass-through status for taxation purposes (although this is a partial pass-through). The consequence is that long-term capital gains on sale of units as well as dividends received by the

REIT and distributed to the investor shall be tax exempt. Interest income received by the REIT is tax exempt and foreign investors shall be subject to a low withholding tax of 5 percent on interest payouts.

A trust can be set up either as:

1. ***Revocable.*** A trust that can be revoked (canceled) by its settlor at any time during this life.
2. ***Irrevocable.*** A trust will not come to an end until the term/purpose of the trust has been fulfilled.
3. ***Discretionary.*** An arrangement where the trustee may choose, from time to time, who (if anyone) among the beneficiaries is to benefit from the trust and to what extent.
4. ***Determinate.*** The entitlement of the beneficiaries is fixed by the settlor at the time of settlement or by way of a formula, the trustees having little or no discretion.
5. ***Combination trusts.*** Namely (1)–(3)/(4), (2)–(3)/(4).

Public charitable or Religious trust. A public trust is created for the benefit of an uncertain and fluctuating body of persons who cannot be ascertained at any point of time, for instance: the public at large or a section of the public following a particular religion, profession, or faith. A public trust is normally permanent or at least indefinite in duration.

As regards public trusts, there is no central act governing the formation and administration of such trusts. But various states such as Bihar, Maharashtra, Madhya Pradesh, and Orissa have enacted their own legislations prescribing conditions and procedures for the administration of public trusts. These acts are more or less similar in nature though there may be certain variations.

A public trust is generally a nonprofit venture with charitable purposes and in such cases it is also referred to as the charitable trust.

A trust created for religious purposes is termed a religious trust and can be either a private or a public trust. A religious endowment made via trustees to a specified person is a private trust and the one to the general public or a section thereof is a public trust. The creation of religious charitable trusts is governed by relevant personal laws. The administration of these religious trusts can either be left to the trustees as per the dictates of the personal law or it can be regulated to a greater or lesser degree by statute such as the Maharashtra Public Trusts Act, 1950. In case of Hindus, the personal law provisions regulating religious trusts have not been codified and are found dispersed in various religious books.

There are four essential requirements for creating a valid religious or charitable trust under Hindu law, which are as follows:

1. Valid religious or charitable purpose of the trust as per the norms of Hindu law.
2. Capability of the author of the trust to create such a trust.
3. The purpose and property of the trust must be indicated with sufficient precision.
4. The trust must not violate any law of the country.

TAXATION OF TRUSTS

Income tax in India is governed by the Income Tax Act, 1961 ("ITA"), which lays down provisions with respect to chargeability to tax, determination of residence, computation of income, transfer pricing, etc. Residents are ordinarily subjected to tax on their worldwide income, whereas nonresidents are taxed only on their Indian source income, that is, income that accrues or arises to them in India.

Private Trust

For the purpose of Indian taxes, a private trust is not regarded as a separate taxable unit. However, a trustee under the ITA acquires the status of the beneficiaries and is taxed in the role of the beneficiaries in a representative capacity. The provisions relating to taxation of trusts are laid out in Sections 161–64 of the ITA.

Irrevocable determinate (specific) trust. In such a trust, the beneficiaries are identifiable and their shares are determinate, a trustee can be assessed as a representative assessee and tax is levied and recovered from him or her in a like manner and to the same extent as it would be leviable upon and recoverable from the person represented by him (i.e., the beneficiary). The tax authorities can alternatively raise an assessment on the beneficiaries directly, but in no case can tax be collected twice. While the income tax officer is free to levy tax either on the beneficiary or on a trustee in his or her capacity as a representative assessee, the taxation in the hands of a trustee must be in the same manner and to the same extent that it would have been levied on the beneficiary, that is, in the role of the beneficiaries. Thus, in a case where a trustee is assessed as a representative assessee, he or she would generally be able to avail all the benefits/deductions, etc. available to the beneficiary, with respect to that beneficiary's share of income. There is no further tax in the hands of the beneficiary on the distribution of income from a trust.

Irrevocable discretionary trust. A trust is regarded as a discretionary trust when a trustee has the power to distribute the income of a trust at its discretion amongst the set of beneficiaries.

In case of an onshore discretionary trust, with both resident and nonresident beneficiaries, a trustee will be regarded as the representative assessee of the beneficiaries and subject to tax at the maximum marginal rate, that is, 30 percent.

In case of an offshore discretionary trust with both resident and nonresident beneficiaries, a trustee should not be subject to Indian taxes or reporting obligations. However, if all the beneficiaries of such discretionary trust are Indian residents, then a trustee may be regarded as the representative assessee of the beneficiaries and can be subject to Indian taxes (on behalf of the beneficiaries) at the maximum marginal rate, that is, 30 percent.

In this regard, an offshore charitable organization can also be one of the beneficiaries to the offshore discretionary trust. As a matter of precaution, it would be preferable if the selected charitable organizations neither originated in India, nor were created to benefit Indian residents as a compulsory class, and were applied toward a cause which is not specific to India.

Revocable trust. Under the ITA, a transfer shall be deemed to be revocable if it contains any provision for the retransfer directly or indirectly of the whole or any part of the income or assets to the transferor or if it in any way gives the transferor a right to reassume power directly or indirectly over the whole or any part of the income or assets. Thus, where a settlement is made in a manner that a settlor is entitled to recover the contributions over a specified period, and is entitled to the income from the contributions, the trust is disregarded for the purposes of tax and the income thereof taxed as though it had directly arisen to the settlor. Alternatively, even in a situation where a settlor has the power to reassume power over the assets of a trust, the trust is disregarded and the income is taxed in the hands of the settlor. In the case of a revocable trust, income shall be chargeable to tax only in the hands of the settlor. If there are joint settlors to a revocable trust, the income of the trust will be taxed in the hands of each settlor to the extent of assets settled by them in the trust. This arrangement is not specifically required to be recorded in a trust deed.

Public Trusts

Subject to conditions, income from property held in trust or other legal obligations, for a religious or charitable purpose, is tax exempt.[19] "Chariable purpose" as defined in Section 2(15) of the ITA includes relief of the poor, education, medical relief, preservation of environment, monuments, places, or objects of artistic or historic interest, and the advancement of any other object of general public utility.

However, when the aggregate value of receipts is ₹25 lakh or more, the advancement of any other object of general public utility is not regarded as a charitable purpose if it involves the carrying on of any

[19] Section 11 of ITA.

activity in the nature of trade, commerce, or business—or any activity of rendering any service in relation to any trade, commerce, or business—for a cess or fee or any other consideration irrespective of the nature of use or application, or retention, of the income from such activity.[20]

Also, income of a revocable charitable or religious trust is chargeable to income tax in the hands of the settlor.[21] Income derived by such a trust from voluntary contributions, not being contributions made with a specific direction that it shall form part of the corpus of the trust or institution, is also tax exempt.[22]

The above-mentioned exemptions are allowed only to the trusts which are registered in accordance with the provisions given in the ITA.[23] The ITA also provides certain grounds on which the exemption to the income of such trusts is not allowed, for example, income from property held under a trust is for private religious purposes and not for the benefit of the public or in the case of a charitable trust established after the commencement of the ITA, any income thereof if the trust is established for the benefit of any particular religious community or caste, etc.[24]

Further, subject to the fulfillment of certain conditions, any income of an institution constituted as a public charitable trust or registered under the Societies Registration Act, 1860, or under any law corresponding to the ITA and existing solely for the development of khadi or village industries or both and not for the purposes of profit—to the extent such income is attributable to the business of production, sale, or marketing, of khadi or products of village industries—is not included in the total income of the trust.[25]

Section IV: Taxation Issues

ESTATE DUTY IN INDIA: REINTRODUCTION AND CONSEQUENCES

Background

Estate duty in India was introduced in 1953 under the Estate Duty Act, 1953 ("Act") with the object of imposing estate duty on property passing or deemed to pass on the death of a person. The Act provided for the imposition of estate duty at certain specified rates upon the ascertained principal value of the property owned by each deceased person, whether or not such property was settled, including upon any agricultural land situated in certain territories in India.

The levy started at a threshold of ₹1 lakh with a rate of 7.5 percent. The maximum rate was 40 percent of the principal value of the estate in excess of ₹20 lakh. However, certain exemptions exist, such as: (a) movable and immovable property owned and situated outside of India, (b) delay on the imposition of estate duty on property jointly owned by spouses until the death of both spouses, and (c) property held by the deceased as a trustee for another person where the deceased person had made a bona fide disposition to a beneficiary at least two years prior to the deceased person's death. Further, exemption was also given to one residential house, subject to a limit of ₹100,000.

Abolition of Estate Duty

Estate duty was abolished on June 16, 1985. The government cited excessive administrative costs as against the actual tax yields (only about 20 crore) as the primary reason for abolishing estate duty. Consequently, estate duty was not payable in respect of the estate of a person who died after March 16, 1985.

[20] Section 2(15) of ITA.
[21] Section 11 and 61 of ITA.
[22] Section 12 of ITA.
[23] Sections 12A and 12AA of ITA.
[24] Section 13 of ITA.
[25] Section 10(23B) of ITA.

At that time, the exemption limit was only ₹150,000 and the rate of estate duty was on a progressive basis, with a maximum rate of 85 percent for estate exceeding ₹2,000,000.

Present Position

It is pertinent to note that even though estate duty has been abolished, India continues to impose "wealth tax" at the rate of 1 percent in case the value of the "net wealth" (total value of assets minus total debt related to such assets) exceeds ₹3,000,000. However, productive assets are out of the purview of wealth tax.

Under the Direct Taxes Code Bill 2010, the wealth tax net is proposed to be spread wider, which arguably should achieve at least part of the objective behind the levy of an inheritance tax. Property passing to heirs on succession is subject to stamp duty and also probate/succession fees and tax thereon being collected not by the central government but by the state governments.

Justification for Reintroduction and Consequences

With the reintroduction of estate duty, the government expects to raise a considerable amount of revenue than when the earlier Act was in force because of the immense amount of wealth generated after the removal of India's License Raj in early 1990s. It also expects that by reintroducing estate duty, it will reduce income disparity (and, therefore, inequality) between two different generations and also between members of the same generation; consequently bridging the widening gap between the "possessed" and the "dispossessed."

Apart from the risk of India losing its momentum of investment generation (both domestic and foreign), the imposition of an estate tax in India will lead to a flight of capital (and along with it, entrepreneurs) to more tax-friendly jurisdictions offshore. Therefore, this move is unlikely to help the government achieve its objectives of greater revenue and economic equality. The objective driving the reintroduction of estate duty may not necessarily be revenue compulsions but the reduction of disparities, which is laudable. However, given India's dismal growth rate, this would be a difficult proposition.

The reintroduction of estate duty may actually impact philanthropy. What happens if estate duty is levied when a large part of the wealth is left for charity? Would that mean that a significantly lower amount would go to charity?

Net financial savings of households was only 7.8 percent of the gross domestic product (GDP) in 2011–12 as compared to the 12.2 percent in 2009–10. It may thus be worthwhile for policymakers to consider employing tax breaks to incentivize savings in financial assets. However, this problem is further compounded by increasing imports of gold, since Indian households seem to be wanting to hedge by buying gold against rapidly rising prices. An estate duty would mean a further disincentivization for investing in financial savings.

Concerns That the New Legislation Should Address

If estate duty is reintroduced, it should provide for appropriate exemptions for financial assets. Estate duty would clearly be a disincentive for investments in financial assets, the small quantum of which, in any case, is a worry for the government. One residential house should not fall within the ambit of estate duty, and the rate at which estate duty is applicable should also be reasonable.

If shares/financial assets are included within the ambit of estate duty, then it could cause serious upheavals in shareholding structures and the running of companies. Notably, the earlier Act did contemplate that assets could be sold to pay estate duty and, indeed, provided a set-off of capital gains against estate duty payments. The new legislation should aim to integrate estate duty, gift tax, and the concept of exit tax. The government should also carefully consider the time when estate duty should be reintroduced.

GIFT TAX IN INDIA

An Introduction to Notional Income

Taxation, as a general rule, is on the accrual/receipt of income. However, with the objective of taxing incomes that would otherwise go untaxed, taxing statutes have evolved the concept of "notional income." Notional income is a legal fiction by which the law deems/presumes certain kinds of income to have accrued to a taxpayer (as it could have potentially accrued) although there is no actual accrual of income.[26] The tax legislation in India uses this legal fiction to tax certain gifts.

History of Gift Tax in India

The Gift Tax Act was first introduced in 1958 and was subsequently repealed in 1998. Under the 1958 Act, gifts that were worth more than ₹25,000 were subject to tax. For the purpose of gift tax, cash, checks, and drafts received from someone who was not a blood relative were reckoned as gifts. The Finance Act (No. 2) 2004 introduced a tax on any sum of money exceeding ₹25,000 received without consideration under the head "income from other sources."

Income from Other Sources

The ITA, 1961, imposes tax under various heads, one of which is "income from other sources" provided for under Section 56. The Finance Act, 2009, introduced clause (vii) to Section 56(2) with a view to check avoidance of tax on transfer of assets without consideration which was in respect of taxation of individuals and HUF.

Money consideration. Under the ITA, where a sum of money exceeding ₹50,000 is received without consideration; the entire sum of money is liable to tax in the hands of the recipient as income from other sources.

Immovable property. In respect of immovable property, where an individual or HUF receives immovable property (having a stamp duty value exceeding ₹50,000) without consideration, the recipient would be taxed on the stamp duty value of the immovable property. The position in respect of immovable property was revised by the Finance Act, 2013. As per the revised law, any immovable property that is received for a consideration that is less than the stamp duty value of the immovable property by an amount exceeding ₹50,000, the difference between the stamp duty value and the consideration would be taxed in the hands of the recipient.

Moveable property. Similar rules are applicable to moveable property. Where an individual or HUF receives moveable property whose aggregate fair market value ("FMV") exceeds ₹50,000 without consideration, the whole of the aggregate FMV of the moveable property will be taxed as income from other sources. Where moveable property is received for a consideration that falls short of the aggregate FMV by more than ₹50,000, the difference between the aggregate FMV and the consideration will be taxed as income from other sources.

Exemptions. There are certain exceptions to the application of Section 56(2) (vii). For instance, money or property that is received from specified relatives or on the occasion of marriage will not be taxed as income from other sources. Similarly, money or property that is received under a will or by inheritance

[26] The constitutionality of bringing such notional income to tax has been upheld by the Supreme Court of India in *Bhagwan Das Jain v. Union of India* (1981) 128 ITR 315.

or in contemplation of the death of the payer is exempt from tax under Section 56(2) (vii). Further, money or property that is received from any local authority [as defined under Section 10(20)] or from any fund/foundation/university or any trust/institution referred to in Section 10(23C) or registered under Section 12AA will not be taxed as income from other sources.

Relative. As mentioned earlier, money or property received from specified relatives will not be taxed as income from other sources. For the purpose of Section 56(2) (vii), relatives are defined differently in the case of individuals and in the case of HUF. In the case of individuals, relatives include spouse, brothers, sisters, parents, uncles, aunts, lineal ascendants, or descendants among others. In the case of an HUF, a relative includes any member of the HUF.

Distribution on Trust Dissolution Not Subject to Tax

In view of Section 56(2) (vii) being designed to tax any income received by individuals/HUFs without consideration, there was some debate about whether distributions received by the beneficiary of a private discretionary trust could be taxed as income from other sources. In *Ashok C. Pratap v. Additional Commissioner of Income Tax*,[27] the Income-Tax Appellate Tribunal held that any money received by a beneficiary on the dissolution of a trust would not be taxed as income from other sources. The Tribunal took the view that the distribution received by the beneficiary would constitute consideration for the dissolution of the trust and, thus, would not attract Section 56. This, however, is not a **settled** position till date.

Unlisted Shares Transferred without Consideration or without Adequate Consideration

A new clause was added to Section 56 by the Finance Act, 2010, to expand the coverage of persons under the provision. The Memorandum to the Finance Bill, 2010, states that under the anti-abuse provisions contained in Section 56 (as it then stood), there were measures to check avoidance only in the case of property received by an individual or an HUF. In other words, the transfer of shares of a company to a firm or a company would not attract the anti-abuse provision even though the consideration for the shares is nil or lower than the FMV.

Accordingly, Section 56(2) was amended to insert a new clause (viia) to remedy the mischief of transferring shares for inadequate or no consideration. However, the amendment was careful to exclude transfer of shares that arise because of a business reorganization, amalgamation, or demerger. Further, Section 56(2) (viia) was limited to cases where the receiver firms/companies are closely held companies and receive shares of a closely held company.

Taxation of Share Premium in Excess of FMV as Income from Other Sources

A new sub-clause (viib) was added to Section 56(2) by the Finance Act, 2012. The Memorandum explaining the provisions of the Finance Bill, 2012, does not state the reason for introducing the amendment but classifies the amendment under the heading "Measures to Prevent Generation and Circulation

[27] [2012] 139 ITD 533 (Mum). This decision sparked some discussion in view of the fact that a trust is not an independent taxable entity and the income of the trust is effectively taxed in the hands of the trustee as a representative assessee or in the hands of the beneficiaries. Accordingly, once tax has already been paid on the income of the trust, any distribution to the beneficiaries should not be subject to further tax.

of Unaccounted Money." This provision seeks to curb the practice of setting up a closely held company and issuing shares at a hefty premium to legitimize unaccounted money.

The operation of Section 56(2) (viib) is subject to certain limitations. The proviso to clause (viib) expressly states that the clause shall not apply where the consideration for the issue of shares is received by a venture capital undertaking from a venture capital company or a venture capital fund or by a company from a class, or classes of persons, that may be notified by the central government.

> *In this chapter, we presented the basic structure of estate planning and the planning practices currently prevailing in India. Details of more advanced estate planning practices in the USA can be found in Practicing Financial Planning for Professionals by Mittra, Sahu, and Starn, Jr.*

Index